1993/94
The Complete Directory for
People with
Learning Disabilities

Products	Resources
Books	Services

A One-Stop Sourcebook
for Individuals
and Professionals

Grey House Publishing

LAKEVILLE, CT 06039

Publisher/Editor : Leslie Mackenzie
Associate Editors : Cathy Hutchings
Amy Lignor
Lyndee Stalter

Grey House Publishing

Published by:
Grey House Publishing, Inc.
Pocket Knife Square
Lakeville, CT 06039
203 • 435 • 0868
FAX 203 • 435 • 0867

Copyright © 1993 Grey House Publishing, Inc.

Library of Congress Cataloging in Publication Data Available

ISBN 0-939300-24-9

Introduction

This is the first edition of Grey House Publishing's newest directory **The Complete Directory for People with Learning Disabilities.** It is the first comprehensive reference book covering the wide range of learning disabilities resources available nationwide.

The directory covers the schools, learning centers, vocational training programs, associations and organizations, and government agencies involved in learning disabilities. In addition, there are comprehensive chapters on teaching materials, assistive devices, technology resources, magazines, newsletters and workshops that are specifically designed to meet the needs of individuals with learning disabilities as well as those who work with them. You will find material for parents and siblings of individuals with learning disabilities and the wide range of information and support services available to that group.

The Table of Contents on the following pages is your guide to this database in print form. In addition, there is an entry name index and a subject index, organized by major learning disability, that refers to entries throughout the directory.

With the publication of this directory important information can now be accessed at every school and library and not just at state special education resource centers or at district level special education offices. Now every special education teacher, student, or parent can have at his or her fingertips a wealth of information on the resources that are available to help individuals achieve in school.

This is the third directory that Grey House Publishing has published in the disability field. In 1992 the company produced **The Complete Directory for People with Disabilities** which is now in its second edition and covers the broad range of resources available to people with physical and/or mental disabilities. Grey House also publishes **The National Housing Directory for People with Disabilities** with 50 state chapters on groups homes, apartments, institutions and referral agencies for people with disabilities.

Following the Table of Contents is a questionnaire for adding listings to our database or up-dating a current listing. Please make copies of the questionnaire and send additions to us throughout the year. We also welcome any suggestions on areas you would like to see included in the next edition of **The Complete Directory for People with Learning Disabilities.**

Leslie E. Mackenzie
Publisher

Acknowledgement

The Directory of for People with Learning Disabilities was made possible with the support and enthusiasm for the project that we received from professionals in the learning disabilities field.

We would particularly like to thank the following: Dr. Thomas Inkpen from the State Education Department of New York; Sally Grimes from the Landmark School in Beverly, Massachusetts; Dr. Richard Cooper from The Center for Alternative Learning in Bryn Mawr, Pennsylvania; Nonnie Starr, C.S.W. from Woodmere, New York; and Stephen Krasner of the Special Education Resource Center in Middletown, Connecticut.

The Complete Directory for People with Learning Disabilities
TABLE OF CONTENTS

Education

Programs For The Learning Disabled

Mailing List Information

This directory is available in mailing list form. Please call 800-562-2139 and we will provide counts and label information at your request. There are a number of ways we can segment the database to meet your mailing list requirements.

Computerized Version of
The Complete Directory for People with Learning Disabilities

The Complete Directory for People with Learning Disabilities is available in a computerized version that can be merged with most database software programs. Again, please call for details on licensing information.

Up-Dating Listings

We have included a questionnaire with this directory so that new listings can easily be added to our database along with updates to keep listings current. Please make copies of the questionnaire and forward additions to us throughout the year. **The Complete Directory for People with Learning Disabilities** will be published annually.

Directories available from Grey House Publishing

The Directory of Mail Order Catalogs, 1993 Edition
Details over 7,000 consumer catalog companies with 44 different product chapters from animal to travel. Contains important business details such as employee size, years in business, sales volume, catalog size, number of catalogs mailed, and more. Published since 1981, this annual directory is the standard in its field.
ISBN 0-939300-18-4

The Directory of Business to Business Catalogs, 1993 Edition
Details 6,000 suppliers to businesses in 40 different industry chapters from agricultural and aviation to tools and machinery with office supplies and maintenance supplies in between. Provides details on company size, executive contacts, catalog size as well as sales volume. *ISBN 0-939300-16-8*

The Directory of Business Information Resources, 1993 Edition
Contains in a single directory information every business needs to stay current and competitive. Organized alphabetically by major industry groups, this new directory provides information on each industry's associations, newsletters, magazines and trade shows.
ISBN 0-939300-26-5 (Softcover); ISBN 0-939300-27-3 (Hardcover)

The Complete Directory for People with Disabilities, 1993 Edition
Provides a single information resource for people with disabilities, their families and the professionals who work with them. Details on organizations and associations, government agencies that serve people with disabilities, as well as an annotated bibliography on over 800 books, information on over 1000 assistive devices, 600 computer programs as well as adaptive hardware. Plus professional texts and programs, foundations and grants, rehabilitative centers and schools as well as newsletters and journals. Information that used to be buried in multiple directories and databases is now in one easy-to-use 800 page volume.
ISBN 0-939300-19-2

The National Housing Directory for People with Disabilities
With this new directory health care professionals and individuals have easy access to basic information such as which government agencies have responsibilities for housing in each state, the names of the local agencies that handle referrals as well as detailed information on the housing units themselves from the large intensive care facilities to independent living apartments and houses.
1,500 pages, 25,000+ entries. ISBN 0-939300-13-3

The Directory for People with Learning Disabilities
Details programs, books, schools, learning centers, organizations and associations, help lines and support groups, counseling programs, newsletters, and journals available to people with learning disabilities and their families, and counselors.
ISBN 0-939300-24-9

Free Listing Questionnaire
for
The Complete Directory for People with Learning Disabilities

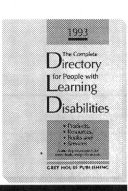

Grey House Publishing
Pocket Knife Square
Lakeville, CT 06039
(203) 435-0868
(800) 562-2139

ENTRY INFORMATION

Entry Name (Book Title, Organization Name or Product Name) _____

Company Name (If different from Entry) _____

Address _____

City _____ State _____ Zip _____

Phone _____ TDD# _____

800# _____ Fax# _____

Profile (Up to 75 words) _____

_____

_____

_____

_____

_____

_____

If the above entry is a publication, please fill out the following: Author/Editor _____

ISBN# _____ Number of Pages _____

Type: ❑ Hardcover   ❑ Paperback   ❑ Video Tape   ❑ Newsletter   ❑ Magazine

Frequency: ❑ Yearly   ❑ Quarterly   ❑ Monthly   ❑ Bi-Annually   ❑ Weekly

ORGANIZATIONS

Please provide list of publications and conference information:

1) _____ Circulation _____ Price _____

   Description _____ Editor _____

2) _____ Circulation _____ Price _____

   Description _____ Editor _____

3) _____ Circulation _____ Price _____

   Description _____ Editor _____

4) _____ Circulation _____ Price _____

   Description _____ Editor _____

5) Conference Information: _____ # Attendees _____ Dates _____

   Description _____

CONTACT NAMES

Name _____ Title _____

Name _____ Title _____

Thank you! Our 800 fax number is 800-248-0115 if you would like to fax this information back to us, or if you prefer, just drop it in the mail.

National

1 AACLD, Association's Adult Committee for Children with Learning Disabilities

4156 Library Road   412-341-1515
Pittsburgh, PA 15234

An organization of learning disabled adults who work within the Association for Children with Learning Disabilities.

2 Access Ability Resource Center

1056 East 19th Avenue, Box 410   303-861-6250
Denver, CO 80218   FAX 303-861-6411

Ann Grady, Director

A resource center providing evaluation, information and support to families with children with disabilities.

3 ACCESS ERIC

1600 Research Blvd.   800-LET-ERIC
Rockville, MD 20850   FAX 301-251-5212

Coordinates ERIC's outreach, dissemination and systemwide activities; develops new ERIC publications and provides reference and referral services. Staffs toll-free information line is available where callers are referred to 16 subject-specific ERIC Clearinghouses and more than 350 education organizations for customized assistance. Free brochures on ERIC and general education themes available, such as parent involvement.

4 ACTION

1100 Vermont Avenue NW   202-606-5135
Washington, DC 20525

The ACTION agency supports the development of creative, effective and lasting solutions to the challenges of crime, hunger, poverty, illiteracy and homelessness. The mission is to stimulate and expand voluntary citizen participation through the coordination of its efforts with public and private sector organizations and other government agencies.

5 AHEAD

P.O. Box 21192   614-488-4972
Columbus, OH 43221

A professional organization for educators committed to promoting full participation of individuals with disabilities in college.

6 Alliance for Parental Involvement in Education

P.O. Box 59
East Chatham, NY 12060

A non-profit organization to encourage and assist parental involvement in education, public, private and home.

7 Alliance for Technology Access

1128 Solano Avenue   510-528-0747
Albany, CA 94706   FAX 510-528-0746

Jacquelyn Brand, Executive Director

Organization providing resource information and services to parents and practitioners working with the disabled learner. Offers forty-six centers in thirty-five states.

8 Alternative Communication Technology

Central Michigan University
441 Moore Hall   517-774-3472
Mt. Pleasant, MI 48859

Lynn Sweeney

Maintains a clinic for assessment and consultation for individuals needing special communication technology and/or augmentative communication strategies. Provides personnel preparation and in-servicing for professionals in practice.

9 American Academy of Pediatrics

141 Northwest Point Blvd.   312-228-5005
Elk Grove Village, IL 60009   800-433-9016

A professional association providing two pamphlets for parents entitled "Learning Disabilities and Children" and "Learning Disabilities and Young Adults".

10 American Alliance for Health, Phys. Ed. Recreation and Dance

1900 Association Drive   703-476-3400
Reston, VA 22091

A membership organization in the fields of physical education, recreation, health and safety and dance.

11 American Art Therapy Association

1202 Allanson Road   708-949-6064
Mundelein, IL 60060

Established to improve the standards of art therapy training and practice and to widen employment opportunities for art therapists.

12 American Association for Adult and Continuing Education

1112 16th Street NW, Ste. 420   202-463-6333
Washington, DC 20036

The largest individual member international organization that promotes learning as a lifelong process.

13 American Association for Counseling and Development

5999 Stevenson Avenue   703-823-9800
Alexandria, VA 22304

The parent organization for counselors from educational and social service settings across the country.

14 American Association for Rehabilitation Therapy

P.O. Box 93
North Little Rock, AR 72116

Offers national and regional educational seminars, publishes brochures on careers and training in each of the rehabilitation specialty areas, and offers a newsletter of its services.

15 American Association for the Advancement of Science

1333 H Street NW   202-326-6667
Washington, DC 20005

Addresses the concerns of scientists and engineers with disabilities.

16 American Association of Collegiate Registrars and Admissions Officers

One Dupont Circle, Ste. 330   202-293-9161
Washington, DC 20036

An educational, professional association of degree-granting, postsecondary institutions, government agencies and private educational organizations.

17 American Association of Disability Communicators

National Easter Seal Society
70 East Lake Street   312-726-6200
Chicago, IL 60601

An information network among communicators who address issues relevant to people with disabilities.

18 American Camping Association

Bradford Woods
5000 State Road 67 North   317-342-8456
Martinsville, IL 46151   800-428-2267

Melody A. Sruder, Bookstore Coord.

Accredits camps throughout the country according to standards of health, safety and program. An annual guide is offered listing camps that mainstream the physically disabled and others that serve children with learning disabilities.

19 American Council of Rural Special Education

Western Washington University
Miller Hall 359   206-676-3576
Bellingham, WA 98225

A membership organization for persons interested in improving services for disabled students living in rural areas. ACRES sponsors a national conference and members participate in action task forces.

20 American Council of the Blind

1155 15th St., Ste. 720   202-467-5081
Washington, DC 20005

Oral Miller, Nat'l Representative

Provides free information on all aspects of blindness: legislation, civil rights, social security and supplemental income, national health insurance, rehabilitation, eye research and technology.

21 American Counseling Association

5999 Stevenson Avenue   703-823-9800
Alexandria, VA 22304

Dr. Theodore Remley, Jr., Executive Director

Provides a variety of programs and services that support the personal, professional and program development goals of its members.

22 American Dance Therapy Association

2000 Century Plaza, Ste. 108   301-997-4040
Columbia, MD 21044

Offers free information on educational programs, guidelines for dance therapy training and internship, professional registration requirements and regional professional contacts.

23 American Federation of Teachers

AFT Teachers' Network for Education of Handicapped
555 New Jersey Avenue NW   202-879-4460
Washington, DC 20001

Facilitates the ability of regular education teachers to work effectively with disabled children.

24 American Occupational Therapy Association

1383 Piccard Drive, P.O. Box 1725   301-948-9626
Rockville, MD 20849   800-366-9799

Refers employers and individuals with disabilities to occupational therapists with expertise on the ADA, for help with performing job analyses, identifying job accommodations and modifications, developing job descriptions, modifying job sites, identifying adaptive devices and equipment.

25 American Printing House for the Blind

1839 Frankfort Avenue   502-895-2405
Louisville, KY 40206   800-223-1839
          FAX 502-895-1509

Non-profit and private organization that offers large print, braille, or recorded format books for the blind and learning disabled.

26 American Psychological Association

750 First Street NE   202-336-5500
Washington, DC 20002

A major organization representing psychology in the United States. Since its founding, the Association has been working toward the advancement of psychology as a science, a profession, and a means of promoting human welfare.

27 American Public Welfare Association

810 First Street NE, #500   202-682-0100
Washington, DC 20002

Lee Partridge

A bi-partisan non-profit organization that promotes effective policies and programs to benefit low-income and disabled individuals.

28 American Red Cross

National Headquarters
17th & D Streets, NW   202-737-8309
Washington, DC 20006

Offers disaster services, military and social services, and heatlh and safety services. Disabled persons are given priority transportation, shelter, food, clothing and medical assistance in case of disaster.

29 American Rehabilitation Counseling Association

5999 Stevenson Avenue   703-823-9800
Alexandria, VA 22304

An organization of professional rehabilitation counselors who work in educational, health care, residential, private practice, community agency, government and business/industry settings.

30 American Speech-Language-Hearing Association

10801 Rockville Pike   301-897-5700
Rockville, MD 20852

A certifying body for professionals providing speech, language and hearing services to the public. It is an accrediting agency for college and university graduate school programs in speech-language pathology and audiology.

31 Association for Disabled Students

P.O. Box 21192   614-488-4972
Columbus, OH 43221

This is a national association of professionals working on college campuses with disabled students.

32 Association for Individually Guided Education

Hutchinson United School District - 308
P.O. Box 1908   316-665-4400
Hutchinson, KS 67504

Dedicated to the individual needs of all educable children and adults.

33 The Association for Persons in Supported Employment

5001 West Broad St., Ste. 34   804-282-3655
Richmond, VA 23230   FAX 804-282-2513

Helps employers utilize subsidized "supported employment" programs by matching individuals with severe disabilities to employers after careful evaluations of the needs of each.

34 Association for the Care of Children's Health

7910 Woodmont Avenue, Ste. 300 301-654-6549
Bethesda, MD 20814   FAX 301-986-4553

William Sciarillo, Sc.D., Executive Director

Offers important books, journals, assistive technology, support, information and referrals for professionals and parents.

35 Association of Birth Defect Children

5400 Diplomat Circle, Ste. 270   407-629-1466
Orlando, FL 32810

Provides information and support to families of children with birth defects of a nongenetic nature.

36 Association of Educational Therapists

P.O. Box 946   818-344-4712
Woodland Hills, CA 91365

National professional association that works with youth and adults blending counseling and special education skills.

37 Association of Higher Education Facilities Officers

1446 Duke Street   703-684-1446
Alexandria, VA 22314

An international association whose purpose is to promote excellence in the administration, care, operation, planning and development of higher education facilities.

38 Association of Medical Rehabilitation Administrators

1733 Forest Hills Drive   304-485-5842
Vienna, WV 26105

A professional organization of administrators, physicians, department directors and educators associated with rehabilitation facilities, programs or agencies.

39 Attention Deficit Disorder Association

2620 Ivy Place   508-462-0495
Toledo, OH 43613

The primary focus of this organization is to provide a national network for all ADD support groups and individuals.

40 Autism Research Institute

4182 Adams Avenue   619-281-7165
San Diego, CA 92116

Bernard Rimland

A clearinghouse for research on autism ajnd related disorders of learning and behavior. Conducts and compiles research findings to provide people with the latest research available.

41 Autism Society of America

8601 Georgia Avenue, Ste. 503   301-565-0433
Silver Spring, MD 20901   FAX 301-565-0834

Veronica Zysk, Administrative Asst.

Founded in 1965, the Society exists to promote public awareness of autism. Both the national office and a network of over 185 chapters in 48 states, works with parents, professionals and the general public. Provides information refererrals and advocacy and also publishes a quarterly newsletter.

42 Autism Support Center

64 Holten Street   508-777-9135
Danvers, MA 01923

A resource library and guidance center for issues of autism.

43 AVKO Educational Research Foundation, Inc.

3084 West Willard Road   313-686-9283
Birch Run, MI 48415

Comprised of teachers and individuals interested in helping others learn to read and spell. Aims to develop reading training materials for individuals with dyslexia or other learning disabilities using a method involving audio, visual, kinesthetic and oral diagnosis and remediation. Conducts research into the causes of reading, spelling and writing disabilities.

44 Boy Scouts of America

Scouting for the Handicapped Services
1325 Walnut Hill Lane   214-580-2000
Irving, TX 75038

A national voluntary organization with expertise in specific handicapping conditions offering special programs and materials.

45 Center for Family Resources

384 Clinton Street   516-489-4323
Hempstead, NY 11550   FAX 516-489-3880

Liz Gold, Resource Coordinator

A non-profit organization that provides technical assistance to school and community professionals throughout NY State including program planning, information on trainers and training, programs, resources, information and referrals.

46 Center on Postsecondary Education for Students with Learning Disabilities

The University of Connecticut U-64/School of Ed.
249 Glenbrook Road   203-486-0178
Storrs, CT 06269

Joan McGuire, PhD, Director
Patricia Anderson, Coordinator

Offers technical assistance on developing support services for students with learning disabilities.

47 C.H.A.D.D. - Children with Attention Deficit Disorders

499 NW 70th Avenue, Ste. 308   305-587-3700
Plantation, FL 33317

A non-profit support group for parents of children with attention deficit disorders. As an organization, the primary objectives are: to maintain support groups for parents who have children with ADD; to provide a forum for continuing education of both parents and professionals about ADD; to be a community resource for information about ADD; and to foster objectives that the best educational experiences should be available to children with ADD.

48 CHILD FIND

25 Industrial Park Road   800-842-8678
Middletown, CT 06457

A service under the direction of The State Department of Education and operated by the Special Education Resource Center. The primary goal is the identification, diagnosis and programming of all unserved disabled children.

49 Clearinghouse Depository for Handicapped Students

P.O. Box 944272   916-445-5103
Sacramento, CA 94244

This group provides specialized instructional material, aids and equipment.

50 Clearinghouse on Adult Education and Literacy

U.S. Department of Education
400 Maryland Avenue SW   202-732-2270
Washington, DC 20202

The Clearinghouse can provide the adult education community with resources in adult education, including putting adults in contact with the Office of Adult Education within their state.

51 Clearinghouse on Disability Information

U.S. Department of Education, Office of Special Ed
Room 3132, Switzer Bldg.   202-205-8241
Washington, DC 20202

Responds to inquiries, provides referrals, and disseminates information about services for individuals with disabilities at the national, state and local levels. The Clearinghouse offers information in the areas of Federal funding for programs serving individuals with disabilities, Federal legislation and Federal programs benefiting people with disabilities.

52 Collaboration Among Parent & Professional, National Parent Resource Center

Federation for Children with Special Needs
95 Berkeley Street, Ste. 104   617-482-2915
Boston, MA 02116   800-331-0688

To develop a parent organized, nationally coordinated system that will maintain and strengthen parent and family involvement in health care. The project is built upon the recognition that understanding the needs of families is central to achieving this nation's agenda for family-centered, community-based coordinated care.

53 Commission on Accreditation of Rehabilitation Facilities

101 North Wilmot Road, Ste. 500   602-748-1212
Tucson, AZ 85711

The recognized authority for organizations serving people with physical, developmental and mental disabilities.

54 The Council for Exceptional Children

1920 Association Drive   703-620-3660
Reston, VA 22091

Established to advance the education of exceptional children and youth, both handicapped and gifted. CEC Information Services act as an information broker for teachers, administrators, students, parents and others, serving as a comprehensive literature depository for English language materials.

55 Council for Learning Disabilities

P.O. Box 40303   913-492-8755
Overland Park, KS 66204

Kristen McBride, Executive Secretary

Provides services to professionals who work with individuals with learning disabilities including conferences and publications.

56 Council on Rehabilitation Education

P.O. Box 1680   217-333-6688
Champaign, IL 61824

Seeks to provide effective delivery of rehabilitation services to individuals with disabilities by stimulating and fostering continuing review and improvement of master's degree-level programs.

57 Counseling and Personnel Services

University of Michigan School of Education
610 East University Street   313-764-9492
Ann Arbor, MI 48109

58 Disability Information and Referral Service

Rocky Mountain Resource and Training Institute
6355 Ward Road, Ste. 310   303-420-2942
Arvada, CO 80004   800-255-3477
          FAX 303-420-8675

This service provides information and referral services available to people with disabilities.

59 The Disabled Reader Group

International Reading Association
800 Barksdale Rd., P.O. Box 8139   302-731-1600
McMurray, PA 15317

Gerald Kochinski, Treasurer
Veronica Kochinski, Treasurer

A Special Interest Group of the International Reading Association composed of individuals who are concerned with the diagnosis and remediation of reading disabilities. The purpose of the DRG are to improve the quality of instruction for reading disabled individuals, to develop better awareness of the significance of the problem, and to promote understanding and cooperation with other professionals groups involved with reading and learning disabilities.

60 Disabled USA

President's Committee for Employment of Disabled
1111 20th Street NW, Ste. 636   202-653-5044
Washington, DC 20036

61 Division for Learning Disabilities

The Council for Exceptional Children
1920 Association Drive   703-620-3660
Reston, VA 22091   FAX 703-264-9494

Serves a membership of over 14,000 professional personnel, students, parents and others interested in promoting the education and general welfare of children and adults with learning disabilities. Members receive the quarterly journal and the newsletter as well. The division sponsors many activities that promote professional growth, including a full schedule of sessions focusing on learning disabilities.

62 Educational Equity Concepts

114 East 32 Street, Ste. 701   212-725-1803
New York, NY 10016   FAX 212-725-0947

Ellen Rubin, Coord. Dis. Programs

Furthers educational opportunities for women and girls through publications which are available to educational institutions, organizations and individuals. Write or call for a brochure with listing of publications and price list.

63 Educational Referral Services

2222 Eastlake Avenue East   206-323-1838
Seattle, WA 98102

Specializes in matching children with the learning environments that are best for them and works with families to help them identify concerns and establish priorities about their child's education.

64 ERIC Clearinghouse on Handicapped and Gifted Children

The Council for Exceptional Children
1920 Association Drive   703-620-3660
Reston, VA 22091

Fred Weintraub, Director

Makes available the following publications on learning disabilities: Digest on Learning Disabilities and an annotated bibliography called Digest on Readings about Learning Disabilities. Both of theses publications are provided free of charge and other information on learning disabilities is also available. The Clearinghouse delves into all aspects of disabled and gifted children, including identification, assessment, intervention and enrichment, both in special settings & within the mainstream.

65 ERIC Clearinghouse on Reading and Communication Skills

2805 East 10th Street, Suite 150   812-855-5847
Bloomington, IN 47408   800-759-4723

Melinda Hamilton, User Services Coord.
Ellie Macfarlane, Associate Director

Concerned with the acquisition of functional competence in reading, writing, speaking and listening at all educational levels in all social contexts. Catalogue of publications available for free, ERIC bibliographic searches performed for clients for a small fee.

66 Estate Planning for Persons with Disabilities

National Office
3100 Arapahoe Avenue, Ste. 112   800-448-1071
Boulder, CO 80303   FAX 303-449-6003

Richard W. Fee, Executive Director

Organized to provide a model team approach to the problem of comprehensive life and estate planning. EPPD is not a legal firm, investment or insurance compa-

ny. However EPPD will work with the appropriate professionals and agencies to help put together an effective comprehensive plan. Serving as a national clearinghouse for parents and professionals on this highly specialized topic and presents two hour educational seminars sponsored by local groups to teach families estate planning.

67 Federation for Children with Special Needs

95 Berkeley Street, Ste. 104   617-482-2915
Boston, MA 02173   800-331-0688
    FAX 617-695-2935

A coalition of parent groups representing children with a variety of disabilities, the Federation offers a Parent Center which offers a variety of services to parents, parent groups and other who are concerned with children with special needs.

68 Foundation for Children with Learning Disabilities

99 Park Avenue   212-687-7211
New York, NY 10016   FAX 212-697-7350

Shirley Cramer, Director

Information referral service providing newsletter, seminars, some public acvocacy and a wide array of materials on learning disabilities, many for parents of children with learning disabilities.

69 Group Health Association of America

1129 Twentieth Street NW, Ste. 600   202-778-3200
Washington, DC 20036

Represented the health maintenance organization industry since 1959. Membership is open to all prepaid health care organizations that meet the associations' standards for quality assurance, financial solvency and comprehensiveness of benefits.

70 Handicapped Infant Intervention Project

1900 Massachusetts Ave. SE, 4th Fl.   202-727-3868
Washington, DC 20003

A hands on treatment program which provides infant and young children screening services in the areas of speech, audiology, cognitive and motor skills.

71 HEATH Resource Center

One Dupont Circle, Suite 800   202-939-9320
Washington, DC 20036   800-544-3284
    FAX 202-833-4760

Rhona Hartman, Director

The national clearinghouse on post-secondary education for individuals with disabilities. Support from the US Department of Education enables HEATH to serve as an information exchange about educational support services, policies, procedures and opportunities on American campuses.

72 Human Resources Center

201 I.U. Willets Road West   516-747-5400
Albertson, NY 11507

A pioneer in rehabilitation and special education fields, this nonprofit organization is dedicated to providing educational, vocational, social and recreational opportunities for persons with disabilities.

73 Institute for Child Behavior Research

4182 Adams Avenue   619-281-7165
San Diego, CA 92116

Ongoing projects include investigation of adequate diagnostic methods, the study of biomechanical defects in autistic children, treatment for autism, and operant conditioning as a method of teaching autistic children.

74 Institute for Educational Leadership

1001 Connecticut Ave. NW, Ste. 310   202-822-8405
Washington, DC 20036   FAX 202-872-4050

Michael C. Usdan, President

The Institute's list of publications on educational trends and policies is available to the public.

75 Institute for Research in Learning Disabilities

The University of Kansas
3060 Robert J. Dole   913-864-4780
Lawrence, KS 66045

Although the focus of the Institute's research is children, they have a sizeable publication list with some of their research having relevance for adults.

76 The International Council for Learning Disabilities

National Office
P.O. Box 40303   913-492-8755
Overland Park, KS 66204

Purpose is to aid all learning disability professionals in the exchange of information.

77 International Reading Association

800 Barksdale Road, P.O. Box 8139   302-731-1600
Newark, DE 19714   FAX 302-731-1057

Cindy Kirkpatrick, Public Info. Coord.

Mission is to improve the quality of reading instruction through the study of the reading process and teaching techniques; to serve as a clearinghouse for the dissemination of reading research through conferences, journals and other publications; and to help increase literacy levels worldwide.

78 LAUNCH, Inc.

Department Of Special Education   214-886-5932
Commerce, TX 75428

An organization that provides resources for learning disabled individuals, coordinates efforts of other local, state and national LD organizations.

79 Learning Disabilities Association of America

4156 Library Road   412-341-1515
Pittsburgh, PA 15234

Jean Petersen, Executive Director

Has 50 state affiliates with more than 775 local chapters. The national office has a resource center of over 500 publications for sale and also operates a film rental service.

80 Learning Disabilities Network

25 Accord Park Drive   617-982-8100
Rockland, MA 02370

A nonprofit, charitable organization dedicated to providing educational and support services to learning disabled individuals, their families and the professionals who work on their behalf.

81 Learning Independence Through Computers

LINC, Inc.
28 East Ostend Street   410-659-5462
Baltimore, MD 21230   800-772-7372
          FAX 410-539-2087

Mary Salkever, Executive Director
Susan Pomp, Dir. Of Program Mgmt

A resource center that offers specially adapted computer technology to children and adults with a variety of disabilities. State-of-the-art systems allow consumers to achieve their potential for productivity and independence at home, school, work and in the community. Also offers a quarterly newsletter called "Connections".

82 Literacy Volunteers of America, Inc.

5795 Widewaters Parkway   315-445-8000
Syracuse, NY 13214

Sharon Hachey, Pub. Director

A national organization designed to combat iliteracy through a network of community volunteer literacy programs.

83 Mainstream, Inc.

3 Bethesda Metro Center, Ste. 830   301-654-2400
Bethesda, MD 20814

Provides on-site accessibility surveys and job analyses, and offers advice on cost-effective training for employers and assists in the development of nondiscriminatory employment policies.

84 MATRIX a Parent Network and Resource Center

320 Nova Albion Way   415-499-3877
San Rafael, CA 94903

A place where parents can turn to when they discover that their child has a special need or disability and a place for parents to find emotional support and information from parents who have "been there".

85 Moving Forward

1689 East Delamo Road   310-603-9923
Carson, CA 90746

An association offering information, referrals, resources, counseling, newspapers and more for persons with disabilities.

86 National Association for Hearing and Speech Action

10801 Rockville Pike   301-897-8682
Rockville, MD 20852   800-638-8255

Committed to encouraging quality services for persons with special hearing, speech and language needs, increasing public awareness of communication problems and stimulating consumer advocacy.

87 National Association of Protection and Advocacy Systems

900 Second Street NE, Ste. 211   202-408-9514
Washington, DC 20002

Provides clients with support from technical assistance for attorneys to providing legal counsel and litigation services for the disabled.

88 National Association of Rehabilitation Agencies

1600 Wilson Blvd., Ste. 905   703-525-1191
Arlington, VA 22209

The purpose of this organization is to foster interest in and provide for the growth of medicare certified rehabilitation agencies.

89 National Captioning Institute

5203 Leesburg Pike, Ste. 1500   703-998-2400
Falls Church, VA 22041   800-533-9673

A non-profit corporation whose goal is to expand the captioned television service.

90 National Center for Education in Maternal and Child Health

2000 15th Street N, Ste. 701   703-524-7802
Arlington, VA 22201   FAX 703-524-9335

Olivia Kredel Pickett, Dir. Info. Services

Provides information to health professionals and the public about maternal, infant, child, and adolescent health; nutrition, injury/violence prevention, genetics, chronic diseases and disabling conditions, children with special health needs and public health programs and services. It focuses on projects funded by the Maternal and Child Health Bureau, U.S. Department of Health and Human Services.

91 National Center for Family Literacy

401 South 4th Avenue, Ste. 610   502-584-1133
Louisville, KY 40202

A private corporation with a purpose to expand the efforts to solve the nation's literacy problems.

92 National Center for Learning Disabilities

99 Park Avenue   212-687-7211
New York, NY 10016   FAX 212-697-7350

Shirley Cramer, Executive Director

Provides information, referral, public education and outreach programs on learning disabilities. Provides technical assistance on school to work transition, and referral to state employment services, job training partnership act programs and rehabiliation services.

93 National Clearinghouse on Literacy Education

Center for Applied Linguistics
1118 22nd Street NW   202-429-9292
Washington, DC 20037

The only national clearinghouse for adult English as a second language and literacy information.

94 National Committee for Citizens in Education

10840 Little Patuxent, Ste. 301   301-997-9300
Columbia, MD 21044   800-638-9675

An organization devoted to improving the quality of public schools through increased public involvement.

95 National Contact Hotline

Contact Center, Inc.
P.O. Box 81826   800-228-8813
Lincoln, NE 68501

A 25 year-old information and referral agency, this hotline helps individuals with literacy problems. This organization mainatins a database of over 7,000 literacy programs across the country and the hotline operates seven days a week.

96 National Council of State Directors of Adult Education

200 West Baltimore Street   410-685-7971
Baltimore, MD 21201

Comprised of state level leaders of adult education from each of the state adult education agencies.

97 National Council on Disability

800 Independence Ave. SW, Ste. 814   202-267-3846
Washington, DC 20591

An independent federal agency comprised of 15 members appointed by the President and confirmed by the Senate.

98 National Council on Rehabilitation Education

Emporia State University
1200 Commercial - VH 334   316-343-5220
Emporia, KS 66801

An organization which has its purpose promoting the improvement of rehabilitation services available to people with disabilities through quality education and rehabilitation research.

99 National Data Bank for Disabled Student Services

University of Maryland - Shoemaker Bldg.
Room 0126   301-314-7682
College Park, MD 20742

Provides the means for accessing statistics related to services, staff, budget and other components of disabled student services programs across the country.

100 National Diffusion Network

U.S. Department of Education
555 New Jersey Avenue NW   202-219-2134
Washington, DC 20208

A nationwide system established to promote educational programs in public and private schools through adoption or adaptation of effective, validated programs.

101 National Early Childhood Technical Assistance Center

NECTAS, Frank Porter Graham Development Center
Univ. Of NC At Chapel Hill   919-962-2001
Chapel Hill, NC 27599

Assists states and other designated governing jurisdictions as they develop multidisciplinary, coordinated and comprehensive services for children with special needs.

102 National Easter Seal Society

70 East Lake Street   312-726-6200
Chicago, IL 60601   800-22106827
    FAX 312-726-1494

James Williams, President

The mission of the Society is to help people with disabilities achieve maximum independence. Provides rehabilitation services, technical assistance, prevention programs, advocacy and public education programs.

103 National Education Association

1201 16th Street NW   202-822-7350
Washington, DC 20036

Deals with the question of pratice, policy, research and standards as relating to the quality of schools for all students including those with learning disabilities.

104 National Foundation for Dyslexia

4801 Hermitage Road   804-262-0586
Richmond, VA 23227   800-SOS-READ

Jo Powell, Executive Director

Provides screenings for schools or individuals and assists individuals with IEP's. Provides information about support groups and organizations and teacher training workshops.

105 National Head Injury Foundation

1776 Mass Avenue NW, Ste. 100   202-296-6443
Washington, DC 20036   800-444-NHIF
    FAX 202-296-8850

George Zitnay, President, CEO

Promotes the quality of life for people with head injuries as well as their families. A network of forty-four state associations work on research projects related to head injuries, provides information to the public and generate major prevention projects.

106 National Home Study Council

1601 18th Street NW   202-234-5100
Washington, DC 20009

A voluntary association of accredited home study councils.

107 National Information Center for Handicapped Children and Youth

P.O. Box 1492   800-999-5599
Washington, DC 20013   FAX 703-893-8614

Services include: personal responses to specific questions, referrals to other organizations, prepared information packets, publications on current issues, technical assistance to family and professional groups. Provides free information to assist parents, educators, caregivers, advocates and others in helping children and youth with disabilities become participating members of the community.

108 National Institute of Art and Disabilities

551 23rd Avenue   415-620-0290
Richmond, CA 94804

Ronald Wray, Executive Director
Elias Katz, President

An organization which operates a demonstration visual arts program, provides professional training and consultations, helps establish art centers and art programs for children and adults with disabilities, and conducts research. Books, videos, artwork and other items available.

109 The National Institute of Child Health and Human Development

Office of Research Reporting
Building 31, Room 2A32   301-496-5133
Bethesda, MS 20892

The organization develops reseach to solve problems that occur in the physical and mental evolution of development. These include some of the most emotionally draining disorders, learning disabilities, behavioral disabilities, birth defects and infant mortality. Acts as a clearinghouse of materials, information and referrals and more.

110 National Institute of Child Health and Human Development

9000 Rockville Pike, Bldg. 31   301-496-5133
Washington, DC 20040

Supports many studies designed to determine how most children learn to read and what may interfere with or prevent some children from acquiring this important skill. The ultimate goal is the complete prevention of dyslexia as well as other specific learning disabilities.

111 National Institute on Disability and Rehabilitation Research

330 C Street SW   202-732-5066
Washington, DC 20202

Funds 31 state technology assistance projects providing information and technical assistance on technology, related services and devices for individuals with disabilities.

112 National Lekotek Center

2100 Ridge Avenue   708-328-0001
Evanston, IL 60201   800-366-PLAY
     FAX 708-328-5514

Marilyn Lederer, Executive Director
Diana Mines Nielander, Dir. Special Events

A nonprofit organization which provides play-centered programs for children with disabilities and their families. Lekotek uses the universal language of play to help parents see their child's abilities. In 50 centers in the U.S. children with learning disabilities, Down Syndrome, Cerebral Palsy, Developmental Dealy come to Lekotek for play sessions, access to its extensive toy libraries, play groups, consultation and training. Compuplay also provides play experiences through adapted hardware.

113 National Library Service for the Blind and Physically Handicapped

1291 Taylor Street NW   202-707-5100
Washington, DC 20542   800-424-8567

Administers a national library service that provides braille and recorded books and magazines on free loan to anyone who cannot read standard print because of visual or learning disabilities. Eligible residents of the United States or American citizens living abroad may apply.

114 National Maternal and Child Health Bureau

5600 Fisher Lane, Park Lawn Bldg.   301-443-1080
Rockville, MD 20857

Dr. Merle McPherson

Focus is on the health-related concerns of mothers and children primarily with those of low-income and those who do not have access to health coverage. The National Bureau administers state title 5 block grants and funds research and projects of regional and national significance. The Bureau has specific responsbility for facilitating development of community based coordinated systems of care.

115 National Network of Learning Disabled Adults

P.O. Box 716   215-275-7211
Bryn Mawr, PA 19010

Organization formed to provide support, assistance and information to learning disabled adults and self-help groups for learning disabled adults nationwide.

116 National Organization on Disability

910 16th Street NW, Ste. 600   202-293-5960
Washington, DC 20006   800-248-ABLE

Administers a community-based network of more than 2, 200 towns, cities, and counties established to improve the participation of people with disabilities in community life.

117 National Parent Network on Disabilities

1600 Prince Street, Suite 115   703-684-6763
Alexandria, VA 22314   FAX 703-548-6191

Patricia McGill Smith, Executive Director
Kate Murphy

A coalition of parent organizations and parents that has been established to provide a presence and national voice for parents of persons with disabilities. The NPND shares information and resources. It also supports the power of parents to influence and affect policy issues concerning the needs of people with disabilities and their families.

118 National Rehabilitation Association

633 South Washington Street   703-836-0850
Alexandria, VA 22314

Comprised of persons with disabilities, professional rehabilitation workers and others from the fields of education, medicine, business and industry.

119   National Rehabilitation Information Center

8455 Colesville Road, Ste. 935   301-588-9284
Silver Spring, MD 20910   800-346-2742

A library and information center on disability and rehabilitation.

120   National Resource Center for Paraprofessionals in Special Ed.

New Careers Training Laboratory-University of NY
33 West 42nd Street   212-840-1278
New York, NY 10036

Disseminates information for the use of employers, program managers and trainers on such issues as skills and competencies needed by paraprofessionals.

121   National Resource Institute on Children with Handicaps

University of Washington
CDMRC WJ-10   206-543-2213
Seattle, WA 98195

Provides resources to professionals who serve children and youth with disabilities and their families.

122   National Special Education Alliance

2025 Mariani Avenue   408-974-7910
Cupertino, CA 95014   800-732-3131

A resource center providing local service, information and hands-on training for individuals with disabilities, their families and others interested in applying technology for persons with disabilities.

123   National Technical Information Service

U.S. Department of Commerce
5285 Port Royal Road   703-487-4600
Springfield, VA 22161

An agency created by Congress in 1950 to provide technical reports and other information products of specialized interest to business, educators, government and the public.

124   Orton Dyslexia Society

Chester Bldg., Ste. 382   410-296-0232
Baltimore, MD 21286   800-222-3123
                                        FAX 410-321-5069

Gary Ulrich, Executive Director

The only national organization solely concerned with dyslexia. The Society provides a packet of basic information on various topics dealing with dyslexia as well as information and referral services both generally and locally.

125   PACER Center

4826 Chicago Avenue South   612-827-2966
Minneapolis, MN 55417   800-53-PACER

Paula Goldberg, Co-Director
Marge Goldberg, Co-Director

A coalition of organizations founded on the concept of Parents Helping Parents. PACER strives to improve and expand opportunities that enhance the quality of life for children and young adults with disabilities and their families. PACER's programs help parents become informed and effective representatives for their children in early childhood, school-age and vocational settings. families become better equipped to work with agencies to obtain appropriate services for their children.

126   Pappanikov Center

1776 Ellington Road   203-648-1205
South Windsor, CT 06074   FAX 203-644-2031

Orv Karan, Director

The center aims to improve the quality of life for individuals with disabilities and their families both directly through a variety of services and indirectly through training, technical assistance, dissemination of information and research.

127   Parents, Let's Unite for Kids

1500 North 30th Street   406-657-2055
Billings, MT 59101

128   Pathfinder Family Center, Parent Training

1600 Second Avenue SW   701-852-9426
Minot, ND 58701   800-245-5840
                                        FAX 710-838-9324

A member of the National Parent Training and Information Program which helps parents to better understand their child's disability and to obtain information about the programs, services and resources available. The center provides refgerrals through their Identa-Net program, support for educational programs for children with disabilities and helps parents learn to communicate more effectively with those involved in their child's program.

129   P.R.I.D.E. Foundation

391 Long Hill Road, Box 1293   203-445-1448
Groton, CT 06340

Primary objective is to provide assistance for disabled and elderly persons in the areas of homemaking, independence in dressing, personal grooming and fashionable apparel. Also offers various publications in these areas.

130   Project Literacy U.S.

WQED
4802 Fifth Avenue   412-622-1320
Pittsburgh, PA 15213

Operates a partnership of television's PBS and ABC. The goal of this organization is to eliminate illiteracy in the United States.

131 Rehabilitation International

25 East 21st Street   212-420-1500
New York, NY 10010

An organization for disability prevention and rehabilitation with more than 135 member organizations in 83 countries and 10 international member organizations.

132 RESNA

1101 Connecticut Ave. NW, Ste. 700   202-857-1199
Washington, DC 20036   FAX 202-223-4579

Nel Bailey, Project Manager

An interdisciplinary association for the advancement of rehabilitation and assistive technologies. The association has 14 specific interest groups, one of which is special education. RESNA is a federally funded project providing technical assistance to states and origins in the area of technology related assistance.

133 Rural Education and Small Schools

Appalachia Educational Laboratory
1031 Quarrier Street   800-344-6646
Charleston, WV 25325

Economic, cultural, social or other factors related to educational programs and practices for rural residents.

134 Search to Serve/Child Find

Learning Disabilities Association of America
11225 East Stetson Place   602-230-7188
Tucson, AZ 85749   800-352-4558

Trains volunteer advocates to understand the federal and state laws and regulations, parental rights and responsibilities, non-adversarial advocacy strategies and supportive resources.

135 Sertoma International/Sertoma Foundation

1912 East Meyer Blvd.   816-333-8320
Kansas City, MO 64132

Activities focus on helping people with speech and hearing problems, but they also have programs in the areas of youth, national heritage, drug awareness and community services.

136 Sibling Information Network

1776 Ellington Road   203-648-1205
South Windsor, CT 06074

Lisa Glidden

Offers information, referrals, support and a newsletter that deals with the many issues surrounding a brother/sister with a disability. The Network serves as a clearinghouse of information relating to brothers/sisters with disabilities.

137 Siblings of Disabled Children

Parents Helping Parents
535 Race St., Ste. 220   408-288-5010
San Jose, CA 95126

A program for Parents Helping Parents with the objective to give siblings special attention relating to their needs around being a member of an exceptional family.

138 Specialized Training of Military Parents

12208 Pacific Highway SE   206-588-1741
Tacoma, WA 98499

Provides individual assistance to families, workshops, assistance and site visits to other Parent Training and Information centers.

139 Stuttering Resource Foundation

123 Oxford Road   914-632-3925
New Rochelle, NY 10804   800-232-4773

Ellin Rind, President
Patricia Rind, Vice President

Publishes books in the areas of stuttering rehabilitation, organizes groups for parents of children who stutter or at risk of stuttering and offers information to parents and professionals who work with individuals who stutter, including a directory of programs and therapists in the U.S. and Canada.

140 Synergy - Adaptive Technology Services

66 Hale Road   508-668-7424
East Walpole, MA 02032   FAX 508-668-4134

Dedicated to empowering persons with physical, language and learning disabilities through the use of technology. Technology can assist persons with disabilities to overcome barriers in education, employment and independent living.

141 TASK Team of Advocates for Special Kids

100 West Cerritos   714-533-TASK
Anaheim, CA 92805

Suzanne Galindo, Info. Specialist

A parent training and information center serving families of children with disabilities. Provides support, legal rights information, phone advocacy, workshops and referral services. Conducts assistive technology assessments for ages 12 months through adulthood and workshops on adapted toys, adaptive hardware and specialized software.
  Provides specialized service for families of Vietnam Veterans' children with disabilities.

142 Technology and Media

Box U-64, University Of Connecticut   203-486-0165
Storrs, CT 06269   FAX 203-486-0210

Chauncy Rucker, President

Membership organization specializing in the education of people with special needs through technology and media.

143 Very Special Arts

1331 F Street NW, Ste. 800   202-678-2800
Washington, DC 20004   800-933-8721
    FAX 202-737-0725

Shelly Shultz, Information Systems

An international organization that provides programs in creative writing, dance, drama, literature, music and the visual arts for individuals with physical and mental disabilities. Founded in 1974 by Joan Kennedy Smith, OS, an educational affiliate of the John F. Kennedy Center for the Performing Arts, Very Special Arts seek to promote worldwide awareness of the educational and cultural benefits of the arts for all people.

144 Vocational Education and Work Adjustment Association

Div. of the National Rehabilitation Association
1910 Association Drive, Ste. 205   703-636-9306
Reston, VA 22901

Provides a Registry of ADA Consultants consisting of vocational evaluators and work adjustment specialists throughout the United States and Canada. Makes referrals to local ADA consultants who may provide information and assistance on identifying employment barriers, worksite or tool modifications, performing accessibility surveys, job analysis and skills assessments.

145 World Institute on Disability

510 16th Street   510-763-4100
Oakland, CA 94612   FAX 510-763-4109

Identifies solutions to problems faced by people with disabilities focusing on areas such as public education, service systems consultation and independent living.

Alabama

146 Alabama Learning Disabilities Association

6055 Red Hollow Road   205-681-0033
Birmingham, AL 35215

Pat Orr

Alaska

147 Alaska Learning Disabilities Association

108 West Cook Avenue   907-279-1662
Anchorage, AK 99501

Mavis Hancock

Arizona

148 Arizona Center for Law in the Public Interest

3724 North 3rd Street, Ste. 300   602-274-6287
Phoenix, AZ 85012   800-927-2260
    FAX 602-274-6779

Timothy Hogan, Executive Director

A non-profit public interest law firm which provides protection and advocacy services for persons with mental or developmental disabilities and those seeking services under the Rehabilitation Act.

149 Association for Retarded Citizens of Arizona

5610 South Central Avenue   602-243-1787
Phoenix, AZ 85040   800-252-9054

150 The Learning Disabilities Association of Arizona

P.O. Box 15525   602-230-7188
Phoenix, AZ 85060

Janet Hand, Office Manager
Cinda Fisher, President

Offers information and referral services, pamphlets and support for the learning disabled.

151 Phoenix Chapter of Adult LDA

815 East Camelback Road, Ste. 108   602-230-7188
Phoenix, AZ 85060

Local chapters meeting on a monthly basis throughout the school year offering speakers and topics of particular interest to those concerned with learning disabilities.

152 Recording for the Blind - Phoenix

Western Psychological Services Corporation
3627 East Indian School Road   602-478-2061
Phoenix, AZ 85018

Offers information on recordings of books on audio cassette and computer disc.

153 Sunshiners of Arizona

P.O. Box 15525   602-840-3192
Phoenix, AZ 85060

A group of individuals with average or above average intelligence who appear incapable of learning things the way others do. This group consists of 3% to 10% of the general population and hold meetings at least once a month. It is a chapter of the Learning Disabilities Association of Arizona.

Arkansas

154 Arkansas Learning Disabilities Association

28 Longmeadow   501-535-3050
Pine Bluff, AR 71603

Brenda Gullett

155 Increasing Capabilities Access Network (ICAN)

2201 Brookwood Drive, Ste. 117   501-666-8868
Little Rock, AR 72202   800-828-2799
                    FAX 501-666-5319

Sue Gaskin, Project Director
A federally funded program of the Department of Human Services, Division of Rehabilitation Service, is designed to make technology information or as ICAN calls it "tools for living, learning and working" available and accessible for all who need it. The program provides information on new and existing technology free to any person regardless of age or disability.

California

156 Bay Area Adult Dyslexic Support Group

239 Whitelem   415-493-3497
Palo Alto, CA 94306

Lynne Stietzel
A support group for any adults with "learning differences" interested in sharing or listening.

157 California Association of Private Specialized Education & Services

Dubnoff Center
10526 Dubnoff Way   213-877-5678
North Hollywood, CA 91606

Dr. Gil Freitag
The purposes are to: serve as a liaison between the public and private sectors and to lend support for continuum of programs and objectives which improve the delivery of services provided to the exceptional individual.

158 California Learning Disabilities Association

655 Lewelling Blvd., #355   818-355-9361
San Leandro, CA 94579

Jane Bagley, President
Support and advocacy for children and adults with learning disabilities.

159 Central California Branch - the Orton Dyslexia Society

P.O. Box 924   408-624-1456
Pebble Beach, CA 93953

Sally Poile, President

160 Foundation on Employment and Disability

3820 Del Amo Blvd. #201   213-214-3430
Torrance, CA 90503
Through multilingual toll-free information lines, pamphlets, articles in local publications and presentations to community organizations, will provide written and oral information on the ADA that is understandable, linguistically and culturally, to minority communities in Los Angeles, Orange County and San Francisco, California.

161 Inland Empire California Branch the Orton Dyslexia Society

190 E. Big Springs Road   714-686-9837
Riverside, CA 92507

Regina Richards, President

162 Los Angeles California Branch - the Orton Dyslexia Society

4379 Tujunga Avenue   818-506-8866
Studio City, CA 91604

Wynne Good, President

163 Northern California Branch - the Orton Dyslexia Society

300 Frederick Street   415-328-7667
San Francisco, CA 94117

Nancy Cushen White, President

164 Orange County Branch - the Orton Dyslexia Society

2905 Miraloma, Suite 9   714-630-4621
Anaheim, CA 92806

Virginia Hunt, President

165 Pacific Coast Disability and Business Technical Assistance Center

440 Grand Avenue, Ste. 500   510-465-7884
Oakland, CA 94610
Provides information, training and technical assistance to employers, people with disabilities and other entities with responsibilities under the ADA. These centers act as a one-stop central source of information, direct technical

assistance, training and referral on ADA issues in employment, public accommodations, public services and communications.

166 Recording for the Blind - Los Angeles

Western Psychological Services Corporation
5022 Hollywood Blvd.   213-478-2061
Los Angeles, CA 90027   800-499-5525
                              FAX 213-664-1881

Carol Smith, Executive Director
Karen Parti, Studio Director

A national, non-profit organization providing recorded textbooks, library services and other educational resources at no charge to people who cannot read standard print because of a visual, physical or learning disability.

167 Recording for the Blind - Manhattan Beach

Western Psychological Services Corporation
1230 Rosecrane Avenue   213-478-2061
Manhattan Beach, CA 90266

Offers information on recordings of books on audio cassette and computer disc.

168 Recording for the Blind - Palo Alto

Western Psychological Services Corporation
488 West Charleston Road   213-478-2061
Palo Alto, CA 94306

Offers information on recordings of books on audio cassette and computer disc.

169 Recording for the Blind - Peoria

Western Psychological Services Corporation
9449 North 99th Avenue   213-478-2061
Peoria, CA 95345

Robert Briscoe, Studio Director

Offers information on recordings of books on audio cassette and computer disc.

170 Recording for the Blind - Santa Barbara

Western Psychological Services Corporation
3970 La Colina Road   213-478-2061
Santa Barbara, CA 93110

Offers information on recordings of books on audio cassette and computer disc.

171 Recording for the Blind - Upland

Recording for the Blind
1844-C West 11th Street   909-949-4316
Upland, CA 91786   800-221-4792

Fisela O'Loughlin, Studio Director

Records texts on audio cassettes and computer disk for the visually, physically and perceptually disabled.

172 San Diego Branch - the Orton Dyslexia Society

530 B Street, Ste. 915   619-234-8139
San Diego, CA 92101

Linda M. Altes, PhD, President

173 Tri-County Branch the Orton Dyslexia Society

P.O. Box 30484   805-687-8993
Santa Barbara, CA 93130

Pam Boswell, President

Colorado

---

174 Colorado Branch - the Orton Dyslexia Society

P.O. Box 102092   303-721-9425
Denver, CO 80250

Ellen Hunter, President

175 Colorado Learning Disabilities Association

1045 Lincoln Street #106   303-894-0992
Denver, CO 80203

Penny Dustin, President

LDAC is an affiliate of the learning Disabilities Association of America. A non-profit, volunteer organization dedicated to enhancing the quality of life for all individuals with learning disabilities. LDA seeks to accomplish this through advocacy, education, research and services.

176 High Plains Easter Seal Society, Inc.

P.O. Box 1885, 209 Ash Street   303-522-5858
Sterling, CO 80751

Sharon Unrein

177 Recording for the Blind - Denver

Western Psychological Services Corporation
2696 South Colorado Blvd., Ste. 330   213-478-2061
Denver, CO 80222

Offers information on recordings of books on audio cassette and computer disc.

178 Rocky Mountain Disability and Business Technical Assistance Center

3630 Sinton Road, Ste. 103   719-444-0252
Colorado Springs, CO 80907

Provides information, training and technical assistance to employers, people with disabilities and other entities with responsibilities under the ADA. These centers act as a one-stop central source of information, direct technical assistance, training and referral on ADA issues in employment, public accommodations, public services and communications.

Connecticut

---

179 Association for Children and Adults with Learning Disabilities of CT

139 North Main Street   203-236-3953
West Hartford, CT 06107

180 Bureau of Rehabilitation Services

10 Griffin Road North   203-298-2032
Windsor, CT 06095   800-537-2549

Offers vocational rehabilitation and independent living services to individuals who are physically or mentally disabled.

181 Connecticut Association of Private Special Education Facilities

Children's Center
1400 Whitney Avenue   203-248-2116
Hamden, CT 06517

Michael MacDonal, President

Providing a basis for unity and common action to serve the common interests among all private education facilities, including cost reporting, the state approval process and the private special education community.

182 Connecticut Learning Disabilities Association

260 Constitution Plaza   203-277-8669
Hartford, CT 06103   FAX 203-277-8673

Harriet Clark, Board President
Elaine Coleman, Executive Director

A non-profit organization that provides the following services to children and youth: information and referrals, lengthy consultations with parents and complete educational advocacy services up to due process hearings. Also provide transition services to youth. With respect to adults, LDA provides information and referral services.

LDA has ten active chapters throughout the state that provide monthly meetings with speakers and support. One for parents, one for adults, remainder for children.

183 Parent-to-Parent Network of Connecticut

The Family Center At Newington Children's Hospital
181 East Cedar Street   203-667-5288
Newington, CT 06111

Laura Glomb, Network Director

A group of trained parent volunteers who help other parents who are seeking professional information and emotional support. Parent volunteers attend a series of training workshops designed to prepare them to provide support and information to other parents.

184 Programs for Children with Special Health Care Needs

Health Services for Disabled Children's Section
150 Washington Street   203-566-2057
Hartford, CT 06106

Rosario Palmeri, Medical Director

185 Recording for the Blind - New Haven

Western Psychological Services Corporation
205-209 Orange Street   213-478-2061
New Haven, CT 06510

Anne Fortunato, Studio Director
Loren D'Amato, Borrower Services

Offers information on recordings of books on audio cassette and computer disc. As of January 1993, more than 8,000 tests-on-tape are available from the Amster Library for immediate shipment to qualified users (vision-impaired, learning disabled and/or physically disabled students of all ages anywhere in the U.S.A. if properly qualified in the RFB Service).

Delaware

---

186 Delaware Learning Disabilities Association

117 East Sutton Place   302-529-9411
Wilmington, DE 19810

Janet Walton, President

District of Columbia

---

187 Learning Disabilities Association of DC

P.O. Box 6350   202-244-5177
Washington, DC 20015

188 Recording for the Blind of Metropolitan Washington

Western Psychological Services Corporation
5225 Wisconsin Avenue NW, Ste. 312   213-478-2061
Washington, DC 20015   FAX 202-244-1346

Kay Marshall, Deputy Director

A nonprofit organization that loans educational books, free-of-charge to people with print disabilities. RFB serves those who are blind, dyslexic or have other disabilities that affect reading. Our national office maintains a library of 80,000 taped textbooks. Washington RFB records books not already in the library for local students.

Florida

189 Broward County Easter Seal Society, Inc.

6951 West Sunrise Blvd.   305-792-8772
Plantation, FL 33313

Barbara Oliver

The Learning Disability Diagnostic/Intervention Program serves individuals 5 years old and above. It has a two-fold purpose: 1) to conduct diagnostic evaluations on individuals who are experiencing learning difficulties; and 2) to provide individualized intervention therapy as well as other appropriate recommendations.

190 Bureau of Education for Exceptional Children

Knott Building   904-488-1461
Tallahassee, FL 32399

Provides consultative services for the establishment and operation of school programs for the visually impaired and learning disabled students.

191 Easter Seal Society of Broward County

6951 West Sunrise Blvd.   305-792-8772
Plantation, FL 33313   FAX 305-791-8275

Barbara Oliver, Program Director

Testing, evaluation and intensive individual consultation for people with learning disabilities of all ages. An LD specialist will provide free in-school training of teachers and screening of students with fees being determined on a sliding scale.

192 Florida ACLD

11046 SW 133rd Place   305-388-3967
Miami, FL 33186

Marilyn McGonigal, President

193 Florida Branch - the Orton Dyslexia Society

3550 Wilkinson Road   813-361-6544
Sarasota, FL 34231

Sandra Soper, President

194 Florida Unit, Recording for the Blind

Recording for the Blind
6704 SW 80th Street   305-666-0552
Miami, FL 33143   800-535-0552
                          FAX 305-667-2505

Christine McCarthy, Executive Director
Kathleen Craynock, Assistant Director

Provides recorded textbook material free, on loan, on request for the print disabled; computer disk texts also available.

Georgia

195 Georgia Branch - the Orton Dyslexia Society

776 Windsor Parkway   404-256-5500
Atlanta, GA 30342

Richard Kaplan, President

196 Georgia Learning Disabilities Association

1959 Spencer Oaks Alne   404-732-5600
Lithonia, GA 30058

Helen White, President

197 Recording for the Blind - Athens

Western Psychological Services Corporation
120 Florida Avenue   213-478-2061
Athens, GA 30605

Offers information on recordings of books on audio cassette and computer disc.

198 Southeast Disability and Business Technical Assistance Center

1776 Peachtree Street, Ste. 310 N   404-888-0022
Latlanta, GA 30309

Provides information, training and technical assistance to employers, people with disabilities and other entities with responsibilities under the ADA. These centers act as a one-stop central source of information, direct technical assistance, training and referral on ADA issues in employment, public accommodations, public services and communications.

199 West Georgia Easter Seal Society

P.O. Box 5789
Columbus, GA 31906

Sharon Borger

Hawaii

200 Hawaii Branch - the Orton Dyslexia Society

P.O. Box 61610   808-988-5164
Honolulu, HI 96839

Roseyn Devlin, Co-President
Jane Anderson, Co-President

201 Learning Disability Association of Hawaii

200 North Vineyard Blvd. #103   800-536-9684
Honolulu, HI 96817

Offers support group counseling, newsletters, advocacy and more.

Idaho

202 Idaho Learning Disabilities Association

12160 N. Forrest Road   208-762-3170
Hayden, ID 83835

Michelle Arnold, President

Illinois

203 Child Care Association of Illinois

Juvenile Protective Association
1707 North Halsted   217-528-4409
Chicago, IL 60614

Richard Calica, Executive Director

A private organization that represents non-profit child welfare agencies in Illinois.

204 Easter Seal Rehabilitation Center of Illinois

212 Barney Drive
Joliet, IL 60435

205 Great Lakes Disability and Business Technical Assistance Center

1640 West Roosevelt Road   312-413-1407
Chicago, IL 60608

Provides information, training and technical assistance to employers, people with disabilities and other entities with responsibilities under the ADA. These centers act as a one-stop central source of information, direct technical assistance, training and referral on ADA issues in employment, public accommodations, public services and communications.

206 Illinois Branch - the Orton Dyslexia Society

40357 N. Sunset Drive   312-472-9933
Antioch, IL 60002

Grant B. Farrell, President

207 Illinois Learning Disabilities Association

12 Beau Meade   708-554-9368
Oswego, IL 60543

Connie Parr, President

208 Learning Disabilities Association of Chicago

P.O. Box 42888   312-445-5830
Chicago, IL 60642

Judy O'Connell, President

Improves special educational opportunities, better professional care and greater understanding of children and young adults.

209 Palos-Orlando Recording for the Blind

Recording for the Blind
LaGrange Road & 143rd Street   708-349-9356
Orland Park, IL 60462

Marge Quinlan, Studio Director

A unit of Recording for the Blind, the volunteers record textbooks on Master tapes. Cassettes are copied from these tapes and mailed to the borrowers. Recordings are made from the 4th grade level thru college/professional material. This service is provided for any visual, perceptual and physically disabled person. The national headquarters houses an 80,000 volume library and application kits are available upon request.

210 Recording for the Blind - Champaign

Western Psychological Services Corporation
1207 South Oak Street   213-478-2061
Champaign, IL 61820

Offers information on recordings of books on audio cassette and computer disc.

211 Recording for the Blind - Chicago

Western Psychological Services Corporation
18 South Michigan Avenue   213-478-2061
Chicago, IL 60603

Offers information on recordings of books on audio cassette and computer disc.

212 Recording for the Blind - Illinois

Western Psychological Services Corporation
University Of Chicago   213-478-2061
Chicago, IL 60637

Offers information on recordings of books on audio cassette and computer disc.

213 Recording for the Blind - Naperville

Western Psychological Services Corporation
30 North Brainard Street   213-478-2061
Naperville, IL 60540

Offers information on recordings of books on audio cassette and computer disc.

214 Recording for the Blind - Winnetka

Western Psychological Services Corporation
708 Oak Street   213-478-2061
Winnetka, IL 60093

Offers information on recordings of books on audio cassette and computer disc.

Indiana

215 Indiana Branch - the Orton Dyslexia Society

1514 Prestwick Circle   317-844-4259
Carmel, IN 46032

Susan Noble, President

216 Indiana Learning Disabilities Association

809 Rewill Drive   219-432-4537
Fort Wayne, IN 46804

217 The North Central Indiana Easter Seal

C/O Bonavista Programs
1220 East Laguna
Kokomo, IN 46902

Johanna Ridenour

218 Southeast Indiana Rehabilitation Center Goodwill Industries

C/O Rehabilitation Center
1329 Applegate Lane, P.O. Box 2117   812-283-7405
Clarksville, IN 47129

Gary Durlee, Asst. Exec. Director

The purpose is to assist the community by providing services which allow individuals to maximize their potential and to participate in work, family and the community. To do this we will provide rehabilitation, education and training.

219 Southwestern Indiana Easter Seal

The Reahbilitation Center
3701 Bellemeade Avenue
Evansville, IN 47714

Elizabeth Sankoviter

Iowa

220 Iowa Branch - the Orton Dyslexia Society

Box 56   319-396-5111
Mt. Auburn, IA 52313

Diane Brazell, President

221 Iowa Learning Disabilities Association

516 Maple   319-296-2316
Washburn, IA 50706

Mary Ann Toothman, President

Kansas

222 Kansas Learning Disabilities Association

1749 Trowman Way   316-383-5801
Emporia, KS 66801

John Schwenn, President

Kentucky

223 Kentucky Learning Disabilities Association

608 Pine Grove Court   606-325-7366
Ashland, KY 41101

Helen Ashworth, President

224 Recording for the Blind - Louisville

Western Psychological Services Corporation
240 Haldeman Avenue   213-478-2061
Louisville, KY 40206

Offers information on recordings of books on audio cassette and computer disc.

Louisiana

225 Louisiana Branch - the Orton Dyslexia Society

Gay Hess Special Education & Learning Center
P.O. Box 7070   318-942-6978
Opeloussa, LA 70571

Gay Hess, President

226 Louisiana Learning Disabilities Association

Route 6, Box 878   318-357-6288
Matchitoches, LA 71497

Jean Keuker, President

Maine

227 Maine Learning Disabilities Association

32 Ware Street   207-784-2413
Lewiston, ME 04240

Sue Hollinger, President

228 New England Disability and Business Technical Assistance Center

145 Newbury Street   207-874-6535
Portland, ME 04101

Provides information, training and technical assistance to employers, people with disabilities and other entities with responsibilities under the ADA. These centers act as a one-stop central source of information, direct technical assistance, training and referral on ADA issues in employment, public accommodations, public services and communications.

Maryland

229 D.C. Capital Branch - the Orton Dyslexia Society

6224 Goodview Street   301-320-3596
Bethesda, MD 20817

Marcia Jeffries, President

230 Maryland Association of Nonpublic Special Education Facilities

Villa Maria School
2300 Dulaney Valley Road   410-252-6343
Timonium, MD 21093

Jack Pumphrey

Responsible for informing public and acting as spokesperson on issues affecting nonpublic special education schools in Maryland.

231 Maryland Branch - the Orton Dyslexia Society

3214 Hearthstone Road   410-461-9564
Ellicott City, MD 21043

Susan Horn, President

232 Maryland Learning Disabilities Association

2314 Birch Drive   410-265-6193
Baltimore, MD 21207

Irene Spencer, President

Massachusetts

233 Children in Hospitals

31 Wilshire Park   617-444-3877
Needham, MA 02192

Barbara Popper

Parents and health care professionals concerned withe needs and rights of hospitalized children and adults.

234 Massachusetts Association of 766 Approved Private Schools

Robert F. Kennedy Action Corporation
11 Bracon Street, Ste. 325   617-227-4183
Boston, MA 02108

Edward Kelley

235 Massachusetts Learning Disabilities Association

23 Connolly Street   617-963-9476
Randolph, MA 02368

Ruth Glazerman, President

236 Recording for the Blind - Cambridge

Western Psychological Services Corporation
43 Thorndike Street   213-478-2061
Cambridge, MA 02141

Offers information on recordings of books on audio cassette and computer disc.

237 Recording for the Blind - Lenox

Western Psychological Services Corporation
Lenox Library, Second Floor   213-478-2061
Lenox, MA 01240

Offers information on recordings of books on audio cassette and computer disc available to registered borrowers.

238 Recording for the Blind - Pittsfield

Western Psychological Services Corporation
Berkshire Community College   213-478-2061
Library
Pittsfield, MA 01201

Offers information on recordings of books on audio cassette and computer disc.

239 Recording for the Blind - Williamstown

Western Psychological Services Corporation
T. Greylock Regional School   213-478-2061
Williamstown, MA 01267

Offers information on recordings of books on audio cassette and computer disc.

Michigan

240 Michigan Branch - the Orton Dyslexia Society

248 Morris Avenue SE   616-392-6398
Grand Rapids, MI 49503

Nanette Clatterbuck, President

241 Michigan Learning Disabilities Association

244 Little Station Road   616-399-5947
Holland, MI 49423

Linda Ries, President

242 Recording for the Blind - Troy

Western Psychological Services Corporation
5600 Rochester Road   213-478-2061
Troy, MI 48098

Jean Lowmaster, Director
Lena Fraasson, Studio Director

Offers information on recorded textbooks on audio cassette and computer disc. Also records textbooks for local students.

Minnesota

243 Learning Disabilities Association Step-by-Step

2104 Park Avenue   612-871-9011
Minneapolis, MN 55404   FAX 612-871-2081

Multisensory instruction books and materials for the hard-to-teach learner for use by volunteers or the experienced professional. Effective with students of all ages with reading or spelling problems. Appropriate for beginning to higher level readers. Includes training video.

244 Minnesota Learning Disabilities Association

Griggs Midway Building, Suite 494-N
1821 University Avenue   612-646-6136
St. Paul, MN 55104   800-488-4395

An organization of caring families and concerned citizens who are committed to action and mutual support on behalf of individuals with learning, attention and interpersonal challenges.

245 Upper Midwest Branch - the Orton Dyslexia Society

Rt. 4, Box 300   612-450-7589
Owatonna, MN 55060

David Winters, President

Mississippi

246 Mississippi Learning Disabilities Association

214 S. 37th Avenue   601-266-5163
Hattiesburg, MS 39402

Camille Yates, President

Missouri

247 Great Plains Disability and Business Technical Assistance Center

4816 Santana Drive   314-882-3600
Columbia, MO 65203

Provides information, training and technical assistance to employers, people with disabilities and other entities with responsibilities under the ADA. These centers act as a one-stop central source of information, direct technical assistance, training and referral on ADA issues in employment, public accommodations, public services and communications.

248   Missouri Learning Disabilities Association

416 North 36th Terrace   816-228-1541
Blue Springs, MO 64015

Linda Alwes, President

Montana

249   Montana Learning Disabilities Association

4026 Pine Cove Road   406-656-7138
Billings, MT 59106

Maureen Ferrell, President

250   Recording for the Blind Research and Development Department

Western Psychological Services Corporation
37 Corbin Hall, P.O. Box 7068   213-478-2061
Missoula, MT 59807

Offers information on recordings of books on audio cassette and computer disc.

Nebraska

251   Nebraska Branch - the Orton Dyslexia Society

6407 Crooked Creek   402-423-7901
Lincoln, NE 68516

Mary Fritz, President

252   Nebraska Learning Disabilities Association

2045 Hazel Street   402-727-9250
Fremont, NE 68025

Kathy Rayburn, President

Nevada

253   Reno Center Easter Seal Society

3959 South McCarren Blvd.
Reno, NV 89502

Charlotte Serline

New Hampshire

254   Easter Seal Intervention Program

44 Birch Street
Derry, NH 03038

Carol Fryer

255   Easter Seal Society Brock Home

New Jersey Easter Seal Society
44 Fairview Street
Pittsfield, NH 03263

Ann Smith

256   Easter Seal Society of New Hampshire

555 Auburn Street
Manchester, NH 03103

Paul Boynton

257   New Hampshire Learning Disabilities Association

4 Sheffield Road   603-888-4694
Nashua, NH 03062

Kathy Reilly, President

New Jersey

258   Family Resource Associates, Inc.

Family Resource Associates, Inc.
35 Haddon Avenue   908-747-5310
Shrewsbury, NJ 07702

Private, non-profit agency servicing children with disabilities and their families. Sibling support services are provided via newsletters and sibling groups.

259   New Jersey Branch - the Orton Dyslexia Society

3297 Route 66   908-922-2126
Neptune, NJ 07753

Nancy Hennessy, President

260   New Jersey Learning Disabilities Association

305 North Lancaster Avenue   609-823-5608
Margate, NJ 08402

Ronee Groff, President

261 Northeast Disability and Business Technical Assistance Center

354 South Broad Street 609-392-4004
Trenton, NJ 08608

Provides information, training and technical assistance to employers, people with disabilities and other entities with responsibilities under the ADA. These centers act as a one-stop central source of information, direct technical assistance, training and referral on ADA issues in employment, public accommodations, public services and communications.

262 Recording for the Blind - Princeton

Western Psychological Services Corporation
36-A Hibben Road 213-478-2061
Princeton, NJ 08540

Offers information on recordings of books on audio cassette and computer disc.

New Mexico

263 New Mexico Learning Disabilities Association

55301 Camino Arbustos 505-294-0268
Albuquerque, NM 87111

Cindy Soo Hoo, President

264 Southwest Branch - the Orton Dyslexia Society

1331 Park Avenue SW #307 505-255-8234
Albuquerque, NM 87102

Robert Wengrod, President

New York

265 Branch Council Chair of the Orton Dyslexia Society

301 East 48th #15E
New York, NY 10017

Dr. Stanley Antonoff

266 Buffalo Branch - the Orton Dyslexia Society

1054 Colvin Blvd. 716-839-2918
Kenmore, NY 14223

Linda Clark, President

267 New York ALD

1605 Genesee Street 315-797-1253
Utica, NY 13502

Lynn Altamura, President

268 The New York Branch of the Orton Dyslexia Society, Inc.

71 West 23rd Street, Ste. 1500 212-691-1930
New York, NY 10010

Iris Spano, Executive Admin.

Provides professional courses and workhops, parent programs, adult dyslexic workshops, a referral service and dispenses information on dyslexia.

269 New York Easter Seal Society

845 Central Avenue
Albany, NY 12206

Nikki Vulgaris, Director

270 Parent Network Center

1443 Main Street 716-885-1004
Buffalo, NY 14209 800-724-7408

Joan Watkins, Executive Director

Views parents as full partners in the educational process and a significant source of support and assistance to each other. These programs provide training and information to parents to enable such individuals to participate more effectively with professionals in meeting the educational needs of disabled children, and ongoing needs as they "age out" of mandated services and require independent help to live inclusive lives and experience full citizenship.

271 Recording for the Blind - New York

Western Psychological Services Corporation
545 5th Avenue, Ste. 204 213-478-2061
New York, NY 10017

Provides recordings of textbooks and other educational materials on audio cassette and computer disc.

272 Suffolk Branch - the Orton Dyslexia Society

23 Meadowbrook Road 516-271-2202
Syosset, NY 11791

Mary Jane Tamulinas, President

North Carolina

273 North Carolina Branch - the Orton Dyslexia Society

3229 Debbie Drive   704-697-6761
Hendersonville, NC 28739

Jo Ann Crawford, President

274 North Carolina Learning Disabilities Association

P.O. Box 26053   919-715-0543
Raliegh, NC 26053

Arlene Stewart, Transition Project

North Dakota

275 North Dakota Learning Disabilities Association

1527 Northview Lane   701-258-2747
Bismarck, ND 58501

Jane Greer, President

Ohio

276 Central Ohio Branch - the Orton Dyslexia Society

Marburn Academy
1860 Walden Drive   614-898-2538
Columbus, OH 43229

Earl Oremus, President

277 Northern Ohio Branch - the Orton Dyslexia Society

29060 Naylor Drive   216-349-3430
Solon, OH 44139

Ellen Brick, President

278 Ohio Learning Disabilities Association

6610 Masefield Street   614-593-2043
Worthington, OH 43085

Rose Rossiter, President

279 Ohio Valley Branch - the Orton Dyslexia Society

7700 Asbury Hills Drive   513-723-0891
Cincinnati, OH 45255

Diana L. Sauter, President

280 Youngstown Easter Seal Society

299 Edwards Street   216-743-1168
Youngstown, OH 44502   FAX 216-743-1616

Andrew Douglas, Director
Occupational, physical and speech therapy available.

Oklahoma

281 Oklahoma Branch - the Orton Dyslexia Society

2538 NW 19th Street   405-943-7348
Oklahoma City, OK 73107

Sherrie Grunow, President

282 Oklahoma Learning Disabilities Association

711 Timberridge   918-225-1882
Cushing, OK 74023

Debra Murphy, President

Oregon

283 Eugene Easter Seal Service Center

3575 Donald Street
Eugene, OR 97405

284 Oregon Branch - the Orton Dyslexia Society

3035 SE Martins Street   503-774-4995
Portalnd, OR 97202

Dorothy B. Whitehead, President

Pennsylvania

285 Easter Seal Society of Beaver County

Dutch Ridge Road
Beaver, PA 15009

286 Easter Seal Society of Hazelton Area

301 Rocky Road & Poplar Street
Hazelton, PA 18201

Mary Lou Steppling

287   Easter Seal Society of Huntingdon County

307 10th Street   814-643-5724
Huntington, PA 16652

Kathryn Long, Executive Director

Speech evaluation and therapy, hearing screenings, family support services, advocacy, equipment loans and various newsletters available on related topics.

288   Fayette County Easter Seal Society

141 Oakland Avenue   412-437-4047
Uniontown, PA 15401

Alice G. Young, President, CEO

Speech, language and learning therapies and evaluations available for people with learning disabilities of all ages. Licensed pre-schoool on the premises with occupational and physical therapies provided.

289   Pennsylvania Easter Seal Society

940 West Chestnut Street
Washington, PA 15301

290   Pennsylvania Learning Disabilities Association

214 West Spruce Street   814-827-1978
Titusville, PA 16354

Jackie Thompson, President

291   Philadelphia Branch - the Orton Dyslexia Society

P.O. Box 251   215-527-1548
Bryn Mawr, PA 19010

Anne H. Van Arkel, Co-President
Jean Bay, Co-President

292   Recording for the Blind - Philadelphia

Western Psychological Services Corporation
3550 Market Street, Ste. 201   213-478-2061
Philadelphia, PA 19104

Offers information on recordings of books on audio cassette and computer disc.

293   University of Pennsylvania National Center for Adult Literacy

700 Walnut Street   215-898-1925
Philadelphia, PA 19104

The Center strives to enhance the knowledge based on adult literacy and improve the quality of research and developments in the field.

Rhode Island

294   Rhode Island Learning Disabilities Association

103 Harris Avenue   401-461-0820
Johnston, RI 02919

Norma Veresko, President

South Carolina

295   South Carolina Branch - the Orton Dyslexia Society

Department of Education
The Citadel   803-577-7485
Charleston, SC 29409

Maureen Laundry, Contact
Col. Gordon Wallace, President

296   South Carolina Learning Disabilities Association

103 Essex Court   803-229-8382
Greenwood, SC 29649

Sheila Marino, President

South Dakota

297   South Dakota Learning Disabilities Association

4022 Helen Sourt   605-342-4320
Rapid City, SD 57701

Dixie Davis, President

Tennessee

298   East Tennessee Beanch - the Orton Dyslexia Society

P.O. Box 3503 CRS   615-928-7477
Johnson City, TN 37602

Claire Oldham, President

299   Tennessee Learning Disabilities Association

P.O. Box 114   901-323-1430
Pocahontas, TN 38061

William Byrne

300 Tennessee Unit of Recording for the Blind

Recording for the Blind
205 Badger Road
Oak Ridge, TN 37830
615-482-3496

Peggy Meier, Executive Director
Carol Plasil, Development Spec.

Part of the national, non-profit organization which records educational and career-related materials for print impaired students and professionals. The special focus is educational books. Blind and other print impaired students at every level, from elementary through graduate school, depend on RFB tapes for the texts they need.

301 West/Middle Tennessee Branch - the Orton Dyslexia Society

2679 Kingham
Memphis, TN 38119
901-754-1441

Rosemary Williams, President

Texas

302 Austin Texas Branch the Orton Dyslexia Society

3105 Mistywood Circle
Austin, TX 78746
512-452-7658

Gayle Anglin, President

303 Capital Area Easter Seal Society and Rehabilitation Center

919 West 28-1/2 Street
Austin, TX 78705
512-478-2581
800-492-5555
FAX 512-476-1638

Dr. Susan Bucklund, President

Testing, evaluations and individual consultation for people with learning disabilities of all ages.

304 Dallas Branch - the Orton Dyslexia Society

Southern Methodist University
SMU Box 382
Dallas, TX 75275
214-768-7323

Jamie Williams, President

305 Easter Seal Society of the Permian

620 North Allgheny
Odessa, TX 79761

306 Easter Seal Trinity Center

5701 Maple Avenue
Dallas, TX 75235

307 Houston Branch - the Orton Dyslexia Society

5434 Darnell
Houston, TX 77096
713-529-1975

Suzanne Carreker, President

308 Learning Disabilities Association of Texas

1011 West 31st Street
Austin, TX 78705
512-458-8234
FAX 512-458-3826

Ann Robinson, State Coordinator

State affiliate of the national learning Disabilities Association. Provides information, referral to services and support to those with learning disabilities.

309 North Texas Easter Seal Rehabilitation

1005 Midwestern Parkway East
Wichita Falls, TX 76302

Thomas King

310 Recording for the Blind - Austin

Western Psychological Services Corporation
404 West 30th Street
Austin, TX 78705
213-478-2061

Offers information on recordings of books on audio cassette and computer disc.

311 Southwest Disability and Business Technical Assistance Center

2323 S. Shepherdblvd., Ste. 1000
Houston, TX 77019
713-520-0232

Provides information, training and technical assistance to employers, people with disabilities and other entities with responsibilities under the ADA. These centers act as a one-stop central source of information, direct technical assistance, training and referral on ADA issues in employment, public accommodations, public services and communications.

312 UAP of Texas

The University of Texas At Austin
Department Of Special Education
Austin, TX 78712
512-471-7621

Utah

313 Utah Learning Disabilities Association

10715 South 1300 West   801-254-3929
South Jordan, UT 84065

Bonnie Hussey, President

Vermont

314 New England Branch - the Orton Dyslexia Society

Pineridge School
1075 Williston Road   802-434-2161
Williston, VT 05495

Jean Foss, President

315 Vermont Learning Disabilities Association

P.O. Box 1041   802-362-3127
Manchester Center, VT 05255

Christina Thurston, President

Virginia

316 Mid-Atlantic Disability and Business Technical Assistance Center

2111 Wilson Blvd., Ste. 400   703-525-3268
Arlington, VA 22201

Provides information, training and technical assistance to employers, people with disabilities and other entities with responsibilities under the ADA. These centers act as a one-stop central source of information, direct technical assistance, training and referral on ADA issues in employment, public accommodations, public services and communications.

317 Parent Educational Advocacy Training Center

228 South Pitt Street, Rm. 300   703-836-2953
Alexandria, VA 22314   800-869-6782

Deidre Hayden, Executive Directo

Views parents as full partners in the educational process and a significant source of support and assistance to each other. The parent training and information center serving Virginia and is funded by the Office of Special education Programs, US Department of Education. The Center provides training and information to parents to enable them to participate more effectively with professionals in meeting the educational needs of children with dsiabilities.

318 Recording for the Blind - Virginia

Western Psychological Services Corporation
1021 Millmont Street   213-478-2061
Charlottesville, VA 22901

Offers information on recordings of books on audio cassette and computer disc.

319 Virginia Branch - the Orton Dyslexia Society

P.O. Box 5362   804-371-7572
Richmond, VA 23220

Harley Tomey, President

320 Virginia Learning Disabilities Association

505 John Street   804-798-3200
Ashland, VA 23005

Tom Bass, President

Washington

321 Northwest Disability and Business Technical Assistance Center

605 Woodview Drive   206-438-3168
Lacey, WA 98503

Provides information, training and technical assistance to employers, people with disabilities and other entities with responsibilities under the ADA. These centers act as a one-stop central source of information, direct technical assistance, training and referral on ADA issues in employment, public accommodations, public services and communications.

322 Puget Sound Branch - the Orton Dyslexia Society

25430 127th Avenue SE   206-382-1020
Kent, WA 98031

Ken Heikkila, President

323 Washington Learning Disabilities Association

U.S. West Cellular
3350 161st Avenue SE, Box 7329   206-562-5760
Bellevue, WA 98008

Sylvia Bushnell, President

324 Washington PAVE - Parent Training Project

6316 South 12th   206-565-2266
Tacoma, WA 98265   800-5-PARENT

Exists to help parents understand their child's school program and to help them become their child's best advocate. The Parent Resource Coordinators on staff, all of whom are parents of children with disabilities, help other parents learn about the rights of children with special learning needs.

West Virginia

325 Job Accommodation Network

P.O. Box 6123, 809 Allen Hall 800-526-7234
Morgantown, WV 26506

Free consultant service with professional human factors counselors. This service provides information and advice to employers and people with disabilities on custom job and worksite accommodations. Performs individualized searches for workplace accommodations, based on the job's functional requirements, the functional limitations of individual, environmental factors and other pertinent information.

326 Project G.L.U.E.

Children's Therapy Clinic
2345 Chesterfield Avenue 304-342-6501
Charleston, WV 25304

327 West Virginia Learning Disabilities Association

24 Heather Drive 304-599-7922
Morgantown, WV 26505

Barbara O'Donnell, President

Wisconsin

328 Easter Seal Society of Milwaukee

3090 North 53rd Street 414-449-4444
Milwaukee, WI 53210 FAX 414-449-4447

Suericia Wells, Director

Three programs are provided: The Child Development Center, which provides educational, therapeutic and social services to disabled children from birth to age 3; The recreation Program, which offers social and recreational activities to disabled adults; and The Equipment Loan Program.

329 Wisconsin Branch - the Orton Dyslexia Society

7915 Hillcrest Drive 414-258-2133
Wauwatosa, WI 53213

Janet Lauerman, President

330 Wisconsin Learning Disabilities Association

1821 Eagle Drive 414-727-4636
Neenah, WI 54956

Pat Hollenberg, President

331 Administration for Children, Youth and Families

330 C Street SW　　　　　　202-205-8347
Washington, DC 20201　　　　FAX 202-205-9721

Joseph Mottola, Acting Deputy Comm.

Programs under the Administration include the Children's Bureau, Headstart, The National Center on Child Abuse and Neglect, and The Family Youth Services Bureau.

332 Civil Rights Office, U.S. Department of Education

U.S. Department of Education
400 Maryland Avenue SW　　　202-732-1213
Washington, DC 20202

Enforces Section 504 provisions that prohibit discrimination on the basis of disability in programs and activities funded by the Department of Education. Investigates complaints and provides technical assistance to individuals and entities with rights and responsibilities under Section 504.

333 Council of State Administrators of Vocational Rehabilitation

1055 Thomas Jefferson St. NW,　202-638-4634
#401
Washington, DC 20007

Composed of the chief administrators of rehabilitation agencies in the States, the District of Columbia and the United States territories. In addition to providing a forum for discussion on relevant issues to its member administrators, the council serves as an advisory body to the Rehabilitation Services Administration.

334 Department of Labor, U.S. Employment Service

Employment and Training Administration
200 Constitution Avenue NW　　202-535-0189
Washington, DC 20210

Through more than 1,700 state and local offices nationwide, provides employment services to job seekers, including employability assessments, job counseling, occupational training referral, job placement, and trained specialists to work with the specific needs of job-seekers with disabilities.

335 Employment Standards Administration

Department of Labor
200 Constitution Avenue NW　　202-523-6666
Washington, DC 20210

Develops policy and implements legislation for all workers in the Nation.

336 Federal Information Service

800-422-2776

Document retrieval, federal information and court cases obtained through this agency.

337 Office of Civil Rights, U.S. Department of Education

U.S. Department of Education
400 Maryland Avenue SW　　　202-732-1213
Washington, DC 20202

Responsible for investigating discrimination on the basis of race, color, national origin, sex, and age in programs and activities that receive Federal financial assistance from the Department of Education.

338 Office of Civil Rights/U.S. Department of Health and Human Services

U.S. Department of Health & Human Services
Room 5410, Cohen Bldg.　　　202-619-0403
Washington, DC 20201

Responsible for investigating discrimination on the basis of race, color, national origin and religion in programs receiving financial assistance from the U.S. Department of Health and Human Services.

339 Office of Federal Contract Compliance Programs, US Department of Labor

200 Constitution Avenue NW　　202-523-9501
Washington, DC 20210

Enforces Section 503 which prohibits discrimination on the basis of disability and required federal contractors and sub-contractors with contracts of $2,500 or more to take affirmative action to employ and advance individuals with disabilities. Investigates complaints and provides technical assistance to individuals with rights and responsibilities under the Act.

340 Office of Special Education Programs, U.S. Department of Education

U.S. Department of Education
330 C Street SW　　　　　　202-732-1241
Washington, DC 20202

Enforces the Individuals with Disabilities Education Act of 1990 which gives funds to state and local school systems to provide special education services to children adn youth with disabilities, and for the removal of architectural barriers.

341 Office of Vocational Rehabilitation

Department of Vocational Rehabilitation
1323 Forbes Avenue　　　　　412-471-2600
Pittsburgh, PA 15219

A federal agency that helps disabled persons prepare for and keep a job.

342 The President's Committee on Employment of People with Disabilities

1331 F Street NW   202-376-6200
Washington, DC 20004

Provides information and advice on employment of people with disabilities. Conducts training conferences on ADA, and an annual meeting which offers training opportunities on many aspects of employing people with disabilities.

343 Project Head Start

U.S. Department of Health & Human Services
P.O. Box 1182   202-245-0562
Washington, DC 20013

Local head start programs are the main source of information about specific services and eligibility.

344 Protection and Advocacy for Individual Rights (PAIR)

U.S. Department of Education
330 C Street SW
Washington, DC 20202

Program established by the Rehabilitation Act of 1973 to protect the rights of individuals with severe disabilities receiving services from federally-funded independent living centers who are not eligible for services provided by other protection and advocacy programs, and whose request for services cannot be addressed by a Client Assistance Program.

345 Protection and Advocacy for Persons with Developmental Disabilities

U.S. Department of Health and Human Services
200 Independence Ave SW   202-245-2890
Washington, DC 20201

Protects the rights of individuals with developmental disabilities under federal and state statutes. Provides legal, administrative and other appropriate remedies to individual problems, including those involving employment discrimination and accessibility issues.

346 Region I: Office for Civil Rights US Department of Education

U.S. Department of Education
P.O. And Courthouse, Room 222   617-223-9662
Boston, MA 02109

These regional offices of agencies enforce laws prohibiting employment discrimination on the basis of disability.

347 Region I: US Department of Health & Human Services, Office for Civil Rights

U.S. Department of Health & Human Services
JFK Federal Bldg., Rm. 1203A   617-565-1340
Boston, MA 02203

These regional offices of agencies enforce laws prohibiting employment discrimination on the basis of disability.

348 Region I: US Department of Labor, Office of Federal Contract Compliance

U.S. Department of Labor
One Congress Street, 11th Floor   617-565-2055
Boston, MA 02114

These regional offices of agencies enforce laws prohibiting employment discrimination on the basis of disability.

349 Region I: US Small Business Administration

155 Federal Street, 9th Floor   617-451-2023
Boston, MA 02110

These regional offices of agencies enforce laws prohibiting employment discrimination on the basis of disability.

350 Region II: US Department of Education, Office for Civil Rights

U.S. Department of Education
26 Federal Plaza, 33rd Floor   212-264-4633
New York, NY 10278

These regional offices of agencies enforce laws prohibiting employment discrimination on the basis of disability.

351 Region II: US Department of Health and Human Services, Civil Rights

U.S. Department of Health & Human Services
26 Federal Plaza, Ste. 3312   212-264-3313
New York, NY 10278

These regional offices of agencies enforce laws prohibiting employment discrimination on the basis of disability.

352 Region II: US Department of Labor, Office of Federal Contract Compliance

U.S. Department of Labor
201 Varick Street, Rm. 750   212-337-2007
New York, NY 10014

These regional offices of agencies enforce laws prohibiting employment discrimination on the basis of disability.

353 Region II: US Small Business Administration

26 Federal Plaza, Rm. 31-08   212-264-7772
New York, NY 10278

These regional offices of agencies enforce laws prohibiting employment discrimination on the basis of disability.

354 Region III: US Department of Education, Office of Civil Rights

U.S. Department of Education
3535 Market Street, Rm. 6300   215-596-6791
Philadelphia, PA 19104

These regional offices of agencies enforce laws prohibiting employment discrimination on the basis of disability.

355 Region III: US Department of Health and Human Services, Civil Rights Office

U.S. Department of Health & Human Services
3535 Market Street, Rm. 6350   215-596-5831
Philadelphia, PA 19101

These regional offices of agencies enforce laws prohibiting employment discrimination on the basis of disability.

356 Region III: US Department of Labor, Office of Federal Contract Compliance

Gateway Building
3535 Market Street, Rm. 15340   215-596-6168
Philadelphia, PA 19104

These regional offices of agencies enforce laws prohibiting employment discrimination on the basis of disability.

357 Region III: US Small Business Administration

475 Allendale Road, Ste. 201   215-962-3700
King Of Prussia, PA 19406

These regional offices of agencies enforce laws prohibiting employment discrimination on the basis of disability.

358 Region IV: US Department of Education, Office for Civil Rights

U.S. Department of Education
101 Marietta Tower, 27th Floor   404-331-2806
Atlanta, GA 30301

These regional offices of agencies enforce laws prohibiting employment discrimination on the basis of disability.

359 Region IV: US Department of Health and Human Services, Civil Rights Office

U.S. Department of Health & Human Services
101 Marietta Tower, Rm. 1502   404-331-2779
Atlanta, GA 30323

These regional offices of agencies enforce laws prohibiting employment discrimination on the basis of disability.

360 Region IV: US Department of Labor, Office of Federal Contract Compliance

U.S. Department of Labor
1375 Peachtree Street NE, Ste. 678   404-347-3200
Atlanta, GA 30367

These regional offices of agencies enforce laws prohibiting employment discrimination on the basis of disability.

361 Region IV: US Small Business Administration

1375 Peachtree Street NE, 5th Floor   404-347-2797
Atlanta, GA 30367

These regional offices of agencies enforce laws prohibiting employment discrimination on the basis of disability.

362 Region IX: US Department of Education, Office of Civil Rights

U.S. Department of Education
50 United Nations Plaza   415-556-7000
San Francisco, CA 94102

These regional offices of agencies enforce laws prohibiting employment discrimination on the basis of disability.

363 Region IX: US Department of Health and Human Services, Civil Rights Office

U.S. Department of Health & Human Services
50 United Nations Plaza   415-556-8586
San Francisco, CA 94102

These regional offices of agencies enforce laws prohibiting employment discrimination on the basis of disability.

364 Region IX: US Department of Labor, Office of Federal Contract Compliance

U.S. Department of Labor
71 Stevenson Street, Ste. 1700   415-744-6986
San Francisco, CA 94105

These regional offices of agencies enforce laws prohibiting employment discrimination on the basis of disability.

365 Region IX: US Small Business Administration

71 Stevenson Street, 20th Floor   415-744-6402
San Francisco, CA 94105

These regional offices of agencies enforce laws prohibiting employment discrimination on the basis of disability.

366 Region V: US Department of Education, Office for Civil Rights

U.S. Department of Education
401 South State Street, Rm. 700-C   312-353-2520
Chicago, IL 60605

These regional offices of agencies enforce laws prohibiting employment discrimination on the basis of disability.

367 Region V: US Department of Health and Human Services, Civil Rights Office

U.S. Department of Health & Human Services
105 West Adams, 16th Floor   312-886-2359
Chicago, IL 60603

These regional offices of agencies enforce laws prohibiting employment discrimination on the basis of disability.

368 Region V: US Department of Labor, Office of Federal Contract Compliance

U.S. Department of Labor
230 S. Dearborn St., Rm. 570   312-353-0335
Chicago, IL 60604

These regional offices of agencies enforce laws prohibiting employment discrimination on the basis of disability.

369 Region V: US Small Business Administration

300 S. Riverside Plaza, Ste. 1975 S   312-353-0359
Chicago, IL 60606

These regional offices of agencies enforce laws prohibiting employment discrimination on the basis of disability.

370 Region VI: US Department of Education, Office of Civil Rights

U.S. Department of Education
1200 Main Tower Bldg., Ste. 2260   214-767-3936
Dallas, TX 75202

These regional offices of agencies enforce laws prohibiting employment discrimination on the basis of disability.

371 Region VI: US Department of Health and Human Services, Civil Rights Office

U.S. Department of Health & Human Services
1200 Main Tower Bldg., Rm. 1360   214-767-4056
Dallas, TX 75202

These regional offices of agencies enforce laws prohibiting employment discrimination on the basis of disability.

372 Region VI: US Department of Labor, Office of Federal Contract Compliance

U.S. Department of Labor
525 South Griffin Street, Rm. 840   214-767-4771
Dallas, TX 75202

These regional offices of agencies enforce laws prohibiting employment discrimination on the basis of disability.

373 Region VI: US Small Business Administration

8625 King George Drive, Bldg. C   214-767-7643
Dallas, TX 75235

These regional offices of agencies enforce laws prohibiting employment discrimination on the basis of disability.

374 Region VII: US Department of Education, Office of Civil Rights

U.S. Department of Education
10220 N. Executive Hills Blvd.   816-891-8026
Kansas City, MO 64153

These regional offices of agencies enforce laws prohibiting employment discrimination on the basis of disability.

375 Region VII: US Department of Health and Human Services, Civil Rights Office

U.S. Department of Health & Human Services
601 East 12th Street, Rm. 248   816-426-7277
Kansas City, MO 64106

These regional offices of agencies enforce laws prohibiting employment discrimination on the basis of disability.

376 Region VII: US Department of Labor, Office of Federal Contract Compliance

U.S. Department of Labor
911 Walnut Streeet, Rm. 2011   816-426-5384
Kansas City, MO 64106

These regional offices of agencies enforce laws prohibiting employment discrimination on the basis of disability.

377   Region VII: US Small Business Administration

911 Walnut Street, 13th Floor   816-426-3608
Kansas City, MO 64106

These regional offices of agencies enforce laws prohibiting employment discrimination on the basis of disability.

378   Region VIII: US Department of Education, Office of Civil Rights

U.S. Department of Education
1244 Speer Blvd., Ste. 310   303-844-5695
Denvewr, CO 80204

These regional offices of agencies enforce laws prohibiting employment discrimination on the basis of disability.

379   Region VIII: US Department of Health and Human Services, Civil Rights Office

U.S. Department of Health & Human Services
1961 Stout Street, Rm. 1185   303-844-4774
Denver, CO 80294

These regional offices of agencies enforce laws prohibiting employment discrimination on the basis of disability.

380   Region VIII: US Department of Labor, Office of Federal Contract Comp.

U.S. Department of Labor
1961 Stout Street, Rm. 1480   303-844-5011
Denver, CO 80294

These regional offices of agencies enforce laws prohibiting employment discrimination on the basis of disability.

381   Region VIII: US Small Business Administration

999 18th Street, Ste. 701   303-294-7001
Denver, CO 80202

These regional offices of agencies enforce laws prohibiting employment discrimination on the basis of disability.

382   Region X: US Department of Education, Office for Civil Rights

U.S. Department of Education
915 2nd Avenue, Rm. 3310   206-553-1636
Seattle, WA 98174

These regional offices of agencies enforce laws prohibiting employment discrimination on the basis of disability.

383   Region X: US Department of Health and Human Services, Civil Rights Office

U.S. Department of Health & Human Services
2201 Sixth Ave., Mail-Stop RX-11   206-553-7483
Seattle, WA 98121

These regional offices of agencies enforce laws prohibiting employment discrimination on the basis of disability.

384   Region X: US Department of Labor, Office of Federal Contract Compliance

U.S. Department of Labor
1111 Third Avenue, Ste. 610   206-442-4508
Seattle, WA 98101

These regional offices of agencies enforce laws prohibiting employment discrimination on the basis of disability.

385   Region X: US Small Business Administration

2615 4th Avenue, Room 440   206-553-5676
Seattle, WA 98121

These regional offices of agencies enforce laws prohibiting employment discrimination on the basis of disability.

386   Rehabilitation Services Administration State Vocational Program

U.S. Department of Education
330 C Street SW   202-732-1282
Washington, DC 20202

State and local vocational rehabilitation agencies provide comprehensive services of rehabilitation, training and job-related assistance to people with disabilities and assists employers in recruiting, training, placing, accommodating and meeting other employment-related needs of people with disabilities.

387   Social Security Administration

U.S. Department of Health & Human Services
          800-234-5772

Local offices of SSA across the country have pamphlets about benefits relating to disability.

388   U.S. Bureau of the Census

Customer Services   301-763-4100
Washington, DC 20233

The principal statistical agency of the Federal Government. It publishes data on persons with disabilities, as well as other demographic data derived from censuses and surveys.

389   U.S. Department of Commerce, National Technical Information Service

U.S. Department of Commerce
5285 Port Royal Road   703-487-4650
Springfield, VA 22161

Maintains worldwide database or research, development and engineering reports on a range of topics, including architectural barrier removal, employing individuals with disabilities, alternative testing formats, job accommodations, school-to-work transition for students with disabilities, rehabilitation engineering, disability law and transportation.

390   U.S. Department of Education, Office of Program Operations

U.S. Department of Education
330 C Street SW   202-732-1406
Washington, DC 20202

Programs in each state provide information and assistance to individuals seeking or receiving services under the Rehabilitation Act of 1973.

391   U.S. Department of Health and Human Services, Developmental Disability

U.S. Department of Health & Human Services
200 Independence Ave SW, Rm 349-F   202-245-2890
Washington, DC 20201

Councils in each state provide training and technical assistance to local and state agencies, employers and the public improving services to people with developmental disabilities.

392   U.S. Department of Justice, Civil Rights Division

Coordination and Review Section
P.O. Box 66118   202-307-2222
Washington, DC 20035

Coordinates the reinforcement of Section 504 which prohibits discrimination on the basis of disability in all federally conducted programs and activities, and in the programs and activities that receive federal financial assistance.

393   U.S. Equal Employment Opportunity Commission

1801 L Street NW   202-663-4515
Washington, DC 20507

Enforces Section 501 which prohibits discrimination on the basis oif disability in Federal employment, and requires that all Federal agencies establish and implement affirmative action programs for hiring, placing and advancing individuals with disabilities. Also oversees federal sector equal employment opportunity complaint processing system.

394   U.S. Small Business Administration, Office of Civil Rights Compliance

409 Third St., SW   202-205-6751
Washington, DC 20416

Enforces Section 504 provisions that prohibit discrimination on the basis of disability by recipients of financial assistance from the Small Business Administration.

395   Youth Services Administration

U.S. Department of Education
717 14th Street NW   202-727-9098
Washington, DC 20005   FAX 202-727-9534

Alabama

396   Alabama Department of Economic and Community Affairs

P.O. Box 250347   205-284-8700
Montgomery, AL 36125

397   Alabama Department of Education

P.O. Box 11586   205-281-8780
Montgomery, AL 36111

398   Alabama Department of Industrial Relations

649 Monroe Street, Rm. 204   205-242-8003
Montgomery, AL 36130

399   Alabama Rehabilitation Services

P.O. Box 11586   205-281-8780
Montgomery, AL 36111

Alaska

400   Alaska Center for Adaptive Technology

700 Katlian Avenue, Ste. B   907-747-6962
Sitka, AK 99835   800-478-6962

401   Alaska Department of Community and Regional Affairs

333 West 4th Avenue, Ste. 220   907-269-4500
Anchorage, AK 99501

402 Alaska Department of Education

801 West 10th Street, Ste. 200   907-465-2900
Juneau, AK 99801

Vince Barry, Director, EPS

403 Alaska Department of Labor Employment Security Division

Department of Labor
P.O. Box 25509   907-465-2712
Juneau, AK 99802

404 Alaska Vocational Rehabilitation

801 West 10th Street, Ste. 200   907-465-2814
Juneau, AK 99801

405 Assistive Technology of Alaska

Division of Vocational Rehabilitation
400 D Street, Ste. 230   907-274-0138
Anchorage, AK 99501   800-770-0138
                                    FAX 907-274-0516

Joyce Palmer, Program Manager
Information and referral to Alaska residents with disabilities about adaptive aids and equipment that will better their lives.

Arizona

406 Arizona Department of Economic Security

Rehabilitation Services Administration
1789 West Jefferson, 271 NW Wing   602-542-3332
Phoenix, AZ 85007

407 Arizona Department of Education

1535 West Jefferson   602-255-3183
Phoenix, AZ 85007

Diane Peterson, Superintendent

408 Arizona Governor's Committee on Employment of the Handicapped

Samaritan Rehabilitation Institute
1812 East Willette   602-239-4762
Phoenix, AZ 85006

409 Governor's Council on Developmental Disabilities of Arizona

1717 West Jefferson, Room 112   602-542-4049
Phoenix, AZ 85007

Arkansas

410 Arkansas Assistive Technology Projects

Increasing Capabilities Access Network
2201 Brookwood #117   501-666-8868
Little Rock, AR 722-2

A consumer responsive statewide program promoting assistive technology devices and sources for persons of all ages with disabilities.

411 Arkansas Department of Human Services Division of Rehabilitation Services

Department of Human Services
P.O. Box 3781   501-682-6708
Little Rock, AR 72203

412 Arkansas Department of Special Education

54 Capitol Mall   501-371-2161
Little Rock, AR 72201

Dr. Diane Sydoriak, Associate Director

413 Arkansas Employment Security Department

P.O. Box 2981   501-682-2121
Little Rock, AR 72203

California

414 California Department of Fair Employment and Housing

2014 T Street, Ste. 210   916-739-4616
Sacramento, CA 95814

415 California Department of Rehabilitation

830 K Street Mall   916-445-3971
Sacramento, CA 95814

416 California Department of Special Education

721 Capitol Mall   916-323-4768
Sacramento, CA 94244

417 California Disability Determination Services - Social Security

P.O. Box 60999   213-965-3008
Los Angeles, CA 90060

418 California Employment Development Department

P.O. Box 826880   916-654-8210
Sacramento, CA 94280

Colorado

419 Adaptive Technology Computerized Bulletin Board of Colorado

Rocky Mountain Resource and Training Institute
6355 Ward Road, Ste. 310   303-420-2942
Arvada, CO 80004   800-374-4245

Information is available via electronic modem on topics such as Colorado's Assistive Technology Project and The RMRTI's Resource Library.

420 Colorado Civil Rights Division

1560 Broadway, Ste. 1050   303-894-7805
Denver, CO 80202

421 Colorado Department of Education

201 East Colfax Avenue   303-866-6694
Denver, CO 80203

Buck Schrotberger, Senior Consultant

422 Colorado Department of Labor and Employment

600 Grant Street, Ste. 900   303-837-3801
Denver, CO 80203

423 Colorado Department of Social Services Rehabilitation Services

Department of Social Services
1575 Sherman Street, 4th Floor 303-866-5196
Denver, CO 80203

424 Colorado Governor's Job Training Office

720 South Colorado Blvd., Ste. 550 303-758-5020
Denver, CO 80222

425 Colorado's Assistive Technology Project

Rocky Mountain Resource and Training Institute
6355 Ward Road, Ste. 310   303-420-2942
Arvada, CO 80004   800-444-KNOW

Developing a state wide information and referral system focusing on devices, services and resources in the field of assistive technology. Maintains updated information about a variety of other state and national projects affecting people with disabilities.

Connecticut

426 Connecticut Department of Human Resources Board of Education

Department of Human Resources
170 Ridge Road   203-566-5800
Wethersfield, CT 06109

427 Connecticut Early Childhood Unit/Departmen Education

P.O. Box 2219   203-566-5658
Hartford, CT 06145

Kay Halverson, Coordinator
Offers programs for children, infants and toddlers with disabilities.

428 Connecticut Governor's Commitee on Employment of the Handicapped

Labor Department Building
200 Folly Brook Blvd.   203-566-1513
Wethersfield, CT 06109

429 Connecticut State Board of Education Division of Rehabilitation

10 Griffin Road North   203-289-2003
Windsor, CT 06095

430 Connecticut State Department of Education

Division of Rehabilitation Services
600 Asylum Avenue   203-566-3317
Hartford, CT 06105

Karen Palma-Halliday, Transition Director

431 Connecticut State Department of Human Resoruces

Bureau of Rehabilitation Services
1049 Asylum Avenue   203-566-3318
Hartford, CT 06105

432 Office of State Coordinator of Vocational Education for Disabled Students

Vocational Prgs. for the Disabled & Disadvantaged
P.O. Box 2219   203-638-4059
Hartford, CT 06145

433 Protection and Advocacy Agency

Office of P&A for Persons with Disabilities
60 B Weston Street   203-297-4300
Hartford, CT 06120   800-842-7303

Eliot Dober, Executive Director

434 State Agency for the Visually Impaired

Board of Education and Services for the Blind
170 Ridge Road   203-249-8525
Wethersfield, CT 06109

George Precourt, Executive Director

435 State Department of Education - Bureau of Special Education & Pupil Services

Department of Education
25 Industrial Park Road   203-638-4274
Middletown, CT 06457

Offers information on educational programs and services. The Complaint Resolution Process Office answers and processes parent complaints regarding procedural violations by local educational agencies and facilities. The Due Process Office is responsible for the management of special education and due process proceedings which are available to parents and school districts.

436 State Developmental Disabilities Planning Council

Developmental Disabilities Council
90 Pitkin Street   203-725-3829
East Hartford, CT 06108

Edward Preneta, Director

437 State Office of Protection and Advocacy Foer Persons with Disabilities

State Office of P&A
60B Weston Street   203-297-4300
Hartford, CT 06120   800-842-7303

Promotes and protects the rights of children and adults with disabilities through advocacy, outreach, education, and information.

438 State Vocational Rehabilitation Agency

Div. of Rehabilitation Services/Board of Education
10 Griffin Road North   203-298-2003
Windsor, CT 06095

Marilyn Campbell, Director

Delaware

439 Delaware Assistive Technology Initiative Applied Science & Engineering Labs

P.O. Box 269   301-651-6834
Wilmington, DE 19899

440 Delaware Department of Labor

Anti-Discrimination Section
820 North French Street, 6th Floor   302-577-3929
Wilmington, DE 19801

441 Delaware Department of Labor/ Division of Vocational Rehabilitation

Department of Labor
Elwyn Bldg, 4th Fl., 321 East 11th   302-577-2850
Wilmington, DE 19801

442 Delaware Division of Employment and Training

P.O. Box 9499   302-368-6810
Newark, DE 19714

District of Columbia

443 D.C. Department of Employment Services

500 C Street NW, Rm. 600   202-639-1000
Washington, DC 20001

444 D.C. Department of Human Services Rehabilitation Services Admin.

Commission on Social Services
605 G Street NW, Rm. 1101   202-727-3227
Washington, DC 20001

445 D.C. Division of Special Education

10th & H Streets NW   202-724-4018
Washington, DC 20001

Doris Woodson, Asst. Superintendent

446 D.C. Office of Human Rights

2000 14th Street NW, 3rd Floor   202-939-8780
Washington, DC 20009

Florida

447 Florida Commission on Human Relations

325 John Knox Road, Bldg. F   904-488-5291
Tallahassee, FL 32303

448 Florida Department of Education

Tallahassee, FL 32399

449 Florida Department of Labor and Employment Security

2012 Capital Circle, SE   904-488-4398
Tallahassee, FL 32399

450 Florida Division of Vocational Rehabilitation

Department of Labor & Employment Security
1709-A Mahan Drive   904-488-6210
Tallahassee, FL 32399

Georgia

451 Georgia Assistive Technological Programs

878 Peachtree Street NE, Rm. 172   404-894-7593
Atlanta, GA 30309

452 Georgia Department of Human Resources

Division of Rehabilitation Services
878 Peachtree Street NE, Rm. 706   404-894-6670
Atlanta, GA 30309

453 Georgia Department of Labor

148 International Blvd NE, Ste. 600   404-656-3011
Atlanta, GA 30303

454 Georgia Office of Fair Employment Practices

156 Trinity Avenue SW, Ste. 208   404-656-1736
Atlanta, GA 30303

455 Georgia State Department of Education

1970 Twin Towers East   404-656-6317
Atlanta, GA 30334

Hawaii

456 Aloha Special Technology Access Center

1750 Kalakaua Avenue #1008   808-955-4464
Honolulu, HI 96826

Ruth Akiona, Program Coordinator

A private, non-profit group of volunteers, parents of disabled children, adults with disabilities and professionals in the field of health and education. The aim of the center is to increase the awareness and use of computers by disabled people through a program of educational activities and events. This technology empowers people through communication, access to information and markets, and entry to new job opportunities.

457 Hawaii Civil Rights Commission

888 Miliani Street, 2nd Floor   808-548-7625
Honolulu, HI 96813

458 Hawaii Department of Education

4697 Kilauea Avenue   808-737-5694
Honolulu, HI 96816

Fay Ikei, District Specialist

459 Hawaii Department of Labor and Industrial Relations

830 Punchbowl Street, Rm. 320   808-586-8844
Honolulu, HI 96813

Idaho

460 Idaho Department of Employment

317 Main Street   208-334-6110
Boise, ID 83735

461 Idaho Division of Vocational Rehabilitation

Len B. Jordan Building, Room 150
650 West State Street   208-334-3390
Boise, ID 83720

462 Idaho Human Rights Commission

450 West State Street   208-334-2873
Boise, ID 83720

463 Idaho State Program for Technology-Related Assistance for the Disabled

University of Idaho
129 West Third Street
Moscow, ID 83843

Illinois

464 Board of Education of Chicago

1819 West Pershing Rd., 6th Floor   312-535-8000
Chicago, IL 60609

Ted Kimbrough, Superintendent

Offers instruction services, information services, curriculum information and government relations advocacy.

465 Illinois Affiliation of Private Schools for Exceptional Children

Lawrence Hall Youth Services
4833 North Francisco Avenue   312-769-3500
Chicago, IL 60625

Pamela Barnet

466 Illinois Department of Commerce and Community Affairs

JTPA Programs Division
620 East Adams, 6th Floor   217-785-6006
Springfield, IL 62701

467 Illinois Department of Employment Security

401 South State Street, Rm. 615   312-793-5700
Chicago, IL 60605

468 Illinois Department of Human Rights

100 W. Randolph, 10th Fl, Ste. 100   312-814-6245
Chicago, IL 60601

469 Illinois Department of Rehabilitation Services

P.O. Box 19429   217-782-2093
Springfield, IL 62794

470 Illinois State Board of Education

100 North First Street   217-782-6601
Springfield, IL 62777

471 Illinois Technology-Related Assistance Project for the Disabled

411 East Adams   217-522-7985
Springfield, IL 62701

Indiana

472 Indiana ATTAIN Project

Indiana Family and Social Services Administration
402 West Washington #W453   317-233-3394
Indianapolis, IN 46207

Iowa

473 Iowa Program for Assistive Technology

University Hospital School
Iowa City, IA 52242   319-353-6386

Kansas

474 Kansas Department of Human Resources

401 Topeka Blvd.   913-296-7474
Topeka, KS 66604

475 Kansas Department of Social and Rehabilitation Services

300 Southwest Oakley Street
Topeka, KS 66606

476 Kansas Division of Special Education

120 East Tenth Street   913-296-4945
Topeka, KS 66612

477 Kansas Human Rights Commission

900 Jackson Street   913-296-3206
Topeka, KS 66612

Kentucky

478 Kentucky Assistive Technology Service Network

427 Versailles Road   502-564-4665
Frankfort, KY 40601   800-327-5287

479 Kentucky Bureau of Education

Capital Plaza Towers   502-564-4970
Frankfort, KY 40601

480 Kentucky Department for Employment Services

275 East Main Street, 2nd West 502-564-5331
Frankfort, KY 40621

481 Kentucky Department of Vocational Rehabilitation

500 Mero St., Capitol Plaza Tower 502-564-4440
Frankfort, KY 40601

Louisiana

482 Louisiana Assistive Technology Projects

P.O. Box 3455 504-342-6804
Baton Rouge, LA 70821

483 Louisiana Department for Employment and Training

P.O. Box 94094 504-342-3011
Baton Rouge, LA 70804

484 Louisiana Department of Social Services Division of Rehabilitation Services

Department of Social Services
P.O. Box 94371
Baton Rouge, LA 70804 504-765-2310

Maine

485 Maine Bureau of Employment and Training Programs

Statehouse Station 55 207-289-3377
Augusta, ME 04333

486 Maine Department of Educational and Rehabilitation Services

State House Station #23 207-289-5811
Augusta, ME 04333

487 Maine Department of Human Services/ Bureau of Rehabilitation

Department of Human Services
35 Anthony Avenue 207-624-5300
Augusta, ME 04333

488 Maine Department of Labor

Bureau of Employment Security
20 Union Street 207-289-2411
Augusta, ME 04330

489 Maine Human Rights Commission

Statehouse Station 51 207-289-2326
Augusta, ME 04333

Maryland

490 Maryland Commission on Human Relations

20 East Franklin Street 301-333-5518
Baltimore, MD 21202

491 Maryland Department of Economic and Employment Development

Office of Employment Services
1100 North Eutaw Street, Rm. 600 410-333-5070
Baltimore, MD 21201

492 Maryland Division of Vocational Rehabilitation

Administrative Offices
2301 Argonne Drive 410-554-3000
Baltimore, MD 21218

493 Maryland State Department of Education

300 West Preston Street, Ste. 205 410-333-7251
Baltimore, MD 21201

494 Maryland Technology Assistance Program

300 West Lexington Street, Box 10 410-333-3098
Baltimore, MD 21201

Massachusetts

495 Massachusetts Assistive Technology Partnership

MATP Center
300 Longwood Avenue 617-735-7820
Boston, MA 02115

Provides information and referral on assistive technology products and services for all Massachusetts residents.

496 Massachusetts Commission Against Discrimination

One Ashburton Place, Rm. 601 617-727-3990
Boston, MA 02108

497 Massachusetts Department of Education

Beaman Street, Rte. 140 617-835-6266
West Boynton, MA 01583

498   Massachusetts Department of Employment and Training

19 Staniford Street, 3rd Floor   617-727-6600
Boston, MA 02114

499   Massachusetts Rehabilitation Commission

Fort Point Pl., 27-43 Wormwood St.   617-727-2172
Boston, MA 02210

500   Massachusetts Special Technology Access Center

12 Mudge Way 1-6   617-275-2446
Bedford, MA 01730

A public service group of the Boston Computer Society, MASTAC serves as a resource and activity care center for those interested in learning about the use of technology for indiviausl with special needs. The services include a software lending library of over 15,000 pieces, classes on using technology , a toy leanding library and a resource directory of other local services.

Michigan

---

501   Michigan Coaltion for Staff Development and School Improvement

P.O. Box 755   313-467-1564
Wayne, MI 48184

502   Michigan Department of Education Rehabilitation Services

P.O. Box 30010   517-373-3391
Lansing, MI 48909

503   Michigan Department of Labor

P.O. Box 30015   517-373-9600
Lansing, MI 48909

504   Michigan Employment Secutiry Commission

7310 Woodward Avenue   313-876-5500
Detroit, MI 48202

Minnesota

---

505   Minnesota Community Based Division of Jobs and Training

150 E. Kellogg   612-296-8004
St. Paul, MN 55101

506   Minnesota Department of Education

812 Capitol Square Building   612-296-4163
St. Paul, MN 55101

507   Minnesota Department of Human Rights

500 Bremer Tower, 5th Floor   612-296-5665
St. Paul, MN 55101

508   Minnesota Department of Jobs and Training

390 N. Roberts Street   612-296-3711
St. Paul, MN 55101

509   Minnesota STAR Program

300 Centennial Bldg., 58 Cedar St.   612-296-2771
St. Paul, MN 55155   800-331-3027
                                        FAX 612-297-7200

Susan Asplund, Program Specialist

Funded under PL 100-407 through NIDRR, provides the following: opportunities for public education through brochures and workshops; assistance for individuals of all ages with disabilities seeking funding for assistive technology devices and services; analyzes policies and makes recommendations for change; grants funds to organizations seeking to develop of expand technology-related programs; and, provides information, through Infotech 800 number on commercially available products for MN & Iowa.

Mississippi

---

510   Mississippi Department of Economic and Community Development

Employment Training Division
301 Pearl Street   601-949-2234
Jackson, MS 39203

511   Mississippi Department of Education

Sillers State Office Bldg.   601-359-3513
Jackson, MS 39205

512   Mississippi Department of Vocational Rehabilitation Services

P.O. Box 1698   601-354-6825
Jackson, MS 39215   800-443-1000

513   Mississippi Employment Security Commission

P.O. Box 1699   601-961-7400
Jackson, MS 39215

514 Mississippi Project START

Division of Rehabilitation Services
P.O. Box 1000   601-354-6891
Jackson, MS 39215

Missouri

515 Missouri Assistive Technology Project

University of Missouri - Kansas City
5100 Rockhill Road   816-235-5337
Kansas City, MO 64110

516 Missouri Commission on Human Rights

3315 West Truman Blvd.   314-444-7590
Jefferson City, MO 65102

517 Missouri Department of Economic Development

Division of Job Development and Training
221 Metro Drive   314-751-7796
Jefferson City, MO 65109

518 Missouri Department of Education

P.O. Box 480   314-751-4909
Jefferson City, MO 65102

519 Missouri Division of Employment Security

P.O. Box 59   314-751-2976
Jefferson City, MO 65104

520 Missouri State Department of Elementary and Secondary Education

Division of Vocational Rehabilitation
2401 East McCarty Street   314-751-3251
Jefferson City, MO 65101

Montana

521 Montana Assistive Technology Projects

111 Sanders   406-444-3889
Helena, MT 59604

William Lamb

A statewide program promoting assistive devices and services for perons of all ages with disabilities.

522 Montana Department of Educational Services

State Capitol, Room 106   406-444-4429
Helena, MT 59620

523 Montana Department of Labor & Industry

P.O. Box 1728   406-444-3555
Helena, MT 59624

524 Montana Department of Social and Rehabilitation Services

P.O. Box 4210, 111 Sanders   406-444-2590
Helena, MT 59604

Nebraska

525 Nebraska Assistive Technology Project

Department of Education
301 Centennial Mall South   402-471-0735
Lincoln, NE 68509

526 Nebraska Department of Education

P.O. Box 94987   402-471-2471
Lincoln, NE 68509

527 Nebraska Department of Labor

550 South 16th Street   402-471-3405
Lincoln, NE 68509

528 Nebraska Equal Opportunity Commission

P.O. Box 94934   402-471-2024
Lincoln, NE 68509

529 Nebraska State Department of Education/ Vocational Rehabilitation Services

Department of Education
301 Centennial Mall S., 6th Floor   402-471-3649
Lincoln, NE 68509

Nevada

530 Assistive Technology Project

Rehabilitation Division
505 East King Street, Rm. 502   702-687-4452
Carson City, NV 89710

531   Nevada Department of Education

400 West King Street   702-885-3140
Carson City, NV 89710

532   Nevada Department of Human Resources/ Rehabilitation Division

Department of Human Resources
505 East King Street, 5th Floor   702-687-4440
Carson City, NV 90710

533   Nevada Employment Security Department

500 East 3rd Street   702-687-4635
Carson City, NV 89713

534   Nevada Equal Rights Commission

1515 East Tropicana, Ste. 590   702-486-7161
Las Vegas, NV 89158

535   Nevada State Job Training Office

Capitol Complex, 400 West King   702-687-4310
Carson City, NV 89710

New Hampshire

---

536   New Hampshire Assistive Technology Projects

Department of Education
State Of New Hampshire   603-862-4320
Concord, NH 03824

Jan Nisbet
A statewide program promoting assistive technology for all persons with disabilities.

537   New Hampshire Commission for Human Rights

163 Loudon Road   603-271-2767
Concord, NH 03301

538   New Hampshire Department of Education

101 Pleasant Street   603-271-3741
Concord, NH 03301

539   New Hampshire Department of Employment Security

32 South Main Street   603-228-4000
Concord, NH 03301

540   New Hampshire Job Training Coordinating Council

64 Old Suncook Road   603-228-9500
Concord, NH 03301

541   New Hampshire State Department of Education/ Vocational Rehabilitation

Department of Education
78 Regional Drive, Bldg. #2   603-271-3471
Concord, NH 03301

New Jersey

---

542   New Jersey Department of Labor and Industry

Division of Vocational Rehabilitation Services
John Fitch Plaza, CN 398   609-292-5987
Trenton, NJ 08625

543   New Jersey Department of Law and Public Safety

New Jersey Division on Civil Rights
CN 089, 31 Clinton Street   201-648-2700
Newark, NJ 07102

544   New Jersey Division of Special Education

225 West State Street   609-292-0147
Trenton, NJ 08625

Jeffrey Osowski, Directyor

New Mexico

---

545   New Mexico Department of Labor

P.O. Box 1928   505-841-8409
Albuquerque, NM 87103

546   New Mexico Human Rights Commission

1596 Pacheo Street, Aspen Plaza   505-827-6838
Santa Fe, NM 87502

547   New Mexico State Department of Education

300 Don Gaspar Street   505-827-6541
Santa Fe, NM 87501

548 New Mexico State Department of Education/ Div. of Vocational Rehabilitation

Department of Education
604 West San Mateo   505-827-3511
Santa Fe, NM 87503

549 New Mexico Technology-Related Assistance Program

Department of Education
435 St. Michael Drive   505-827-3533
Santa Fe, NM 87505

New York

550 New York Assistive Technology Projects

One Empire State Plaza, 10th Floor   518-473-4129
Albany, NY 12223

Deborah Buck, Project Manager

A statewide program promoting assistive technology devices and services to persons of all ages with all disabilities.

551 New York State Department of Education

One Commerce Plaza, Room 1606   518-474-2714
Albany, NY 12234

Lawrence Gloeckler, Deputy Commissioner

552 New York State Department of Human Rights

55 West 125th Street, 13th Fl.   212-870-8566
New York, NY 10027

553 New York State Department of Labor

State Office Building Campus
Bldg. 12, Room 592   518-457-2270
Albany, NY 12240

554 New York State Office of Advocate for the Disabled

1 ESP 10th Floor   518-473-4129
Albany, NY 12223   800-522-4369
                         FAX 518-473-6005

Catherine Gilboe, Info/Referral Svcs.

Information and referral service to residents of NYS regarding issues related to disability.

555 New York State Office of Advocate for the Disabled TRIAD

1 Empire State Plaza, 10th Floor   518-473-4129
Albany, NY 12223

556 Organization to Assure Services for Exceptional Students

OASES
136-25 218th Street   718-525-3414
Springfield Gardens, NY 11413   FAX 718-525-0982

Thomas Darnowski, President

North Carolina

557 North Carolina Assistive Technology Project

1110 Navaho Drive, Ste. 101   919-850-2787
Raleigh, NC 27609

558 North Carolina Department of Economic and Community Development

Division of Employment and Training
111 Seaboard Avenue   919-733-6383
Raleigh, NC 27604

559 North Carolina Department of Education

116 West Edenton Street   919-733-3921
Raleigh, NC 27603

E. Lowell Harris, Director

560 North Carolina Department of Human Resources

Division of Vocational Rehabilitation Services
P.O. Box 26053   919-733-3364
Raleigh, NC 27611

561 North Carolina Division of Vocational Rehabilitation Services

P.O. Box 26053   919-733-3364
Raleigh, NC 27611

562 North Carolina Employment Security Commission

P.O. Box 25903   919-733-7546
Raleigh, NC 27611

563   North Carolina Office of Administrative Hearings/Civil Rights Division

P.O. Drawer 27447
Raleigh, NC 27611

919-733-0431

North Dakota

564   Job Service of North Dakota

P.O. Box 1537
Bismarck, ND 58502

701-224-2836

565   North Dakota Department of Education

State Capitol
Bismarck, ND 58505

701-224-2277

Gary Gronberg, Director

566   North Dakota Department of Human Services

Office of Vocational Rehabilitation
400 East Broadway
Bismarck, ND 58501

701-224-3970

567   North Dakota Department of Labor

State Capitol Building
600 East Blvd.
Bismarck, ND 58505

701-224-2660

Ohio

568   Ohio Bureau of Employment Services

145 South Front Street
Columbus, OH 43215

614-466-2100

569   Ohio Civil Rights Commission

220 Parsons Avenue
Columbus, OH 43226

614-466-7637

570   Ohio Department of Education

933 High Street
Worthington, OH 43085

614-466-2650

Frank New, Director

571   Ohio Rehabilitation Services Commission

400 E. Campus View Blvd.
Columbus, OH 43235

614-438-1210

572   Ohio Rehabilitative Services Commission

Division of Public Affairs
400 East Campus View Blvd.
Columbus, OH 43235

614-438-1236

Oklahoma

573   Oklahoma Department of Human Services

P.O. Box 25352
Oklahoma City, OK 73125

405-424-4311

574   Oklahoma Department of Human Services/ Rehabilitation Services Division

Department of Human Services
2409 North Kelley
Oklahoma City, OK 73111

405-424-6006

575   Oklahoma Employment Security Commission

2401 North Lincoln
Oklahoma City, OK 73105

405-557-7200

576   Oklahoma Human Rights Commission

2101 N. Lincoln Blvd., Rm. 480
Oklahoma City, OK 73105

405-521-3441

577   Oklahoma State Department of Education

2500 North Lincoln
Oklahoma City, OK 73105

405-521-3351

J.L. Prickett, Director

Oregon

578   Oregon Assistive Technology Projects

2045 Silverton Road NE
Salem, OR 97310

503-378-3830

Joy Rostson

A statewide program promoting services and assistive devices for the disabled.

579   Oregon Bureau of Labor and Industry

Civil Rights Division
P.O. Box 800
Portland, OR 97207

503-229-6601

580 Oregon Department of Education

700 Pringle Parkway   503-378-3136
Salem, OR 97301

581 Oregon Department of Human Resources

Vocational Rehabilitation Division
2045 Silverton Road NE   503-378-3830
Salem, OR 97310

582 Oregon Employment Division

875 Union Street NE   503-378-3208
Salem, OR 97311

583 Oregon Job Training Partnership Act Administration

775 Summer Street NE   503-373-1995
Salem, OR 97310

584 Oregon Outback

Technology Access Center
111 Elm, P.O. Box 2916   503-962-7258
La Grade, OR 97850

585 Vocational Rehabilitation Department of Oregon/TALN Project

Department of Human Resources
500 Summer Street NE   503-378-3830
Salem, OR 97310

Pennsylvania
---

586 Pennsylvania Department of Education

Box 911, 333 Market Street   717-783-6913
Harrisburg, PA 17108

Dr. Gary Makuck, Director

587 Pennsylvania Department of Labor and Industry

Labor & Industry Bldg., Rm. 1708   717-787-1745
Harrisburg, PA 17120

588 Pennsylvania Department of Labor Office of Vocational Rehabilitation

Department of Labor
7th & Forster Sts.   717-787-5244
Harrisburg, PA 17120

589 Pennsylvania Human Rights Commission

101 S Second Street, Ste. 300   717-787-4412
Harrisburg, PA 17101

590 Pennsylvania's Initiative on Assistive Technology

Temple University
423 Ritter Annex   215-787-1356
Philadelphia, PA 19122

Rhode Island
---

591 Rhode Island Commission for Human Rights

10 Abbott Park Place   401-277-2661
Providence, RI 02903

592 Rhode Island Department of Education

22 Hayes Street   401-277-2031
Providence, RI 02908

J. Troy Earhart, Commissioner

593 Rhode Island Department of Employment and Training

101 Friendship Street   401-277-3732
Providence, RI 02903

594 Rhode Island Department of Human Services/ Office of Vocational Rehabilitation

Department of Human Resources
40 Fountain Street   401-421-7005
Providence, RI 02903

South Carolina
---

595 South Carolina Assistive Technology Program

South Carolina Vocational Rehabilitation Depart.
1410-C Boston Avenue, P.O. Box 15   803-822-5404
West Columbia, SC 29171   FAX 803-822-4301

LaNelle C. Durant, Project Director
Cheri R. Coleman, Tech. Services

A statewide project established to provide an opporunity for individuals with disabilities to lead the fullest, most productive lives possible. Specifically, Assistive Technology is adapted toys, computers, seating systems, powered mobility, augmentative communication devices, special switches and thousands of other commercially availabel or adapted solutions.

596 **South Carolina Department of Education**

311 Rutledge Street 803-758-7432
Columbia, SC 29201

Robert Black, Director

597 **South Carolina Employment Security Commission**

P.O. Box 995 803-737-2617
Columbia, SC 29202

598 **South Carolina Human Affairs Commission**

2611 Forest Street 803-737-6570
Columbia, SC 29240

599 **South Carolina Vocational Rehabilitation Department**

P.O. Box 15, 1410 Boston Avenue 8-3734-4300
West Columbia, SC 29171

South Dakota

600 **South Dakota Department of Human Services**

East Highway 34 605-773-3195
Pierre, SD 57501

601 **South Dakota Department of Labor**

700 Governors Drive 605-773-3101
Pieere, SD 57501

602 **South Dakota Division of Human Rights**

C/O Capitol Building
222 E Capitol Street, Ste. 11 605-773-4493
Pierre, SD 57501

603 **South Dakota Division of Rehabilitation Services**

700 Goernors Drive 605-773-3195
Pierre, SD 57501

604 **South Dakota Division of Special Education**

700 Governors Drive 605-773-3315
Pierre, SD 57501

Dean Myers, Director

Tennessee

605 **Tennessee Department of Education**

132 Cordell Hull Building 615-741-2851
Nashville, TN 37219

Bob McElrath, Commissioner

606 **Tennessee Department of Employment Security**

500 James Robertson Pkwy. 615-741-2131
Nashville, TN 37245

607 **Tennessee Department of Human Services Div. of Vocational Rehabilitation**

Department of Human Services
400 Deaderick Street 615-741-2521
Nashville, TN 37219

608 **Tennessee Department of Labor**

501 Union Bldg. 615-741-2582
Nashville, TN 37219

609 **Tennessee Technology Access Project**

706 Church Street, Ste. 300 615-741-7441
Nashville, TN 37243

Texas

610 **Texas Commission on Human Rights**

8100 Cameron Road #525 512-837-8534
Austin, TX 78711

611 **Texas Department of Commerce, Work Force Development Division**

P.O. Box 12728 512-320-9801
Austin, TX 78711

612 **Texas Department of Education**

1701 North Congress Avenue 512-463-9414
Austin, TX 78701

Jill Gray, Program Director

613 **Texas Employment Commission**

15th & Congress Ave., Rm. 656 512-463-2652
Austin, TX 78778

614 Texas Rehabilitation Commission

4900 N. Lamar Blvd., Rm. 7102   512-483-4001
Austin, TX 78751

Utah
---

615 Utah Assistive Technology Program

Utah State University
UMC 6855   801-750-1982
Logan, UT 84322

616 Utah Department of Employment Security

P.O. Box 11249   801-536-7401
Salt Lake City, UT 84147

617 Utah Labor and Anti-Discrimination Division

160 East 300 South   801-530-6801
Salt Lake City, UT 84114

618 Utah Office of Job Training for Economic Development

324 South State St., Ste. 500   801-538-8750
Salt Lake City, UT 84114

619 Utah State Office of Education

250 East Fifth South   801-533-5982
Salt Lake City, UT 84111

Elwood Pace, Coordinator

620 Utah State Office of Rehabilitation

250 East 500 South   801-538-7530
Salt Lake City, UT 84111

Vermont
---

621 Vermont Agency of Human Services/ Vocational Rehabilitation Division

Department of Human Services
103 South Main Street   802-241-2189
Waterbury, VT 05671

622 Vermont Assistive Technology Project

Agency of Human Services
103 South Main Street   802-241-2620
Waterbury, VT 05671   800-639-1522
                                      FAX 802-241-3052

Christine Pellegrino, Project Director

Provides a revolving loan fund for assistive technology and five regional consultants who provide advocacy and help obtaining technology. Also provides training and starting a recycle program.

623 Vermont Attorney General's Office

Public Protection Division
109 State Street   802-828-3171
Montpelier, VT 05602

624 Vermont Department of Employment and Training

P.O. Box 488   802-229-0311
Montpelier, VT 05601

625 Vermont Special Education

120 State Street   802-828-3141
Montpelier, VT 05602

Theodore Riggen, Executive Director

Washington
---

626 Washington State Human Rights Commission

711 S. Capitol Way, Ste. 402   206-753-6770
Olympia, WA 98504

627 Washington Technology Access Center for Resources and Training

257 100th Avenue NE   206-637-9848
Bellevue, WA 98004

West Virginia
---

628 West Virginia Bureau of Employment Programs

112 California Avenue   304-348-9180
Charleston, WV 25305

629 West Virginia Department of Education

1900 Washington Street   304-348-2696
Charleston, WV 25305

William Capehart, Director

630 West Virginia Human Rights Commission

1321 Plaza East, Rm. 106   304-348-2616
Charleston, WV 25301

631 West Virginia State Board of Rehabilitation Services

State Capitol Complex   304-766-4601
Charleston, WV 25305

Wisconsin

632 Wisconsin Assistive Technology Projects

State Grants Program
1 West Wilson St., 8th Floor   608-266-2179
Madison, WI 53707

Kathy McCleave
A statewide progrma promoting assistive technology and services for the disabled.

633 Wisconsin Department of Health & Social Services/ Vocational Rehabilitation

Department of Health Services
P.O. Box 7852   608-266-2168
Madison, WI 53707

634 Wisconsin Department of Industry, Labor, and Human Relations

'p.O. Box 79436   608-266-7552
Madison, WI 53702

635 Wisconsin Equal Rights Division

P.O. Box 53708   608-267-9678
Madison, WI 537-2

Wyoming

636 Wyoming Department of Education

2300 Capitol Avenue   307-777-7414
Cheyenne, WY 82002

Lynn Simons, Superintendent

637 Wyoming Department of Employment

100 West Midwest   307-235-3611
Casper, WY 82602

638 Wyoming Employment Security Commission

P.O. Box 2760   307-235-3650
Casper, WY 82602

639 Wyoming Fair Employment Commission

122 West 25th Street, 2nd Fl. East   307-777-7261
Cheyenne, WY 82002

Associations

640 ADA Clearinghouse and Resource Center National Center for State Courts

300 Newport Avenue 804-253-2000
Williamsburg, VA 23185

Will disseminate information on ADA compliance to State and local court systems. Will develop a diagnostic checklist, strategies for compliance specifically relevant to the State and local courts, and a model curriculum for use in the education of future judges and court administrators.

641 American Arbitration Association

140 West 51st Street 212-484-4000
New York, NY 10020

Provides information on mediation, arbitration and other dispute resolution alternatives. Makes referrals to local American Arbitration Association offices, and publishes a directory of mediators and arbitrators with subject matter expertise.

642 American Bar Association

1800 M Street, NW, Ste. 200 202-331-2250
Washington, DC 20036

Howard Davidson, Executive Director

A professional organization for lawyers, through its commission on the Mentally Disabled, formulates policy on mental disability issues and monitors legal developments affecting mentally disabled, developmentally disabled, and physically disabled persons.

643 Community Alliance for Special Education

1031 Franklin Street #B5 415-928-2273
San Francisco, CA 94109 FAX 415-928-2289

Legal and paralegal support and services.

644 Disability Rights Education and Defense Fund, Inc.

2212 6th Street 415-644-2555
Berkeley, CA 94710

A national disability rights law and policy center dedicated to furthering the civil rights of persons with disabilities.

645 Fund for Equal Access to Society

7945 MacArthur Blvd., Ste. 204 301-320-6185
Cabin John, MS 20818

A non-profit corporation that advocates for full and equal access for individuals precluded from effective participation in various aspects of society.

646 Legal Services for Children, Inc.

1254 Market Street, 3rd Floor 415-863-3762
San Francisco, CA 94102 FAX 415-863-7708

Christopher N. Wu, Executive Director

Provides comprehensive legal and related support services to children and youth under age 18.

647 National Center for Youth Law

114 Sansome Street 510-542-3307
San Francisco, CA 94104 FAX 510-946-9024

Litigation and support center for the disabled.

648 National Council of Juvenile and Family Court Judges

P.O. Box 8978 702-784-6012
Reno, NV 89507

649 National Institute for Dispute Resolution

1901 L Street NW, Ste. 600 202-466-4764
Washington, DC 20036

Serves as a clearinghouse for information on alternative dispute resolution. Makes referrals to local providers of alternative dispute resolution services.

650 Public Interest Law Center of Philadelphia

125 South 9th Street, Ste. 700 215-627-7100
Philadelphia, PA 19107

A public interest law firm with a Disabilities Project specializing in class action by individuals and organizations.

Information Sources

651 Access to Institutions of Higher Education for Disabled Students

One Dupont Circle, Ste. 620 202-833-8390
Washington, DC 20036

$ 6.50

652 Administration for Children and Families Fact Sheet

U.S. Dept. of Health & Human Services
370 L'Enfant Promenade SW 202-401-9215
Washington, DC 20447

Offers information on the major programs offered by the Association such as Head Start, Child Support Enforcement, Job Opportunities and Aid to Families with Dependent Children, just to name a few.

653 Advocacy Manual: a Parents' How-to Guide for Special Education Services

Learning Disabilities Association of America
4156 Library Road   412-341-1515
Pittsburgh, PA 15234

654 Americans with Disabilities Act Management Training Program

RPM Press, Inc.
P.O. Box 31483   602-886-1990
Tucson, AZ 85751

Jan Stonebraker, Operations Manager

Provides authoritative information on the Americans with Disabilities Act and compliance requirements for employers schools and other entities which provide employment, education or related opportunities to persons with disabilities.

655 Approaching Equality

Frank Bowe, Author

T-J Publishers
817 Silver Spring Avenue, Ste. 206   301-585-4440
Silver Spring, MS 20910   800-999-1186
    FAX 301-585-5930

Public education laws guarantee special education for all deaf and learning disabled children, but many find the special education system confusing, or are unsure of their rights under current laws. For anyone with interest in education, advocacy and the disabled community, this book reviews dramatic developments in education of special children, youth and adults.

$ 12.95

656 Attorneys' Fees

Special Education Resource Center
25 Industrial Park Road   203-632-1485
Middletown, CT 06457

J.J. Jennings
C.L. Weatherly

Analyzes provisions for the recovery of attorneys' fees by parents who are the "prevailing party" in any action or proceeding involving the provision of a free appropriate public education to a student with a disability.

657 Beyond Separate Education

Dorothy Kerzner Lipsky, Author

Paul H. Brookes Publishing Company
P.O. Box 10624   410-337-8539
Baltimore, MD 21285   800-638-3775
    FAX 410-337-8539

This timely volume addresses the mission of PL 94-142 in its second decade of implementation.

$ 32.00

658 California School Law Digest

Whitaker Newsletters
313 South Avenue   908-889-6336
Fanwood, NJ 07023

Joel Whitaker, Publisher

News and administrative/court decisions pertaining to the law.

$ 108.00

659 The Civil Rights of Students with Hidden Disabilities Under Section 504

U.S. Department of Education
400 Maryland Avenue South   202-732-2270
Washington, DC 20202

Describes the disabilities covered by the legislation and identifies what hidden disabilities are and discusses the responsibilities of federal fund recipients.

660 Clues on Learning Disability for the Juvenile Justice System

Learning Disabilities Association of America
4156 Library Road   412-341-1515
Pittsburgh, PA 15234

661 Committee on Patient's Rights and Education

7742 Golf Drive   708-448-2349
Palos Heights, IL 60463

Advocacy, education, information and publications concerning patient's rights when dealing with the medical community.

662 Digest of Judicial Decisions of the N.Y. State Commissioner of Education

Advocates for Children
24-16 Bridge Plaza South   718-729-8866
Long Island City, NY 11103   FAX 718-729-8931

Galen D. Kirkland, Executive Director

A journal describing laws and legislation involving students with disabling conditions.

$ 25.00

663 Disability Rights

Disability Rights Education & Defense Fund
2212 Sixth Street   510-644-2555
Berkeley, CA 94710

Offers information on law and legislation for the disabled.

664 Discipline

Special Education Resource Center
25 Industrial Park Road   203-632-1485
Middletown, CT 06457

J.J. Jennings
C.L. Weatherly

A general analysis of the problems encountered in the discipline of students with disabilities. Discussion of the legal principles of discipline that have evolved pursuant to Public Law 94-142.

665 Due Process in Special Education

Milton Budoff, Author

Brookline Books
P.O. Box 1046   617-868-0360
Cambridge, MA 02238

The only comprehensive study of special education appeals hearings: What happens at a hearing, why parents choose to appeal, how schools respond and how hearing officers decide cases.
> *"... of use and interest to parents in any state who wish to be involved in their child's education."*
> -Rehabilitation Literature
$ 21.95

666 Early Services for Children with Special Needs

Alfred Healy, Author

Special Needs Project
1482 East Valley Road, #A-121   805-565-1914
Santa Barbara, CA 93108   800-333-6867

Summarizes the 14 steps of PL 99-457 in highly readable language with quotes from parents and professionals.

667 Education of the Handicapped: Laws

Bernard D. Reams, Jr., Author

William Hein & Co., Inc.
1286 Main Street   716-882-2600
Buffalo, NY 14209

Focuses on elementary and secondary Education Act of 1965 and its amendment, Education For All Handicapped Children Act of 1975 and its amendments and acts providing services for the disabled.

668 Ethical and Legal Issues in School Counseling

American Association for Counseling & Development
5999 Stevenson Avenue   703-823-9800
Alexandria, VA 22304   800-347-6647

Contains answers to many of the most controversial and challenging questions school counselors face every day.
$ 29.95

669 Evaluation of the Association for Children with Learning Disabilities

National Center for State Courts
300 Newport Avenue   804-253-2000
Williamsburg, VA 23187

Final report on children with learning disabilities training institute.
$ 6.96

670 Free Appropriate Public Education

H. Rutherford Turnbull, III, Author

Love Publishing Company
1777 South Bellaire Street   303-757-2579
Denver, CO 80222   FAX 303-757-6912

Information on significant legislation regarding the disabled. Laws are discussed with attention to their impact on the child, the parents, the public schools and higher education.
$ 39.95

671 A Guide to the Employment Section of the Americans with Disabilities Act

Jamie Satcher, Author

Department of Counselor Education
Mississippi State, MS

Primarily written in a question and answer format, this booklet presents information to assist employers.
$ 1.75

672 How to Write An IEP

NICHCY
P.O. Box 1492   703-893-6061
Washington, DC 20013   800-999-5599

Offers all the information needed to write an IEP and the laws parents and professionals need to understand when working with a disabled child.

673 Implementing the Americans with Disabilities Act

Lawrence Gostin, Author

Paul H. Brookes Publishing Company
P.O. Box 10624   410-337-8539
Baltimore, MD 21285   800-638-3775

Designed to inform and inspire all persons involved with implementing the ADA, this guide offers an understanding of the statuatory and regulatory requirements of the law.

674 Learning Disabilities and Juvenile Delinquency

Learning Disabilities Association of America
4156 Library Road   412-341-1515
Pittsburgh, PA 15234

675 Learning Disabilities and the Young Offender

Learning Disabilities Association of America
4156 Library Road   412-341-1515
Pittsburgh, PA 15234

676 Least Restrictive Environment

Special Education Resource Center
25 Industrial Park Road   203-632-1485
Middletown, CT 06457

J.J. Jennings
C.L. Weatherly

A general discussion and analysis of the mandate to educate students with disabilities to the maximum extent appropriate with nondisabled students.

677 Legal Notes for Education

Data Research, Inc.
4635 Nichols Road #100   612-452-8267
Eagan, MN 55122

Summaries of court decisions dealing with education law.

$ 89.00

678 Legal Rights of Persons with Disabilities: An Analysis of Federal Law

LRP Publications
747 Dresher Road   800-341-7874
Horsham, PA 19044

This book will provide professionals working with the disabled a comprehensive analysis of the issues involved.

$ 95.00

679 Mainstreaming in Massachusetts

Brookline Books
P.O. Box 1046   617-868-0360
Cambridge, MA 02238   FAX 617-868-1772

This book explains how commitments, made bny law, are extended and reinforced by the shared involvement of students, teachers, parents and other professionals.

680 Modern Consumer Education: You and the Law

Educational Design, Inc.
47 West 13th Street   800-221-9372
New York, NY 10011

An instructional program to teach independent living, with emphasis on legal resources and survival skills.

$ 58.00

681 New Directions

Association of State Mental Retardation Directors
113 Oronoco Street   703-683-4202
Alexandria, VA 22314

A newsletter offering information on laws, amendments, and legislation affecting the disabled.

$ 55.00

682 New IDEA Amendments: Assistive Technology Devices and Services

Special Education Resource Center
25 Industrial Park Road   203-632-1485
Middletown, CT 06457

J.J. Jennings
C.L. Weatherly

A discussion of new mandates created by the 1990 Amendments to Public Law 94-142. An overview of the requirement for the provision of assistive technology devices and services as well as a discussion on the transition services that are to be provided to disabled adolescents.

683 New Jersey Education Law Report

Whitaker Newsletters
313 South Avenue   908-322-7797
Fanwood, NJ 07023

Joel Whittaker, Publisher

Court decisions and rulings on employment in New Jersey schools.

$ 169.00

684 New York Education Law Report

Whitaker Newsletters
313 South Avenue   908-889-6336
Fanwood, NJ 07023

Joel Whitaker, Publisher

News and administrative decisions pertaining to the law, the courts and public schools.

$ 108.00

685 Numbers That Add Up to Eduational Rights for Children with Disabilities

Children's Defense Fund
25 E Street NW   202-628-8787
Washington, DC 20001

Information on the laws 94-142 and 504.

686 A Parent's Guide to the Social Security Administration

Eden Programs
One Logan Drive   609-987-0099
Princeton, NJ 08540   FAX 609-987-0243

David Holmes, EdD, Executive Director
Anne Holmes, M.S., C.C.C., Outreach Director

687 P.L. 99-457: the Next Step Forward for Disabled Children

The Council for Exceptional Children
1920 Association Drive   703-620-3660
Reston, VA 22091

A multimedia training program for parents and professionals presenting the significant changes in education of disabled children and youth created by Public Law 99-457.

688 A Pocket Guide to Federal Help for Individuals with Disabilities

Clearinghouse on Disability Information
US Department Of Education
Washington, DC 20202

Robert Davila, Asst. Secretary

A pamphlet offering persons with disabilities, their families and service providers information on government wide benefits and services for which individuals with disabilities may be eligible.

689 Procedural Due Process

Special Education Resource Center
25 Industrial Park Road   203-632-1485
Middletown, CT 06457

J.J. Jennings
C.L. Weatherly

Analyzes the importance of the procedural safeguards afforded to parents and their children with disabilities by the Public Law 94-142. Safeguards are discussed and possible legal implications are addressed.

690 Public Law 94-142: An Overview

Special Education Resource Center
25 Industrial Park Road   203-632-1485
Middletown, CT 06457

J.J. Jennings
C.L. Weatherly

An overview of the general provisions of the Individuals with Disabilities Education Act, commonly referrred to as Public Law 94-142. Designed to provide the less-experienced viewer with a fundamental understanding of the Public Law and its significance.

691 Purposeful Integration... Inherently Equal

Steven Taylor, Author
Federation for Children with Special Needs
95 Berkeley Street, Ste. 104   617-482-2915
Boston, MA 02116   800-331-0688

This publication covers integration, mainstreaming, and least restrictive environments.

$ 5.00

692 Representing Learning Disabled Children: a Manual for Attorneys

Learning Disabilities Association of America
4156 Library Road   412-341-1515
Pittsburgh, PA 15234

693 Section 504 - Help for the Learning Disabled College Student

Joan Sedita, Author
Connecticut Association for Children with LD
18 Marshall Street   203-838-5010
South Norwalk, CT 06854   FAX 203-866-6108

Provides a review of Section 504 of the Vocational Rehabilitation Act as it relates specifically to the learning disabled.

$ 3.25

694 Section 504 of the Rehabilitation Act

Special Education Resource Center
25 Industrial Park Road   203-632-1485
Middletown, CT 06457

J.J. Jennings
C.L. Weatherly

A general overview of the legal implications of the Rehabilitation Act and its implementing regulations, a law that is often forgotten in the process of appropriately educating children with disabilities.

695 So You're Going to a Hearing - Preparing for a Public Law 94-142

Learning Disabilities Association of America
4156 Library Road   412-341-1515
Pittsburgh, PA 15234

696 Special Education and the Handicapped

Data Research, Inc.
4635 Nichols Road #100   612-452-8267
Eagan, MN 55122

Summaries of court decisions dealing with special education law.

$ 88.00

697 Special Education in Juvenile Corrections

Peter E. Leone, Robert B. Rutherford, Jr., Author
The Council for Exceptional Children
1920 Association Drive   703-620-3660
Reston, VA 22091

This topic is of incerasing concern. This book describes the demographics of incarcerated youth and suggests some promising pratices that are being used.

698   Special Law for Special People

Fortson and White
3333 Peachtree Road NE   404-239-1900
Atlanta, GA 30326

Julie J. Jennings
A pamphlet offering information on the passage of the Education for All Handicapped Children Act affecting 8 million children in the classroom.

699   Stories Behind Special Education Case Law

Ree Martin, Author
Special Needs Project
1482 East Valley Road, #A-121   805-565-1914
Santa Barbara, CA 93108   800-333-6867

The personal stories behind ten leading court cases that shaped the basic principles of special education law.

$ 12.95

700   Students with Disabilities and Special Education - 9th Edition

Data Research, Inc.
4635 Nichols Road #100   617-452-8267
Eagan, MN 55122

701   Summary of Existing Legislation Affecting People with Disabilities

U.S. Department of Education
Room 3132, Switzer Bldg.   202-205-8241
Washington, DC 20202

702   Taking the First Step...to Solve Learning Problems

Learning Disabilities Association of America
4156 Library Road   412-341-1515
Pittsburgh, PA 15234

A pamphlet offering information on the legal aspects, parents rights and tax information on the learning disabled.

703   U.S. Department of Justice - Public Access Section

P.O. Box 66738   202-514-0301
Washington, DC 20035

Information concerning the rights people with learning disabilities have under the American With Disabilities Act.

Adult Education

704 Adults Who Feel Stupid But Aren't

Walt Murray, Author
Connecticut Association for Children with LD
18 Marshall Street   **203-838-5010**
South Norwalk, CT 06854   **FAX 203-866-6108**
An eye opener into the "real world" of the adult with ADHD.
2 Pages

$ .50

705 Can't Read, Write Or Add: the Secret Hell of Millions of Americans

Rocky Mountain Resource and Training Institute
6355 Ward Road, Ste. 310   **303-420-2942**
Arvada, CO 80004   **FAX 303-420-8675**
A brief treatment of issues facing the adult with undiagnosed learning disabilities and how being diagnosed can change one's life.

706 For You - Adults with Learning Disabilities

Cathy Smith, Author
Connecticut Association for Children with LD
18 Marshall Street   **203-838-5010**
South Norwalk, CT 06854   **FAX 203-866-6108**
82 Pages

$ 6.95

707 Forming a New Reader Support Group

Anna Mae Kuchta, Author
Pittsburgh Literacy Initiative/Goodwill Industries
2600 East Carson Street   **412-481-9005**
Pittsburgh, PA 15203

$ 10.00

708 How to Get Services By Being ASSERTIVE

Learning Disabilities Association of America
4156 Library Road   **412-341-1515**
Pittsburgh, PA 15234

709 Learning Intervention Strategies: Handbook for Learning Disabled Adults

M. Massey-Henderson, Author
Connecticut Association for Children with LD
18 Marshall Street   **203-838-5010**
South Norwalk, CT 06854   **FAX 203-866-6108**

Designed to help high school and college students learn how to learn. Theses study strategies are designed in a step-by-step format.
80 Pages

$ 25.00

710 Learning Strategies for Adults: Compensations for LD

Sandra Crux, Author
Connecticut Association for Children with LD
18 Marshall Street   **203-838-5010**
South Norwalk, CT 06854   **FAX 203-866-6108**
Written for professionals who work with adults who have a learning disability.
130 Pages

$ 14.25

711 You Don't Outgrow It

Marnell Hayes, EdD, Author
Academic Therapy Publications
20 Commercial Blvd.   **415-883-3314**
Novato, CA 94949   **800-422-7249**
Offers information to help the learning disabled adult.
240 Pages

$ 16.00

712 You Mean I'm Not Lazy, Stupid Or Crazy?

Peggy Ramundo & Kate Kelly, Author
Tyrell & Jerem Press
P.O. Box 20089   **800-622-6611**
Cincinnati, OH 45220
A new self-help book is the first written by ADD adults for ADD adults. This comprehensive guide provides accurate information, practical "how-to's" and moral support.

$ 24.95

Children

713 The Best Way Out

Karyn Follis Cheatham, Author
Harcourt Brace Jovanovich, Inc.
6277 Sea Harbor Drive   **407-345-2000**
Orlando, FL 32887
A fictional story of thirteen year old Haywood Romby who faces the same real life academic and social problems faced daily by teenagers with learning disabilities.
168 Pages

714 The Don't Give-Up Kid

Verbal Images Press
19 Fox Hill Drive   **716-377-3807**
Fairport, NY 14450   **FAX 716-377-5401**

A picture book for children with dyslexia and other learning differences gives a clear understanding of their difficulties and the necessary courage to live with them.
Softcover

$ 8.95

715　Josh: a Boy with Dyslexia

Caroline Janover, Author

Waterfront Books
98 Brookes Avenue　　802-658-7477
Burlington, VT　05401

This is an adventure story for kids with a section in the back of facts about learning disabilities and a list of resources for parents and teachers.
100 Pages

$ 7.95

716　Jumpin' Johnny Get Back to Work - a Child's Guide to ADHD/Hyperactivity

Michael Gordon, PhD, Author

Connecticut Association for Children with LD
18 Marhshall Street　　203-838-5010
South Norwalk, CT　06854　　FAX 203-866-6108

Written primarily for elementay age youngsters with ADHD, this book helps them to understand their disability. Also valuable as an educational tool for parents, siblings, friends and classmates. The author's text reflects his sensitivity toward children with ADHD.

$ 10.95

717　Just One Friend

Lynne Hall, Author

Charles Scribner & Sons
866 Third Avenue　　212-702-2000
New York, NY　10022　　800-257-5755
　　　　FAX 212-319-1216

Dory, a learning disabled teenager, wanted pretty, smart Robin for her friend. Scared of being mainstreamed into the regular school, she decided that if Meredith were out of the way.
118 Pages

718　Kevin's Story

Dvora Levinson, Author

Connecticut Association for Children with LD
18 Marshall Street　　203-838-5010
South Norwalk, CT　06854　　FAX 203-866-6108

$ 7.65

719　Kiss the Clown

C.S. Adler, Author

Clarion Books
215 Park Avenue South
New York, NY　10003　　212-420-5800

Joel and Marc are brothers. Marc achieves honors in school while Joel struggles against his learning disability in special education classes. This book is a sensitive portray-

al which realistically shows the sometimes difficult times faced by families with children who have learning disabilities.
178 Pages

720　Leo the Late Bloomer

Robert Kraus, Author

Connecticut Association for Children with LD
18 Marshall Street　　203-838-5010
South Norwalk, CT　06854　　FAX 203-866-6108

$ 6.50

721　Liking Myself

Pat Palmer, Author

Connecticut Association for Children with LD
18 Marshall Street　　203-838-5010
South Norwalk, CT　06854　　FAX 203-866-6108

$ 5.50

722　The Magic Feather

Special Needs Project
1482 East Valley Road, #A-121　　805-565-1914
Santa Barbara, CA　93108　　800-333-6867

Offers information, from one viewpoint, on how the special education system can fail for the learning disabled child.
272 Pages

$ 9.95

723　Me and Einstein

Rose Blue, Author

Human Science Press
72 Fifth Avenue　　212-243-6000
New York, NY　10011

Bobby had been able to hide his reading disability from everyone. He fooled his teacher in school by clowning around and finally by being delinquent. The family could not figure out what was happening and agreed to place Bobby in a class for the retarded.
62 Pages

724　The Mountain Song

Dave Fullen, Author

Mountain Books
P.O. Box 21-1104　　800-876-MNTN
Columbus, OH　43221

A story about courage and how the ability to climb and reach goals is essential. This book for children with learning disabilities is about self-esteem and how they can grow with each step in the climb to the peak of the mountain.
16 Pages

$ 14.95

725　A Nest in the Gale

Dave Fullen, Author

Mountain Books
P.O. Box 21-1104   800-876-MNTN
Columbus, OH 43221

A story for learning disabled children about finding the safe harbor in the midst of the constant changes in their lives. It uses the North Atlantic Puffin as an analogy for learning to build nests wherever you may find yourself.
80 Pages

$ 18.95

726   No One to Play with - the Social Side of Learning Disabilities

Betty Osman, Author

Connecticut Association for Children with LD
18 Marshall Street   203-838-5010
South Norwalk, CT 06854   FAX 203-866-6108

Your child suffers from a learning disability and you have read reams on how to improve on her academic skills and now want to address his or her social needs.

$ 11.00

727   Rosey - the Imperfect Angel

Sandra Lee Peckinpah, Author

Special Needs Project
1482 East Valley Road, #A-121   805-565-1914
Santa Barbara, CA 93108   800-333-6867

This fable for young children emphasizes "the beauties that lie hidden beneath the defects" of "abnormal" angels.
Cloth

$ 15.95

728   Secrets Aren't Always for Keeps

Barbara Aiello, Author

Twenty-First Century Books
38 South Market Street   301-698-0210
Frederick, MD 21701

Jennifer Hauser is embarrassed to tell her visiting pen-pal about her learning disabilities, she is afraid she will think she is "retarded or something". Jennifer's difficulty and shame of being learning disabled eventually goes away, through the support of her parents and her friend, to the realization that she is still a capable person despite her disability.
48 Pages

729   Shelley, the Hyperactive Turtle

Deborah Moss, Author

Woodbine House
5615 Fishers Lane   301-468-8800
Rockville, MD 20852   800-843-7323

Carol Schwartz, Illustrator

Entertaining picture book for use with very young children. Sensitive text and colorful illustrations help children understand ADHD.
20 Pages

$ 12.95

730   Silent Words

Oliver-Pate
P.O. Box 2017
Ottawa, Ontario, Canada, K1 S 5B1
236 Pages

$ 20.50

731   Someone Special, Just Like You

Tricia Brown, Author

Special Needs Project
1482 East Valley Road, #A-121   805-565-1914
Santa Barbara, CA 93108   800-333-6867

A handsome photo-essay including a range of youngsters with disabilities at four preschools in the San Francisco Bay area.
19 Pages   Cloth   Ages 3-7

$ 14.95

732   Stories About Children Regardless of Ability, Learning Side-by-Side

Donna Bracewell, Author

Special Needs Project
1482 East Valley Road, #A-121   805-565-1914
Santa Barbara, CA 93108   800-333-6867

A collection of wonderful stories about children who have successfully integrated into regular classrooms in their neighborhood.
48 Pages

$ 5.00

733   Trouble with Explosives

Sally Kelley, Author

Bradbury Press
866 Third Avenue   212-702-2000
New York, NY 10022   800-257-5755

Polly moved regularly with her family, changing schools almost every year. This was especially difficult as she couldn't pronounce her explosive name, Polly Banks without stuttering.
117 Pages

734   Unicorns Are Real!

Learning Disabilities Association of America
4156 Library Road   412-341-1515
Pittsburgh, PA 15234

Major Catalogs

735 APA Books

American Psychological Association
Order Dept., P.O. Box 2710   202-336-5510
Hyattsville, MD 20784   800-374-2721
     FAX 202-336-5502

A catalog offering a variety of books and resources on various aspects of psychology, from clinical psychology to teaching aids.
47 Pages

736 Barrington House Publishing Company

1119 Lorne Way   408-241-8422
Sunnyvale, CA 94087   800-333-8731

737 Basic Educational Books

420 Bell Street   206-775-4710
Edmonds, WA 98020

738 Books on Special Children

P.O. Box 305   914-638-1236
Congers, NY 10920   FAX 914-638-0847

A newsletter offering information on books, resources, videos and more for parents, professionals and gifted children.
Monthly

739 Books on Tape, Inc.

P.O. Box 7900   800-626-3333
Newport Beach, CA 92660

Distributes fiction and non-fiction books on cassette tapes.

740 Bookwinkle's Children's Books

Kasten & Albion Streetes   707-937-KIDS
Mendocino, CA 95460

741 Brookline Books

P.O. Box 1046   617-868-0360
Cambridge, MA 02238   FAX 617-868-1772

Offers books for teachers and parents on law and legislation, education, integration and mainstreaming.

742 Brooks/Cole Publishing Company

511 Forest Lodge Road   408-373-0728
Pacific Grove, CA 93950   FAX 408-375-6414

Human services, counseling and social work books and videos.

743 Charles C. Thomas Publisher

2600 South First Street
Springfield, IL 62794

Offers books for professional, educators, clinicians, paraprofessionals, psychologists and more who work with the disabled.

744 Dog-Eared Publications

P.O. Box 863   608-831-1410
Middleton, WI 53562

745 Educator's Publishing Services

75 Moulton Street   617-547-6706
Cambridge, MA 02138   800-225-5750

Specializes in publishing materials for students grades K-12. The catalog offered includes several multisensory methods of teaching which are recommended for use with children and adults with learning disabilities. In addition, we have specialized student books in spelling, handwriting, vocabulary building, phonics and English review exercises designed particularly for children with learning disabilities.

746 Farnsworth's Books

1923 San Diego Avenue   619-299-4041
San Diego, CA 92110

747 Fearon/Janus/Quercus Publishers for Special Needs

500 Harbor Blvd.   800-877-4283
Belmont, CA 94002   FAX 415-595-8143

Offers a variety of information on special education, adult education, remedial programs, vocational/transitional education, libraries and literacy programs for the learning disabled and special needs individual.
97 Pages

748 Fun Publishing Company

5860 Miami Road   513-272-3672
Cincinnati, OH 45243

749 George Wahr Publishing Company

304 1/2 South State Street   313-668-6097
Ann Arbor, MI 48104

750 High Noon Books

20 Commercial Blvd.   415-883-3314
Novato, CA 94949   800-422-7249
     FAX 415-883-3720

Offers high interest reading and learning materials.

751 Kids' Favorite Books: Children's Choices 1989-1991

International Reading Association
800 Barksdale Rd., P.O. Box 8139   302-731-1600
Newark, DE 19714   800-336-READ
     FAX 302-731-1057

A compilation of the Children's Choices lists from the past three years, complete with annotations and cumulative indexes of the books' authors, illustrators and titles.
$ 8.00

752 NICHCY Publications List

NICHCY
P.O. Box 1492   703-893-6061
Washington, DC 20013   800-999-5599

Offers information on some of the brochures, books and resource material available from the organization.

753 Oryx Press

4041 North Central   800-279-4663
Phoenix, AZ 85012

754 Partners in Publishing

P.O. Box 50347
Tulsa, OK 74150

Offer directories of college programs for the learning disabled students and handbooks of free and inexpensive aids to college and career.

755 Quarterly Update

Lawrence Erlbaum Associates, Inc.
365 Broadway   201-666-4110
Hillsdale, NJ 07642   FAX 201-666-2394

Sharon Levy, Library Mktg. Mgr.
Publishers of books, journals, software, videos and alternative media.
37 Pages   Quarterly

756 Woodbine House

5615 Fishers Lane   301-468-8800
Rockville, MD 20852   800-843-7323

Books on disabilities for parents, professionals and kids with various disabilities.

Parents

---

757 After the Tears

Robin Simons, Author
Connecticut Association for Children with LD
18 Marshall Street   203-838-5010
South Norwalk, CT 06854   FAX 203-866-6108
                                      $ 7.75

758 Attention Deficit Disorders: Hyperactivity and Associated Disorders

Wendy S. Coleman, Author
Connecticut Association for Children with LD
18 Marshall Street   203-838-5010
South Norwalk, CT 06854   FAX 203-866-6108

A handbook for parents and professionals offering a comprehensive introduction to ADHD. Includes chapters on associated disorders and medication. Also outlines 38 realistic management techniques for parents.
70 Pages

                                      $ 6.00

759 Believe the Heart

Elizaebth Fleming, Author
Strawberry Hill Press
3848 SE Division Street   503-235-5989
Portland, OR 97202

This story is written by a mother whose five children were all diagnosed as having hereditary dyslexia. Personal and engaging, her story describes the challenge facing her own dyslexia in order to help her children cope with theirs.
180 Pages

760 Beyond the Rainbow

Patricia Dodds, Author
Learning Disabilities Association of America
4156 Library Road   412-341-1515
Pittsburgh, PA 15234

A guide for parents with children with dyslexia and other disabilities.

                                      $ 15.00

761 Building a Child's Self-Image - a Guide for Parents

Learning Disabilities Association of America
4156 Library Road   412-341-1515
Pittsburgh, PA 15234

762 Can What a Child Eat Make Him Dull, Stupid/Hyperactive?

Learning Disabilities Association of America
4156 Library Road   412-341-1515
Pittsburgh, PA 15234

763 Care of the Neurologically Handicapped Child

Arthur Prensky, Author
Special Needs Project
1482 East Valley Road, #A-121   805-565-1914
Santa Barbara, CA 93108   800-333-6867

This book describes normal and abnormal development, what to expect from the various specialists parents may consult, and seven of the most common neurological disorders.
331 Pages   Cloth

                                      $ 32.95

764 Children with Autism

Michael Powers, Author
Special Needs Project
1482 East Valley Road, #A-121   805-565-1914
Santa Barbara, CA 93108   800-333-6867

Recommended as the first book that parents should read, this book provides a complete introduction to autism, while easing a family's fears and concerns as they adjust and cope with their child's disorders.

"This guide clears away...misconceptions and offers straightforward advice from parents..."

-Booklist

368 Pages

$ 14.95

765 Children with Learning and Behavioral Disorders

Learning Disabilities Association of America
4156 Library Road   **412-341-1515**
Pittsburgh, PA 15234

766 Children with Tourette Syndrome

Tracy Haerle, Author
Woodbine House
5615 Fishers Lane   **301-468-8800**
Rockville, MD 20852   **800-843-7323**

This book explains the Syndrome including its symptoms, causes and medications as well as other disorders which are commonly linked with it.
340 Pages

$ 14.95

767 Common Sense About Dyslexia

Ann Marshall Huston, Author
Special Needs Project
1482 East Valley Road, #A-121   **805-565-1914**
Santa Barbara, CA 93108   **800-333-6867**

Offers important, need-to-know information about dyslexia.
300 Pages Paper

$ 16.95

768 ConverSations: the Go Anywhere Speech Book

Janet Shaw, Author
The Speech Bin
1965 Twenty-Fifth Avenue   **407-770-0007**
Vero Beach, FL 32960   **FAX 407-770-0006**

Jan J. Binney, Editor In Chief
Barbara Hector, Office Manager

Conversational activities that parents and kids love to do together. Includes 40 results-oriented conversation scripts that can be done anywhere.
48 Pages ISBN 0-937857-00-9

$ 16.95

769 Diamonds in the Rough

Peggy S. Dias, Author
Slosson Educational Publications, Inc.
P.O. Box 280
East Aurora, NY 14052   **800-828-4800**

Infancy to college reference guide on the learning disabled child.

770 The Difficult Child

Stanley Turecki, Author
Connecticut Association for Children with LD
18 Marshall Street   **203-838-5010**
South Norwalk, CT 06854   **FAX 203-866-6108**

Describes a step-by-step program for managing a "hard-to-raise child".
258 Pages

$ 10.95

771 Discipline and Self-Esteem to Helping Your Family Adjust

Learning Disabilities Association of America
4156 Library Road   **412-341-1515**
Pittsburgh, PA 15234

772 Dr. Cott's Help for Your Learning Disabled Child

Learning Disabilities Association of America
4156 Library Road   **412-341-1515**
Pittsburgh, PA 15234

773 Dr. Larry Silver's Advice to Parents on AD-HD

Dr. Larry B. Silver, Author
Learning Disabilities Association of America
4156 Library Road   **412-341-1515**
Pittsburgh, PA 15234

$ 17.95

774 Early Childhood Special Education: Birth to Three

J. Jordan, Author
Connecticut Association for Children with LD
18 Marshall Street   **203-838-5010**
South Norwalk, CT 06854   **FAX 203-866-6108**

$ 29.74

775 Endangered Minds: Why Our Children Dont Think

J. Healy, Author
Learning Disabilities Association of America
4156 Library Road   **412-341-1515**
Pittsburgh, PA 15234

$ 13.00

776 Getting Through

Elizabth Ostuni, Author

The Speech Bin
1965 Twenty-Fifth Avenue
Vero Beach, FL 32960
407-770-0007
FAX 407-770-0006

Jan J. Binney, Editor In Chief
Barbara Hector, Office Manager

Practical, realistic guidelines to facilitate and maintain communication in dementia. Written in clear, down-to-earth style, this unique book explains how parents and family can help slow the agonizing affects of Alzheimer's Disease.
100 Pages

$ 16.95

777 A Guide for Parents on Hyperactivity in Children

Klaus K. Minde, Author

Learning Disabilities Association of America
4156 Library Road
Pittsburgh, PA 15234
412-341-1515

Describes difficulties faced by a child with ADHD. Elaborates on types of management and ends with a section called "A Day With A Hyperactive Child: Possible Problems".
23 Pages

$ 3.25

778 Guidelines and Recommended Practices for Individualized Family Service Plan

B. Johnson, Author

Association for the Care of Children's Health
7910 Woodmont Avenue, Ste. 300
BethesdaPark, MD 20814
301-654-6549
FAX 301-986-4553

Presents a growing consensus about best practices for comprehensive family-centered early intervention services as required by Part H of the Individuals with Disabilities Education Act.
208 Pages

$ 15.00

779 A Handbook for Implementing Workshops for Siblings of Special Needs Children

Donald Meyer, Author

Special Needs Project
1482 East Valley Road, #A-121
Santa Barbara, CA 93108
805-565-1914
800-333-6867

Based on three years of professional experience working with siblings ages 8 through 13 and their parents, this handbook provides guidelines and technologies for those who wish to start and conduct workshops for siblings.
65 Pages

$ 40.00

780 Handbook of Parent Training - Parents As Cotherapists for Children

Charles Schaefer, Author

Books on Special Children
P.O. Box 305
Congers, NY 10920
914-638-1236
FAX 914-638-0847

Teaches parents techniques to supervise their home based implementation of positive changes in child behavior.
498 Pages

$ 66.95

781 Help Build a Brighter Future - Children At Risk for LD in Child Care Centers

Learning Disabilities Association of America
4156 Library Road
Pittsburgh, PA 15234
412-341-1515

782 Help for the Hyperactive Child - a Good Sense Guide for Parents

Learning Disabilities Association of America
4156 Library Road
Pittsburgh, PA 15234
412-341-1515

783 Help Me to Help My Child - a Sourcebook for Parents of LD Children

Learning Disabilities Association of America
4156 Library Road
Pittsburgh, PA 15234
412-341-1515

$ 10.00

784 Helping Children Overcome Learning Disabilities

Jerome Rosner, Author

Special Needs Project
1482 East Valley Road #A-121
Santa Barbara, CA 93108
805-565-1914
800-333-6867

This book is for parents and teachers offering them meaty and detailed programs for teaching the fundamentals of learning at home and school, with a strong admonition to work together.
377 Pages   Paper

$ 16.95

785 Helping the Hyperactive Child

Department of Health and Human Services
National Institute Of Mental Health
Rockville, MD 20857
301-763-1896
9 Pages

786 Helping the Learning Disabled Student with Homework

S.H. Stevens, Author

Learning Disabilities Association of America
4156 Library Road   412-341-1515
Pittsburgh, PA 15234

$ 5.00

787 Helping Your Child Achieve in School

B. Johnson, Author

Connecticut Association for Children with LD
18 Marshall Street   203-838-5010
South Norwalk, CT 06854   FAX 203-866-6108

$ 10.95

788 Helping Your Child Learn At School

R. Maloney, Author

Connecticut Association for Children with LD
18 Marshall Street   203-838-5010
South Norwalk, CT 06854   FAX 203-866-6108

$ 2.00

789 Helping Your Child with Attention-Deficit Hyperactivity Disorder

Learning Disabilities Association of America
4156 Library Road   412-341-1515
Pittsburgh, PA 15234

790 Helping Your Hyperactive Child

John Taylor, Author

Connecticut Association for Children with LD
18 Marshall Street   203-838-5010
South Norwalk, CT 06584   FAX 203-866-6018

A large, comprehensive book for parents, covering everything from techniques pertaining to sibling rivalry to coping with marital stresses. Contains thorough discussions of various treatments: nutritional, medical and educational. Also is an excellent source of advice and information for parents of kids with ADHD.
483 Pages

$ 21.95

791 The Hidden Child

Jeanne Simons, Author

Woodbine House
5615 Fishers Lane   301-468-8800
Rockville, MD 20852   800-843-7323

Offers inforrmation on a successful treatment program used in the Linwood Children's Center for reaching the autistic child.

792 How to Cure Low Self-Esteem

R. Maloney, Author

Connecticut Association for Children with LD
18 Marshall Street   203-838-5010
South Norwalk, CT 06854   FAX 203-866-6108

$ 8.75

793 How to Organize An Effective Parent/ Advocacy Group

C. DesJardins, Author

Connecticut Association for Children with LD
18 Marshall Street   203-838-5010
South Norwalk, CT 06854   FAX 203-866-6108

$ 6.50

794 How to Organize Your Child and Save Your Sanity

Brown/Connelly, Author

Learning Disabilities Association of America
4156 Library Road   412-341-1515
Pittsburgh, PA 15234

795 How to Own and Operate An Attention Deficit

Learning Disabilities Association of America
4156 Library Road   412-341-1515
Pittsburgh, PA 15234

Clear, informative and sensitive introduction to ADHD. Packed with practical things to do at home and school, the author offers her own insight being a professional and mother of a son with ADHD.
43 Pages

$ 6.95

796 How to Raise Your Child to Be a Winner

Hawes, Weiss & Weiss, Author

Learning Disabilities Association of America
4156 Library Road   412-341-1515
Pittsburgh, PA 15234

$ 11.50

797 Hyperactivity, Attention Deficits, and School Failure: Better Ways

Learning Disabilities Association of America
4156 Library Road   412-341-1515
Pittsburgh, PA 15234

798 Identification and Treatment of Attention Deficit Disorders

Nancy Nussbaum, Author

Therapro, Inc.
225 Arlington Street   508-872-9494
Framingham, MA 01701   FAX 508-875-2062

This handbook contains information that is based on research yet offers practical suggestions for parents, teachers and other professionals.

$ 10.00

799   If Your Child Stutters

Speech Foundation of America
P.O. Box 11749   800-992-9392
Memphis, TN 38111

A guide that enables parents to provide appropriate help to children who stutter.

$ 1.00

800   Importance of Play

Department of Health and Human Services
National Institute Of Mental Health   301-763-1896
Rockville, MD 20857
16 Pages

801   The Impossible Child: a Guide for Caring Teachers and Parents

D. Bamberg, Author

Learning Disabilities Association of America
4156 Library Road   412-341-1515
Pittsburgh, PA 15234

$ 13.00

802   In Their Own Way: Discovering and Encouraging You Child's Learning

Dr. Thomas Armstrong, Author

Special Needs Project
1482 East Valley Road #A-121   805-565-1914
Santa Barbara, CA 93108   800-333-6867

An unconventional teacher has written a very popular book for a wide audience. It's customary to be categorical about youngsters who learn conventionally/are normal/ are OK - and those who don't/who need special ed/are learning disabled.
224 Pages   paper

$ 8.95

803   In Time and with Love

Special Needs Project
1482 East Valley Road, #A-121   805-565-1914
Santa Barbara, CA 93108   800-333-6867

Play and parenting techniques for children with disabilities.
19 Pages   Ages 0-3

$ 12.95

804   Labelled Autistic

Temple Grandin, Author

Special Needs Project
1482 East Valley Road, #A-121   805-565-1914
Santa Barbara, CA 93108   800-333-6867

A recovered autistic individual shares her history, and includes her own suggestions for parents and professionals.
184 Pages

$ 8.95

805   Language and Speech Disorders in Children

J. Eisenson, Author

Connecticut Association for Children with LD
18 Marshall Street   203-838-5010
South Norwalk, CT 06854   FAX 203-866-6108

$ 16.50

806   The Language of Toys

Sue Schwartz, Author

Woodbine House
5615 Fishers Lane   301-468-8800
Rockville, MD 20852   800-843-7323

Teaches parents how to improve their child's communication skills at home with fun, easy-to-follow exercises.
280 Pages

$ 14.95

807   Learning Disabilities - a Family Affair

B. Osman, Author

Connecticut Association for Children with LD
18 Marshall Street   203-838-5010
South Norwalk, CT 06854   FAX 203-866-6108

$ 6.00

808   Learning Disabilities and Your Child

L.J. Greene, Author

Learning Disabilities Association of America
4156 Library Road   412-341-1515
Pittsburgh, PA 15234

$ 9.95

809   Learning Disabilities: National Information/Advocacy Organizations

Library Service for the Blind/Physically Disabled
The Library Of Congress   202-707-5100
Washington, DC 20542

810   Learning Disabled Child

Suzanne H. Stevens, Author

John F. Balir, Publisher
1406 Plaza Drive   919-768-1374
Winston-Salem, NC 27103

Book about learning disabilities available to parents. Stvens cuts through the jargon and complex theories which usually characterize books on the subject to present effective and practical techniques that parents can employ to help their child succeed at home and school.

"Stevens' book should be on the desk of every elementary and middle school teacher"
-Dr. William M. Cruickshank
196 Pages

$ 7.95

811 Learning While Growing: Cognitive Development

Department of Health and Human Services
National Institute Of Mental Health 301-763-1896
Rockville, MD 20857
14 Pages

812 Living with a Learning Disability

Barbara Cordoni, Author
Southern Illinois University Press
P.O. Box 3697 618-453-6619
Carbondale, IL 62902

Written by a mother and special educator, this general guide to learning disabilities stresses problems and skills needed for the life outside school.
140 Pages

813 Living with a Learning Disability: Revised Edition

B. Cordoni, Author
Southern Illinois University Press
P.O. Box 3697 618-453-6619
Carbondale, IL 62901 FAX 618-453-1221

Drawing on decades of research, training and the parenting of her learning disabled son and daughter, Cordoni presents techniques, counsel and case studies to guide counselors, teachers and parents in their efforts to assist their learning disabled person.
176 Pages Paper ISBN 0-809316-68-4

$ 15.95

814 Looking Through the "I"'s of the Learning Disabled

The Churchill School
1035 Price School Lane 314-997-4343
St. Louis, MO 63124 FAX 314-997-2760

Sandra K. Gilligan, Director
Thsi book was writen by learning disabled teenagers for learning disabled teenagers.
paperback

$ 6.50

815 Management of Children and Adolescents with AD-HD

Friedman/Royal, Author

Learning Disabilities Association of America
4156 Library Road 412-341-1515
Pittsburgh, PA 15234

$ 24.00

816 Maybe You Know My Kid: a Parent's Guide to Identifying ADHD

M.C. Fowler, Author
Birch Lane Press
120 Enterprise Avenue 800-447-2665
Secaucus, NJ 07094

The author writes about her family exeriences with their son, David, who has attention deficit disorder. Contains a comprehensive review of important issues plus descriptions of some helpful management techniques.
222 Pages

$ 13.25

817 The Misunderstood Child

L.B. Silver, Author
Connecticut Association for Children with LD
18 Marshall Street 203-838-5010
South Norwalk, CT 06854 FAX 203-866-6108

A guide for parents of learning disabled children.

$ 8.95

818 Mothers Talk About Learning Disabilities

Elizabeth Weiss, Author
Learning Disabilities Association of America
4156 Library Road 412-341-1515
Pittsburgh, PA 15234

In this book, the mother of two learning disabled boys seeks to give mothers in similar circumstances encouragement, support and everyday advice.

$ 17.95

819 Negotiating the Special Education Maze: a Guide for Parents and Teachers

Anderson, Chitwood & Hayden, Author
Learning Disabilities Association of America
4156 Library Road 412-341-1515
Pittsburgh, PA 15234

820 The New Read-Aloud Handbook

Jim Trelease, Author
International Reading Association
800 Barksdale Rd., P.O. Box 8139 302-731-1600
Newark, DE 19714 800-336-READ
FAX 302-731-1057

This handbook tells teachers and parents why and how to read aloud, suggests what and what not to do, and connects reading aloud to home, school and library settings.
352 Pages   ISBN 0-140468-81-1

$ 9.95

821   No Easy Answers (The Learning Disabled Child At Home and School)

Sally L. Smith, Author

Special Needs Project
1482 East Valley Road, #A-121   805-565-1914
Santa Barbara, CA 93108   800-333-6867

The author, director of the Lab School of the Kingsbury Center in Washington, DC, provides a clearly written description of the child with learning disabilities and positive suggestions for the parent and teacher.
Paper

$ 4.95

822   Parenting the Learning Disabled: a Realistic Approach

R.W. Cummings, Author

Charles C. Thomas Publisher
2600 South First Street   217-789-8980
Springfield, IL 62794

$ 27.00

823   Parents Assistance Program - a Bridge Between Parents and School Systems

Learning Disabilities Association of America
4156 Library Road   412-341-1515
Pittsburgh, PA 15234

$ 3.50

824   Parent's Guide to the Montessori Classroom

Aline D. Wolf, Author

Alliance for Parental Involvement in Education
P.O. Box 59   518-392-6900
East Chatham, NY 12060

This guide gives concise explanations of the meaning of Montessori. It describes in detail the program for children between ages of three to six.
Ages 3-6

$ 5.00

825   Parents Organizing to Improve Schools

Learning Disabilities Association of America
4156 Library Road   412-341-1515
Pittsburgh, PA 15234

$ 4.75

826   Please Doctor - If Someone Should Mention Learning Disabilities

Mahoney/Resnick, Author

Learning Disabilities Association of America
4156 Library Road   412-341-1515
Pittsburgh, PA 15234

$ 4.50

827   Preparing Children with Disabilities for School

ERIC Clearinghouse on Disabled and Gifted Children
1920 Association Drive   703-620-3660
Reston, VA 22091

828   Preschool Services for Children with Handicaps

ERIC Clearinghouse on Disabled and Gifted Children
1920 Association Drive   703-620-3660
Reston, VA 22091

829   Profiles of the Other Child - a Sibling Guide for Parents

P. McCaffrey, Author

Connecticut Association for Children with LD
18 Marshall Street   203-838-5010
South Norwalk, CT 06854   FAX 203-866-6108

$ 2.75

830   A Reader's Guide

Cory Moore, Author

Woodbine House
5615 Fishers Lane   301-468-8800
Rockville, MD 20852   800-843-7323

An indispensable tool for parents, teachers and librarians who need to find the most current, authoritative information in print about children with disabilities.
   "This is an outstanding and most useful book... In sum: a masterpiece."

-Library Journal
248 Pages

$ 14.95

831   Reading Is for Everyone: a Guide for Parents and Teachers of Children

Prentice-Hall
Englewood Cliffs, NJ 07632

Designed for parents and teachers, this book presents practical information on helping children with learning disabilities learn to read.
154 Pages

832 Recreation for Children with Learning Disabilities

Ripley/Cvach, Author

Learning Disabilities Association of America
4156 Library Road   **412-341-1515**
Pittsburgh, PA 15234

$ 2.00

833 Securing An Appropriate Education for Children with Disabling Conditions

Advocates for Children
24-16 Bridge Plaza South   **718-729-8866**
Long Island City, NY 11103   **FAX 718-729-8931**

Galen D. Kirkland, Executive Director

A guide to parents effective advocacy.

$ 10.00

834 Securing An Appropriate Education for Your Preschool Disabled Child

Advocates for Children
24-16 Bridge Plaza South   **718-729-8866**
Long Island City, NY 11103   **FAX 718-729-8931**

Galen D. Kirkland, Executive Director

A guide for parents on education and advocacy for their child with a disabling condition.

$ 2.50

835 Sensory Integration and the Child

A. Jean Ayers, Author

Therapro, Inc.
225 Arlington Street   **508-872-9494**
Framingham, MA 01701   **FAX 508-875-2062**

Designed to educate parents, students and beginning therapists in sensory integration treatment.

$ 24.00

836 Smart Kids with School Problems

Priscilla Vail, Author

NCLD
99 Park Avenue   **212-687-7211**
New York, NY 10016

837 So Your Child Has a Learning Problem: Now What?

Wallbrown/Wallbrown, Author

Learning Disabilities Association of America
4156 Library Road   **412-341-1515**
Pittsburgh, PA 15234

Designed for parents of children who are encountering learning problems in the classroom.

$ 23.00

838 Solving the Puzzle of Your Hard-to-Raise Child

William G. Crook & Laura Stevens, Author

Learning Disabilities Association of America
4156 Library Road   **412-341-1515**
Pittsburgh, PA 15234

The authors, a pediatrician and a mother, one convinced that allergies are a major cause of behavior and learning problems. Discussions include the child with allergies in today's world, how to recognize their symptoms and what can be done about them.
368 Pages

$ 17.95

839 SOS! Help for Parents

Lynn Clark, Author

Connecticut Association for Children with LD
18 Marshall Street   **203-838-5010**
South Norwalk, CT 06854   **FAX 203-866-6108**

This guide gives parents a number of specific methods to use to help children improve behavior.
241 Pages

$ 10.95

840 Special Populations

YMCA of USA
Box 181
Longview, WA 98632

Grace Reynolds, Director

841 Successful Parenting: a Guide to Stronger Families for Mothers and Fathers

Ducharme, Author

Learning Disabilities Association of America
4156 Library Road   **412-341-1515**
Pittsburgh, PA 15234

$ 3.00

842 Teaching Social Skills to Young Children

Sheri Searcy, Author

Connecticut Association for Children with LD
18 Marshall Street   **203-838-5010**
South Norwalk, CT 06854   **FAX 203-866-6108**

$ 8.50

843 Teaching the Young Child with Motor Delays : a Guide for Parents

Therapro, Inc.
225 Arlington Street   508-872-9494
Framingham, MA 01701   FAX 508-875-2062

Provides teaching strategies and therapy activities for movement impaired children.
228 Pages   Ages 0-3

$ 27.50

844 To Play Is to Learn

Learning Disabilities Association of America
4156 Library Road   412-341-1515
Pittsburgh, PA 15234

845 Trouble with School a Family Story About Learning Disabilities

Allison Boesel Dunn, Author

Woodbine House
5615 Fishers Lane   301-468-8800
Rockville, MD 20852   800-843-7323

A book explaining the process of identifying and understanding a child's learning disability.
32 Pages   Grades 1-5

$ 9.95

846 The Unconventional Child: a Book for Parents of Children with LD

Learning Disabilities Association of America
4156 Library Road   412-341-1515
Pittsburgh, PA 15234

847 Understanding Adolescents and Young Adults with Learning Disabilities

Learning Disabilities Association of America
4156 Library Road   412-341-1515
Pittsburgh, PA 15234

848 Understanding Learning Disabilities: a Parent Guide and Workbook

LD Council
P.O. Box 8451   804-748-5012
Richmond, VA 23226

Provides practical, easy to understand information for parents and teachers, workbook pages at the end of each chapter helps parents apply concepts to their child. Topics include characteristics of learning disabilities, coping as a parent, helping your child at home, the LD student at

school and planning for the future. Appendices include case studies, glossaries of terms, lists of other resources and support groups.
181 Pages   Paperback   ISBN 0-963630-50-4

849 When Snow Turns to Rain

Craig Schulze, Author

Woodbine House
5615 Fishers Lane   301-468-8800
Rockville, MD 20852   800-843-7323

A story of one family's struggle to solve the riddle of autism.
250 Pages

$ 14.95

850 Without Reason, a Family Copes with Autism

Charles Hart, Author

Books on Special Children
P.O. Box 305   914-638-1236
Congers, NY 10920

The author discovers his son haas autism. He delves into problems of the autistic person and explains reasons for their actions.
292 Pages

$ 20.95

851 You Can Encourage Your High School Student to Read

Jamie Myers, Author

International Reading Association
800 Barksdale Rd., P.O. Box 8139   302-731-1600
Newark, DE 19714   800-336-READ
                                        FAX 302-731-1057

Offers parents subtle suggestions that will help their teens discover the joy of reading while improving their sense of family community.

$ 1.75

852 You Can Help Your Young Child with Writing

Marcia Baghban, Author

International Reading Association
800 Barksdale Rd., P.O. Box 8139   302-731-1600
Newark, DE 19714   800-336-READ
                                        FAX 302-731-1057

Shows how parents can encourage and support preschoolers as they learn to write.

$ 1.75

853 You, Your Child and "Special" Education

Barbara Coyle Cutler, Author

Paul H. Brookes Publishing Company
P.O. Box 10624   410-337-8539
Baltimore, MD 21285   800-638-3775

This inspiring resource enables parents of children with disabilities to make sense out of often bewildering educational systems.
256 Pages

$ 22.00

854 Your Child's Growing Mind

NCLD
99 Park Avenue   212-687-7211
New York, NY 10016

A parents guide to learning from birth to adolescence.

855 Your Child's Vision Is Important

Caroline Beverstock, Author

International Reading Association
800 Barksdale Rd., P.O. Box 8139   302-731-1600
Newark, DE 19714   800-336-READ
FAX 302-731-1057

Offers parents and teachers a concise yet detailed guide to monitoring their child's vision.

$ 1.75

Young Adult/Adult

856 About Dyslexia - Unraveling the Myth

Priscilla Vail, Author

Connecticut Association for Children with LD
18 Marshall Street   203-838-5010
South Norwalk, CT 06854   FAX 203-866-6108

This book focuses on the communication patterns of strength and weaknesses in dyslexic people from early childhood through adulthood.
49 Pages

$ 7.95

857 Adapted Physical Education for Students

Kimberly Davis, Author

Exceptional Parent Press
2600 South First Street   217-789-8980
Springfield, IL 62794   FAX 217-789-9130

Focuses on the physical education needs and curriculum for autistic children.
142 Pages

$ 29.75

858 Adolescence and the Learning Disabled

W. Cruikshank, Author

Learning Disabilities Association of America
4156 Library Road   412-341-1515
Pittsburgh, PA 15234

$ 1.00

859 The Assertive Option

1990 Research Press Catalog
217-352-3273

A self-instructional book with many exercises and self-tests.

$ 18.95

860 Attention Deficit Disorder in Teenagers and Young Adults

Mark Sloane, Author

Connecticut Association for Children with LD
18 Marshall Street   203-838-5010
South Norwalk, CT 06854   FAX 203-866-6108

Social immaturity, diagnostic procedures and management techniques are among some of the topics explored.
12 Pages

$ 2.00

861 Body and Soul: Ten American Women

Carolyn Corman, Author

Hill & Company Publishers
754 Main Street   207-764-7188
Presque Isle, ME 04769

A powerful book about ten women whose lives make strong statements of individuality, freedom and creativity. One of which, Doreen Lopes, the single mother of three children, struggles with Dyslexia. Despite the odds, Doreen learns to read and eventually enters college. Doreen's true story serves as an excellent example for those coping with learning disabilities and even those who are not, of the power of courage and determination.
134 Pages

862 Clothing and Grooming Manual for Special Young Men

Bebe Antell, Author

Connecticut Association for Children with LD
18 Marshall Street   203-838-5010
South Norwalk, CT 06854   FAX 203-866-6108

A practical guide to help young men dress appropriately and to appear well groomed.
18 Pages

$ 3.00

863 College and the High School Student with Learning Disabilities

Carol Wren, Author

Project Learning Strategies, DePaul University
Room 220, 2323 N. Seminary
Chicago, IL 60614

This booklet has been written for high school students as well as their teachers and counselors. It discusses the nature of learning disabilities and the impact of a disability at both high school and college levels.

864 Defeating Dyslexia

Paris Innes, Author
Trafalgar Square
Box 257   **802-457-1911**
N. Pomfret, VT 05053

Paris Innes, an otherwise normal 14-year old boy suffers from word blindness or dyslexia. While teachers constantly assessed him as average, his father recognized Paris' problems were not normal. While his written work remains severely substandard, this inspiring book will offer hope to dyslexic persons.

    $ 10.95

865 Developing Self-Advocacy

Robert Valenti, Author
Connecticut Association for Children with LD
18 Marshall Street   **203-838-5010**
South Norwalk, CT 06854   **FAX 203-866-6108**
    $ 19.25

866 The Education of Students with Disabilities: Where Do We Stand?

National Council on Disability
800 Independence Ave. SW, Ste. 814
Washington, DC 20591

867 Emergence-Labeled Autistic

Temple Grandin, Author
Therapro, Inc.
225 Arlington Street   **508-872-9494**
Framingham, MA 01701   **FAX 508-875-2062**

Describes what it is like to be autistic and what can be done to help this population.

    $ 10.00

868 Improving Social Skills: a Guide for Teen, Young Adults and Parents

Connecticut Association for Children with LD
18 Marshall Street   **203-838-5010**
South Norwalk, CT 06854   **FAX 203-866-6108**
103 Pages
    $ 8.50

869 Is This Kid Crazy? Understanding Unusual Behavior

Margaret O. Hyde, Author
Westminster Press
925 Chestnut Street   **215-928-2700**
Philadelphia, PA 19107   **800-523-1631**

Helps young people understand unusual behavior stemming from a disabling conidtion. Discusses the possible symptoms, and treatments of autism, schizophrenia, depression and other emotional problems.
96 Pages   Ages 12-15

870 Keeping a Head in School: a Students Book About Learning Abilities/Disorders

Mel Levine, Author
Educators Publishing Service, Inc.
75 Moulton Street   **800-225-5750**
Cambridge, MA 02138

A book for students with learning disabilities. It helps them to gain a better understanding of their personal strengths and weaknesses.

    $ 20.35

871 Lessons Learned

Dave Fullen, Author
Mountain Books
P.O. Box 21-1104   **800-876-MNTN**
Columbus, OH 43221

Children and young adults with learning disabilities share what they have learned about life and learning so far. They also share what they say when asked what its like to have a learning disability.
100 Pages

    $ 4.95

872 Out of Darkness

Connecticut Association for Children with LD
18 Marshall Street   **203-838-5010**
South Norwalk, CT 06854   **FAX 203-866-6108**
Article by an adult who discovers at age 30 that he has ADD.
4 Pages

    $ 1.00

873 Please Don't Say Hello: Living with Childhood Autism

Phyllis Gold, Author
Human Science Press
72 Fifth Avenue   **212-243-6000**
New York, NY 10011

An absorbing, sensitive introduction to autism.
47 Pages   Paper   Ages 9-12

    $ 5.75

874 Reflections on Growing Up Disabled

The Council for Exceptional Children
1920 Association Drive   **703-620-3660**
Reston, VA 22091

R.L. Jones, Editor
Understand how it feels to be a disabled person in school by tuning in to the first-hand accounts of people who

experienced it. Contributors are disabled with learning disabilities, orthopedic impairments, hearing loss and deafness/blindness. These accounts are good for teachers to read, but they are also appropriate for sharing with students at a secondary level.
111 Pages   Paperback

875   Roots and Wings: a Manual About Self-Advocacy

TAPP Project
312 Stuart Street, 2nd Floor   **617-482-2915**
Boston, MA 02116

Why self-advocacy is important and where it begins.

876   The School Survival Guide for Kids with Learning Disabilities

Rhoda Cummings & Gary Fisher, Author
Free Spirit Publishing, Inc.
400 First Avenue North, Ste. 616   **612-338-2068**
Minneapolis, MN 55401   **800-735-7323**
                                         FAX 612-337-5050

Judy Galbraith, Publisher/President
Maurice Prater, Marketing Manager

Helps kids who have been identified as learning disabled succeed in school. Chapters include: You Can Get Organized, You Can Use a Computer, You Can Handle Testing, Ten Ways to be a Better Reader, Ten Steps To Better Writing, Eight Ways to be a Better Speller, How to Solve your Math Problems, You Can Get Along With Others, You Can Stick up For Yourself, and You Can Stay Out Of Trouble.
176 Pages

$ 10.95

877   Scouting and the Learning Disabled - a Manual for Scouting Leaders

Boy Scouts of America
1325 Walnut Hill Lane   **214-580-2000**
Irving, TX 75038

878   Skills for Living

1990 Research Press Catalog
                                         217-352-3273

Group activities for young adolescents.

$ 19.95

879   Speaking for Themselves: Ethnographic Interviews with LD Adults

P.J. Gerber, Author
University of Michigan Press
P.O. Box 1104   **313-764-4392**
Ann Arbor, MI 48106   **FAX 313-936-0456**

In this book, nine adults with learning disabilities tell the "inside story" of how they deal with a very real handicap

that the outside world does not see. The interviews in this volume demonstrate that, for many, learning disabilities do not preclude successful adjustment to adult life.
176 Pages

880   A Student's Guide to Good Grades

Learning Disabilities Association of America
4156 Library Road   **412-341-1515**
Pittsburgh, PA 15234

                                          $ 14.00

881   Succeeding Against the Odds: Strategies & Insights From the Learning Disabled

S. l. Smith, Author
Publishers Book and Audio
P.O. Box 120159   **800-288-2131**
Staten Island, NY 10312

882   A Survival Manual: Case Studies and Suggestions for the LD Teenager

Helen Girandes Weiss, Author
Connecticut Association for Children with LD
18 Marshall Street   **203-838-5010**
South Norwalk, CT 06854   **FAX 203-866-6108**
154 Pages

                                          $ 10.00

883   Tuned-In Book About Learning Disabilities

Marnell L. Hayes, Author
Foothills Educational Materials
#250, 200 Rivercrest Drive SE   **403-236-1655**
Calgary, AB, Canada, T2 C 2X5

Takes the mystery and negative elements out of the term learning disability and speaks directly to LD youngsters in an honest, straightforward manner.

                                          $ 9.00

884   What Do I Do Tomorrow?

A. Stan-Spence, Author
Connecticut Association for Children with LD
18 Marshall Street   **203-838-5010**
South Norwalk, CT 06854   **FAX 203-866-6108**
                                          $ 10.95

885   You Dont Have to Be Dyslexic

Joan M. Smith, Author
Melvin-Smith Learning Center
4436 Engle Road   **916-483-6417**
Sacramento, CA 95821   **800-637-2256**

Provides the first hope for individuals with a dyslexic learning style. It describes individuals, children and adults, who experience these unique learning styles. The challenges, frustration and failures that these individuals experience are changed as they learn to read and to be successful in learning. This book provides assistance in identifying the challenges created by this unique learning style. It is important for parents who wonder why their children are having reading problems.

205 Pages   Paperback

$ 19.95

Children

886 Chickadee Magazine

P.O. Box 11314   416-868-6001
Des Moines, IA 50340

Sylvia Funston, Editor
A "hands-on" science and nature publication designed to entertain and educate 4-9 year olds.
32 Pages

$ 12.95

887 Children's Album

P.O. Box 6086   415-671-9852
Concord, CA 94520

Kathy Madsen, Editor
Emphasizes creative writing and arts and crafts. Featured are original fiction, poetry and artwork by children ages 8-14.

$ 12.00

888 Children's Magic Window

J Publishing Company
1008 West 80th Street
Bloomington, MN 55420   612-881-6112

Mary Morse, Editor
A general interest magazine for children ages 6-12.
98 Pages   Bi-Monthly

$ 16.95

889 Cobblestone: the History Magazine for Young People

Cobblestone Publishing
30 Grove Street   603-924-7209
Peterborough, NH 03458

Carolyn P. Yoder, Editor
American history magazine for children ages 8-14 offering historical accuracy and original approaches to the issue theme.
Monthly

$ 21.95

890 Creative Kids

100 Pine Avenue   800-476-8711
Holmes, PA 19043

Fay L. Gold, Editor
A magazine for kids, by kids. The material includes stories, poetry, artwork, music, games and photography. Aims to motivate and encourage children to strive for results good enough for publication and to experience pride in seeing their work in an international magazine.

$ 17.97

891 Cricket: the Magazine for Children

P.O. Box 51144   800-827-0227
Boulder, CO 80321

Marianna Carus, Editor
Introduces children to some of the best literature and art from all over the world. Featuring a variety of stories and articles coupled with a hearty sense of humor.
Ages 6-12

$ 22.50

892 For Siblings Only

Family Resource Associates, Inc.
35 Haddon Avenue   908-747-5310
Shrewsbury, NJ 07702

Susan Levine, Editor
Newsletter for siblings ages 4-10 with brothers or sisters with disabilities.
Quarterly

$ 6.00

893 Highlights for Children

P.O. Box 269   800-848-8922
Columbus, OH 43272

Kent L. Brown, Jr., Editor
A general interest magazine whose motto is "Fun For Purpose". Each issues has crafts, verses and thinking features interspersed among short stories and factual articles.
Ages 2-12

$ 19.95

894 Jack and Jill

P.O. Box 10003   317-636-8881
Des Moines, IA 50340

Steve Charles, Editor
Contains a variety of short stories that blend humor, adventure and intellect.
48 Pages

$ 11.95

895 Jellybean Jamboree

Xerox Education Publishers
4343 Equity Drive   614-771-0006
Columbus, OH 43228

Robert Quigley, Publisher
Practice in reading and thinking skills for children during summer.
Grades K-1

$ 3.00

896   Junior Scholastic

Scholastic
2931 E. McCarthy Street   314-636-8890
Jefferson City, MO 65102

Lee Baier, Editor

A classroom magazine for students, used as a supplement to the classroom special studies curriculum.
Grades 6-8

$ 19.50

897   Kid City

Children's Television Workshop
One Lincoln Plaza   212-875-6379
New York, NY 10023

Maureen Hunter-Bone, Editor

A general interest magazine with an emphasis on reading and writing. It uses theme such as disguise, treasure, flight and space to interest readers.
Ages 6-10

$ 15.97

898   Kids Life and Times

Kid Life
P.O. Box D   516-447-2853
Bellport, NY 11713

William R. Hulmes, III, Editor

Attempts to motivate parent/child and child/child participation. The various activities and stories are chosen with education and moral content prerequisites.
Grades 1-6

$ 11.95

899   KIND News

NAHEE
P.O. Box 362   203-434-8666
East Haddam, CT 06423   FAX 203-434-9579

Patty Finch, Director

Published by NAHEE, the youth education division of the Humane Society of the United States. Four page color periodical with games, puzzles and entertaining, informative articles designed to teach children to be kind to each other, animals and the earth. Effective as a teaching tool for LD children due to its controlled vocabulary in an easy to read format.

$ 20.00

900   Koala Club News

San Diego Zoo Membership Department
P.O. Box 271   619-231-1515
San Diego, CA 92112

Georgeanne Irvine, Editor

A magazine about animals going to kids who are members of the Zoological Society of San Diego Koala Club.
Ages 0-15

$ 9.00

901   Lady Bug Magazine

P.O. Box 51144   800-827-0227
Boulder, CO 80321

Marianne Carus, Editor

A monthly magazine featuring stories, songs, poems, games and activities for children ages 2-6.
Monthly   Ages 2-6

902   Let's Find Out

Scholastic
2931 E. McCarthy Street   314-636-8890
Jefferson City, MO 65102

Jean Marzollo, Editor

A magazine with a learning program based on monthly themes such as the child, school, transporation, animals and plants.
8 x annually

$ 4.25

903   Letterbug

Letterbug
111 Hillcrest Avenue   412-847-3327
Beaver Falls, PA 15010

Shandel Gilbert, Editor

Available in English and Spanish and emphasizes reading, writing and thinking skills.
4 Pages   Ages 3-6

904   Muppet Magazine

Muppet Magazine
P.O. Box 10176   515-247-7500
Des Moines, IA 50340

Kaly Dobbs, VP/Editorial Dir.

A humor and entertainment magazine featuring the Muppets.
Per Issue   Ages 8-12

$ 3.00

905   Owl Magazine

P.O. Box 11314   416-868-6001
Des Moines, IA 50340

Sylvia Funston, Editor

A discovery magazine for children over the age of eight. readers can explore the world around them, with topics ranging from animals to late-breaking high-tech developments.
32 Pages

$ 19.95

906   Pennywhistle Press

Gannett Publishing
P.O. Box 500-P   703-276-3780
Washington, DC 20044

Anita Sama, Editor

A national children's newspaper supplement for young readers established to help stir children's interests in reading the newspaper.
Ages 4-14

907   Ranger Rick

National Wildlife Foundation/Membership Services
8925 Leesburg Pike   703-790-4000
Vienna, VA   22180

Gerry Bishop, Editor

Dedicated to helping students gain a greater understanding and appreciation of nature.
Ages 6-12

$ 14.00

908   Read Magazine

Field Publications
4343 Equity Drive   800-999-7100
Columbus, OH   43216

Lynell Johnson, Editor

Designed for use in English and reading classes. Every issue contains a play and a short story, word games, logic puzzles and ideas for students poems.
Graddes 6-9

$ 6.25

909   Scholastic News

Scholastic
2931 E. McCarthy Street   314-636-8890
Jefferson City, MO   65102

John Lent, Editor

A weekly classroom newspaper, published in six separate editions for children in grades 1-6. Each edition is planned and written at the level to help students understand major world and national news.
Grades 1-6

$ 1.95

910   Sesame Street Magazine

P.O. Box 52000   212-595-3456
Boulder, CO   80321

Marge Kennedy, Editor

A publication featuring stories, games and activities that introduce the alphabet, numbers and single problem-solving skills and reinforce positive social skills.
Ages 2-6

$ 13.97

911   Snoopy Magazine

P.O. Box 10570   515-247-7500
Des Moines, IA   50340

Katy Dobbs, VP/Editorial Dir.

A publication for preschoolers and their parents starring Charles Schultz' Peanuts characters. The kids pages feature stories and activities for children and the parents pages include a variety of features of interest to parents.
Per Issue   Preschool

$ 3.00

912   Sports Illustrated for Kids

Time, Inc. Magazine Company
P.O. Box 830067   800-632-1300
Birmingham, AL   35283

John Papanek, Editor

Presents sports-oriented subjects and, in a 4-color magazine format, introduces young readers to professional and amateur sports figures.
Monthly   Ages 8-13

$ 15.95

913   Stone Soup: the Magazine for Children

P.O. Box 83   408-426-5557
Santa Cruz, CA   95063

Gerry Mandel, Editor

A literary magazine publishing fiction, poetry, book reviews and art by children through age 13.
Bi-Monthly   Ages 6-13

914   Stork Magazine

P.O. Box 10003   317-636-8881
Des Moines, IA   50340

Deborah Block, Editor

A new publication designed to teach love of reading in children ages 3 months to 3 years. Focuses on early developmental concepts and health in its poems, stories and activities.
ages 0-3

$ 11.95

915   Turtle Magazine for Preschool Kids

P.O. Box 10003   317-636-8881
Des Moines, IA   50340

Beth Wood Thomas, Editor

Created to meet the intellectual and developmental needs of children, with special emphasis placed on health.
48 Pages   Ages 2-5

$ 11.95

916   U*S* Kids

Field Publications
4343 Equity Drive   800-999-7100
Columbus, OH   43216

Nancy Webb, Managing Editor

A magazine with a "real-world" focus. It has four editorial objectives; to help children understand the world

around them, to interest them in learning, to develop creativity and imagination, and to develop better reading skills and vocabulary.
Ages 5-10

$ 18.95

917　Weekly Reader

Field Publications
P.O. Box 16630　　　　　　800-999-7100
Columbus, OH　43216

Lyneel Johnson, Executive Editor

A graded series of classroom newspapaers. Provides current information and recreational reading material.
Pre-K - 6

$ 3.25

918　Weekly Reader Summer Editions A, B and C

Field Publications
4343 Equity Drive　　　　　800-999-7100
Columbus, OH　43216

Lynell Johnson, Executive Editor

Extend the classroom periodicals purposes - to connect children to their world and to provide skill-based learning activities. This is done through news features, true-life adventures, and activities selected and written to appeal to readers at each grade level.
Pre-K - 6

Parents

919　ACTTion News

ACTT - Western Illinois University
27 Horabin Halle　　　　　309-298-1014
Macomb, IL　61455

Offers articles and information for families, teachers, parents and professionals working with young learning disabled children.

920　ADHD/Hyperactivity: a Consumers Guide

Connecticut Association for Children with LD
18 Marshall Street　　　　203-838-5010
South Norwalk, CT　06854　　FAX 203-866-6108

Sifts through a sea of information about the assessment and treatment of ADHD in children.
178 Pages

$ 16.50

921　The Bridge

Statewide Parent Advocacy Network, Inc.
516 North Avenue, East　　908-654-7726
Westfield, NJ　07090　　　800-654-SPAn
　　　　　　　　　　　　FAX 908-654-7880

Provides updates on educational laws, model programs and a calendar of events of interest to parents.
Quarterly

922　Exceptional Children

The Council for Exceptional Children
1920 Association Drive　　　703-620-3660
Reston, VA　22091

Articles include research, literature surveys and position papers concerning exceptional children, special education and mainstreaming.

$ 35.00

923　Exceptional Parent

Psy-Ed Corporation
1170 Commonwealth Avenue, 3rd Fl.　617-730-5800
Boston, MA　02134

Offers information on products, services, news and technology for parents, professionals and the learning disabled.
Monthly

$ 18.00

924　First Steps

Parents Union for Public Schools in Philadelphia
311 S. Juniper Street, Rm. 602　　215-546-1166
Philadelphia, PA　19107　　FAX 215-731-1688

A handbook for parents of children with disabilities 0-3 years of age.

925　How Does Your Child Hear and Talk?

American Speech-Language-Hearing Association
10801 Rockville Pike　　　301-897-5700
Rockville, MD　20852　　　800-638-8255

Offers information charting your child's age and what they should be doing in the areas of hearing and speaking. Also offered in a Spanish version.

926　Letting Go

National Stuttering Project
4681 Irving Street　　　　415-566-5324
San Francisco, CA　91364

Contains informal articles sharing experiences and ideas on stuttering.
Monthly

927　Next Step

Parents Union for Public Schools in Philadelphia
311 S. Juniper Street, Rm. 602　　215-546-1166
Philadelphia, PA　19107　　FAX 215-731-1688

A handbook for parents of children with disabilities 3-5 years of age.

928　A Parents Guide

NICHCY
P.O. Box 1492　　　　　　703-893-6061
Washington, DC　20013　　800-999-5599

Offers information on accessing programs for infants, toddlers and preschoolers with disabilities.

Young Adult/Adult

929 American Girl

Pleasant Company Publications
P.O. Box 620896   608-836-4848
Middleton, WI 53562   800-233-0264

Nancy Holyoke, Editor

Contains fictional, stories of the "American Girl" as well as entertaining articles of current topics relevant to girls.
Bi-Monthly   Ages 7-12

$ 19.95

930 Bear Essential News for Kids

2406 South 24th Street   602-244-2527
Phoenix, AZ 85034

An education/entertainment publication that welcomes children's creative writing and advertises products and services geared to families.
Pre-K - 7

931 Boy's Life

Boy's Life Subscription Service
1325 Walnut Hill Lane   214-580-2512
Irving, TX 75015

William B. McMorris, Editor

Seeks to provide entertainment for boys ages 7-17 with subject matter including outdoor activities, hobbies, sports, history and the dangers of drugs and alcohol.

932 Disabled Outdoors Magazine

2052 West 23rd Streetue   708-358-4160
Chicago, IL 60608

John Kopchik, Publisher
Carolyn Dohme, Editor

A publication for sports persons with disabilities. Covers hunting, fishing, mountaineering, aviation, travel, new products and places to go for people of all ages with all types of disabilities covering the United States and Canada.
32-40 Pages

933 The Goldfinch

State Historical Society of Iowa
402 Iowa Avenue   319-335-3916
Iowa City, IA 52240

Carolyn Hardesty, Editor

A history magazine for children ages 9-13. Offers play, games, puzzles and contests.
Ages 9-13

$ 10.00

934 Know Your World Extra

Field Publications
4343 Equity Drive   800-999-7100
Columbus, OH 43216

Scott Ingram, Editor

A special education periodical presenting a wide variety of high-interest topics to students with their interests and abilities in mind.
Ages 11-16

$ 6.99

935 Literary Cavalcade

Scholastic
2931 E. McCarthy Street   314-636-8890
Jefferson City, MO 65102

A language arts magazine used in advance placement English classrooms.
48 Pages   Monthly   Grades 9-12

$ 5.95

936 Magazines for Children

Donald Stoll, Author

International Reading Association
800 Barksdale Rd., P.O. Box 8139   302-731-1600
Newark, DE 19714   800-336-READ
                                       FAX 302-731-1057

This award winning volume is a guidebook to more than 120 worthwhile children's periodicals, aimed at infants on up to teenagers.
48 Pages

$ 5.25

937 Moving Forward

1689 E. Del Amo Blvd.   310-603-9923
Carson, CA 90746   FAX 310-603-9932

Paul Aziz, Publisher/Editor
Agena Aziz, Publisher/Bus. Mgr.

A national newspaper for persons with disabilities offering convention information, book reviews, assistive technology, law and legislation information and more.
Bi-Monthly

$ 11.50

938 National Association for Adults with Special Learning Needs

NAASLN Membership/SCI-Hab Unit
4546 Broad River Road   803-896-1859
Columbia, SC 29210

Mitch Townley, NAASLN Membership
Jay Creteila, NAASLN President

Offers brief articles on topics of interest, task force reviews, information on national conference and activities and other items relative to the NAASLN mission..
Quarterly

$ 45.00

939   National Geographic World

P.O. Box 2330   202-857-7000
Washington, DC 20077

Pat Robbins, Editor

Features factual stories on outdoor adventures, natural
history, sports, science and history. Special features
include posters, games, crafts and mazes.
32 Pages   Ages 8-14

$ 10.95

940   New Mobility

Spinal Network
P.O. Box 4162   303-449-5412
Boulder, CO 80306   800-338-5412
                                            FAX 303-449-5817

Sam Maddox, Publisher
Barry Corbet, Editor

The award-winning, lifestyle magazine for people with
disabilities. New Mobility provides hard-hitting coverage
of personalities, medical issues, civil rights, equipment
sports and recreation, travel, sexuality, and family issues.
72 Pages   Bi-Monthly

$ 18.00

941   NICHCY News Digest

NICHCY
P.O. Box 1492   703-893-6061
Washington, DC 20013   800-999-5599

Offers articles and various information for the disabled.

942   OnCenter

Department of Veterans Affairs, Medical Center
3801 Miranda Avenue/153   415-493-5000
Palo Alto, CA 94304

A newsletter offering information on technology, assistive
devices, evaluations, tests and more for the disabled and
elderly.
Bi-Annual

943   Options in Learning

Alliance for Parental Involvement in Education
P.O. Box 59   518-392-6900
East Chatham, NY 12060

Association newsletter offering information on referral
services, letters from readers, resources for families and
notices of special events.
Quarterly

944   PIP College "HELPS"

Partners in Publishing
1419 West First   918-584-5906
Tulsa, OK 74127

P.M. Fielding, Editor

A publication written for learning disabled parents and
service providers that includes timely information and
"first person" articles.
13 issues

$ 33.00

945   Scholastic Action

Scholastic
2931 E. McCarthy Street   314-636-8890
Jefferson City, MO 65102

Patrick Daley, Editor

A classroom magazine created for students in grades 7-9
whose reading level is grades 4-7. It is used as a motivating and timely teen-oriented reading supplement for special education students in language arts programs.
32 Pages   Grades 7-9

$ 5.75

946   Scholastic Math

Scholastic
2931 E. McCarthy Street   314-636-8890
Jefferson City, MO 65102

John Lent, Editor

A classroom magazine used as a supplement to the math
curriculum.
Bi-Weekly   Grades 7-9

$ 5.95

947   Scholastic Scope

Scholastic
2931 E. McCarthy Street   314-636-8890
Jefferson City, MO 65102

David Goddy, Editor

A classroom magazine for students in grades 8-12 who
have reading levels of grades 4-7. Used as a supplement
for a language arts class.
Grades 8-12

$ 5.95

948   Scholastic Search

Scholastic
2931 E. McCarthy Street   314-636-8890
Jefferson City, MO 65102

Jeff Kisseloff, Editor

A classroom magazine written at an easy reading level. It
is used as a supplement to US History classes.
32 Pages   Grades 8-12

$ 6.50

949   Scholastic Sprint

Scholastic
2931 E. McCarthy Street   314-636-8890
Jefferson City, MO 65102

Karen Glenn, Editor

A classroom magazine for students with a reading level of grades 2-3. It is used as a supplement for language arts classes for students with special learning needs.
Grades 4-6

$ 5.95

950   Scholastic Update

Scholastic
2931 E. McCarthy Street   314-636-8890
Jefferson City, MO 65102

Lee Kravitz, Editor

A classroom magazine created as a supplement for social studies students. This publication includes articles on national and global affairs presented in terms of history, sociology, economics and world studies.
32 Pages   Grades 8-12

$ 5.95

951   Scholastic Voice

Scholastic
2931 E. McCarthy Street   314-636-8890
Jefferson City, MO 65102

Forrest Stone, Editor

Designed to be a supplement for language arts classes during the school year. It features high-interest, on-level critical reading and response writing activities.
32 Pages   Grades 8-12

$ 5.95

952   Seedling Stories: Short Story International

P.O. Box 405   516-466-4166
Great Neck, NY 11022

Sylvia Tankel, Editor

Contains worldwide short stories with application to language arts and social studies.
64 Pages   Ages 9-12

$ 14.00

953   Shoe Tree

Membership Services
P.O. Box 3000   505-982-8596
Denville, NJ 07834

Sheila Cowing, Editor

The literary magazine by and for young writers, presents stories, poems, book reviews and personal narratives contributed by writers and illustrators.
Ages 6-14

$ 15.00

954   Sibling Forum

Family Resource Associates, Inc.
35 Haddon Avenue   908-747-5310
Shrewsbury, NJ 07702

Susan Levine, Editor

Newsletter for siblings ages 10 and up with brothers or sisters with disabilities.
Quarterly

$ 6.00

955   The Source

CRW Publications
P.O. Box 878   414-255-9077
Menomonee Falls, WI 53051   FAX 414-255-3388

Wendy Loerch, Editor
Jeff Schlax, Account Executive

A paper for people with disabilities offering information, resources and articles on the latest technology for persons with disabilities.
24 Pages   Monthly

956   Student Series: Short Story International

Short Story International
P.O. Box 405   516-466-4166
Great Neck, NY 11022

Sylvia Tankel, Editor

A publication carrying about 10 unabridged, contemporary stories by living authors throughout the world. The goal of the magazine is to help promote and strengthen the reading habit and provide insights into other cultures as well as our own.
96 Pages   Ages 13-18

$ 16.00

957   Their World 1993

National Center for Learning Disabilities
TW-93, NCLD, 99 Park Avenue   212-687-7211
New York, NY 10016

The only comprehensive publication in the field describing true life stories about ways children and adults cope with learning disabilities.

$ 10.00

958   3-2-1 Contact

P.O. Box 53051   212-595-3456
Boulder, CO 80322

Jonathan Rosenbloom, Editor

A science and teachnology magazine. It aims to make readers aware of the science around them. Includes articles on animals and nature, sociology and psychology and scientists' tasks.
Ages 8-14

$ 15.97

959   Wombat: a Journal of Young People's Writing and Art

Wombat
745 Prince Avenue   404-549-4875
Athens, GA 30603

Jacqueline Howe, Editor

A national magazine devoted entirely to the poetry, short stories, artwork, nonfiction, cartoons and puzzles created by young people.

32 Pages   Ages 6-16

$ 14.95

960   Writing!

Field Publications
4343 Equity Drive
Columbus, OH 43216

800-999-7100

Alan Lenhoff, Editor

The continuing guide to written communication. Its goal is to motivate students to write. Focuses on articles addressing writing problems or challenges. Includes practical writing exercises, examples of student writing and interviews with successful authors.

Grades 7-12

$ 5.60

961 About Learning Disabilities

Learning Disabilities Association of America
P.O. Box 15525   602-230-7188
Phoenix, AZ 85060

A pamphlet about what everyone should know about learning disabilities.

962 About the Americans with Disabilities Act

Learning Disabilities Association of America
4156 Library Road   412-341-1515
Pittsburgh, PA 15234

A booklet which provides a clear description of the Americans with Disabilities Act and the right it offers to persons with disabilities.

$ 2.00

963 Activities to Help Develop Motor and Perceptual Skills

Learning Disabilities Association of America
P.O. Box 15525   602-230-7188
Phoenix, AZ 85060

Offering hints on how to increase coordination and strengthen hand muscles.

964 ADHD

Larry B. Silver, M.D., Author
ACLD
4156 Library Road   412-341-1515
Pittsburgh, PA 15234

A booklet for parents offering information on Attention Deficit-Hyperactivity Disorders and learning disabilities.

965 Adult Dyslexia in Remediation: the ABC's and Much More

Joan Knight, Author
Connecticut Association for Children with LD
18 Marshall Street   203-838-5010
South Norwalk, CT 06854   FAX 203-866-6108
$ .75

966 Advocacy Services for Families of Children in Special Education

Arizona Department of Education
1535 West Jefferson   602-542-3852
Phoenix, AZ 85007   800-352-4558

967 All About ERIC

United States Department of Education
Washington, DC 20208   202-293-2450

A pamphlet offering information on The Educational Resources Information Center.

968 An Introduction to Your Child Who Has Hyperkinesis

Siegried Centerwall, Author
Connecticut Association for Children with LD
18 Marshall Street   203-838-5010
South Norwalk, CT 06854   FAX 203-866-6108

A short, but impressive general introduction to ADHD written specifically for parents.
12 Pages

$ 2.00

969 Answers & Questions About Adult Aphasia

American Speech-Language-Hearing Association
10801 Rockville Pike   301-897-5700
Rockville, MD 20852   800-638-8255

Offers information regarding aphasia.

970 Answers & Questions About Articulation Problems

American Speech-Language-Hearing Association
10801 Rockville Pike   301-897-5700
Rockville, MD 20852   800-638-8255

Offers information on articulation problems in children and adults.

971 Answers & Questions About Assistive Listening Devices

American Speech-Language-Hearing Association
10801 Rockville Pike   301-897-5700
Rockville, MD 20852   800-638-8255

Offers information about hearing assistive devices.

972 Answers & Questions About Child Language

American Speech-Language-Hearing Association
10801 Rockville Pike   301-897-5700
Rockville, MD 20852   800-638-8255

Offers information on speech, language, and what certain indications are in the learning disabled child.

973 Answers & Questions About Noise and Hearing Loss

American Speech-Language-Hearing Association
10801 Rockville Pike   301-897-5700
Rockville, MD 20852   800-638-8255

Gives information on how noise can affect hearing loss.

974 Answers & Questions About Otitis Media, Hearing and Language Development

American Speech-Language-Hearing Association
10801 Rockville Pike   301-897-5700
Rockville, MD 20852   800-638-8255

Answers questions about Otitis Media and the effects it has on language development.

975 Answers & Questions About Stuttering

American Speech-Language-Hearing Association
10801 Rockville Pike   **301-897-5700**
Rockville, MD 20852   **800-638-8255**

Offers information on the causes and indications of stuttering.

976 Answers & Questions About Tinnitus

American Speech-Language-Hearing Association
10801 Rockville Pike   **301-897-5700**
Rockville, MD 20852   **800-638-8255**

Offers answers to various questions on tinnitus.

977 Answers & Questions About Voice Problems

American Speech-Language-Hearing Association
10801 Rockville Pike   **301-897-5700**
Rockville, MD 20852   **800-638-8255**

Offers information on what a "normal" voice and what a "problem" voice is.

978 Attention Deficit and the MacIntosh

Bob Margolies, Author
Connecticut Association for Children with LD
18 Marshall Street   **203-838-5010**
South Norwalk, CT 06854   **FAX 203-866-6108**

Discusses the fascination of children and adolescents with ADHD, in video related activities and the reason for that intense involvement.
11-13 Pages

$ 3.25

979 Attention Deficit Disorder

Learning Disabilities Association of America
4156 Library Road   **412-341-1515**
Pittsburgh, PA 15234

Well organized, scholarly outline covering terminology, definition, characteristics, physical and emotional aspects, chronological patterns, diagnosis, treatment adn prognosis. Somewhat a technical text aimed at professionals and informed parents.
4 Pages

$ 1.00

980 Attention Deficit-Hyperactivity Disorder: It It a Learning Disability?

Larry Silver, Author

Georgetown University, School of Medicine
3800 Reservoir Road NW
Washington, DC 20007

Larry Silver, M.D.
Offers information on learning disabilities and related disorders.

981 Audiology Sample Packet

American Speech-Language-Hearing Association
10801 Rockville Pike   **301-897-5700**
Rockville, MD 20852   **800-638-8255**

Offers 12 brochures on communication disorders.
12 brochures

$ 1.50

982 Augmentative Communication Booklets

American Speech-Language-Hearing Association
10801 Rockville Pike   **301-897-5700**
Rockville, MD 20852   **800-638-8255**

Briefly explains augmentative communication systems with specific readers in mind.
15-35 Pages   Set of 5

$ 6.00

983 Common Ground: the National Council of Teachers of English and the IRA

International Reading Association
800 Barksdale Rd., P.O. Box 8139   **302-731-1600**
Newark, DE 19714   **800-336-READ**
                        FAX 302-731-1057

This informative pamphlet outlines four principles on intellectual freedom in education.
100 Copies

$ 7.00

984 The Confusion Relating to Ritalin

Learning Disabilities Association of America
P.O. Box 15525   **602-230-7188**
Phoenix, AZ 85060

Offers information on the problems occurring when drugs are used to modify behavior.

985 Dear Parent

Learning Disabilities Association of America
4156 Library Road   **412-341-1515**
Pittsburgh, PA 15234

Set of seven pamphlets.

986 Do Your Health Benefits Cover Audiology and Speech-Language Pathology?

American Speech-Language-Hearing Association
10801 Rockville Pike   301-897-5700
Rockville, MD 20852   800-638-8255
Answers all important questions about health benefits.

987 Dyslexia and Severe Reading Disability

K. Ngandu, Author
Connecticut Association for Children with LD
18 Marshall Street   203-838-5010
South Norwalk, CT 06854   FAX 203-866-6108
                                          $ .75

988 Dyslexia: Especially for Parents

Connecticut Association for Children with LD
18 Marshall Street   203-838-5010
South Norwalk, CT 06854   FAX 203-866-6108
                                          $ 2.00

989 Dyslexia - the Language Disability That Can Be Overcome

Connecticut Association for Children with LD
18 Marshall Street   203-838-5010
South Norwalk, CT 06854   FAX 203-866-6108
                                          $ 2.25

990 The Dyslogic Syndrome

Learning Disabilities Association of America
1011 West 31st Street   512-458-8234
Austin, TX 78705
Offers information to parents and teachers on how to cope with and treat children with this specific behavioral disorder.

991 Educating Children with Disabilities

Learning Disabilities Association of America
P.O. Box 15525   602-230-7188
Phoenix, AZ 85060
Pamphlet describing educational testing and resources offered to the disabled student.

992 Educational Technology and Learning Disabilities

Learning Disabilities Association of America
4156 Library Road   412-341-1515
Pittsburgh, PA 15234
A resource directory of software and hardware products for the learning disabled.
23 Pages

993 Effective Discipline: a Guide to Child Management for Parents

J. Windell & E. Windell, Author
Learning Disabilities Association of America
4156 Library Road   412-341-1515
Pittsburgh, PA 15234
                                          $ 3.00

994 Facing the Invisible Disability

Steven Shulman, Author
Connecticut Association for Children with LD
18 Marshall Street   203-838-5010
South Norwalk, CT 06854   FAX 203-866-6108
5 Pages
                                          $ 1.50

995 Fact Sheet - Attention Deficit-Hyperactivity Disorder

Learning Disabilities Association of America
P.O. Box 15525   602-230-7188
Phoenix, AZ 85060
A pamphlet offering factual information on ADHD.

996 Facts About Dyslexia

National Inst. of Child Health/Human Development
P.O. Box 29111   301-496-5133
Washington, DC 20040
A brief, informative packet that includes a definition of dyslexia, common symptoms, possible causes, treatments and listings of other sources of information.
13 Pages

997 Finally! Rehabilitation and Remediation for the Learning Disabled Soldier

Major Judith Riggan, Author
Connecticut Association for Children with LD
18 Marshall Street   203-838-5010
South Norwalk, CT 06854   FAX 203-866-6108
2 Pages

998 General Information About Autism

NICHCY
P.O. Box 1492   703-893-6061
Washington, DC 20013   800-999-5599
Offers information, in pamphlet form, about Autism.

999 General Information About Disabilities

NICHCY
P.O. Box 1492   703-893-6061
Washington, DC 20013   800-999-5599
A fact sheet offering information on the Education of the Handicapped Act.

1000 General Information About Speech and Language Disorders

NICHCY
P.O. Box 1492   703-893-6061
Washington, DC 20013   800-999-5599

Offers characterisitcs, educational implications and association in the area of speech and language disorders.

1001 Have You Ever Known a Perceptually Handicapped Child?

L. Lethinen, Author

Learning Disabilities Association of America
4156 Library Road   412-341-1515
Pittsburgh, PA 15234

$ .50

1002 Helping Learning Disabled Music Students

Learning Disabilities Association of America
4156 Library Road   412-341-1515
Pittsburgh, PA 15234

$ .75

1003 Here's Help for Your Most Distractible Students

Robert McNergney, Author

Connecticut Association for Children with LD
18 Marshall Street   203-838-5010
South Norwalk, CT 06854   FAX 203-866-6108

Teacher manual on improving attention with self-monitoring.
1 Pages

1004 How to Choose a College

Association on Higher Education and Disability
P.O. Box 21192   614-488-4972
Columbus, OH 43221

A guide for students with a disability.
16 Pages

$ .95

1005 A Learning Disabilities Digest for Service Providers

Connecticut Association for Children with LD
18 Marshall Street   203-838-5010
South Norwalk, CT 06854   FAX 203-866-6108
22 Pages

$ 3.00

1006 Learning Disabilities: Why Some Smart People Can't Learn

L. Duncan, Author

Learning Disabilities Association of America
4156 Library Road   412-341-1515
Pittsburgh, PA 15234

$ 1.00

1007 Learning Disability: Unsure Social Behavior/Insecure Relationships

Dale Brown, Author

Connecticut Association for Children with LD
18 Marshall Street   203-838-5010
South Norwalk, CT 06854   FAX 203-866-6108
4 Pages

1008 Let's Talk

American Speech-Language-Hearing Association
10801 Rockville Pike   301-897-5700
Rockville, MD 20852   800-638-8255

Contains brief information on a variety of interesting speech-language-hearing topics to inform and educate the public.
100 copies

$ 24.00

1009 Parenting Attention Deficit Disordered Teens

Connecticut Association for Children with LD
18 Marshall Street   203-838-5010
South Norwalk, CT 06854   FAX 203-866-6108

A small pamphlet with amazingly detailed outline of the various problems of adolescents with ADHD.
14 Pages

$ 3.25

1010 Plain Talk About Children with Learning Disabilities

Learning Disabilities Association of America
P.O. Box 15525   602-230-7188
Phoenix, AZ 85060

Offers information on how to cope and understand with the learning disabled child.

1011 Public Agencies Fact Sheet

NICHCY
P.O. Box 1492   703-893-6061
Washington, DC 20013   800-999-5599

General information on public agencies that serve the disabled individual.

1012 Questions About

American Speech-Language-Hearing Association
10801 Rockville Pike   301-897-5700
Rockville, MD 20852   800-638-8255

Various brochures on stuttering, aphasia, voice problems, tinnitus, assistive learning devices and more.
100 copies

$ 20.00

1013 Questions Often Asked About Special Education Services

NICHCY
P.O. Box 1492   703-893-6061
Washington, DC 20013   800-999-5599

Offers information regarding special education.

1014 Ready, Set, Go!!!

HEATH Resource Center
One Dupont Circle NW   202-939-9329
Washington, DC 20036   800-544-3284

A pamphlet helping learning disabled students prepare for college.

1015 Recognizing Communication Disorders

American Speech-Language-Hearing Association
10801 Rockville Pike   301-897-5700
Rockville, MD 20852   800-638-8255

Offers information on common speech and communication disorders and how a speech-language pathologist can help.

1016 Specific Learning Disabilities in the Adult Years

ACLD, Inc.
4156 Library Road   412-341-1515
Pittsburgh, PA 15234

Offers information and suggestions on learning disabilities.

1017 Speech and Language Disorders and the Speech-Language Pathologist

American Speech-Language-Hearing Association
10801 Rockville Pike   301-897-5700
Rockville, MD 20852   800-638-8255

Offers information on speech and language disorders, some various types, and answers some important questions on the disorders and how they affect learning.

1018 Speech-Language Pathology Packet

American Speech-Language-Hearing Association
10801 Rockville Pike   301-897-5700
Rockville, MD 20852   800-638-8255

Includes 13 brochures on speech-language pathology.
13 brochures

$ 1.50

1019 Suggestions to Parents

Learning Disabilities Association of America
P.O. Box 15525   602-230-7188
Phoenix, AZ 95060

Offers helpful hints to parents to help modify behavior exhibited by the learning disabled child in the home and to help the child cope with his/her environment.

1020 What Are Learning Disabilities

Mary Banbury, Author
Connecticut Association for Children with LD
18 Marshall Street   203-838-5010
South Norwalk, CT 06854   FAX 203-866-6108

A brief, but informative booklet which provides a concise definition of various learning disabilities.

$ .75

1021 What Every Parent Should Know About Learning Disabilities

C.L. Bete Co., Author
Connecticut Association for Children with LD
18 Marshall Street   203-838-5010
South Norwalk, CT 06854   FAX 203-866-6108

$ 1.50

1022 The ABC's of Learning Disabilities

American Federation of Teachers
555 New Jersey Avenue NW   202-879-4458
Washington, DC 20001

This film illustrates the case histories of four learning disabled students with various learning disabilities.

1023 ADHD in Adulthood: a Clinical Perspective

A.L. Robin, Author

Professional Advancement Seminars
No. 1 Dix Street   508-792-2408
Worcester, MA 01609

A video providing mental health professionals and their clients with information which can be used to better understand how attention deficit hyperactivity disorder manifests itself in adults.
Video

1024 ADHD: What Can We Do?

R.A. Barkley, Author

Guilford Publications
72 Spring Street   212-431-9800
New York, NY 10012

Illustrates the many avenues for helping persons with attention deficit hyperactivity disorder.
Video

1025 ADHD: What Do We Know?

R.A. Barkley, Author

Guilford Publications
72 Spring Street   212-431-9800
New York, NY 10012

Providing an overview of attention deficit hyperactivity disorder and introduces viewers to three young children who have ADHD. Discusses how ADHD affects the lives of chldren and adults, causes of the disorder, associated problems, and outcomes in adulthood.
Video

1026 Adolescent Language Disorders: Modeule V

Thinking Publications
P.O. Box 163   715-832-2488
Eau Claire, WI 54702

A video designed to identify the ways in which language of instruction negatively affects the academic performance of language-disordered adolescents.
Video

1027 Adults with Learning Problems

Learning Disabilities Resources
P.O. Box 716   215-525-8336
Bryn Mawr, PA 19010   800-869-8336
Video

$ 12.00

1028 All in a Lifetime

Mohawk Council on Educational TV
WMHT TV   518-356-1700
Schnectady, NY

The four sessions present interviews with children, parents and other young adults who discuss their perceptions of mainstreaming.
Video

$ 20.00

1029 America's Disability Channel

ADC
1777 NE Loop 410, Ste. 1401   512-824-SIGN
San Antonio, TX 78217   FAX 512-829-1388

A national cable television channel featuring entertainment and informational programming "Focusing on Disability." Designed to be a "Telecommunications Cooperative" for people with disabilities, their families and the organizations and professionals who work with them.

1030 Andreas - Outcomes of Inclusion

The University Affiliated Program of Vermont
499 C. Waterman Bldg.   802-656-4031
Burlington, VT 05405

Portrays the academic, occupational, and social inclusion of a student with severe disability in a high school. Includes commentary of parents, administrators, teachers, support personnel and classmates.
Video

1031 The Anger Within: Programs 1-4

N.A. Klotz, Author

NAK 1 Productions
1422 Fenwick Lane   301-565-0355
Silver Spring, MD 20910

Two videos focusing on parental and professional perspectives, understanding of children's feelings, treatment models and techniques and skills for working with students with emotional problems.
Video

1032 Another Page

KET, the Kentucky Network Enterprise Division
560 Cooper Drive   800-354-9067
Lexington, KY 40502   FAX 606-258-7396

This video series develops and delivers practical instruction in reading comprehension using a whole language approach, emphasizing consumer and life skills.
Video

1033 The Art of Communication

B. Wagonseller, Author

United Learning
6633 West Howard Street   708-647-0600
Niles, IL 60714

Designed for parents and professionals, this video focuses on: effective parent-child communication; nonverbal communication in children; effective listening; effects of negative and critical messages; and deterrents limiting child/parent communication.
Video

1034 Arts Express

KET, the Kentucky Network Enterprise Division
560 Cooper Drive   800-354-9067
Lexington, KY 40502   FAX 606-258-7396

A delightful way to introduce elementary students to the visual arts, music and dance.
Video

1035 ASCD Cooperative Learning Series

R.E. Slavin, Author

Association for Supervision/Curriculum Development
1250 North Pitt Street   703-549-9110
Alexandria, VA 22314

A facilitator's manual, book and five videotapes focusing on the following goals: providing a fundamental knowledge of cooperative learning and the benefits derived from its use; provides a basic understanding of how to plan and teach cooperative lessons; and provide resources to use to expand and refine the above knowledge and skills.
Video

1036 Assessing Infants and Toddlers: a Family Focus Videoconference

American Speech-Language-Hearing Association
10801 Rockville Pike   301-897-5700
Rockville, MD 20852   800-638-8255

Designed for speech-language pathologists and audiologists, 2 videotapes to improve clinical skills in assessing infants, toddlers and their families.
Video

1037 Assessment

Hubbard Scientific
P.O. Box 760   800-323-8368
Chippewa Falls, WI 54729

A video familiarizing viewers with the process and the materials for determining the learning potential of individual students.
Video

1038 Attention Deficit Disorder

D.R. Jordan, Author
Pro-Ed
8700 Shoal Creek Road   512-451-3246
Austin, TX 78758

A video and book providing helpful suggestions for both home and classroom management of students with attention deficit disorder.
Video

1039 Attention Disorders: the School's Votal Role

3 C's of Childhood, Inc.
5395 Roswell Rd. NE, Ste. 3046   404-986-9054
Atlanta, GA 30342

A manual and 2 videotapes dramatizing life of children, adolescents and adults with attention disorders.
Video

1040 Breaking the Unseen Barrier: Teaching the Student with Learning Disabilities

Agency for Instructional Technology
1111 West 17th Street   812-339-2203
Bloomington, IN 47404

A series of eight videotapes designed to train regular classroom teachers, parents and other caring adults to instruct individuals with learning disabilities.
Video-Set of 8

1041 Catch Them Being Good: Reinforcement in the Classroom

Association for Supervision/Curriculum Development
1250 North Pitt Street   703-549-9110
Alexandria, VA 22314

A facilitator's manual and videotapes designed for teachers K-12. A proactive, preventive approach to managing student behavior problems based on the principles of positive reinforcement, extinction, negative reinforcement, punishment, cursing and modeling.
Video

1042 Chance to Be

National Audiovisual Center
1618 Orrington Avenue   301-763-1896
Washington, DC 60201

A video focusing on career education programs for physically disabled, the gifted, minorities and women. It addresses the total issue of education as a prerequisite for work.
Video

1043 Characteristics of the Learning Disabled Adult

Special Education Nazareth
College Of Rochester   716-586-2525
New York, NY 14610

An awareness interactive video recognizing characteristics and instructional needs of learning disabled adults.

1044 Child Management

B. Wagonseller, Author
United Learning
6633 West Howard Street   708-647-0600
Niles, IL 60714

Designed for parents and professionals, this video focuses on: causes for behavioral problems; discipline strategies, a plan for behavior management and more.
Video

1045 Children with Special Needs: Cognitive Development

J.M. Levy, Author

Young Adult Institute
460 West 34th Street   212-563-7474
New York, NY 10001

Designed for parents and professionals involved with developmentally disabled infants and preschoolers, a video of milestones as well as activities parents can do to foster their child's cognitive development.
Video

1046 Children with Special Needs: Diagnosis

J.M. Levy, Author

Young Adult Institute
460 West 34th Street   212-563-7474
New York, NY 10001

Designed for parents and professionals involved with developmentally disabled infants and preschoolers, a video featuring assessment in progress, with early childhood specialists joining parents in various discussions.
Video

1047 Children with Special Needs: Early Intervention

J.M. Levy, Author

Young Adult Institute
460 West 34th Street   212-563-7474
New York, NY 10001

Designed for parents and professionals involved with developmentally disabled infants and preschoolers, this video features a discussion between early childhood specialists and parents focusing on selecting and monitoring programs with examples of home-based and school-based programs.
Video

1048 Children with Special Needs: Emotional Development

J.M. Levy, Author

Young Adult Institute
460 West 34th Street   212-563-7474
New York, NY 10001

Designed for parents and professionals involved with developmentally disabled infants and preschoolers, this video of milestones as well as activities parents can do to foster their child's emotional development.
Video

1049 Children with Special Needs: Language Development

J.M. Levy, Author

Young Adult Institute
460 West 34th Street   212-563-7474
New York, NY 10001

Designed for parents and professionals this video of milestones as well as activities parents can do to foster their child's language developmentt.
Video

1050 Children with Special Needs: Motor Development

J.M. Levy, Author

Young Adult Institute
460 West 34th Street   212-563-7474
New York, NY 10001

This video tape offers milestones as well as activities parents can do to foster their child's motor development.
Video

1051 Child's Play: the World of Learning

Educational Productions
7412 SW Beaverton, Ste. 210   503-292-9234
Portland, OR 97225

A video for administrators, teachers, aides and parents designed to illustrate the connection between play, academic learning, thinking and skill development in language, gross and fine motor performance and readiness for reading.
Video

1052 Classroom Management: a Proactive Approach to a Creative Learning Environment

P. Wolfe, Author

Association for Supervision/Curriculum Development
1250 North Pitt Street   703-549-9110
Alexandria, VA 22314

A facilitator's manual and video designed to provide teachers with a comprehensive framework for organizing and managing the classroom environment.
Video

1053 Client Rights Are Human Rights

Young Adult Institute
460 West 34th Street   212-563-7474
New York, NY 10001

A video and workbook to assist staff who work with developmentally disabled persons by: clarifying what human rights are; addressing the importance of respecting human rights; presenting a five step system to ensure appropriate interventions; and utilizing four role playing situations to reinforce learning.
Video

1054 Collaboration in the Schools: the Problem-Solving Process

L. Idol, Author

Pro-Ed
8700 Shoal Creek Road   512-451-3246
Austin, TX 78758

An inservice/preservice video that demonstrates the stages of the consultative/collaborative process, as well as many of the various communicative/interactive skills and collaborative problem solving skills.
Video

1055   College: a Viable Option

HEATH Resource Center
One Dupont Circle NW, Ste. 800   202-939-9320
Washington, DC 20036   800-544-3284

A video discussing what a learning disability is, learning strategies and compensatory techniques.
Video

$ 23.00

1056   College Transition

Central Piedmont Community College
P.O. Box 35009   704-342-6621
Charlotte, NC 28235

A video developed for facilitators to show to audiences of high school students, college transfer students and college freshman.

1057   Communicating on the Job

Educational Design, Inc.
47 West 13th Street   800-221-9372
New York, NY 10011

Teaches career/vocational education and independent living, with emphasis on vocational adjustment, work attitudes, telephone skills, communication skills, writing skills and listening skills.

$ 145.00

1058   Concentration Video

Learning Disabilities Resources
P.O. Box 716   215-525-8336
Bryn Mawr, PA 19010   800-869-8336

An instructional video which provides a perspective about attention problems, possible causes and solutions.
Video

$ 19.95

1059   Concrete Career Counseling

Learning Disabilities Resources
P.O. Box 716   215-525-8336
Bryn Mawr, PA 19010   800-869-8336
Video

$ 12.00

1060   Considerations When Selecting a Speech Output Communication Device

Prentke Romich Company
1022 Heyl Road   216-262-1984
Wooster, OH 44691   FAX 216-263-4829

Looks at the issues one must consider in the selection process. These include hardware, software and service and support.

1061   Cooperative Discipline: Classroom Management Promoting Self-Esteem

L. Albert, Author

AGS
7201 Woodland Road   612-786-4343
Circle Pines, MN 55014   800-328-2560

A leader's guide, teacher's guide, set of 23 blackline masters, 2 scripts and 2 videotapes comprise this comprehensive discipline training program that helps teachers achieve control and order in their classroom.
Video   Grades K-12

1062   Counseling Parents

Hubbard Scientific
P.O. Box 760   800-323-8368
Chippewa Falls, WI 54729

An inservices training module to assist teachers in acquiring and implementing effective techniques in counseling parents of disabled children.
Video

1063   The Creative Curriculum for Early Childhood

D.T. Dodge, Author

Teaching Strategies
P.O. Box 42243   202-362-7543
Washington, DC 20015

Focuses on the developmentally appropriate program in early childhood education. Illustrates how preschool and kindergarten teachers set the stage for learning, and how children and teachers interact and learn in various interest areas.
Video

1064   Dare to Be Different: Resisting Drug Related Peer Pressure

Guidance Associates
P.O. Box 1000   914-666-4100
Mt. Kisco, NY 10549

A video depicting an enduring friendship between two high school students which helps them keep their values in perspective and avoid becoming members of a group who use drugs.
Video

1065   Degrees of Success: Conversations with College Students with LD

New York University
566 LaGuardia Place #701   212-998-4980
New York, NY 10012   FAX 212-995-4114

A new video which features college students with learning disabilities speaking in their own words about: making the decision to attend college, developing effective learning strategies, coping with frustrations and utilizing college support services.

1066 Delivering Family-Centered, Homebased Services

L. Edelman, Author

Kennedy Krieger Institute
2911 East Biddle   410-550-9750
Baltimore, MD 21213

A facilitator's guide and video designed to train service providers in home-based programs for families whose children have special needs by illustrating a variety of family-centered care principles, including communication skills, parent/professional collaboration, and individualized family support plan development.
Video

1067 Determined to Succeed

Books on Special Children
P.O. Box 305   914-638-1236
Congers, NY 10920   FAX 914-638-0847

A video about two young adults, one with learning disability and the other autistic, with their parents who discuss experiences while they struggle for self-esteem and independence.

$ 125.00

1068 Different...But the Same

Resources in Special Education
6580 Howe Avenue, Ste. 300
Sacramento, CA 95825   916-641-5925

A video showing the overview of children and adults with disabilities.
Video   Grades 4-8

1069 Direct Link, May I Help You?

Direct Link for the Disabled
P.O. Box 1036   805-688-1603
Solvang, CA 93464

Introduces Direct Link and demonstrates practical ideas to include those with disabilities in the work force.
Video

$ 25.00

1070 Discipline with Dignity

R.L. Curwin, Author

National Educational Services
1610 West 3rd Street   812-336-7701
Bloomington, IN 47402

A set of three videotapes and a 12-page guide providing teachers, administrators, and counselors with an overview of effective discipline methods.
Video

1071 Dyslexia: the Challenge and the Promise

Emi Flynn Hamilton School At Wheeler
216 Hope Street   401-421-8100
Providence, RI 02906

A group of adults and one child explain their personal experiences as dyslexics.

1072 Dyslexia, the Hidden Disability

Grand Rapids Community College
143 Bostwick NE   616-771-3830
Grand Rapids, MI 49503

This is a documentary that examines the history, symptoms, probable causes and successful techniques for dealing with this widespread learning disability.

1073 Early Childhood STEP: Systematic Training for Effective Parenting

AGS
7201 Woodland Road   612-786-4343
Circle Pines, MN 55014   800-328-2560

A leader's guide, parent handbook, publicity materials, and a videotape to educate parents of children under age six.
Video

1074 Early Intervention with Special Needs Children

3830 E. Bellevue   602-323-7500
Tucson, AZ 85733

Marsha TeBockhorst

Provides a wealth of resources and training materials for parents and caregivers.

$ 179.00

1075 Educating Inattentive Children: a Guide for the Classroom

S. Goldstein, Author

Neurology: Learning & Behavior Center
230 South 500th Street, Ste. 1000   801-532-1484
Salt Lake City, UT 84102

A 2 hour videotape provides regular and special educators with information necessary to identify and evaluate classroom problems caused by inattention.
Video

1076 Electronic "Town Meeting" on Students with Serious Emotional Disturbance

The Council for Exceptional Children
1920 Association Drive   703-620-3660
Reston, VA 22091

A video and discussion guide depicting a teleconference designed to develop a national agenda for achieving better results for educating children and youth with serious emotional disturbance.
Video

1077 Employment Initiatives Model: Job Coach Training Manual and Tape

Young Adult Institute
460 West 34th Street   212-563-7474
New York, NY 10001

A video and manual providing an overview and orientation for staff members involved in transition services to ensure that they are well-grounded in the concepts, responsibilities, and activities that are required to provide quality supported employment services.
Video

1078 Enhancing the Communication Abilities of Disabled Infants and Toddlers

M.J. Wilcox, Author

Purdue University Continuing Education
1586 Stewart Center   317-494-7231
West Lafayette, IN 47907

Focuses on communication as one of the key needs of most infants and toddlers with disabilities, this videotape provides: a brief young population; an overview of approaches to intervention; and strategies for using children's interactive partners in order to enhance or facilitate their acquisition of communication skills.
Video

1079 Environmental Words Reading Video

Learning Disabilities Resources
P.O. Box 716   215-525-8336
Bryn Mawr, PA 19010   800-869-8336

A video for non or weak readers to provide them with sample environmental words which they can use to develop their reading vocabulary and learn how to find their own environmental words.

1080 Equal Access Video

CAST, Inc.
39 Cross Street   508-531-8555
Peabody, MA 01960

Filmed on site in severeal Massachusetts schools which participated in CAST's Equal Access project. This research project addressed integration of children with diverse learning needs through a combination of technology, cooperative learning, collaborative teaching and restructured roles.

$ 29.95

1081 Facilitated Communication Personal Training Video

New Breakthroughs, Inc.
P.O. Box 25228   503-741-5070
Eugene, OR 97401

$ 35.00

1082 Faculty Training Session

Learning Disabilities Resources
P.O. Box 716   215-525-8336
Bryn Mawr, PA 19010   800-869-8336
Video

$ 12.00

1083 First Jobs: Entering the Job World

Educational Design, Inc.
47 West 13th Street   800-221-9372
New York, NY 10011

Career/vocational education with emphasis on job search skills, job interviews and survival skills.

$ 129.00

1084 First Jobs: Five First Jobs

Educational Design, Inc.
47 West 13th Street   800-221-9372
New York, NY 10011

Instructional material to teach job search skills, job interviews and service occupations.

$ 145.00

1085 Getting Started with Facilitated Communication

D. Biklen, Author

Syracuse University, Institute on Communication
805 South Krouse   315-443-2693
Syracuse, NY 13244

Describes in detail how to help individuals with autism and/or severe communication difficulties to get started with facilitated communication.
Video

1086 Gifts of Greatness: a Positive Look At Learning Differences

J. Bulifant, Author

Learning Disabilities Foundation
Culver City, CA   818-355-0240

Designed to inform and entertain, as well as educate and inspire teachers, parents and students by presenting a musical drama with well-known entertainers portraying the lives of four famous people who overcame dyslexia.
Video

1087 Going to School with Facilitated Communication

D. Biklen, Author

Syracuse University, School of Education
805 South Krouse   315-443-2693
Syracuse, NY 13244

A video in which students with autism and/or severe disabilities illustrate the use of facilitated communication focusing on basic principles fostering facilitated communication.
Video

1088 He Comes From Another Room

National Audiovisual Center
1618 Orrington Avenue   301-763-1896
Washington, DC 60201

A video of one school's approach to mainstreaming and what happens when a disabled child moves from a special education program to a regular third grade class.
Video

1089 Heart to Heart: Autism and the Parent's Quest

New Breakthroughs, Inc.
P.O. Box 25228   503-741-5070
Eugene, OR 97401

$ 50.00

1090 Help! This Kid's Driving Me Crazy!

L. Adkins, Author

Pro-Ed
8700 Shoal Creek Road   512-451-3246
Austin, TX 78758

Designed for parents and professionals working with children up to five years old, this videotape and booklet offers information about the nature, special needs, and typical behavioral characteristics fo young children with attention deficit disorder.
Video

1091 Helping Adults Learn: Adult Learning Disabilities

Audio-Visual Services
1127 Fox Hill Road   814-865-6314
University Park, PA 16803   800-826-0132

One of the most perplexing issues for educators dealing with learning disabled adults is that most of the research and recommendations for practice are from a child-based perspective.

1092 Helping Adults Learn - Learning Disabled Viewer's Guide

PENN State Audio/Visual Services
Special Services Building   814-865-6314
University Park, PA 16802   800-826-0132
                            FAX 814-863-2574

Intended for people who deal with adult learners. Focuses on the special needs of adults with learning disabilities. A printed guide accompanies this video package.
28 minutes

$ 140.00

1093 How Difficult Can This Be? a Learning Disabilities Workshop

R. Lavoie, Author

WETA-TV, Department of Educational Activities
2700 South Quincy, Ste. 440   703-998-2600
Arlington, VA 22206

This video for parents and professionals illustrates the frustration, anxiety and tension that learning disabled children face through a workshop where participants experience learning disabilities firsthand.
Video

1094 How Not to Contact Employers

National Clearinghouse of Rehab. Training Material
Oklahoma State University   405-744-5000
Stillwater, OK

A single vingette of what not to do when visiting perspective employers to secure positions for clients.
Videos

$ 10.00

1095 Identifying Learning Problems

Learning Disabilities Resources
P.O. Box 716   215-525-8336
Bryn Mawr, PA 19010   800-869-8336
Video

$ 12.00

1096 I'm Not Autistic on the Typewriter

D. Biklen, Author

Syracuse University, School of Education
805 South Krouse   315-443-2693
Syracuse, NY 13244

A video introducing facilitated communication, a method by which persons with autism express themselves. Focuses on the following elements: physical support; progression from initial training to practice, and finally to fluency; maintenance of focus on task; emotional support; and fading physical support.
Video

1097 I'm Not Stupid

Learning Disabilities Association of America
4156 Library Road   412-341-1515
Pittsburgh, PA 15234

This video depicts the constant battle of the learning disabled child in school.

1098 I'm Special

L. Bowers, Author

University of Florida, Educational Resources Div.
4202 East Fowler Avenue   813-974-2011
Tampa, FL 33620

A series of 15 modules and 4 videotapes presenting a comprehensive look at a developmental physical education program for physically and mentally disabled children.
Video

1099   Imagine That

KET, the Kentucky Network Enterprise Division
560 Cooper Drive   800-354-9067
Lexington, KY 40502   FAX 606-258-7396

A 10-part video series designed to release, channel and focus creative expression in fourth and fifth graders.
Video

1100   Instructional Strategies for Learning Disabled Community College Students

The Graduate School and University Center
New York, NY 10036
      212-642-2942

For working with a cross-section of types of individuals with learning problems.

$ 47.50

1101   It's Just Attention Disorder: a Video Guide for Kids

S. Goldstein, Author

Neurology: Learning & Behavior Center
230 South 500th Street East   801-532-1484
Salt Lake City, UT 84102

A user's manual/study guide and video designed to help parents, teachers, and counselors assist students with attention deficit hyperactivity disorders.
Video

1102   Jamie's Great Discovery: a Curriculum Guide

American Speech-Language-Hearing Association
10801 Rockville Pike   301-897-5700
Rockville, MD 20852   800-638-8255

Video dramatization designed to sensitize 3rd and 4th graders to classmates with communication problems.
Grades 3-4

$ 25.00

1103   Jenny's Story

L'institute Roeher Institute
91 Granton Drive   416-661-9611
Richmond Hill, ON, Canada, L4 B 2N5

Jenny, a teenager who has challenging needs which include an intellectual impairment, lives at home and goes to a regular school in her area. Parents and friends describe their roles in the support network which enables Jenny to participate fully in her school and community.
Film

$ 55.00

1104   Job Coaching Video Training Series

RPM Press, Inc.
P.O. Box 31483   602-886-1990
Tucson, AZ 85751

Jan Stonebraker, Operations Manager

Multi-media professional training program designed for training educators, counselors, vocational rehabilitation personnel, employment specialists and paraprofessional staff in job coaching methods such as speed training, time sampling, fading, behavior observation and other methods.

$ 225.00

1105   Job Interview Reality Seminar

Texas Commission for the Blind
Austin, TX   512-459-2500

These tapes include job interview and "feedback" to the interviewee about his/her performance.
Video

$ 20.00

1106   Job Placement Success for Counselors and Clients

Juliet Swieczkowski, Author

Texas Rehabilitation Commission
Austin, TX   512-483-4000

Materials developed to assist the rehabilitation counselor to work effectively with clients and potential employers.
Videos

1107   Job Seeking Skills

Massachusetts Rehabilitation Commission
Boston, MA   617-727-2183

Vignettes of interviews involving disabled persons enable trainers to identify productive and non-productive behaviors in seeking employment.
Video

$ 35.00

1108   Kathy: on My Own

Film Ideas, Inc.
Northbrook, IL   708-480-5760

A video of an enthusiastic and determined teenager with osteogenesis imperfecta facing interpersonal and environmental roadblocks as she integrates herself into her school and society.
Video

1109 The KET Basic Skills Series

KET, the Kentucky Network Enterprise Division
560 Cooper Drive   800-354-9067
Lexington, KY 40502   FAX 606-258-7396

Offers an independent learning system for workers who need retraining or help with basic skills.
Video

1110 The KET Foundation Series

KET, the Kentucky Network Enterprise Division
560 Cooper Drive   800-354-9067
Lexington, KY 40502   FAX 606-258-7396

A highly effective basic skills series that is tailor-made for the needs of proprietary and vocational schools.
Video

1111 The KET/GED Series

KET, the Kentucky Network Enterprise Division
560 Cooper Drive   800-354-9067
Lexington, KY 40502   FAX 606-258-7396

This nationally accalimed instructional series helps adults prepare for the GED test.
Video

1112 The KET/GED Series Transitional Spanish Edition

KET, the Kentucky Network Enterprise Division
560 Cooper Drive   800-354-9067
Lexington, KY 40502   FAX 606-258-7396

This award-winning series offers ESL students effective preparation for the GED test.
Video

1113 Kids Belong Together

L.J. Hutchinson-Maclean, Author

Inclusion Press
Toronto, Ontario, Canada

A video providing perspectives of parents and school personnel regarding the inclusion of a variety of students with moderate to severe disabilities into regular classrooms.
Video

1114 Learn to Read

KET, the Kentucky Network Enterprise Division
560 Cooper Drive   800-354-9067
Lexington, KY 40502   FAX 606-258-7396

Offers 30 half-hour programs tailored for the adult student.
Video

1115 Learning Problems in Language

Learning Disabilities Resources
P.O. Box 716   215-525-8336
Bryn Mawr, PA 19010   800-869-8336
Video

$ 12.00

1116 Legal Challenges in Special Education: Tapes 1-11

Reed Martin, Author

Carle Media
110 West Main Street   217-384-4838
Urbana, IL 61801

A set of eleven videocassettes and resource guides designed for parents and professionals who need assistance in understanding current special education law. Reed Martin, a noted special education legal authority presents his views.
Video

1117 Let Me Try

Alan P. Sloan, Author

Britannica Software
345 Fourth Street   415-597-5555
San Francisco, CA 94107   FAX 415-546-1887

When the gang decided to build a tree house at one of their grandma's. Billy brought along his sister, Wendy who learn's slowly. The afternoon a learning adventure for all of them.
Films

1118 Letting Go: Views on Integration

Iowa University Affiliated Programs
100 University Hospital School   319-356-1616
Iowa City, IA 52242

A video designed for parents and professionals involved in special education, illustrating the fears that parents of special needs children have of letting go, of allowing their children to experience life.
Video

1119 Life After High School for Students with Moderate and Severe Disabilities

Beech Center on Families and Disability
3111 Haworth Hall   913-864-7600
Lawrence, MA 66045

A set of three videotapes and a participant handbook document , and a teleconference in which family members, people with disabiltieis, teachers, rehabilitation specialists, program administrators and policy makers focus on improving the quality of services in high school and supported employment programs.
Video

1120 Literature, Literacy and Learning

International Reading Association
800 Barksdale Rd., P.O. Box 8139   302-731-1600
Newark, DE 19714   800-336-READ
                                                                 FAX 302-731-1057

Video with supplementary text presents new and revitalized approaches to language arts and examines the key principles and characteristics each approach.

$ 125.00

1121 Lost Dreams & Growth: Parents' Concerns

K. Moses, Author
Resource Networks, Inc.
Evanston, IL   708-964-4522

A video designed for professionals and parents of children with developmental disabilities.
Video

1122 Mainstreaming Students with Learning Disabilities

Learning Disabilities Resources
P.O. Box 716   215-525-8336
Bryn Mawr, PA 19010   800-869-8336
Video

$ 12.00

1123 Making Meaning: Integrated Language Arts Series

International Reading Association
800 Barksdale Rd., P.O. Box 8139   302-731-1600
Newark, DE 19714   800-336-READ
                                    FAX 302-731-1057

This new staff development video program includes five videocassettes, a comprehensive Facilitator's Guide and the book "When Writers Read" by Jane Hansen. Learn how to teach children reading, writing, listening and speaking by using the element of natural language learning in the classroom.

$ 965.00

1124 Math Country

KET, the Kentucky Network Enterprise Division
560 Cooper Drive   800-354-9067
Lexington, KY 40502   FAX 606-258-7396

This 30-program video series is designed to make the ideas clear and to show how mathematics is needed in everyday living.
Video   Grades 2-3

1125 Motivating Staff

Young Adult Institute
460 West 34th Street   212-563-7474
New York, NY 10001

A video and workbook designed for use by supervisors of staff working with developmentally disabled persons.
Video

1126 Motivation to Learn: How Parents and Teachers Can Help

Association for Supervision/Curriculum Development
1250 North Pitt Street   703-549-9110
Alexandria, VA 22314

Two videos intended for all those concerned about how educators and families can develop student motivation to learn, solve motivational problems, and effectively participate in parent-teacher conferences.
Video

1127 National Audiovisual Center/ National Archives Multimedia & Publications

National Archives Multimedia & Publications Div.
8700 Edgeworth Ddrive   301-763-1896
Capitol Heights, MD 20743   800-788-6282

The central information and distribution source for more than 8,000 videos, slide sets and films produced by the US Government.

1128 New Directions in Teacher Education

Center on Education and Training for Employment
Ohio State - 1900 Kenny Road   614-292-4353
Columbus, OH 43210   800-848-4815

Discusses the historical trands in teacher education from the 1770's. This video outlines a proposed three-stage differentiated work force of instructors, professional teachers and career professional teachers.

$ 150.00

1129 The New Room Arrangement As a Teaching Strategy

Teaching Strategies
P.O. Box 42243   202-362-7543
Washington, DC 20015

A manual and video present the impact of the early childhood classroom environment on how children learn, how they relate to others and how teachers teach.
Video

1130 A New Way of Thinking

TASH
11201 Greenwood Avenue North   206-361-8870
Seattle, WA 98133

A video based on the understanding that people with developmental disabilities, like all other people, need to have real homes, learn real skills, work at real jobs, and have real friends.
Video

1131 Now You're Talking: Techniques That Extend Conversations

C. Sharp, Author

Educational Productions
7412 SW Beaverton, Ste. 210   503-292-9234
Portland, OR 97225

A video, teachers in a language-based preschool and speech-language pathologists model effective techniques that focus and extend conversations.
Video

1132 Oh Say What They See: An Introduction to Indirect Language Stimulation

Educational Productions
7412 SW Beaverton, Ste. 210   503-292-9234
Portland, OR 97225

A video illustrating indirect language stimulation techniques to teachers, parents, students, child care staff, and other adult caregivers working with children.
Video   Ages 1-4

1133 On Our Own Transition Series

Young Adult Institute
460 West 34th Street   212-563-7474
New York, NY 10001

Designed for parents and professionals, this series of 15 videotapes examines innovative transitional approaches that help create marketable skills, instill self-esteem and facilitates successful transition for individuals with developmental disabilities.
Video

1134 Overview of Assistive Technology

Department of Special Education
229 Taylor Education Bldg.   606-257-4713
Lexington, KY 40506

Marcia Bowling
Slides on videotapes.
$ 35.00

1135 Parent Teacher Meeting

Learning Disabilities Resources
P.O. Box 716   215-525-8336
Bryn Mawr, PA 19010   800-869-8336

Discusses learning differences and instructional techniques.
Video
$ 12.00

1136 Phonologic Level Speech Development

D. Ling, Author
McGill University
Instructional Communications Centre
Montreal, QC, Canada

Examines the problems of generalizing phonetic level speech skills into meaningful spoken language.
Video

1137 Pioneering New Breakthroughs

New Breakthroughs, Inc.
P.O. Box 25228   503-741-5070
Eugene, OR 97401
$ 100.00

1138 The Prevention of Voice Problems in Children

B.S.W. Solomon, Author
Purdue University Continuing Education
1586 Stewart Center   317-494-7231
West Lafayette, IN 47907

A videotape focusing on: the incidence of voice problems in children; the vocally abusive child; and a vocal abuse checklist.
Video

1139 Problems with Social Skills

Learning Disabilities Resources
P.O. Box 716   215-525-8336
Bryn Mawr, PA 19010   800-869-8336
Video
$ 12.00

1140 A Question of Learning

L'institute Roeher Institute
91 Granton Drive   416-661-9661
Richmond Hill, ON, Canada, L4 B 2N5

This is the story of one family's struggle and the vision of community integration, friendship and learning which inspires their activism to get two learning disabled children into a neighborhood school.
Film
$ 20.00

1141 Reach for the Stars

Learning Disabilities Association of America
4156 Library Road   412-341-1515
Pittsburgh, PA 15234

An inspiring story for people with learning disabilities.
$ 22.00

1142 Read to Me

International Reading Association
800 Barksdale Rd., P.O. Box 8139   302-731-1600
Newark, DE 19714   800-336-READ
FAX 302-731-1057

Introduces parents to the importance of reading aloud to their children.
$ 30.00

1143 Reading and Young Children: a Practical Guide for Childcare Providers

International Reading Association
800 Barksdale Rd., P.O. Box 8139   302-731-1600
Newark, DE 19714   800-336-READ
FAX 302-731-1057

Provides general, practical information for anyone working with young children on the importance of making reading a part of every child's day.

$ 30.00

1144 Reading, Thinking and Concept Development: a Professional Development Series

International Reading Association
800 Barksdale Rd., P.O. Box 8139   302-731-1600
Newark, DE 19714   800-336-READ
FAX 302-731-1057

Illustrates how teachers and students can work together to improve students' ability to construct meaning, apply ideas and think critically.
Six Videotapes

$ 295.00

1145 Regular Lives

D.P. Biklen, Author

WETA-TV, Department of Educational Activities
2700 South Quincy, Ste. 440   703-998-2600
Arlington, VA 22206

Designed to show the successful integration of handicapped students in school, work and community settings. Demonstrates that sharing the ordinary routines of learning and living is essential for people with disabilities.
Video

1146 Restructuring America's Schools

M. D'Arcangelo, Author

Association for Supervision/Curriculum Development
1250 North Pitt Street   703-549-9110
Alexandria, VA 22314

A leader's guide and videotape designed for administrators, teachers, parents, school board members, and community leaders.
Video

1147 School Days

B. Wagonseller, Author

United Learning
6633 West Howard Street   708-647-0600
Niles, IL 60714

Designed for parents and professionals, this videotape clarifies parental roles and defines parental expectations of the educational system to assist their children in reaching their highest potential.
Video

1148 Section 504

Carle Center for Health Law and Ethics
110 West Main
Urbana, IL 61501

Expanding schools' responisbilities to special education students.

1149 Sign Language Training for the Developmentally Delayed, Part II

Therapy Skill Builders
3830 East Bellevue   602-323-7500
Tucson, AZ 85733

A video designed to teach developmentally disabled individuals 69 sign lanaguage words and combinations focusing on colors, clothing, and the alphabet.
Video

1150 The Skillstreaming Video: How to Teach Students Prosocial Skills

A.P. Goldstein, Author

Research Press
2612 North Mathis Avenue   217-352-3273
Champaign, IL 61821

A video and 2 books providing an overview of a training procedure for teaching elementary and secondary level students the skills they need for coping with typical social and interpersonal problems.
Video

1151 The SLP in the Collaborative Role

C. Simon, Author

Communication Skill Builders
3830 East Bellevue   602-323-7500
Tucson, AZ 85733

An instructional manual and two videotapes designed for use by speech-language pathologists and classroom teachers who are collaborating on development of communication programs.
Video

1152 Social Skills on the Job: a Transition to the Workplace for Special Needs

Ameircan Guidance Service
Circle Pines, MN 55014   612-786-4343

Presents 28 simulations to help students learn and practice 14 basic social skills that will allow them to compete successfully with their peers in the job market.
Video

1153 Someday's Child: a Focus on Special Needs Children and Their Families

L.L. Pletcher, Author

Educational Productions
7412 SW Beaverton, Ste. 210   503-292-9234
Portland, OR 97225

A video for parents and professionals working with young children with special needs.
Video

1154 Specific Learning Disabilities in Adolescence

Davidson Films
231 East Street   FAX 916-753-3719
Davis, CA 95616

A video focusing on research pertaining to adolescents with learning disabilities.
Video

1155 Speech-Language Pathology and Audiology: Careers That Make a Difference

American Speech-Language-Hearing Association
10801 Rockville Pike   301-897-5700
Rockville, MD 20852   800-638-8255

Designed for prospective speech-language pathologists and audiologists, this video highlights career functions in this field.
Video

1156 Spelling Workbook Video

Learning Disabilities Resources
P.O. Box 716   215-525-8336
Bryn Mawr, PA 19010   800-869-8336

An instructional video which works through the spelling workbooks for teachers and students.

1157 STEP/teen: Systematic Training for Effective Parenting of Teens

D. Dinkmeyer, Author

AGS
7201 Woodland Road   612-786-4343
Circle Pines, MN 55014   800-328-2560

A parent training program designed to help parents of teenagers in the following areas: understanding misbehavior; improving communication and family relationships; understanding and expressing emotions and feelings and discipline.
Video

1158 Strategic Planning and Leadership

Association for Supervision/Curriculum Development
1250 North Pitt Street   703-549-9110
Alexandria, VA 22314

Designed to explain and illustrate effective approaches to dealing with change through strategic planning.
Video

1159 Strategies Intervention Program

A. Marks, Author

Special Education Resource Center
25 Industrial Park Road   203-632-1485
Middletown, CT 06457

A video illustrating through an interview with five eighth grade students, the effectiveness of a program designed to develop specific learning strategies for adolescents with learning disabilities.
Video

1160 Strengths and Weaknesses: College Students with Learning Disabilities

Altschul Group
930 Piner Avenue   312-326-6700
Evanston, IL 60202

Four students share their feelings and four professionals explore possible adjustment and compensation relative to learning disabilities.

1161 Study Skills: How to Manage Your Time

Guidance Associates
P.O. Box 1000   914-666-4100
Mt. Kisco, NY 10549

Describes how to create a personal schedule that will help users get more accomplished each day and waste less time.
Video

1162 Talking From Infancy: How to Nurture and Cultivate Early Language

W. Fowler, Author

Brookline Books
P.O. Box 1046   617-868-0360
Cambridge, MA 02238

A video, book, and video guide designed for parents and child care providers interacting with children from 2 months to 3 years.
Video

1163 Talking Is Sharing: Videotape

Rae Banigan, Author

The Speech Bin
1965 Twenty-Fifth Avenue   407-770-0007
Vero Beach, FL 32960   FAX 407-770-0006

Jan J. Binney, Editor In Chief
Barbara Hector, Office Manager

Demonstrates techniques adults can use to help young children to talk, listen and think.
Ages 0-5

$ 49.95

1164 Tapes 13-17: Legal Challenges in Special Education

Reed Martin, Author

Carle Media
110 West Main Street　　　　217-384-4838
Urbana, IL 61801

A set of five videotapes designed for parents and professionals who need assistance in understanding current special education law.
Video

1165 Teach An Adult to Read

KET, the Kentucky Network Enterprise Division
560 Cooper Drive　　　　800-354-9067
Lexington, KY 40502　　　　FAX 606-258-7396

A video series for reading tutors and tutor trainers that will help your program solve problems and give insight on how to teach an adult to read.

1166 Teaching: a Problem Solving Venture - Observation and Collaboration

Pro-Ed
8700 Shoal Creek Road　　　　512-451-3246
Austin, TX 78758

Portrays collaboration between regular and special education teachers. This program illustrates how teachers can assess and remediate childrens' academic and behavior problems in classroom settings using a problem solving process.
Video

1167 Teaching Math

Learning Disabilities Resources
P.O. Box 716　　　　215-525-8336
Bryn Mawr, PA 19010　　　　800-869-8336

A video for educational professionals teaching math to disabled children.
Video

$ 12.00

1168 Teaching Mildly Handicapped Students

A. Archer, Author

The Council for Exceptional Children
1920 Association Drive　　　　703-620-3660
Reston, VA 22091

Designed for preservice and special education teachers, 2 videos and training materials illustrating how effective teaching principles can be applied to elementary and secondary school situations.
Video

1169 Teaching People with Developmental Disabilities

Research Press
2612 North Mathis Avenue　　　　217-352-3273
Champaign, IL 61821

A set of four videotapes and accompanying participant workbooks designed to help teachers, staff, volunteers, or family members master the following behavioral techniques: task analysis, prompting, reinforcement and error correction.
Video

1170 Teaching Reading: Strategies From Successful Classrooms

International Reading Association
800 Barksdale Rd., P.O. Box 8139　　　302-731-1600
Newark, DE 19714　　　　800-336-READ
　　　　FAX 302-731-1057

A series of six videotapes designed as simulated field experiences for use in college-level education courses for preservice teachers and in inservice workshops for teachers.

$ 200.00

1171 Teaching Strategies Library: Research Based Strategies for Teachers

H.F. Silver, Author

Association for Supervision/Curriculum Development
1250 North Pitt Street　　　　703-549-9110
Alexandria, VA 22314

A trainer's manual and five videotapes designed for inservice education of teachers K-12 focusing on four different types of learning expected of students: mastery, understanding, synthesis and involvement.
Video

1172 Teaching Students Through Their Individual Learning Styles

R. Dunn, Author

St. John's University, Learning Styles Network
Grand Central And Utopa Park　　　718-990-6161
Hwys.
Jamaica, NY 11439

A set of six videotapes introducing the Dunn and Dunn learning styles model. Explains the environmental, emotional, sociological, physical and psychological elements of style.
Video

1173 Teaching the Hard-to-Reach Adolescent, Module 3: Secondary Curriculum

D.D. Lund, Author

Simplot/Micron Teachnology Center
1910 University Drive　　　　208-385-1011
Boise, ID 83725

Designed for secondary regular and special educators, a notebook and 3 videotapes providing the means to: evalu-

ate curriculum for hard-to-reach students, write and use curriculum based assessments and implement adapted curriculum for subjects at the secondary level.
Video

1174 Technology in the Classroom Kit

American Speech-Language-Hearing Association
10801 Rockville Pike   **301-897-5700**
Rockville, MD 20852   **800-638-8255**
      FAX 301-571-0457

Cameron Werker, Mktg. Coordinator
This kit includes a collection of four written modules and a videotape designed to help families and professionals implement assistive technology in the education programs of young children. Each module provides a brief background in assistive technology and covers specific topics in great detail. The technology is geared for children.
Ages 2-7

      $ 35.00

1175 Telling Tales

KET, the Kentucky Network Enterprise Division
560 Cooper Drive   **800-354-9067**
Lexington, KY 40502 **FAX 606-258-7396**
KET's popular video series is an outstanding resource for teachers, librarians and drama departments at all levels of instruction.
Video

1176 Time Together: Learning to Play with Young Children

Educational Productions
7412 SW Beaverton, Ste. 210 **503-292-9234**
Portland, OR 97225
A video for beginning childhood teachers, aides and parents illustrating when to join a child's play and when to step back.
Video

1177 Together We're Better

M. Forest, Author
Comforty Mediaconcepts
613 Michigan Avenue   **708-475-0791**
Evanston, IL 60202
A set of three videotapes that provide highlights of an inclusion workshop conducted by three noted inclusion specialists.
Video

1178 Tomorrow's Children

E. Brower, Author
Vallejo City Unified School District
211 Valle Vista   **707-644-8921**
Vallejo, CA 94590
Addresses the needs for early intervention and comprehensive services for high risk and handicapped infants and preschool children.
Video

1179 Tools for Transition: Preparing Students with Learning Disabilities

E.P. Aune, Author
AGS
7201 Woodland Road   **612-786-4343**
Circle Pines, MN 55014 **800-328-2560**
Designed for learning disabled high school juniors and seniors, this program will prepare them for postsecondary education by focusing on: learning styles, study skills, learning accommodations, self advocacy, career exploration, interpersonal relationships and choosing and applying to postsecondary schools.
Video Grades 11-12

1180 Tutor Training Session

Learning Disabilities Resources
P.O. Box 716   **215-525-8336**
Bryn Mawr, PA 19010 **800-869-8336**
Video

      $ 12.00

1181 Understanding Attention Deficit Disorder

Connecticut Association for Children with LD
18 Marshall Street   **203-838-5010**
Norwalk, CT 06854
A video in an interview format for parents and professionals providing the history, symptoms, methods of diagnosis and three approaches used to ease the effects of attention deficit disorder.
Video

1182 Understanding Developmental Disabilities

Young Adult Institute
460 West 34th Street   **212-563-7474**
New York, NY 10001
A video and workbook providing a concise overview of developmental disabilities.
Video

1183 Understanding Hyperactivity

L. Ripley, Author
Psychiatric Support Services, Inc.
Houston, TX
Designed for parents and teachers, a video explaining the symptoms and consequences of attention deficit hyperactivity disorder.
Video

1184 Universe & I

KET, the Kentucky Network Enterprise Division
560 Cooper Drive   **800-354-9067**
Lexington, KY 40502 **FAX 606-258-7396**

Offers the subject of science in an exciting human way based on growing, evolving body of knowledge through dramatization, music and animation.
Video

1185   Vocabulary Workbook Video

Learning Disabilities Resources
P.O. Box 716   215-525-8336
Bryn Mawr, PA 19010   800-869-8336

An instructional video which demonstrates how to use the Vocabulary Development Workbook.

1186   What About Me? Brothers and Sisters of Children with Disabilities

S. Butrille, Author

Educational Productions
7412 SW Beaverton, Ste. 210   503-292-9234
Portland, OR 97225

Designed for siblings, parents, professionals, community members and students about two teenagers who share their perspectives, their worries, concerns and histories about living with a sibling with a disability.
Video

1187   What Did You Say?

The Speech Bin
1965 Twenty-Fifth Avenue   407-770-0007
Vero Beach, FL 32960   FAX 407-770-0006

Jan J. Binney, Editor In Chief
Barbara Hector, Office Manager

This innovative videotape presents five everyday situations interesting to clients from third garde to adult levels.
Ages 5-Up

$ 99.00

1188   Wherever We Find Them

National Audiovisual Center
1618 Orrington Avenue   301-763-1896
Washington, DC 60201

A video featuring disabled men and women of all ages participating and competing in almost every type of athletic and recreational activity.
Video

1189   Whole Language: a New Zealand Approach

International Reading Association
800 Barksdale Rd., P.O. Box 8139   302-731-1600
Newark, DE 19714   800-336-READ
                                          FAX 302-731-1057

Four-part videotape and accompanying booklet covering various aspects of whole language instruction.

$ 160.00

1190   Word Feathers

KET, the Kentucky Network Enterprise Division
560 Cooper Drive   800-354-9067
Lexington, KY 40502   FAX 606-258-7396

An activity-oriented language arts video series.
Grades 1-2

1191   Working I: Attitudes and Habits for Getting and Holding a Job

James Stanfield and Company
Santa Monica, CA   805-897-1188

Designed for adolescents with mild disabilities, includes a teacher's guide and test, 3 videotapes illustrate behaviors and attitudes important to job acquisition.
Video

1192   Working II: Interpersonal Skills Assessment and Training

G. Foss, Author

James Stanfield and Company
Santa Monica, CA   805-897-1188

Designed for adolescents with mild disabilities. Contains a teacher's guide and test, with 3 videotapes focusing on 24 seperate interpersonal skills that have been identified as important for maintatining a job.
Video

1193   Working with Families: What Professionals Need to Know

Young Adult Institute
460 West 34th Street   212-563-7474
New York, NY 10001

A video and workbook designed to help professionals to explore the differences between raising a child with a disability and a child without a disability.
Video

Language Arts

1194 Acquire: Answer-Comprehend-Question-interpret-Reason-Express

Linda Collins, Author
The Speech Bin
1965 Twenty-Fifth Avenue   **407-770-0007**
Vero Beach, FL 32960   **FAX 407-770-0006**

Jan J. Binney, Editor In Chief
Barbara Hector, Office Manager

Uses game format to teach the difficult concept of how to ask questions in three levels of cognitive-linguistic difficulty and increases vocabulary comprehension and use.

$ 34.95

1195 Analogies I

Arthur Liebman, Author
Educators Publishing Service, Inc.
75 Moulton Street   **800-225-5750**
Cambridge, MA 02138

Combine practice in solving analogy problems with opportunities for vocabulary study.

1196 Angling for Words

Carolyn C. Bowen, Author
Educators Publishing Service, Inc.
5 Moulton Street
Cambridge, MA 02138

This multisensory approach to teaching reading and spelling to students with specific learning disabilities can be used by tutors or classroom teachers with individuals or small classes.

$ 12.00

1197 Apple Tree Language Program

Edmark Corporation
P.O. Box 3218   **206-746-3900**
Redmond, WA 98073   **800-362-2890**

This program helps students develop written language skills by sequentially introducing them to the construction of ten basic sentence structures.

$ 69.00

1198 Articu-Action

Denise Grigas, Author
The Speech Bin
1965 Twenty-Fifth Avenue   **407-770-0007**
Vero Beach, FL 32960   **FAX 407-770-0006**

Jan J. Binney, Editor In Chief
Barbara Hector, Office Manager

Hands-on, action-oriented games and activities to enhance children's speech and language learning.

$ 14.95

1199 Articulation Calendars

The Speech Bin
1965 Twenty-Fifth Avenue   **407-770-0007**
Vero Beach, FL 32960   **FAX 407-770-0006**

Jan J. Binney, Editor In Chief
Barbara Hector, Office Manager

Offers 12 months of reproductible daily activities for home practice.

$ 24.95

1200 Articulation Curriculum

The Speech Bin
1965 Twenty-Fifth Avenue   **407-770-0007**
Vero Beach, FL 32960   **FAX 407-770-0006**

Jan J. Binney, Editor In Chief
Barbara Hector, Office Manager

Offers more than 1,000 appealing illustrations for practicing the consonant phonemes in words, sentences and careful speech.

$ 29.95

1201 Articulation Curriculum II

The Speech Bin
1965 Twenty-Fifth Avenue   **407-770-0007**
Vero Beach, FL 32960   **FAX 407-770-0006**

Jan J. Binney, Editor In Chief
Barbara Hector, Office Manager

Offers clever materials that stimulate hours of practice on beginning and advanced levels.

$ 29.95

1202 Articulation Plus

The Speech Bin
1965 Twenty-Fifth Avenue   **407-770-0007**
Vero Beach, FL 32960   **FAX 407-770-0006**

Jan J. Binney, Editor In Chief
Barbara Hector, Office Manager

Focuses on earlier-developing sounds and auditory skills.

$ 29.95

1203 Asking Good Questions

Jean DeGaetano, Author
The Speech Bin
1965 Twenty-Fifth Avenue   **407-770-0007**
Vero Beach, FL 32960   **FAX 407-770-0006**

Jan J. Binney, Editor In Chief
Barbara Hector, Office Manager

20 illustrated lessons that teach children how to ask good questions.

$ 18.95

1204 Avery Articulation Cards

Erica Avery, Author

The Speech Bin
1965 Twenty-Fifth Avenue 407-770-0007
Vero Beach, FL 32960 FAX 407-770-0006

Jan J. Binney, Editor In Chief
Barbara Hector, Office Manager
Colorful and attractive articulation cards.

1205 Biking for Better Voice

Julie Blonigan, Author
The Speech Bin
1965 Twenty-Fifth Avenue 407-770-0007
Vero Beach, FL 32960 FAX 407-770-0006

Jan J. Binney, Editor In Chief
Barbara Hector, Office Manager
Games and activities to remediate vocal hoarseness.

$ 39.95

1206 Boredom RX

Kristel Aderholdt, Author
The Speech Bin
1965 Twenty-Fifth Avenue 407-770-0007
Vero Beach, FL 32960 FAX 407-770-0006

Jan J. Binney, Editor In Chief
Barbara Hector, Office Manager
Based on the premise that kids like to have fun, and fun is the best anecdote for school-based frustration. It is a wonderful collection of activities designed to help children achieve success in the critical language skills of listening, paying attention and remembering what was said.

$ 27.95

1207 Born to Talk

Lloyd Hulit, Author
The Speech Bin
1965 Twenty-Fifth Avenue 407-770-0007
Vero Beach, FL 32960 FAX 407-770-0006

Jan J. Binney, Editor In Chief
Barbara Hector, Office Manager
Offers critical information on morphology, syntax, phonology, semantics and pragmatics.

$ 39.00

1208 A Bridge to Carryover

The Speech Bin
1965 Twenty-Fifth Avenue 407-770-0007
Vero Beach, FL 32960 FAX 407-770-0006

Jan J. Binney, Editor In Chief
Barbara Hector, Office Manager
A comprehensive collection of 45 reproducible games that kids will ask for again and again that teach correct speech sounds, complete sentences and good listening skills.

$ 24.95

1209 Bugaboo Words

Noreen Briggs, Author
The Speech Bin
1965 Twenty-Fifth Avenue 407-770-0007
Vero Beach, FL 32960 FAX 407-770-0006

Jan J. Binney, Editor In Chief
Barbara Hector, Office Manager
Exercises and activities to improve speech production of difficult-to-say problem words.

$ 25.00

1210 Building Thinking Skills

The Speech Bin
1965 Twenty-Fifth Avenue 407-770-0007
Vero Beach, FL 32960 FAX 407-770-0006

Jan J. Binney, Editor In Chief
Barbara Hector, Office Manager
Engaging activities to develop cognitive skills and analytic reasoning.

$ 20.95

1211 Calendar Capers: Year-Round Speech & Language in English & Spanish

Pamela Meza Steckbeck, Author
The Speech Bin
1965 Twenty-Fifth Avenue 407-770-0007
Vero Beach, FL 32960 FAX 407-770-0006

Jan J. Binney, Editor In Chief
Barbara Hector, Office Manager
Stimulating activities to facilitate oral langauge development and correct speech sound production in both English and Spanish. Cleverly illustrated instructional games.

$ 22.95

1212 Caps, Commas and Other Things

S. Pastorek, Author
Connecticut Association for Children with LD
18 Marshall Street 203-838-5010
South Norwalk, CT 06854 FAX 203-866-6108

$ 18.00

1213 Carolina Picture Vocabulary Test

Thomas Layton, Author
Pro-Ed
8700 Shoal Creek Blvd. 512-451-3246
Austin, TX 78758 FAX 512-451-8542
A norm-referenced, validated, receptive sign vocabulary test for deaf and hearing-impaired children.

$ 18.00

1214 Chatty Hats and Other Props

Denise Manilone, Author
The Speech Bin
1965 Twenty-Fifth Avenue   407-770-0007
Vero Beach, FL 32960   FAX 407-770-0006

Jan J. Binney, Editor In Chief
Barbara Hector, Office Manager

Thematic activities and costume patterns for 20 familiar occupations and extensive suggestions to help young children improve pragmatic language and speech skills.

$ 22.95

1215 The Child - Childhood Inventory of Language and Development

Chris Bauman, Author
The Speech Bin
1965 Twenty-Fifth Avenue   407-770-0007
Vero Beach, FL 32960   FAX 407-770-0006

Jan J. Binney, Editor In Chief
Barbara Hector, Office Manager

Behaviors and indicators of cognitive, speech and language, social and motor skill development in children birth to 5 years of age.

$ 7.50

1216 Classroom Language Builders

Carolyn Weiner, Author
The Speech Bin
1965 Twenty-Fifth Avenue   407-770-0007
Vero Beach, FL 32960   FAX 407-770-0006

Jan J. Binney, Editor In Chief
Barbara Hector, Office Manager

A perfect answer for classroom teachers who need language building materials.

$ 26.95

1217 Cognitive-Linguistic Improvement Program

Deborah Ross-Swain, Author
The Speech Bin
1965 Twenty-Fifth Avenue   407-770-0007
Vero Beach, FL 32960   FAX 407-770-0006

Jan J. Binney, Editor In Chief
Barbara Hector, Office Manager

How to treat neuropathologies of speech, language and learning disabilities including effective strategies and techniques for improving skills in memory, judgement and reasoning.

$ 45.00

1218 Communication Cartoons

Cathy Hazelton, Author
The Speech Bin
1965 Twenty-Fifth Avenue   407-770-0007
Vero Beach, FL 32960   FAX 407-770-0006

Jan J. Binney, Editor In Chief
Barbara Hector, Office Manager

This comprehensive program teaches oral language concepts to preschool and elementary age children. More than 400 black and white line drawings.

$ 24.95

1219 The Communication Curriculum

Linda Collins, Author
The Speech Bin
1965 Twenty-Fifth Avenue   407-770-0007
Vero Beach, FL 32960   FAX 407-770-0006

Jan J. Binney, Editor In Chief
Barbara Hector, Office Manager

A practical curriculum of treatment goals and objectives, implementation strategies and evaluation criteria for a wide variety of communication disorders in school-age children. Covers language, phonology, articulation, stuttering and voice problems.

$ 39.95

1220 The Communication Program Planning Book

Linda Collins, Author
The Speech Bin
1965 Twenty-Fifth Avenue   407-770-0007
Vero Beach, FL 32960   FAX 407-770-0006

Jan J. Binney, Editor In Chief
Barbara Hector, Office Manager

This book will help professionals manage all the administration-trivia.

$ 21.95

1221 Comprehension Workbooks

The Speech Bin
1965 Twenty-Fifth Avenue   407-770-0007
Vero Beach, FL 32960   FAX 407-770-0006

Jan J. Binney, Editor In Chief
Barbara Hector, Office Manager

Reproducible workbooks carefully sequence activities that build skill and confidence.

$ 5.95

1222 Concepts for Learning

Julie Blonigen, Author
The Speech Bin
1965 Twenty-Fifth Avenue   407-770-0007
Vero Beach, FL 32960   FAX 407-770-0006

Jan J. Binney, Editor In Chief
Barbara Hector, Office Manager

A comprehensive program for teaching basic language concepts to preschool and early elementary age children that includes more than 200 learning activities.

$ 24.95

1223 Countless Categories

Monica Gustafson, Author

The Speech Bin
1965 Twenty-Fifth Avenue   **407-770-0007**
Vero Beach, FL 32960   **FAX 407-770-0006**

Jan J. Binney, Editor In Chief
Barbara Hector, Office Manager

A wonderful book of reproductible activities to teach word associations, characterizations, vocabulary and problem solving.

$ 21.00

1224 Critical Thinking Activities

The Speech Bin
1965 Twenty-Fifth Avenue   **407-770-0007**
Vero Beach, FL 32960   **FAX 407-770-0006**

Jan J. Binney, Editor In Chief
Barbara Hector, Office Manager

Two challenging books of cooperative activities that improve critical communication skills in enjoyable ways.

$ 9.95

1225 Cut 'N Color Language Development Activity Book

Carolyn Weiner, Author

The Speech Bin
1965 Twenty-Fifth Avenue   **407-770-0007**
Vero Beach, FL 32960   **FAX 407-770-0006**

Jan J. Binney, Editor In Chief
Barbara Hector, Office Manager

High-interest reproductible language activities for four stages of language development, including encoding experiences.

$ 17.95

1226 Don't Take It So Literally!

Danielle Legler, Author

The Speech Bin
1965 Twenty-Fifth Avenue   **407-770-0007**
Vero Beach, FL 32960   **FAX 407-770-0006**

Jan J. Binney, Editor In Chief
Barbara Hector, Office Manager

Offers illustrations teaching sixty idioms in a delightful way.

$ 16.95

1227 Dormac Easy English Dictionary

Edmark Corporation
P.O. Box 3218   **206-746-3900**
Redmond, WA 98073   **800-362-2890**

Provides simply worded definitions for more than 5,000 words.

$ 29.00

1228 Dormac Idiom Series

Edmark Corporation
P.O. Box 3218   **206-746-3900**
Redmond, WA 98073   **800-362-2890**

Each idiom is presented within the context of a short paragraph, which is followed by five exercises that cover the idiom's definition.

$ 59.00

1229 Dotbot Language Activities

Cathie Roberts Mulder, Author

The Speech Bin
1965 Twenty-Fifth Avenue   **407-770-0007**
Vero Beach, FL 32960   **FAX 407-770-0006**

Jan J. Binney, Editor In Chief
Barbara Hector, Office Manager

Wonderful little robots that teach colors, numbers, shapes, sizes and more.

$ 32.95

1230 Double Talk

AGS
7201 Woodland Road   **612-786-4343**
Circle Pines, MN 55014   **800-328-2560**

Helps children develop awareness and understanding of idioms in everday speech.

$ 29.95

1231 Exercises in Grammar: Books I and II

Educators Publishing Service, Inc.
75 Moulton Street   **800-225-5750**
Cambridge, MA 02138

These two grammar books provide a convenient reference source and an excellent set of practice exercises.

1232 The Expression Collection

Joan Klecan-Aker, Author

The Speech Bin
1965 Twenty-Fifth Avenue   **407-770-0007**
Vero Beach, FL 32960   **FAX 407-770-0006**

Jan J. Binney, Editor In Chief
Barbara Hector, Office Manager

Offers a way to evaluate and treat language-disabled children who experience difficulty expressing themselves in organized ways.

$ 39.95

1233 Facilitating Early Language: Handouts

Sherrill Howard, Author

The Speech Bin
1965 Twenty-Fifth Avenue   407-770-0007
Vero Beach, FL 32960   FAX 407-770-0006

Jan J. Binney, Editor In Chief
Barbara Hector, Office Manager

Handouts for parents and teachers that describe normal language development and provide ways to improve speech and language skills.

$ 52.00

1234 Fast Progress

Eva Schmidler, Author

The Speech Bin
1965 Twenty-Fifth Avenue   407-770-0007
Vero Beach, FL 32960   FAX 407-770-0006

Jan J. Binney, Editor In Chief
Barbara Hector, Office Manager

Offers a chance for children to learn language skills such as classifying, describing, vocabulary-learning, expressing and conversation.

$ 25.00

1235 Finishing Touches

Noreen Briggs, Author

The Speech Bin
1965 Twenty-Fifth Avenue   407-770-0007
Vero Beach, FL 32960   FAX 407-770-0006

Jan J. Binney, Editor In Chief
Barbara Hector, Office Manager

Stimulating practice exercises to facilitate improved language and speech production.

$ 16.95

1236 First Language Taught and Learned

E.L. Moerk, Author

Books on Special Children
P.O. Box 305   914-638-1236
Congers, NY 10920   FAX 914-638-0847

Offers information on language development through careful attention of verbal interactions involving one child.

$ 42.00

1237 Functional Instructional Materials

Rosalind Olson, Author

The Speech Bin
1965 Twenty-Fifth Avenue   407-770-0007
Vero Beach, FL 32960   FAX 407-770-0006

Jan J. Binney, Editor In Chief
Barbara Hector, Office Manager

Speech and language materials designed to provide intensive language stimulation and use at a low cost.

1238 Gameway Card Games

The Speech Bin
1965 Twenty-Fifth Avenue   407-770-0007
Vero Beach, FL 32960   FAX 407-770-0006

Jan J. Binney, Editor In Chief
Barbara Hector, Office Manager

Each deck has 24 paired color pictures of target phoneme words - essential speech sound cards you'll use over and over.

$ 84.00

1239 Here's How to Handle

Carolyn Weiner, Author

The Speech Bin
1965 Twenty-Fifth Avenue   407-770-0007
Vero Beach, FL 32960   FAX 407-770-0006

Jan J. Binney, Editor In Chief
Barbara Hector, Office Manager

An outstanding set of popular workbooks that help you quickly establish an effective treatment program for the misarticulated phonemes.

$ 39.95

1240 Holiday Potpourri

M. Sherry Smith, Author

The Speech Bin
1965 Twenty-Fifth Avenue   407-770-0007
Vero Beach, FL 32960   FAX 407-770-0006

Jan J. Binney, Editor In Chief
Barbara Hector, Office Manager

Language development games with five major holiday themes.

$ 16.95

1241 Holidays

The Speech Bin
1965 Twenty-Fifth Avenue   407-770-0007
Vero Beach, FL 32960   FAX 407-770-0006

Jan J. Binney, Editor In Chief
Barbara Hector, Office Manager

Offers over 145 delightful worksheets for carryover practice in conversational speech.

$ 34.95

1242 How to Teach Spelling and How to Spell 1, 2, 3, 4

Laura Toby Rudginsky, Author
Educators Publishing Service, Inc.
75 Moulton Street   **800-225-5750**
Cambridge, MA 02138

A comprehensive resource manual based on the Orton-Gillingham approach to reading and spelling.

1243 I Love Lists

Linda Schwartz, Author
The Speech Bin
1965 Twenty-Fifth Avenue   **407-770-0007**
Vero Beach, FL 32960   **FAX 407-770-0006**

Jan J. Binney, Editor In Chief
Barbara Hector, Office Manager

Offers nearly 200 vocabulary-building word lists with intriguing topics ranging from symbols to comets.

$ 19.95

1244 Idiom Workbooks

Myra Austin, Author
The Speech Bin
1965 Twenty-Fifth Avenue   **407-770-0007**
Vero Beach, FL 32960   **FAX 407-770-0006**

Jan J. Binney, Editor In Chief
Barbara Hector, Office Manager

Workbooks suitable for children or adults that teach idioms enjoyably and memorably.

$ 59.00

1245 Idiom's Delight

John Arena, Author
The Speech Bin
1965 Twenty-Fifth Avenue   **407-770-0007**
Vero Beach, FL 32960   **FAX 407-770-0006**

Jan J. Binney, Editor In Chief
Barbara Hector, Office Manager

Offers 75 idioms and accompanying reproductible activities.

$ 10.00

1246 I'm Good At Speech

The Speech Bin
1965 Twenty-Fifth Avenue   **407-770-0007**
Vero Beach, FL 32960   **FAX 407-770-0006**

Jan J. Binney, Editor In Chief
Barbara Hector, Office Manager

A unique musical speech and language kit.

$ 55.00

1247 The Junior Question Collection

Linda Schwartz, Author
The Speech Bin
1965 Twenty-Fifth Avenue   **407-770-0007**
Vero Beach, FL 32960   **FAX 407-770-0006**

Jan J. Binney, Editor In Chief
Barbara Hector, Office Manager

An exciting collection of knowledge questions-a great motivator for practicing expressive language.

$ 7.95

1248 Language Making Action Cards

The Speech Bin
1965 Twenty-Fifth Avenue   **407-770-0007**
Vero Beach, FL 32960   **FAX 407-770-0006**

Jan J. Binney, Editor In Chief
Barbara Hector, Office Manager

Set of 600 full color language picture cards including beautifully illustrated action verbs, plurals, comparatives and stories.

$ 98.00

1249 Language Rehabilitation

Jame Martinoff, Author
Pro-Ed
8700 Shoal Creek Blvd.   **512-451-3246**
Austin, TX 78758   **FAX 512-451-8542**

Offers practical exercises for developing language in older children or rebuilding language in aphasic adults.

1250 Language-Related Learning Disabilities

Adele Gerber, Author
The Speech Bin
1965 Twenty-Fifth Avenue   **407-770-0007**
Vero Beach, FL 32960   **FAX 407-770-0006**

Jan J. Binney, Editor In Chief
Barbara Hector, Office Manager

A comprehensive look at the relationship between learning disabilities and language disabilities.

$ 46.00

1251 Learning Disabilities, Academic Areas

Pro-Ed
8700 Shoal Creek Blvd.   **512-451-3246**
Austin, TX 78758   **FAX 512-451-8542**

A Dormac english dictionary that meets the needs of those who have limited reading and comprehension abilities.

1252 Mad As a Wet Hen

Marvin Terban, Author
The Speech Bin
1965 Twenty-Fifth Avenue   **407-770-0007**
Vero Beach, FL 32960   **FAX 407-770-0006**

Jan J. Binney, Editor In Chief
Barbara Hector, Office Manager

This book provides entertaining explanations of each idiom from body parts to dogs.

$ 13.95

1253 Make-A-Games

Fran Colberg, Author

The Speech Bin
1965 Twenty-Fifth Avenue
Vero Beach, FL 32960
407-770-0007
FAX 407-770-0006

Jan J. Binney, Editor In Chief
Barbara Hector, Office Manager

Offers ten gameboards you can adapt for virtually any speech of language game.

$ 8.50

1254 The Many Voices of Paws

Julie Reville, Author

The Speech Bin
1965 Twenty-Fifth Avenue
Vero Beach, FL 32960
407-770-0007
FAX 407-770-0006

Jan J. Binney, Editor In Chief
Barbara Hector, Office Manager

Appealing story and treatment materials for use with young stuttering children.

$ 25.00

1255 Multiple Meanings

Edmark Corporation
P.O. Box 3218
Redmond, WA 98073
206-746-3900
800-362-2890

Intended for use by students in the elementary grades and above who have limited understanding of words having more than one meaning.

$ 21.00

1256 My First Word Book

The Speech Bin
1965 Twenty-Fifth Avenue
Vero Beach, FL 32960
407-770-0007
FAX 407-770-0006

Jan J. Binney, Editor In Chief
Barbara Hector, Office Manager

Superb full-color photographs of real-life objects teaching the 1,000 most essential words used by young children.

$ 12.95

1257 My Speech Workbooks

The Speech Bin
1965 Twenty-Fifth Avenue
Vero Beach, FL 32960
407-770-0007
FAX 407-770-0006

Jan J. Binney, Editor In Chief
Barbara Hector, Office Manager

Books of speech articulation materials.

$ 64.00

1258 The Newspaper: Subscription to Success

Lisa Cabiale O'Connor, Author

The Speech Bin
1965 Twenty-Fifth Avenue
Vero Beach, FL 32960
407-770-0007
FAX 407-770-0006

Jan J. Binney, Editor In Chief
Barbara Hector, Office Manager

A practical new tool, based on a whole language approach.

$ 31.00

1259 No-Bos Games

The Speech Bin
1965 Twenty-Fifth Avenue
Vero Beach, FL 32960
407-770-0007
FAX 407-770-0006

Jan J. Binney, Editor In Chief
Barbara Hector, Office Manager

Wonderful games that encourage environmental awareness while they expand and enrich children's language development.

$ 15.50

1260 101 Categories

Marilyn Toomey, Author

The Speech Bin
1965 Twenty-Fifth Avenue
Vero Beach, FL 32960
407-770-0007
FAX 407-770-0006

Jan J. Binney, Editor In Chief
Barbara Hector, Office Manager

101 diverse categories effectively stimulating language development.

$ 21.95

1261 PALS: Pragmatic Activities in Language and Speech

Betty Davis, Author

The Speech Bin
1965 Twenty-Fifth Avenue
Vero Beach, FL 32960
407-770-0007
FAX 407-770-0006

Jan J. Binney, Editor In Chief
Barbara Hector, Office Manager

Offers 180 lessons relevant to kids that deal with the speech of the here-and-now, the language of thought, purposeful styles of speaking and verbal give-and-takes.

$ 59.00

1262 Pick a Picture - Select a Story

Linda Schwartz, Author

The Speech Bin
1965 Twenty-Fifth Avenue
Vero Beach, FL 32960
407-770-0007
FAX 407-770-0006

Jan J. Binney, Editor In Chief
Barbara Hector, Office Manager

Instant ideas for creative expression.

$ 9.95

1263 Play and Say Cards

The Speech Bin
1965 Twenty-Fifth Avenue   407-770-0007
Vero Beach, FL 32960   FAX 407-770-0006

Jan J. Binney, Editor In Chief
Barbara Hector, Office Manager

Offers sixteen decks of bright, full-color playing cards.

$ 69.00

1264 Playing with Idioms

Danielle Legler, Author

The Speech Bin
1965 Twenty-Fifth Avenue   407-770-0007
Vero Beach, FL 32960   FAX 407-770-0006

Jan J. Binney, Editor In Chief
Barbara Hector, Office Manager

Reproductible card games and gameboards teach 60 idioms in everday speech.

$ 16.95

1265 Potpourri: a Bouquet of Language Activities

M. Sherry Smith, Author

The Speech Bin
1965 Twenty-Fifth Avenue   407-770-0007
Vero Beach, FL 32960   FAX 407-770-0006

Jan J. Binney, Editor In Chief
Barbara Hector, Office Manager

Language development activities for learning vocabulary, analogies, categorization, rhyming and syntax.

$ 16.95

1266 Practical Language Activities

JoAnn Jeffries, Author

The Speech Bin
1965 Twenty-Fifth Avenue   407-770-0007
Vero Beach, FL 32960   FAX 407-770-0006

Jan J. Binney, Editor In Chief
Barbara Hector, Office Manager

Highly practical book offering exciting activities and reproductible worksheets for 60 language skills in semantics.

$ 30.95

1267 Primary Thinking Skills

Merle Karnes, Author

The Speech Bin
1965 Twenty-Fifth Avenue   407-770-0007
Vero Beach, FL 32960   FAX 407-770-0006

Jan J. Binney, Editor In Chief
Barbara Hector, Office Manager

Imaginative activities fostering language skills.

$ 23.95

1268 Programmed Materials for Articulation Therapy

Bob McKee, Author

The Speech Bin
1965 Twenty-Fifth Avenue   407-770-0007
Vero Beach, FL 32960   FAX 407-770-0006

Jan J. Binney, Editor In Chief
Barbara Hector, Office Manager

A wealth of materials to provide your articulation clients with great success.

$ 15.00

1269 Quantitative Concepts Workbook

Learning Disabilities Resources
P.O. Box 716   215-525-8336
Bryn Mawr, PA 19010   800-869-8336

A workbook which helps students whose quantitative concepts are weak, especially those with a yearning to learn, understand and use math concepts.

1270 Read-The-Picture Stories

The Speech Bin
1965 Twenty-Fifth Avenue   407-770-0007
Vero Beach, FL 32960   FAX 407-770-0006

Jan J. Binney, Editor In Chief
Barbara Hector, Office Manager

Offers six stories built around a single phoneme; words pictured all begin with that sound.

$ 49.00

1271 Recall

Linda Collins, Author

The Speech Bin
1965 Twenty-Fifth Avenue   407-770-0007
Vero Beach, FL 32960   FAX 407-770-0006

Jan J. Binney, Editor In Chief
Barbara Hector, Office Manager

A wealth of materials to help clients improve their word finding skills.

$ 62.50

1272 Remember with Me

Michael Edson, Author

The Speech Bin
1965 Twenty-Fifth Avenue   407-770-0007
Vero Beach, FL 32960   FAX 407-770-0006

Jan J. Binney, Editor In Chief
Barbara Hector, Office Manager

An excellent tool to encourage dialogue and communication.

$ 19.95

1273 Retell Stories: From Words to Conversation with Meaning

Laura Goepfert, Author

The Speech Bin
1965 Twenty-Fifth Avenue   **407-770-0007**
Vero Beach, FL 32960   **FAX 407-770-0006**

Jan J. Binney, Editor In Chief
Barbara Hector, Office Manager

Reproducible, cleverly illustrated stimulus pictures and re-tell stories use semantically potent words for phonoly training and language development.

$ 16.95

1274 Reversals and Rotations

Edmark Corporation
P.O. Box 3218   **206-746-3900**
Redmond, WA 98073   **800-362-2890**

Two illustrated workbooks for students to practice letters, words and numbers most commonly reversed or rotated.

$ 13.90

1275 Roots, Prefixes, Suffix Spelling Patterns and Syllable Plus

Educators Publishing Service, Inc.
75 Moulton Street   **800-225-5750**
Cambridge, MA 02138

Four programs written for the Apple Commodore 64 and IBM PC to review and reinforce basic concepts in reading, spelling and vocabulary development.

1276 Rules of the Game: Grammar Through Discovery

Mary Page, Author

Educators Publishing Service, Inc.
75 Moulton Street   **800-225-5750**
Cambridge, MA 02138

This series teaches grammar with examples and directed questions that hep students to see that rules and definitions begin with language.

1277 Rules: Remediating Unintelligible Linguistic Expressions of Speech

Jane Webb, Author

The Speech Bin
1965 Twenty-Fifth Avenue   **407-770-0007**
Vero Beach, FL 32960   **FAX 407-770-0006**

Jan J. Binney, Editor In Chief
Barbara Hector, Office Manager

A comprehensive treatment program for remediating the unintelligible speech of preschool and early elementary age children. Delightful cartoon illustrations depict hundreds of words; extensive instructions.

$ 39.95

1278 Search and Say

Shirley McPherson, Author

The Speech Bin
1965 Twenty-Fifth Avenue   **407-770-0007**
Vero Beach, FL 32960   **FAX 407-770-0006**

Jan J. Binney, Editor In Chief
Barbara Hector, Office Manager

Set of 60 word search articulation puzzles giving you high-interest materials that target ten different sounds.

$ 17.95

1279 Sentence Tracking: High Frequency Words

Learning Disabilities Association of America
4156 Library Road   **412-341-1515**
Pittsburgh, PA 15234

1280 Sequencing Practice

Edmark Corporation
P.O. Box 3218   **206-746-3900**
Redmond, WA 98073   **800-362-2890**

Motivating exercises help students practice story sequencing and creative writing skills in these seven reproductible workbooks.

$ 35.65

1281 Sight/Sound System

Learning Disabilities Resources
P.O. Box 716   **215-525-8336**
Bryn Mawr, PA 19010   **800-869-8336**

This publication and video provides explanations in how to use the system for students just learning to read or reading on a very low level.

$ 14.95

1282 Slice: Speech-Language In-services for Colleagues in Education

Denise Mantione, Author

The Speech Bin
1965 Twenty-Fifth Avenue   **407-770-0007**
Vero Beach, FL 32960   **FAX 407-770-0006**

Jan J. Binney, Editor In Chief
Barbara Hector, Office Manager

A comprehensive resource that features unique in-service programs ready for you to present to teachers, parents and others who work with pre-school and school age children.

$ 22.95

1283 Speaking Ace

Franklin Learning Resources
122 Burrs Road   **800-525-9673**
Mt. Holly, NJ 08060

Offers state-of-the-art speech technology in the palm of your hand. The Ace gives you the correct pronunciation for over 80,000 words.

$ 59.00

1284 Speaking Dictionary Companion

Franklin Learning Resources
122 Burrs Road   **800-525-9673**
Mt. Holly, NJ 08060

Uses speech technology to pronounce over 50,000 words at the touch of a button. This combination of speech, spelling, and reference skills allows students to learn and integrate new words into their working vocabularies at their own pace.

$ 89.00

1285 Speaking Language Master - LM 6000

Franklin Learning Resources
122 Burrs Road   **800-525-9673**
Mt. Holly, NJ 08060

The all-in-one English language resource with electronic grammar handbook.

$ 199.00

1286 Speaking Language Master - LM-4000

Franklin Learning Resources
122 Burrs Road   **800-525-9673**
Mt. Holly, NJ 08060

Clearly pronounces over 83,000 words to help strengthen language skills and broaden vocabulary and writing skills.

$ 149.00

1287 Speaking Language Master Special Edition

Franklin Learning Resources
122 Burrs Road   **800-525-9673**
Mt. Holly, NJ 08060

The only portable language reference for people who are blind or visually impaired, learning disabled or speech impaired. Offers pronunciation, spelling correction, complete thesaurus, dictionary and grammar handbook.

$ 500.00

1288 Speech and Language Rehabilitation

Robert Keith, Author

Pro-Ed
8700 Shoal Creek Blvd.   **512-451-3246**
Austin, TX 78758   **FAX 512-451-8542**

A workbook for the neurologically impaired and language delayed.

$ 21.00

1289 Speech Class Goes Home

Carolyn Tayzel, Author

The Speech Bin
1965 Twenty-Fifth Avenue   **407-770-0007**
Vero Beach, FL 32960   **FAX 407-770-0006**

Jan J. Binney, Editor In Chief
Barbara Hector, Office Manager

Worksheets for home practice of speech sounds with simple instructions on each sheet, letters to parents and award certificates.

$ 19.00

1290 Speech Illustrated Cards

Dale Stryker, Author

The Speech Bin
1965 Twenty-Fifth Avenue   **407-770-0007**
Vero Beach, FL 32960   **FAX 407-770-0006**

Jan J. Binney, Editor In Chief
Barbara Hector, Office Manager

The classic card set for treatment of language impairments.

$ 122.00

1291 Speech Lingo

The Speech Bin
1965 Twenty-Fifth Avenue   **407-770-0007**
Vero Beach, FL 32960   **FAX 407-770-0006**

Jan J. Binney, Editor In Chief
Barbara Hector, Office Manager

Offers a set of 12 sturdy boards and 192 matching picture cut-outs for target sounds.

$ 24.00

1292 Speech Rehabilitation

W. Chad Nye, Author

The Speech Bin
1965 Twenty-Fifth Avenue   **407-770-0007**
Vero Beach, FL 32960   **FAX 407-770-0006**

Jan J. Binney, Editor In Chief
Barbara Hector, Office Manager

Treats disorders of apraxia, dysarthria, esophageal speech, cleft palate and articulation of adolescents and adults.

$ 59.00

1293 Speech Sports

Janet Shaw, Author

The Speech Bin
1965 Twenty-Fifth Avenue   407-770-0007
Vero Beach, FL 32960   FAX 407-770-0006

Jan J. Binney, Editor In Chief
Barbara Hector, Office Manager

An exciting collection of sports activities that lets you make every child in your caseload a shining sports star.

$ 23.95

1294   Speech Stations: the One-Stop Speech Book

Janet Shaw, Author

The Speech Bin
1965 Twenty-Fifth Avenue   407-770-0007
Vero Beach, FL 32960   FAX 407-770-0006

Jan J. Binney, Editor In Chief
Barbara Hector, Office Manager

Stimulating activities that facilitate oral and written language skills and cleverly illustrated reproducible games and worksheets.

$ 24.95

1295   Speech Takes Off

Cathy Ann Boudreau, Author

The Speech Bin
1965 Twenty-Fifth Avenue   407-770-0007
Vero Beach, FL 32960   FAX 407-770-0006

Jan J. Binney, Editor In Chief
Barbara Hector, Office Manager

Activities and games for parents to use for speech and language stimulation.

$ 24.95

1296   Speech Therapy Workbooks

The Speech Bin
1965 Twenty-Fifth Avenue   407-770-0007
Vero Beach, FL 32960   FAX 407-770-0006

Jan J. Binney, Editor In Chief
Barbara Hector, Office Manager

Offers 24 reproducible blackline masters of creative activities to help children practice speech sound production in a way they find interesting and motivating.

$ 11.00

1297   Spelling Simplified

Franklyn Peterson, Author

Contemporary Books, Inc.
180 N. Michigan   312-782-9161
Chicago, IL 60601   800-691-1918
                       FAX 312-782-3987

Part of the Study Aids Series. This book contains easy to understand strategies for spelling successfully.

$ 6.95

1298   Spelling Tutor

Franklin Learning Resources
122 Burrs Road   800-525-9673
Mt. Holly, NJ 08060

Contains all of the same features found in the ES-90, in a more mature format for older students. Helps teach and reinforce basic reference skills.

$ 35.00

1299   Spelling Workbooks

Learning Disabilities Resources
P.O. Box 716   215-525-8336
Bryn Mawr, PA 19010 800-869-8336

These workbooks are designed for students with learning problems. They do not contain spelling words but allow the students to collect the words they need for their written expression.

1300   Spellmaster

Franklin Learning Resources
122 Burrs Road   800-525-9673
Mt. Holly, NJ 08060

Offers spelling correction capability, vocabulary enrichment activities and sound-alikes.

$ 29.00

1301   Sticks

The Speech Bin
1965 Twenty-Fifth Avenue   407-770-0007
Vero Beach, FL 32960   FAX 407-770-0006

Jan J. Binney, Editor In Chief
Barbara Hector, Office Manager

700 different four-color, self-adhesive stickers to appeal to kids of all ages.

1302   Super Science Fiction

The Speech Bin
1965 Twenty-Fifth Avenue   407-770-0007
Vero Beach, FL 32960   FAX 407-770-0006

Jan J. Binney, Editor In Chief
Barbara Hector, Office Manager

Offers clever stories and comprehension activities.

$ 5.95

1303   Talking Time

Jeanette Stickel, Author

The Speech Bin
1965 Twenty-Fifth Avenue   407-770-0007
Vero Beach, FL 32960   FAX 407-770-0006

Jan J. Binney, Editor In Chief
Barbara Hector, Office Manager

Activities and guidelines for facilitating language development in children birth to age three years.

$ 13.95

1304 Think on Your Feet

The Speech Bin
1965 Twenty-Fifth Avenue   407-770-0007
Vero Beach, FL 32960 FAX 407-770-0006

Jan J. Binney, Editor In Chief
Barbara Hector, Office Manager

Offers kids a chance to organize their thoughts and express their ideas.

$ 7.95

1305 Thinking Speech

Roberta Hill Fehling, Author

The Speech Bin
1965 Twenty-Fifth Avenue   407-770-0007
Vero Beach, FL 32960 FAX 407-770-0006

Jan J. Binney, Editor In Chief
Barbara Hector, Office Manager

Challenging practice materials for older children and adults. It is designed for clients who are ready for the practical day-to-day application of their new communication skills.

$ 16.95

1306 Unisets

The Speech Bin
1965 Twenty-Fifth Avenue   407-770-0007
Vero Beach, FL 32960 FAX 407-770-0006

Jan J. Binney, Editor In Chief
Barbara Hector, Office Manager

Sets of peel-off/stick-on plastic pieces that adhere to a coated background sceneboard. Theses great language learning tools are offered in various sets (farm, beach, classroom, circus, kitchen, calendar, supermarket, department store, house, zoo, ballet and busy sets).

1307 Vocabulary Workbooks

Learning Disabilities Resources
P.O. Box 716   215-525-8336
Bryn Mawr, PA 19010 800-869-8336

This new addition to the language development series provides the student with a systematic way to sharpen and expand his or her vocabulary.

$ 6.00

1308 Word Elements - How They Work Together

Alan Riese, Author

Educators Publishing Service, Inc.
75 Moulton Street   800-225-5750
Cambridge, MA 02138

This vocabulary workbook teaches students to recognize common word elements.

1309 Word Making Cards

The Speech Bin
1965 Twenty-Fifth Avenue   407-770-0007
Vero Beach, FL 32960 FAX 407-770-0006

Jan J. Binney, Editor In Chief
Barbara Hector, Office Manager

Teaches articulation basics with 600 full color wood word picture boards.

1310 Wordmaster

Franklin Learning Resources
122 Burrs Road   800-525-9673
Mt. Holly, NJ 08060

Electronic thesaurus with 496,000 synonyms from Merriam-Webster.

$ 45.00

1311 Words That Name, Tell Action, Describe and Connect

Alan Riese, Author

Educators Publishing Service, Inc.
75 Moulton Street   800-225-5750
Cambridge, MA 02138

Teaches recognition of nouns and pronouns, verbs and verb phrases in sentences, identifies adjectives and adverbs and includes conjunctions and prepositions that compund and complex sentences.

1312 Workbook for Word Retrieval

Beth M. Kennedy, Author

The Speech Bin
1965 Twenty-Fifth Avenue   407-770-0007
Vero Beach, FL 32960 FAX 407-770-0006

Jan J. Binney, Editor In Chief
Barbara Hector, Office Manager

Word retrieval and vocabulary building exercises and activities.

$ 39.95

Life Skills

1313 About Me

Britannica Books and Reference Materials
310 South Michigan Avenue   800-554-9862
Chicago, IL 60604 FAX 312-347-7903

Offers colorful and fun stories about siblings growing up together and the various antics they create.

$ 32.20

1314 All Kinds of Minds

Dr. Mel Levine, Author

Educators Publishing Service, Inc.
75 Moulton Street   800-225-5750
Cambridge, MA 02138

Enables students with learning disorders to understand their difficulties and behavior. Prevents children from losing motivation and developing behavior problems stemming from their learning difficulties and helps children to understand and respect all kinds of minds.

1315 Basic Skills for Everyone

Edmark Corporation
P.O. Box 3218   206-746-3900
Redmond, WA 98073   800-362-2890

Teaches students essential skills to function in today's world.

$ 25.90

1316 Check Writing Program

Edmark Corporation
P.O. Box 3218   206-746-3900
Redmond, WA 98073   800-362-2890

Simulates real-life situations and procedures on how to write a check.

$ 95.00

1317 Community-Based Curriculum

Edmark Corporation
P.O. Box 3218   206-746-3900
Redmond, WA 98073   800-362-2890

Broadens understanding of the common concepts of community integration.

$ 31.00

1318 Daily Dilemmas

Elisabeth Wilig, Author
The Speech Bin
1965 Twenty-Fifth Avenue   407-770-0007
Vero Beach, FL 32960   FAX 407-770-0006

Jan J. Binney, Editor In Chief
Barbara Hector, Office Manager

Reproductible skits to help young children learn to cope with social and educational aspects of learning disabilities in their daily lives.

$ 39.00

1319 Daily Living Skills: Using a Telephone

Edmark Corporation
P.O. Box 3218   206-746-3900
Redmond, WA 98073   800-362-2890

Helps students with basic telephone communication skills.

$ 79.00

1320 Food & Nutrition

Edmark Corporation
P.O. Box 3218   206-746-3900
Redmond, WA 98073   800-362-2890

Teaches basic cooking techniques and meal planning guidelines.

$ 65.00

1321 Go for It!

Judy Zerafa, Author
Unlimited, Inc.
P.O. Box 4349
Traverse City, MI 49684

This is a book with accompanying audio tapes designed to show you how to discover and develop personal talents and abilities, to face problems and learn how to solve them, and to develop self-respect.

1322 Home Cooking

Edmark Corporation
P.O. Box 3218   206-746-3900
Redmond, WA 98073   800-362-2890

Provides new tools for independent meal preparation.

$ 219.00

1323 Keeping House

Edmark Corporation
P.O. Box 3218   206-746-3900
Redmond, WA 98073   800-362-2890

Establishes and practices the sequential steps necessary to keep a personal living space clean.

$ 179.00

1324 Leisure Programs for Disabled Persons

Edmark Corporation
P.O. Box 3218   206-746-3900
Redmond, WA 98073   800-362-2890

Teaches skills to enhance independent leisure-time activities.

$ 28.00

1325 Life Centered Career Education: Daily Living Skills

Donn E. Brolin, Author
The Council for Exceptional Children
1920 Association Drive   703-620-3660
Reston, VA 22091

Competency in Daily Living Skills Domain increasaes the probability that students will be able to function as independent and productive family members and citizens.

$ 400.00

1326 Life Skills

Edmark Corporation
P.O. Box 3218   206-746-3900
Redmond, WA 98073   800-362-2890

Hands-on experience helps develop skills needed to live independently. This set of nine reproductible books provides worksheets for use as pre-tests, study guides and review.

$ 80.95

1327 Look 'n Cook

Edmark Corporation
P.O. Box 3218   206-746-3900
Redmond, WA 98073   800-362-2890

Encourages nonreaders to discover basic cooking skills.

$ 125.00

1328 Looking Good

Edmark Corporation
P.O. Box 3218   206-746-3900
Redmond, WA 98073   800-362-2890

Focuses on self-care routines critical for successful independent living.

$ 179.00

1329 Making Choices

Britannica Books and Reference Materials
310 South Michigan Avenue   800-554-9862
Chicago, IL 60604   FAX 312-347-7903

This series will face children with dramatic stories and situations and offer solutions to the problems.

$ 87.90

1330 Project MORE: Personal Care Series

Edmark Corporation
P.O. Box 3218   206-746-3900
Redmond, WA 98073   800-362-2890

Comes with complete guides that contain all the procedures and tips you need to help a student or client master these important personal care skills.

$ 149.00

1331 Project MORE: Taking Care of Simple Injuries Series

Edmark Corporation
P.O. Box 3218   206-746-3900
Redmond, WA 98073   800-362-2890

Comes with complete guides that contain all the procedures and tips you need to help a student or a client take care of simple injuries.

$ 149.00

1332 Select-A-Meal

Edmark Corporation
P.O. Box 3218   206-746-3900
Redmond, WA 98073   800-362-2890

Assists independent dining out with colorful picture cards.

$ 45.00

1333 Shopping Smart

Edmark Corporation
P.O. Box 3218   206-746-3900
Redmond, WA 98073   800-362-2890

Offers programs on how to simplify shopping experiences.

$ 45.00

1334 Simply Cooking

Edmark Corporation
P.O. Box 3218   206-746-3900
Redmond, WA 98073   800-362-2890

Prepare delicious meals with this step-by-step illustrated cooking guide.

$ 14.95

1335 Skills for Living

Britannica Books and Reference Materials
310 South Michigan Avenue   800-554-9862
Chicago, IL 60604   FAX 312-347-7903

This series explores the joys of reading, writing and research. Each volume shows students how they can increase their proficiency in, or best develop the basic skills essential to success in school.

$ 43.00

1336 Special Day Books

Britannica Books and Reference Materials
310 South Michigan Avenue   800-554-9862
Chicago, IL 60604   FAX 312-347-7903

This series offers students and teachers creative and engaging ideas for holiday classroom projects.

$ 134.55

1337 A Special Picture Cookbook

Edmark Corporation
P.O. Box 3218   206-746-3900
Redmond, WA 98073   800-362-2890

A simple manual offering information to students on how to prepare basic food items.

$ 18.00

1338 Successful Living

Britannica Books and Reference Materials
310 South Michigan Avenue   800-554-9862
Chicago, IL 60604   FAX 312-347-7903

This series of books will teach children how to relate to others as they develop into well-adjusted adults.

$ 67.30

1339 Survival Guides

Edmark Corporation
P.O. Box 3218   206-746-3900
Redmond, WA 98073   800-362-2890

Provides experience with typical information resources available to students or clients who are transitioning to independent living or making independent decisions.

$ 53.10

1340 Survival Vocabularies

Edmark Corporation
P.O. Box 3218   206-746-3900
Redmond, WA 98073   800-362-2890

Teaches 80 important words or phrases necessary for interacting successfully in stores, restaurants, offices and other public places.

$ 43.00

1341 Teaching Functional Academics

Edmark Corporation
P.O. Box 3218   206-746-3900
Redmond, WA 98073   800-362-2890

Helps students become more capable in basic reading, writing and math.

$ 34.00

1342 Understanding Myself Picture Books

Britannica Books and Reference Materials
310 South Michigan Avenue   800-554-9862
Chicago, IL 60604   FAX 312-347-7903

This series of books helps students understand important events that happen in childhood and the emotions that often accompany them.

$ 107.65

1343 Value Tales

Britannica Books and Reference Materials
310 South Michigan Avenue   800-554-9862
Chicago, IL 60604   FAX 312-347-7903

This series of books takes wonderfully creative animal stories and combines them with lessons on morals and values.

$ 107.65

1344 Values

Britannica Books and Reference Materials
310 South Michigan Avenue   800-554-9862
Chicago, IL 60604   FAX 312-347-7903

This series deals with the everyday problems of growing up, such as listening to others, learning self-control and showing good manners.

$ 40.35

1345 Values to Live By?

Britannica Books and Reference Materials
310 South Michigan Avenue   800-554-9862
Chicago, IL 60604   FAX 312-347-7903

Sometimes it seems that negative values are everywhere. This series of books will help children identify various situations and define the type of values they should adapt.

$ 322.90

1346 What Does It Mean?

Britannica Books and Reference Materials
310 South Michigan Avenue   800-554-9862
Chicago, IL 60604   FAX 312-347-7903

A series helping students understand their feelings and live with all their complex emotions.

$ 139.85

Math

1347 Attack Math

Carole Greenes, Author
Educators Publishing Service, Inc.
75 Moulton Street   800-225-5750
Cambridge, MA 02138

Teaches the four arithmetic operations.

1348 Beginning Math and Science Concepts

Britannica Books and Reference Materials
310 South Michigan Avenue   800-554-9862
Chicago, IL 60604   FAX 312-347-7903

This popluar series helps students learn beginning math and science concepts in a highly appealing and creative way.

$ 296.00

1349 Big Money Math Kit

Edmark Corporation
P.O. Box 3218   206-746-3900
Redmond, WA 98073   800-362-2890

Combines the above two sets to teach money math skills.

$ 42.00

1350 Classroom Cash

Edmark Corporation
P.O. Box 3218   206-746-3900
Redmond, WA 98073   800-362-2890

Satisfies an entire classroom of enthusiastic money handlers.

$ 39.95

1351 Coin Skills Curriculum, Revised

Edmark Corporation
P.O. Box 3218   206-746-3900
Redmond, WA 98073   800-362-2890

Teaches self-sufficiency through money handling skills.

$ 24.95

1352 Instructional Guide of Alternative Math Techniques

Dr. Richard Cooper, Author
Learning Disabilities Resources
P.O. Box 716   215-525-8336
Bryn Mawr, PA 19010   800-869-8336

A collection of alternative techniques which Dr. Cooper has found useful in teaching arithmetic to individuals with learning problems.

1353 Keyboarding Math

Diana Hanbury King, Author

Educators Publishing Service, Inc.
75 Moulton Street   800-225-5750
Cambridge, MA 02138

This innovative touch typing method enables students of all ages to learn to type quickly and easilyw.

1354   Math and Writing I & II

Robert Pauker, Author

Educators Publishing Service, Inc.
75 Moulton Street   800-225-5750
Cambridge, MA 02138

For students who are good at math but reluctant to write, these books offer practice in important language arts skills.

1355   Math in Action: Word Problems

Edmark Corporation
P.O. Box 3218   206-746-3900
Redmond, WA 98073   800-362-2890

Advance reading levels helping students learn computation skills.

$ 49.10

1356   Money Math Kit: Buying and Making Change

Edmark Corporation
P.O. Box 3218   206-746-3900
Redmond, WA 98073   800-362-2890

Teaches everyday money math skills.

$ 22.00

1357   Money Math Kit: Counting and Finding Exact Amounts

Edmark Corporation
P.O. Box 3218   206-746-3900
Redmond, WA 98073   800-362-2890

Uses coin and currency to teach counting and place value concepts.

$ 22.00

1358   My Number Books

Britannica Books and Reference Materials
310 South Michigan Avenue   800-554-9862
Chicago, IL 60604   FAX 312-347-7903

This series allows children to learn beginning number concepts.

$ 134.55

1359   Number Facts Mastery Program

Edmark Corporation
P.O. Box 3218   206-746-3900
Redmond, WA 98073   800-362-2890

Teaches basic number facts systematically and completely. Through the memorization of number facts, students create a foundation on which to build more complex computation math skills.

$ 69.95

1360   Real-Life Math

Edmark Corporation
P.O. Box 3218   206-746-3900
Redmond, WA 98073   800-362-2890

Teaches basic arithmetic skills through personal money management role-playing activities.

$ 198.00

1361   Tic-Tac-Toe Math Instructional Guide and Video

Dr. Richard Cooper, Author

Learning Disabilities Resources
P.O. Box 716   215-525-8336
Bryn Mawr, PA 19010   800-869-8336

This guide and video teaches Tic-Tac-Toe math which can be used wither by a teacher or the student.

$ 19.95

1362   Tic-Tac-Toe Math Workbook III: Guide and Video

Dr. Richard Cooper, Author

Learning Disabilities Resources
P.O. Box 716   215-525-8336
Bryn Mawr, PA 19010   800-869-8336

This third set teaches the students how to use the Tic Tac Toe Math to do fractions.

$ 20.25

Pre-School

1363   Color Cards

The Speech Bin
1965 Twenty-Fifth Avenue   407-770-0007
Vero Beach, FL 32960   FAX 407-770-0006

Jan J. Binney, Editor In Chief
Barbara Hector, Office Manager

The best language stimulation cards you can buy. Various sets are offered such as: Adjectives; Prepositions; Basic Sequences; Everday Objects; Verbs; Clothes; Possessions; Foods; Social Situations; Daily Living Skills and more.

1364   Communication Disorders in Infants and Toddlers

Frances Billeaud, Author

The Speech Bin
1965 Twenty-Fifth Avenue   407-770-0007
Vero Beach, FL 32960   FAX 407-770-0006

Jan J. Binney, Editor In Chief
Barbara Hector, Office Manager

Offers service delivery models, interdisciplinary functioning, neonatal intensive care and feeding issues.

$ 29.95

1365 A Curriculum for Infants and Toddlers with Cleft Palate

Joan Lynch, Author

The Speech Bin
1965 Twenty-Fifth Avenue   407-770-0007
Vero Beach, FL 32960   FAX 407-770-0006

Jan J. Binney, Editor In Chief
Barbara Hector, Office Manager

Outstanding text covering social use of language, language comprehension skills and speech, voice, resonance production for young children with cleft palates.

$ 49.00

1366 Early Communication Skills

Charlotte Lynch, Author

The Speech Bin
1965 Twenty-Fifth Avenue   407-770-0007
Vero Beach, FL 32960   FAX 407-770-0006

Jan J. Binney, Editor In Chief
Barbara Hector, Office Manager

Ready-to-use ideas for activities that foster preverbal skills, vocalization, listening and awareness skills.

$ 44.00

1367 Early Language Intervention

Alice Warren, Author

The Speech Bin
1965 Twenty-Fifth Avenue   407-770-0007
Vero Beach, FL 32960   FAX 407-770-0006

Jan J. Binney, Editor In Chief
Barbara Hector, Office Manager

Ready-to-use language program for preschool and elementary children has 300 worksheets plus pre/post test, profiles, awards and a daily planner to facilitate learning vocabulary, concepts and grammar.

$ 24.95

1368 Help for Special Preschoolers

The Speech Bin
1965 Twenty-Fifth Avenue   407-770-0007
Vero Beach, FL 32960   FAX 407-770-0006

Jan J. Binney, Editor In Chief
Barbara Hector, Office Manager

Provides a practical criterion-referenced tool to assess over 600 skills in communication, self-help, social and learning.

$ 43.95

1369 Infants and Toddlers with Special Needs

The Speech Bin
1965 Twenty-Fifth Avenue   407-770-0007
Vero Beach, FL 32960   FAX 407-770-0006

Jan J. Binney, Editor In Chief
Barbara Hector, Office Manager

Using this curriculum, teachers can create a program tailored specifically to the special strengths and weaknesses of each child.

$ 40.00

1370 The Language of Toys

Sue Schwartz, Author

The Speech Bin
1965 Twenty-Fifth Avenue   407-770-0007
Vero Beach, FL 32960   FAX 407-770-0006

Jan J. Binney, Editor In Chief
Barbara Hector, Office Manager

Tells parents how to use toys, both store-bought and homemade, to improve children's communication skills.

$ 14.95

1371 Let's Take a Walk Books

Britannica Books and Reference Materials
310 South Michigan Avenue   800-554-9862
Chicago, IL 60604   FAX 312-347-7903

Helps children discover the wonders of the world around them with these specialized walk books. Children learn how to use all of their senses and sharpen their observation skills.

$ 53.80

1372 Polka-Dot Puppy Books

Britannica Books and Reference Materials
310 South Michigan Avenue   800-554-9862
Chicago, IL 60604   FAX 312-347-7903

A friendly spotted dog introduces important beginning concepts to young children.

$ 53.80

1373 Preschool Language Intervention

Adele Gerber, Author

The Speech Bin
1965 Twenty-Fifth Avenue   407-770-0007
Vero Beach, FL 32960   FAX 407-770-0006

Jan J. Binney, Editor In Chief
Barbara Hector, Office Manager

Preschool language program focusing on small-group language intervention in a natural setting.

$ 24.95

1374 Preschoolers with Special Needs

The Speech Bin
1965 Twenty-Fifth Avenue   407-770-0007
Vero Beach, FL 32960   FAX 407-770-0006

Jan J. Binney, Editor In Chief
Barbara Hector, Office Manager

A comprehensive curriculum covering cognition, communication, social adaptation, and fine and gross motor development.

$ 38.75

1375 Program for the Assessment and Instruction of Swallowing

Virginia Mulpeter, Author

The Speech Bin
1965 Twenty-Fifth Avenue   407-770-0007
Vero Beach, FL 32960   FAX 407-770-0006

Jan J. Binney, Editor In Chief
Barbara Hector, Office Manager

Diagnostic procedures for dysphagic swallowing evaluation and videofluroscopic examination in modified barium swallow plus instructional materials for patients with disorders of swallowing.

$ 55.00

1376 Sequence Books

Britannica Books and Reference Materials
310 South Michigan Avenue   800-554-9862
Chicago, IL 60604   FAX 312-347-7903

Youngsters will appreciate this fun series that explains in simple ways how some of their favorite things are made from start to finish.

$ 67.30

1377 Speech Language In-Services Colleagues in Education

Denise A. Mantione, Author

The Speech Bin
1965 Twenty-Fifth Avenue   407-770-0007
Vero Beach, FL 32960   FAX 407-770-0006

Jan J. Binney, Editor In Chief
Barbara Hector, Office Manager

Ten in-service presentations about language development and communication disorders in preschool-age children.

$ 22.95

1378 Talk-Along Books

Britannica Books and Reference Materials
310 South Michigan Avenue   800-554-9862
Chicago, IL 60604   FAX 312-347-7903

These books increase reading readiness and teach basic concepts to your class.

$ 67.30

1379 Transdisciplinary Play-Based Assessment

Toni Linder, Author

The Speech Bin
1965 Twenty-Fifth Avenue   407-770-0007
Vero Beach, FL 32960   FAX 407-770-0006

Jan J. Binney, Editor In Chief
Barbara Hector, Office Manager

Uses play to assess communicative, cognitive, social, emotional and sensorimotor developmental levels of nondisabled, at risk children.

$ 39.00

Reading

1380 Access to Learning Series

LinguiSystems, Inc.
3100 4th Avenue   800-PRO-IDEA
East Moline, IL 61244   FAX 309-755-2377

Programs for learners with special needs. Each Student Book comes complete with a Teacher Guide. The Student book provides the student with activities to help them learn through prior knowledge and experience, visual clues, practice and repitition plus the teacher's guide offering strategies for reaching the hardest to teach, lesson goals, progress charts and more. There are six series in all touching the reading, language arts and literature curriculums for skill grades 2-6.

1381 Alphabet Books

Britannica Books and Reference Materials
310 South Michigan Avenue   800-554-9862
Chicago, IL 60604   FAX 312-347-7903

Students will enjoy this series of books where individual letters "star" in their own scenarios while inviting other letters to play along.

$ 67.30

1382 Beginning Reasoning and Reading

Joanne Carlisle, Author

Educators Publishing Service, Inc.
75 Moulton Street   800-225-5750
Cambridge, MA 02138

Develops basic language and thinking skills that build the foundation for good reading comprehension.

1383 Big Book Reading Units

Saddleback Educational, Inc.
711 West 17th Street, Ste. F-12   714-650-4010
Costa Mesa, CA 92627   FAX 714-650-1108

Offers various Big Books ranging from the classics, Goldilocks and the Three Bears to ABC Adventures, Farm Animals, etc. There are twelve categories to choose from and each unit consists of a big book, a read-along cassette, one teacher's guide and eight student-sized versions of the same title.

$ 47.00

1384 By Myself Books

Edmark Corporation
P.O. Box 3218   206-746-3900
Redmond, WA 98073   800-362-2890

Intended to motivate primary grade students to read independently and with pleasure.

$ 21.00

1385 Caught Reading

Edmark Corporation
P.O. Box 3218   206-746-3900
Redmond, WA 98073   800-362-2890

Series of seven workbooks for students giving them the opportunity to read stories created from interviews with teenage students.

$ 80.00

1386 Children's Choices

International Reading Association
800 Barksdale Rd., P.O. Box 8139   302-731-1600
Newark, DE 19714   800-336-READ
                                       FAX 302-731-1057

A wonderful source for classroom reading instruction and for introducing books to children for recreational reading.

$ 4.25

1387 The Child's World Library

Britannica Books and Reference Materials
310 South Michigan Avenue   800-554-9862
Chicago, IL 60604   FAX 312-347-7903

A series of books encouraging and fostering the idea of reading. A simple code on each book indicates the suggested reading skill level for each story, from beginning-to-read to more advanced reading.

$ 279.70

1388 Clues to Meaning

Ann Staman, Author
Educators Publishing Service, Inc.
75 Moulton Street   800-225-5750
Cambridge, MA 02138

A new and different beginning reading series that can be incorporated into any reading program.

1389 Dilemmas and Decisions

Edmark Corporation
P.O. Box 3218   206-746-3900
Redmond, WA 98073   800-362-2890

Motivates adolescent readers with simple vocabulary stories.

$ 59.00

1390 Direct Instruction Reading

Books on Special Children
P.O. Box 305   914-638-1236
Congers, NY 10920   FAX 914-638-0847

Teaches reading skills.

$ 54.00

1391 Dyslexia Training Program

Educators Publishing Service, Inc.
5 Moulton Street   800-225-5130
Cambridge, MA 02138

Introduces reading and writing skills to dyslexic children through a two-year, cumulative series of daily one-houe videotaped lessons and accompanying student's books and tacher's guides.

$ 5.00

1392 Early Readers

Edmark Corporation
P.O. Box 3218   206-746-3900
Redmond, WA 98073   800-362-2890

An excellent introduction to reading beginning stories. Each reader focuses on a simple theme and is accompanied by creative full-page illustrations.

$ 18.00

1393 Explode the Code Series

Educators Publishing Service, Inc.
75 Moulton Street   800-225-5750
Cambridge, MA 02138

For use in the primary and elementary grades, teaches basic phonics concepts necessary for beginning through intermediate reading.

1394 A First Course in Phonic Reading

Lida Helson, Author
Educators Publishing Service, Inc.
75 Moulton Street   800-225-5750
Cambridge, MA 02138

1395 Ghostwriter

Children's Television Workshop
One Lincoln Plaza   212-875-6379
New York, NY 10023

Designed to be read and used by students and teachers together, and in conjunction with the "Ghostwriter" TV program. Its main objective is to encourage reading and writing.

1396 Great Unsolved Mysteries

Steck-Vaughn Company
P.O. Box 26015   800-531-5015
Austin, TX 78755

20 intriguing titles of fascinating literature motivating even the most reluctant readers.

$ 19.95

1397 Helping Anyone Overcome Reading/Spelling Problems

AVKO
3084 West Willard Road
Birch Run, MI 48415

313-686-9283

Don McCabe, Research Director

A tutor's book designed to be used by anyone who can read this paragraph.

1398 I Can Read Program Series

Teddy Bear Press
3265 East Tropicana, Ste. E-149
Las Vegas, NV 89121

702-435-8026

Offers 7 books and workbooks, charts and a placement test using a sight-word approach to teach 52 pre-primmer words to beginning readers.

$ 65.00

1399 The I Love to Read Collection

Britannica Books and Reference Materials
310 South Michigan Avenue
Chicago, IL 60604

800-554-9862
FAX 312-347-7903

Created with the whole language reading concept in mind, this series is easy-to-read with each story introducing young readers to a host of quirky and delightful characters.

$ 193.30

1400 Let's Read

Leonard Bloomfield, Author

Educators Publishing Service, Inc.
75 Moulton Street
Cambridge, MA 02138

800-225-5750

A series of nine books and nine accompanying workbooks used a linguistic approach to teaching reading skills.

1401 Look and Learn

Edmark Corporation
P.O. Box 3218
Redmond, WA 98073

206-746-3900
800-362-2890

A comprehensive program for visual reading readiness skills.

$ 49.95

1402 Magic Castle Readers

Britannica Books and Reference Materials
310 South Michigan Avenue
Chicago, IL 60604

800-554-9862
FAX 312-347-7903

Children will delight in the fanciful world of dragons and dinosaurs. The vocabulary in each book is built around one category of words such as color words, number words or feeling words. Also the back of each book lists key words from the story and features simple activities that show students how to use the new words that they've learned.

$ 363.30

1403 Meg and Max Books

Britannica Books and Reference Materials
310 South Michigan Avenue
Chicago, IL 60604

800-554-9862
FAX 312-347-7903

Readers of all ages will love the adventures of Meg and Max, two well-intentioned elephants offering stories to children at beginning reading levels.

$ 28.70

1404 Megawords, Books 1-8

Educators Publishing Service, Inc.
75 Moulton Street
Cambridge, MA 02138

800-225-5750

A series of systematic, multisensory approach to learning the longer words encountered from fourth grade on.

1405 More Primary Phonics

Barbara Makar, Author

Educators Publishing Service, Inc.
75 Moulton Street
Cambridge, MA 02138

800-225-5750

Reinforces and expands skills developed in Primary Phonics. Workbooks and storybooks contain essentially the same phonetic elements, sight words and phonetic sequences.

1406 Most Loved Classics Series

Edmark Corporation
P.O. Box 3218
Redmond, WA 98073

206-746-3900
800-362-2890

Provides classic American and European literature in a low level vocabulary format. Offers opportunity for special education students in mainstream classrooms to read the same books as their peers.

$ 24.95

1407 Pacemaker Classics

Edmark Corporation
P.O. Box 3218
Redmond, WA 98073

206-746-3900
800-362-2890

Timeless stories and characters from the classics that are just the answer to get many students interested in reading.

$ 64.20

1408 Phonetic Primers

Carolyn Smith, Author

Educators Publishing Service, Inc.
75 Moulton Street
Cambridge, MA 02138

800-225-5750

This series of six storybooks with controlled vocabularies can be used as a supplement to a developmental or remedial reading program.

1409 Primary Phonics

Barbara Makar, Author

Educators Publishing Service, Inc.
75 Moulton Street
Cambridge, MA 02138

800-225-5750

A reading series with a structured phonetic approach.

1410 R.A.T. Pack

Dr. Suzanne Ruth Butler, Author

Learning Center, Psychology & Special Education
University Of Sydney   **011-692-3793**
Sydney 2006, NSW   **FAX 011-358-5560**

A remedial, integrated and innovative reading program that has been developed on recent research findings. Despite current remedial technique, the poorer reader tends to remain so throughout the school years. With The R.A.T. Pack series, the activities involved will enable the reader to experience motivating and reinforcing properties of success through all stages of reading skills development.

$ 40.00

1411 Readiness Resource Books

Edmark Corporation
P.O. Box 3218   **206-746-3900**
Redmond, WA 98073   **800-362-2890**

Developed for teachers, this set of five books provides children with enjoyable activities and games.

$ 28.75

1412 Reading Comprehension in Varied Subject Matter

Jane Ervin, Author

Educators Publishing Service, Inc.
75 Moulton Street   **800-225-5750**
Cambridge, MA 02138

Ten workbooks that present a wide range of people and situations.

1413 Reading for Content and Speed

Carol Einstein, Author

Educators Publishing Service, Inc.
75 Moulton Street   **800-225-5750**
Cambridge, MA 02138

High-interest selections are written about such subjects as sports, hobbies, science and more. The student is asked to read the selections followed by four questions on what they just read.

1414 Reading Is Fun Program Series

Teddy Bear Press
3265 E. Tropicana, Ste. E-149   **702-435-8026**
Las Vegas, NV 89121

Offers 6 books and workbooks teaching 54 primer level basic words. This program uses both visual-motor and fine motor discrimination. The small books promote a feeling of success as the child moves through them quickly.

$ 65.00

1415 Reading Mastery Program

Edmark Corporation
P.O. Box 3218   **206-746-3900**
Redmond, WA 98073   **800-362-2890**

A 60-lesson instructional program teaching basic reading skills by introducing the most frequently used sounds first.

$ 69.95

1416 Reading, Rhymes and Riddles

Britannica Books and Reference Materials
310 South Michigan Avenue   **800-554-9862**
Chicago, IL 60604   **FAX 312-347-7903**

Humorous, rhyming text and full color illustrations pose riddles about nature, animals, colors, food and clothing, helping children open their eyes and ears to the sights and sounds all around them.

$ 69.95

1417 Reading - the Right Start

Toni Gould, Author

Educators Publishing Service, Inc.
75 Moulton Street   **800-225-5750**
Cambridge, MA 02138

Uses the Structural Reading approach, which emphasizes the relationship between letters and sounds.

1418 Reasoning and Reading

Joanne Carlisle, Author

Educators Publishing Service, Inc.
75 Moulton Street   **800-225-5750**
Cambridge, MA 02138

These workbooks focus on the kinds of thinking students need to do both to understand and to evaluate what they read.

1419 School-Day Books

Britannica Books and Reference Materials
310 South Michigan Avenue   **800-554-9862**
Chicago, IL 60604   **FAX 312-347-7903**

This series encourages children to read along as Word Bird discovers the fun of going to museums, writing, making new friends and doing all of the things that early learners like to do.

$ 67.30

1420 Short and Long Vowels Play a Game

Britannica Books and Reference Materials
310 South Michigan Avenue   **800-554-9862**
Chicago, IL 60604   **FAX 312-347-7903**

Each book features two delightful characters, one representing the short vowel and one representing the long vowel. The characters have a contest to determine which of them can find the most words containing their individual sounds. Who will win? Let your students decide.

$ 67.30

1421 Short Vowel Adventures

Britannica Books and Reference Materials
310 South Michigan Avenue   800-554-9862
Chicago, IL 60604   FAX 312-347-7903

Join in the fun as Word Bird and his animal friends take part in exciting adventures, all based on words with the five short vowels.

$ 67.30

1422 Simple English Classics Series

Edmark Corporation
P.O. Box 3218   206-746-3900
Redmond, WA 98073   800-362-2890

Allows young readers access to the classics, this series provides a valuable introduction to our literary heritage.

$ 49.95

1423 Sociolinguistics of the Deaf Community

Books on Special Children
P.O. Box 305   914-638-1236
Congers, NY 10920   FAX 914-638-0847

Book offering articles on defining special linguistic and social issues of the deaf community.

$ 48.00

1424 Sound Box Books

Britannica Books and Reference Materials
310 South Michigan Avenue   800-554-9862
Chicago, IL 60604   FAX 312-347-7903

Used in thousands of classrooms across the country, these books are filled with objects that have names beginning with a particular sound. A good way for children to learn vocabulary and preliminary reading skills.

$ 349.85

1425 Sound Workbook

Mary Briggs, Author

Educators Publishing Service, Inc.
75 Moulton Street   800-225-5750
Cambridge, MA 02138

This workbook reinforces the teaching of specific vowel combinations.

1426 Speech Synthesis

A.D.N. Edwards, Author

Books on Special Children
P.O. Box 305   914-638-1236
Congers, NY 10920   FAX 914-638-0847

Describes mechanics of human speech and computer adapters.

$ 35.00

1427 A Spelling Dictionary

Gregory Hurray, Author

Educators Publishing Service, Inc.
75 Moulton Street   800-225-5750
Cambridge, MA 02138

This book gives children a means of spelling words correctly without depending exclusively on their teacher.

1428 SporTellers

Edmark Corporation
P.O. Box 3218   206-746-3900
Redmond, WA 98073   800-362-2890

Builds reading interest with athletic adventure stories.

$ 37.50

1429 Start to Read!

Edmark Corporation
P.O. Box 3218   206-746-3900
Redmond, WA 98073   800-362-2890

Simulates reading with beautifully illustrated story books.

$ 54.00

1430 Understanding Me

The Churchill School
1035 Price School Lane   314-997-4343
St. Louis, MO 63124   FAX 314-997-2760

Sandra K. Gilligan, Director

A student workbook of activities that have been developed to reinforce the language and vocabulary found in "Keeping Ahead in School" by Dr. Melvin levine. The workbook is comprised of blackline masters which can be reproduced.

$ 19.95

1431 Vocabulary Building Exercises for the Young Adult

Edmark Corporation
P.O. Box 3218   206-746-3900
Redmond, WA 98073   800-362-2890

Designed for the student who needs to build useful, meaningful vocabulary for successful everyday life.

$ 59.00

1432 Wilson Reading System

Wilson Language Training
162 West Main Street   508-865-5699
Millbury, MA 01527   800-899-8454
    FAX 508-865-9644

Edward Wilson, Publisher

A remedial reading and writing program for individuals with language-based learning disabilities. Based on Orton-Gillingham philosophy and procedures, WRS teaches the structure of words so that students master the phonological coding system for reading and spelling. The material is presented in 12 steps in a systematic, sequential and cumulative manner.

1433 Word Bird Readers

Britannica Books and Reference Materials
310 South Michigan Avenue   800-554-9862
Chicago, IL 60604   FAX 312-347-7903

With colorful illustrations, simple text and engaging animal characters, this series helps build basic vocabulary for early-bird readers.

$ 161.45

1434 Word House Words

Britannica Books and Reference Materials
310 South Michigan Avenue   800-554-9862
Chicago, IL 60604   FAX 312-347-7903

Everyone's favorite bird creates vocabularies of seasonal and holiday words, putting words on vocabulary cards and making a special word house.

$ 121.10

1435 Word Mastery

Florence Akin, Author

Educators Publishing Service, Inc.
75 Moulton Street   800-225-5750
Cambridge, MA 02138

This phonics classic, reprinted in soft cover, supplements any reading series with its straightforward phonics series.

1436 Word, Sentence, Paragraph Meanings and Reasoning Skills

Joanne Carlisle, Author

Educators Publishing Service, Inc.
75 Moulton Street   800-225-5750
Cambridge, MA 02138

Eight workbooks offering improtant additional exercises to help students think clearly about the meaning of what they read.

1437 Wordly Wise

Kenneth Hodkinson, Author

Educators Publishing Service, Inc.
75 Moulton Street   800-225-5750
Cambridge, MA 02138

Vocabulary workbook series employs crossword puzzles, riddles, word games and a sense of humor to make the learning of new words an interesting experience.

1438 Wordly Wise A,B, and C

Kenneth Hodkinson, Author

Educators Publishing Service, Inc.
75 Moulton Street   800-225-5750
Cambridge, MA 02138

Each book in the ABC series contains approximately one hundred vocabulary words.

1439 Wordly Wise Reading

Kenneth Hodkinson, Author

Educators Publishing Service, Inc.
75 Moulton Street   800-225-5750
Cambridge, MA 02138

Each of these two workbooks contains three original stories, with each story followed by writing and comprehension exercises.

1440 Your Personal Smart Profile

Lynda Miller, Author

Smart Alternatives, Inc.
P.O. Box 5849   512-836-8212
Austin, TX 78763   800-453-9226
    FAX 512-836-8212

Lynda Miller Program Director

Self-journaling workbook guides the reader (with or without assistance) in generating a self-profile of strengths across 8 thinking patterns: interpersonal, spatial, linguistic, mathematical, logical, counseling, musical and self-development.

Science

1441 Activities in Science, Math and English for Persons with Disabilities

Lawrence Scadden & Mary Kohlerman, Author

National Science Foundation
1800 G Street NW   202-357-7562
Washington, DC 20550

Lawrence Scadden, Senior Program Dir.
Mary Kohlerman, Program Director

Education and Human Resources activities for persons with disabilities are designed to complement other special education efforts with two types of projects: those that can produce significant and immediate changes (Model Projects) and those that develop and test comprehensive models to make long-term changes in the infrastructure of science, engineering and mathematics education for persons with disabilities.

1442 Science and Math Series

Britannica Books and Reference Materials
310 South Michigan Avenue   800-554-9862
Chicago, IL 60604   FAX 312-347-7903

This engaging series answers various questions about our earth.

$ 118.25

Social Skills

1443 Augmentative Communication Resource Manuals

Carol Goosens, Author

Don Johnston Developmental Equipment, Inc.
P.O. Box 639, 1000 N. Rand Road   708-526-2682
Wauconda, IL 60084   800-999-4660

Two excellent resource manuals of field-tested assessment and training strategies for children and adolescents in need of augmentative communication systems.

$ 80.00

1444   Life Centered Career Education: Personal- Social Skills

Donn E. Brolin, Author

The Council for Exceptional Children
1920 Association Drive   703-620-3660
Reston, VA 22091

Mastery of the competencies in the Personal-Social Skills Domain increases the probability that students will function more adequately in interpersonal relationships and problem-solving areas.

$ 400.00

1445   Life Management Skills Series

Kathy Korb, Author

Therapro, Inc.
225 Arlington Street   508-872-9494
Framingham, MA 01701   FAX 508-875-2062

Two books that are great for individual or group activities on life management. They can also be used for cognitive retraining with functional activities.

$ 34.95

1446   Life Skills Activities for Special Children

Learning Disabilities Association of America
4156 Library Road   412-341-1515
Pittsburgh, PA 15234

1447   Life Skills Mastery for Students with Special Needs

ERIC Clearinghouse on Disabled and Gifted Children
1920 Association Drive   703-620-3660
Reston, VA 22091

1448   Safety Cards: in and Around the House

Imaginari Photographics, Author

The Speech Bin
1965 Twenty-Fifth Avenue   407-770-0007
Vero Beach, FL 32960   FAX 407-770-0006

Jan J. Binney, Editor In Chief
Barbara Hector, Office Manager

Stimulate discussion and thinking skills with these top quality photographs.

$ 36.00

1449   Social Competence of Young Children with Disabilities

Samuel Odom, Author

The Speech Bin
1965 Twenty-Fifth Avenue   407-770-0007
Vero Beach, FL 32960   FAX 407-770-0006

Jan J. Binney, Editor In Chief
Barbara Hector, Office Manager

This book gives you a multitude of intervention strategies to promote meaningful relations with peers in their classrooms and other contexts.

$ 31.00

1450   Teaching Behavioral Self Control to Students

Edmark Corporation
P.O. Box 3218   206-746-3900
Redmond, WA 98073   800-362-2890

Shows students how to modify their own behavior.

$ 19.00

1451   Thinking, Feeling, Behaving: An Emotional Education Curriculum for Children

Edmark Corporation
P.O. Box 3218   206-746-3900
Redmond, WA 98073   800-362-2890

Teaches positive mental health skills.

$ 25.95

1452   The Walker Social Skills Curriculum: the ACCEPTS Program

Edmark Corporation
P.O. Box 3218   206-746-3900
Redmond, WA 98073   800-362-2890

Encourages integration into less restrictive environments through social skill development.

$ 39.00

1453   Why Is It Always Me?

Polly Behrmann, Author

849 Seabrooke Court
Englewood, FL 34223

Polly Behrmann, Author

A social skills handbook written by a special education teacher who is also the mother of two children with learning disabilities. It is designed for teens and young adults with learning disabilities who want to improve their social skills.

$ 7.90

Social Studies

1454 Biographies From American History

Edmark Corporation
P.O. Box 3218   206-746-3900
Redmond, WA 98073   800-362-2890

Books introducing students to famous Americans.

$ 96.50

1455 Hopes and Dreams

Edmark Corporation
P.O. Box 3218   206-746-3900
Redmond, WA 98073   800-362-2890

Introduces older readers to the experience of multicultural immigrants.

$ 48.00

1456 The Story of the U.S.A.

Franklin Escher, Jr., Author
Educators Publishing Service, Inc.
75 Moulton Street   800-225-5750
Cambridge, MA 02138

A series for four, easy to read workbooks that present basic topics in American history.

1457 The Story of Western Civilization

Alan Riese, Author
Educators Publishing Service, Inc.
75 Moulton Street   800-225-5750
Cambridge, MA 02138

A series of four illustrated reading workbooks that have carefully controlled language levels so that the readers will not be frustrated.

Speech

1458 Acquired Speech and Language Disorders

B.E. Murdoch, Author
Books on Special Children
P.O. Box 305   914-638-1236
Congers, NY 10920   FAX 914-638-0847

Offers an introduction of anatomy of nervous systems and speech/language centers of the brain to show symptoms and neurological mechanisms in speech/language disorders.

$ 37.00

1459 Straight Speech

Jane Folk, Author

The Speech Bin
1965 Twenty-Fifth Avenue   407-770-0007
Vero Beach, FL 32960   FAX 407-770-0006

Jan J. Binney, Editor In Chief
Barbara Hector, Office Manager

A lisp treatment program for use by speech-language pathologists.

$ 14.95

1460 Winning in Speech

Michelle Waugh, Author
The Speech Bin
1965 Twenty-Fifth Avenue   407-770-0007
Vero Beach, FL 32960   FAX 407-770-0006

Jan J. Binney, Editor In Chief
Barbara Hector, Office Manager

Worksheets and activities to facilitate fluent speech in young schoolage stuttering children.

$ 16.95

1461 Your Child's Speech and Language

The Speech Bin
1965 Twenty-Fifth Avenue   407-770-0007
Vero Beach, FL 32960   FAX 407-770-0006

Jan J. Binney, Editor In Chief
Barbara Hector, Office Manager

Provides information for parents about speech and language development of their child.

$ 13.00

Study Skills

1462 Landmark Study Guide

Joan Sedita, Author
Connecticut Association for Children with LD
18 Marshall Street   203-838-5010
South Norwalk, CT 06854   FAX 203-866-6108

A "bible" based on Landmark Schools extensive experience in providing instruction for study skills.

$ 16.50

1463 Study Skills and Learning Strategies for Transition

HEATH Resource Center
One Dupont Circle NW, Ste. 800   202-939-9320
Washington, DC 20036   800-544-3284

The curriculum guide provides students with learning disabilities the skills and strategies they will need to increase their level of success with high school curriculum.

$ 15.00

1464   Study Smarts: How to Learn More in Less Time

Franklyn Peterson, Author

Contemporary Books, Inc.
180 N. Michigan Avenue   312-782-9181
Chicago, IL 60601   800-691-1918
                                FAX 312-782-3987

Part of the Study Aids Series. Contains excellent step-by-step study strategies.

$ 6.95

1465   The Survey of Problem-Solving and Educational Skills

Lynn Meltzer, Author

Educators Publishing Service, Inc.
75 Moulton Street   800-225-5750
Cambridge, MA 02138

Designed to characterize the problem-solving and learning strategies of students in middle childhood.

1466   Test Taking Strategies

Franklyn Peterson, Author

Contemporary Books, Inc.
180 N. Michigan   312-782-9181
Chicago, IL 60601   800-691-1918
                                FAX 312-782-3987

Part of the Study Aids Series, this book contains easy to understand tips on successful test taking.

$ 6.95

1467   The Think Aloud Series: Increasing Social and Cognitive Skills

Edmark Corporation
P.O. Box 3218   206-746-3900
Redmond, WA 98073   800-362-2890

Develops problem-solving capabilities in children.

$ 49.95

Writing

1468   Itl

AGS
7201 Woodland Road   612-786-4343
Circle Pines, MN 55014   800-328-2560

This writing program is an integrated total language approach, with developmentally appropriate lessons and activities.

$ 125.00

1469   Learning Grammar Through Writing

Sandra Bell, Author

Educators Publishing Service, Inc.
75 Moulton Street   800-225-5750
Cambridge, MA 02138

This manual contains grammar and composition rules explained and reference-numbered.

1470   Learning to Use Manuscript Handwriting and Cursive Handwriting

Beth Slingerland, Author

Educators Publishing Service, Inc.
75 Moulton Street   800-225-5750
Cambridge, MA 02138

This multisensory handwriting program is divided into two parts, manuscript and cursive, which can be used either consecutively or independently.

1471   Type It

Joan Duffy, Author

Educators Publishing Service, Inc.
75 Moulton Street   800-225-5750
Cambridge, MA 02138

A linguistically oriented beginning touch-systemed typing manual.

1472   The Writing Center/Children's Writing and Publishing Center

Edmark Corporation
P.O. Box 3218   206-746-3900
Redmond, WA 98073   800-362-2890

Produces student sory books and teaching materials in your classroom.

$ 89.95

1473 ABLEDATA - National Rehabilitation Information Center

Newington Children's Hospital
181 East Cedar Street   203-667-5405
Newington, CT 06111   800-344-5405

Maintains a computerized database of commercially available products for learning disabilities and other types of disabilities.

1474 Access Unlimited

3535 Briarpark Drive, Ste. 102   713-781-7441
Houston, TX 77042   800-848-0311
    FAX 713-781-3550

Polly Buenger, Tech. Consultant

Assists educators, health care providers and parents in discovering how personal computers can help children and adults with disabilities compensate for some of the barriers imposed by their conditions.

1475 ACTT (Activating Children Through Technology)

Western Illinois University
27 Horrabin Hall   309-298-1634
Macomb, IL 61455   FAX 309-298-2305

Joyce Johnson, Co-Ordinator

Goal is to integrate assistive technology into early childhood services for children from birth to 8 years old with disabilities to help them gain control over their environment, develop autonomy, communicate, develop problem-solving skills and participate in an inclusive environment.

1476 Adaptive Technology Laboratory

Southern Connecticut State University
501 Crescent Street   203-397-4791
New Haven, CT 06515

Helps individuals with visual, orthopedic and learning disabilities to gain computer access through the use of the latest technology.

1477 American Foundation for Technology Assistance

Route 14, Box 230   704-438-9697
Morganton, NC

Maintains a database of providers of adaptive and assistive technology for individuals with disabilities, and sources of financial aid for procuring "essential and special needs" products.

1478 Apple Computer, Inc.

Worldwide Disability Solutions Group
20525 Mariani Ave., Mail Stop 36SE   408-974-7910
Cupertino, CA 95014

Dr. Alan Brightman, Manager

Offers a wide variety of materials, in print, electronic and video form, that describe how personal computers can constructively influence the experience of being learning disabled.

1479 ARTIC Technologies

55 Park Street, Suite 2   313-588-7370
Troy, MI 48083

Manufacturers of speed boards for the blind and visually impaired.

1480 Artificial Language Laboratory

Michigan State University
405 Computer Center   517-353-5399
East Lansing, MI 48824

A multidisciplinary teaching and research center involved in basic and applied research concerning the computer processing of formal linguistic structures.

1481 Assistive Technology Information Network

InfoTech - Iowa Program for Assistive Technology
The University Of Iowa   800-331-3027
Iowa City, IA 52242

Provides free, up-to-date product information on adaptive equipment for people with disabilities.

1482 Association for Educational Communications and Technology

1126 16th Street NW   202-466-4780
Washington, DC 20036

1483 ATA Computer Resource Center

Pathfinder Services of North Dakota, Inc.
1600 Second Avenue SW   701-852-9426
Minot, ND 58701   800-245-5840

Diana Spencer, Program Support
Kathryn Erickson, Executive Director

Offers the opportunity for children, parents and teachers to learn more about personal computers and gain hands-on experience with a variety of special programs. Specialized software, adaptive devices and resources are on site for exploring. The Center has a video learning library, a book sending library and a software lending library.

1484 AT&T Accessible Communication Product Center

5 Woodhollow Road   800-233-1222
Parsippany, NJ 07054

Selss AT & T equipment for customers who have difficulty using their phones because of hearing, speech, vision of motion impairments.

1485 AT&T National Needs Center

2001 Route 46, Ste. 310   800-233-1222
Parsipanny, NJ 07054

Offers specially trained customer representatives who can recommend appropriate solutions to many communications needs.

1486 Birmingham Alliance for Technology Access Center

Birmingham Independent Living Center
206 13th Street South   205-251-2223
Brimingham, AL 35233

1487 Blue Grass Technology Center for People with Disabilities

169 North Limestone   606-255-9951
Lexington, KY 40507   FAX 606-255-0059

Beth McKinney, Director

A resource center serving Eastern Kentucky where a variety of assistive devices and equipment can be previewed. Equipment loans, family support groups and referral services are also available.

1488 BRS Information Technologies

A Division of Mazwell Online, Inc,
800 Westpark Drive   703-442-0900
McLean, VA 22102   800-955-0906

A complete library of 150 data bases covering virtually every major discipline. Data bases include current and historical information from journal articles, books, dissertations and government reports.

1489 Carolina Computer Access Center

Metro School
700 East Second Street   704-342-3004
Charlotte, NC 28202

Beth McKinney, Director

Demonstration, referral, workshop training, and information on assistive technology.

1490 CAST

39 Cross Street   508-531-8555
Peabody, MA 01960   FAX 508-531-0192

A non-profit organization whose mission is to expand educational opportunities for all children through innovative uses of computer technology. CAST provides direct services to individuals, offers consultation and training organizations, conducts research and develops software and implementation models for education.

1491 The Center for Enabling Technology

9 Whippany Road   201-428-1455
Whippany, NJ 07981

1492 Center for Information Resources and Handi-Soft Foundation

4212 Chestnut Street   215-898-8108
Philadelphia, PA 19104   FAX 215-222-4111

John Connolly, Jr., CEO

A computer learning center for people with disabilities. Helps the person with a disability obtain a job in computer related fields.

1493 Closing the Gap

P.O. Box 68   612-248-3294
Henderson, MN 56044   FAX 612-248-3810

Evaluates hardware and software for handicapped users, including the learning disabled.

1494 CMECSU Technology Project for Learners with Low Incidence Disabilities

3335 West St. Germaine Street   612-255-4913
St. Cloud, MN 56301

Dixie Waller Anderson

A regional educational organization that works within a nine county region. Maintains a demonstration center with about 500 public domain software programs. Offers specialized equipment for loan to students.

1495 Compuplay

711 East Colfax   219-233-4366
South Bend, IN 46617

1496 Computer Access Center

2425 16th Street, Rm. 23   310-450-8827
Santa Monica, CA 90405

Donna Dutton, Director

Computer resource center serving primarily as a place where people with all types fo disabilities can preview equipment, workshops, seminars, afterschool clubs for children and individual consultation are provided.

1497 Computer Accommodation Lab

Woodrow Wilson Rehab Center
Box W-28   703-332-7228
Fishersville, VA 22939

1498 Computer Center for Citizens with Disabilities

401 Twelfth Avenue, Ste. 114   801-321-5770
Salt Lake City, UT 84103

Craig Boogaard, Director

The fundamental goal is to improve the lives of children and adults with disabilities by introducing them and their families to the many ways in which microcomputers technology can enhance their jobs, careers and education.

1499 Computer CITE

215 East New Hampshire Street   407-898-2483
Orlando, FL 32804

1500 The Computer Club

Box 278   914-723-6563
Scarsdale, NY 10583

A technology resource center for individuals with special needs. The mission of the organization is to assist disabled individuals, their families, teachers and other support personnel in obtaining access to new technologies that will improve the quality of life for individuals with special needs.

1501 Computer Use in Social Services Network

University of Texas At Arlington
UTA Box 19129   817-273-3964
Arlington, TX 76019

1502 DCCG: Technology Resources for People with Disabilities

2547 Eighth Street, 12-A   510-841-3224
Berkeley, CA 94710   FAX 510-841-7956

Lisa Wahl, Executive Director

Resource and demonstration center that provides access to technology for people with disabilities. Seminar series, equipment loans, and toy lending provided. A newsletter "Real Times" is free with membership.

1503 Dialog Information Services, Inc.

3460 Hillview Avenue   800-3-DIALOG
Palo Alto, CA 94304

Offers access to over 390 data bases containing information on various aspects of disabling conditions and services to disabled individuals.

1504 DIRECT LINK for the Disabled, Inc.

P.O. Box 1036   805-688-1603
Solvang, CA 93464

Linda Harry, Executive Director

Provides technical assistance for making job accommodations and worksite adaptations for individuals with disabilities. Maintains database providing information on financial assistance, attendant care services, adaptive equipment, transportation, job training, job placement services and vocational rehabilitation.

1505 Disabled Children's Computer Group

2547 8th Street, 12-A   510-841-3224
Berkeley, CA 94710

Lisa Lahl, Director

A resource center for parents, professionals, developers and individuals with disabilities, filled with computers, software, adapted toys and adaptive technology.

1506 Disabled Citizens Computer Center

Fourth And York Streets   502-561-9637
Louisville, KY 40203

1507 Eastern Tennessee Special Technology Access Center

5719 Kingston Pike   615-584-4465
Knoxville, TN 37919

Louis Symington, Director

Resource and information center for individuals with disabilities, their families and professionals who work with them. Workshops, consultations, tutoring, information and product reviews available.

1508 Foundation for Technology Access

1307 Solano Avenue   415-528-0747
Albany, CA 94706

Provides information, consultation and technical assistance on assistive technology for people with disabilities, including computer hardware and software technology, and adaptive and assistive equipment.

1509 High Tech Center for the Disabled California Community Colleges

Foothill-DeAnza Community College
21050 McClellan Road   408-996-4636
Cupertino, CA 95014

1510 IBM Corporation Rehabilitation Training Programs

IBM, Federal Systems Division
4111 Northside Pkwy.   404-238-2805
Atlanta, GA 30327

1511 Learning Independence Through Computers, Inc.

28 East Ostend Street, Ste. 140   410-659-5462
Baltimore, MD 21230

1512 Learning Systems Technologies

48 Tioga Way, P.O. Box 15   617-639-0114
Marblehead, MA 01945

Offers clients total customization of software, employs the latest technology in writing programs and provides consultants to work with schools in the implementation of hardware and software.

1513 Micro Abilities

98 Main Street, Ste. 232   415-435-2966
Tiburon, CA 94920

1514 Moonlight

P.O. Box 164   203-537-0217
Colchester, CT 06415

A business that interfaces with schools, institutions, other businesses and parents to provide adaptations on microcomputers for people with special needs.

1515 National Information Center for Educational Media

P.O. Box 40130   800-421-8721
Albuquerque, NM 87196

Maintains a database with information on types of instructional materials (audio recordings, talking books, filmstrips) for special education.

1516 National Technology Center

American Federation for the Blind
15 West 16th Street   212-620-2080
New York, NY 10011   800-232-5463
    FAX 212-620-2137

Elliot Schreier, Director
Mark Uslan, Mgr. Of Tech Service

Demonstrates and evaluates equipment and publishes evaluations in the "Journal of Visual Impairment & Blindness".

1517 New Breakthroughs

P.O. Box 25228   503-741-5070
Euegene, OR 97042   FAX 503-896-0123

Carol Lee Berger

Facilitated communication and information in all areas of assistive, alternative communication. Technological education materials, workshops and training in new special education advancements are available.

1518 Northern Illinois Center for Adaptive Technology

3615 Louisiana Road   815-229-2163
Rockford, IL 61108

A nonprofit computer and adaptive devices resource center operated by parents, consumers, volunteers and professionals dedicated to providing information, seminars and individual needs technology. It is the goal of the center to help people with disabilities reach their full potential by providing them with information on the latest technology and by matching adaptive devices to their disabilities allowing them to more effectively interface with their environment.

1519 On-Board Computer Solutions

103 East Third Street   302-645-9159
Lewes, DE 19958

1520 Project AIMS CoPlanner

Department of Education of Exceptional Children
College Of Education   306-966-5262
Saskatoon, SK, Canada, S7 N 0W0 FAX 306-966-8719

Designed for Macintosh computers using System 7 operating software.

1521 Project TECH

Massachusetts Easter Seal Society
484 Main Street, 6th Floor   508-757-2756
Worcester, MA 01608

1522 Special Awareness Computer Center

Rehabilitation Center
2975 North Sycamore Drive   805-582-1881
Simi Valley, CA 93065

Suzanne Feit, Director

Non-profit resource center helping people with disabilities to learn how technology can lead them to more independent lives. Offers workshops, training and community presentations.

1523 Special Education Preview Center

Ruth Eason School
648 Old Mill Road   301-987-9505
Millersville, MD 21108

1524 Special Technology Center

590 Castro Street   415-961-6789
Mountain View, CA 94041

Lisa Cohn, Executive Director

A non-profit computer access center for children and adults with disabilities. The consumer can learn about current computer technology in a supportive environment with a professional staff. STC is part of a network of 45 Alliance for Technology Access centers across the United States. The Center offers consultations and classess that introduce people to the latest hardware and software for persons with disabilities.

1525 SpeciaLink

36 West Fifth Street   606-491-2464
Covington, KY 41011   FAX 606-491-2495

Elaine Hackett, Technical Director

Operates and enabling technology resource center for persons with disabilities. It provides access to law and high-tech devices which can help children and adults with disabilities reach their potential and maximize their independence. SpecialLink is a member of the Alliance for Technology Access, a coalition of centers operating across the nation.

1526   Synthesis

27 Hillsdale Road   617-395-3440
Medford, MA 02155

Provides tutoring/training on the use of computer for children or adults with disabilities and can assist in implementing the recommendations from an evaluation. Synthesis also provides inservice training and technical support to schools and other institutions.

1527   Tech-Able

1040 Irwin Bridge Road   404-922-6768
Conyers, GA 30207

Computer technology center offering hands-on computers and software. Fabrication of special-order assistive items, resources, referrals and adaptive toy leanding is offered.

1528   Technical Aids and Assistance for the Disabled Center

1950 West Roosevelt   312-421-3373
Chicago, IL 60608   FAX 312-421-3464

A resource center for disabled clients who visit and work with the staff in various areas, such as education, employment, daily living skills.

1529   Technology Access Center of Middle Tennessee

2222 Metro Center Blvd., Ste. 126   615-248-6733
Nashville, TN 37228   800-368-4651
                             FAX 615-259-2536

Serves the community as a resource center and carries out specific projects related to assistive technology.

1530   Technology Assistance for Special Consumers

P.O. Box 443   205-532-5996
Huntsville, AL 35804

1531   Technology for Language and Learning

P.O. Box 327
East Rockaway, NY 11518

An organization dedicated to advancing the use of computers and technology with children and adults with special language and learning needs.

1532   Technology Resources for People with Disabilities

One Plymouth Meeting Mall   215-8250-929
Plymouth Meeting, PA 19462

1533   Technology Resources for Special People

1710 West Schilling Road   913-827-9383
Salina, KS 67401

Shiela Nelson-Stout, Director

Provides technological assistance and training for children and adults with all disabilities.

1534   Technology Utilization Program

National Aeronautics and Space Administration
500 Independence Avenue SW   202-755-2420
Washington, DC 20546

Adapts aerospace technology to the development of equipment for the disabled, sick and elderly persons.

1535   Tidewater Center for Technology Access

Special Education Annex
273 North Witchdick Avenue   804-473-5136
Virginia Beach, VA 23462

1536   TRACE R&D Center

1500 Highland Avenue   608-262-6966
Madison, WI 53705   FAX 608-262-8848

Gregg Vanderheiden, Director

Provides information on access to computers for people with disabilities. Publishes TRACE ResourceBook, listing available products on the market.

1537   Washington Apple Pi

7910 Woodmont Avenue, Ste. 190   301-654-8060
Bethesda, MD 20814

Lorin Evans, Director

Largest user group on the east coast. Assists people with special needs to select, install and use computers with adaptive firmware.

1538   West Tennessee Special Technology Resource Center

P.O. Box 3683   901-424-9089
Jackson, TN 38303   800-464-5619

1539   WVU Augmentative Communication Center

805 Allen Hall   304-293-4242
Morgantown, WV 26506

1540   YES Family Learning and Computer Centers

435 North Elizabeth Street   419-222-0373
Lima, OH 45801

Dianne Wright, Owner
Kandy Takas, Ed. Computer Spec.

Sells hardware and software and accessories for the IBM, APPLE II and MAC computers. The organization is comprised of certified teachers who can assist the disabled in choosing the best software.

Assistive Devices

1541 Adaptive Technology Training

Jackson Hole High School
1855 High School Road   307-638-2610
Jackson, WY

Courses offered in computer and technology training.

1542 Arkenstone Head Scanner

Arkenstone, Inc.
1185 Bordeaux Drive, Ste. D   408-752-2200
Sunnyvale, CA 94089

Enables Arkenstone users to have a portable Arkenstone reader when combined with a portable talking computer and TrueScan recognition card.

$ 895.00

1543 Arkenstone Reader

Arkenstone, Inc.
1185 Bordeaux Drive, Ste. D   408-752-2200
Sunnyvale, CA 94089

An optical character recognition system for the learning disabled and visually impaired.

$ 4295.00

1544 Audapter Speech System

Personal Data Systems, Inc.
P.O. Box 1008   408-866-1126
Campbell, CA 95009

A speech output system for converting alpha numeric text to speech.

$ 895.00

1545 BASS Switches

Don Johnston Developmental Equipment, Inc.
1000 N. Rand Road   708-526-2682
Wauconda, IL 60084

A low profile switch for the learning disabled and physically disabled.

1546 Chroma CCD

TeleSensory
455 N. Bernardo Avenue   415-960-0920
Mountain View, CA 94039   800-227-8418
                                 FAX 415-969-9064

Adds sharp, realistic color to TeleSensory's family of video magnifiers. Provides low vision people with magnifiction up to 60 times and is invluable for reading maps, textbooks, catalogs, instructions and forms in color.

1547 Compu-Lenz

AbleTech Connection
P.O. Box 898   614-899-9989
Westerville, OH 43081

A powerful freznel lens which will more than double the size of computer screen characters without distortion of light refraction.

$ 199.95

1548 Computer Magnification Systems

TSI-Jack Stollman
194-B Kinderkamack Road   201-391-8171
Park Ridge, NJ 07656

Allows a person with low vision to magnify computer screens and print documents while easily navigating around a screen and manipulating text or graphics.

1549 Concept Keyboard

Hach Associates
P.O. Box 10849   919-744-7280
Winston On Salem, NC 27108

Alternative input device to the standard keyboard.

$ 495.00

1550 Consultants for Communication Technology

508 Bellevue Terrace   412-761-6062
Pittsburgh, PA 15202   FAX 412-761-7336

Kathleen Miller, PhD, Speech Pathologist

Manufactures and distributes the Handy Speech Communication Aide, a state of the art augmentative communication device for persons with speech impairments. In addition we have software products for environmental control, word processing and phone management. All products can be used with only one muscle movement or from the full keyboard. Telephone number interface allows two way communications over the telephone for the hearing impaired without the use of a TTY.

1551 DAC

Adaptive Communication Systems, Inc.
1400 Lee Drive   412-264-2288
Coraopolis, PA 15108

A digital augmentative communicator. A portable communication device with human capabilities that can be programmed with up to 72 minutes of human voice.

1552 Desktop PC Family

GW Micro
310 Racquet Drive   219-483-3625
Fort Wayne, IN 46825

Desktop PC computer system for the learning disabled.

$ 2495.00

1553 DOS Helper

Aristo Computers, Inc.
6700 SW 105th Ave., Ste. 307   503-626-6333
Beaverton, OR 97005

An on-line help system for MS DOS that can eliminate the need for manual referrals.

$ 35.00

1554 DoubleTalk PC

RC Systems, Inc.
121 W. Winesap Road   206-672-6909
Bothell, WA 98012

Contains four speech synthesizers on a half-length card.

$ 279.00

1555 Echo II

Street Electronics Corporation
6420 Via Real   805-684-4593
Carpintera, CA 93013

A speech output system for the learning disabled and speech impaired.

$ 116.95

1556 Echo II Synthesizer with Western Center Modifications

Western Center for Microcomputers in Special Ed.
1259 El Camino Real, Ste. 275   415-326-6997
Menlo Park, CA 94025

A speech synthesizer providing external volume control and pitch control.

$ 269.00

1557 Echo II with Textalker and Textalker-GS

American Printing House for the Blind
P.O. Box 6085   502-895-2405
Louisville, KY 40206

A complete speech synthesis system that gives a voice to Apple IIe and IIGS computers.

$ 144.13

1558 Echo LC

Street Electronics Corporation
6420 Via Real   805-684-4593
Carpintera, CA 93013

A new external speech output device for the Macintosh LC.

$ 116.95

1559 Echo MC

Street Electronics Corporation
6420 Via Real   805-684-4593
Carpintera, CA 93013

A plug-in speech synthesizer card for IBM PS/2 micro-channel architecture computers.

$ 179.00

1560 Echo PC II

Street Electronics Corporation
6420 Via Real   805-684-4593
Carpintera, CA 93013

A synthesizer card for PC's and compatibles.

$ 99.95

1561 Enlarged Alpha/Numeric Keytop Labels

Hooleon Corporation
P.O. Box 230   602-634-7515
Cornville, AZ 86325

Adhesive keytop labels increased to 38 point.

1562 Execusheet

Hearsay, Inc.
307-76 Street   718-836-0990
Brooklyn, NY 11209

Advanced voice recognition system for IBM PCs and compatibles.

$ 499.95

1563 EZ Keys/Key Wiz

Words, Inc.
P.O. Box 1229   800-869-8521
Lancaster, CA 93584

An assistance program that provides keyboard control, dual word prediction, abbreviation-expansion and speech output while running standard software.

$ 695.00

1564 Governor

TASH
70 Gibson Dr., Unit 12   416-475-2212
Markham, ON, Canada, L3 R 4C2

A speed control card to slow down computer games for Apple IIe and II computers.

$ 250.00

1565 HandiCODE

Synergy-Adaptive Innovations
66 Hale Road   508-668-7424
East Walpole, MA 02032   FAX 508-668-4134

Software providing Morse Code access to the computer for writing and/or speaking.

1566 HandiKEY

Synergy-Adaptive Innovations
66 Hale Road   508-668-7424
East Walpole, MA 02032   FAX 508-668-4134

Software providing non-keyboard access to computers for writing and/or speaking.

1567 HandiWORD

Synergy-Adaptive Innovations
66 Hale Road   508-668-7424
East Walpole, MA 02032   FAX 508-668-4134

Provides word prediction and abbreviation expansion to increase the speed at which you can "type" words and sentences, as well as offer assistance for limited spelling skills.

1568   Handy Speech Telephone Interface

Consultants for Communication Technology
508 Bellevue Terrace   412-761-6062
Pittsburgh, PA 15202

This option allows a message to be directly transmitted from the "Handy Speech" speech synthesizer through the telephone.

1569   Hearsay VIP

Hearsay, Inc.
307-76 Street   718-836-0990
Brooklyn, NY 11209

A speech input/output device that includes all the screen reader and review functions of the most popular VIP programs.

$ 599.95

1570   Hearsay 1000

Hearsay, Inc.
307-76 Street   718-836-0990
Brooklyn, NY 11209

A plug-in card for IBM PCs or Commodore with built-in controlling software.

$ 199.95

1571   Home Row Indicators

Hooleon Corporation
P.O. Box 230   602-634-7515
Cornville, AZ 86325

A plastic adhesive label with a raised bump in the center allowing the user to designate home row keys, or any other key, for quick recognition.

$ 4.95

1572   InLARGE

Berkeley Systems, Inc.
2095 Rose Street   510-540-5535
Berkeley, CA 94709

Magnifies everything, including graphics and the cursor by 2 to 16 times and follows typing and mouse movements.

$ 95.00

1573   IntelliKeys

Learning Disabilities Association of America
4156 Library Road   412-341-1515
Pittsburgh, PA 15234

The award-winning Intellikeys keyboard is an easy-to-use computer keyboard with a changing face.

$ 395.00

1574   Key Largo

Don Johnston Developmental Equipment, Inc.
P.O. Box 639, 1000 N. Rand Road   708-526-2682
Wauconda, IL 60084   800-999-4660

A new expanded membrane keyboard with a totally new look, design and size.

$ 320.00

1575   Keyboard Overlays for Apple and Laser

MarbleSoft
12301 Central Ave. NE   612-755-1402
Baline, MN 55434

Keyboard overlay made of molded flexible plastic strips that cover rows of keys on the computer keyboard while still allowing the keys to be pressed.

$ 50.00

1576   Keynote Gold

Humanware, Inc.
6245 King Road   916-652-7253
Loomis, CA 95650

A speech synthesizer for the learning disabled.

$ 1545.00

1577   Koala Pad Plus

Koala Acquistions, Inc.
16055 Caputo Drive, Unit H   408-776-8181
Morgan Hill, CA 95037

A touch sensitive graphics tablet that is designed to allow the user to construct graphic images on the monitor screen, save a disk and print the images.

$ 139.95

1578   LightningScan 400

Thunderware, Inc.
21 Orinda Way   415-254-6581
Orinda, CA 94563

A hand-held scanner with external termination, push button SCSI addressing and a detachable SCSI cable.

$ 495.00

1579   Little-Jack Headphones

Access Unlimited
3535 Briarpark Dr., #102   713-781-7441
Houston, TX 77042

A set of stereo headphones with an adaptor for school use.

$ 29.95

1580   Loc Dots

Arts Computer Products, Inc.
121 Beach Street, Ste. 400   800-343-0095
Boston, MA 02111

Adhesive-backed, raised dots that can be applied to any keys on any keyboard.

$ 3.00

1581 MAGIC

Synergy-Adaptive Innovations
66 Hale Road   508-668-7424
East Walpole, MA 02032   FAX 508-668-4134

Software that enlarges the size of any text or graphics on your screen.

1582 Make It Series Pack

Don Johnston Developmental Equipment, Inc.
P.O. Box 639, 1000 N. Rand Rd.   708-526-2682
Wauconda, IL 60084   800-999-4660
                                   FAX 708-526-4177

All of the games in the "Make It" programs are designed for motor training. Ass the complete "Make It" series to your library.

$ 150.00

1583 MatchBox Keyboard Covers

Don Johnston Developmental Equipment, Inc.
P.O. Box 639, 1000 N. Rand Road   708-526-2682
Wauconda, IL 60084   800-999-4660

Snap these covers over your computer keyboard and insert your own pictures.

$ 99.00

1584 Micro IntroVoice

Voice Connection
17835 Skypark Circle, Ste. C   714-261-2366
Irvine, CA 92714

A complete voice input/output system which provides voice recognition of 1,000 words with accuracy of 98 percent and unlimited text-to-speech synthesis.

$ 1495.00

1585 Microtek Scanner and Omnitype OCR

Synergy-Adaptive Innovations
66 Hale Road   508-668-7424
East Walpole, MA 02032   FAX 508-668-4134

"optics" reading materials, such as books and articles, into a computer format. The software interprets the "copied" text so that a computer can identify it as words.

1586 Mini Keyboard

Don Johnston Developmental Equipment, Inc.
P.O. Box 639, 1000 N. Rand Road   708-526-2682
Wauconda, IL 60084   800-999-4660

For users with limited range of motion but good fine motor control.

$ 375.00

1587 Modified Joystick

Don Johnston Developmental Equipment, Inc.
1000 N. Rand Road   708-526-2682
Wauconda, IL 60084

Combines the cursor of a mouse with the speed and convenience of a joystick.

$ 85.00

1588 OutSPOKEN

Berkeley Systems, Inc.
2095 Rose Street   510-540-5535
Berkeley, CA 94709

Gives the blind and learning disabled persons access to mainstream Macintosh software via speech output.

$ 395.00

1589 Parallel Keyboard 101

Genovation, Inc.
17741 Mitchell N.   714-833-3355
Irvine, CA 92741

A full 101 key tactile feel keyboard that works with any laptop or portable computer.

$ 199.95

1590 Parallel Keypad II

Genovation, Inc.
17741 Mitchell N.   714-833-3355
Irvine, CA 92741

A numerical keypad that connects to the parallel printer port between the port and the printer cable.

$ 139.95

1591 PC Lens

Arts Computer Products, Inc.
1212 Beach Street, Ste. 400   800-343-0095
Boston, MA 02111

Enlarges and enhances the standard PC screen image.

$ 180.00

1592 PC Private Eye

Reflection Technology, Inc.
230 Second Avenue   617-890-5905
Waltham, MA 02154

An ultra-miniature virtual display which creates the full size image of a 12 inch monitor.

$ 795.00

1593 Personal Communicating Device

ABOVO
96 Rhinebeck Avenue   413-594-5279
Springfield, MA 01129   FAX 413-594-5809

A portable, handheld electronic device designed for "single finger" communication by people who wish to communicate through typing.

1594 Phonic Ear Auditory Trainers

Phonic Ear, Inc.
3880 Cypress Drive   707-769-1110
Petaluma, CA 94954   FAX 707-769-9624

A line of learning disabled communication equipment.

1595   Picture Switch Kit

ComputAbility Corporation
40000 Grand River, #109   313-477-6720
Novi, MI 48375

Allows up to eight switches to be connected to the computer for direct selection input.

$ 99.95

1596   PowerPad

Dunamis, Inc.
3620 Highway 317   404-932-0485
Suwanee, GA 30174

A touch-sensitive alternative input device which allows users with special needs to use the computer without the limitations associated with keyboards.

$ 199.95

1597   PowerPad Overlays

MarbleSoft
12301 Central Ave. NE   612-755-1402
Baline, MN 55434

$ 30.00

1598   PowerPad Starter Kit (Apple)

Dunamis, Inc.
3620 Highway 317   404-932-0485
Suwanee, GA 30174

Allows the user to define the active areas of the Power Pad with this speech synthesizer.

$ 249.95

1599   PowerPad Starter Kit (IBM)

Dunamis, Inc.
3620 Highway 317   404-932-0485
Suwanee, GA 30174

A game port input unit for the IBM computer.

$ 279.95

1600   PowerPort

Dunamis, Inc.
3620 Highway 317   404-932-0485
Suwanee, GA 30174

A PowerPad cable and an external game port all in one.

$ 39.95

1601   Prose Synthesizer

Henter-Joyce, Inc.
816-75 Ave. N.   813-576-5658
St. Petersburg, FL 33716

A speech output device for the learning disabled.

1602   QuicKeys

CE Software, Inc.
P.O. Box 66580   515-224-1995
West Des Moines, IA 50625

Assigns Macintosh functions to one keystroke.

$ 149.95

1603   RDS Speech and Learning Center System

Royal Data Systems
Rt. 14, Box 230   704-433-5909
Morganton, NC 28655

A peripheral platform upon which stock and custom learning applications can be designed and operated.

$ 999.00

1604   Response Optimizer

Icon Peripherals
2901 Independence Avenue South   612-933-7986
St. Louis Park, MN 55426

A single circuit board and control box that plugs into an Apple IIe.

$ 98.50

1605   SCAT

RC Systems, Inc.
121 W. Winesap Roadad   206-672-6909
Bothell, WA 98012

Designed to be used with a multi-function card that enables students to gain access to many programs through automatic keyboard and program oral feedback.

$ 19.95

1606   Scooter Zero Force Game Ports

OHM Electronics
746 Vermont Street   800-323-2727
Palatine, IL 60067

An extension cord bringing the 16-pin game connector from inside the Apple to the outside.

$ 24.50

1607   Slotbuster II

RC Systems, Inc.
121 W. Winesap Road   206-672-6909
Bothell, WA 98012

Multi-function card which can be configured with a speech synthesizer printers, modem ports and more.

$ 165.00

1608   Small Talk PC Family

GW Micro
310 Racquet Drive   219-483-3625
Fort Wayne, IN 46825

Offers various products from speech synthesizers to software packages compatible to IBM.

$ 1749.00

1609   Speaking Ace - 200

Tiger Communication Systems, Inc.
155 E. Broad Street   716-454-5134
Rochester, NY 14604

A keyboard designed as a spelling checker and word game player, that pronounces over 90,000 words.

$ 134.95

1610 Speaqualizer

American Printing House for the Blind
P.O. Box 6085   502-895-2405
Louisville, KY 40206

A speech output device designed for IBM and compatible PC's.

$ 825.60

1611 Speech Synthesizers

Synergy-Adaptive Innovations
66 Hale Road   508-668-7424
East Walpole, MA 02032   FAX 508-668-4134

Offers a line of speech activated computer cards for IBM full-size and IBM lap-top computers.

1612 Speech Thing

Covox, Inc.
675 Conger Street   503-342-1271
Eugene, OR 97402

A speech output device.

1613 Study Buddy

Access Unlimited
3535 Briarpark Dr., #102   713-781-7441
Houston, TX 77042

Allows user to enter words followed by a definition or concept description.

$ 50.00

1614 Switch PowerPad Boc

Lekotek of Georgia, Inc.
1955 Cliff Valley Way, Ste. 102   404-633-3430
Atlanta, GA 30329

A modification of the PowerPad that allows access to PowerPad software through switch activation.

$ 150.00

1615 Synergy PC Computer System

Synergy-Adaptive Innovations
66 Hale Road   508-668-7424
East Walpole, MA 02032   FAX 508-668-4134

A portable computer system with available options such as optical disk drives, environmental control systems, access to standard software and hardware and more.

$ 5875.00

1616 Syntha-Voice Model I

Syntha-Voice Computers, Inc.
125 Gailmont Drive   800-263-4540
Hamilton, ON, Canada, L8 K 4B8

A half-length, 8 bit accessory card for the IBM family of personal computers.

$ 695.00

1617 Syntha-Voice Model S

Syntha-Voice Computers, Inc.
125 Gailmont Drive   800-263-4540
Hamilton, ON, Canada, L8 K 4B8

A hand-held, rechargeable battery version of the Syntha-Voice Model I synthesizer.

$ 895.00

1618 Text2000

American Printing House for the Blind
1839 Frankfort Avenue   502-895-2405
Louisville, KY 40206   800-223-1839
                                    FAX 502-895-1509

Allows students to read textbooks in a number of ways, including synthetic speech, large type sized to the screen and refreshable braille.

1619 Toshiba Portable Keyguard

Kennedy Institute Design Systems
2925 East Biddle Street   800-685-5437
Baltimore, MD 21213

A removable keyguard designed to allow users top take advantage of Toshiba's portables.

$ 110.00

1620 TouchWindow

Edmark Corporation
P.O. Box 3903   206-746-3900
Bellevue, WA 98009

A transparent, pressure senstive screen pad that can be used as a touch screen, a graphics tablet and an input pad.

$ 275.00

1621 Type N' Talk

Vysion, Inc.
30777 Schoolcraft Road   313-542-3300
Livonia, MI 48150

A text-to-speech synthesizer converts computer data into unlimited speech.

$ 299.00

1622 Ufonic Voice System

Jostens Learning Systems, Inc.
7878 N. 16th St., Ste. 100   800-852-1925
Phoenix, AZ 85020

Consists of the interface card, amplifier/speaker with dual headphones and volume control, and provides human sounding speech in instructional software developed for this use.

$ 245.00

1623 Unicorn Expanded Keyboard Model II

Unicorn Engineering, Inc.
5221 Central Ave. #205   415-528-0670
Richmond, CA 94804

Alternative keyboard for the learning disabled.

$ 315.00

1624 Unicorn Keyboard Model 510

Unicorn Engineering, Inc.
5221 Central Ave. #205   415-528-0670
Richmond, CA 94804

Alternative keyboard.

$ 250.00

1625 The Unicorn Smart Keyboard

Unicorn Engineering, Inc.
5221 Central Ave. #205   415-528-0670
Richmond, CA 94804   800-899-6687

Works with any standard keyboard and offers seven overlays and a cable for one type of computer.

1626 Unitone Speaker

Access Unlimited
3535 Briarpark Dr., #102   713-781-7441
Houston, TX 77042

Offers external volume control on the rear of the speaker and an earphone connection on the side of the speaker.

$ 25.00

1627 Up and Running

Unicorn Engineering, Inc.
5221 Central Ave. #205   415-528-0670
Richmond, CA 94804

A custom overlay kit for the Unicorn Keyboard that provides instant access to a wide range of software including over 60 popular educational programs.

$ 69.95

1628 Verbal Operating Systems

Computer Conversations
6297 Worthington Road SW   614-924-2885
Alexandria, OH 43001

Interactive software that speaks both screen and keyboard output.

$ 350.00

1629 Verbette Mark I and II

Computer Conversations
6297 Worthington Road SW   614-924-2885
Alexandria, OH 43001

Speech output systems.

$ 329.95

1630 VersiColor CCTV System

TeleSensory
455 N. Bernardo Avenue   415-960-0920
Mountain View, CA 94039   800-227-8418
    FAX 415-969-9064

Brings clarity and comfort to reading and writing. Since many people with low vision find that specific color combinations enhance legibility, VersiColor offers 24 customized foreground and background color combinations to choose from.

1631 VISTA

TeleSensory
455 N. Bernardo Ave.   415-960-0920
Mountain View, CA 94039

An image enlarging system that magnifies the print and graphics on the screen from three to 16 times.

$ 2495.00

1632 Vocal-Eyes

GW Micro
310 Racquet Drive   219-483-3625
Fort Wayne, IN 46825   FAX 219-484-2510

A voice access system for IBM PC's and compatibles.

1633 Voice Navigator

Don Johnston Developmental Equipment, Inc.
P.O. Box 639, 1000 N. Rand Road   708-526-2682
Wauconda, IL 60084   800-999-4660

A voice recognition system.

1634 Voice Navigator II

Don Johnston Developmental Equipment, Inc.
P.O. Box 639, 1000 N. Rand Road   708-526-2682
Wauconda, IL 60084   800-999-4660
    FAX 708-526-4177

Voice recognition technology systems offering hands free word processing.

1635 Voice Navigator SW

Don Johnston Developmental Equipment, Inc.
P.O. Box 639, 1000 N. Rand Road   708-526-2682
Wauconda, IL 60084   800-999-4660
    FAX 708-526-4177

Eliminates extra hardware for Macs with built-in sound digitizers.

$ 399.00

1636 WiViK

Synergy-Adaptive Innovations
66 Hale Road   508-668-7424
East Walpole, MA 02032   FAX 508-668-4134

Software providing non-keyboard access to any software runnign under Microsoft Windows.

Books & Periodicals

1637 Apple Works Education

AACE
Box 2966   804-973-3987
Charlottesville, VA 22902

Gary Marks, Publisher
Covers educational uses of Appleworks software.

$ 25.00

1638 Assistive Technology Sourcebook

Alexandra Enders, Author
Special Needs Project
1482 East Valley Road, #A-121   805-565-1914
Santa Barbara, CA 93108   800-333-6867

Practical information on all aspects of assistive technology for individuals with functional and learning limitations.

$ 60.00

1639 Bibliography of Journal Articles on Microcomputers & Special Education

Special Education Resource Center
25 Industrial Park Road   203-632-1485
Middletown, CT 06457

Stephen Kramer, Compiler

This pamphlet offers information on a wide variety of professional journals in the fields of microcomputers and special education.

1640 Catalyst

Western Center for Microcomputers in Special Ed.
1259 El Camino Real, Ste. 275   415-326-6997
Menlo Park, CA 94025

Digest of news and information on the use of computers in special education.

1641 The Catalyst

Western Center for Microcomputers in Special Ed.
1259 El Camino Real, Ste. 275   415-326-6997
Menlo Park, CA 94025

A newsletter offering information on computer technology, books and resources for the learning disabled.

1642 Closing the Gap

P.O. Box 68   612-248-3294
Henderson, MN 56044

Jan Larzke, Subscription Manager

A magazine offering information on hardware and software for persons with disabilities.

$ 26.00

1643 Computer Access/Computer Learning

Ginny LaVine, Author
Special Needs Project
1482 East Valley Road, #A-121   805-565-1914
Santa Barbara, CA 93108   800-333-6867

A resource manual in adaptive technology.

$ 22.50

1644 Computer Assistance Model for Learning Disabled

Wyoming Division of Vocational Rehabilitation
University Station   307-766-6189
Laramie, WY 82071

A cooperative research model combining the office of Disabled Student Services of the University of Wyoming.

$ 9.25

1645 Computer Disability News

National Easter Seal Society
70 East Lake Street   312-726-6200
Chicago, IL 60601

Provides general information about computers and disability in education, the workplace and independent living.

$ 10.00

1646 Computers in Head Start Classrooms

Compiled By IBM, Author
Learning Disabilities Association of America
4156 Library Road   412-341-1515
Pittsburgh, PA 15234

$ 7.00

1647 Facilitated Communication Technology Guide

New Breakthroughs, Inc.
P.O. Box 25228   503-741-5070
Eugene, OR 97401

Offers a list of computer programs used successfully to teach math, reading and spelling.

$ 20.00

1648 Using Computers and Speech

Linda Burkhart, Author
Don Johnston Developmental Equipment, Inc.
P.O. Box 639, 1000 N. Rand Road   708-526-2682
Wauconda, IL 60084   800-999-4660

Ideas and strategies for interactive communication using speech synthesis which provides verbal feedback and voice control that is beneficial to children who are developing skills to attract attention.

$ 27.50

1649 The Works Curriculum Packs

MindPlay
Unit F92, P.O. Box 36491   602-322-6365
Tucson, AZ 85740   800-221-7911

Offers data disks with workbooks for practice on various subjects.

$ 69.00

Games

1650 Blazing Paddles

BAUDVILLE
5380 52nd Street SE   616-698-0888
Grand Rapids, MI 49508

A graphic design program that allows the user to print illustrations with ease.

$ 34.95

1651 Bozon's Quest

Edmark Corporation
P.O. Box 3218   206-746-3900
Redmond, WA 98073   800-362-2890

Explores cognitive challenges in a game format.

$ 65.00

1652 Creature Antics

Edmark Corporation
P.O. Box 3218   206-746-3900
Redmond, WA 98073   800-362-2890

Animated characters teach cause and effect, taking turns and the use of a single switch in the Laureate Learning Systems software.

$ 65.00

1653 Creature Capers

Edmark Corporation
P.O. Box 3218   206-746-3900
Redmond, WA 98073   800-362-2890

Offers the student fun while learning and reinforcing cause and effect concepts.

$ 65.00

1654 Creature Chorus

Edmark Corporation
P.O. Box 3218   206-746-3900
Redmond, WA 98073   800-362-2890

Engages students in practicing basic computer-using skills.

$ 85.00

1655 Creature Features

Edmark Corporation
P.O. Box 3218   206-746-3900
Redmond, WA 98073   800-362-2890

Provides the opportunity to learn through discovery.

$ 75.00

1656 God Bless America

Dunamis, Inc.
3620 Highway 317   404-932-0485
Suwanee, GA 30174   800-828-2443
                             FAX 404-932-0486

Game that can be played by pressing PowerPad buttons, which represent lines of song.

$ 24.95

1657 Micro Illustrator

Dunamis, Inc.
3620 Highway 317   404-932-0485
Suwanee, GA 30174

Allows students to create, revise, adapt and combine basic shapes.

$ 69.95

1658 Moose Caboose

Dunamis, Inc.
3620 Highway 317   404-932-0485
Suwanee, GA 30174

Simialr to pin the tail on the donkey.

$ 19.95

1659 Motor Training Games

Don Johnston Developmental Equipment, Inc.
1000 N. Rand Road0 N. Rand Rd.   708-526-2682
Wauconda, IL 60084   800-999-4660
                             FAX 708-526-4177

A collection of fourteen games which utilize single switch input.

$ 35.00

1660 Pitch Explorer

Electronic Courseware Systems, Inc.
1210 Lancaster Drive   217-359-7099
Champaign, IL 61821

Enables a computer to detect pitches produced by voice or instruments.

$ 295.00

1661 Ted Bear's Rain Day Games

Edmark Corporation
P.O. Box 3218   206-746-3900
Redmond, WA 98073   800-362-2890

Game offering the ability for students to concentrate and use strategy skills.

$ 29.95

Language Arts

1662 Academic Skill Builders in Language Arts

DLM Teaching Resources
One DLM Park   214-248-6300
Allen, TX 75002

Six programs providing drill and practice in vital language arts areas.

$ 46.00

1663 Ace Reporter

MindPlay
3130 N. Dodge Road   602-322-6365
Tucson, AZ 85716

Practice reading for main ideas and details by reading teletypes and conducting telephone interviews.

$ 49.99

1664　Action/Music Play

PEAL Software
P.O. Box 8188　　　　818-883-7849
Calabasas, CA 93172

A computer-enhanced language intervention activity for severly visually impaired children with developmental disabilities.

$ 150.00

1665　Adventures of Jimmy Jumper: Prepositions

Exceptional Children's Software
P.O. Box 487　　　　913-625-9281
Hays, KS 67601

A video storybook about a small rabbit named Jimmy. The story is read while Jimmy displays different preposi-tional concepts.

$ 29.95

1666　AFC: Literacy Setups

Don Johnston Developmental Equipment, Inc.
1000 N. Rand Road　　　　708-526-2682
Wauconda, IL 60084

More than 100 ready-to-use AFC setups for popular programs.

$ 99.00

1667　Alpha Series Alphabetizing Skills

Lexia Learning Systems, Inc.
P.O. Box 466　　　　617-259-8751
Lincoln, MA 01773　　　　800-435-3942

Offers ABC Race and Alpha Rocket: two programs for learning alphabetizing skills.

$ 50.00

1668　Alphabet Blocks

Bright Star Technology, Inc.
1450 114th Avenue SE, Ste. 200　　　　206-451-3697
Bellevue, WA 98004

A reading education product for children incorporating Hyper/Animation technology on the Macintosh.

$ 59.95

1669　Alphabetizing

Aquarius Instructional
P.O. Box 128　　　　813-595-7890
Indian Rocks Bch., FL 34635

Teaches language arts skills to early childhood students.

$ 45.00

1670　Analogies Tutorial

Software to Go - Galluadet University
800 Florida Avenue NE　　　　202-651-5705
Washington, DC 20002

1671　APH/SEI Talking Software

American Printing House for the Blind
P.O. Box 6085　　　　502-895-2405
Louisville, KY 40206

Talking programs that test students knowledge of subjects ranging from SAT preparation to the history of space flight.

$ 38.38

1672　AppleWorks Companion

RC Systems, Inc.
121 W. Winesap Road　　　　206-672-6909
Bothell, WA 98012

Offers keyboards and screen speech capabilities.

$ 49.95

1673　Arcademic Skill Builders in Language Arts: Spelling Wiz

Jerry Chaffin, Author
DLM Teaching Resources
One DLM Parkhany　　　　214-248-6300
Allen, TX 75002

A program using an arcade game format to assist students in mastering over 300 commonly misspelled words.

1674　Auditory Skills

Psychological Software Services, Inc.
6555 Carrolton Avenue　　　　317-257-9672
Indianapolis, IN 46220

Four computer programs designed to aid in the remediation of audiotry discrimination problems.

$ 50.00

1675　Author! Author!

MindPlay
Unit F92, P.O. Box 36491　　　　602-322-6365
Tucson, AZ 85740　　　　800-221-7911

The complete tool kit for writing plays.
　　"Let's hear applause! applause! for Author! Author!"

-Famliy Computing
$ 59.99

1676　Bake & Taste

MindPlay
Unit F92, P.O. Box 36491　　　　602-322-6365
Tucson, AZ 85740　　　　800-221-7911

With tasty recipes, delicious ingredients and guided in-structions, this program teaches users to follow directions, builds math skills in a "real-life" setting and encourages creative solutions to challenging problems.

$ 49.99

1677 Basic Concepts Package

Vocational and Rehabilitation Research Institute
3304 33rd St. NW 403-284-1121
Calgary, AB, Canada, T2 L 2A6

Program designed to develop, through a frill and practice format.

$ 50.00

1678 Basic Language Units: Grammar

Continental Press, Inc.
520 East Bainbridge 800-847-0656
Elizabethtown, PA 17022

Sentences disks include sentence types, subjects and predicates and phrases and clauses.

$ 120.00

1679 Basic Sentence Comprehension

Linda Huntress, Author

The Speech Bin
1965 Twenty-Fifth Avenue 407-770-0007
Vero Beach, FL 32960 FAX 407-770-0006

Jan J. Binney, Editor In Chief
Barbara Hector, Office Manager

Easy-to-operate software presents 650 stimulus tasks to treat a variety of morphological and syntactic difficulties.

$ 110.00

1680 Be a Writer

Sunburst Communications, Inc.
39 Washington Ave. 914-769-5030
Pleasantville, NY 10570

An initial response to word processing.

$ 59.00

1681 Beamer

Data Command, Inc.
P.O. Box 548 800-528-7390
Kankakee, IL 60901

Students learn to idntify prefixes, roots or suffixes.

$ 38.95

1682 BearJam

Dunamis, Inc.
3620 Highway 317 404-932-0485
Suwanee, GA 30174

Originally designed as a reading readiness program for small children.

$ 59.95

1683 Best Faces

Dunamis, Inc.
3620 Highway 317 404-932-0485
Suwanee, GA 30174

A series of games that revolve around the elements of the face.

$ 59.95

1684 Big Book Maker: Favorite Fairy Tales and Nursery Rhymes

Pelican Software, Inc.
768 Farmington Ave. 203-674-8221
Farmington, CT 06032

Write your own fairy tales or recreate traditional ones to encourage writing.

$ 49.95

1685 Big Book Maker: Feeling Good About Yourself

Pelican Software, Inc.
768 Farmington Ave. 203-674-8221
Farmington, CT 06032

A program designed to motivate self-expression through writing and illustrating books.

$ 49.95

1686 Big Book Maker: Letters, Numbers and Shapes

Pelican Software, Inc.
768 Farmington Ave. 203-674-8221
Farmington, CT 06032

Offers hundreds of graphics to teach basic skills.

$ 49.95

1687 Big Book Maker: Tall Tales and American Folk Heros

Pelican Software, Inc.
768 Farmington Ave. 203-674-8221
Farmington, CT 06032

This program uses art based on traditional tales to motivate creative writing skills.

$ 49.95

1688 Big/Little I

UCLA Intervention Program for Disabled Children
1000 Veteran Ave., #23-10 301-825-4821
Los Angeles, CA 90024

Program for one to four players in which a little bear scans big and little objects commonly seen by young children.

$ 35.00

1689 Blackout! a Capitalization Game

Software to Go - Galluadet University
800 Florida Avenue NE 202-651-5705
Washington, DC 20002

1690 Boppie's Great Word Chase

Stephen Schlapp, Author

DLM Teaching Resources
One DLM Parkhany   214-248-6300
Allen, TX 75002

A program that helps refine spelling and word recognition skills.

1691   Breakthrough to Language, Volume 1: Multisensory Curriculum

Barbara Schacker, Author

Crative Learning/Up-Grade Systems
Hilton Head, SC

A series of 8 diskettes to reinforce beginning reading and spelling programs for students.

1692   Breakthrough to Language, Volume 2

Creative Learning, Inc.
P.O. Box 829   916-292-3001
N. San Juan, CA 95960

A talking-making series for pre-readers offering the same multi-sensory learning techniques, program features and options.

$ 500.00

1693   Breakthrough to Writing

Creative Learning, Inc.
P.O. Box 829   916-292-3001
N. San Juan, CA 95960

This program allows users to trace large clear letters and pictures on the TouchWindow while hearing the human voice pronounce phonic sounds of leatters and words.

$ 125.00

1694   Bubblegum Machine

Heartsoft, Inc.
P.O. Box 691381   800-285-3475
Tulsa, OK 74169   800-285-3475

A vocabulary enrichment program that challenges students to rhyme, build words out of provided vocabulary or a user-created one.

$ 49.95

1695   Build-a-Scene

R.J. Cooper and Associates
24843 DelPrado, #283   714-240-1912
Dana Point, CA 92629

This software builds from a blank screen to a colorful scene with every switch hit.

$ 75.00

1696   Capitalization Machine

SouthWest Ed Psych Services, Inc.
2001 W. Silvergate Dr.   602-253-6528
Chandler, AZ 85224

Covers capitalization skills.

$ 49.95

1697   Capitalization Plus

Software to Go - Galluadet University
800 Florida Avenue NE   202-651-5705
Washington, DC 20002

1698   Cat N' Mouse

MindPlay
3130 North Dodge Blvd.   602-322-6365
Tucson, AZ 85716

Learn picture/word or word/word associations and relationships as you guide your mice through a series of mazes occupied by hungry cats.

$ 49.99

1699   Cause and Effect

Hartley Courseware, Inc.
P.O. Box 431   517-646-6458
Dimondale, MI 48821

A two disk program offering information and instructions, the student must decide which is cause or effect phrases.

$ 39.95

1700   Charlotte's Web

Sunburst Communications, Inc.
39 Washington Ave.   914-769-5030
Pleasantville, NY 10570

Students re-live this Newberry favorite as they participate with Charlotte the spider and Wilbur the pig.

$ 65.00

1701   Children's Carrousel

Nancy Delaney, Author

Dynacomp, Inc.
178 Phillips Road   716-671-6167
Webster, NY 14580

Nine games for children teaching shape discrimination and colors.

1702   Children's Writing & Publishing Center

The Learning Company
6493 Kaiser Drive   415-792-2101
Fremont, CA 94555

Features sophisticated word processing, picture selection and page design capabilities.

$ 89.95

1703   Children's Writing & Publishing Center, School Edition

Janet Joers, Author

The Learning Company
6493 Kaiser Drive   510-792-2101
Freemont, CA 94555

A program to develop written communication skills for students.

1704   Cloze Plus

Instructional/Communications Technology
10 Stepar Place   516-549-3000
Huntington Station, NY 11746

Uses structured cloze and vocabulary in context activities to help students see word relationships and to drive meaning from context clues.

$ 160.00

1705   Cloze Thinking

A/V Concepts Corporation
30 Montauk Blvd.   516-567-7227
Oakdale, NY 11769

Designed to aid in the development of reading comprehension skills through the use of a variety of modified cloze techniques.

$ 190.00

1706   Cloze Vocabulary and More

A/V Concepts Corporation
30 Montauk Blvd.   516-567-7227
Oakdale, NY 11769

Aids in the development of word-changing skills involving multiple meaning and word usage.

$ 190.00

1707   Clozemaster

Research Design Associates
10 Boulevard Ave.   516-754-5280
Greenlawn, NY 11740

Program allows the generation and authoring of Cloze reading passages.

$ 59.95

1708   Cognitive Disorders

The Speech Bin
1965 Twenty-Fifth Avenue   407-770-0007
Vero Beach, FL 32960   FAX 407-770-0006

Jan J. Binney, Editor In Chief
Barbara Hector, Office Manager

Offers fifteen different software programs comprising Parrot's great Cognitive Disorders series.

$ 99.50

1709   Cognitive Rehabilitation

Technology for Language and Learning
P.O. Box 327   516-625-4550
East Rockaway, NY 11518

A series of public domain programs that strengthen cognitive skills, memory, language and visual motor skills.

$ 20.00

1710   Communication Skills

ComputAbility Corporation
40000 Grand River, #109 109   313-477-6720
Novi, MI 48375   800-433-8872

High interest, low vocabulary program aids individuals in building effective communication skills.

1711   CommuniKeys

MECC
3490 Lexington Ave. N   612-481-3611
St. Paul, MN 55126

Students are reporters-in-training for an international agency.

$ 59.00

1712   Complete Spelling Program

SLED Software
P.O. Box 16322   612-926-5820
Minneapolis, MN 55416

Designed to meet the special needs of anyone with spelling deficits or specific language learning disabilities.

$ 230.00

1713   The Complete Spelling Program

SLED Software
P.O. Box 16322   612-926-5820
Minneapolis, MN 55416

A set of 4 diskettes providing a comprehensive, self-contained spelling program for students.

1714   Comprehension Connection

Milliken Publishing
P.O. Box 21579   314-991-4220
St. Louis, MO 63132

Designed to improve students' reading skills.

$ 150.00

1715   Comprehension Power

Instructional/Communications Technology
10 Stepar Place   516-549-3000
Huntington Station, NY 11746

Reading program consisting of 180 reading selections designed to improve comprehension and study skills.

$ 160.00

1716   Computer CUP

Amidon Publications
1966 Benson Avenue   612-690-2401
St. Paul, MN 56116

Covers the 50 concepts tested by the Boehm Test of Basic Concepts.

$ 39.95

1717   Computer Managed Language Treatment

Communication Skill Builders
P.O. Box 42050   602-323-7500
Tucson, AZ 42050

Contains individual sets of lessons for colors, numbers, prepositions and mean length of utterance.

$ 85.00

1718 Computer Managed Screening Test

Communication Skill Builders
P.O. Box 42050   602-323-7500
Tucson, AZ 42050

Presents 32 items for articulation, receptive language, voice and fluency.

$ 85.00

1719 Computerized Test of Pragmatic Skills

Communication Skill Builders
P.O. Box 42050   602-323-7500
Tucson, AZ 42050

This is a test scoring system to use with the Test of Pragmatic Skills.

$ 39.95

1720 Concentrate! on Words & Concepts

Laureate Learning Systems, Inc.
110 E. Spring St.   802-655-4755
Winooski, VT 05404

A series of educational games that reinforces the lessons of the Words & Concepts series while developing short term memory skills.

$ 95.00

1721 Consonant Capers

Hartley Courseware, Inc.
P.O. Box 431treet   517-646-6458
Dimondale, MI 48821

A 4-diskette set teaching initial conconant sounds. Used with a speech synthesizer, this program helps students hear initial consonants in meaningful contexts by participating in make-believe trips to a farm, jungle, circus and zoo.

1722 Consonants

Hartley Courseware, Inc.
P.O. Box 431   517-646-6458
Dimondale, MI 48821

This program uses a multimedia format to help the child discriminate between the different consonants.

$ 49.95

1723 Construct-a-Word I, II

DLM Teaching Resources
One DLM Park   214-248-6300
Allen, TX 75002

Students blend beginnings and endings to create words.

$ 99.00

1724 Contained Reading Series

A/V Concepts Corporation
30 Montauk Blvd.   516-567-7227
Oakdale, NY 11769

Designed to develop more fluent and efficient reading through a controlled left-to-right presentation.

$ 189.00

1725 Create PR/CCD Lessons

Hartley Courseware, Inc.
P.O. Box 431   517-646-6458
Dimondale, MI 48821

Authoring programs for writing tutorials, drills and tests with synchronized, natural voice.

$ 39.95

1726 Credit: the First Steps

MCE, a Division of Lawrence Productions
1800 S. 35th St.   616-665-7075
Galesburg, MI 49078

Students are helped to a fuller understanding of the complex issues in the use of credit.

$ 59.95

1727 Crossword Magic

MindPlay
1345 Diversey Pkwy.   312-525-1500
Chicago, IL 60614

User can create, arrange, edit and print crossword puzzles.

$ 59.95

1728 Crozzzwords

MindPlay
Unit F92, P.O. Box 36491   602-322-6365
Tucson, AZ 85740   800-221-7911

Work ready-to-play puzzles on various subjects or create your own puzzles.

"...excellent teaching tool for supplementing any subject."

-Software Reports
$ 44.99

1729 Crypto Cube

Software to Go - Galluadet University
800 Florida Avenue NE   202-651-5705
Washington, DC 20002

1730 Cue Write

Communication Skill Builders
P.O. Box 42050   602-323-7500
Tucson, AZ 42050

A word processing program to increase literacy skills by learning and practicing words they cannot spell spontaneously.

$ 49.00

1731 Decisions, Decisions

Tom Snyder Productions
90 Sherman Street   617-876-4433
Cambridge, MA 02140

Students engage in simulations which provoke thought and encourage informed decision-making.

$ 119.95

1732   Dinosaur Days Plus

Pelican Software, Inc.
768 Farmington Ave.   203-674-8221
Farmington, CT 06032

Choose from hundreds of dinosaur body parts to create a prehistoric scene.

$ 49.95

1733   Dinosaur Discovery Kit

First Byte
19840 Pioneer Ave.ue   800-523-2983
Torrance, CA 90503   800-523-2983

Offers children help with reading and pre-reading skills.

$ 49.95

1734   Disney Comic Strip Maker

Mary S. Balcer, Author

Disney Educational Software
238 Nanuet Mall   914-627-1304
Ny 10954

Designed for students to use existing comic strips in the program or create new ones using Disney graphics.

1735   Disney Design Studio

Mary S. Balcer, Author

Disney Educational Software
238 Nanuet Mall   914-627-1304
Thornwood, NY 10954

A program allowing one to create party decorations using existing Disney comic strips, encouraging creative writing and other language arts skills.

1736   Double-Up

Research Design Associates
10 Boulevard Ave.   516-754-5280
Greenlawn, NY 11740

Takes one or two sentences and puts words in alphabetical order.

$ 139.95

1737   EasyDraw

Focus Media
839 Stewart Avenue   516-794-8900
Garden City, NY 11530

A drawing and writing program that children can use with the PowerPad to create and draw pictures.

$ 129.00

1738   Echo Programmer's Toolkit

Street Electronics Corporation
6420 Via Real   805-684-4593
Carpintera, CA 93013

Includes a collection of tools for the BASIC or assembly language programmer for use with the Echo speech synthesizer.

$ 19.95

1739   Echo Sensible Speller

Access Unlimited
3535 Briarpark Dr., #102   713-781-7441
Houston, TX 77042

A talking spelling checker for text files created by most commonly used word processing programs.

$ 150.00

1740   Eco-Saurus

First Byte
19840 Pioneer Ave.   800-523-2983
Torrance, CA 90503

Introduces children to the concepts of ecology.

$ 49.95

1741   Edmark LessonMaker

Edmark Corporation
P.O. Box 3903   206-746-3900
Bellevue, WA 98009

Lets users make their own talking, interactive and multi-layered TouchWindow lessons.

$ 199.95

1742   Edmark Reading Program (Level 1)

Edmark Corporation
P.O. Box 3903   206-746-3900
Bellevue, WA 98009

A beginning reading and language development program that teaches 150 words plus endings.

$ 450.00

1743   Edmark Reading Program (Level 2)

Edmark Corporation
P.O. Box 3903   206-746-3900
Bellevue, WA 98009

A beginning reading and language program that teaches 200 new words and reinforces the 150 words taught in Level 1.

$ 450.00

1744   Eighth Through Tenth Grade Reading and Language Arts Competencies

Aquarius Instructional
P.O. Box 128   813-595-7890
Indiana Rocks Beach, FL 34635   800-338-2644
                             FAX 813-595-2685

Offers information on everyting from reading signs to indentifying words in daily living.

$ 250.00

1745 Electric Crayon

Merit Software
13635 Gamma Road   214-385-2353
Dallas, TX 75244

A tool to help preschool and primary aged children learn about and enjoy the computer.

$ 14.95

1746 Electronic Bilingual English Speaking Dictionaries

Franklin Learning Resources
122 Burrs Road   800-525-9673
Mt. Holly, NJ 08060

Offers complete translations, spelling corrections, complete conjugations, electronic grammar guides and a personal word list.

$ 179.00

1747 Elementary: Volume 11 - Phonet

Minnesota Educational Computing Consortium
6160 Summit Drive North   612-569-1500
St. Paul, MN 55430

Drill and practice in phonetic skills.

1748 Elephant Ears: English with Speech

Ballard & Tighe, Inc.
480 Atlas Street   800-321-4332
Brea, CA 92621

Features instruction and assessment of prepositions in a 3-part diskette.

$ 49.00

1749 Elmentary School Grade Builder 3 Pack

Britannica Software
345 Fourth Street   415-597-5555
San Francisco, CA 94107

Includes Math Maze, Spellicopter and Designasaurus.

$ 29.95

1750 Emerging Literacy

Technology for Language and Learning
P.O. Box 327   516-625-4550
East Rockaway, NY 11518

A five volume set of stories.

$ 25.00

1751 English

Aquarius Instructional
P.O. Box 128   813-595-7890
Indiana Rocks Beach, FL 34635   800-338-2644
                                    FAX 813-595-2685

Offers informational disks on teaching nouns, pronouns, adjectives and more.

$ 350.00

1752 English Master

Franklin Learning Resources
122 Burrs Road   800-525-9673
Mt. Holly, NJ 08060

English/Korean dictionary that is designed for the student studying English as a second language.

$ 349.95

1753 English 4-Pack

Dataflo Computer Services, Inc.
HC 32, Box 1   603-448-2223
Enfield, NH 03748

These programs provide various spelling problems through word scrambling, letter substitution and spelling bee simulation.

$ 39.95

1754 Essay Ease

MindPlay
Unit F92, P.O. Box 36491   602-322-6365
Tucson, AZ 85740   800-221-7911

The complete tool kit for writing essays.
"New dimension for essay writing."
                                    -Curriculum Product News
$ 59.00

1755 Exploratory Play

Learning Disabilities Association of America
4156 Library Road   412-341-1515
Pittsburgh, PA 15234

Language play activities using real toys.

$ 150.00

1756 Explore-A-Classics Series

Wm. K. Bradford Publishing Company
310 School Street   508-263-6996
Acton, MA 01720

Presents stduents with familiar stories and involve them in reading, thinking and storytelling.

$ 75.00

1757 Explore-a-Folktale Series

Wm. K. Bradford Publishing Company
310 School Street   508-263-6996
Acton, MA 01720

A series of animated writing adventures based on three folk tales.

$ 75.00

1758 Explore-a-Science Series

Wm. K. Bradford Publishing Company
310 School Street   508-263-6996
Acton, MA 01720

Introduces students to science topics through discovery and inquiry and creative imagination.

$ 75.00

1759 Explore-a-Story Series

Wm. K. Bradford Publishing Company
310 School Street   **508-263-6996**
Acton, MA 01720

Engages children in storytelling as well as writing.

$ 75.00

1760 Fact Or Opinion

Hartley Courseware, Inc.
P.O. Box 431   **517-646-6458**
Dimondale, MI 48821

In each lesson a statement is given to the student: the student must then decide if it is fact or opinion.

$ 39.95

1761 Fay's Word Rally

Didatech Software, Ltd.
3812 William St.   **604-299-4435**
Burnaby, BC, Canada, V5 C 3H9

Designed to teach reading comprehension and vocabulary skills within a car rally format that encourages children to move from simple words to more challenging reading.

$ 52.00

1762 Fifth Through Seventh Grade Reading and Language Arts Competencies

Aquarius Instructional
P.O. Box 128   **813-595-7890**
Indiana Rocks Beach, FL 34635   **800-338-2644**
    FAX 813-595-2685

Offers information on everything from using maps and graphs to indetifying punctuation marks used to punctuate sentences.

$ 675.00

1763 Five Little Ducks

KidTECH
21274 Oak Knoll   **805-822-1663**
Tehachapi, CA 93561

This classic children's song uses rhyme, rhythm and repetition to build vocabulary and beginning number concepts.

$ 30.00

1764 Flash Spelling/Scrambled Letters/Word Editor

Stefan Irving, Author
Educational Activities
P.O. Box 392venue   **516-223-4666**
Freeport, Long Island, NY 11520

Drill and practice on 99 spelling words and 48 scrambled words, along witha word editor for filing and storing additional spelling words.

1765 Freddy's Puzzling Adventure

DLM Teaching Resources
One DLM Park   **214-248-6300**
Allen, TX 75002

Helps students acquire problem solving and logical thinking skills with three activities.

$ 32.95

1766 Functional Vocabulary

The Speech Bin
1965 Twenty-Fifth Avenue   **407-770-0007**
Vero Beach, FL 32960   **FAX 407-770-0006**

Jan J. Binney, Editor In Chief
Barbara Hector, Office Manager

This program focuses on real life pictures and their functional aspects.

$ 129.50

1767 Game Power for Phonics

Spin-A-Test Publishing Company
3177 Hogarth Drive   **916-369-2032**
Sacramento, CA 95827

Program caters to the aural and verbal rehabilitation needs of the reading, speech, hearing impaired or to the ESl student.

$ 35.00

1768 Game Power for Phonics, Plus

Spin-A-Test Publishing Co.
3177 Hogarth Drive
Sacramento, CA 95827

This program caters to aural and verbal rehabilitation needs of the reading, speech, hearing impaired or to the ESL student.

$ 75.00

1769 Game Show

Advanced Ideas, Inc.
680 Hawthorne Drive   **415-425-5086**
Tiburon, CA 94920

A popular quiz show format with animated graphics, flashing lights and cheering teammates to build vocabularies, and develop essential thinking skills.

$ 39.95

1770 Getting Ready to Read and Add

Sunburst Communications, Inc.
39 Washington Ave.   **914-769-5030**
Pleasantville, NY 10570

Sound, color and animation help the primary student identify and match shapes, upper and lowercase letters and numbers in a series of programs.

$ 65.00

1771 Goldilocks and the Three Bears

Diane Fantaskey, Author

Microcomputer Applications
Selingrove, PA   717-225-4291

Using this famous children's story to teach grammatic closure by having students fill in missing verbs, nouns, pronouns and more on each page.

1772   Grammar Examiner

Software to Go - Galluadet University
800 Florida Avenue NE   202-651-5705
Washington, DC 20002

1773   Grammar Gremlins

Santa Barbara Softworks
Torrance, CA

A suplemental grammar program containing rules of grammar and over 600 practice sentences focusing on abbreviations, agreement, capitalization, contractions, parts of speech, plurals, possessives, punctuation and sentence structure.

1774   Grammar Study Center

Teach Yourself By Computer Software
3400 Monroe Avenue   716-381-5450
Rochester, NY 14618

Drill and text learning game program which comes with question and answer files for working with a variety of English grammar topics.

$ 39.95

1775   Grammar Toy Shop

Software to Go - Galluadet University
800 Florida Avenue NE   202-651-5705
Washington, DC 20002

1776   Great Beginnings

Teacher Support Software
1035 NW 57th Street   904-332-6404
Gainesville, FL 32605

From a broad selection of topics and descriptive words, students may create their own stories and illustrate them with colorful graphics.

$ 99.95

1777   Guided Reading

Instructional/Communications Technology
10 Stepar Place   516-549-3000
Huntington Station, NY 11746

Contains 264 reading selections that provide for development of silent reading proficiency and fluency.

$ 160.00

1778   High Frequency Vocabulary

Technology for Language and Learning
P.O. Box 327   516-625-4550
East Rockaway, NY 11518

Each volume of the series has 10 stories that teach specific vocabulary.

$ 35.00

1779   Hint and Hunt I, II

DLM Teaching Resources
One DLM Park   214-248-6300
Allen, TX 75002

With these programs, students can actually see and hear how changing vowels can make a new word.

$ 99.00

1780   Homonyms

Software to Go - Galluadet University
800 Florida Avenue NE   202-651-5705
Washington, DC 20002

1781   Hyperlingua

Research Design Associates
10 Boulevard Ave.   516-754-5280
Greenlawn, NY 11740

Allows teachers to create on-screen printing language drills.

$ 69.95

1782   HyperStudio Stacks

Technology for Language and Learning
P.O. Box 327   516-625-4550
East Rockaway, NY 11518

Offers various volumes in language arts, social studies and reading.

$ 10.00

1783   I Can Write!

Sunburst Communications, Inc.
39 Washington Ave.   914-769-5030
Pleasantville, NY 10570

This book-building program provides a complete writing curriculum for the second grade.

$ 59.00

1784   I Love You in the Sky, Butterfly

Hartley Courseware, Inc.
P.O. Box 431treet   517-646-6458
Dimondale, MI 48821   800-247-1380
                                   FAX 517-646-8451

Telaina Eriksen

This 50-disk set is language based and presented in seperate units that focus on a theme, such as emotions or animals.

$ 297.00

1785   IDEA Cat I, II and III

Ballard & Tighe, Inc.
480 Atlas Street   800-321-4332
Brea, CA 92621

Computer assisted teaching of English language lessons reinforces skills of Level I, II, and III of the IDEA Oral Program.

$ 142.00

1786 If You're Happy and You Know It

UCLA Intervention Program for Disabled Children
1000 Veteran Ave., #23-10   301-825-4821
Los Angeles, CA 90024

A nursery school song with five verses depicted in picture form.

$ 35.00

1787 In/Out Concepts Package

Vocational and Rehabilitation Research Institute
3304 33rd St. NW   403-284-1121
Calgary, AB, Canada, T2 L 2A6

Tutorials and drill and practice programs are used to teach the basic concepts of in and out featuring the integration of speech, graphics and text.

$ 55.00

1788 Jumblezzz

MindPlay
Unit F92, P.O. Box 36491   602-322-6365
Tucson, AZ 85740   800-221-7911

A puzzle game for playing and creating scrambled word puzzles.

> *"...marvelous way to practice your spelling words - or words revolving around a particular theme."*
> -InCider

$ 44.99

1789 Katie's Farm

MCE, a Division of Lawrence Productions
1800 S. 35th St.   616-665-7075
Galesburg, MI 49078

Designed to encorage exploration and language development.

$ 39.95

1790 Key Words

Humanities Software
P.O. Box 950   800-245-6737
Hood River, OR 97031

Uses words, phrases and rhymes to teach keyboarding.

$ 49.00

1791 Keyboarder

Sunset Software
9277 E. Corrine Dr.   602-451-0753
Scottsdale, AZ 85260

This drill program helps orientate users to the position of letter and number keys on the computer keyboard.

$ 29.95

1792 Keys to Success: Computer Keyboard Skills for Blind Children

Life Science Associates
1 Fenimore Road   516-472-2111
Bayport, NY 11705

A talking program that provides keyboard tutorial, keyboard practice, timed keyboard practice and a timed game for two players.

$ 35.00

1793 Kid Pix

Broderbund Software
500 Redwood Blvd.   415-382-4400
Novato, CA 94948

A painting program that combines special effect art tools, sounds and magic screen transformations.

$ 59.95

1794 Kinder Keyboard

EBSCO Curriculum Materials
Box 1943   205-991-6600
Birmingham, AL 35201

Assists young children in learning the correct fingering position as well as encourging accuracy and speed.

$ 39.95

1795 Knock-Knock Jokes

Dunamis, Inc.
3620 Highway 317   404-932-0485
Suwanee, GA 30174

Offers a speech variation between the voice of the joker and the joke hearer.

$ 19.95

1796 KRS: Keyboarding/Reading/ Spelling

Instructional/Communications Technology
10 Stepar Place   516-549-3000
Huntington Station, NY 11746

Provides intensive keyboarding practice to develop computer literacy.

$ 180.00

1797 Language Activities Courseware

Houghton Mifflin School Division
One Memorial Drive   617-725-5022
Cambridge, MA 02178

Activities for grammar and study skills which use full color graphics and sound.

$ 126.00

1798 Language Activities of Daily Living Series

Laureate Learning Systems, Inc.
110 E. Spring St.treet
Winooski, VT 05404

802-655-4755
800-562-6801
FAX 802-655-4757

Mary Sweig Wilson, President
Bernard Fox, Vice President

Functional language stimulation programs specifically designed for communicatively low-functioning clients.

$ 175.00

1799 Language Arts: the Rules and the Partner

Morning Star Software
P.O. Box 5364
Madison, WI 53705

608-233-5056

A two-disk program to assist teachers in the instruction of spelling.

$ 75.00

1800 Language Carnival I

David Ertmer, Author

DLM Teaching Resources
One DLM Parkhany
Allen, TX 75002

214-248-6300

A diskette of four games using humor to help students develop language and thinking skills.

1801 Language Carnival II

David Ertmer, Author

DLM Teaching Resources
One DLM Parkhany
Allen, TX 75002

214-248-6300

A diskette of four games using humor to help students develop language and thinking skills.

1802 Language Experience Recorder Plus

Teacher Support Software
1035 NW 57th Street
Gainesville, FL 32605

904-332-6404

This program provides students with the opportunity to read, write and hear their own experience stories.

$ 99.95

1803 Language Experience Series

Teacher Support Services
1035 NW 57th Street
Gainesville, FL 32605

904-332-6404

A talking multi-sized print and graphics combination which invites children's involvement through reading, writing and listening.

$ 479.95

1804 Language L.A.B.

James Stanfield and Company
P.O. Box 41058
Santa Barbara, CA 93140

805-897-1188
800-421-6534

A set of programs designed to help teach receptive and expressive language skills in many curriculum areas.

$ 199.00

1805 Language Master - LM-3000

Franklin Learning Resources
122 Burrs Road
Mt. Holly, NJ 08060

800-525-9673

A language master without speech defining over 83,000 words, spelling correction capability, pick/edit feature, vocabulary enrichment activities and advanced word list.

$ 85.00

1806 Learn About Insects

Wings for Learning, Inc.
1600 Green Hills Rd.
Scotts Valley, CA 95067

408-438-5502

Students may learn identification, growth, homes and movement of insects.

$ 65.00

1807 Learn About Plants

Wings for Learning, Inc.
1600 Green Hills Rd.
Scotts Valley, CA 95067

408-438-5502

In this interactive eight-part program, students begin by planning an on-screen garden and watching their seeds grow.

$ 65.00

1808 Learn to Match

Technology for Language and Learning
P.O. Box 327
East Rockaway, NY 11518

516-625-4550

Ten volume set of picture-matching disks.

$ 50.00

1809 Lessons in Syntax

Pro-Ed
8700 Shoal Creek Road
Austin, TX 78758

512-451-3246

Developing skills with Eight English structures.

$ 360.00

1810 Letter Recognition

Hartley Courseware, Inc.
P.O. Box 431
Dimondale, MI 48821

517-646-6458

A first porgram for a child who is just beginning to learn the location of the letters and numbers on the keyboard.

$ 29.95

1811 Letter Recognition SkillBuilder Series

Edmark Corporation
P.O. Box 3218   206-746-3900
Redmond, WA 98073   800-362-2890

Teaches letter names, associates letters with the sounds they make at the beginning of a word and more.

1812 Letter SkillBuilders Series

Edmark Corporation
P.O. Box 3903   206-746-3900
Bellevue, WA 98009

All units include exploration and question and answer exercises.

$ 129.95

1813 Letters and First Words

C & C Software
5713 Kentfor Circle   316-682-2699
Wichita, KS 67208

Helps children learn to identify letters and recognize their associated sounds.

$ 60.00

1814 Letters and Words

Methods & Solutions, Inc.
Northbrook, IL

A reading readiness game program focusing on alphabetical order, matching upper and lower case letters and reinforcement of sight vocabulary and picture word matching.

1815 Lexia I - Consonants & Short Vowels

Lexia Learning Systems, Inc.
P.O. Box 466   617-259-8751
Lincoln, MA 01773   800-435-3942

Five various programs teaching language arts skills.

$ 250.00

1816 Lexia II - Short Vowels and Long Vowels/ Silent E & Consonant Diagraphs

Lexia Learning Systems, Inc.
P.O. Box 466   617-259-8751
Lincoln, MA 01773   800-435-3942

Five programs offering language arts skills.

$ 250.00

1817 Lexia III - Short Vowel and Long Vowel/ Silent E Review & More

Lexia Learning Systems, Inc.
P.O. Box 466   617-259-8751
Lincoln, MA 01773   800-435-3942

Five programs offering language arts skills.

$ 250.00

1818 Literacy Mapper

Teacher Support Software
1035 NW 57th Street   904-332-6404
Gainesville, FL 32605

Allows students to work with action, settings and characters from various stories.

$ 159.95

1819 Livewriter

Research Design Associates
10 Boulevard Ave.   516-754-5280
Greenlawn, NY 11740

Gives the ability to log on to a student's work for live interactive editing by means of a message window.

$ 349.00

1820 Logo Writer for Special Needs

Logo Computer Systems, Inc.
3300 Cole Vertu, Ste. 201
Montreal, PQ, Canada, H4 R 2B7   514-331-7090

Students can write or draw by simply using a single key of a paddle/switch.

$ 199.00

1821 LogoWriter

Logo Computer Systems, Inc.
3300 Cole Vertu, Ste. 201
Montreal, PQ, Canada, H4 R 2B7   514-331-7090

Enables students to write and illustrate stories, create animation and design crossword puzzles.

$ 199.00

1822 Magic Slate/Magic Slate II

Sunburst Communications, Inc.
39 Washington Ave.   914-769-5030
Pleasantville, NY 10570

A word processing package with a three-level format that grows as students skills increase.

$ 129.00

1823 Magic Spells

Leslie Grimm, Author

The Learning Company
6493 Kaiser Drive   510-792-2101
Freemont, CA 94555

A program for teaching essential spelling skills to students. Children unscramble words or reproduce flashed words. Contains over 500 words as well as an editor for creating/ printing customized spelling word lists.

1824 Make It Go

KidTECH
21274 Oak Knoll   805-822-1663
Tehachapi, CA 93561

A collection of seven original cause and effect programs.
$ 20.00

1825 Make-a-Flash

Teacher Support Software
1035 NW 57th Street   904-332-6404
Gainesville, FL 32605

A flash card program displaying and printing large, easy-to-read letters or numbers.
$ 59.95

1826 Marblesoft Crosswords, Special Access and the Edmark Reading Program Disk

Edmark Corporation
P.O. Box 3218   206-746-3900
Redmond, WA 98073   800-362-2890

Makes conventional crossword puzzles, spelling tests and jumbled word puzzles to supplement your students' work in the classroom and the Edmark Reading Program.
$ 100.00

1827 MarbleSoft Crosswords 3.5

MarbleSoft
12301 Central Ave. NE   612-755-1402
Baline, MN 55434

Puzzles may be used in any of four crossword and word search formats.
$ 100.00

1828 Mark Up

Research Design Associates
10 Boulevard Ave.   516-754-5280
Greenlawn, NY 11740

A sentence reconstruction program which presents learners with four options for the study of grammar.
$ 49.95

1829 MasterType

MindPlay
1345 Diversey Pkwy.   312-525-1500
Chicago, IL 60614

A game for learning to type and improve keyboard skills.
$ 39.95

1830 Max's Library: Beginning to Read and Understand

Society for Visual Education, Inc.
1345 Diversey Parkway   312-525-1500
Chicago, IL 60614

Readers join Max the mouse in his library for hands-on introduction to basic comprehension skills.
$ 144.00

1831 Maze-o

Software to Go - Galluadet University
800 Florida Avenue NE   202-651-5705
Washington, DC 20002

1832 McGee

MCE, a Division of Lawrence Productions
1800 S. 35th St.   616-665-7075
Galesburg, MI 49078

An independent exploration with no words.
$ 39.95

1833 Me Too!

Pugliese, Davey and Associates
5 Bessom Street, Ste. 175 617-639-1930
Marblehead, MA 01945

A software utility, that helps non-technical Adaptive Filmware Card users access the story writing series Explore-a-Story.
$ 95.00

1834 Mickey's Magic Reader

Sunburst Communications, Inc.
39 Washington Ave.   914-769-5030
Pleasantville, NY 10570

This beginning reading program is designed to entice students into building comprehension skills.
$ 65.00

1835 Microcomputer Language Assessment and Development System

Laureate Learning Systems, Inc.
110 E. Spring St.treet   802-655-4755
Winooski, VT 05404   800-562-6801
                          FAX 802-655-4757

Mary Sweig Wilson, President
Bernard Fox, Vice President

A series of seven diskettes designed to teach over 45 fundamental syntatic rules. Students are presented two or three pictures, depending on the grammatical construction being trained with optional speech and/or text and asked to select the picture which represents the correct construction.
$ 775.00

1836 Micro-LABS: Microcomputer Language Assessment and Development System

Mary S. Wilson, Author

Laureate Learning Systems, Inc.
110 E. Spring Street   802-655-4755
Winooski, VT 05404

A program to train auditory and/or reading comprehension of the fundamental syntatic rules of grammar to handicapped children.

1837   Monsters and Make Believe

Pelican Software, Inc.
768 Farmington Ave.   203-674-8221
Farmington, CT 06032

Make a monster choosing from hundreds of cute and
creepy body parts.

$ 49.95

1838   Monsters & Make-Believe

Queue, Inc.
338 Commerce Drive   203-335-0906
Fairfield, CT 06430   800-232-2224
                             FAX 203-336-2481

Children of all ages will love making monsters from over
100 body parts. Use the text processor to write about
characters and even adds speech bubbles and type to the
dialogue.

$ 49.95

1839   Monty Plays Scrabble

Software to Go - Galluadet University
800 Florida Avenue NE   202-651-5705
Washington, DC 20002

1840   Moptown Hotel

The Learning Company
6493 Kaiser Drive   510-792-2101
Freemont, CA 94555

Seven games for testing hypotheses, using analogies and
developing thinking skills.

1841   Mount Murdoch

Kidsview Software
P.O. Box 98   603-927-4428
Warner, NH 03278

Contains the master disk and the Mount Murdoch adventure.

$ 49.95

1842   Muppet Word Book

Sunburst Communications, Inc.
39 Washington Ave.   914-769-5030
Pleasantville, NY 10570

Introduces children to letters, words, reading and writing.

$ 65.00

1843   Mutanoid Word Challenge

Learning Disabilities Association of America
4156 Library Road   412-341-1515
Pittsburgh, PA 15234

A combination Scrabble and crossword game designed to
reinforce spelling and word meaning.

$ 49.95

1844   My Action Book

KidTECH
21274 Oak Knoll   805-822-1663
Tehachapi, CA 93561

Designed to teach familiar action vocabulary through live
voice, song and animation.

$ 30.00

1845   Natural Language Processing Program

Educational Audiology Programs, Inc.
1077 South Gilpin Street   908-745-9675
Milltown, NJ 08850

Uses stories and short lessons to train semantic and
syntactic rules with natural language context.

$ 159.00

1846   Number SkillBuilder Series

Edmark Corporation
P.O. Box 3218   206-746-3900
Redmond, WA 98073   800-362-2890

Recognizes numerals 1 to 20, associates a set of objects
with its corresponding numerals and develops simple
addition skills.

1847   The O'Brien Vocabulary Placement Test

Janet O'Brien, Author
Educational Activities
P.O. Box 392venue   516-223-4666
Freeport, Long Island, NY 11520

An independent reading level test in which students must
select the appropriate antonym from four choices.

1848   Old MacDonald II

UCLA Intervention Program for Disabled Children
1000 Veterans Avenue, Rm. 23-10   301-825-4821
Los Angeles, CA 90024

An early preposition program involving in, on top, behind, infront of, next to and between depicted in a farm
scence.

$ 35.00

1849   Once Upon a Time Volume II

Compu-Teach
14924 21st Srive SE   800-448-3224
Mill Creek, WA 98012

Children can design and publish their own illustrated
books.

$ 49.95

1850   Padded Food

UCLA Intervention Program for Disabled Children
1000 Veteran Ave., #23-10   301-825-4821
Los Angeles, CA 90024

Program overlay depicts familiar foods and can be used as
a matching or categorizing program.

$ 35.00

1851 Paint with Words

MECC
3490 Lexington Ave. N   612-481-3611
St. Paul, MN 55126

Enables early readers to create color pictures while learning new words.

$ 49.00

1852 Parachute Parts of Speech

SouthWest Ed Psych Services, Inc.
2001 W. Silvergate Dr.   602-253-6528
Chandler, AZ 85224

Transforms identification of parts of speech into a challenging game.

$ 34.99

1853 Parrot Easy Language Sample Analysis

The Speech Bin
1965 Twenty-Fifth Avenue   407-770-0007
Vero Beach, FL 32960   FAX 407-770-0006

Jan J. Binney, Editor In Chief
Barbara Hector, Office Manager

Gives easy entry, editing and storgae of up to 20 different language samples at a time.

$ 159.50

1854 PEACEbook

Tiger Communication Systems, Inc.
155 E. Broad Street   716-454-5134
Rochester, NY 14604

An expandable, comprehensive picture communication book which may be adapted to include an electronic keyboard.

$ 89.95

1855 Peek and Speak

ACTT Activating Children Through Technology
West Illinois University   309-298-1014
Macomb, IL 61455

A beginning communication board for reading skills.

$ 49.95

1856 Peptalk: Take-a-Turn

Communication Skill Builders
P.O. Box 42050   602-323-7500
Tucson, AZ 42050

A second program of three modules that parallel the stages of speech therapy.

$ 99.00

1857 Peptalk: Tell Pep

Communication Skill Builders
P.O. Box 42050   602-323-7500
Tucson, AZ 42050

The third program of three modules that parallel the stages of speech therapy.

$ 99.00

1858 Phonics Prime Time: Initial Consonants

MECC
3490 Lexington Ave. N   612-481-3611
St. Paul, MN 55126

When students correctly match consonants with illustrations that represent words starting with those consonants.

$ 59.00

1859 Phonics Round-Up

Access Unlimited
3535 Briarpark Dr., #102   713-781-7441
Houston, TX 77042

Helps students learn phonics by sorting words according to their vowel and consonant sounds.

$ 39.95

1860 Picture Chompers

MECC
3490 Lexington Ave. N   612-481-3611
St. Paul, MN 55126

Young children move teeth around the gameboard to "chomp" various objects that have the same color, size, design or use.

$ 59.00

1861 Planning Individualized Speech and Language Intervention Programs

Communication Skill Builders
P.O. Box 42050   602-323-7500
Tucson, AZ 42050

Write, store, revise, retrieve and print individualized programs for infants, children and adolescents.

$ 99.00

1862 Podd

Sunburst Communications, Inc.
39 Washington Ave.   914-769-5030
Pleasantville, NY 10570

Helps students become familiar with action verbs to find words that make Podd perform.

$ 65.00

1863 Poetry Express

Carole Kidder, Author
MindPlay
1345 Diversey Pkwy.   312-525-1500
Chicago, IL 60614

This program allows students to write any of eight styles of poetry as well as edit, store and print what they write.

1864 Poetry Palette

MindPlay
Unit F92, P.O. Box 36491   602-322-6365
Tucson, AZ 85740   800-221-7911

The complete tool kit for writing poetry.

"Students will be encouraged to develop their own poems through this easy-to-use program."
-Florida Center Instructional Computing

$ 59.00

1865 Power Talker

UCLA Intervention Program for Disabled Children
1000 Veteran Ave., #23-10   301-825-4821
Los Angeles, CA 90024

An entry level communication board.

$ 45.00

1866 PowerPad Communication Series

Dunamis, Inc.
3620 Highway 317   404-932-0485
Suwanee, GA 30174   800-828-2443
    FAX 404-932-0486

Four programs that combine graphics and speech and deal with specific themes. Needs, Wants, Free Time and Emotions and Feelings.

1867 Preschool Activities for Learning

Werner Meserth, Author
Educational Activities
P.O. Box 392venue   516-223-4666
Freeport, Long Island, NY 11520

A program focusing on the following math and readiness skills: number and alphabet letter discrimination, number sets and phonetic analysis of 100 simple words.

1868 Primer 83

Dynacomp, Inc.
178 Phillips Road   716-671-6167
Webster, NY 14580

Learning package containing several program modules designed for individuals with dyslexia.

$ 99.95

1869 Proofreader

Elaine David, Author
E. David Associates
Storrs, CT

An English language exercise program concerned with critical reading, grammar, punctuation and spelling errors.

1870 Punctuation Rules

Richard Hefter, Author

Optimum Resource, Inc.
10 Station Place   203-542-5553
Norfolk, CT 06058

A diskette and user's guide to teach students the correct placement of periods, commas, apostrophes, colons and hyphens.

1871 Quick Talk

Educational Activities
P.O. Box 392   516-223-4666
Freeport, Long Island, NY 11520

A model voice introduces illustrated vocabulary words followed by sentences and questions using the words.

$ 299.00

1872 Railroad Snoop

Sunburst Communications, Inc.
39 Washington Ave.   914-769-5030
Pleasantville, NY 10570

A comprehensive short story writing project for students 5th through 7th grades.

$ 59.00

1873 RAPID

Krell Software
Flowerfield Bldg. #7   516-584-7900
St. James, NY 11788

Pinpoints specific reading problem areas, analyzes results, profiles student strengths and weaknesses.

$ 199.95

1874 Read Along Series By Bertamax

Access Unlimited
3535 Briarpark Dr., #102   713-781-7441
Houston, TX 77042

Beginning readers need only to type their names, press the space bar and enter key to operate this program.

$ 24.95

1875 Reader Rabbit and the Fabulous Word Factory

Leslie Grimm, Author
The Learning Company
6493 Kaiser Drive   510-792-2101
Freemont, CA 94555

A program of 4 games for children teaching them to recognize over 200 three-letter words through phonetic analysis, spelling and the matching of words to pictures.

1876 Reading Around Words

Instructional/Communications Technology
10 Stepar Place   516-549-3000
Huntington Station, NY 11746

Develops vocabulary through structured, context-analysis strategies.

$ 160.00

1877 Relational Concepts Package

Vocational and Rehabilitation Research Institute
3304 33rd St. NW   403-284-1121
Calgary, AB, Canada, T2 L 2A6

A training program for learning basic quantitative and seriation concepts.

$ 55.00

1878 Representational Play

Learning Disabilities Association of America
4156 Library Road   412-341-1515
Pittsburgh, PA 15234

Language activity using real toys.

$ 150.00

1879 Rhubarb

Research Design Associates
10 Boulevard Ave.   516-754-5280
Greenlawn, NY 11740

Allows teachers to quickly and easily enter reading passages tailored to needs of their classes.

$ 69.95

1880 Rhymes & Riddles

Mark Cross, Author

Spinnaker Software Corporation
201 Broadway   508-494-1200
Cambridge, MA 01239

Three games in which children guess letters to spell out famous nursery rhymes and sayings, and answer clever riddles.

1881 Robot Writer

Pelican Software, Inc.
768 Farmington Ave.   203-674-8221
Farmington, CT 06032

Assemble a family of robots by choosing parts from the Body Shop.

$ 49.95

1882 School Speller 40, 80 Column

Sunburst Communications, Inc.
39 Washington Ave.   914-769-5030
Pleasantville, NY 10570

A spelling checker.

$ 75.00

1883 Sense Or Nonsense

Hartley Courseware, Inc.
P.O. Box 431treet   517-646-6458
Dimondale, MI 48821

A program for teaching sentence comprehension to students, by having them decide which sentences make sense.

1884 Sentence Fun

Richard Hefter, Author

Optimum Resource, Inc.
10 Station Place   203-542-5553
Norfolk, CT 06058

Designed for students, this diskette and user's guide helps students learn parts of speech by creating comical sentences and stories.

1885 Sequencer

Teacher Support Software
1035 NW 57th Street   904-332-6404
Gainesville, FL 32605

Improves comprehension by sequencing basic stories or children's literature.

$ 99.95

1886 Sharon's Program Series

Access Unlimited
3535 Briarpark Dr., #102   713-781-7441
Houston, TX 77042

A collection of 15 color, musical programs are motivating and help teach or reinforce readiness skills with large print and menu options.

$ 325.00

1887 Show Time

Software to Go - Galluadet University
800 Florida Avenue NE   202-651-5705
Washington, DC 20002

1888 SimpleCom I: Yes/No Communication

Dunamis, Inc.
3620 Highway 317   404-932-0485
Suwanee, GA 30174

Designed as a step toward more sophisticated communication for nonverbal individuals and as a yes/no discrimination teaching tool.

$ 59.95

1889 SimpleCom II: Needs/Wants Communication

Dunamis, Inc.
3620 Highway 317   404-932-0485
Suwanee, GA 30174

A yes/no response system for nonverbal users.

$ 59.95

1890 SocOrder: Sequencing Games

Bill Maxwell, Author

AGS
7201 Woodland Road   612-786-4343
Circle Pines, MN 55014   800-328-2560

A diskette to help students to use logical thinking skills to put words, sentences, numbers and letters in proper sequence.

1891 Sound Ideas: Consonants, Vowels, Word Attack and Word Structure

Houghton Mifflin School Division
One Memorial Drive 617-725-5022
Cambridge, MA 02178

A four-set series designed to build effective strategies for mastering phonics and word identification.

$ 165.00

1892 Speak Up

Mary S. Wilson, Author

Laureate Learning Systems, Inc.
110 E. Spring St.treet 802-655-4755
Winooski, VT 05404

Designed for children and adults with language impairments, an electronic dictionary of 349 audible words, with room for building, editing and storing words, phrases and augmentative communication systems.

1893 Special Needs: Volume I

Duane Loewan, Author

Minnesota Educational Computing Consortium
6160 Summit Drive North 612-569-1500
St. Paul, MN 55430

A program to teach beginning students spelling words.

1894 Speech and Sound Mechanic

CAST, Inc.
39 Cross Street 508-531-8555
Peabody, MA 01960

A utility that installs synthesized speech and digitized sound resources into HyperCard stacks.

$ 10.00

1895 Speech/Language Database

Barbara Polckoff, Author

The Speech Bin
1965 Twenty-Fifth Avenue 407-770-0007
Vero Beach, FL 32960 FAX 407-770-0006

Jan J. Binney, Editor In Chief
Barbara Hector, Office Manager

Contains over 1,000 goals and objectives in areas such as auditory skills, pragmatics, voice, fluency and syntax.

$ 99.50

1896 Spell Bound

Andrew Halvorsen, Author

World Book, Inc.
P.O. Box 1192 800-621-8202
Elk Grove Village, IL 60009

A program for children using an interactive game format at four levels to develop skills in using vocabulary and building verbal analogies.

1897 Spell It!

Jancie Davidson, Author

Davidson & Associates, Inc.
19840 Pioneer Avenue 213-534-4070
Torrancealo Verdes, CA 90503

Using an arcade game format, this program for teaching 1000 of the most commonly misspelled words and the spelling rules that go with them.

1898 S-P-E-L-L: the Reading/ Writing Connection

Eric Grubbs, Author

Sunburst Communications, Inc.
39 Washington Ave.et 914-769-5030
Pleasantville, NY 10570

A set of three diskettes with backups designed as a 30-week course to teach 4th grade spelling.

1899 Spellagraph

Software to Go - Galluadet University
800 Florida Avenue NE 202-651-5705
Washington, DC 20002

1900 Spell-a-Saurus

First Byte
19840 Pioneer Ave. 800-523-2983
Torrance, CA 90503

Children enter their own spelling lists, and with limited test-to-speech, play four challenging games to reinforce learning.

$ 54.95

1901 Spelling: Pre-Primer Through Second Grade

Barbara Johnson, Author

Communication Skill Builders
P.O. Box 42050evue 602-323-7500
Tucson, AZ 42050

Drill and practice in spelling 280 words for special needs students.

1902 Spelling Rules

Richard Hefter, Author

Optimum Resource, Inc.
10 Station Place 203-542-5553
Norfolk, CT 06058

A diskette and user's guide presents a series of practice exercises which are designed to help students improve their spelling skills.

1903 Spelling Sorcery

SouthWest Ed Psych Services, Inc.
2001 W. Silvergate Dr. 602-253-6528
Chandler, AZ 85224

Contains four color graphics programs which teach spelling to children.

$ 34.95

1904 Spelling Speechware, Levels 1-6

Houghton Mifflin School Division
One Memorial Drive   617-725-5022
Cambridge, MA 02178

Incorporates computer-generated speech, tutorials and motivational lessons for supplemental practice on spelling lessons.

$ 390.00

1905 Spelling Tutor

Access Unlimited
3535 Briarpark Dr., #102   713-781-7441
Houston, TX 77042

Main menu offering flexibility to those who modify the spelling file and to those who take the spelling tests it provides.

$ 50.00

1906 Spelling: Volume I

Minnesota Educational Computing Consortium
6160 Summit Drive North   612-569-1500
St. Paul, MN 55430

Designed to teach primary spelling words, a series of 20 spelling drills, each with 20 words.

1907 Spelling: Volume 2

Minnesota Educational Computing Consortium
6160 Summit Drive North   612-569-1500
St. Paul, MN 55430

Designed for upper elementary students or older students seeking remedial assistance, a series of 30 spelling drills, each with 20 spelling words.

1908 Spin N' Spell

Access Unlimited
3535 Briarpark Dr., #102   713-781-7441
Houston, TX 77042

Teacher creates word lists.

$ 45.00

1909 Stickybear ABS

Steve Worthington, Author

Newfield Publications
245 Long Hill Road   203-638-2400
Middletown, CT 06457

A program for children with colorful and animated pictures of objects representing words beginning with each letter of the alphabet.

1910 Stickybear Parts of Speech

Richard Hefter, Author

Optimum Resource, Inc.
10 Station Place   203-542-5553
Norfolk, CT 06058

Designed for students this diskette provides reinforcement in recognizing parts of speech in word lists, sentences and paragraphs.

1911 Stickybear Reading: Word and Sentence Fun for Children

Richard Hefter, Author

Optimum Resource, Inc.
10 Station Place   203-542-5553
Norfolk, CT 06058

A primary level program for developing vocabulary and reading comprehension.

1912 Stickybear Spellgrabber

Richard Hefter, Author

Optimum Resource, Inc.
10 Station Place   203-542-5553
Norfolk, CT 06058

Learn to spell over 4,000 words and develop keyboard skills in three animated games in which they spell the names of objects they see, unscramble letters to make words and guess words in the computer's memory.

1913 Story Sketcher

MindPlay
Unit F92, P.O. Box 36491   602-322-6365
Tucson, AZ 85740   800-221-7911

The complete tool kit for writing short stories.
> *"...great software to introduce story writing to an entire class."*

-Booklist
$ 59.99

1914 The Storyteller

Mary Roessler, Author

Educational Activities
P.O. Box 392venue   516-223-4666
Freeport, Long Island, NY 11520

An interactive fiction program that integrates the computer with language arts, reading and creative writing.

1915 Storytime Tales

Don Johnston Developmental Equipment, Inc.
P.O. Box 639, 1000 N. Rand Road   708-526-2682
Wauconda, IL 60084   800-999-4660
                                 FAX 708-526-4177

Paula Kwit, Vice President
Ruth Ziolowski, Sales Manager

Entertaining and interactive tales introduce beginning literacy activities and are well-suited for early cognitive and communication development.

$ 95.00

1916 StoryTree

George Bracket, Author
Scholastic Software
730 Broadway   212-505-6006
New York, NY 10003

A creative writing program for students focusing on reading, writing, editing and printing interactive stories.

1917 Super Spellicopter

Britannica Software
345 Fourth Street   415-597-5555
San Francisco, CA 94107

A sequel to the Spellicopter game, this program utilizes the 400 most frequently-used words in the school curriculum.

$ 34.95

1918 Superlead

Helen Grush, Author
Superlead Associates
Lexington, MA

A set of 6 diskettes providing a sequential, linguistic, phonetic approach to the teaching of spelling adn reading.

1919 Survival Words

Conover Company
P.O. Box 155   800-800-933-
Omro, WI 54963

There are three disks to the system offering basic living skills and cognitive training.

$ 149.95

1920 Symbol Writer

Don Johnston Developmental Equipment, Inc.
P.O. Box 639, 1000 N. Rand Road   708-526-2682
Wauconda, IL 60084   800-999-4660

A language discovery program for children beginning to control the computer.

$ 75.00

1921 Syntax Study Center

Teach Yourself By Computer Software
3400 Monroe Avenue   716-381-5450
Rochester, NY 14618

A drill-and-test learning game program which comes with question and answer files for working with adverbs, adjectives, verbs and subjects.

$ 39.95

1922 Talking Junior Writer

Technology for Language and Learning
P.O. Box 327   516-625-4550
East Rockaway, NY 11518

The individual letters are named as they are typed, and each line is spoke when it is completed.

$ 5.00

1923 Talking Riddles

Cross Educational Software
P.O. Box 1536   318-255-8921
Ruston, LA 71270

Contains three programs in Hangman format.

$ 24.95

1924 Talking Text Library

Scholastic Software
730 Broadway   212-505-6006
New York, NY 10003

Designed especially for beginning and struggling readers.

$ 62.45

1925 Talking Touch Window

ComputAbility Corporation
40000 Grand River, #109 109   313-477-6720
Novi, MI 48375   800-433-8872

Step by step instructions for creating your own lessons that TALK!.

1926 Talking Writer

Cross Educational Software
P.O. Box 1536   318-255-8921
Ruston, LA 71270

A text editor that speaks everything on the screen and prints it in double-sized letters.

$ 24.95

1927 Teacher's Puzzle Center

MindPlay
Unit F92, P.O. Box 36491   602-322-6365
Tucson, AZ 85740   800-221-7911

Available as a series, this program allows you to make your own puzzles, build vocabluary, improves reading skills and spelling, encourages creativity and encourages thinking skills.

$ 99.00

1928 Text Tiger

MindPlay
Unit F92, P.O. Box 36491   602-322-6365
Tucson, AZ 85740   800-221-7911

A word processor with introductory skills in word processing, practicing keyboarding skills, editing and more.
  "Only the Best!"

-Educational News Service
$ 39.00

1929 That's My Story: Creative Writing

Methods & Solutions, Inc.
Northbrook, IL

A program with 2 diskettes providing 12 story starters to encourage students to create, edit and rpint their own stories.

1930 Third and Fourth Grade Reading and Language Arts Competencies

Aquarius Instructional
P.O. Box 128   813-595-7890
Indiana Rocks Beach, FL 34635   800-338-2644
                                 FAX 813-595-2685

Offers various programs from following directions to the subject of synonyms and antonyms.

$ 925.00

1931 Tic-Tac-Spell

SouthWest Ed Psych Services, Inc.
2001 W. Silvergate Dr.   602-253-6528
Chandler, AZ 85224

Combines strategy and spelling to create a captivating educational game.

$ 34.99

1932 Time Terminal

Communication Skill Builders
P.O. Box 42050   602-323-7500
Tucson, AZ 42050

This game provides drill and practice plus stresses time vocabulary, morphological endings and comprehension skills.

$ 39.95

1933 Toltec Pyramid Game for English Usage

David Herzog, Author
Educational Activities
P.O. Box 392venue   516-223-4666
Freeport, Long Island, NY 11520

A tutorial and practice program with five activities in which students select the proper part of speech to complete a sentence.

1934 Touch Window

ComputAbility Corporation
40000 Grand River, #109 109   313-477-6720
Novi, MI 48375   800-433-8872

A simple, direct way for users to operate the computer especially helpful for individuals who point to the screen.

1935 TouchCom

Don Johnston Developmental Equipment, Inc.
P.O. Box 639, 1000 N. Rand Road 708-526-2682
Wauconda, IL 60084   800-999-4660

For beginning literacy. This program lets you design your own talking word boards and vocabularies for the PowerPad.

$ 128.00

1936 Twenty Categories

Mary S. Wilson, Author

Laureate Learning Systems, Inc.
110 E. Spring St.treet   802-655-4755
Winooski, VT 05404

Designed to use with children and adults, these two diskettes provide instruction in both abstracting the correct category for a noun and placing a noun in the appropriate category.

1937 Type to Learn

Sunburst Communications, Inc.
39 Washington Ave.   914-769-5030
Pleasantville, NY 10570

Language-based keyboarding program filled with teacher change-options including choice in vocabulary level, type, size and accuracy.

$ 75.00

1938 Type-Talk

Access Unlimited
3535 Briarpark Dr., #102   713-781-7441
Houston, TX 77042

Teaches keyboarding skills including awareness of the more obscure symbols and control characters frequently used in software applications.

$ 49.95

1939 Typing Well

Learning Well
2200 Marcus Avenue   516-326-2101
New Hyde Park, NY 11040

Five games players a chance to have fun while practicing touch-typing competence and speed building.

$ 49.95

1940 Understanding Questions II: More Questions

Sunset Software
9277 E. Corrine Dr.   602-451-0753
Scottsdale, AZ 85260

Questions that contrast the selected pair of question words are randomly presented.

$ 49.95

1941 Vocabulary Development

Richard Hefter, Author
Optimum Resource, Inc.
10 Station Place   203-542-5553
Norfolk, CT 06058

A diskette giving practice at recognizing synonyms, antonyms, homophones, multiple meanings, prefixes, suffixes and context clues through vocabulary study.

1942 Vocabulary Tutor

MindPlay
Unit F92, P.O. Box 36491   602-322-6365
Tucson, AZ 85740   800-221-7911

Users learn vocabulary skills while investigating and compiling lingustic information.

$ 99.00

1943 Voice Interactive Software

Learning Disabilities Association of America
4156 Library Road   412-341-1515
Pittsburgh, PA 15234

Students respond to graphic and spoken instructions, speaking into a microphone.

$ 65.00

1944 Whole Neighborhood

Pelican Software, Inc.
768 Farmington Ave.   203-674-8221
Farmington, CT 06032

Program to introduce the wide diversity of a community: occupations, locations and the differing needs of individuals.

$ 49.95

1945 Who-What-Where-When-Why

Hartley Courseware, Inc.
P.O. Box 431treet   517-646-6458
Dimondale, MI 48821

A program to provide an easy way for students to practice discrimination between commonly confused words and concepts they represent.

1946 Winning with Vowels

Hartley Courseware, Inc.
P.O. Box 431treet   517-646-6458
Dimondale, MI 48821

This diskette program enables students to hear and learn the sounds of both short and long vowels as they experience the excitement of summer and winter sports.

1947 Wizard of Words

Anita Neely, Author

Advanced Ideas, Inc.
591 Redwood Highway, Ste. 2325   415-425-5086
Mill Valley, CA 94941

A program that teaches reading, spelling, vocabulary and dictionary skills.

1948 Word Attack

Janice Davidson, Author

Davidson & Associates, Inc.
19840 Pioneer Avenue   213-534-4070
Torrancealos Verdes, CA 90503

A program using arcade game format to master the meanings and usages of 675 words.

1949 Word Attack Plus!

Jan Davidson, Author

Davidson & Associates, Inc.
19840 Pioneer Avenue   213-534-4070
Torrance, CA 90503

A diskette containing a five-part vocabulary program for learning 700 vocabulary words, their meanings and usages.

1950 Word Invasion: Arcademic Skill Builders in Language Arts

Jerry Chaffin, Author

DLM Teaching Resources
One DLM Parkhany   214-248-6300
Allen, TX 75002

A program using an arcade game format to provide practice in identifying words represnting six parts of speech: nouns, pronouns, verbs, adjectives, adverbs and prepositions.

1951 Word Master: Arcademic Skill Builders in Language Arts

Jerry Chaffin, Author

DLM Teaching Resources
One DLM Parkhany   214-248-6300
Allen, TX 75002

A program using arcade game format to provide practice in identifying parts of antonyms, synonyms or homonyns at three difficulty levels.

1952 Word Scrambler and Spelling Tutor

Brad Evans, Author

Avant-Garde Publishing Company
Eugene, OR

A program for students that offers drill and practice with flashing words and scrambled words.

1953 Word Search

Hartley Courseware, Inc.
P.O. Box 431treet   517-646-6458
Dimondale, MI 48821

A program to develop and print up to 90 wordfind puzzles each containing up to 22 words.

1954 Word Spinner

Dale Disharoon, Author

The Learning Company
6493 Kaiser Drive   510-792-2101
Freemont, CA 94555

A program to help students learn word patterns and develop critical vocabulary and spelling skills by making three- and four- letter words.

1955 Word Study Center

Teach Yourself By Computer Software
3400 Monroe Avenue   716-381-5450
Rochester, NY 14618

Flexible drill-and-test learning game program which comes with question/answer files.

$ 39.95

1956 Word Wise I and III: Better Comprehension Through Vocabulary

Isabel Beck, Author

DLM Teaching Resources
One DLM Parkhany   214-248-6300
Allen, TX 75002

A series of two software programs for developing and improving reading comprehension by building vocabulary knowledge.

1957 Wordzzzearch

MindPlay
Unit F92, P.O. Box 36491   602-322-6365
Tucson, AZ 85740   800-221-7911

Students find words hidden in the puzzles.

"...great teaching tools for building vocabulary, reading skills, and motivating students."
-Booklist
$ 44.99

1958 The Writing Adventure

Robert Caldwell, Author

DLM Teaching Resources
One DLM Parkhany   214-248-6300
Allen, TX 75002

A program using motivating pictures and stories to encourage studens to think creatively, observe details, take notes, write, proofread and print up a story.

Life Skills

1959 Alphabet Circus

DLM Teaching Resources
One DLM Park   214-248-6300
Allen, TX 75002

Software to teach letter recognition.
$ 32.95

1960 Aphasia Programs

The Speech Bin
1965 Twenty-Fifth Avenue   407-770-0007
Vero Beach, FL 32960   FAX 407-770-0006

Jan J. Binney, Editor In Chief
Barbara Hector, Office Manager

Helps aphasic individuals and others with reading and comprehension problems.
$ 99.50

1961 Bake and Taste

MindPlay
3130 N. Dodge Road   602-322-6365
Tucson, AZ 85716

A life skills program that simulates the baking process.
$ 49.99

1962 Big Book Maker

Queue, Inc.
338 Commerce Drive   203-335-0906
Fairfield, CT 06430   800-232-2224
     FAX 203-336-2481

Enables teachers and students to create customized stories that fulfill individual needs. Enlarged text and appealing graphics make it easy to capitalize on the "read together" storytime experience. Offers many various programs with everything from Favorite Fairy Tales & Nursery Rhymes to a program on Letters, Numbers & Shapes.

"...One of the most exciting whole language software packages available..."
Instructor Magazine, January 1991
$ 49.95

1963 Blueprint for Decision Making

MCE, a Division of Lawrence Productions
1800 S. 35th St.   616-665-7075
Galesburg, MI 49078

Teaches basic life skills and problem solving for at-risk students.
$ 69.95

1964 The Boars Tell Time

Queue, Inc.
338 Commerce Drive   203-335-0906
Fairfield, CT 06430   800-232-2224
     FAX 203-336-2481

The Boars help youngsters to learn both analog and digital time.
$ 39.95

1965 The Boars 1, 2, 3! Counting with the Boars

Queue, Inc.
338 Commerce Drive   203-335-0906
Fairfield, CT 06430   800-232-2224
     FAX 203-336-2481

The Boars teach young learners basic keyboard skills while they identify numbers from 1-10 and count familiar objects in a variety of colorful scenes.
$ 39.95

1966 Body Awareness

Methods & Solutions, Inc.
Northbrook, IL

A program providing practice and reinforcement in these areas of early childhood learning.

1967 The Body in Focus

Neosoft, Inc.
Northbrook, IL

Two diskettes for students providing animated explorations of eight major body systems and the functions of their organs, glands and bones.

1968 Braille-Talk

GW Micro
310 Racquet Drive   219-483-3625
Fort Wayne, IN 46825   FAX 219-484-2510

A grade two braille translating program.

1969 Buddy's Body

UCLA Intervention Program for Disabled Children
1000 Veteran Ave., #23-10   301-825-4821
Los Angeles, CA 90024

A body parts program containing two levels with animation.

$ 35.00

1970 Calendar Fun with Lollipop Dragons

Society for Visual Education, Inc.
1345 Diversey Parkway   312-525-1500
Chicago, IL 60614

Young students learn the calendar basics.

$ 84.00

1971 Captain's Log Cognitive Training System

BrainTrain, Inc.
727 Twin Ridge Lanbe   804-320-0105
Richmond, VA 23235

Includes 32 programs designed to train attention, concentration memory, visual-motor skills, basic numeric concepts, problem solving and resoning skills.

1972 Car Builder

Richard Hefter, Author

Optimum Resource, Inc.
10 Station Place   203-542-5553
Norfolk, CT 06058

A scientific graphic simulation program for designing, constructing, modifying and testing cars.

1973 Career Surveys

Conover Company
P.O. Box 155
Omro, WI 54963   800-800-933-

Contains four seperate, yet related, career programs.

$ 69.95

1974 Castaway's Dilemma

SouthWest Ed Psych Services, Inc.
2001 W. Silvergate Dr.   602-253-6528
Chandler, AZ 85224

A simulation of cooperation and competition which allows students to explore the ramifications of cooperation-competition problems.

$ 39.95

1975 Certificates and More!

Pelican Software, Inc.
768 Farmington Ave.   203-674-8221
Farmington, CT 06032

Designed for students and teachers enabling users to write, design and print checklists, calendars, game boards, certificates, greeting cards and other printed materials.

1976 Choices, Choices: on the Playground

Tom Snyder Productions
90 Sherman Street   617-876-4433
Cambridge, MA 02140

A teacher-centered discussion generator that provides a structured context that teaches critical thinking skills.

$ 89.95

1977 Choices, Choices: Taking Responsibility

Tom Snyder Productions
90 Sherman Street   617-876-4433
Cambridge, MA 02140

Provides a structured context that teaches critical thinking skills.

$ 89.95

1978 Clock

Hartley Courseware, Inc.
P.O. Box 431treet   517-646-6458
Dimondale, MI 48821

A program for students designed to teach the relationship between digital time and clock time by means of a graphic clock.

1979 Codes and Cyphers

Richard Hefter, Author

Optimum Resource, Inc.
10 Station Place   203-542-5553
Norfolk, CT 06058

A program for students in which they create and break secret codes, send and receive secret messages and construct encode-decode machines for others.

1980 Coin Changer

Heartsoft, Inc.
P.O. Box 691381   800-285-3475
Tulsa, OK 74169   800-285-3475

Uses large coin graphics which help teach money skills.

$ 49.00

1981 Coins N' Keys

Castle Special Computer Services, Inc.
9801 San Gabriel NE   505-293-8379
Albuquerque, NM 87111

Set of six game-like programs teaching recognition of real coins.

$ 45.00

1982 Community Activity SkillBuilder Series

Edmark Corporation
P.O. Box 3903   206-746-3900
Bellevue, WA 98009

Helps introduce or review vocabulary and procedures for community activities.

$ 179.95

1983 Community Signs

ComputAbility Corporation
40000 Grand River, #109 109   313-477-6720
Novi, MI 48375   800-433-8872

A new program for teaching survival skills. 8 disks focus on signs commonly found within the community.

1984 Computer Parts

Dunamis, Inc.
3620 Highway 317   404-932-0485
Suwanee, GA 30174   800-828-2443
                                             FAX 404-932-0486

Helps introduce the various parts of the computer.

$ 24.95

1985 Contemporary Living

Aquarius Instructional
P.O. Box 128   813-595-7890
Indian Rocks Bch., FL 34635

Through the use of high interest, low-reading levels, these programs promote self concept.

$ 115.00

1986 CORE: Computer Oriented Record Keeping Enabler

Macomb Projects
27 Horrabin Hall   209-298-1634
Macomb, IL 61455

Addresses developmental domains.

$ 89.95

1987 Counting and More Counting

Hartley Courseware, Inc.
P.O. Box 431treet   517-646-6458
Dimondale, MI 48821   800-247-1380
                                             FAX 517-646-8451

Telaina Eriksen

Expands the skills of counting and mathematics.

$ 49.95

1988 Critical Thinking for Contemporary Lifestyles

Aquarius Instructional
P.O. Box 128   813-595-7890
Indiana Rocks Beach, FL 34635   800-338-2644
                                             FAX 813-595-2685

This program of 14 titles offers to help improve employment, independent living, and community life skills.

$ 825.00

1989 Daily Living Skills

Looking Glass Learning Products, Inc.
276 Howare Avenue   800-545-5457
Des Plaines, IL 60018

Four programs that emphasize reading skills as the key to functional literacy.

$ 49.00

1990 Dinosaur Days

Queue, Inc.
338 Commerce Drive   203-335-0906
Fairfield, CT 06430   800-232-2224
                                             FAX 203-336-2481

Students can create their own unique dinosaurs choosing from hundreds of prehistoric parts.

$ 49.95

1991 Drivin'

Learning Disabilities Association of America
4156 Library Road   412-341-1515
Pittsburgh, PA 15234

Designed to supplement a full driver's education curriculum, emphasizes responsible, defensive driving.

$ 650.00

1992 Early Childhood Series

Learning Well
2200 Marcus Avenue   516-326-2101
New Hyde Park, NY 11040

Five programs offering information on visual discrimination and shapes and patterns.

$ 229.00

1993 Early Discoveries: Size and Logic

Software to Go - Galluadet University
800 Florida Avenue NE   202-651-5705
Washington, DC 20002

1994 Edmark

Don Johnston Developmental Equipment, Inc.
1000 N. Rand Road0 N. Rand Rd.   708-526-2682
Wauconda, IL 60084   800-999-4660
                                             FAX 708-526-4177

Creates your own talking lessons using the TouchWindow.

$ 79.95

1995 Emerging Occupations Interest Inventory

ComputAbility Corporation
40000 Grand River, #109 109   313-477-6720
Novi, MI 48375   800-433-8872

This unique program matches user interest against the characteristics of nearly 100 occupations.

1996 Employment Signs

Conover Company
P.O. Box 155   800-800-933-
Omro, WI 54963

The subject matter focuses around common funtional signs found in the workplace.

$ 179.95

1997 English on the Job

Conover Company
P.O. Box 155   800-800-933-
Omro, WI 54963

Developed to allow special needs and at-risk students an opportunity to explore careers and pratice basic English skills.

$ 1695.00

1998 Explorer Metros

Sunburst Communications, Inc.
39 Washington Ave.   914-769-5030
Pleasantville, NY 10570

Coloful games teaching estimation skills of mere capacity, mass, length and temperature.

$ 65.00

1999 Exploring Tables and Graphs: Level 1

Stephen Bannasch, Author

Weekly Reader Software
4343 East Gentry Drive   614-771-2741
Columbus, OH 43216

A diskette for learning about tables as well as picture, area and bar graphs through games, interesting examples and quizzes.

2000 Exploring Tables & Graphs: Level 2

Optimum Resource, Inc.
10 Station Place   203-542-5553
Norfolk, CT 06058

Designed for learning about tables, picture graphs, bar graphs, area graphs and line graphs through computer games.

2001 Facemaker

Clark Quinn, Author

Spinnaker Software Corporation
201 Broadway   508-494-1200
Cambridge, MA 01239

A program for children allowing them to create and animate faces while improving their memory, concentration skills and knowledge of computers.

2002 Family Fun

UCLA Intervention Program for Disabled Children
1000 Veteran Ave., #23-10   301-825-4821
Los Angeles, CA 90024

A program with family members and household items represented graphically on an overlay.

$ 35.00

2003 Fast Food/Restaurant Words

Edmark Corporation
P.O. Box 3218   206-746-3900
Redmond, WA 98073   800-362-2890

Teaches students to read 100 words for ordering a meal from a fast food establishment or a restaurant.

$ 179.00

2004 Feelings

UCLA Intervention Program for Disabled Children
1000 Veteran Ave., #23-10   301-825-4821
Los Angeles, CA 90024

Includes six feelings: happy, mad, sad, scared, loved and tired.

$ 35.00

2005 First R

Milliken Publishing
P.O. Box 21579   314-991-4220
St. Louis, MO 63132

A phonetically-based word recognition program with emphasis on comprehension.

$ 325.00

2006 Fish Scales

DLM Teaching Resources
One DLM Park   214-248-6300
Allen, TX 75002

Graphics, animation and sound will capture players' attention as they learn how things are measured for height, length and distance.

$ 32.95

2007 Following Directions

ComputAbility Corporation
40000 Grand River, #109 109   313-477-6720
Novi, MI 48375   800-433-8872

For users with learning disabilities or Attention Deficit Disorders.

2008 Following Directions: Behind the Wheel

MindPlay
1345 Diversey Pkwy.   312-525-1500
Chicago, IL 60614

An auto race challenges students to follow directions and to remeber details.

$ 49.95

2009 Following Directions: Left and Right

Laureate Learning Systems, Inc.
110 E. Spring St.treet   802-655-4755
Winooski, VT 05404   800-562-6801
                                 FAX 802-655-4757

Mary Sweig Wilson, President
Bernard Fox, Vice President

Provides practice in following directions and exercises short term memory while reinforcing left/right discrimination concepts.

$ 165.00

2010 Following Directions: One and Two Level Commands

Eleanor Semel, Author

Laureate Learning Systems, Inc.
110 E. Spring St.treet   802-655-4755
Winooski, VT 05404

Designed for a broad range of students experiencing difficulty in processing, remembering and following oral commands, a program of exercises on short and long term memory highlighting specific spatial, directional and ordinal vocabulary.

2011 Following Directions: 1 and 2

Laureate Learning Systems, Inc.
110 E. Spring St.treet   802-655-4755
Winooski, VT 05404   800-562-6801
                                 FAX 802-655-4757

Mary Sweig Wilson, President
Bernard Fox, Vice President

This two-disk program provides practice in following one and two step directions and exercises short term memory while teaching spatial relations and directional terms.

$ 235.00

2012 Food for Thought

Marshware, Inc.
P.O. Box 8082   816-523-1059
Shawnee Mission, KS 66208

Nutritional information, including the five food groups and facts about 30 different foods.

$ 55.95

2013 Food Group Puzzles

Marshware, Inc.
P.O. Box 8082   816-523-1059
Shawnee Mission, KS 66208

Two computer games uses colorful, high resolution graphics to review and reinforce group facts and concepts.

$ 55.95

2014 Further Adventures of Jimmy Jumper: Perseverance

Exceptional Children's Software
P.O. Box 487   913-625-9281
Hays, KS 67601

A short story that is read by an Echo.

$ 39.95

2015 Grocery Words

Edmark Corporation
P.O. Box 3218   206-746-3900
Redmond, WA 98073   800-362-2890

Provides students with 100 words necessary to read and write grocery lists and find items in a grocery store.

$ 179.00

2016 Guidance and Counseling Software

Conover Company
P.O. Box 155   800-933-1933
Omro, WI 54963

A series of programs that allows students to gain a better insight into their own personal values, self-concept and relationships.

$ 460.00

2017 Handling Money

Aquarius Instructional
P.O. Box 128   813-595-7890
Indian Rocks Beach, FL 34635

This program teaches students how to count money and make change in paper and coin.

$ 75.00

2018 How to Read for Everyday Living

Educational Activities
P.O. Box 392   516-223-4666
Freeport, Long Island, NY 11520

Students learn to read want ads, job ads, lables, forms and other items.

$ 139.00

2019 How to Write for Everyday Living

Educational Activities
P.O. Box 392   516-223-4666
Freeport, Long Island, NY 11520

Students use the reading/writing connection to achieve literacy competency.

$ 159.00

2020 Information Signs

ComputAbility Corporation
40000 Grand River, #109 109   313-477-6720
Novi, MI 48375   800-433-8872

Four disks teaching 40 words which assist in functioning in the community setting.

2021   Information Station

Society for Visual Education, Inc.
1345 Diversey Parkway   312-525-1500
Chicago, IL 60614

Students who boot up this software will find themselves floating miles above the earth orbiting the planet in an information station satellite.

$ 144.00

2022   Introduction to Business Office

ComputAbility Corporation
40000 Grand River, #109 109   313-477-6720
Novi, MI 48375   800-433-8872

Explores personal qualifications needed by office workers while examining the importance of telephone manners, record-keeping and accuracy in an office job.

2023   Jack and the Beanstalk

Software to Go - Galluadet University
800 Florida Avenue NE   202-651-5705
Washington, DC 20002

2024   Job Readiness

ComputAbility Corporation
40000 Grand River, #109 109   313-477-6720
Novi, MI 48375   800-433-8872

The best selling series helps develop the skills necessary to gain employment.

2025   Job Readiness Software

MCE, a Division of Lawrence Productions
1800 S. 35th St.   616-665-7075
Galesburg, MI 49078

Four programs: Job Attitudes: Assessment and Improvement, Filing Out Job Applications, Successful Job Interviewing and Resumes Made Easy.

$ 249.95

2026   Job Success Series

ComputAbility Corporation
40000 Grand River, #109 109   313-477-6720
Novi, MI 48375   800-433-8872

Helps users prepare for that first job with this complete 4 disk package.

2027   Jobs in Today's World

ComputAbility Corporation
40000 Grand River, #109 109   313-477-6720
Novi, MI 48375   800-433-8872

Helps non-college bound individuals prepare for work in today's job market.

2028   Job/Work Words

Edmark Corporation
P.O. Box 3218   206-746-3900
Redmond, WA 98073   800-362-2890

Teaches students 100 words to help them get and keep a job.

$ 179.00

2029   Keyboard: Keyboard Training Program

Barbara Johnson, Author
Communication Skill Builders
P.O. Box 42050evue   602-323-7500
Tucson, AZ 42050

Independent drill and practice in keyboard training for special needs students.

2030   KidDesk

Edmark Corporation
P.O. Box 3218   206-746-3900
Redmond, WA 98073   800-362-2890

Gives students creative control over their computing environment, without putting the professionals at risk. Turns all interaction into graphical choices, no reading or typing is required.

2031   Krell's SAT Vocabulary Builder

Krell Software
Flowerfield Bldg. #7   516-584-7900
St. James, NY 11788

Using both tutorial and game formats, this program provides practice in mastering the words which are important for tests, course work and job interviews.

$ 69.95

2032   Learning Left and Right

Eleanor Semel, Author
Laureate Learning Systems, Inc.
110 E. Spring St.treet   802-655-4755
Winooski, VT 05404

A program using drill and practice to develop laterality concepts ranging from simple to complex.

2033   Learning to Count Change

Life Science Associates
1 Fenimore Road   516-472-2111
Bayport, NY 11705

An instruction package to assist those who have trouble dealing with money and making change.

$ 49.95

2034   Lesson Maker

ComputAbility Corporation
40000 Grand River, #109 109   313-477-6720
Novi, MI 48375   800-433-8872

Creates individualized multi-layered basic skill lessons using Lesson maker's 50 graphics and 1500 digitized words.

2035 Let's Go Shopping I and II

UCLA Intervention Program for Disabled Children
1000 Veteran Ave., #23-10   301-825-4821
Los Angeles, CA 90024

Game in which items are selected to go in the appropriate store by pressing a switch.

$ 35.00

2036 Little Shoppers Kit

Tom Snyder Productions
90 Sherman Street   617-876-4433
Cambridge, MA 02140

Promotes cooperative learning and introduces early math skills and money denominations.

$ 109.95

2037 Living Alone

ComputAbility Corporation
40000 Grand River, #109 109   313-477-6720
Novi, MI 48375   800-433-8872

High interest, low vocabulary program encourages users to make carefully considered decisions regarding personal goals and values in daily living.

2038 MacKids Series

Nordic Software, Inc.
917 Carlos R   402-466-6502
Lincoln, NE 68505

A series of four programs to teach problem solving and basic living skills.

$ 59.95

2039 The Magic Cash Register

Daniel Barstow, Author

Metacomet Software
P.O. Box 231337   203-666-8854
Hartford, CT 06123

A program to teach students how to handle money by using simulated cash registers that display sales, calculate change and prints receipts.

2040 Make It Happen

Don Johnston Developmental Equipment, Inc.
P.O. Box 639, 1000 N. Rand Road   708-526-2682
Wauconda, IL 60084   800-999-4660

Cause/effect program designed as a first step to using a switch with a computer.

$ 60.00

2041 Make It in Time

Don Johnston Developmental Equipment, Inc.
P.O. Box 639, 1000 N. Rand Road   708-526-2682
Wauconda, IL 60084   800-999-4660

Introduces visual-motor and timing features in a fun format.

$ 60.00

2042 Make It Scan

Don Johnston Developmental Equipment, Inc.
P.O. Box 639, 1000 N. Rand Road   708-526-2682
Wauconda, IL 60084   800-999-4660

Builds visual-motor and timing skills learned in previous games, players now make choices from scanning options.

$ 60.00

2043 Mariner Home

Intellimation, Library for the Macintosh
Box 219   800-346-8355
Santa Barbara, CA 93116

An all purpose customization, organizing and presentation tool. Personalize home cards with a wide array of icons and color or monochrome pictures.

$ 42.00

2044 Math Concepts

Hartley Courseware, Inc.
P.O. Box 431treet   517-646-6458
Dimondale, MI 48821   800-247-1380
          FAX 517-646-8451

Telaina Eriksen

This package provides extra practice with concepts such as before/after; odd/even; counting by twos, threes, fours, fives and tens; less than/greater than; ordinal numbers; prime numbers; place values and more.

$ 49.95

2045 Memory: a First Step in Problem Solving

Software to Go - Galluadet University
800 Florida Avenue NE   202-651-5705
Washington, DC 20002

2046 Memory Match

Software to Go - Galluadet University
800 Florida Avenue NE   202-651-5705
Washington, DC 20002

2047 MicroSoc Thinking Games

AGS
7201 Woodland Road   612-786-4343
Circle Pines, MN 55014   800-328-2560

Six-program series helps develop critical thinking skills in the areas of classification, association and identification of common relationships.

$ 295.00

2048 Microzine 10

Dan Klassen, Author

Scholastic
730 Broadway   212-505-6006
New York, NY 10003

A program focusing on a Revolutionary War adventure story, a sailing simulation, an electronic billboard, puzzles and an electronic comic strip.

2049 Microzine 6

Dan Klassen, Author

Scholastic
730 Broadway   212-505-6006
New York, NY 10003

A program on a prehistoric adventure story, and electronic newspaper simulation on the Olympics, 40 sound effects and a data base of free or inexpensive mail-order items.

2050 Microzine 7

Dan Klassen, Author

Scholastic
730 Broadway   212-505-6006
New York, NY 10003

A program for students on an outer space story, a survey tool, a graphic design of a city and puzzles.

2051 Microzine 8

Dan Klassen, Author

Scholastic
730 Broadway   212-505-6006
New York, NY 10003

A program focusing on a fantasy adventure story involving creative writing, a secret journal, a graphic drawing board, puzzles and an electronic comic strip.

2052 Microzine 9

Dan Klassen, Author

Scholastic
730 Broadway   212-505-6006
New York, NY 10003

A program focusing on a detective story, budgeting, a quiz making/taking option, puzzles and an electronic comic strip.

2053 Mind Over Matter

Michael Heins, Author

Learning Well
2200 Marcus Avenue   516-326-2101
New Hyde Park, NY 11040

A game program that challenges students to solve 185 visual word puzzles or create their own puzzles, using symbols and graphics.

2054 Money Matters

ComputAbility Corporation
40000 Grand River, #109   313-477-6720
Novi, MI 48375   800-433-8872

Reinforces the development of money concepts such as identifying bills and coins, counting money and making change.

2055 My House: Language Activities of Daily Living

Laureate Learning Systems, Inc.
110 E. Spring St.   802-655-4755
Winooski, VT 05404

A language-simulation program designed for communicatively low-functioning clients.

$ 175.00

2056 Normal Growth and Development: Performance Prediction

Love Publishing Company
1777 South Bellaire Street   303-757-2579
Denver, CO 80222

Teaches the age at which skills are normally achieved by children ages 0 to 48 months.

$ 140.00

2057 Pacesetter Projects I

MindPlay
3130 N. Dodge Road   602-322-6365
Tucson, AZ 85716

For students who need extra motivation and reinforcement.

$ 24.99

2058 PEANUTS Maza Marathon

Queue, Inc.
338 Commerce Drive   203-335-0906
Fairfield, CT 06430   800-232-2224
                                FAX 203-336-2481

Helps develop hand/eye coordination, logic skills and directionality with these wonderful mazes.

$ 29.95

2059 PEANUTS Picture Puzzlers

Queue, Inc.
338 Commerce Drive   203-335-0906
Fairfield, CT 06430   800-232-2224
                                FAX 203-336-2481

Animated jigsaw puzzles come to life. Solve these delightful puzzles featuring the PEANUTS gang and let the computer create the picture or choose your favorite character to star in the puzzles.

$ 39.95

2060 Personal Information for Independence

ComputAbility Corporation
40000 Grand River, #109 109   313-477-6720
Novi, MI 48375   800-433-8872

Easy to use menu driven program allowing the individual user to learn personal information important for daily living.

2061 PhraseIT

Synergy-Adaptive Innovations
66 Hale Road   508-668-7424
East Walpole, MA 02032   FAX 508-668-4134

Software bringing a new meaning to the word assistive technology. In addition to augmentative communication and adaptive access, this software provides assistance for linguistic and memory difficulties.

2062 The Pond: Strategies in Problem Solving

Marge Kosel, Author
Sunburst Communications, Inc.
39 Washington Ave.et   914-769-5030
Pleasantville, NY 10570

A program for students providing six levels of practice and a game focusing on their use of pattern recognition, logic and generalization from raw data to help a lost frog cross a pond.

2063 Preschool IQ Builder

John Victor, Author
Program Design, Inc.
Greenwich, CT

A program to teach children to discriminate shapes, colors, alphabet letters and similarities and differences.

2064 The Print Shop

David Valsam, Author
Broderbund Software
P.O. Box 6121   415-382-4400
Novato, CA 94948

A program allowing the user to automatically design and print greeting cards, letterhead stationery, banners, signs and other graphic designs on regular computer paper.

2065 The Print Shop Companion

Roland Gustafsson, Author
Broderbund Software
P.O. Box 6121   415-382-4400
Novato, CA 94948

A program designed to expand the capabilities of The Print Shop with 12 new printing fonts, 50 new borders, additional graphic design options, custom calendar production and more.

2066 The Print Shop Graphics Library

David Balsam, Author
Broderbund Software
P.O. Box 6121   415-382-4400
Novato, CA 94948

Designed to be used with The Print Shop, this program with 120 additional graphic designs focusses on holidays, zodiac signs, animals, sports, school children and creative patterns.

2067 The Print Shop Graphics Library: Disk 2

David Balsam, Author
Broderbund Software
P.O. Box 6121   415-382-4400
Novato, CA 94948

Designed to supplement The Print Shop, this diskette with 120 additional graphics and a graphic editor focuses on graphics used on the job, as hobbies, places, travel, health, animals, sports and musci.

2068 Quiz Castle

Software to Go - Galluadet University
800 Florida Avenue NE   202-651-5705
Washington, DC 20002

2069 Reading for Understanding: That's Life!

Focus Media
839 Stewart Avenue   516-794-8900
Garden City, NY 11530

A collection of high-interest, low-readability programs for students reading between a fourth and sixth grade level.
$ 159.00

2070 Reasoning Skills on the Job

Conover Company
P.O. Box 155   800-800-933-
Omro, WI 54963

Focuses on the critical thinking and reasoning competencies necessary to function within an occupational area and assesses how well students can handle those competencies.
$ 1995.00

2071 Regrouping

Sunburst Communications, Inc.
39 Washington Ave.   914-769-5030
Pleasantville, NY 10570

Students learn how reclassifying items according to common attributes can be a powerful memory tool.
$ 65.00

2072 Resumes Made Easy

George Spengler, Author
MCE, a Division of Lawrence Productions
1800 S. 35th St.   616-665-7075
Galesburg, MI 49078

An interactive program covering what a resume is, how a resume is prepared, what to include in a resume, and the two most common types.

2073 The Right Job

Janet Brawner, Author
Sunburst Communications, Inc.
39 Washington Ave.et   914-769-5030
Pleasantville, NY 10570

An interactive, career exploration program for the mildly handicapped students to develop skills in the job search process, research, decision making, computer literacy and identifying personal interests.

2074 Safety Signs

ComputAbility Corporation
40000 Grand River, #109 109   313-477-6720
Novi, MI 48375   800-433-8872

Similar in purpose and format to Information Signs.

2075 Set the Table

Dunamis, Inc.
3620 Highway 317   404-932-0485
Suwanee, GA 30174

The overlay features a table place showing the fork, knife, plate and spoon to teach basic eating skills.

$ 19.95

2076 Signs Around You

Edmark Corporation
P.O. Box 3218   206-746-3900
Redmond, WA 98073   800-362-2890

Enables students to read more than 100 informational and protection words such as: Telephone, Restrooms, Fire and Do Not Enter.

$ 179.00

2077 Skills for Living I & II

Hartley Courseware, Inc.
P.O. Box 431treet   517-646-6458
Dimondale, MI 48821   800-247-1380
                                     FAX 517-646-8451

Telaina Eriksen

These programs emphasize basic life skills.

$ 350.00

2078 SocSort: Games for Developing Classification Skills

Bill Maxwell, Author
AGS
7201 Woodland Road   612-786-4343
Circle Pines, MN 55014   800-328-2560

A diskette to teach students to understand what words have in common by selecting and classifying 17 categories and 93 subcategories of words.

2079 Stickybear Music

Richard Hefter, Author

Optimum Resource, Inc.
10 Station Place   203-542-5553
Norfolk, CT 06058

A program for creating, editing, playing, saving and printing songs while practicing music notation.

2080 Stickybear Music Library 1

Janie Worthington, Author

Optimum Resource, Inc.
10 Station Place   203-542-5553
Norfolk, CT 06058

A diskette with more than 30 songs tro be used in conjunction with the Stickybear Music program who want to create and play songs while practicing music notation skills.

2081 Stickybear Printer

Richard Hefter, Author

Optimum Resource, Inc.
10 Station Place   203-542-5553
Norfolk, CT 06058

A utility program for students to use in designing and printing greeting cards, pictures of towns, stories, invitations, posters and signs.

2082 Stickybear Printer Picture Library 1

Richard Hefter, Author

Optimum Resource, Inc.
10 Station Place   203-542-5553
Norfolk, CT 06058

Designed for use with Stickybear Printer, these 2 diskettes provide hundreds of additional pictures, backgrounds, typefaces, frames and patterns for creating graphic designs.

2083 Stickybear Shapes

Richard Hefter, Author

Optimum Resource, Inc.
10 Station Place   203-542-5553
Norfolk, CT 06058

A program to help children identify circles, squares, triangles, rectangles and diamonds.

2084 Stickybear Town Builder

Richard Hefter, Author

Optimum Resource, Inc.
10 Station Place   203-542-5553
Norfolk, CT 06058

Students learn to read maps, build towns, take trips and use a compass with this diskette.

2085 Stickybear Typing

Richard Hefter, Author

Optimum Resource, Inc.
10 Station Place   203-542-5553
Norfolk, CT 06058

Three animated games for children and adults, the first focusing on keyboard training, the second on building typing skills and the third for practicing with text in a choice of categories.

2086 Study Skills

Arlene Isaacson, Author

C.C. Publications, Inc.
Tigard, OR

A program with 8 diskettes to teach students reading at or above 4th grade level how to research and write a theme through a task sequence.

2087　Teddy Barrels of Fun

DLM Teaching Resources
One DLM Parkhany　　　214-248-6300
Allen, TX 75002

A graphic design program that includes over 200 pieces of art for creating pictures, posters and labels, and word processing capabilities to develop writing skills and creative thinking.

2088　Teddy's Playground

Donna Stanger, Author

Sunburst Communications, Inc.
39 Washington Ave.et　　　914-769-5030
Pleasantville, NY 10570

Two diskettes to help children identify attributes while playing any of three games. Color monitor is required.

2089　Test Master Basic Skills Software

Test Master, Inc.
Washington, DC

An instructional and management computer system for students that includes 58 diskettes providing tutorial lessons, quizzes, tests and various summary report options focusing on over 200 basic skill areas.

2090　The Three Bears: An Interactive Fairy-Tale Classic

Laura Boxer, Author

Millenium
New York, NY

A program allowing children to control the progress, graphics and ending of this famous children's story.

2091　Thw Comic Book Maker

Queue, Inc.
338 Commerce Drive　　　203-335-0906
Fairfield, CT 06430　　　800-232-2224
　　　　　　　　　　FAX 203-336-2481

Designs your own comic books and share them in the classroom or at home. Comics provide a unique writing environment for combining text and graphics to communicate ideas.

$ 49.95

2092　Type to Learn: a New Approach to Keyboarding

Wendy Ashlock, Author

Sunburst Communications, Inc.
39 Washington Ave.et　　　914-769-5030
Pleasantville, NY 10570

A complete keyboard training course using language-based formats to reinforce and strengthen spelling, grammar, composition and punctuation skills.

2093　Ultimate Banker

Access Unlimited
3535 Briarpark Dr., #102　　　713-781-7441
Houston, TX 77042

Permits users to keep track of all banking transactions whether they bechecking or savings accounts.

$ 40.00

2094　What I Wannabe

Dunamis, Inc.
3620 Highway 317　　　404-932-0485
Suwanee, GA 30174　　　800-828-2443
　　　　　　　　　FAX 404-932-0486

This program teaches children about occupations.

$ 24.95

Math

2095　Academic Drill Builders: Wiz Works

Jerry Chaddin, Author

DLM Teaching Resources
One DLM Parkhany　　　214-248-6300
Allen, TX 75002

A program using an arcade game format for the creation, editing, pacing and monitoring of 36 drill and practice games.

2096　Academic Skill Builders in Math

DLM Teaching Resources
One DLM Park　　　214-248-6300
Allen, TX 75002

Offers a fast-action game format and colorful graphics.

$ 46.00

2097　Access to Math

Don Johnston Developmental Equipment, Inc.
1000 N. Rand Road　　　708-526-2682
Wauconda, IL 60084

Software offering help in subtraction, addition, multiplication and division problems.

2098　Adventure with Fractions

Lois Edwards, Author

Minnesota Educational Computing Consortium
6160 Summit Drive North　　　612-569-1500
St. Paul, MN 55430

Three tutorial math programs that teach two methods of comparing unlike fractions.

2099 Alien Addition

Software to Go - Galluadet University
800 Florida Avenue NE   202-651-5705
Washington, DC 20002

2100 Allen Addition: Arcademic Skill Builders in Math

Jerry Chaffin, Author
DLM Teaching Resources
One DLM Parkhany   214-248-6300
Allen, TX 75002

A program using an arcade game format to provide practice in addition of numbers 0 through 9.

2101 Alpine Tram Ride

Merit Software
13635 Gamma Road   214-385-2353
Dallas, TX 75244

Teaches cognitive redevelopment skills.

$ 12.95

2102 America, An Early History

Aquarius Instructional
P.O. Box 128   813-595-7890
Indiana Rocks Beach, FL 34635   800-338-2644
FAX 813-595-2685

This tutorial program takes students into historical settings, allowing them to become active participants in the past.

$ 195.00

2103 Analytic Learning Disability Assessment

UNITED Educational Services, Inc.
P.O. Box 1099   800-458-7900
Buffalo, NY 14224

This program facilitates interpretation and application of the various aspects of this evaluation tool.

$ 195.00

2104 Arithmetic Critters

MECC
3490 Lexington Ave. N   612-481-3611
St. Paul, MN 55126

Four programs help to master simple math skills.

$ 59.00

2105 Balancing Bear

Sunburst Communications, Inc.
39 Washington Ave.   914-769-5030
Pleasantville, NY 10570

Offers basic math skills for the learning disabled.

$ 65.00

2106 Basic Math Competency Skill Building

Michael Conlon, Author
Educational Activities
P.O. Box 392   516-223-4666
Freeport, Long Island, NY 11520

An interactive, tutorial and practice program to teach competency with arithmetic operations, decimals, fractions, graphs, measurement and geometric concepts.

2107 Basic Math Facts

Houghton Mifflin School Division
One Memorial Drive   617-725-5022
Cambridge, MA 02178

Gives teachers a systematic way to provide students with supplemental practice on basic facts in addition, subtraction and division.

$ 99.00

2108 Basic Number Facts Practice

Bonnie Seiler, Author
Control Data Publishing Company
San Diego, CA   619-279-1941

A program using an animated race track format to improve elementary students' speed and accuracy in calculating basic number facts in addition, subtraction, multiplication and division.

2109 The Boars Store

Queue, Inc.
338 Commerce Drive   203-335-0906
Fairfield, CT 06430   800-232-2224
FAX 203-336-2481

Shopping at the Boars Store offers students an exciting way to learn to count money and make change.

$ 39.95

2110 Bumble Games

Leslie Grimm, Author
The Learning Company
6493 Kaiser Drive   510-792-2101
Freemont, CA 94555

Six games designed to teach children the basics of numbers and number plotting through the use of number pairs.

2111 Calc-Talk

GW Micro
310 Racquet Drive   219-483-3625
Fort Wayne, IN 46825

Speech synthesizer for speech output that turns the standard Apple keyboard into a fully featured scientific calculator keypad.

$ 95.00

2112   Calcworthy

GW Micro
310 Racquet Drive   219-483-3625
Fort Wayne, IN 46825   FAX 219-484-2510

A "pop-up" calculator for the IBM and compatibles.

2113   Campaign Math

MindPlay
Unit F92, P.O. Box 36491   602-322-6365
Tucson, AZ 85740   800-221-7911

Introduces the American Election Process and Optional
Practice with Arithmetic.

> *"...highly motivated and innovative program!"*
> -The Wright Selection
> **$ 49.99**

2114   Challenge Math

Jon Sweedler, Author

Sunburst Communications, Inc.
39 Washington Ave.et   914-769-5030
Pleasantville, NY 10570

Three game programs for students to give them practice in
calculating and estimating with whole numbers and
decimals while building their inductive reasoning skills.

2115   Charlie Brown's 1, 2, 3's

Queue, Inc.
338 Commerce Drive   203-335-0906
Fairfield, CT 06430   800-232-2224
                                        FAX 203-336-2481

Strengthen numbers and counting skills with the PEA-
NUTS gang.

$ 29.95

2116   Clock

Software to Go - Galluadet University
800 Florida Avenue NE   202-651-5705
Washington, DC 20002

2117   Clock Works

Software to Go - Galluadet University
800 Florida Avenue NE   202-651-5705
Washington, DC 20002

2118   Code Quest

Sunburst Communications, Inc.
39 Washington Ave.   914-769-5030
Pleasantville, NY 10570

Sharpens thinking skills by breaking a series of secret
codes that reveal clues to the identities of mystery items.

$ 65.00

2119   Comparison Kitchen

DLM Teaching Resources
One DLM Park   214-248-6300
Allen, TX 75002

Strengthens students visual perception of sizes and
amounts as well as their visual discrimination of objects
by color, shape and size.

$ 32.95

2120   Computer Courseware for the Exceptional Student: Arithmetic

Barbara Johnson, Author

Communication Skill Builders
P.O. Box 42050evue   602-323-7500
Tucson, AZ 42050

A drill and practice program in addition, subtraction,
multiplication and division of whole numbers 0-99.

2121   Conceptual Skills

Psychological Software Services, Inc.
6555 Carrolton Avenue   317-257-9672
Indianapolis, IN 46220

12 programs designed to enhance skills involved in relationships, comparisons and number concepts.

$ 50.00

2122   Conquering Fractions

MECC
3490 Lexington Ave. N   612-481-3611
St. Paul, MN 55126

Students develop the ability to add and subtract fractions
as they complete a series of exercises.

$ 59.00

2123   Dinosaurs

Advanced Ideas, Inc.
680 Hawthorne Drive   415-425-5086
Tiburon, CA 94920

A child can match, sort or count creatures including the
tyrannosaurus rex.

$ 39.95

2124   DLM Math Fluency Program

DLM Teaching Resources
One DLM Park   214-248-6300
Allen, TX 75002

Designed for children in special and remedial education
who need additional help prior to the customary drill and
practice.

$ 29.95

2125   DLM Math Fluency Program: Division Facts

Ted Hasselbring, Author

DLM Teaching Resources
One DLM Park   214-248-6300
Allen, TX 75002

A series of 10-minute sessions in this diskette program
easily retrieves answers to basic division facts up to 144
divided by 12.

2126 DLM Math Fluency Program: Multiplication Facts

Ted Hasselbring, Author

DLM Teaching Resources
One DLM Park   214-248-6300
Allen, TX 75002

A series of 10-minute sessions easily retrieves answers to basic multiplication facts up to 12 x 12.

2127 DLM Math Fluency Program: Subtraction Facts

Ted Hasselbring, Author

DLM Teaching Resources
One DLM Park   214-248-6300
Allen, TX 75002

A series of 10-minute sessions that easily retrieve answers to basic subtraction facts up to 24-12.

2128 DLM Math Fluency Programs: Addition Facts

Ted Hasselbring, Author

DLM Teaching Resources
One DLM Park   214-248-6300
Allen, TX 75002

A program using drill and practice, arcade games, student record keeping, worksheet production and testing to develop the ability to recall basic addition math facts.

2129 Dr. Seuss Fix-up the Mix-up Puzzler

Coleco Industries, Inc.
Greenwich, CT

A diskette providing practice in problem solving, sequencing, object and pattern recognition and memory skills.

2130 Dragon Mix: Arcademic Skill Builders in Math

Jerry Chaffin, Author

DLM Teaching Resources
One DLM Parkhany   214-248-6300
Allen, TX 75002

A program providing practice in multiplication of numbers 0 through 9 and division of problems with answers 0 through 9.

2131 Early Learning II

MarbleSoft
12301 Central Ave. NE   612-755-1402
Baline, MN 55434

Uses sight and sound to teach early addition and number sequencing.

$ 57.00

2132 Early Learning III

MarbleSoft
12301 Central Ave. NE   612-755-1402
Baline, MN 55434

Teaches subtraction and number comparison with the aid of objects presented on the screen for the student to count.

$ 57.00

2133 Edmark Time Telling

Edmark Corporation
P.O. Box 3218   206-746-3900
Redmond, WA 98073   800-362-2890

Designed for students not yet able to tell time, this book teaches the basics required to read a standard or digital clock.

$ 79.95

2134 Eighth Through Tenth Grade Math Competencies

Aquarius Instructional
P.O. Box 128   813-595-7890
Indiana Rocks Beach, FL 34635   800-338-2644
                                 FAX 813-595-2685

Offers 59 disks on reading numerals and comparing, solving word problems with fractions, word problems, measurement, averages, geometry, graphs and more.

$ 1775.00

2135 Elementary Volume 1: Mathematics

American Printing House for the Blind
P.O. Box 6085   502-895-2405
Louisville, KY 40206

This program has been adapted for speech output and contains the assortment of math games, puzzles and drills.

$ 18.57

2136 Equations

Software to Go - Galluadet University
800 Florida Avenue NE
Washington, DC 20002   202-651-5705

2137 Excelling in Mathematics

Aquarius Instructional
P.O. Box 128   813-595-7890
Indiana Rocks Beach, FL 34635   800-338-2644
                                 FAX 813-595-2685

A series of tutorial math programs designed to provide instruction for above average math students to prepare them for college math.

$ 795.00

2138 Factory

Wings for Learning, Inc.
1600 Green Hills Rd.   408-438-5502
Scotts Valley, CA 95067

Using color graphics and animation, this three-level program challenges students to create geometric shaped and products.

$ 65.00

2139 The Factory: Strategies in Problem Solving

Mike Fish, Author

Sunburst Communications, Inc.
39 Washington Ave.et   914-769-5030
Pleasantville, NY 10570

A program using color graphics and animation to challenge students to create geometric products while developing indictive reasoning and perceptual motor skills.

2140 Fast-Track Fractions

DLM Teaching Resources
One DLM Park   214-248-6300
Allen, TX 75002

Students solve problems that compare, add, subtract, multiply and divide fractions.

$ 46.00

2141 Fay: That Math Woman

Didatech Software, Ltd.
3812 William St.   604-299-4435
Burnaby, BC, Canada, V5 C 3H9

Learn how and why arithmetic works.

$ 42.00

2142 Fifth Through Seventh Grade Math Competencies

Aquarius Instructional
P.O. Box 128   813-595-7890
Indiana Rocks Beach, FL 34635   800-338-2644
                                    FAX 813-595-2685

Offers 32 disks on reading money values, ordering numers, multiplying whole number, dividing whole numbers, adding and subtracting decimals and more.

$ 995.00

2143 Fingerspeller/Fingernumbers

Steven Longacre, Author

Specialsoft
Santa Monica, CA

A program designed to provide drill and practice for nonverbal and hearing impaired students in recognizing and reproducing the Manual Alphabet.

2144 Fraction Fairy Tales with the Boars

Queue, Inc.
338 Commerce Drive   203-335-0906
Fairfield, CT 06430   800-232-2224
                                    FAX 203-336-2481

The Boars teach students about fractions in their favorite fairy tale surroundings.

$ 39.95

2145 Fraction Fuel-Up

DLM Teaching Resources
One DLM Park   214-248-6300
Allen, TX 75002

Players practice reducing, renaming, finding equivalent fractions and adding/subtracting fractions.

$ 46.00

2146 Fraction Munchers

Software to Go - Galluadet University
800 Florida Avenue NE   202-651-5705
Washington, DC 20002

2147 Fraction-Oids

MindPlay
Unit F92, P.O. Box 36491   602-322-6365
Tucson, AZ 85740   800-221-7911

This math game for fractions offers practice in the fundamentals of fractions.

"A superior program combining fun and learning in a format that students enjoy..."

-Software Reports

$ 39.00

2148 Guessing and Thinking

Software to Go - Galluadet University
800 Florida Avenue NE   202-651-5705
Washington, DC 20002

2149 Hey, Taxi!

Queue, Inc.
338 Commerce Drive   203-333-7268
Fairfield, CT 06430

Children manuever their cab through the city streets to pick up passengers that solve basic math facts problems to collect their fares.

$ 39.95

2150 Hop to It!

Sunburst Communications, Inc.
39 Washington Ave.   914-769-5030
Pleasantville, NY 10570

This math program helps students strengthen their addition and subtraction skills using a number line.

$ 65.00

2151 Juggles' Rainbow

Ann Piestrup, Author

The Learning Company
6493 Kaiser Drive   510-792-2101
Freemont, CA 94555

Three games using colorful graphics to teach reading and math readiness skills to children.

2152 KidSoft Works

The KidSoft Company
718 University Avenue, Ste. 112   800-354-6150
Los Gatos, CA 95034

A great first business application for kids, teaching them to manage different kinds of information. Integrates a word processor, a database and a spreadsheet for the inquisitive business mind.

$ 49.95

2153 Kieran

OHM Electronics
746 Vermont Street   800-323-2727
Palatine, IL 60067

Preschool educational software with eight learning functions.

$ 39.95

2154 Kinderlogo

Terrapin Software, Inc.
400 Riverside Street   207-878-8200
Portland, ME 04103

A curriculum based on single keystroke commands.

$ 49.95

2155 Kindermath II

Houghton Mifflin School Division
One Memorial Drive   617-725-5022
Cambridge, MA 02178

Teaches fundamentals of math to young children.

$ 276.00

2156 Knowing Numbers

Methods & Solutions, Inc.
Northbrook, IL

A mathematics readiness game program focusing on the numbers 1 to 10, the concepts of greater than, less than and equal to.

2157 Krell's Math Diagnostic

Krell Software
Flowerfield Bldg. #7   516-584-7900
St. James, NY 11788

Evaluates student skills and performance in 46 key areas tested by standardized exams.

$ 199.95

2158 Language of Math

Krell Software
Flowerfield Bldg. #7   516-584-7900
St. James, NY 11788

A 23-disk set full of stories, tutorials, drill and practice and quizzes aimed at providing a sequenced approach for children who learn slowly.

$ 299.95

2159 Learning About Numbers

C&C Software
5713 Kentford Circle   316-682-2699
Wichita, KS 67208

Three segments use computer graphics to provide students with an experience in working with numbers.

$ 50.00

2160 Learning Activity Packets

Conover Company
P.O. Box 155   800-800-933-
Omro, WI 54963

Provide exposure to the math and English competencies necessary to funtion within a general vocational areas.

$ 995.00

2161 Letter Find

Exceptional Children's Software
P.O. Box 487   913-625-9281
Hays, KS 67601

Five programs designed for and field tested with preschoolers.

$ 19.95

2162 Logo Plus

Terrapin Software, Inc.
400 Riverside Street   207-878-8200
Portland, ME 04103

An enhanced version offering features such as the original language.

$ 119.00

2163 Logo TouchTools for PowerPad

Dunamis, Inc.
3620 Highway 317   404-932-0485
Suwanee, GA 30174

A collection of flexible utility programs for adaptation by teachers and clinicians to give persons, with a wide variety of disabilities, access to a computer.

$ 29.95

2164 Logo Works: Lessons in Logo

Terrapin Software, Inc.
400 Riverside Street   207-878-8200
Portland, ME 04103

Curriculum support materials designed to integrate Logo into the classroom.

$ 29.95

2165 Long Division

Philip Hessmer, Author
Educational Activities
P.O. Box 392   516-223-4666
Freeport, Long Island, NY 11520

An elementary level tutorial with drill and reinforcement intended to supplement classroom instruction on the mechanics of long division.

2166   Math Across the Curriculum

Learning Disabilities Association of America
4156 Library Road   412-341-1515
Pittsburgh, PA 15234

A new approach to math problem solving skills using writing across the curriculum.

2167   Math and Me/Talking Math and Me

Davidson & Associates, Inc.
19840 Pioneer Avenue   213-534-4070
Torrance, CA 90503

Introduces the student to math readiness concepts and builds beginning math skills.

$ 39.95

2168   Math Baseball

Richard Panneitz, Author

Educational Activities
P.O. Box 392   516-223-4666
Freeport, Long Island, NY 11520

A program using a baseball game format to motivate students to practice the skills of addition, subtraction, multiplication and division.

2169   Math Blaster

Janice Davidson, Author

Davidson & Associates, Inc.
19840 Pioneer Avenue   213-534-4070
Torrancealo Verdes, CA 90503

A program designed for students to help them master basic math facts in addition, sibtraction, multiplication, division, fractions, decimals and percents.

2170   Math Facts: II

Morning Star Software
P.O. Box 5364   608-223-5056
Madison, WI 53705

Teaches the basic math facts of addition, subtraction, multiplication and division utilizing the principles of Direct Instruction.

$ 95.00

2171   Math for All Ages a Sequential Math Program

Aquarius Instructional
P.O. Box 128   813-595-7890
Indiana Rocks Beach, FL 34635   800-338-2644
                                  FAX 813-595-2685

Offers 16 disks on adding, subtracting, multiplication and division.

$ 250.00

2172   Math for Everyday Living

Ann Edson, Author

Educational Activities
P.O. Box 392venue   516-223-4666
Freeport, Long Island, NY 11520

Designed for secondary students, a tutorial and practice program with simulated activities for applying math skills in making change, working with sales slips, unit pricing, computing gas mileage and sales tax.

2173   Math Machine

Software to Go - Galluadet University
800 Florida Avenue NE   202-651-5705
Washington, DC 20002

2174   Math Magic

MindPlay
3130 N. Dodge Road   602-322-6365
Tucson, AZ 85716

Beginners' lessons feature counting objects with the space bar and progress in steps in adding and subtracting numbers as they collect their monsters or presents.

$ 49.99

2175   Math Marvels

Doug Super, Author

Houghton Mifflin School Division
One Memorial Drive   617-725-5022
Cambridge, MA 02178

Three math games for teaching decimals.

2176   Math Masters

Doug Super, Author

Houghton Mifflin School Division
One Memorial Drive   617-725-5022
Cambridge, MA 02178

Three math games for teaching fractions, percentages and ratios to children.

2177   Math Masters: Addition and Subtraction

Jerry Chaffin, Author

DLM Teaching Resources
One DLM Parkhany   214-248-6300
Allen, TX 75002

Designed to supplement math curriculum, this program covers addition and subtraction for all numbers from 0 through 25.

2178   Math Masters: Multiplication and Division

Jerry Chaffin, Author

DLM Teaching Resources
One DLM Parkhany   214-248-6300
Allen, TX 75002

Designed to supplement math curriculum, this program covers multiplication and division for all numbers from 0 through 25.

2179   Math Rabbit

Teri Perl, Author

The Learning Company
6493 Kaiser Drive   510-792-2101
Freemont, CA 94555

A set of 4 games to develop skills in counting, adding, subtracting, recognizing number relationships, and identifying equalities and inequalities.

2180   Math Shop

Software to Go - Galluadet University
800 Florida Avenue NE   202-651-5705
Washington, DC 20002

2181   Math Skill Games

Software to Go - Galluadet University
800 Florida Avenue NE   202-651-5705
Washington, DC 20002

2182   Math Spending and Saving

Paul Edwards, Author

Media Materials
111 Kane Street   410-633-0730
Baltimore, MD 21224

Designed for secondary students and adults, this program focuses on personal financial management, comparison shopping and calculation of essential banking transactions.

2183   Math Study Center

Teach Yourself By Computer Software
3400 Monroe Avenue   716-381-5450
Rochester, NY 14618

Flexible drill-and-test learning game program which comes with question/answer files on math skills appropriate for each grade level.

$ 39.95

2184   M*A*T*H: the Fundamentals

Krell Software
Flowerfield Bldg. #7   516-584-7900
St. James, NY 11788

Six disks covering the basics from beginning addition and carrying through exponents.

$ 99.95

2185   Math Word Problems

Richard Hefter, Author

Optimum Resource, Inc.
10 Station Place   203-542-5553
Norfolk, CT 06058

A program for students with four levels of arithmetic word problems requiring one to three operations for answers.

2186   Mathematics: Volume 2

Minnesota Educational Computing Consortium
6160 Summit Drive North   612-569-1500
St. Paul, MN 55430

Designed for students offering nine tutorial/drill and practice programs on the English measurement system.

2187   Measure Works

MECC
3490 Lexington Ave. N   612-481-3611
St. Paul, MN 55126

Shows how to compare sizes and heights, measure with whole units and recognize perimeter and area measurements.

$ 59.00

2188   Milicent's Math House

Edmark Corporation
P.O. Box 3903   206-746-3900
Bellevue, WA 98009

Children can explore six interactive activities, each of which has educational foundations.

$ 79.95

2189   Millie's Math House

Edmark Corporation
P.O. Box 3218   206-746-3900
Redmond, WA 98073   800-362-2890

A dynamic supplement to your daily curriculum. This program, full of lively characters and colorful graphics captures children's imaginations while teaching fundamental skills and concepts in six interactive activities.

$ 64.95

2190   Money! Money!

Hartley Courseware, Inc.
P.O. Box 431treet   517-646-6458
Dimondale, MI 48821

A program involving counting money, making change or solving simple word problems about money.

2191   The Money Series: Counting Rosie Bogo

Hartley Courseware, Inc.
P.O. Box 431treet   517-646-6458
Dimondale, MI 48821

Using moving graphics and verbal feedback, this money counting program focuses on recognition and addition of combinations of coins and use of decimal points.

2192   The Money Series: More Counting

Phil Mansour, Author

Hartley Courseware, Inc.
P.O. Box 431treet   517-646-6458
Dimondale, MI 48821

Designed for students and an adult literacy program, this diskette focuses on the counting of coins and dollars. Includes simple problems requiring the student to determine if she or he has enough money to pay for a given time.

2193　Money Skills

MarbleSoft
12301 Central Ave. NE　　612-755-1402
Baline, MN　55434

Teaches students to count money and make change.

$ 47.00

2194　MouseMath Counting and Comparing Kit

Edmark Corporation
P.O. Box 3218　　　　　206-746-3900
Redmond, WA　98073　　800-362-2890

Links language arts and math while you encourage your students to talk about their math problems.

$ 45.00

2195　Multiply with Balancing Bear

Sunburst Communications, Inc.
39 Washington Ave.　　　914-769-5030
Pleasantville, NY　10570

As students select sets of various-priced balloons for the bear's balancing beams, they increase their understanding of multiplication.

$ 65.00

2196　Multisensory Math

Creative Learning, Inc.
P.O. Box 829　　　　　916-292-3001
N. San Juan, CA　95960

A challenging talking math series.

$ 600.00

2197　Number Concepts Package

Vocational and Rehabilitation Research Institute
3304 33rd St. NW　　　403-284-1121
Calgary, AB, Canada, T2　L 2A6

11 programs designed to teach number and money concepts.

$ 55.00

2198　Number Farm

Software to Go - Galluadet University
800 Florida Avenue NE　　202-651-5705
Washington, DC　20002

2199　Number Munchers

MECC
3490 Lexington Ave. N　　612-481-3611
St. Paul, MN　55126

Students hunt for number or numerical expressions.

$ 59.00

2200　Number SkillBuilder Series

Edmark Corporation
P.O. Box 3903　　　　　206-746-3900
Bellevue, WA　98009

Numerals are presented with corresponding pictures of objects.

$ 129.95

2201　Number Stumper

Software to Go - Galluadet University
800 Florida Avenue NE　　202-651-5705
Washington, DC　20002

2202　Number Words, Level I

Hartley Courseware, Inc.
P.O. Box 431　　　　　517-646-6458
Dimondale, MI　48821

Program to teach beginning students to match numerals to their appropriate number words.

$ 29.95

2203　Numeric Concepts with Memory Skills I and II

BrainTrain, Inc.
727 Twin Ridge Road　　804-320-0105
Richmond, VA　23235

Designed to train and evaluate basic math concepts and memory skills.

$ 149.00

2204　Odd One Out

Donna Stanger, Author
Sunburst Communications, Inc.
39 Washington Ave.et　　914-769-5030
Pleasantville, NY　10570

Students develop classification, discrimination and problem solving skills in 5 animated, colorful programs.

2205　Olympic Learnathon

K-12 MicroMedia Publishing
6 Arrow Road　　　　　201-825-8888
Ramsey, NJ　07446

Teaches number and letter recognition skills for preschool or remedial students.

$ 39.95

2206　Path Tactics

Software to Go - Galluadet University
800 Florida Avenue NE　　202-651-5705
Washington, DC　20002

2207　Pond

Wings for Learning, Inc.
1600 Green Hills Rd.　　408-438-5502
Scotts Valley, CA　95067

As students send a frog leaping through a maze of lily pads, they develop skills in pattern recognition, prediction and logic.

$ 65.00

2208 Prescriptive Math Drill

Hartley Courseware, Inc.
P.O. Box 431treet   **517-646-6458**
Dimondale, MI 48821

A program for students providing drill and practice in all four basic operations at difficulty and mastery levels set by the teacher.

2209 Problem Solving Basics

Learning Disabilities Association of America
4156 Library Road   **412-341-1515**
Pittsburgh, PA 15234

Helps adults develop practical mathematics skills through applications and problem solving.

$ 695.00

2210 Problem Solving Basics I, II & III

Hartley Courseware, Inc.
P.O. Box 431treet   **517-646-6458**
Dimondale, MI 48821   **800-247-1380**
    FAX 517-646-8451

Telaina Eriksen

This comprehensive math curriculum covers applications of problem solving at levels 4-11.

$ 695.00

2211 Race Car 'rithmetic

Software to Go - Galluadet University
800 Florida Avenue NE   **202-651-5705**
Washington, DC 20002

2212 Read and Solve Math Problems #1

Ann Edson, Author
Educational Activities
P.O. Box 392venue   **516-223-4666**
Freeport, Long Island, NY 11520

A tutorial and practice program for students which focuses on recognition of key words in solving arithmetic word problems, writing equations and solving word problems.

2213 Read and Solve Math Problems #2

Ann Edson, Author
Educational Activities
P.O. Box 392venue   **516-223-4666**
Freeport, Long Island, NY 11520

A tutorial and practice program for students which focuses on recognition of key words in solving two-step arithmetic problems, writing equations and solving two-step word problems.

2214 Read and Solve Math Problems #3 - Fractions: Two-Step Problems

Ann Edson, Author
Educational Activities
P.O. Box 392venue   **516-223-4666**
Freeport, Long Island, NY 11520

Designed for students, this tutorial and practice program provides initial instruction and experience in critical thinking and problem solving using fractions and mixed numbers.

2215 Robomath

MindPlay
Unit F92, P.O. Box 36491   **602-322-6365**
Tucson, AZ 85740   **800-221-7911**

A math game offering drills and practice in multiplication and division, improves regrouping skills and offers practice with whole numbers.
> *"...can be tailor made for all ability levels."*
> -School Science and Mathematics

$ 49.99

2216 Schoolcraft Math I

Kidsview Software
P.O. Box 98   **603-927-4428**
Warner, NH 03278

Five sub-systems culled from a large charactermenu and with large character display/printout.

$ 49.95

2217 Schoolcraft Miscellaneous I

Kidsview Software
P.O. Box 98   **603-927-4428**
Warner, NH 03278

Several games and topics culled from a large character menu with large character display.

$ 49.95

2218 Ships Ahoy

Software to Go - Galluadet University
800 Florida Avenue NE   **202-651-5705**
Washington, DC 20002

2219 Smart Shaper

Psychological Software Services, Inc.
6555 Carrolton Avenue   **317-257-9672**
Indianapolis, IN 46220

Eight programs that provide basic low level exercises in matching, shape recognition and counting.

$ 25.00

2220 Snoopy to the Rescue

Queue, Inc.
338 Commerce Drive   **203-335-0906**
Fairfield, CT 06430   **800-232-2224**
    FAX 203-336-2481

Thrilling game starring Snoopy offering exciting math challenges.

$ 29.95

2221 Solving Word Problems

Aquarius Instructional
P.O. Box 128
Indiana Rocks Beach, FL 34635

813-595-7890
800-338-2644
FAX 813-595-2685

Offers 3 disks on how to solve word problems.

$ 115.00

2222 Special Needs: Volume 2

Minnesota Educational Computing Consortium
6160 Summit Drive North
St. Paul, MN 55430

612-569-1500

Designed for students with motor impairments, this diskette offers five programs: a drill on four basic arithmetic operations, a drill on making change, two food web simulations, and a drill comparing written and performed pitch patterns to find the incorrect musical note.

2223 Stickybear Math: An Addition and Subtraction Program for Children

Richard Hefter, Author

Optimum Resource, Inc.
10 Station Place
Norfolk, CT 06058

203-542-5553

Individualized drill and practice in addition and subtraction at 20 levels of difficulty.

2224 Stickybear Math 2

Richard Hefter, Author

Optimum Resource, Inc.
10 Station Place
Norfolk, CT 06058

203-542-5553

An animated drill and practice program on basic multiplication and division for children.

2225 Stickybear Numbers: Counting Fun for Children

Optimum Resource, Inc.
10 Station Place
Norfolk, CT 06058

203-542-5553

A program for children designed to introduce them to computers, encourage their sense of exploration and discovery and teach them counting and number recognition skills, using colorful moving graphics.

2226 Student Pack

Don Johnston Developmental Equipment, Inc.
1000 N. Rand Road0 N. Rand Rd.
Wauconda, IL 60084

708-526-2682
800-999-4660
FAX 708-526-4177

Sets of five additional Student Workbook disks for students to work independently at home.

$ 65.00

2227 Success with Math: Addition & Subtraction

Don Ross, Author

MindPlay
1345 Diversey Pkwy.
Chicago, IL 60614

312-525-1500

A diskette for students providing drill and practice in addition with carrying and subtraction with or without borrowing.

2228 Survival Math

Sunburst Communications, Inc.
39 Washington Ave.
Pleasantville, NY 10570

914-769-5030

Shopping, making travel plans, building a playroom and running a hotdog stand give practice in calculating prices.

$ 65.00

2229 Third and Fourth Grade Math Competencies

Aquarius Instructional
P.O. Box 128
Indiana Rocks Beach, FL 34635

813-595-7890
800-338-2644
FAX 813-595-2685

Offers various programs of 40 disks on geometry, money, measurement, adding whole numbers, subtracting whole numbers and more.

$ 1175.00

2230 Timekeeper

Edmark Corporation
P.O. Box 3903
Bellevue, WA 98009

206-746-3900

Four activities designed to enhance students ability to tell time.

$ 39.95

Pre-School

2231 Alphabet with Tom and Andy

ComputAbility Corporation
40000 Grand River, #109 109
Novi, MI 48375

313-477-6720
800-433-8872

Three programs designed to teach the letters of the alphabet through exploration and discovery while making extensive use of large print and colorful graphics.

2232 Bear Jam for Exceptional Children

ComputAbility Corporation
40000 Grand River, #109 109
Novi, MI 48375

313-477-6720
800-433-8872

A lively software program emphasizing color and shape identification, matching, spatial relationships and sequencing.

2233 BearJam Body Parts

Dunamis, Inc.
3620 Highway 317   404-932-0485
Suwanee, GA 30174

Cause and effect software cues the user to find and touch various body parts on the BearJam Panda.

$ 19.95

2234 Berenstein Bears Junior Jigsaw

Britannica Software
345 Fourth Street   415-597-5555
San Francisco, CA 94107

A colorful program introducing children to shape and pattern recognition.

$ 24.95

2235 Captain's Log: Attention Skills Module

BrainTrain, Inc.
727 Twin Ridge Lane   804-320-0105
Rochmond, VA 23235

Designed to train basic cognitive functions in treatment of individuals with head injuries, learning disabilities and mental retardation.

$ 495.00

2236 Choice Board

Don Johnston Developmental Equipment, Inc.
1000 N. Rand Road0 N. Rand Rd.   708-526-2682
Wauconda, IL 60084   800-999-4660
                                   FAX 708-526-4177

Makes functional communication displays.

$ 60.00

2237 Color Find

Exceptional Children's Software
P.O. Box 487   913-625-9281
Hays, KS 67601

Helps students work with colors.

$ 19.95

2238 Color N' Canvas

Wings for Learning, Inc.
1600 Green Hills Road   408-438-5502
Scotts Valley, CA 95067

Offers various colors and palettes rather then just the standard primary colors.

$ 99.00

2239 Color Track

Easter Seals & Lehigh Valley Comp. Project
P.O. Box 3337   215-866-8092
Kulpsville, PA 19443

Suitable for the visual training of very young, disabled and cortically blind children.

$ 2.00

2240 Cotton Plus & Cotton Works

MindPlay
Unit F92, P.O. Box 36491   602-322-6365
Tucson, AZ 85740   800-221-7911

Part of the Cotton Tales Series, these two accessories offer 50 prepared worksheets containing lessons for: matching, labeling, categorizing, sorting, sequencing, phonics, math and more. They feature automatic integration, picture to word translator, colorful graphics and color printing options.

$ 99.00

2241 Cotton Tales

MindPlay
Unit F92, P.O. Box 36491   602-322-6365
Tucson, AZ 85740   800-221-7911

This program comes along with a bunny cursor guiding children through the program and helps youngsters read and write, builds basic reading skills, builds self-expression skills and improves spelling.

$ 49.99

2242 Cotton's First Files

MindPlay
Unit F92, P.O. Box 36491   602-322-6365
Tucson, AZ 85740   800-221-7911

With the help of the bouncing bunny, this program introduces database concepts-categorizing and sorting, offers practice for working with files, allows students to create personal study tools and teaches early learners to build their own files.

$ 139.00

2243 Counters

Software to Go - Galluadet University
800 Florida Avenue NE   202-651-5705
Washington, DC 20002

2244 Counting Criters

Software to Go - Galluadet University
800 Florida Avenue NE   202-651-5705
Washington, DC 20002

2245 Creature Series

Laureate Learning Systems, Inc.
110 E. Spring St.treet   802-655-4755
Winooski, VT 05404   800-562-6801
                                FAX 802-655-4757

Mary Sweig Wilson, President
Bernard Fox, Vice President

Programs designed to improve visual and auditory attention and teach cause and effect, turn taking, and switch use.

$ 65.00

2246　Curious George Visits the Library

Software to Go - Galluadet University
800 Florida Avenue NE　　　202-651-5705
Washington, DC 20002

2247　Dial Scan

Don Johnston Developmental Equipment, Inc.
1000 N. Rand Road0 N. Rand Rd.　708-526-2682
Wauconda, IL 60084　　　　　800-999-4660
　　　　　　　　　　　　FAX 708-526-4177

A rotary scanning communication aid for people who need a switch-activated communication device.

　　　　　　　　　　　$ 195.00

2248　Dinosaur Game

UCLA Intervention Program for Disabled Children
1000 Veteran Ave., #23-10　　301-825-4821
Los Angeles, CA 90024

Similar in format to Rockets to the Moon involving one to four players.

　　　　　　　　　　　$ 35.00

2249　Early and Advanced Switch Games

R.J. Cooper and Associates
24843 DelPrado, #283　　　714-240-1912
Dana Point, CA 92629

13 single switch games that start at cause/effect, work through timing and selection and graduate with matching and manipulation tasks.

　　　　　　　　　　　$ 75.00

2250　The Early Discoveries Series

Hartley Courseware, Inc.
P.O. Box 431treet　　　　517-646-6458
Dimondale, MI 48821　　　800-247-1380
　　　　　　　　　　　FAX 517-646-8451

Telaina Eriksen

This delightful series features colorful, highly interactive programs created to provide activities which stimulate early growth and development.

　　　　　　　　　　　$ 45.95

2251　Early Games for Young Children

Software to Go - Galluadet University
800 Florida Avenue NE　　　202-651-5705
Washington, DC 20002

2252　Early Learning 3.5

Don Johnston Developmental Equipment, Inc.
1000 N. Rand Road0 N. Rand Rd.　708-526-2682
Wauconda, IL 60084　　　　　800-999-4660
　　　　　　　　　　　　FAX 708-526-4177

Includes all programs from Early Learning I, II & III.

2253　Early Music Skills

Electronic Courseware Systems, Inc.
1210 Lancaster Drive　　　　217-359-7099
Champaign, IL 61821

Covers four basic music reading skills.

　　　　　　　　　　　$ 39.95

2254　Edustar's Early Childhood Special Education Programs

Edustar America, Inc.
6220 S Orange Blossom Trail #186　407-859-7059
Orlando, FL 32819　　　　　800-952-3041
　　　　　　　　　　　　FAX 407-859-7144

David Zeldin, Marketing Manager
Stewart Holtz, Curriculum Director

Integrated software program that incorporates manipulatives and special tables for learning early childhood subjects. Features include an illuminated six key keyboard,a special U-shaped "touch" table for the physically challenged and changeable mats and keys for different subject areas.

2255　Electric Coloring Book

Heartsoft, Inc.
P.O. Box 691381　　　　　800-285-3475
Tulsa, OK 74169

Teaches young students the alphabet, numbers and basic keyboarding skills by using a graphic coloring concept.

　　　　　　　　　　　$ 39.95

2256　Exploratory Play

Don Johnston Developmental Equipment, Inc.
1000 N. Rand Road0 N. Rand Rd.　708-526-2682
Wauconda, IL 60084　　　　　800-999-4660
　　　　　　　　　　　　FAX 708-526-4177

Software for Muppet Learning Keys.

　　　　　　　　　　　$ 150.00

2257　E-Z Pilot II Authoring System

Hartley Courseware, Inc.
P.O. Box 431　　　　　　　517-646-6458
Dimondale, MI 48821

Authoring language can be used to develop interactive tutorials for any subject.

　　　　　　　　　　　$ 79.95

2258　Garden Series 1 and 2

Focus Media
839 Stewart Avenue　　　　516-794-8900
Garden City, NY 11530

Provides an integrated learning approach to promote reading and math readiness by combining stories, songs, dicussions and art projects.

　　　　　　　　　　　$ 249.00

2259   Interaction Games

Don Johnston Developmental Equipment, Inc.
1000 N. Rand Road0 N. Rand Rd.   708-526-2682
Wauconda, IL 60084   800-999-4660
                                                     FAX 708-526-4177

The original leisure time program written for two switch users to play at the same time.

$ 65.00

2260   Interaction Games II

Don Johnston Developmental Equipment, Inc.
1000 N. Rand Road0 N. Rand Rd.   708-526-2682
Wauconda, IL 60084   800-999-4660
                                                     FAX 708-526-4177

Two players improve their single switch skills with six new games.

$ 65.00

2261   Join the Circus

Don Johnston Developmental Equipment, Inc.
1000 N. Rand Road0 N. Rand Rd.   708-526-2682
Wauconda, IL 60084   800-999-4660
                                                     FAX 708-526-4177

This exciting program takes place in the center ring with single switch input controlling the action.

$ 49.95

2262   Joystick Games

Technology for Language and Learning
P.O. Box 327   516-625-4550
East Rockaway, NY 11518

Five volumes of public domain joystick programs.

$ 28.50

2263   Kid Fun - Songs for Children

MindPlay
Unit F92, P.O. Box 36491   602-322-6365
Tucson, AZ 85740   800-221-7911

Cindy the songlady, teacher, children's recording artist and performer, brings youngsters her lively music that enhances self-esteem, sparks imagination and stimulates creativity.
"...helps children learn that they can choose to be happy...Their attitudes affect other people."
-Early Childhood News
$ 10.95

2264   Kidsview

Kidsview Software
P.O. Box 98   603-927-4428
Warner, NH 03278

Utility that allows all normal functions of the computer to operate with large print display.

$ 39.95

2265   Kindercomp Gold

Software to Go - Galluadet University
800 Florida Avenue NE   202-651-5705
Washington, DC 20002

2266   Learn to Scan

Don Johnston Developmental Equipment, Inc.
1000 N. Rand Road0 N. Rand Rd.   708-526-2682
Wauconda, IL 60084   800-999-4660
                                                     FAX 708-526-4177

Teach elements of scanning with a single switch.

$ 60.00

2267   Leo's Lectric Paintbrush

Dunamis, Inc.
3620 Highway 317   404-932-0485
Suwanee, GA 30174

As the student touches the PowerPad, a mark is registered on the monitor screen.

$ 29.95

2268   Math Magic - Elementary Math Skills

MindPlay
Unit F92, P.O. Box 36491   602-322-6365
Tucson, AZ 85740   800-221-7911

This program builds elementary math skills, teaches basic counting, builds addition and subtraction skills, offers drill and practice, encourages working with two or three-part questions, teachers working with horizontal and vertical presentation of math problems and lets you choose to work with or without graphics.
"One of the most versatile educational programs."
-USA Today
$ 49.99

2269   Mouse in the Toy Box

Don Johnston Developmental Equipment, Inc.
1000 N. Rand Road   708-526-2682
Wauconda, IL 60084

A collection of nine activities that specifically train for use of the mouse.

2270   Multiple Choices

MindPlay
1345 Diversey Pkwy.   312-525-1500
Chicago, IL 60614

Adapts to any subject matter, any grade level, or any learning style.

$ 59.95

2271   Muppetville

Sunburst Communications, Inc.
39 Washington Ave.   914-769-5030
Pleasantville, NY 10570

Travel to scenic Muppetville and learn about shapes, colors and letters.

$ 65.00

2272 Number Words Level I

Software to Go - Galluadet University
800 Florida Avenue NE   202-651-5705
Washington, DC 20002

2273 Old MacDonald I

UCLA Intervention Program for Disabled Children
1000 Veteran Ave., #23-10   301-825-4821
Los Angeles, CA 90024

Six farm animals are depicted on a PowerPad overlay in a familiar nursery school song.

$ 35.00

2274 Old MacDonald's Farm

KidTECH
21274 Oak Knoll   805-822-1663
Tehachapi, CA 93561

Utilizes the all-time favorite children's song to teach vocabulary and animal sounds to young children.

$ 30.00

2275 One Banana More

Data Command, Inc.
P.O. Box 548   800-528-7390
Kankakee, IL 60901

Program teaches matching shapes, sizes, letter recognition, word recognition and counting objects.

$ 39.95

2276 Padded Vehicles

UCLA Intervention Program for Disabled Children
1000 Veteran Ave., #23-10   301-825-4821
Los Angeles, CA 90024

Program for one to six players identifying 10 vehicles.

$ 35.00

2277 Pick 'n Stick Color Packs, Primary Packs and Food Packs

Don Johnston Developmental Equipment, Inc.
1000 N. Rand Road0 N. Rand Rd.   708-526-2682
Wauconda, IL 60084   800-999-4660
        FAX 708-526-4177

Full color illustrations for communication boards.

2278 PICSYMS

Don Johnston Developmental Equipment, Inc.
1000 N. Rand Road0 N. Rand Rd.   708-526-2682
Wauconda, IL 60084   800-999-4660
        FAX 708-526-4177

Open-ended visual language system, flexible enough to incorporate customized symbols for specific vocabulary needs.

$ 25.00

2279 Picture Communication Symbols

Don Johnston Developmental Equipment, Inc.
1000 N. Rand Road0 N. Rand Rd.   708-526-2682
Wauconda, IL 60084   800-999-4660
        FAX 708-526-4177

Simple, clear drawings for individual communication aids.

2280 Picture Perfect

MindPlay
Unit F92, P.O. Box 36491   602-322-6365
Tucson, AZ 85740   800-221-7911

While helping students create pretty pictures or poetic paragraphs, Picture Perfect also introduces computer graphics, builds self-expression skills, improves writing and illustration skills, develops spelling and creative writing skills, improves language art skills and allows users to make original coloring or story books.

$ 49.99

2281 Pictures Program

The Speech Bin
1965 Twenty-Fifth Avenue   407-770-0007
Vero Beach, FL 32960   FAX 407-770-0006

Jan J. Binney, Editor In Chief
Barbara Hector, Office Manager

Three different programs with two levels of operation. One teaches the names and the other functions of the six picturs displayed.

$ 99.50

2282 Play and Match

Easter Seals & Lehigh Valley Comp. Project
P.O. Box 3337   215-866-8092
Kulpsville, PA 19443

This software requires a small extended keyboard to be constructed.

$ 2.00

2283 Power Pad Early Learning Package

ComputAbility Corporation
40000 Grand River, #109 109   313-477-6720
Novi, MI 48375   800-433-8872

A complete early learning tool with large clear graphics, bold overlays and speech reinforcement.

2284 PuzzleMaker

Edmark Corporation
P.O. Box 3903   206-746-3900
Bellevue, WA 98009

Students unscramble puzzle pieces to build a picture.

$ 39.95

2285 Rabbit Scanner

Don Johnston Developmental Equipment, Inc.
1000 N. Rand Road0 N. Rand Rd.   708-526-2682
Wauconda, IL 60084   800-999-4660
                                    FAX 708-526-4177

Implements goals of left to right scanning, introducing the timing aspect of scanning and one-to-one correspondence.
$ 39.95

2286 Race the Clock

MindPlay
Unit F92, P.O. Box 36491   602-322-6365
Tucson, AZ 85740   800-221-7911

Offers children colorful animated graphics and hidden words improving communication skills, memorization skills and builds quick response.
"Recommended...can be used by students with a wide range of skills."
-Electronic Learning
$ 49.99

2287 Reactions

Don Johnston Developmental Equipment, Inc.
1000 N. Rand Road0 N. Rand Rd.   708-526-2682
Wauconda, IL 60084   800-999-4660
                                    FAX 708-526-4177

This program presents cause-effect principles in six colorful games.
$ 60.00

2288 Reading Starters

Houghton Mifflin School Division
One Memorial Drive   617-725-5022
Cambridge, MA 02178

Provides beginning reading students with supplemental early reading experiences to develop the skills needed to become a more proficient readers.
$ 135.00

2289 Representational Play

Don Johnston Developmental Equipment, Inc.
1000 N. Rand Road0 N. Rand Rd.   708-526-2682
Wauconda, IL 60084   800-999-4660
                                    FAX 708-526-4177

Software for Muppet Learning Keys offering games of Doll Play and Car Play.
$ 150.00

2290 Run Rabbit Run

Don Johnston Developmental Equipment, Inc.
1000 N. Rand Road0 N. Rand Rd.   708-526-2682
Wauconda, IL 60084   800-999-4660
                                    FAX 708-526-4177

This program concentrates on choice-making and visual tracking skills.
$ 29.95

2291 School Activity SkillBuilder Series

Edmark Corporation
P.O. Box 3903   206-746-3900
Bellevue, WA 98009

Programs introduce or review the steps, procedures and vocabulary of school-based activities.
$ 339.95

2292 Shape and Color Rodeo

DLM Teaching Resources
One DLM Park   214-248-6300
Allen, TX 75002

Children learn recognition and identification of common shapes and color discriminations.
$ 32.95

2293 Shutterbug's Patterns

MCE, a Division of Lawrence Productions
1800 S. 35th St.   616-665-7075
Galesburg, MI 49078

Helps develop pattern recognition skills.
$ 69.95

2294 Silly Sandwich

UCLA Intervention Program for Disabled Children
1000 Veteran Ave., #23-10   301-825-4821
Los Angeles, CA 90024

Build a silly sandwich selecting from six to twelve different items depicted on a PowerPad overlay.
$ 35.00

2295 Simon Says

Sunburst Communications, Inc.
39 Washington Ave.   914-769-5030
Pleasantville, NY 10570

Students practice a memory strategy called chaining, remembering items in a sequence.
$ 65.00

2296 Star-U-Are

MindPlay
Unit F92, P.O. Box 36491   602-322-6365
Tucson, AZ 85740   800-221-7911

Guided visualization audio tapes builds childrens self-esteem and teaches them to love themselves.
"A laudable concept which could be easily integrated into elementary classrooms by teachers."
-Media Evaluation Service
$ 39.00

2297 Stickybear Opposites

Software to Go - Galluadet University
800 Florida Avenue NE   202-651-5705
Washington, DC 20002

2298 Switch It-Change It

UCLA Intervention Program for Disabled Children
1000 Veteran Ave., #23-10   301-825-4821
Los Angeles, CA 90024

Cause and effect program presents color, animated common objects.

$ 35.00

2299 There's a Mouse in the Toybox

Don Johnston Developmental Equipment, Inc.
1000 N. Rand Road0 N. Rand Rd.   708-526-2682
Wauconda, IL 60084   800-999-4660
                                  FAX 708-526-4177

A delightful mouse training program for the Apple IIGS, learners can master "point and click" and "click and drag" with this assortment of colorful activities.

$ 60.00

2300 Touch 'n Match

Don Johnston Developmental Equipment, Inc.
1000 N. Rand Road0 N. Rand Rd.   708-526-2682
Wauconda, IL 60084   800-999-4660
                                  FAX 708-526-4177

Teach and drill basic matching, association and discrimination skills.

$ 29.95

2301 Touch 'n See

Don Johnston Developmental Equipment, Inc.
1000 N. Rand Road0 N. Rand Rd.   708-526-2682
Wauconda, IL 60084   800-999-4660
                                  FAX 708-526-4177

Practice concentration skills in this memory game.

$ 39.95

2302 Touch Window Early Learning Package

ComputAbility Corporation
40000 Grand River, #109 109   313-477-6720
Novi, MI 48375   800-433-8872

An early learning tool with programs designed at the Handicapped Children's Computer Center.

2303 Visual Communication Naming

The Speech Bin
1965 Twenty-Fifth Avenue   407-770-0007
Vero Beach, FL 32960   FAX 407-770-0006

Jan J. Binney, Editor In Chief
Barbara Hector, Office Manager

This program offers 60 pictures and it can be updated by adding new pictures from the list of Real Life Picture Programs offered.

$ 129.50

2304 Word Pieces

Software to Go - Galluadet University
800 Florida Avenue NE   202-651-5705
Washington, DC 20002

Problem Solving

2305 Essential Learning Systems

Creative Education Institute
P.O. Box 7306   817-751-1188
Waco, TX 76714   800-234-7319

Enables the special education, learning disabled and dyslexic student to develop the skills they need to learn. Using computer exercises to appropriately stimulate the brain's language areas, the lagging learning skills can be developed and patterns of correct language taught.

2306 Fun with Directions

MindPlay
1345 Diversey Pkwy.   312-525-1500
Chicago, IL 60614

The three activities in this program provide ways for students to develop the concepts of directionality.

$ 49.95

2307 Gremlin Hunt

Merit Software
13635 Gamma Road   214-385-2353
Dallas, TX 75244

Gremlins test visual discrimination and memory skills at three levels.

$ 9.95

2308 Learning Improvement Series

MCE, a Division of Lawrence Productions
1800 S. 35th St.   616-665-7075
Galesburg, MI 49078

Three programs assisting in the development of skills necessary for success in learning.

$ 189.95

2309 Lego

Krell Software
Flowerfield Bldg. #7   516-584-7900
St. James, NY 11788

A method of learning math, computer literacy and thinking skills.

$ 74.95

2310 Leo's Links

Dunamis, Inc.
3620 Highway 317   404-932-0485
Suwanee, GA 30174

This game allows a student to draw a golf course on the PowerPad complete with fairway, traps and putting surface.

$ 39.95

2311   LogicMaster

Dunamis, Inc.
3620 Highway 317
Suwanee, GA 30174   404-932-0485

A problem solving game for more cognitively-mature students.

$ 39.95

2312   Magic Music Balloon

Temporal Acuity Products, Inc.
300-120th Avenue NE   206-462-1007
Bellevue, WA 98005

Provides the first steps in melodic discrimination, determining whether a brief melody goes up, down or stays the same.

$ 30.00

2313   Master Match

Advanced Ideas, Inc.
680 Hawthorne Drive   415-425-5086
Tiburon, CA 94920

Enhances visual memory skills by letting the user find matches in images and words under numbered mystery squares.

$ 39.95

2314   Memory Building Blocks

Sunburst Communications, Inc.
39 Washington Ave.   914-769-5030
Pleasantville, NY 10570

Students discover the power of memory strategies in meeting the challenges of five concentration-type games.

$ 65.00

2315   Memory Castle

Sunburst Communications, Inc.
39 Washington Ave.   914-769-5030
Pleasantville, NY 10570

This adventure game introduces students to several memory strategies designed to help them remeber instructions and follow directions.

$ 65.00

2316   Memory I

Psychological Software Services, Inc.
6555 Carrolton Avenue   317-257-9672
Indianapolis, IN 46220

Consists of four computer programs designed to provide verbal and nonverbal memory exercises.

$ 110.00

2317   Memory II

Psychological Software Services, Inc.
6555 Carrolton Avenue   317-257-9672
Indianapolis, IN 46220

These programs allow for work with encoding, categorizing and organizing skills.

$ 150.00

2318   Memory Machine

Sunburst Communications, Inc.
39 Washington Ave.   914-769-5030
Pleasantville, NY 10570

Asks students to view, study and recall, through memeory strategies what they have read and seen.

$ 65.00

2319   Monkey Business

Merit Software
13635 Gamma Road   214-385-2353
Dallas, TX 75244

Choose one of the three levels of difficulty and play until a minimum score is reached.

$ 10.95

2320   The Moon and Its Phases

SouthWest Ed Psych Services, Inc.
2001 W. Silvergate Dr.   602-253-6528
Chandler, AZ 85224

Explains the moon's phase cycle and is self-pacing and interactive with graphics, memory aids and techniques for dealing with sequencing, directionality and attention problems.

$ 39.95

2321   Mosaix/VGA

Data Assist
651 Lakeview Plaza Blvd.   614-888-8088
Columbus, OH 43085

An electronic jigsaw puzzle program that uses digitized photographic images as its puzzles.

$ 59.00

2322   Number Please

Merit Software
13635 Gamma Road   214-385-2353
Dallas, TX 75244

Students are challenged to remember combinations of 4, 7 and 10 digit numbers.

$ 9.95

2323   Problem Solving

Psychological Software Services, Inc.
6555 Carrolton Avenue   317-257-9672
Indianapolis, IN 46220

Nine computer programs designed to challenge high functioning patients/students with tasks requiring logic.

$ 150.00

2324   Puzzle Storybook

First Byte
19840 Pioneer Ave.   800-523-2983
Torrance, CA 90503

Helps students build early problem solving skills.

$ 49.95

2325 Same Or Different

Merit Software
13635 Gamma Road   214-385-2353
Dallas, TX 75244

Requires students to make important visual discriminations which involve shape, color and whole/part relationships.

$ 9.95

2326 Scrambled Eggs

Merit Software
13635 Gamma Road   214-385-2353
Dallas, TX 75244

Deductive logic and problem solving are the primary skills developed in the variation of the game MASTERMIND.

$ 9.95

2327 Sebastian II

Temporal Acuity Products, Inc.
300-120th Ave. NE   206-462-1007
Bellevue, WA 98005

Develops aural and visual discrimination through melodic error detection.

$ 125.00

2328 Sliding Block

Merit Software
13635 Gamma Road   214-385-2353
Dallas, TX 75244

Learners rearrange one of the four pictures which can be scrambled at five seperate levels to test visual discrimination and problem solving skills.

$ 9.95

2329 Soft Tools '90, '91

Psychological Software Services, Inc.
6555 Carrolton Avenue   317-257-9672
Indianapolis, IN 46220

Menu-driven disk versions of the computer programs published in the Cognitive Rehabilitation Journal.

$ 50.00

2330 Sound Match

Enable/Schneier Communication Unit
1603 Court Street   315-455-7591
Syracuse, NY 13208

Presents a variety of sounds/noises requiring gross levels of auditory discrimination and matching.

$ 25.00

2331 Teddy and Iggy

Sunburst Communications, Inc.
39 Washington Ave.   914-769-5030
Pleasantville, NY 10570

Students use chaining to remember the items in sequence.

$ 65.00

2332 Teenage Switch and TouchWindow Progressions

R.J. Cooper and Associates
24843 DelPrado, #283   714-240-1912
Dana Point, CA 92629

Five activities for teenage persons working on switch training, attention training, life skills simulation and following directions.

$ 75.00

2333 What's in a Frame

Sunburst Communications, Inc.
39 Washington Ave.   914-769-5030
Pleasantville, NY 10570

Brightly colored objects appear in a frame and students must remeber what they saw, using two memory strategies.

$ 65.00

2334 Worksheet Generator

Creative Learning, Inc.
P.O. Box 829   916-292-3001
N. San Juan, CA 95960

A creative tool that allows teachers to create instructional materials in large type.

$ 89.95

Professional

2335 Assistive Device Information Network

University Hospital School
The University Of Iowa   800-331-3027
Iowa City, IA 52242

2336 Attention/Selective Attention

ComputAbility Corporation
40000 Grand River, #109 109   313-477-6720
Novi, MI 48375   800-433-8872

Three programs designed to address the arousal, capacity and selectivity components of attention.

2337 AutoEDMS 2.1

ACS Telecom
25825 Eshelman Avenue   310-325-3055
Lomita, CA 90717   FAX 310-325-3059

Automates the job of creating, editing, distributing and storing your documents, drawings, scanned images and files.

2338 Becoming a Champion

CGP - Chronicle Guidance Publications, Inc.
P.O. Box 1190   800-622-7284
Moravia, NY 13118

A motivational tool for positive growth offers a unique skill building program with built-in continuity for positive intervention from kindergarten through grade 12.

2339 Beyond Drill and Practice: Expanding the Computer Mainstream

The Council for Exceptional Children
1920 Association Drive   703-620-3660
Reston, VA 22091

Provides informative guidelines and examples for teachers who want to expand the use of the computer as a learning tool.

$ 18.00

2340 Brunswick Cognitive Programs By EET

ComputAbility Corporation
40000 Grand River, #109 109   313-477-6720
Novi, MI 48375   800-433-8872

Developed by OT's at the Brunswick Hospital Center.

2341 Cambridge Development Laboratory, Inc.

P.O. Box 605   800-637-0047
Newton Lower Falls, MA 02162

2342 Can't Wait to Communicate!

Don Johnston Developmental Equipment, Inc.
1000 N. Rand Road0 N. Rand Rd.   708-526-2682
Wauconda, IL 60084   800-999-4660
                                 FAX 708-526-4177

A collection of fun activities for working with nonspeaking students that belongs on the teacher's reference shelf.

$ 24.00

2343 Captain's Log

ComputAbility Corporation
40000 Grand River, #109 109   313-477-6720
Novi, MI 48375   800-433-8872

A complete evaluation and treatment system for the assessment and remediation of cognitive/perceptual motor deficits.

2344 CE Software

1854 Fuller Road
West Des Moines, IA 50265

2345 Checkmate Technology, Inc.

509 South Rockford Drive   602-966-5802
Tempe, AZ 85281

2346 Claris Corporation

5201 Patrick Nehry Drive   800-334-3535
Santa Clara, CA 95052

2347 Classification Series

Aquarius Instructional
P.O. Box 128   813-595-7890
Indian Rocks Beach, FL 34635

Curriculum-based programs are learning units containing matching, sorting, form and object, and familiar settings.

$ 75.00

2348 Cognitive Disorders Series

ComputAbility Corporation
40000 Grand River, #109 109   313-477-6720
Novi, MI 48375   800-433-8872

This popular 4 diskette series requires limited keyboard usage for reinforcement training in the areas of category discrimination and completion, category naming, visual attention and perception.

2349 The Colorworks Diskette Organizing System

Learning Disabilities Association of America
4156 Library Road   412-341-1515
Pittsburgh, PA 15234

Software and resource storage to custom plan for instruction, check-out and integration into curriculum.

2350 Communication Board Builder

Don Johnston Developmental Equipment, Inc.
1000 N. Rand Road0 N. Rand Rd.   708-526-2682
Wauconda, IL 60084   800-999-4660
                                 FAX 708-526-4177

Constructs communication boards for teachers.

$ 169.00

2351 Compucon

62 Fulton Avenue   516-361-5344
Smithtown, NY 11787

2352 CompuServe Education Forum

LINC Resources, Inc.
4820 Indianola Avenue   614-885-5599
Columbus, OH 43214

2353 Computer Learning Foundation

P.O. Box 60007   415-858-1103
Palo Alto, CA 94306

2354 The Conover Company

P.O. Box 155   414-685-5707
Omro, WI 54963

2355 CRISP

Nat'l Inst. of Health, Division of Research Grants
Westwood Bldg., Room 148   301-496-7543
BethesdaGrove, MD 20892

A Computer Retrieval of Information On Scientific Projects is a major scientific information system containing data on the research programs suppoirted by the US Public Health Service.

2356 D.C. Health and Company

125 Spring Street   800-235-3565
Lexington, MA 02173

2357   Discrimination/Memory

ComputAbility Corporation
40000 Grand River, #109 109   313-477-6720
Novi, MI 48375   800-433-8872

Six programs designed to evaluate and treat deficits in
visual communication and memory skills.

2358   DLM Teaching Resources

One DLM Park   800-527-4747
Allen, TX 75002

2359   Dunamis, Inc.

3620 Highway 317   404-932-0485
Suwanee, GA 30174

2360   EdLINC

P.O. Box 14325   800-736-1405
Columbus, OH 43214

2361   Edmark Corporation

P.O. Box 3903   800-426-0856
Bellevue, WA 98009

2362   The Educational Software Center

P.O. Box 31849   206-784-9226
Seattle, WA 98103

2363   The Educational Software Selector

P.O. Box 246   207-737-4763
Dresden, ME 04342

2364   File-Talk

GW Micro
310 Racquet Drive   219-483-3625
Fort Wayne, IN 46825   FAX 219-484-2510

Talking database and forms processor.

2365   Filling Out Job Applications

Holly Argue, Author

MCE, a Division of Lawrence Productions
1800 S. 35th St.   616-665-7075
Galesburg, MI 49078

Designed for adolescents and adults in basic education
classes providing one-step analyses and completion of
typical job applications.

2366   Hartley Courseware, Inc.

133 Bridge   800-247-1380
Dimondale, MI 48821

2367   Higher Education with Adult Training for People with Handicaps

One DuPont Circle NW, Ste. 800   202-939-9320
Washington, DC 20036   800-544-3284

2368   Hyper-ABLEDATA

Trace Research and Development Cetnter
1500 Highland Avenue   608-262-6966
Madison, WI 53705

A microcomputer based version of ABLEDATA assistive
technology database.

$ 50.00

2369   HyperScreen 2.0

Scholastic
730 Broadway   212-505-6006
New York, NY 10003

Allows teachers to create self-booting, interactive lessons
on the computer.

$ 124.95

2370   IBM/Special Needs Exchange

LINC Resources
P.O. Box 18707   703-439-1492
Washington, DC 20036

2371   Individual Study Center

Teach Yourself By Computer Software
3400 Monroe Avenue   716-381-5450
Rochester, NY 14618

A test and drill program with learning games and activities.

$ 29.95

2372   The Information Center for Special Education Media & Materials

LINC Resources, Inc.
4820 Indianola Avenue   614-885-5599
Columbus, OH 43214   800-772-7372

2373   International Society for Technology in Education

University of Oregon
1787 Agate Street   503-346-4414
Eugene, OR 97403

2374   Keyboard Assessment Program

Assistive Device Center, School of Engineering
California State University   916-278-6422
Sacramento, CA 95819

Program gathers and compiles data about track time,
select time and multiple key selection.

$ 40.00

2375 Laureate Learning Systems, Inc.

110 East Spring Street   802-655-4755
Winowski, VT 05454

2376 The Learning Company

6493 Kaiser Drive   415-792-2101
Fremont, CA 94555   800-852-2255

2377 Macromind, Inc.

410 Townsend Street   415-332-0200
San Francisco, CA 94107

2378 MECC

3490 Lexington Avenue North   612-481-3500
St. Paul, MN 55112   800-228-3504

2379 Mediagenic

3885 Bohannon Drive   415-329-0500
Menlo Park, CA 94025

2380 Microsoft Corporation

One Microsoft Way   206-882-8088
Redmond, WA 98052   800-227-4679

2381 Mindscape, Inc.

3444 Dundee Road   800-999-2242
Northbrook, IL 60062

2382 Multiple Choices

MindPlay
1345 Diversey Pkwy.   312-525-1500
Chicago, IL 60614

Designed for teachers this is a tool program that allows the creation of puzzles, quizzes, games and activity sheets for practice, play, study or testing.

2383 Noteworthy

GW Micro
310 Racquet Drive   219-483-3625
Fort Wayne, IN 46825   FAX 219-484-2510

A "pop-up" notetaker for the IBM and compatibles.

2384 Objectives for the Brigance Diagnostic Comprehensive Inventory of Skills

Albert Brigance, Author

Curriculum Associates, Inc.
5 Esquire Road   508-667-8000
North Billerica, MA 01862   FAX 508-667-5706

Designed for use with Tally Goals and Objective Writer, this diskette with 22 goals and 230 objectives, with room for up to 500 goals and objectives, focuses on readiness, reading, listening, spelling, language, math, research and study skills.

2385 Overlay Express

Don Johnston Developmental Equipment, Inc.
1000 N. Rand Road0 N. Rand Rd.   708-526-2682
Wauconda, IL 60084   800-999-4660
    FAX 708-526-4177

A time-saving tool for those who construct custom paper overlays for the Unicorn Board. Users select pictures, position squares, choose icon size and print overlays.

$ 140.00

2386 PEAL Software

5000 N. Parkway, Ste. 105   818-883-7849
Calabasas, CA 91372

2387 PEAR

Pearamount Educational Products, Inc.
RR 2, Box 811   802-457-3300
Woodstock, VT 05091

Easy-to-use computer program that can cut hours of time it takes professionals to generate Woodcock-Johnson reports, allowing more analysis and interpretation time.

2388 Peripheral Tester

Don Johnston Developmental Equipment, Inc.
1000 N. Rand Road0 N. Rand Rd.   708-526-2682
Wauconda, IL 60084   800-999-4660
    FAX 708-526-4177

Provides a quick way to troubleshoot adaptive computer hardware.

$ 39.95

2389 The Porter

Don Johnston Developmental Equipment, Inc.
1000 N. Rand Road0 N. Rand Rd.   708-526-2682
Wauconda, IL 60084   800-999-4660
    FAX 708-526-4177

Connects up to four peripherals to a multi-port extender.

2390 Print Module

Failure Free
137 Corban Court   800-542-2170
Concord, NC 28025

Includes teacher's manual, instructional readers, flashcards, independent activities and illustrated independent reading booklets.

$ 499.00

2391 Resources for Job Hunting

Florence Taber, Author

MCE, a Division of Lawrence Productions
1800 S. 35th St.   616-665-7075
Galesburg, MI 49078

A program to help secondary and adult special needs students find a job and the places to go for assistance.

2392 Rocky's Boots

Warren Robinett, Author

The Learning Company
6493 Kaiser Drive   510-792-2101
Freemont, CA 94555

Teaches the basics of logic and computer circuitry through any of 39 different games.

2393   Scholastic, Inc.

2931 East McCarty Street   800-541-5513
Jefferson City, MO 65102

2394   Software Ventures Corporation

2907 Claremont Avenue, Ste. 220   415-644-3232
Berkeley, CA 94705

2395   SpecialNet

GTE Education Services, Inc.
8505 Freeport Parkway   800-634-5644
Irving, TX 75063

2396   Spinnaker Software

One Kendall Square
Cambridge, MA 01239

2397   Strategic Simulations

675 Almanor Avenue   408-737-6800
Sunnyvale, CA 94086

2398   Sunburst Communications

39 Washington Avenue   914-769-5030
Pleasantville, NY 10570   800-431-1934

2399   Symmetry Corporation

761 East University Drive #C   800-624-2485
Mesa, AZ 85203

2400   Talley Goals and Objectives Writer

Martha Talley, Author

Curriculum Associates, Inc.
5 Esquire Road   508-667-8000
North Billerica, MA 01862   FAX 508-667-5706

Designed for teacher use in creating and printing individualized education programs.

2401   Tell 'Em Ware

Department TM
1714 Olson Way
Marshalltown, IA 50158

2402   Term-Talk

GW Micro
310 Racquet Drive   219-483-3625
Fort Wayne, IN 46825   FAX 219-484-2510

A talking data communication program.

2403   Test of Language Development - Primary 2 (TOLD-2P)

UNITED Educational Services, Inc.
P.O. Box 1099   800-458-7900
Buffalo, NY 14224

This program allows test users to accurately and quickly score the TOLD-2 Primary.

$ 80.00

2404   Testmaster

Research Design Associates
10 Boulevard Ave.   516-754-5280
Greenlawn, NY 11740

A new concept in question and answer testing with an Exploratory Mode which allows students to explore a range of answers.

$ 199.95

2405   Trace Center

1500 Highland Avenue   608-262-6966
Madison, WI 53705

2406   UCLA/LAUSD Microcomputer Team

1000 Veterns Avenue   213-825-4821
Los Angeles, CA 90024

2407   United Software Industries

22231 Mulholland Highway, Ste.   818-887-5800
212A
Woodland Hills, CA 91364

2408   Visual/Perceptual Diagnostic Testing and Training By EET

ComputAbility Corporation
40000 Grand River, #109 109   313-477-6720
Novi, MI 48375   800-433-8872

An integrated 14 diskette package designed to aid in the diagnosis and treatment of many visual/perceptual problems associated with brain injury.

2409   Voc Report

Conover Company
P.O. Box 155   800-800-933-
Omro, WI 54963

A word processing-type program which summarizes a wide range of vocational, educational and personal data on a person's background.

$ 110.00

2410   WAIS-Riter BASIC

Southern Micro Systems
3545 S. Church Street   919-548-1661
Burlington, NC 27215

Provides the psychologist with a comprehensive client interpretation in less then three minutes.

$ 199.00

2411   Word-Talk

GW Micro
310 Racquet Drive   219-483-3625
Fort Wayne, IN 46825   FAX 219-484-2510

A full-featured word processing program that uses synthe-sized speech as well as the screen.

Reading

2412   Ace Reading Series

MindPlay
Unit F92, P.O. Box 36491   602-322-6365
Tucson, AZ 85740   800-221-7911

Available individual or as a series.   Players become reporters, explorers and detectives and even host their own talk show as they read to uncover clues to succeed in their missions. The Series includes Ace Reporter, Ace Reporter Deluxe, Ace Explorer, Ace Detective and Ace Inquirer.

$ 169.00

2413   Alphabet Sounds

Data Command, Inc.
P.O. Box 548
Kankakee, IL 60901   800-528-7390

An early childhood pre-reading skill software program.

$ 84.95

2414   aMAZEing Ways

Don Johnston Developmental Equipment, Inc.
1000 N. Rand Road0 N. Rand Rd.   708-526-2682
Wauconda, IL 60084   800-999-4660
                                        FAX 708-526-4177

This program has a selection of activities for training the concepts of up, down and sideways.

$ 80.00

2415   An Open Book

Learning Disabilities Association of America
4156 Library Road   412-341-1515
Pittsburgh, PA 15234

A reading tool that works with IBM PC for the person with a disability that affects reading.

$ 995.00

2416   Analogies Tutorial

Hartley Courseware, Inc.
P.O. Box 431treet   517-646-6458
Dimondale, MI 48821   800-247-1380
                                       FAX 517-646-8451

Telaina Eriksen

The content uses simple vocabulary to demonstrate each type of analogy and to teach a step-by-step method of solving analogy problems.

$ 59.95

2417   Aphasia Programs

ComputAbility Corporation
40000 Grand River, #109 109   313-477-6720
Novi, MI 48375   800-433-8872

Set of 8 confidence building diskettes for use by aphasics and others with reading problems.

2418   Basic Reading Skills

Aquarius Instructional
P.O. Box 128   813-595-7890
Indiana Rocks Beach, FL 34635   800-338-2644
                                       FAX 813-595-2685

These programs are designed to encourage students to learn and use critical thinking skills.

$ 550.00

2419   The Boars in Camelot

Queue, Inc.
338 Commerce Drive   203-335-0906
Fairfield, CT 06430   800-232-2224
                                       FAX 203-336-2481

Written in an upbeat and amusing style to capture students' interest as they interact with the story by answering questions about what they have read.

$ 45.00

2420   BookWise

Learning Disabilities Association of America
4156 Library Road   412-341-1515
Pittsburgh, PA 15234

A unique teaching tool for teachers and their students.

$ 7295.00

2421   Bozons' Quest

Laureate Learning Systems, Inc.
110 E. Spring St.treet   802-655-4755
Winooski, VT 05404   800-562-6801
                                       FAX 802-655-4757

Mary Sweig Wilson, President
Bernard Fox, Vice President

A computer game designed to teach cognitive skills and strategies and left/right discrimination skills.

$ 65.00

2422   Brainz-Builder One

ComputAbility Corporation
40000 Grand River, #109 109   313-477-6720
Novi, MI 48375   800-433-8872

Large type, speech supported authoring system.

2423   Brick By Brick

Learning Disabilities Association of America
4156 Library Road   412-341-1515
Pittsburgh, PA 15234

Reading program that helps build a sight vocabulary which is then used to build usage and comprehension.

$ 2975.00

2424 Camelephant

Don Johnston Developmental Equipment, Inc.
1000 N. Rand Road0 N. Rand Rd.   708-526-2682
Wauconda, IL 60084   800-999-4660
                                    FAX 708-526-4177

Start out with cause and effect and move on to decision making with this early learning program.

$ 65.00

2425 CARIS

Looking Glass Learning Products, Inc.
276 Howare Avenue   800-545-5457
Des Plaines, IL 60018

Introduces reading skills to low readiness, very young or learning disabled students.

$ 59.00

2426 Chariots, Cougars & Kings: Building Comprehension II

Janet Goldman, Author

Hartley Courseware, Inc.
P.O. Box 431treet   517-646-6458
Dimondale, MI 48821

A reading comprehension skill building program with 20 stories for students focusing on sequencing events, predicting outcomes, vocabulary, drawing conclusions, making judgements and indentifying pronouns.

2427 Charlie Brown's ABC's

Software to Go - Galluadet University
800 Florida Avenue NE   202-651-5705
Washington, DC 20002

2428 Circletime Tales

Don Johnston Developmental Equipment, Inc.
1000 N. Rand Road0 N. Rand Road   708-526-2682
Wauconda, IL 60084   800-999-4660
                                    FAX 708-526-4177

Paula Kwit, Vice President
Ruth Ziolowski, Sales Manager

Bright and lively group activities brought to life by creative animation.

$ 95.00

2429 Compu-Read

Edu-Ware Services, Inc.
Atlanta, GA

An adjustable reading program for students designed to improve reading speed and recall.

2430 CONCENTRATE! on Words and Concepts

Laureate Learning Systems, Inc.
110 E. Spring St.treet   802-655-4755
Winooski, VT 05404   800-562-6801
                                    FAX 802-655-4757

Mary Sweig Wilson, President
Bernard Fox, Vice President

A series of educational games that reinforces the lessons of the Words and Concepts Series while developing short term memory skills.

$ 95.00

2431 Confusing Words

Richard Wanderman
P.O. Box 1075   203-567-4307
Litchfield, CT 06759

A collection of words that are troublesome to readers and writers. Words are grouped on each card according to the way they are most often confused and misused.

$ 20.00

2432 Core Picture Vocabulary

Don Johnston Developmental Equipment, Inc.
1000 N. Rand Road0 N. Rand Rd.   708-526-2682
Wauconda, IL 60084   800-999-4660
                                    FAX 708-526-4177

Set of realistic line drawings representing 160 words. The word accompanies each picture to promote literacy.

$ 26.00

2433 Cotton's 1st Files

MindPlay
3130 N. Dodge Road   602-322-6365
Tucson, AZ 85716

Three-step progression of puzzle games introduces beginning readers to the rudimentary concepts of categorizing and sorting.

$ 49.99

2434 Create - Spell It!

Hartley Courseware, Inc.
P.O. Box 431   517-646-6458
Dimondale, MI 48821

This program provides a simple way to give students individualized spelling tests.

$ 39.95

2435 Critical Reading

Hartley Courseware, Inc.
P.O. Box 431treet   517-646-6458
Dimondale, MI 48821   800-247-1380
                                    FAX 517-646-8451

Telaina Eriksen

A 144-lesson program designed to build critical reading skills.

$ 695.00

2436 A Day in the Life...

Learning Disabilities Association of America
4156 Library Road   412-341-1515
Pittsburgh, PA 15234

Builds basic skills, life skills, critical thinking and problem-solving.

$ 199.00

2437 Discis Books Multimedia Series

Learning Disabilities Association of America
4156 Library Road   412-341-1515
Pittsburgh, PA 15234

Award-winning, interactive books with a questions and commentary feature for in-depth exploration and understanding of the text.

$ 59.95

2438 Dr. Peet's Talk/Writer

Hartley Courseware, Inc.
P.O. Box 431treet   517-646-6458
Dimondale, MI 48821   800-247-1380
                                 FAX 517-646-8451

Telaina Eriksen

This award-winning program takes the non reader from letter recognition to word processing.

$ 79.95

2439 Early Emerging Rules Series

Laureate Learning Systems, Inc.
110 E. Spring St.treet   802-655-4755
Winooski, VT 05404   800-562-6801
                                 FAX 802-655-4757

Mary Sweig Wilson, President
Bernard Fox, Vice President

Three programs that introduce early developing grammatical constructions using natural sounding speech, pictures and animated characters.

$ 150.00

2440 Early Learning I

MarbleSoft
12301 Central Ave. NE   612-755-1402
Baline, MN 55434

Uses sight and sound to help students recognize letters, numbers and sound using various programs.

$ 75.00

2441 Early Words: Beginning Reading

Merry Bee Communications
Omaha, NE

A program to teach children sight vocabulary.

2442 Early Words Reading Kit

Edmark Corporation
P.O. Box 3218   206-746-3900
Redmond, WA 98073   800-362-2890

Develops a basic sight vocabulary by using 100 magnetic words and pictures to create sentences.

$ 40.00

2443 Easy As ABC

Software to Go - Galluadet University
800 Florida Avenue NE   202-651-5705
Washington, DC 20002

2444 Easy Street

MindPlay
3130 N. Dodge Road   602-322-6365
Tucson, AZ 85716

Playful adventures offering instruction on reading and math awareness.

$ 49.99

2445 Echo II

Edmark Corporation
P.O. Box 3903   206-746-3900
Bellevue, WA 98009   800-426-0856

Engage students with voice interaction. Required for the speech component of the Edmark Reading Program, the Echo Speech Processor easily installs in a slot inside your Apple II or IIGS.

$ 129.99

2446 Edmark Functional Word Series

Edmark Corporation
P.O. Box 3903   206-746-3900
Bellevue, WA 98009   800-426-0856

Teaches 400 words important for promoting independent living skills. Four programs offered include: Job/Work Words, Grocery Words, Fast Food/Restaurant Words and Signs Around You.

$ 475.00

2447 The Edmark Reading Program: Print and Software

Edmark Corporation
P.O. Box 3903   206-746-3900
Bellevue, WA 98009   800-426-0856

A beginning reading and language development program for use with non-readers. Offers a printed game and software programs.

2448 Edmark Reading Program Software

Edmark Corporation
P.O. Box 3903   206-746-3900
Bellevue, WA 98009   800-426-0856

A version for Apple II series featuring human-quality digitized voice which gives directions, leads instruction and provides important feedback.

$ 1200.00

2449   Essential Sight Words

SouthWest Ed Psych Services, Inc.
2001 West Silvergate Drive   602-253-6528
Chandler, AZ 85224

Strengthens word recognition skills and speaks with a digitally-recorded human voice without additional hardware.

$ 39.95

2450   Evelyn Wood Dynamic Reader

Timeworks
444 Lake Cook Road   708-948-9200
Deerfield, IL 60015

An effective and enjoyable way to improve reading comprehension, retention and speed.

$ 39.95

2451   Faces

Don Johnston Developmental Equipment, Inc.
1000 N. Rand Road0 N. Rand Rd.   708-526-2682
Wauconda, IL 60084   800-999-4660
FAX 708-526-4177

This is a program that you can start with cause and effect. A switch or key press, changes hair, eyes or mouth on the face.

$ 65.00

2452   Failure Free Reading

137 Corban Court   704-786-7838
Concord, NC 28025   800-542-2170
FAX 704-786-7838

Bill Sedergren, Vice President
Bob Fowles, V.P. Sales

Curriculum areas covered: Reading for the learning disabilities and moderate mentally disabled/emotionally disabled.

2453   The Failure Free Reading Program

Failure Free
137 Corban Court   800-542-2170
Concord, NC 28025

Offers various modules teaching independent living skills. Some of the programs included are; Getting A Job, Getting A Driver's License, Getting An Apartment and Going To The Mall.

2454   Fantasy Land: Reading Between the Lines- Red Level

Methods & Solutions, Inc.
Northbrook, IL

Designed for students who can search for magic coins to retrieve a "sword of justice" and in the process develop skills in reasoning and reading comprehension.

2455   First Categories

Laureate Learning Systems, Inc.
110 E. Spring St.treet   802-655-4755
Winooski, VT 05404   800-562-6801
FAX 802-655-4757

Mary Sweig Wilson, President
Bernard Fox, Vice President

A program that trains categorization skills with a natural sounding voice and pictures of 60 nouns in six categories.

2456   First Letter Fun

MECC
3490 Lexington Ave. N   612-481-3611
St. Paul, MN 55126

Four programs help young children, preschool through kindergarten, match the beginning sounds of words with the letters that make those sounds.

$ 49.00

2457   First Verbs

Laureate Learning Systems, Inc.
110 E. Spring St.treet   802-655-4755
Winooski, VT 05404   800-562-6801
FAX 802-655-4757

Mary Sweig Wilson, President
Bernard Fox, Vice President

A program that trains and tests 40 early developing verbs using animated pictures and a natural sounding female voice.

$ 200.00

2458   First Words

Laureate Learning Systems, Inc.
110 E. Spring St.treet   802-655-4755
Winooski, VT 05404   800-562-6801
FAX 802-655-4757

Mary Sweig Wilson, President
Bernard Fox, Vice President

A talking program that trains and tests 50 early developing nouns presented within 10 categories.

$ 200.00

2459   First Words II

Laureate Learning Systems, Inc.
110 E. Spring St.treet   802-655-4755
Winooski, VT 05404   800-562-6801
FAX 802-655-4757

Mary Sweig Wilson, President
Bernard Fox, Vice President

Continues the training of First Words with training and testing of an additional 50 early developing nouns presented within the same 10 categories as used in First Words.

$ 200.00

2460 Frogs, Dogs, Kittens and Kids 1

Janet Goldman, Author
Hartley Courseware, Inc.
P.O. Box 431treet   517-646-6458
Dimondale, MI 48821

A set of three diskettes providing practice in the development of inferential and factual comprehension of stories written at or below 1.5 grade level.

2461 Fun From a to Z

MECC
3490 Lexington Ave. N   612-481-3611
St. Paul, MN 55126

Discriminate among letters and lower case forms while helping a lost bird.

$ 49.00

2462 Gateway Stories and Gateway Stories II

Don Johnston Developmental Equipment, Inc.
1000 N. Rand Road0 N. Rand Rd.   708-526-2682
Wauconda, IL 60084   800-999-4660
                                  FAX 708-526-4177

Readers may independently select stories, listen to the text and turn pages with a mouse click or switch input.

2463 Getting Ready to Read and Add: MECC Elementary Volume 7

Sunburst Communications, Inc.
39 Washington Ave.et   914-769-5030
Pleasantville, NY 10570

A program teaching identification and matching of shapes, colors, numbers and upper/lower case alphabet letters.

2464 Hickory Dickory Doc

Dunamis, Inc.
3620 Highway 317   404-932-0485
Suwanee, GA 30174

The three mischievous mice are featured along with the old grandfather clock.

$ 19.94

2465 Hit 'n Time

Don Johnston Developmental Equipment, Inc.
1000 N. Rand Road0 N. Rand Rd.   708-526-2682
Wauconda, IL 60084   800-999-4660
                                  FAX 708-526-4177

This program is designed to improve timing skills.

$ 80.00

2466 Homework Level 1

Edmark Corporation
P.O. Box 3903   206-746-3900
Bellevue, WA 98009   800-426-0856

Lessons are designed for stimulating home involvement.

$ 32.95

2467 Informal Reading Comprehension Placement Test

Eunice Insel, Author
Educational Activities
P.O. Box 392venue   516-223-4666
Freeport, Long Island, NY 11520

Assess students instructional and independent reading comprehension levels.

2468 Integrated Reading and Writing Series

MindPlay
Unit F92, P.O. Box 36491   602-322-6365
Tucson, AZ 85740   800-221-7911

Four award winning programs adopted for students at risk. The programs stimulate students through simulated adventures, offers special hints to make play simple if needed, includes higher interest reading lists and offers stimulating assisgnments for essays.

$ 195.00

2469 KEYTALK

Learning Disabilities Association of America
4156 Library Road   412-341-1515
Pittsburgh, PA 15234

Beginning literacy activity.

$ 99.00

2470 Keytalk

Don Johnston Developmental Equipment, Inc.
1000 N. Rand Road0 N. Rand Rd.   708-526-2682
Wauconda, IL 60084   800-999-4660
                                  FAX 708-526-4177

Students type letters, words and sentences and the ECHO Speech Synthesizer speaks them as they are displayed on the screen.

$ 99.00

2471 Kid-Leidoscope

MindPlay
Unit F92, P.O. Box 36491   602-322-6365
Tucson, AZ 85740   800-221-7911

Features five different issues which focus on five different topics. The reading material will enhance and encourage creative thinking skills, improve typing ability, encourage critical reading and problem-solving skills, and encourages investigation skills.

"Sound and colorful graphics increase the appeal of the games, which build reading skills..."

-Booklist

$ 79.00

2472 Kids Can Read Discis Books Series

Learning Disabilities Association of America
4156 Library Road   412-341-1515
Pittsburgh, PA 15234

Get kids hooked on reading with these award-winning, interactive storybooks.

$ 39.95

2473 Kittens, Kids and a Frog: Building Comprehension I

Janet Goldman, Author
Hartley Courseware, Inc.
P.O. Box 431treet
Dimondale, MI 48821   517-646-6458

Two diskettes providing sequenced practice in the development of inferential and factual reading comprehension.

2474 Language Master

ComputAbility Corporation
40000 Grand River, #109 109   313-477-6720
Novi, MI 48375   800-433-8872

A real definition dictionary "on-line".

2475 Lekotek Software

Lekotek of Georgia, Inc.
1955 Cliff Valley Way, Ste. 102   404-633-3430
Altanta, GA 30329

Includes various programs teaching pre-reading skills.

$ 25.00

2476 Lexia I Reading Series

Lexia Learning Systems, Inc.
P.O. Box 466   617-259-8751
Lincoln, MA 01773   800-435-3942

Offers five programs used for the reading development of the learning disabled.

$ 50.00

2477 Lexia II Reading Series

Lexia Learning Systems, Inc.
P.O. Box 466   617-259-8751
Lincoln, MA 01773   800-435-3942

Offers five programs on the reading and language arts basics.

$ 50.00

2478 Lexia III: Reading Services

Lexia Learning Systems, Inc.
P.O. Box 466   617-259-8751
Lincoln, MA 01773   800-435-3942

Offers five programs on recognition skills, elementary reading and language arts.

$ 50.00

2479 Lion's Workshop

Merit Software
13635 Gamma Road   214-385-2353
Dallas, TX 75244

Presents various objects with parts missing or with like objects to be matched.

$ 9.95

2480 Little Boy Blue

Dunamis, Inc.
3620 Highway 317   404-932-0485
Suwanee, GA 30174

This program features everything in this literary classic and the child gets to choose a new ending for the story.

$ 19.95

2481 Little Miss Muffet

Dunamis, Inc.
3620 Highway 317   404-932-0485
Suwanee, GA 30174

Features our heroine from that crafty nursery rhyme and the child chooses the ending.

$ 19.95

2482 LogoWriter Activities for Readers

Learning Disabilities Association of America
4156 Library Road   412-341-1515
Pittsburgh, PA 15234

A collection of twenty-five activities which work in conjunction with LogoWriter to build reading and writing skills.

$ 99.50

2483 Main Idea Maze

SouthWest Ed Psych Services, Inc.
2001 W. Silvergate Dr.   602-253-6528
Chandler, AZ 85224

Assists students in grasping the main idea of a reading passage.

$ 34.99

2484 Match-on-a-Mac

Teach Yourself By Computer Software
3400 Monroe Avenue   716-381-5450
Rochester, NY 14618

Improves recognition and association skills.

$ 39.95

2485 McGee At the Fun Fair

MCE, a Division of Lawrence Productions
1800 S. 35th St.   616-665-7075
Galesburg, MI 49078

Mom and Dad take McGee and his friend Tony to the Fun Fair at the city park.

$ 24.95

2486   Mix N' Match

MarbleSoft
12301 Central Ave. NE   612-755-1402
Baline, MN 55434

Teaches students to recognize, differentiate and solve problems by color, shape and size.

$ 57.00

2487   Moonlight and Madness Levels 1 and 2

Toby Shaw, Author

Hartley Courseware, Inc.
P.O. Box 431treet   517-646-6458
Dimondale, MI 48821

A set of 5 diskettes presenting carefully abridged and adapted classic short stories for adolescents reading from 3.0 to 5.0.

2488   Mouse Train

CAST, Inc.
39 Cross Street   508-531-8555
Peabody, MA 01960

A HyperCard program that is currently under development at CAST. ResearchWare is developed within CAST's research and development program and Mouse Train is a practice program that isolates the subskills of mouse control and presents them in a structured progressive sequence.

$ 10.00

2489   M-ss-ng L-nks: Young People's Literature

Software to Go - Galluadet University
800 Florida Avenue NE   202-651-5705
Washington, DC 20002

2490   Muppet Learning Keys

Sunburst Communications, Inc.
39 Washington Ave.   914-769-5030
Pleasantville, NY 10570

Designed to introduce young children to the world of the computer as they become familiar with letters, numbers and colors.

$ 129.00

2491   My Words: a Language Experience Approach to Reading and Writing

Ed Herstein, Author

Hartley Courseware, Inc.
P.O. Box 431   517-646-6458
Dimondale, MI 48821

A diskette designed as a talking word processor encourgaing the creation of stories, letters and other forms of written communication using language experience approach.

2492   New Kids on the Block: Building Comprehension III

Hartley Courseware, Inc.
P.O. Box 431   517-646-6458
Dimondale, MI 48821

A set of 4 diskettes to develop advanced reading comprehension skills including an understanding of characterization, mood, word meanings, theme, sequencing and making inferences.

2493   Numberswitch

Easter Seals & Lehigh Valley Comp. Project
P.O. Box 3337   215-866-8092
Kulpsville, PA 19443

Six disks with ten pictures on a disk.

$ 2.00

2494   Oakland Schools Picture Dictionary

Don Johnston Developmental Equipment, Inc.
1000 N. Rand Road0 N. Rand Rd.   708-526-2682
Wauconda, IL 60084   800-999-4660
          FAX 708-526-4177

This picture communication collection contains more than 500 clear, realistic line drawings that can be used effectively for communication boards and language training.

$ 45.00

2495   Opposites

Hartley Courseware, Inc.
P.O. Box 431treet   517-646-6458
Dimondale, MI 48821   800-247-1380
          FAX 517-646-8451

Telaina Eriksen

Uses key words in context to help students when they make errors. It is an excellent way to learn opposites and increase vocabulary.

$ 49.95

2496   PAVE: Perceptual Accuracy

Software to Go - Galluadet University
800 Florida Avenue NE   202-651-5705
Washington, DC 20002

2497   Phonological Series

ComputAbility Corporation
40000 Grand River, #109 109   313-477-6720
Novi, MI 48375   800-433-8872

Three disks for use by speech therapists to assist in analyzing phonetic responses to 59 stimuli.

2498   Pickleface and Other Stories

Software to Go - Galluadet University
800 Florida Avenue NE   202-651-5705
Washington, DC 20002

2499 The Picture of English

Learning Disabilities Association of America
4156 Library Road   412-341-1515
Pittsburgh, PA 15234

Reading and spelling program for special education, ESL, adult literacy and reading classes.

$ 49.95

2500 Picture Programs

ComputAbility Corporation
40000 Grand River, #109 109   313-477-6720
Novi, MI 48375   800-433-8872

Set of three diskettes teaching identification and functions of common nouns.

2501 Project STAR

Hartley Courseware, Inc.
P.O. Box 431treet   517-646-6458
Dimondale, MI 48821   800-247-1380
                                   FAX 517-646-8451

Telaina Eriksen

A comprehensive program designed for adults and secondary students who have minimal reading skills.

2502 Puzzle Works Readiness

Continental Press, Inc.
520 E. Bainbridge Street   800-847-0656
Elizabethtown, PA 17022

This series of five disks uses colorful graphics and reward techniques that are especially suited to the interests and needs of special learners.

$ 49.95

2503 Quotes

Richard Wanderman
P.O. Box 1075   203-567-4307
Litchfield, CT 06759

A collection of quotations from over 1000 authors. Subjects range from: many humorous, some serious and everything in between.

$ 20.00

2504 Read N' Roll

Thomas DeBry, Author

Davidson & Associates, Inc.
19840 Pioneer Avenue   213-534-4070
Torrance, CA 90503

Designed for students this program of two diskettes, for improving reading comprehension skills, focuses on recognizing the main idea, recalling facts, identifying the sequence of events, drawing inferences and building vocabulary.

2505 The Readable Stories Series

Laureate Learning Systems, Inc.
110 E. Spring St.treet   802-655-4755
Winooski, VT 05404   800-562-6801
                                   FAX 802-655-4757

Mary Sweig Wilson, President
Bernard Fox, Vice President

A trio of programs designed to improve reading comprehension in early through intermediate readers. Each program consists of a story diskette and a question diskette.

$ 110.00

2506 Readable Stories: the Birthday Surprise

Laureate Learning Systems, Inc.
110 E. Spring St.   802-655-4755
Winooski, VT 05404

This program is designed to increase reading comprehension in early through intermediate readers.

$ 110.00

2507 Readable Stories: the Hidden Toy

Laureate Learning Systems, Inc.
110 E. Spring St.   802-655-4755
Winooski, VT 05404

This program is designed to increase reading comprehension.

$ 110.00

2508 Readable Stories: the Puppet Show

Laureate Learning Systems, Inc.
110 E. Spring St.   802-655-4755
Winooski, VT 05404

A reading comprehension series.

$ 110.00

2509 Reading Across the Curriculum

Hartley Courseware, Inc.
P.O. Box 431   517-646-6458
Dimondale, MI 48821   800-247-1380
                                   FAX 517-646-8451

Telaina Eriksen

This program focuses on the critical reading skills of comprehension, analysis, evaluation and application.

$ 695.00

2510 Reading and Me

Mark Simonsen, Author

Davidson & Associates, Inc.
19840 Pioneer Avenue   213-534-4070
Torrance, CA 90503

A diskette with 12 games focusing on reading readiness, visual discrimination, alphabet letter recognition and sequencing, beginning and final consonant recognition and beginning word recognition.

2511   Reading Bridge

Edmark Corporation
P.O. Box 3218   206-746-3900
Redmond, WA 98073   800-362-2890

A reading program for intermediate special needs students. Explores a variety of interesting and appealing topics enriched by attractive illustrations and photographs.

2512   Reading Comprehension

Richard Hefter, Author

Optimum Resource, Inc.
10 Station Place   203-542-5553
Norfolk, CT 06058

A diskette designed to teach students how to master skills such as predicting outcomes, recognizing cause and effect, making inferences, sequencing and summarizing by analyzing 30 high-interest stories.

2513   Reading Comprehension: What's Different

Program Design, Inc.
Greenwich, CT

Five programs to help students improve their reading comprehension skills by selecting the word that is different in a group of four words presented.

2514   Reading for Meaning 2 with Mother Goose

Vera Gierman, Author

Hartley Courseware, Inc.
P.O. Box 431treet   517-646-6458
Dimondale, MI 48821

Two diskettes designed to teach reading comprehension skills to students using 55 nursery rhymes.

2515   Reading Genie

Quest Systems, Inc.
P.O. Box 102   316-232-2626
Pittsburg, KS 66762

A flexible, menu-driven reading recognition/comprehension program.

$ 125.00

2516   Reading Magic

Edmark Corporation
P.O. Box 3218   206-746-3900
Redmond, WA 98073   800-362-2890

Provides positive reading experiences with interactive fairy tales.

$ 44.95

2517   Reading Magic Library: Jack and the Beanstalk

Tom Snyder Productions
90 Sherman Street   617-876-4433
Cambridge, MA 02140

This interactive storybook helps students step into the shoes of heroes choosing what will happen next.

$ 44.95

2518   Reading Realities

Teacher Support Software
1035 NW 57th Street   904-332-6404
Gainesville, FL 32605

This low-level reading program was designed for the at risk middle to senior high student who is reading at the 2-6 grade reading level.

$ 489.95

2519   Reading Realities Elementary Series

Teacher Support Software
1035 NW 57th Street   904-332-6404
Gainesville, FL 32605

Real-life stories based on interviews with children about school issues, family issues and personal issues.

$ 489.95

2520   Reading Riddles with the Boars

Queue, Inc.
338 Commerce Drive   203-335-0906
Fairfield, CT 06430   800-232-2224
                                   FAX 203-336-2481

Children are naturally curious about pictures. This program uses pictures to teach over 1,000 vocabulary words.

$ 39.95

2521   Reading Rodeo

Heartsoft, Inc.
P.O. Box 691381   800-285-3475
Tulsa, OK 74169

Utilizes over 100 artist drawn pictures to show students how to distinguish between words beginning with different initial consonant sounds.

$ 49.95

2522   Reading to Learn I-IV

Society for Visual Education, Inc.
1345 Diversey Parkway   312-525-1500
Chicago, IL 60614

Consists of four units: vocabulary development, literal comprehension and interpretive thinking.

$ 104.00

2523   Reading Tutorial Comprehension: Details, Level B

Pamela Broach, Author

Random House
New York, NY

Designed for independent readers this program of tutorial, drill and practice lessons developing the concept of part-to-whole relationships ny focusing on identifying details within a simple, compound, and/or complex sentence.

2524 Reading & Writing with the Boars

Queue, Inc.
338 Commerce Drive   203-335-0906
Fairfield, CT 06430   800-232-2224
    FAX 203-336-2481

Children begin by answering questions, using text and graphics. Answers are used to compose an illustrated story that can be read, changed, saved or printed.

$ 49.95

2525 Ready-Set-Read

Continental Press, Inc.
520 E. Bainbridge Street   800-847-0656
Elizabethtoen, PA 17022

Provides three activities ranging from those involving pictorial and word clues to those requiring contextual awareness.

$ 49.95

2526 Relevant Reading Series

Aquarius Instructional
P.O. Box 128   813-595-7890
Indiana Rocks Beach, FL 34635   800-338-2644
    FAX 813-595-2685

Programs feature maze and cloze tasks, a detailed management system and teacher's guides.

$ 150.00

2527 Remembering Numbers and Letters

Aquarius Instructional
P.O. Box 128   813-595-7890
Indian Rocks Beach, FL 34635

Students work at their own pace and select their own numbers and letters with which to work.

$ 29.95

2528 Scramble

Ahead Designs
1827 Hawk View Drive   619-942-5860
Encinitas, CA 92024

Students are presented with large-character scrambled words and are to type in the correct spelling.

$ 15.95

2529 Scuffy and Friends

Janet Goldman, Author

Hartley Courseware, Inc.
P.O. Box 431treet   517-646-6458
Dimondale, MI 48821

Designed for students, this program with 18 stories providing beginning readers with carefully sequenced practice in the development of inferential and factual comprehension.

2530 Sentence Master - Level 1,2,3,4

Laureate Learning Systems, Inc.
110 E. Spring St.treet   802-655-4755
Winooski, VT 05404   800-562-6801
    FAX 802-655-4757

Mary Sweig Wilson, President
Bernard Fox, Vice President

A system of teaching reading that was uniquely developed for children at risk for reading failure and those who have failed in reading because of difficulties in phonics, oral language, English as a second language and/or impulsive reading styles.

$ 475.00

2531 Slimware

Syntha-Voice Computers, Inc.
125 Gailmont Drive   800-263-4540
Hamilton, ON, Canada, L8 K 4B8

A memory-resident screen review program which responds to the same keystrokes used by sighted computer users without keyboard conflicts.

$ 595.00

2532 Snoopy's Reading Machine

Queue, Inc.
338 Commerce Drive   203-335-0906
Fairfield, CT 06430   800-232-2224
    FAX 203-336-2481

Teaches five word families with 25 words to create and learn.

$ 29.95

2533 SocPix: Classification Games for Prereaders

Bill Maxwell, Author

AGS
7201 Woodland Road   612-786-4343
Circle Pines, MN 55014   800-328-2560

A diskette to help non-readers organize and remember information by selecting and classifying 175 pictures into 7 categories.

2534 Sounder

Edmark Corporation
P.O. Box 3218   206-746-3900
Redmond, WA 98073   800-362-2890

Establishes strong basic reading skills with this systematic, phonics-based reading program.

$ 135.00

2535 Speed Reader

Davidson & Associates, Inc.
19840 Pioneer Avenue   213-534-4070
Torrance, CA 90503

Designed to increase reading speed and improve comprehension.

$ 59.95

2536 Speed Reader II

Jan Davidson, Author

Davidson & Associates, Inc.
19840 Pioneer Avenue   213-534-4070
Torrance, CA 90503

A program designed to help increase reading speed and improve comprehension of students in high school through adult levels. Contains 35 reading selections and lessons focusing on eye movement training, column reading, passage reading, timed reading adn letter and word recall.

2537 Spelling, Level 1 and 2

Edmark Corporation
P.O. Box 3903   206-746-3900
Bellevue, WA 98009   800-426-0856

Practice spelling and writing skills with the Edmark Reading Program words. Level 1 consists of 48 worksheets with activities such as writing the word, filling in a missing letter, completing a sentence, drawing a picture and writing dictionary definition. Level 2 adds 53 worksheets with more activities.

$ 39.95

2538 Spelling Mastery

DLM Teaching Resources
One DLM Park   214-248-6300
Allen, TX 75002

Six animated games offer practice for spelling in grades 1 to 3.

$ 46.00

2539 Stickybear Reading Comprehension

Richard Hefter, Author

Optimum Resource, Inc.
10 Station Place   203-542-5553
Norfolk, CT 06058

A program with a variety of short stories and comprehension questions at 7 difficulty levels.

2540 Supplemental Worksheets, Level 1 and 2

Edmark Corporation
P.O. Box 3903   206-746-3900
Bellevue, WA 98009   800-426-0856

Reproducible worksheets including matching words and pictures with underlining, cutting/pasting, drawing lines or circling words to match illustrations.

$ 89.50

2541 Survival Skills Reading Program

Aquarius Instructional
P.O. Box 128   813-595-7890
Indiana Rocks Beach, FL 34635   800-338-2644
                              FAX 813-595-2685

A vocabulary section introduces each program to familiarize the students with the subject areas to be covered. Students read a fifth grade level paragraph and are asked a comprehension question. If students answer correctly, they advance to the next section.

2542 Syllasearch I, II, III, IV

DLM Teaching Resources
One DLM Park   214-248-6300
Allen, TX 75002

Students learn how to read multi-syllable words accurately and automatically whith this new game that uses actual human speech for instruction and correction.

$ 99.00

2543 Symbols

Richard Wanderman
P.O. Box 1075   203-567-4307
Litchfield, CT 06759

A collection of symbolic clip-art images, Morse Code and Braille alphabets, as well as numerous other symbolic images from diverse categories.

$ 20.00

2544 Talking Nouns

Laureate Learning Systems, Inc.
110 E. Spring St.treet   802-655-4755
Winooski, VT 05404   800-562-6801
                              FAX 802-655-4757

Mary Sweig Wilson, President
Bernard Fox, Vice President

An interactive communication product that helps build expressive language and augmentative communication skills.

$ 115.00

2545 Talking Nouns II

Laureate Learning Systems, Inc.
110 E. Spring St.treet   802-655-4755
Winooski, VT 05404   800-562-6801
                              FAX 802-655-4757

Mary Sweig Wilson, President
Bernard Fox, Vice President

Designed to build expressive language and augmentative communication skills.

$ 115.00

2546 Talking Picture Series

ComputAbility Corporation
40000 Grand River, #109 109   313-477-6720
Novi, MI 48375   800-433-8872

Popular touch window program.

2547 Talking Verbs

Laureate Learning Systems, Inc.
110 E. Spring St.treet   802-655-4755
Winooski, VT 05404   800-562-6801
                                FAX 802-655-4757

Mary Sweig Wilson, President
Bernard Fox, Vice President

Builds expressive language and augmentative communication skills.

$ 115.00

2548 Task Master

Life Science Associates
1 Fenimore Road   516-472-2111
Bayport, NY 11705

Menu-driven programs enable users to design their own tasks in six areas.

$ 195.00

2549 Tennis Anyone?

Software to Go - Galluadet University
800 Florida Avenue NE   202-651-5705
Washington, DC 20002

2550 That's My Job! a Reading Comprehension Program: Level 1

Judy Priven, Author

Hartley Courseware, Inc.
P.O. Box 431treet   517-646-6458
Dimondale, MI 48821

A program developing inferential and literal reading comprehension skills through stories about the following jobs: landscaper, truck driver, fisherman, firefighter, painter, cab driver and janitor.

2551 Tiger's Tale

Sunburst Communications, Inc.
39 Washington Ave.   914-769-5030
Pleasantville, NY 10570

Beginning readers learn to master vocabulary with this series of interactive stories about the adventures of a mischievous cat.

$ 65.00

2552 Tim and the Cat and Jen the Hen

Janet Goldman, Author

Hartley Courseware, Inc.
P.O. Box 431treet   517-646-6458
Dimondale, MI 48821

Designed to teach literal and inferential reading comprehension, this program offers two diskettes presenting a set of stories about Elmo the Cat as he runs away from home and finds new adventures.

2553 Tim and the Cat and the Fish Dish

Janet Goldman, Author

Hartley Courseware, Inc.
P.O. Box 431treet   517-646-6458
Dimondale, MI 48821

Designed to teach literal and inferential reading comprehension.

2554 Tim and the Cat And...(The Big Red Hat... the Fish Dish...Jen the Hen)

Hartley Courseware, Inc.
P.O. Box 431treet   517-646-6458
Dimondale, MI 48821   800-247-1380
                                FAX 517-646-8451

Telaina Eriksen

These colorful, animated reading comprehension programs are written for the beginning reader.

$ 59.95

2555 Touch and Learn Reading Series: 1, 2 & 3

Learning Disabilities Association of America
4156 Library Road   412-341-1515
Pittsburgh, PA 15234

Fun, interactive reading programs reinforce sound-symbol correspondence and focus on decoding skills that are most difficult for beginning readers.

$ 250.00

2556 TouchWindow

Edmark Corporation
P.O. Box 3903   206-746-3900
Bellevue, WA 98009   800-426-0856

Simply point and reach. The TouchWindow allows a student the most natural, direct way to work with a computer.

$ 275.00

2557 ToyStore, JOKUS Software

Don Johnston Developmental Equipment, Inc.
1000 N. Rand Road0 N. Rand Road   708-526-2682
Wauconda, IL 60084   800-999-4660
                                FAX 708-526-4177

Multi-faceted collection of six discovery and learning activities creating simple fairy tales with easy choice-making.

$ 95.00

2558 Understanding Questions I

Sunset Software
9277 E. Corrine Dr.   602-451-0753
Scottsdale, AZ 85260

Questions that contrast the selected pair of question words are randomly presented.

$ 29.95

2559   Velveteen Rabbit

Sunburst Communications, Inc.
39 Washington Ave.   914-769-5030
Pleasantville, NY 10570

Encourages students to listen and think as the story is read to them by the teacher.

$ 59.00

2560   Visagraph Eye-Movement Recording System

Instructional/Communications Technology
10 Stepar Place   516-549-3000
Huntington Station, NY 11746

Measures the efficiency of students' reading abilities.

$ 1800.00

2561   Visual Tracking

Gary Karcz, Author

Hartley Courseware, Inc.
P.O. Box 431treet   517-646-6458
Dimondale, MI 48821

A diskette program which emulates a tachistoscopic reading machine, allowing the user to set the reading speed and the way in which words of the text will be displayed on the screen.

2562   Vocabulary Machine

SouthWest Ed Psych Services, Inc.
2001 W. Silvergate Dr.   602-253-6528
Chandler, AZ 85224

Comtains more than 1,000 words and sentences to expand reading vocabulary skills.

$ 59.95

2563   Vowels

Hartley Courseware, Inc.
P.O. Box 431   517-646-6458
Dimondale, MI 48821

This 53-lesson program uses a multimedia approach to help the beginning reader.

$ 49.95

2564   Who, What, Where, When, Why

Hartley Courseware, Inc.
P.O. Box 431treet   517-646-6458
Dimondale, MI 48821   800-247-1380
                                      FAX 517-646-8451

Telaina Eriksen

This program can help build good reading comprehension by providing carefully sequenced practice on these easily confused concepts.

$ 49.95

2565   Wizard of Words

Software to Go - Galluadet University
800 Florida Avenue NE   202-651-5705
Washington, DC 20002

2566   Word Bank

Software to Go - Galluadet University
800 Florida Avenue NE   202-651-5705
Washington, DC 20002

2567   Word List

Richard Wanderman
P.O. Box 1075   203-567-4307
Litchfield, CT 06759

A simple tool for keeping track of words and their definitions or for general note taking.

$ 20.00

2568   Words & Concepts Series

Laureate Learning Systems, Inc.
110 E. Spring St.treet   802-655-4755
Winooski, VT 05404   800-562-6801
                                      FAX 802-655-4757

Mary Sweig Wilson, President
Bernard Fox, Vice President

A series of three programs that integrate language and concept training using natural sounding speech and pictures of 40 nouns.

$ 200.00

2569   Write

Computers to Help People, Inc.
1221 West Johnson Street   608-257-5917
Madison, WI 53715

Enter up to 20 words/sentences which are displayed in large letters word-by-word for the pupil.

$ 50.00

Science

2570   Animal Photo Fun

Software to Go - Galluadet University
800 Florida Avenue NE   202-651-5705
Washington, DC 20002

2571   Basic Environmental Science

Aquarius Instructional
P.O. Box 128   813-595-7890
Indiana Rocks Beach, FL 34635   800-338-2644
                                      FAX 813-595-2685

These programs provide students with an overview of basic scientific concepts on a sixth through ninth grade level.

$ 275.00

2572 Biology Tutor

MindPlay
Unit F92, P.O. Box 36491   602-322-6365
Tucson, AZ 85740   800-221-7911

Knowledge of biology grows with this lively three-package series.

$ 349.00

2573 Chemistry Tutor

MindPlay
Unit F92, P.O. Box 36491   602-322-6365
Tucson, AZ 85740   800-221-7911

Offers information to students on learning chemistry at a personal pace with this two-package series.

$ 429.00

2574 Exploring Heat

TERC
2067 Massachusetts Ave.   617-547-0430
Cambridge, MA 02140

A combination of lessons, software, temperature probes and activity sheets, specifically designed for the learning disabled child.

$ 160.00

2575 Exploring Matter

TERC
2067 Massachusetts Ave.   617-547-0430
Cambridge, MA 02140

A combination of lessons, temperature probes, software and activity sheets for the learning of scientific matters.

$ 160.00

2576 Fundamental Skills for General Chemistry

Software to Go - Galluadet University
800 Florida Avenue NE
Washington, DC 20002   202-651-5705

2577 The Lab: Experiments in Biology

MindPlay
Unit F92, P.O. Box 36491   602-322-6365
Tucson, AZ 85740   800-221-7911

This self-paced, interactive computer simluation offers important biology experiments, preceded by instructions and explanations.

$ 129.00

2578 The Lab: Experiments in Chemistry

MindPlay
Unit F92, P.O. Box 36491   602-322-6365
Tucson, AZ 85740   800-221-7911

Program offering graphic simulations of chemistry experiments.

$ 129.00

2579 Learn About Animals

Wings for Learning, Inc.
1600 Green Hills Rd.   408-438-5502
Scotts Valley, CA 95067

Students use illustrated, animated programs to explore nature and the natural habitats of animals.

$ 65.00

2580 Milliken Science Series: Circulation and Digestion

Delores Boufard, Author
Milliken Publishing
1100 Research Blvd.   314-991-4220
St. Paul, MO 63132

A program designed to introduce students to two subsystems of the human body. Provides practice using the correct terms for the various organs that make up each system, illustrating how the parts of each subsystem work together, and ensuring that students can explain the functions of the subsystems and their parts.

2581 Mystery Objects

MECC
3490 Lexington Ave. N   612-481-3611
St. Paul, MN 55126

Students text hideen for such physical properties as texture, size, smell, weight and color.

$ 59.00

2582 Operation: Frog

Scholastic
730 Broadway   212-505-6006
New York, NY 10003

A program introducing students to the fundamentals of biology and anatomy as they perform a computer simulation of the dissection of a frog.

2583 Physics Tutor

MindPlay
Unit F92, P.O. Box 36491   602-322-6365
Tucson, AZ 85740   800-221-7911

This four-package series offers a full knowledge of physics at a personalized pace.

$ 699.00

2584 Seasons (Dunamis)

Dunamis, Inc.
3620 Highway 317   404-932-0485
Suwanee, GA 30174

Seasons compares and contrasts the characteristics of the winter, spring, summer and fall seasons.

$ 19.95

2585 Sory Starters: Science

Queue, Inc.
338 Commerce Drive   203-335-0906
Fairfield, CT 06430   800-232-2224
                                  FAX 203-336-2481

Offers students the ability to put together habitats, create food chains or design their own solar system with an abundance of specialized clip art.

$ 49.95

2586   Touchy Subject

Marshware, Inc.
P.O. Box 8082   816-523-1059
Shawnee Mission, KS 66208

This program teaches the user to recognize touch, hot, cold, pressure and pain.

$ 55.95

2587   VisiFrog: Vertebrate Anatomy

Ventura Educational Systems
Newbury Park, CA

A program on the anatomy of a frog focusing on the graphic examination, identification, and study of the structures and functions of various systems.

2588   The Wonders of Science

Steck-Vaughn Company
P.O. Box 26015   800-531-5015
Austin, TX 78755

A complete science program for middle school adn secondary students.

Social Skills

2589   Ace Programmer II

MindPlay
Unit F92, P.O. Box 36491   602-322-6365
Tucson, AZ 85740   800-221-7911

This program teaches commands and functions of BASIC language, improves logic skills, teaches the entering and editing of programs and teaches advanced concepts like arrays, variables and subroutines.

"Highly interactive and supplies very good remedial feedback."

-Software Reports
$ 39.00

2590   Being Gifted: the Gift

MindPlay
Unit F92, P.O. Box 36491   602-322-6365
Tucson, AZ 85740   800-221-7911

A video study kit focusing on identifying and developing the potential of the gifted, identifies characteristics of gifted children and stimulates discussion and offers follow-up activities, educates parents, educates teachers, and increases understanding and empathy for the gifted individual.

$ 129.00

2591   Create with Garfield

DLM Teaching Resources
One DLM Parkhany   214-248-6300
Allen, TX 75002

For students to create cartoons, posters and labels by choosing a variety of backgrounds, props and Garfield characters.

2592   Create with Garfield: Deluxe Edition

Ahead Designes, Author

DLM Teaching Resources
One DLM Parkhany   214-248-6300
Allen, TX 75002

A program to be used by children to create and print cartoons, posters or labels featuring Garfield and his friends.

2593   Garfield Trivia Game

Jerry Chaffin, Author

DLM Teaching Resources
One DLM Parkhany   214-248-6300
Allen, TX 75002

Designed for the students creative side. Students can apply their knowledge to 300 intriguing questions about Garfield and his friends.

2594   Gertrude's Puzzles

The Learning Company
6493 Kaiser Drive   415-792-2101
Fremontark, CA 94555

Design or solve puzzles and in the process of deep logic and abstract thinking skills.

2595   Improving Your Self-Concept

George Spengler, Author

MCE, a Division of Lawrence Productions
1800 S. 35th St.   616-665-7075
Galesburg, MI 49078

An interactive program assessing students strengths, weaknesses, likes, dislikes and roles, focusing on a positive self-concept.

2596   Job Readiness Attitude Assessment

Florence Taber, Author

MCE, a Division of Lawrence Productions
1800 S. 35th St.   616-665-7075
Galesburg, MI 49078

A program to assess attitudes and behaviors necessary job success as well as provide probable consequences of the students' response to each question.

2597   Learning to Cope with Pressure

Hal Meyers, Author

Sunburst Communications, Inc.
39 Washington Ave.et   914-769-5030
Pleasantville, NY 10570

A program for use with emotionally disturbed, learning disabled and text anxious students. Using biofeedback monitors and relaxation exercises, this program helps students learn causes for and techniques to reduce and control stress.

2598 Pic. Building

Richard Hefter, Author

Optimum Resource, Inc.
10 Station Place   203-542-5553
Norfolk, CT 06058

A picture-building program with 40 build-by-numbers pictures and 4 palettes for creating, storing and printing graphics.

2599 Predict It

Don Johnston Developmental Equipment, Inc.
1000 N. Rand Road0 N. Rand Rd.   708-526-2682
Wauconda, IL 60084   800-999-4660
                        FAX 708-526-4177

A word processing program that "predicts" what the user wants to type.

$ 148.00

2600 Story Starters: Social Studies

Queue, Inc.
338 Commerce Drive   203-335-0906
Fairfield, CT 06430   800-232-2224
                    FAX 203-336-2481

With this two-disk package students can recreate actual events or add their own twist to stories and reports. Categories include: Civil War, American Redvolution, Westward Expansion, Colonization and more.

$ 49.95

2601 Three Social Interaction and Decision Making Kits

MindPlay
Unit F92, P.O. Box 36491   602-322-6365
Tucson, AZ 85740   800-221-7911

This multimedia program provides you with a high-interest video plus worksheets, follow-up activities and roel playing practices to teach students the essential skills of decision making, assertive responses, effective communication and conflict resoloution. The series is made up of Peers, Family and Resisting Peer Pressure.

$ 517.00

2602 Zoo Time

UCLA Intervention Program for Disabled Children
1000 Veteran Ave., #23-10   301-825-4821
Los Angeles, CA 90024

Offers five familiar zoo animals to choose from.

$ 35.00

Social Studies

2603 Ace Programmer 1

MindPlay
Unit F92, P.O. Box 36491   602-322-6365
Tucson, AZ 85740   800-221-7911

With easy-to-read instructions and step-by-step guidance through 35 lessons, this program gives introductory knowledge of the BASIC computer language, teaches commands and functions of BASIC and improves logic skills.
  "...excellent taching tool for supplementing any subject."
                -Software Reports
                $ 39.00

2604 Africa

Software to Go - Galluadet University
800 Florida Avenue NE   202-651-5705
Washington, DC 20002

2605 American Coast to Coast

Neosoft, Inc.
Northbrook, IL

Five interactive geography games for students focusing on names, capitals, sizes, mottos and selected industries of the United States.

2606 Creating the U.S. Constitution

Mark Swanson, Author

Educational Activities
P.O. Box 392venue   516-223-4666
Freeport, Long Island, NY 11520

An interactive simulation program focusing on the Constitutional Convention of 1787.

2607 Dyno-Quest

MindPlay
Unit F92, P.O. Box 36491   602-322-6365
Tucson, AZ 85740   800-221-7911

Offers help to students in risk taking, decision making and map reading.
  "...an excellent follow-up activity on dinosaurs while increasing map reading skills..."
                -Software Reports
                $ 49.99

2608 The Earth Moves

Aquarius Instructional
P.O. Box 128   813-595-7890
Indiana Rocks Beach, FL 34635   800-338-2644
                    FAX 813-595-2685

Set of 2 disks offering information on folds and faults and earthquakes.

$ 75.00

2609 EarthQuest

The KidSoft Company
718 University Avenue, Ste. 112   800-354-6150
Los Gatos, CA 95030

Explore the history of inventions and learn more about how people created lasting works of art and literature.

$ 59.95

2610 Geo-Sphere: Earth

MindPlay
Unit F92, P.O. Box 36491   602-322-6365
Tucson, AZ 85740   800-221-7911

Offers information and an inspiring way to put the world into student's hands. The program promotes planetary awareness, reinforces general knowledge of geography and increases visual perception.

$ 19.95

2611 Nigel's World

Lawrence Productions
1800 South 35th Street   616-665-7075
Galesburg, MI 49053

A software game providing children with adventures in geography.

2612 Settling America

William Nelson, Author

World Book, Inc.
P.O. Box 1192   800-621-8202
Chicago, IL 60009

A simulation program for children in which they help decide the fate of a pioneer family living in the Ohio Valley from 1789 through 1793.

2613 States & Traits

DesignWare, Inc.
San Francisco, CA

A game on United States geography with historical information adn current trivia on each state.

2614 Story Tailor

Pelican Software, Inc.
768 Farmington Ave.   203-674-8221
Farmington, CT 06032

Literature-designed to teach basic reading and writing skills.

$ 79.00

2615 U.S. Atlas Action

Jerry Chaffin, Author

DLM Teaching Resources
One DLM Parkhany   214-248-6300
Allen, TX 75002

Diskettes review important geography facts about the nation, regions and individual states. Includes 58 maps, 25 built-in map and geography games and a student record system.

2616 Where in the USA Is Carmen Santiago

Ken Bull, Author

Broderbund Software
P.O. Box 6121   415-382-4400
Novato, CA 94948

A program combining graphic adventures, trivia games, mysteries and arcade animation to teach students about geography, economy and history of the 50 states and the District of Columbia.

2617 World Atlas Action

Software to Go - Galluadet University
800 Florida Avenue NE   202-651-5705
Washington, DC 20002

Word Processing

2618 Abbreviation/Expansion

Zygo Industries
P.O. Box 1008   503-297-1724
Portland, OR 97207

Allows the individual to define and store word/phrase abbreviations to achieve efficiency and accelerated entry rate of text.

$ 95.00

2619 ACCENT

Aicom Corporation
1590 Oakland Road, Ste. B112   408-453-8251
San Jose, CA 95131   FAX 408-453-8255

Offers high quality test-to-speech synthesis and efficiency for the visually impaired.

2620 The Adaptive Device Locator System

Academic Software, Inc.
331 West Second Street   606-233-2332
Lexington, KY 40507

This system describes thousands of devices, cross references over 600 vendors and illustrates devices graphically. The ADLS databases include a full spectrum of living aids, products ranging from specialized eating utensils to dressing aids, electronic switches, computer hardware and software, adapted physical education devices and much more.

$ 195.00

2621 The Adaptive Firmware Card

Don Johnston Developmental Equipment, Inc.
1000 N. Rand Road0 N. Rand Rd.   708-526-2682
Wauconda, IL 60084   800-999-4660
          FAX 708-526-4177

The card is the keyboard and mouse emulator that lets you use you alternate input device to access Apple IIe and IIGS computers. The AFC lets thousands of students with disabilities use input methods and special options.

$ 520.00

2622 Bank Street Writer

Franklin Smith, Author

San Rafael, CA

A word processor with an on-disk tutorial for students allowing them to write, revise, correct, erase, unerase and rearrange words in various forms of written communication.

2623 Co:Writer

Don Johnston Developmental Equipment, Inc.
1000 N. Rand Road, P.O. Box 639   708-526-2682
Wauconda, IL 60084   800-999-4660
                                               FAX 708-526-4177

Paula Kwit, Vice President
Ruth Ziolowski, Sales Manager

A word prediction program that helps improve productivity and quality of written work.

$ 29.00

2624 Co:Writer - Intelligent Word Prediction Software

Don Johnston Developmental Equipment, Inc.
1000 N. Rand Road0 N. Rand Road   708-526-2682
Wauconda, IL 60084   800-999-4660
                                               FAX 708-526-4177

Works with any standard word processor to create work or school documents easier and faster. Grammar-intelligent word prediction helps reduce keystrokes, boost productivity and stimulate creativity.

$ 290.00

2625 Elementary Spelling Ace

Franklin Learning Resources
122 Burrs Road   800-525-9673
Mt. Holly, NJ 08060

Designed for younger students, this machine takes into account the typical phonetic misspelling patterns of younger children and corrects their spelling in seconds.

$ 35.00

2626 The Fast Access Scan Talker

Mary S. Wilson, Author

Laureate Learning Systems, Inc.
110 E. Spring St.treet   802-655-4755
Winooski, VT 05404

A single-switch activated augmentative communication system to help non-vocal persons express themselves quickly and effectively.

2627 Friendly Computer

Software to Go - Galluadet University
800 Florida Avenue NE   202-651-5705
Washington, DC 20002

2628 Ke:nx On:Board An Access Keyboard

Don Johnston Developmental Equipment, Inc.
1000 N. Rand Road, P.O. Box 639   708-526-2682
Wauconda, IL 60084   800-999-4660
                                               FAX 708-526-4177

Paula Kwit, Vice President
Ruth Ziolkowski, Sales Manager

A keyboard with built in Ke:nx 2.0 technology, made especially for the Macintosh computer. Sleek look features a wide wrist rest, low profile and compact design and fits into learning and work environments.

$ 625.00

2629 Keyboard Cadet

Software to Go - Galluadet University
800 Florida Avenue NE   202-651-5705
Washington, DC 20002

2630 Kidsword: Large Character Word Processor

Julie Griffiths, Author

Kidsview Software
P.O. Box 98   603-927-4428
Warner, NH 03278

A word processor in which the screen holds ten lines of large character text. Prints both large and standard characters with a dot matrix printer.

2631 Kidwriter

Jim Pejsa, Author

Spinnaker Software
Cambridge, MA   617-494-1200

Two diskettes encouraging the creation and printing of word and picture stories while introducing the fundamentals of word processing.

2632 Magic Slate: the Word Processor That Grows with You

Donna Stanger, Author

Sunburst Communications, Inc.
39 Washington Ave.et   914-769-5030
Pleasantville, NY 10570

A word processing program fostering proofreading, editing and rewriting skills, using either a 20-column, 40-column, or 80-column format.

2633 Marblesoft

12301 Cental Avenue NE, Ste. 205   612-755-1402
Blaine, MN 55434

2634 Mind Reader

Brown Bag Software, Inc.
2155 South Bascom Ave., Ste. 114   408-559-4545
Campbell, CA 95008

A word processor driven by an artificial intelligence engine.

$ 89.00

2635 Mindplay Works

MindPlay
Unit F92, P.O. Box 36491   602-322-6365
Tucson, AZ 85740   800-221-7911

A complete tool kit for writing, planning and record-keeping.

$ 79.99

2636 Powerama

Syntha-Voice Computers, Inc.
125 Gailmont Drive   800-263-4540
Hamilton, ON, Canada, L8 K 4B8

Integrates software into a fully synchronized method of seeing and hearing to the text on the screen through a speech synthesizer.

$ 895.00

2637 PowerMenu Plus 6.0

Brown Bag Software, Inc.
2155 S. Bascom Ave., Ste. 114   408-559-4545
Campbell, CA 95008

A menuing program that can run any program at the touch of a single key without having to exit to DOS.

$ 89.00

2638 Prewrite

MindPlay
1345 Diversey Pkwy.   312-525-1500
Chicago, IL 60614

Interactive questions and answers will help students brainstorm and produce a printout of concepts for developing a first draft of writing assignments.

$ 49.95

2639 PsycINFO

American Psychological Association
Order Dept., P.O. Box 2710   202-336-5510
Hyattsville, MD 20784   800-374-2721
                               FAX 202-336-5502

An online research tool that provides instant access to citations to the international serial literature in psychology and related disciplines.

2640 PsycLIT on Silver Platter

American Psychological Association
Order Dept., P.O. Box 2710   202-336-5510
Hyattsville, MD 20784   800-374-2721
                               FAX 202-336-5502

A computerized CD-ROM database produced by PsychINFO and provides access to the international journal, book-shapter and book literature in psychology and related disciplines such as education, business, medicine and law.

2641 Public Domain Software

Kentucky Special Education Technology Training Ctr
229 Taylor Education Bldg.
Lexington, KY 40506

Entire collections of Macintosh, MS-DOS or Apple II software.

2642 Qwerty Word Processor

HFK Software
68 Wells Road   617-259-0059
Lincoln, MA 01773

A word processor with Keysaver for boiler plate and highly structured documents, key assignments for use of all keyboards and more.

$ 49.00

2643 Seasons (UCLA Intervention Program for Handicapped Children)

UCLA Intervention Program for Disabled Children
1000 Veteran Ave., #23-10   301-825-4821
Los Angeles, CA 90024

Selects a season from the menu and objects scan across the bottom of the screen.

$ 435.00

2644 Secondary Print Pack

Failure Free
137 Corban Court   800-542-2170
Concord, NC 28025

Thousands of independent activities teaching over 750 words.

$ 1929.00

2645 Sensible Speller, Talking APH Edition

American Printing House for the Blind
P.O. Box 6085   502-895-2405
Louisville, KY 40206

A speech output version of the spelling checker program from Sensible Software, Inc..

$ 96.97

2646 Special Education Public Domain Software

Learning Disabilities Association of America
4156 Library Road   412-341-1515
Pittsburgh, PA 15234

Over 400 volumes: single switch, cause & effect, readiness, language skills, emerging literacy, reading, math, science, social studies and more.

$ 5.00

2647 Special Writer Coach

Tom Snyder Productions
90 Sherman Street   617-876-4433
Cambridge, MA 02140

Designed specifically for a teacher, tutor, aide or professional who is trying to help students who have severe trouble writing.

$ 69.95

2648 Stanford-Binet Computer Report

Southern Micro Systems
3545 S. Church Street   919-548-1661
Burlington, NC 27215

Generates a five-page psychological report based on the student's performance.

$ 295.00

2649 System 2000

Words, Inc.
P.O. Box 1229   800-869-8521
Lancaster, CA 93584   800-869-8521

A personal communication system that offers touch screen, full keyboard or alternate input methods, digitized sound recording and playback capability.

2650 Telesensory

455 North Bernardo Avenue   800-227-8418
Mountain View, CA 94043

Helps visually impaired people become more independent with the most comprehensive products available anywhere for reading, writing, taking notes and using computers.

2651 Ultimate File Cabinet

Access Unlimited
3535 Briarpark Dr., #102   713-781-7441
Houston, TX 77042

A file management package that allows storage adn retrieval of up to 500 files of information on a single floppy disk.

$ 40.00

2652 VELAN Educational Network System

Learning Disabilities Association of America
4156 Library Road   412-341-1515
Pittsburgh, PA 15234

Allows all curriculum software to be installed on a central hard drive, eliminating the need to use floppy disks.

2653 Verbal View

Computer Conversations
6297 Worthington Road SW   614-924-2885
Alexandria, OH 43001

Enlarges the print on the computer screen at a keystroke for reading by computer users.

$ 249.95

2654 VoiceType

IBM - Special Needs Systems
P.O. Box 2150   800-426-2133
Atlantaton, GA 30301   800-426-2133

A flexible speech recognition system that provides an affordable keyboard alternative. It lets the operator control DOS and many popular text-based software programs by speaking.

2655 Write:Outloud

Don Johnston Developmental Equipment, Inc.
P.O. Box 639, 1000 N. Rand Road   708-526-2682
Wauconda, IL 60084   800-999-4660
FAX 708-526-4177

Paula Kwit, Vice President
Ruth Ziolkowski, Sales Manager

Talking word processor for the Macintosh computer. Easy to use and puts file navigation, speech and file management tools in on-screen ribbon buttons. Supports multi-sensory learning with speech output letter-by-letter, word-by-word, sentence-by-sentence or paragraph-by-paragraph.

$ 125.00

2656 Writing Center

The Learning Company
6493 Kaiser Drive   415-792-2101
Fremont, CA 94555

Designed to meet the writing and publishing needs of students, families and social groups.

$ 89.00

Writing

2657 Adventures in Reading Comprehension: the Classics

Queue, Inc.
338 Commerce Drive   203-335-0906
Fairfield, CT 06430   800-232-2224
FAX 203-336-2481

In these exciting programs, student explore and interact with their favorite characters, answer questions, watch animations and listen to sound effects and music. These classic tales are beautifully retold for appropriate reading levels.

$ 49.95

2658 Banner Books

Queue, Inc.
338 Commerce Drive   203-335-0906
Fairfield, CT 06430   800-232-2224
FAX 203-336-2481

This is a format students and teachers will love. Students select a variety of backgrounds and watch as they move by on the screen. Students then add clip art and text to create their own Banner Book pages. Offers various programs.

$ 49.95

2659   Conover Company

P.O. Box 155   800-933-1933
Omro, WI 54963

Survival skills system software assists in the transition
from school to the community and workplace.

2660   Creative Learning, Inc.

P.O. Box 829   800-842-5360
North San Juan, CA 95960

Multisensory Curriculum.

2661   Dr. Peet's Picture Writer

Dr. Peet's Software
71 Laurie Circle   901-668-5812
Jackson, TN 38305   800-354-2950

A talking picture-writer. It guides first writers, regardless
of age, motivation or ability, in creating simple sentences
about things that are interesting and important to them.
$ 499.95

2662   Easy Report Writer

The Speech Bin
1965 Twenty-Fifth Avenue   407-770-0007
Vero Beach, FL 32960   FAX 407-770-0006

Jan J. Binney, Editor In Chief
Barbara Hector, Office Manager

Now create IEP's and treatment plans, evaluation reports
and any other report needed in as little as two minutes.
$ 149.50

2663   Gateway Authoring System

Don Johnston Developmental Equipment, Inc.
1000 N. Rand Road0 N. Rand Rd.   708-526-2682
Wauconda, IL 60084   800-999-4660
                                  FAX 708-526-4177

Convert your lessons and student stories to the Gateway
format. This HyperCard system makes it easy to create
literature that lets your reader independently select, hear
and turn pages with a mouse click.

2664   The Incredible Adventures of Quentin

Queue, Inc.
338 Commerce Drive   203-335-0906
Fairfield, CT 06430   800-232-2224
                                  FAX 203-336-2481

Students can interact with the story on a screen, with
wonderful visual and sound effects, animation and music,
for a multisensory learning experience.
$ 225.00

2665   Judy Lynn Software

278 Dunhams Corner Road   908-390-8845
East Brunswick, NJ 08816

2666   Junior High Writing Series

MindPlay
Unit F92, P.O. Box 36491   602-322-6365
Tucson, AZ 85740   800-221-7911

Sample writings and practice exercises on five specific
topics using a complete word processor.
$ 229.00

2667   Media Magic

Queue, Inc.
338 Commerce Drive   203-335-0906
Fairfield, CT 06430   800-232-2224
                                  FAX 203-336-2481

Students can create their own single concept programs and
dazzling desk top presentations. This one program offers
spectacular, innovative ways to create dynamic computer
programs and presentations with an easy-to-use Mouse or
keyboard interface.
$ 199.95

2668   Modern Writing Skills

Aquarius Instructional
P.O. Box 128   813-595-7890
Indiana Rocks Beach, FL 34635   800-338-2644
                                  FAX 813-595-2685

An interactive approach to writing that coordinates with
required reading and utilizes critical thinking skills.
$ 1250.00

2669   Name Writing

Edmark Corporation
P.O. Box 3218   206-746-3900
Redmond, WA 98073   800-362-2890

Helps special students learn to read and write their names.
$ 69.00

2670   PRD

ComputAbility Corporation
40000 Grand River, #109 109   313-477-6720
Novi, MI 48375   800-433-8872

This IBM computer shorthand program works with your
word processor of other software to allow shortened input
of words and phrases.

2671   Print Shop (new)

Software to Go - Galluadet University
800 Florida Avenue NE   202-651-5705
Washington, DC 20002

2672   Raised Dot Computing

408 South Baldwin Street   800-347-9594
Madison, WI 53703

2673   Realtime Learning Systems

2700 Connecticut Avenue NW   202-483-1510
Washington, DC 20008

2674 Senior High Writing Series

MindPlay
Unit F92, P.O. Box 36491   602-322-6365
Tucson, AZ 85740   800-221-7911

Sample writings and practice exercises on five specific topics using a complete word processor.

$ 229.00

2675 The Sensible Pencil

Edmark Corporation
P.O. Box 3218   206-746-3900
Redmond, WA 98073   800-362-2890

Students learn to form upper and lower case manuscript letters and numbers with this carefully structured program.

$ 49.95

2676 Snoopy Writer

Queue, Inc.
338 Commerce Drive   203-335-0906
Fairfield, CT 06430   800-232-2224
                                  FAX 203-336-2481

To fire a young writer's imagination, this word processing program generates colorful pictures of the PEANUTS gang along with optional story-starter sentences that solve the problems of "what to write about".

"Most highly rated."
-Only The Best, 1989 Edition
$ 29.95

2677 Snoopy's Skywriter Scrambler

Queue, Inc.
338 Commerce Drive   203-335-0906
Fairfield, CT 06430   800-232-2224
                                  FAX 203-336-2481

The Flying Ace soars across the screen, trailing the game word behind him. The goal: to make as many words as possible from Snoopy's challenge word.

$ 39.95

2678 Software and Resources

97 Manchester Road   617-969-2614
Newton Highlands, MA

2679 Story-Ware

Don Johnston Developmental Equipment, Inc.
1000 N. Rand Road0 N. Rand Rd.   708-526-2682
Wauconda, IL 60084   800-999-4660
                                  FAX 708-526-4177

This system lets the writer illustrate an original story, add sound effects and present the creation to others.
"Our students voted Story-Ware their favorite writing program...and so did the teachers."
-Judy Timms/Carolina Computer Access Ctr.

2680 Talking Fingers

Learning Disabilities Association of America
4156 Library Road   412-341-1515
Pittsburgh, PA 15234

Teaches phonics, encoding, writing, typing and word processing by associating each speech sound with a finger stroke on the keyboard.

$ 149.00

2681 Teaching Competence in Written Language

Edmark Corporation
P.O. Box 3218   206-746-3900
Redmond, WA 98073   800-362-2890

Provides a systematic writing program for those with special needs.

$ 49.00

2682 TechWare Corporation

P.O. Box 151085   800-347-3224
Altamonte Springs, FL

2683 Touch N' Write

Edmark Corporation
P.O. Box 3903   206-746-3900
Bellevue, WA 98009

Memory exercises in which students use the TouchWindow to turn cards bearing shapes, upper and lower case letters, numbers and words.

$ 39.95

2684 Typing Is a Ball, Charlie Brown

Queue, Inc.
338 Commerce Drive   203-335-0906
Fairfield, CT 06430   800-232-2224
                                  FAX 203-336-2481

Practice typing and word recognition with the PEANUTS gang.

$ 29.95

2685 Wish Writer

Consultants for Communication Technology
508 Bellevue Terrace   412-761-6062
Pittsburgh, PA 15202

A word processing program designed to be used by single switch users. It's word prediction feature helps the user produce documents with fewer key strokes.

$ 250.00

2686 Write - Right Now!

Edmark Corporation
P.O. Box 3218   206-746-3900
Redmond, WA 98073   800-362-2890

This program develops writing skills with this two-semester program.

$ 125.00

2687 Writing with POWER

Learning Disabilities Association of America
4156 Library Road   412-341-1515
Pittsburgh, PA 15234

A complete curriculum teaching writing and grammar applications.

$ 899.00

General

2688 ACLD - Youth and Adult Section Newsletter

Learning Disabilities Association of America
4156 Library Road   412-341-1515
Pittsburgh, PA 15234

Offers information on the ACLD international conferences, activity suggestions, group news and educational information for the learning disabled.

2689 American College Testing - Activity

ACT Test Administration
P.O. Box 168   319-337-1410
Iowa City, IA 52243

Dr. Patricia Farrant, Assistant VP

Activity newsletter is offered for counselors, administrators, advisors and educators at all levels of education.

2690 American School Board Journal

National School Board Association
1680 Duke Street   703-838-6722
Alexandria, VA 22314   FAX 703-683-7590

Sally Zakariya, Managing Editor

A monthly magazine for school board members and school administrators covering issues such as government, social investments and curriculums.

2691 Annals of Otology, Rhinology and Laryngology

Annals Publishing Company
4507 Lacleded Avenue   314-367-4987
St. Louis, MO 63108   FAX 314-367-4988

Offers clinical research to speech pathologists, surgeons, pathology consultants and more.

2692 ASCD Update

Association for Supervision/Curriculum Development
1250 North Pitt Street   703-549-9110
Alexandria, VA 22314

Ronald Brandt, Executive Editor
Marge Scherer, Managing Editor

News on contemporary education issues and information on ASCD programs.

2693 Autism Bibliography

Kelly MacGregor, Author
TASH
11201 Greenwood Avenue North   206-361-8870
Seattle, WA 98133

300 recent references to publications on autism.

2694 Autism Research Review

Institute of Child Behavior Research
4182 Adams Avenue   619-281-7165
San Diego, CA 92116

A quarterly newsletter that reviews current research pertaining to autism.

$ 16.00

2695 Avant Garde

Rocky Mountain Resource and Training Institute
6355 Ward Road, Ste. 310   303-420-2942
Arvada, CO 80004   FAX 303-420-8675

A national newsletter on integrated services containing valuable information on current trends and best practices on issues related to people with disabilities including learning disabilities.

2696 CABE Journal

Connecticut Association of Boards of Education
309 Franklin Street   203-296-8201
Hartford, CT 06114

Published for school board members and deals with a wide range of issues such as; legal, teaching and learning, finances and resources, at-risk youth and more.

2697 The Case Manager

Systemedic Corporation
10809 Executive Center Dr. #105   501-227-5553
Little Rock, AR 72211   FAX 501-227-8362

Offers articles and information for the case manager working with persons with disabilities.

2698 CASE Newsletter

Council of Administrators of Special Education
615 SW 7th Street   507-285-8738
Rochester, MN 55902

Virginia Dixon, Editor

Information to CASE members on issues pertinent to education of youth with special needs.

$ 48.00

2699 Chalk Talk

Fresno Teachers Association
5334 North Fresno #A   209-224-8430
Fresno, CA 93710

Pat Imperatrice, Editor

Improvement in public education and the condition of the working wnvironment of public school teachers.

$ 2.00

2700 Children and Youth Services Review

Pergamon Press, Inc.
Fairview Park   914-592-7700
Elmsford, NY 10523   FAX 914-592-3625

2701 Classroom Computer Learning

Peter Li, Inc.
2451 East River Road #200
Dayton, OH 45439   513-847-5900

An educational magazine geared toward teachers.

2702 Creative Classroom

Children's Television Workshop
One Lincoln Plaza   212-595-3456
New York, NY 10023

Elaine Israel, Editor-in-Chief
Mina B. Link, Publisher

Classroom ideas, lesson suggestions, materials listings, advice and articles on teaching students current events such as environment issues. Covers all subjects and includes a calendar of special events and suggested projects.

$ 16.95

2703 CYDLINE Reviews

University of Minnesota
Harvard Street At East Road   612-626-2825
Minneapolis, MN 55455   800-333-6293

A series of bibliographies produced by the National Center for Youth with Disabilities.

2704 Disability Issues

Business Publishers
951 Pershing Drive   301-587-6300
Silver Spring, MD 20910   800-274-0122
    FAX 301-585-9075

Linda Hillyer, Editor

Covers a variety of topics relating to a wide range of disabilities. Reviews and information on everything from assistive technology to available resources are offered.

2705 Division for Children with Communication Disorders Newsletter

The Council for Exceptional Children
1920 Association Drive   703-620-3660
Reston, VA 22091

Chad Nye, Editor

Information concerning the welfare and education of children and youth with communication disorders.

2706 The DLD Times Newsletter

The Council for Exceptional Children
1920 Association Drive   703-620-3660
Reston, VA 22091   FAX 703-264-9494

Katherine Garnett, Editor

Includes highlights of current research and programs; DLD position statements; reports of division membership, elections, committee and meeting activities; an event calendar; highlights of CEC/DLD convention evenets and information about new ERIC documents, organizations and publications of interest.

2707 Dyslexia: How Would I Cope?

Michael Ryden, Author
Jessica Kingsley Publishers
118 Pentonville Road   071-833-2307
London, England, N1 9JB   FAX 071-837-2917

Offers information on dyslexia and the rehabilitation process.

$ 5.95

2708 ED LIB - Higher Educational Information Center

Boston Public Library
666 Boylston Street   617-536-0200
Boston, MA 02116   800-442-1171

Newsletter offering information on career counseling, educational opportunities, workshops and programs.

2709 The Education Digest

College of Education
University Of Illinois   217-333-0962
Urbana, IL 61801

2710 Education Technology News

Business Publishers
951 Pershing Drive   301-587-6300
Silver Spring, MD 20910   800-274-0122
    FAX 301-585-9075

David Ritchie, Editor

Newsletter dealing with news, reviews and updates for those using technology for educational purposes.

$ 267.54

2711 Education U.S.A.

National School Public Relations Association
1501 Lee Highway #201   703-528-5840
Arlington, VA 22209

Joseph Scherer, Publisher

Education events, conferences, legislative actions, government policy and curriculum trends.

$ 99.00

2712 Education Week

4301 Connecticut Ave NW #432   202-364-4114
Washington, DC 20008

Offers articles of interest to educators, teachers, professionals and special educators on the latest developments, laws, issues and more in the various fields of education.

$ 59.94

2713 Educational Leadership

Association for Supervision/Curriculum Development
1250 North Pitt Street   703-549-9110
Alexandria, VA 22314

2714 Educational Researcher

American Educational Research Association
1230 17th Street NW   202-223-9485
Washington, DC 20036

2715 Educational Technology

Educational Technology Publications
700 Palisade Avenue   201-871-4009
Englewood Cliffs, NJ 07632

2716 Electronic Learning

Scholastic
730 Broadway   212-505-6006
New York, NY 10003

For curriculum planners and administrators working with grades K-12 offering articles on planning, purchasing, teacher-training, curriculum application and more. Offers a complete buyers guide for software and hardware.

2717 Ethical Principles of Psychologists and Code of Conduct

American Psychological Association
Order Dept., P.O. Box 2710   202-336-5510
Hyattsville, MD 20784   800-374-2721
          FAX 202-336-5502

A journal offering information on ethical principles and standards for persons in the area of psychology.

2718 Exceptionality

Springer International - Exceptionality EXCEET
University Of VA, Ruffner Hall
Charlottesville, VA 22903

A research journal for the Division of Research for the Council of Exceptional Children.

2719 The Exchange

The Learning Disability Network
30 Pond Park Road   617-982-8100
Hingham, MA 02043

Polly Cowen, Administrator
Cynthia Christopher, Asst. Director

A semi-annual forum for the exchange of ideas pertinent to learning disabilities.

$ 20.00

2720 Faculty Inservice Education Kit

Association on Higher Education and Disability
P.O. Box 21192   614-488-4972
Columbus, OH 43221   FAX 614-488-1174

Lists all the handouts and documentation necessary to conduct inservice training for the postsecondary community regarding the inclusion of students with disabilities in campus life.

$ 35.95

2721 Federal Grants & Contracts Weekly

Capitol Publications, Inc.
1101 King Street #444   703-683-4100
Alexandria, VA 22314

Helen Hoart, Publisher

The most timely and complete record of new federal grants and contracts in research, services and training available anywhere.

$ 329.00

2722 Focus on Autistic Behavior

Pro-Ed
8700 Shoal Creek Blvd.   512-451-3246
Austin, TX 78758

Aimed at educators of autistic children.

2723 Gifted Child Today

GCT, Inc.
Box 6448   205-478-4700
Mobile, AL 36660

2724 Headlines

P.O. Box 33
Boston, MA 02117

Advancing the health care professional's knowledge of neurologic injuries and conditions.

2725 The Hidden Handicap

Learning Disabilities Association of America
P.O. Box 15525   602-230-7188
Phoenix, AZ 85060

A professional journal offering information on how to understand learning disabled students.

2726 Hints for Teaching Children with Learning Disabilities

Learning Disabilities Association of America
P.O. Box 15525   602-230-7188
Phoenix, AZ 85060

Offers information and facts on the best methods to teach the learning disabled child.

2727 Information From HEATH

One Dupont Circle, Ste. 800   202-939-9320
Washington, DC 20036   800-544-3284

A newsletter offering information on postsecondary education for individuals with disabilities.

2728 InfoTech Newsletter

InfoTech
University Of Iowa   800-331-3027
Iowa City, IA 52242

A free publication covering topics relating to assistive technology, including announcements from Iowa's IPAT Program and from Minnesota's S.T.A.R. Program as well as Used Equipment Referral Service listing.

2729 Instructor

730 Broadway   212-505-4900
New York, NY 10003

A source for curriculum enrichment, ideas and activities for math, science, language arts and social studies.

2730 Integration Strategies for Students

Robert Gaylord-Ross, Author

Paul H. Brookes Publishing Company
P.O. Box 10624   410-337-8539
Baltimore, MD 21285

This up-to0date textbook provides the practical overviews and detailed strategies needed to understand all facets of integration movements in today's educational, community and work settings.

> *"Structured in an excellent style...actual teaching techniques that can be used in a real classroom"*
> -Journal of Rehab Counseling

$ 35.00

2731 In-The-Mainstream

Mainstream, Inc.
3 Bethesda Metro Center, Ste. 830   301-654-2400
Bethesda, MD 20814   800-424-8089

A newsletter offering information and stories on issues that concern disabled persons.

2732 Journal of Applied Rehabilitation Counseling

National Rehabilitation Association
633 South Washington Street   703-836-0850
Alexandria, VA 22314

Articles on counseling history, research and practice of interest in rehabilitation.

2733 Journal of Learning Disabilities

Pro-Ed
8700 Shoal Creek Blvd.   512-451-3246
Austin, TX 78757   FAX 512-451-8542

J. Lee Wiederholt, EdD, Editor-In-Chief
Judith K. Voress, PhD, Periodicals Director

A multidisciplinary publication containing articles on practice, research and theory related to learning disabilities.

2734 Journal of Postsecondary Education and Disability

Association on Higher Education and Disability
P.O. Box 21192   614-488-4972
Columbus, OH 43227

Provides in-depth examination of research, issues, policies and programs in postsecondary education.

2735 Journal of Rehabilitation

National Rehabilitation Association
633 South Washington Street   800-535-9982
Alexandria, VA 22314

The Journal of the National Rehabilitation Association is dedicated to all disabilities. Included are seventeen major articles written by leaders in the field of learning disabilities.

$ 7.50

2736 Journal of School Health

American School Health Association
P.O. Box 708   216-678-1601
Kent, OH 44240

2737 Journal of Special Education Technology

Peabody College, Box 328
Vanderbilt University
Nashville, TN 37203

2738 LDA Newsbriefs

Learning Disabilities Association of America
4156 Library Road   412-341-1515
Pittsburgh, PA 15234

2739 Learning

Springhouse Corporation
1111 Bethlehem Pike   215-646-8700
Springhouse, PA 19477

Ideas and information for special education teachers.

$ 14.96

2740 Learning Disabilities a Multidisciplinary Journal

Learning Disabilities Association of America
4156 Library Road   412-341-1515
Pittsburgh, PA 15234

Jeannette Fleischner, Editor-in-Chief

A vehicle for disseminating the most current thinking on learning disabilities and to provide information on research, practice, theory, issues and trends regarding learning disabilities.

2741 Learning Disabilities Association of America/ Magazine

4156 Library Road   412-341-1515
Pittsburgh, PA 15234

Jean Petersen, Executive Director

Offers pamphlets, informational guides, educational resources and advocacy for the learning disabled.

$ 13.50

2742 Learning Disabilities Newsletter

Learning Disabilities Consultants
P.O. Box 716   215-252-8336
Bryn Mawr, PA 19010

Offers information on difficulties associated with learning disabilities.

2743 Learning Unlimited Network of Oregon

31960 SE Chin Street   503-663-5153
Boring, OR 97009

Gene Lehman, Editor

Networking newsletter reaching out to all interested in alternatives to traditional thinking about education, schools and government, social instituions and more.

$ 10.00

2744 Learning 90

Springhouse Corporation
1111 Bethlehem Pike   215-646-8700
Springhose, PA 19477

2745 Literacy News

National Institute for Literacy
800 Connecticut Ave., Ste. 200   202-632-1500
Washington, DC 20202

Provides current information on what the Institute is doing (and progress).

2746 Mainstream

Johnson Press
2973 Beech Street   619-234-3138
San Diego, CA 92102

2747 Me! a Curriculum for Teaching Self-Esteem Through An Interest Center

Jo Ellen Hartline, Author

Connecticut Association for Children with LD
18 Marshall Street   203-838-5010
South Norwalk, CT 06854   FAX 203-866-6108

$ 18.50

2748 Media & Methods Magazine

1429 Walnut Street
Philadelphia, PA 19102

2749 National Organization on Disability Report

910 Sixteenth Street NW, Ste. 600   202-293-5960
Washington, DC 20006   FAX 202-293-7999

A newsletter offering information and articles on the organization.

2750 Network Exchange

Learning Disabilities Network
25 Accord Park Drive   617-982-8100
Rockland, MA 02370

Provides a forum for the exchange of ideas pertinent to learning disabilities.

2751 NewsLinks

International Schools Services
15 Roszel Road   609-452-0990
Princeton, NJ 08543

Mea Kaemmerlen, Editor

Articles and information relevant to international and American teachers around the world.

2752 NICHCY Briefing Paper

Nat'l Info. Center for Children/Youth Disabilities
P.O. Box 1492   800-999-5599
Washington, DC 20013

A newsletter offering information, guides, books and reference sources for the learning disabled.

2753 Occupational Outlook Quarterly

U.S. Department of Labor
Bureau Of Labor Statistics   202-272-5298
Washington, DC 20212

Information on new educational and training opportunities, emerging jobs, prospects for change in the work world and the latest research findings.

2754 Occupational Therapy Forum

Suite A-115, 251 W. Dekalb Pike   215-337-0381
King Of Prussia, PA 19406

Newsletter for professionals in the field of occupational therapy.

2755 Occupational Therapy in Health Care

The Haworth Press
12 West 32nd Street   212-279-1200
New York, NY 10001

Each issues focuses on significant practices and concerns involving occupational therapy and therapists.

2756 Packet of ADHD Articles

Connecticut Association for Children with LD
18 Marshall Street 203-838-5010
South Norwalk, CT 06854 FAX 203-866-6108

Contains reprints of seven newspapers and other short articles which discuss various aspects of ADHD including identification, medication and other forms of therapy.

$ 7.00

2757 The PEATC Press

Parent Educational Advocacy Training Center
228 South Pitt Street, Ste. 300 703-836-2953
Alexandria, VA 22314

A newsletter offering information to parents and professionals on the organization.

2758 Perceptions, Inc.

P.O. Box 142 201-376-3766
Millburn, NJ 07041

Bebe Antell, Editor
Offers various professional newsletters.

2759 PLUS - Project Literacy U.S.

WQED
4802 Fifth Avenue 412-622-1320
Pittsburgh, PA 15213

Margot Woodwell, Project Director
Herb Stein, Assistant Director
A newsletter offering information on learning disabilities.

2760 Practical Approaches

Lexia Learning Systems, Inc.
11a Lewis Street, P.O. Box 466 617-259-8751
Lincoln, MA 01773

A newsletter devoted to learning disabilities.

2761 Pure Facts

Feingold Association of the United States
Box 6550 703-768-3287
Alexandria, VA 22306

Jane Hersey, Editor
Explains the relationship between foods and behavior/learning problems.

2762 Rehabilitation Education

Pergamon Press, Inc.
Fairview Park 914-592-7700
Elmsford, NY 10523

Rehabilitation education, curricula and continuing education newsletter.

2763 Rehabilitation Grants and Contracts

RPM Press, Inc.
P.O. Box 31483 602-886-1990
Tucson, AZ 85751

Jan Stonebraker, Operations Manager
Newsletter providing a listing of grants and contracts available in the areas of special education, education, voced special needs, vocational rehabilitation, mental health, job training, housing, transportation and a variety of other human service fields.

$ 97.00

2764 Report on Disability Programs

Business Publishers
951 Pershing Drive 301-587-6300
Silver Spring, MD 20910

Contains information on legislation, regulations and current topics pertaining to the disabled.

$ 253.00

2765 Reporting Classroom Research

Ontario Educational Research Council
979 Finley Avenue 416-428-6622
Ajax, ON, Canada, L1 S 3V5

Dr. Dormer Ellis, Editor
Deals mainly with research related to teaching, learning and school problems.

$ 6.00

2766 Scouting and the Learning Disabled: a Manual for Scouting Leaders

Boy Scouts Of America, Author
Connecticut Association for Children with LD
18 Marshall Street 203-838-5010
South Norwalk, CT 06854 FAX 203-866-6108

$ 5.25

2767 Self-Advocacy Resources for Persons with Learning Disabilities

Learning Disabilities Association of America
4156 Library Road 412-341-1515
Pittsburgh, PA 15234

A newsletter offering information on resources and programs for the learning disabled.

2768 Shortcuts for Teachers

J. Enk, Author
Connecticut Association for Children with LD
18 Marshall Street 203-838-5010
South Norwalk, CT 06854 FAX 203-866-6108

$ 7.75

2769 Special Education Leadership

Sunday School Board Southern Baptist Conv.
127 9th Avenue North   **615-251-2000**
Nashville, TN 37234

Covers special education issues relating to religious education.

$ 7.50

2770 Specialty Guidelines for the Delivery of Services

American Psychological Association
Order Dept., P.O. Box 2710   **202-336-5510**
Hyattsville, MD 20784   **800-374-2721**
                          FAX 202-336-5502

A journal offering clinical psychologists, counseling psychologists, school psychologists and industrial/organizational psychologists information on guidelines, ethics and standards for theis various fields.

2771 Specific Dyslexia Developmental Problems

Lucius Weiss, Author

Educators Publishing Service, Inc.
75 Moulton Street   **800-225-5750**
Cambridge, MA 02138

Reviews eleven kinds of developmental problems the author has dealt with as a medical director.

$ 8.00

2772 Teacher Magazine

Editorial Projects in Education
4301 Connecticut Avenue NW   **202-364-4114**
Washington, DC 20008

Offers articles and information on the newest programs, software, books, classroom materials and more for the teaching professional.

$ 17.94

2773 Teaching Exceptional Children

ERIC Clearinghouse on Disabled and Gifted Children
1920 Association Drive   **703-620-3660**
Reston, VA 22901

A quarterly journal for special education teachers.

2774 Teaching Notes

University of Guelph
Educational Practice   **519-824-4120**
Guelph, ON, Canada, N1 G 2W1

Informs faculty and graduate students of practical or new items in the areas of teaching and learning.

2775 The Texas Key

Learning Disabilities Association of America
1011 West 31st Street   **512-458-8234**
Austin, TX 78705   **FAX 512-458-3826**

Ann Robinson, Editor

Information on the organization and the field of learning disabilities.

2776 Thinking Families

605 Worcester Road
Towson, MD 21204

2777 Try Another Way Training Manual

Dr. Marc Gold, Author

Research Press
P.O. Box 9177   **217-352-3273**
Champaign, IL 61826   **FAX 217-351-1221**

This manual illustrates how to write detailed and extremely functional task analyses for training individuals with developmental disabilities.

2778 Underachieving Gifted

The Council for Exceptional Children
1920 Association Drive   **703-620-3660**
Reston, VA 22091

A collection of annotated references from the ERIC and Exceptional Child Evaluation Resources (171 abstracts). Note: Abstracts only. Not the complete research.

$ 18.00

2779 Whole Literacy: Possibilities and Challenges

Connie Bridge, Author

International Reading Association
800 Barksdale Rd., P.O. Box 8139 **302-731-1600**
Newark, DE 19714   **800-336-READ**
                   FAX 302-731-1057

This special journal issue explores the possibilities and challenges of implementing a holistic, whole literacy approach to elementary education.

$ 3.00

Attention Deficit Disorder

2780 Challenge

Challenge, Inc.
P.O. Box 488   **508-462-0495**
West Newbury, MA 01985

A newsletter focusing on Attention Deficit Disorder published in association with the National Deficit Disorder Association.

$ 20.00

2781 A Description of Youngsters with Organization/Output Difficulties

Elsie Freeman, Author

Connecticut Association for Children with LD
18 Marshall Street   **203-838-5010**
South Norwalk, CT 06854   **FAX 203-866-6108**

Comprehensive general introduction to ADHD.

$ 2.50

Counseling & Psychology

2782 American Psychologist

American Psychological Association
750 First Street NW
Washington, DC 20036

202-336-5500
800-374-2721
FAX 202-336-5502

Raymond Fowler, Editor

Contains articles of broad interest to all psychologists that cut across all domains of the field of psychology. The articles are theoretical in nature.

2783 CAPS Capsule

ERIC Clearinghouse Disabled and Gifted Children
2108 School Of Education
Ann Arbor, MI 48109

313-764-9492

Covers news about ERIC and the latest developments in the field of education and counseling.

2784 Counselor Education and Supervision

American Association for Counseling & Development
5999 Stevenson Avenue
Alexandria, VA 22304

703-823-9800

Covers research, theory development and program applications pertinent to counseling and counselor education.

$ 7.00

2785 Educational Therapist

14852 Ventura Blvd., Ste. 207
Sherman Oaks, CA 91403

818-788-3850

Contains articles on such topics as clinical practice, current theory, research, reviews of testing methods and assessments of materials. A legislative summary is included.

$ 25.00

2786 Epstein Quarterly

Connecticut Association for Children with LD
18 Marshall Street
South Norwalk, CT 06854

203-838-5010
FAX 203-866-6108

A psychiatric newsletter for professionals.

$ 1.00

2787 Journal of Social and Clinical Psychology

72 Spring Street
New York, NY 10012

800-365-7006

Jody Falco, Managing Editor

Examines and reports the burgeoning areas of theory, research and practice. This journal was created to foster interdisciplinary communication and scholarship among practitioners of social and clinical psychology. It concen-

trates on presenting solid clinical and experimental reports on a wide range of topics crucial to the practice and study of mental health.

$ 35.00

2788 Learning Disabilities: Research and Practice

Lawrence Erlbaum Associates, Inc.
365 Broadway
Hillsdale, NJ 07642

201-666-4110
800-9-BOOKS9
FAX 201-666-2394

Hollis Humbouck, Senior Editor
Joe Petrowski, Executive VP

A journal for researchers and practitioners, focusing on the nature and characteristics for learning disabled students; provides great value for professionals in a variety of discipline including school psychology, counseling, reading and medicine.

2789 Psychological Assessment of the Learning Disabled Child

V. Harway, Author

Learning Disabilities Association of America
4156 Library Road
Pittsburgh, PA 15234

412-341-1515

$ 1.00

2790 Psychotherapeutic Issues for the Learning Disabled Adults

Steven Shulman, Author

Connecticut Association for Children with LD
18 Marshall Street
South Norwalk, CT 06854

203-838-5010
FAX 203-866-6108

$ 3.00

Language Arts

2791 American Journal of Speech-Language Pathology: Clinical Practice

ASHA Fulfillment Operations
10801 Rockville Pike
Rockville, MD 20852

301-897-5700

Addressess all aspects of clinical practice in speech-language pathology.

2792 ASHA - the Monthly Magazine

ASHA Fulfillment Operations
10801 Rockville Pike
Rockville, MD 20852

301-897-5700

Pertains to the professional and administrative activities in the fields of speech-language pathology, audiology and the American Speech-Language-Hearing Association.

2793 Communication Outlook

Michigan University/Artificial Langauge Laboratory
405 Computer Center   517-353-0870
East Lansing, MI 48824

Tammy Watt
A magazine focusing on communication aids and techniques.

$ 18.00

2794 English Journal

National Council of Teachers of English
1111 Kenyon Road   217-328-3870
Urbana, IL 61801

2795 Journal of Physical Education, Recreation and Dance

1900 Association Drive   703-476-3475
Reston, VA 22091

2796 Journal of Speech and Hearing Research

ASHA Fulfillment Operations
10801 Rockville Pike   301-897-5700
Rockville, MD 20852

An archival research publication that includes papers pertaining to the processes and disorders of hearing, language, speech and to the diagnosis and treatment of these disorders.

2797 Kaleidoscope, International Magazine of Literature, Fine Arts & Disability

326 Locust Street   216-762-9755
Akron, OH 44302   FAX 216-762-0912

Cheryl Hultman, Publication Director
Darshan Perusek, PhD, Editor-in-Chief

Creatively focuses on the experience of disability through diverse forms of literature and the fine arts. An award-winning magazine unique to the field of disability studies, it is open to writers with or without disabilities. KALEIDOSCOPE strives to express how disability does, or does not affect society and individuals feelings and reactions to disability. Its portrayals of disability reflects a conscious effort to challenge and overcome stereotypical and patronizing attitudes.

2798 Language Arts

National Council of Teachers of English
1111 Kenyon Road   217-328-3870
Urbana, IL 61801

2799 NSSLHA Journal

ASHA Fulfillment Operations
10801 Rockville Pike   301-897-5700
Rockville, MD 20852

Features articles and reports on a variety of current speech-language-hearing topics of special interest to students and practicing clinicians.

Life Skills

2800 Establishing Group Homes for Adults with Autism

Eden Programs
One Logan Drive   609-987-0099
Princeton, NJ 08540   FAX 609-987-0243

David Holmes, EdD, Executive Director
Anne Holmes, M.S., C.C.C., Outreach Director

A practical guide to establishing community-based group homes.

$ 5.00

2801 Faculty Guidebook - Working with Students with Learning Disabilities

HEATH Resource Center
One Dupont Circle NW, Ste. 800   202-939-9320
Washington, DC 20036   800-544-3284

A compilation of articles written by various faculty members of New River Community College. Among others, topics addressed include suggestions for teaching general academic subjects, options for instruction in the social sciences, strategies and suggestions for math and data processing teachers and electrical/electronic technologies.

$ 7.50

2802 Service Operations Manual

HEATH Resource Center
One Dupont Circle NW, Ste. 800   202-939-9320
Washington, DC 20036   800-544-3284

This manual describes the system for delivering services to students with learning disabilities at community colleges.

$ 15.00

2803 Six Training Manuals From the Technical Assistance for Postsecondary Ed.

HEATH Resource Center
One Dupont Circle NW, Ste. 800   202-939-9320
Washington, DC 20036   800-544-3284

The manuals are designed to train community college personnel who work with individuals with learning disabilities.

$ 50.00

2804 Supervision and Evaluation of Support Personnel, CF's and SLP's

American Speech-Language-Hearing Association
10801 Rockville Pike   301-897-5700
Rockville, MD 20852   800-638-8255
                              FAX 301-571-0457

Cameron Werker, Marketing Coord.

Focuses on the issues of large caseloads, the shortage of qualified personnel and the evaluation of the performance of speech-language pathologists and audiologists by those who are not in the profession. Discusses how to handle these issues and provides strategies for implementing quality programs and proceduares in school systems.

2805 Vocational Education Journal

American Vocational Association
1410 King Street   703-683-3111
Alexandria, VA 22314

Pre-School

2806 Day Care and Early Education

Human Science Press
233 Spring Street   212-620-8000
New York, NY 10013   FAX 212-463-0742

Designed for early childhood teachers, program administrators and day care workers and other professionals concerned with the education of young children. This quarterly journal publishes peer reviewed articles covering child care programs, administration, staff development, family/school relationships, infant/toddler issues, advocacy and more.

2807 Early Childhood News

2451 East River Road
Dayton, OH 45439

2808 ERIC/EECE Newsletter

ERIC EECE College of Education
805 West Pennsylvania Avenue   217-333-1386
Urbana, IL 61801

Karen Steiner, Editor

Elementary and early childhood education, day care, parental behavior and child development from the prenatal period to age 12.

$ 5.00

2809 Help for Special Preschoolers: Activities Binder

Therapro, Inc.
225 Arlington Street   508-872-9494
Framingham, MA 01701   FAX 508-875-2062

Provides thousands of tested, effective activities correlated to the 625 checklist assessment skills.

$ 35.95

2810 Teaching Pre-Kindergarten Through 8th Grade

Early Years, Inc.
40 Richards Avenue, 7th Floor   203-855-2650
Norwalk, CT 06854

2811 Young Children

Nat'l Assoc. for the Education of Young Children
1834 Connecticut Avenue NW   202-232-8777
Washington, DC 20009

Reading

2812 Annual Summary of Investigations Relating to Reading

Sam Weintraub, Author

International Reading Association
800 Barksdale Rd., P.O. Box 8139   302-731-1600
Newark, DE 19714   800-336-READ
                                         FAX 302-731-1057

Summarizes reading research published in a given year from July 1 to June 30. These volumes identify and report the research available in periodicals and summarize many additional studies from books, conference proceedings, and other publications related to the field of reading.

$ 23.00

2813 Bringing About Change in Schools Journal of Reading

JoAnne Vacca, Author

International Reading Association
800 Barksdale Rd., P.O. Box 8139   302-731-1600
Newark, DE 19714   800-336-READ
                                         FAX 302-731-1057

These articles describe school-based change to bring about improved literacy instruction.

$ 5.00

2814 The Failure Free Reading Program

137 Corban Court   800-542-2170
Concord, NC 28025

The first and only program to control for the simultaneous use of these three critical elements. This dramatic reading breakthrough takes the mystery out of reading for struggling students by greatly simplfying what it takes to read successfully.

2815 Reading Disabilities: Interaction of Reading Language Deficits

Books on Special Children
P.O. Box 305   914-638-1236
Congers, NY 10920   FAX 914-638-0847

Offers research, theories, classifications and more of reading skills.

$ 57.00

2816   Reading Informer

Reading Reform Foundation
949 Market Street, #436   206-572-9966
Tacoma, WA 98402

Restoration of intensive phonics to beginning reading instruction.

$ 25.00

2817   The Reading Teacher

School of Education, Purdue University
West Lafayette, IN 47907

Study Skills

2818   SMARTS, a Study Skills Resource Guide

Susan Custer, Author
Connecticut Association for Children with LD
18 Marshall Street   203-838-5010
South Norwalk, CT 06854   FAX 203-866-6108

A comprehensive teachers handbook of activities to help students develop study skills.

$ 14.50

General

2819 Academic and Developmental Learning Disabilities

Samuel Kirk, Author
Love Publishing Company
1777 South Bellaire Street   303-757-2579
Denver, CO 80222

This text is intended to serve as a basis for classifying children and to help teachers diagnose and remediate children who have major disabilities in the learning process.

2820 Academic Therapy

Pro-Ed
8700 Shoal Creek Blvd.   512-451-3246
Austin, TX 78758

Features articles and instructional ideas to help teachers and therapists work with students with learning and behavior problems.

$ 20.00

2821 Adapting Early Childhood Curricula for Children with Special Needs

R.E Cook, Author '
Books on Special Children
P.O. Box 305   914-638-1236
Congers, NY 10920   FAX 914-638-0847

Helps child in emotional and behavior challenges especially those abused and drug exposed.

$ 25.95

2822 Adaptive Education Strategies

M.C. Wang, Author
Books on Special Children
P.O. Box 305   914-638-1236
Congers, NY 10920   FAX 914-638-0847

Knowing individual differences in learning can help provide experiences built on their competence then respond to their learning needs. This book offers information on how to develop programs, assessment and implementation planning and staff development.

$ 42.00

2823 Adults with Learning Disabilities: An Overview for the Adult Educator

Center on Education and Training for Employment
1900 Kenny Road   614-292-4353
Columbus, OH 43210   800-848-4815

A comprehensive manual for the adult educator as well as the special educator who serves the young adult with learning disabilities.

$ 7.00

2824 Affect and Creativity

Sandra Walker Russ, Author
Lawrence Erlbaum Associates, Inc.
365 Broadway   201-666-4110
Hillsdale, NJ 07642   FAX 201-666-2394

This volume offers information on the role of affect and play in the creative process. Designed as a required or supplemental text in graduate level courses in creativity, children's play, child development, affective/cognitive development and psychodynamic theory.

$ 36.00

2825 An Introduction to Learning Disabilities

Howard Adelman, Author
Scott, Foresman and Company
1900 East Lake Avenue
Glenview, IL 60025

This text is designed to introduce learning disabilities in a way that clarifies both instructional options and large educational issues.

2826 Art As a Language for the Learning Disabled Child

Learning Disabilities Association of America
4156 Library Road   412-341-1515
Pittsburgh, PA 15234

2827 Assessment in Special and Remedial Education

J. Salvia, Author
Learning Disabilities Association of America
4156 Library Road   412-341-1515
Pittsburgh, PA 15234

This book provides an excellent guide for many different kinds of assessments for learning disabled adults and children.

2828 Assisting College Students with Learning Disabilities: a Tutor's Manual

Association on Higher Education and Disability
P.O. Box 21192   614-488-4972
Columbus, OH 43221   FAX 614-488-1174

This manual is designed for use by service providers and tutors working with students with learning disabilities.

$ 26.00

2829 Auditory Processes

Pamela Gillet, Author
Academic Therapy Publications
20 Commercial Blvd.   415-883-3314
Novato, CA 94949   800-422-7249

Teachers how teachers, educational consultants and parents can identify auditory processing problems, understand their impact and implement appropriate instructional strategies to enhance learning.

$ 12.50

2830 Auditory Rehabilitation

Karlene Stefanakos, Author
The Speech Bin
1965 Twenty-Fifth Avenue   407-770-0007
Vero Beach, FL 32960   FAX 407-770-0006

Jan J. Binney, Editor In Chief
Barbara Hector, Office Manager

Helps adults or adolescents improve their ability to receive, retain and utilize auditory messages.

$ 69.00

2831 Behavioral Objectives for Learning Disabilities

Psychological and Educational Publishers, Inc.
1477 Rollins Road
Burlingame, CA 94010

A curriculum guide to help plan for your students with learning problems in pre-school and high school.

2832 Behavioral Technology Guidebook

Eden Programs
One Logan Drive   609-987-0099
Princeton, NJ 08540   FAX 609-987-0243

David Holmes, EdD, Executive Director
Anne Holmes, M.S., C.C.C., Outreach Director

Practical guide for behavioral modifications and techniques.

$ 45.00

2833 Better Understanding Learning Disabilities

G. Reid Lyon, PhD, Author
Paul H. Brookes Publishing Company
P.O. Box 10624   410-337-8539
Baltimore, MD 21285   800-638-3775
          FAX 410-337-8539

Research-based text provides a comprehensive study of theory, classification and future research directions facing professionals in the fiels of learning disabilities intervention.

$ 35.00

2834 Beyond Separate Education

A. Gartner, Author
Books on Special Children
P.O. Box 305   914-638-1236
Congers, NY 10920   FAX 914-638-0847

Collection of papers on including children who previously were out of the mainstream.

$ 38.00

2835 Bilingualism and Learning Disabilities

Learning Disabilities Association of America
4156 Library Road   412-341-1515
Pittsburgh, PA 15234

2836 Caseload Issues in Schools: Who Should Be Served?

American Speech-Language-Hearing Association
10801 Rockville Pike   301-897-5700
Rockville, MD 20852   800-638-8255

Covers caseload/service delivery issues including options to direct service delivery and procedures for establishing rating scales for case selection.

$ 28.00

2837 Children with Special Needs

Learning Disabilities Association of America
4156 Library Road   412-341-1515
Pittsburgh, PA 15234

2838 Classroom Integration and Collaborative Consultation As Service Models

American Speech-Language-Hearing Association
10801 Rockville Pike   301-897-5700
Rockville, MD 20852   800-638-8255

Describes alternative service delivery models such as integration of services into the classroom and consultation with classroom teachers.

$ 20.00

2839 Classroom Success for the Learning Disabled

Suzanne H. Stevens, Author
Learning Disabilities Association of America
4156 Library Road   412-341-1515
Pittsburgh, PA 15234

Offers valuable suggestions on recognizing the learning disabled child, adjusting teaching techniques and adapting texts and other materials.
   "This volume could be effectively used in a variety of ways from training teachers to parents..."
          -Library Journal
$ 10.50

2840 The Classroom Teachers Guide to Mainstreaming

A.J. Roffman, Author
Learning Disabilities Association of America
4156 Library Road   412-341-1515
Pittsburgh, PA 15234

$ 22.00

2841 Cognitive and Behavioral Characteristics of Learning Disabled Children

Joseph Torgesen, Author
Pro-Ed
8700 Shoal Creek Blvd.   512-451-3246
Austin, TX 78758   FAX 512-451-8542

Offers recent research on the cognitive and behavioral characteristics of children with learning disabilities.

$ 33.00

2842 A Cognitive Approach to Learning Disabilities

D. Kim Reid, Author
Pro-Ed
8700 Shoal Creek Blvd.   512-451-3246
Austin, TX 78758   FAX 512-451-8542

This book is the first to bridge the gap between cognitive psychology and information processing theory in understanding learning disabilities.

$ 38.00

2843 Cognitive Rehabilitation of Closed Head Injured Patients

Brenda Adamovich, Author
The Speech Bin
1965 Twenty-Fifth Avenue   407-770-0007
Vero Beach, FL 32960   FAX 407-770-0006

Jan J. Binney, Editor In Chief
Barbara Hector, Office Manager

Gives comprehensive diagnostic and treatment protocols for patients with closed head injuries.

$ 28.00

2844 Cognitive Retraining Using Microcomputers

Veronica Bradley, Author
Lawrence Erlbaum Associates, Inc.
365 Broadway   201-666-4110
Hillsdale, NJ 07642   FAX 201-666-2394

This text reviews representative examples from the literature relating to the training of cognitive systems with the emphasis on studies describing the use of computerized methods.

$ 69.95

2845 Cognitive Strategy Instruction to Improve Children's Academic Performance

Brookline Books
P.O. Box 1046   617-868-0360
Cambridge, MA 02238   FAX 617-868-1772

A concise and focused work that summarily presents the few procedures for teaching strategies that aid academic subject matter learning that are empirically validated and fit well with the elementary school curriculum.

2846 Competencies for Teachers of Students with Learning Disabilities

Amme Graves, Mary F. Landers, Jean Lockerson, Author
The Council for Exceptional Children
1920 Association Drive   703-620-3660
Reston, VA 22091

Lists 209 specific professional competencies needed by teachers of studens with learning disabilities and provides a conceptual framework for the tean areas in which the competencies are organized.

$ 5.00

2847 Complete Learning Disabilities Handbook

J.M. Hartwell, Author
Learning Disabilities Association of America
4156 Library Road   412-341-1515
Pittsburgh, PA 15234

2848 The Comprehensive Local School - Regular Education for All Disabled Students

J.L. Anderson, Author
Books on Special Children
P.O. Box 305   914-638-1236
Congers, NY 10920   FAX 914-638-0847

Defines "least restrictive environment" and how to integrate all children in regular classrooms.

$ 38.00

2849 Comprehensive Treatment of the Older Disabled Readers

Learning Disabilities Association of America
4156 Library Road   412-341-1515
Pittsburgh, PA 15234

2850 Curriculum Considerations in Inclusive Classrooms

S. Stainbeck, Author
Books on Special Children
P.O. Box 305   914-638-1236
Congers, NY 10920   FAX 914-638-0847

Contributions regarding inclusive schools attempt to be certain that all students are accepted as equal and recognized for what they have to offer.

$ 28.00

2851 Deal Me In: the Use of Playing Cards in Learning and Teaching

M. Golick, Author

Connecticut Association for Children with LD
18 Marshall Street   203-838-5010
South Norwalk, CT 06854   FAX 203-866-6108
                                    $ 9.85

2852 Dictionary of Special Education and Rehabilitation

Glenn A. Vergason, Author

Love Publishing Company
1777 South Bellaire Street   303-757-2579
Denver, CO 80222   FAX 303-757-6912

A valuable basic resource in the field. It incorporates hundreds of additions and changes.

                                    $ 19.95

2853 Disorders of Learning in Childhood

Learning Disabilities Association of America
4156 Library Road   412-341-1515
Pittsburgh, PA 15234

2854 Dysarthia and Apraxia of Speech

C.A. Moore, Author

Books on Special Children
P.O. Box 305   914-638-1236
Congers, NY 10920   FAX 914-638-0847

Offers perspectives, assessments, clinical measurements and case studies of dysarthia.

                                    $ 49.00

2855 Early Adolescence Perspectives on Research, Policy and Intervention

Richard M. Lerner, Author

Lawrence Erlbaum Associates, Inc.
365 Broadway   201-666-4110
Hillsdale, NJ 07642   FAX 201-666-2394

This forthcoming volume brings together a diverse group of scholars to write integratively about sutting-edge research issues pertinent to the study of early adolescence.

                                    $ 99.95

2856 The Early Intervention Dictionary

Jeanine Coleman, Author

Woodbine House
5615 Fishers Lane   301-468-8800
Rockville, MD 20852   800-843-7323

A multidisciplinary guide to terminology.

                                    $ 16.95

2857 Eden Institute Curriculum - Adaptive Physical Education, Volume V

Eden Programs
One Logan Drive   609-987-0099
Princeton, NJ 08540   FAX 609-987-0243

David Holmes, EdD, Executive Director
Anne Holmes, M.S., C.C.C., Outreach Director

Teaching programs in the areas of sensory integration and adaptive physical education.

                                    $ 50.00

2858 Eden Institute Curriculum - Classroom Orientation, Volume II

Eden Programs
One Logan Drive   609-987-0099
Princeton, NJ 08540   FAX 609-987-0243

David Holmes, EdD, Executive Director
Anne Holmes, M.S., C.C.C., Outreach Director

Academic and social skills programs for students with autism.

                                    $ 100.00

2859 Eden Institute Curriculum - Speech and Language, Volume IV

Eden Programs
One Logan Drive   609-987-0099
Princeton, NJ 08540   FAX 609-987-0243

David Holmes, EdD, Executive Director
Anne Holmes, M.S., C.C.C., Outreach Director

Speech and language development programs for students with autism.

                                    $ 170.00

2860 Eden Institute Curriculum - Volume I

Eden Programs
One Logan Drive   609-987-0099
Princeton, NJ 08540   FAX 609-987-0243

David Holmes, EdD, Executive Director
Anne Holmes, M.S., C.C.C., Outreach Director

Teaching programs for students with autism.

                                    $ 200.00

2861 Educating the Learning Disabled

E. Siegel & R. Gold, Author

Learning Disabilities Association of America
4156 Library Road   412-341-1515
Pittsburgh, PA 15234

$ 30.00

2862 Education of Children and Adolescents with Learning Disabilities

Abraham Ariel, Author

Macmillan Publishing Company
866 Third Avenue
New York, NY 10022

This text addresses the full specterum of learning disabled topics with the aim of helping future special educators learn how to provide an optimal learning dituation for individuals who find it difficult to learn in traditional settings.

2863 Educational Assessment

Robert S. Calfee, Author

Lawrence Erlbaum Associates, Inc.
365 Broadway   201-666-4110
Hillsdale, NJ 07642   FAX 201-666-2394

Publish original research and scholarship on the assessment of individuals, groups and programs in educational settings.

2864 Educational Principles for Children with Learning Disabilities

D.J. Johnson, Author

Learning Disabilities Association of America
4156 Library Road   412-341-1515
Pittsburgh, PA 15234

$ 38.00

2865 The Effects of Student-Teacher Ratios on Student Performance in Special Ed

ERIC Clearinghouse on Disabled and Gifted Children
1920 Association Drive   703-620-3660
Reston, VA 22091

2866 Enabling Disorganized Students to Succeed

S. Stevens, Author

Learning Disabilities Association of America
4156 Library Road   412-341-1515
Pittsburgh, PA 15234

$ 5.00

2867 Enhancing Children's Communications

Ann Kaiser, Author

Paul H. Brookes Publishing Company
P.O. Box 10624   410-337-8539
Baltimore, MD 21285   800-638-3775

This groundbreaking book provides helpful insights, unique perspectives and innovative strategies that are needed to intervene successfully with children whose developmental disabilities affect their use of communication and language.

$ 43.00

2868 The Exceptional Child (An Introduction to Special Education)

Susan Ruth Butler, Ph.D., Author

University of Sydney/School Educational Psychology
New South Wales, 2011
Australia

This comprehensive text, the first in Australia, covers all major special education topics. It features special contributions from professionals working with special disabilities. It has been edited to achieve a balance of substantive text (with medical and educational implications for each special need) as well as practical illustrative components and first-hand commentary from professionals and organizations in the field.

$ 36.95

2869 Exceptional Child Education Resources

ERIC Clearinghouse on Disabled and Gifted Children
1920 Association Drive   703-620-3660
Reston, VA 22091

Offers an extensive list of educational materials including those focusing on the learning disabled.

2870 Exceptional Children Introduction to Special Education

D.P. Hallahan, Author

Books on Special Children
P.O. Box 305   914-638-1236
Congers, NY 10920   FAX 914-638-0847

Offers characteristics of classroom practices, psychological, medical and social aspects.

$ 44.00

2871 Exceptional Individuals An Introduction

Bill R. Gearhart, Author

Brooks/Cole
511 Forest Lodge Road   408-373-0728
Pacific Grove, CA 93950

Every chapter highlights current trends and the consensus about issues within the field.

2872 The Exceptional Student in the Regular Classroom

M.W. Weishahn, Author
Books on Special Children
P.O. Box 305   914-638-1236
Congers, NY 10920   FAX 914-638-0847

Defines problems, laws and services available for the learning disabled student.

$ 54.00

2873 Exceptionality

Edward J. Sabornie, Author
Lawrence Erlbaum Associates, Inc.
365 Broadway   201-666-4110
Hillsdale, NJ 07642   FAX 201-666-2394

Devoted to the publication of original research and research reviews pertaining to individuals of all ages and disabilities as well as those who are gifted and talented.

$ 35.00

2874 Extraordinary Children, Ordinary Lives: Stories Behind Special Education

R. Martin, Author
Learning Disabilities Association of America
4156 Library Road   412-341-1515
Pittsburgh, PA 15234

This book tells the personal stories behind 10 of the leading court cases that have shaped and defined the basic principles of special education law.

$ 12.95

2875 Focus on Exceptional Children

Love Publishing Company
1777 S. Bellaire Street   303-757-2579
Denver, CO 80222

Contains research and theory-based articles on special education topics, with an emphasis on application and intervention of interest to teachers, professors and administrators.

2876 Gifted But Learning Disabled: a Puzzling Paradox

ERIC Clearinghouse on Disabled and Gifted Children
1920 Association Drive   703-620-3660
Reston, VA 22091

2877 Handbook for Volunteer Tutors

HEATH Resource Center
One Dupont Circle NW, Ste. 800   202-939-9320
Washington, DC 20036   800-544-3284

Filled with tips for both students and tutors, as well as materials to increease awareness and understanding of learning disabilities.

$ 25.00

2878 Handbook of Learning Disabilities

Pro-Ed
8700 Shoal Creek Blvd.   512-451-3246
Austin, TX 78758   FAX 512-451-8542

These three volumes provide students and practitioners with ready access to the essential sfor understanding and treating learning disabilities.

$ 79.00

2879 HELP Activity Guide

Therapro, Inc.
225 Arlington Street   508-872-9494
Framingham, MA 01701   FAX 508-875-2062

Used in conjunction with the HELP Assessment, this guide provides practical task analyzed curriculum indexed by 650 assessment skills.

$ 20.95

2880 Helping Learning Disabled Gifted Children Learn Through Compensatory Play

Charles C. Thomas Publisher
2600 South First Street   217-789-8980
Springfield, IL 62794   FAX 217-789-9130

About 3% of the school population is gifted and 5-8% of this number suffer from learning disabilities. These children experience a great deal more trauma than the normal child. This text will help educators deal with learning disabilities more effectively.

2881 Helping Students Become Strategic Learners

Karen Scheid, Author
Brookline Books
P.O. Box 1046   617-868-0360
Cambridge, MA 02238   FAX 617-868-1772

The author demonstrates how teachers can implement cognitive theories of instruction in the classroom.

2882 Helping Students Grow

James Humphrey, Author
American College Testing Program
2201 North Dodge Street   319-337-1000
Iowa City, IA 52243

Designed to assist counselors in using the wealth of information generated by the ACT assessment.

2883 Helping Students Succeed in the Regular Classroom

Joseph Zins, Author
Jossey-Bass, Inc.
350 Sansome Street   415-433-1767
San Francisco, CA 94104

The first book in a series from Jossey-Bass on psychoeducational interventions. Shows how to develop programs to help the learning disabled students integrate within the regular classroom situation and avoid costly and often ineffective special education classes.

$ 26.95

2884 Helping the Child with Learning Disabilities: a Volunteer Guide

Ruth Gottesman, Author
Connecticut Association for Children with LD
18 Marshall Street   203-838-5010
South Norwalk, CT 06854   FAX 203-866-6108
$ 4.75

2885 Hidden Youth: Dropouts From Special Education

Donald L. MacMillan, Author
The Council for Exceptional Children
1920 Association Drive   703-620-3660
Reston, VA 22091

Examines the characteristics of students and schools that place students at risk for early school leaving. Discusses the accounting procedures used by different agencies for estimating graduation and dropout rates and cautions educators about using these rates as indicators of eduational quality.

2886 High Order Thinking

Douglas Carmine, Author
Pro-Ed
8700 Shoal Creek Blvd.   512-451-3246
Austin, TX 78758   FAX 512-451-8542

A designed curriculum for mainstreamed students. Intended to be responsive to the educational demands of the 21st Century, to increease the learning and employment options for all students.

$ 24.00

2887 Hot Tips for Teachers

A. Harrison, Author
Connecticut Association for Children with LD
18 Marshall Street   203-838-5010
South Norwalk, CT 06854   FAX 203-866-6108
$ 10.50

2888 How Significant Is Significant? a Personal Glimpse of Life with LD

Carolee Reiling, Author
Association on Higher Education and Disability
P.O. Box 21192   614-488-4972
Columbus, OH 43221   FAX 614-488-1174

Provides a perspective not usually found in learning disability research material.

$ 3.50

2889 How to Help Students Overcome Learning Problems and Learning Disabilities

Rosalie Young, Author
Pro-Ed
8700 Shoal Creek Blvd.   512-451-3246
Austin, TX 78758   FAX 512-451-8542

Using nontechnical language, this text explains how most learning problems from preschool years through adulthood may be overcome.

$ 24.00

2890 How to Overcome Social Deficits in the Learning Disabled Child and Adult

Nonnie Star, Author
Connecticut Association for Children with LD
18 Marshall Street   203-838-5010
South Norwalk, CT 06854   FAX 203-866-6108

2891 How to Rescue At-Risk Students

S. Stevens, Author
Learning Disabilities Association of America
4156 Library Road   412-341-1515
Pittsburgh, PA 15234
$ 8.25

2892 Human Communication Disorders

G.H. Shames, Author
Books on Special Children
P.O. Box 305   914-638-1236
Congers, NY 10920   FAX 914-638-0847

Introduction into speech & hearing pathology and disorders.

$ 49.00

2893 Implementing Cognitive Strategy Instruction Across the School

Irene Gaskins, Author
Brookline Books
P.O. Box 1046   617-868-0360
Cambridge, MA 02238   FAX 617-868-1772

Describes a classroom based program planned and executed by teachers to focus and guide students with serious reading problems to be goal oriented, planful, strategic and self-assessing.

$ 24.95

2894 Individual Program Planning: a Value- Based Approach to Planning Services

Diane Galambos, Author

L'institute Roeher Institute
York University, 4700 Keele St.   416-661-9611
North York, Ontario, M3 J 1P3   FAX 416-661-5701

A clear manual aimed at service providers, it suggests that as services become more personalized, planned and increasingly client-directed, the IPP approach will be transformed.

$ 40.00

2895 Infants and Young Children with Special Needs

S.K. Thurman, Author

Books on Special Children
P.O. Box 305   914-638-1236
Congers, NY 10920   FAX 914-638-0847

Factors contributing to risk of learning disabled persons offersing screening, assessment techniques and role of each on team.

$ 46.00

2896 Instructional Methods for Students

Patrick Joseph Schloss, Author

Allyn & Bacon
160 Gould Street   800-852-8024
Needham Heights, MA 02194

Instructional methods for students with learning and behavior problems.

2897 Integrating Transition Planning Into the IEP Process

Lynda West, Author

The Council for Exceptional Children
1920 Association Drive   703-620-3660
Reston, VA 22091

A joint publication of the Division on Career Development and the Council for Exceptional Children. This book helps students with disabilities make a smooth transition from school to adult life. Learn how to incorporate transition planning into the IEP process, makes students self-advocates, do cooperative planning among schools, community service agencies, private organizations and families and more. Sample IEPs that incorporate transition goals and objectives are also included.

$ 15.70

2898 Integrating Young Children with Disabilities Into Community Program

Charles A. Peck, Author

Paul H. Brookes Publishing Company
P.O. Box 10624   410-337-8539
Baltimore, MD 21285   800-638-3775
FAX 410-337-8539

This textbook chronicles and evaluates the success of research projects and prgrams in community service and integration.

$ 30.00

2899 Interactive Teaming

C.V. Morsink, Author

Connecticut Association for Children with LD
18 Marshall Street   203-838-5010
South Norwalk, CT 06854   FAX 203-866-6108
$ 34.00

2900 Interactive Teaming - Consultation and Collaboration in Special Programs

C.V. Morsink, Author

Books on Special Children
P.O. Box 305   914-638-1236
Congers, NY 10920   FAX 914-638-0847

Offers information on consultation.

$ 38.00

2901 International Handbook of Research and Development of Giftedness & Talent

Kurt A. Heller, Author

Pergamon Press, Inc.
660 White Plains Road   914-524-9200
Tarrytown, NY 10591   FAX 914-333-2444

Contains 53 chapters, drawing on some 15 nations to provide a cross-national perspective that is unique. Written for readers with a sound knowledge base, it is designed as a synthesis and critical review of significant theory and research in all aspects of giftedness, both to help frame more valid research questions and to provide guidance for educational policy and practice.

$ 162.00

2902 Intervention in School and Clinic

8700 Shoal Creek Blvd.
Austin, TX 78758

2903 Issues and Options in Restructuring Schools & Special Education Program

The Council for Exceptional Children
1920 Association Drive   703-620-3660
Reston, VA 22091

This document explores the issues that effect decisions for delivering education to students with disabilities within the context of educational restructuring. Restructuring options examine unified systems, inclusive or heterogeneous schools and categorical programs using a contiuum of placements. Decision making options explore centralized administration vs. school-based management. Options for measuring student outcomes and performance measures for all students with differential outcomes.

$ 10.00

2904 Kids Who Hate School: a Survival Handbook on Learning Disabilities

Lawrence Greene, Author
Fawcett Book Group
201 East 50th Street   212-751-2600
New York, NY 10022

Case studies, anecdotal material and educational data are used to tell parents of children with learning disabilities how to recognize the symptoms of a learning problem and what steps to take to see that their children receive the remediation needed.

$ 12.00

2905 Kraus Curriculum Development Library

Route 100   914-762-2200
Millwood, NY 10546   800-223-8323

Offers a variety of professional texts.

2906 Language Disorders

Robert Owens, Jr., Author
Books on Special Children
P.O. Box 305   914-638-1236
Congers, NY 10920   FAX 914-638-0847

A book for professionals who deal mostly with children's speech disorders.

$ 40.00

2907 Language Minority Students with Disabilities

Leonard M. Baca And Estella Almanza, Author
The Council for Exceptional Children
1920 Association Drive   703-620-3660
Reston, VA 22091

Helps teachers understand prereferral intervention, proper assessment and appropriate instruction can help these at-risk students succeed in school.

2908 Learning and Individual Differences

National Association of School Psychologists
8455 Colesville Road, Ste. 1000   301-608-0500
Silver Spring, MD 20901   FAX 301-608-2514

A multidisciplinary journal in education.

2909 Learning Disabilities: Basic Concepts, Assessment Practices & Strategies

Patricia I Myers, Author
Pro-Ed
8700 Shoal Creek Blvd.   512-451-3246
Austin, TX 78758   FAX 512-451-8542

One of the first and best comprehensive books published in the learning disability field in its fourth edition. The contents focus on the moderate to severe LD student who requires special help that is different from that generally provided in regular classrooms.

$ 39.00

2910 Learning Disabilities: Definitions, Assessment and Eligibility Criteria

ERIC Clearinghouse on Disabled and Gifted Children
1920 Association Drive   703-620-3660
Reston, VA 22091

2911 Learning Disabilities: Educational Strategies

Bill Gearhart, Author
Merrill Publishing Company
Columbus, OH 43216   614-755-4151

Designed for use in an introductory course, the text examines the issues related to learning disabilities.

2912 Learning Disabilities Focus

1920 Association Drive   703-620-3660
Reston, VA 22091

Practitioner-oriented journal devoted to the translation of research in the field of learning disabilities into practice related to identification, assessment, placement and service delivery models.

$ 25.00

2913 Learning Disabilities in High School

Learning Disabilities Association of America
4156 Library Road   412-341-1515
Pittsburgh, PA 15234

$ 2.00

2914 Learning Disabilities Materials Guide - Secondary Level

Learning Disabilities Association of America
4156 Library Road   412-341-1515
Pittsburgh, PA 15234

$ 3.00

2915 Learning Disabilities Research

1920 Association Drive   703-620-3660
Reston, VA 22091

Scholarly journal providing current research in the field of learning disabilities of importance to teachers, educators and researchers.

2916 Learning Disabilities State of the Art and Practice

Kenneth Kavale, Author

Pro-Ed
8700 Shoal Creek Blvd.   512-451-3246
Austin, TX 78758   FAX 512-451-8542

The dynamic nature of the field of learning disabilities causes information to be outdated quickly.

$ 27.00

2917 Learning Disabilities: the Interaction of Learner, Task and Setting

C.R. Smith, Author

Learning Disabilities Association of America
4156 Library Road   412-341-1515
Pittsburgh, PA 15234

2918 Learning Disabilities: the Search for Causes

Learning Disabilities Association of America
4156 Library Road   412-341-1515
Pittsburgh, PA 15234

$ 2.00

2919 Learning Problems & Learning Disabilities Moving Forward

Howard S. Adelman, Author

Brooks/Cole
511 Forest Lodge Road   408-373-0728
Pacific Grove, CA 93950

Advocates a point of view assessing and teaching students with learning disabilities.

2920 Life Centered Education-Complete Set of Instructional Units & Assessments

The Council for Exceptional Children
1920 Association Drive   703-620-3660
Reston, VA 22091

Over 3,500 pages of classroom activities to use with the Life Centered Curriculum Based Approach. The basic text is described and already adopted in several states as the "official" curriculum for teaching life skills, this field-tested set of activities provides teachers with everything they need to develop competencies in 97 skill areas.

2921 Mainstreaming: a Practical Approach for Teachers, Second Edition

Judy W. Wood, Author

Macmillan Publishing Company
866 Third Avenue
New York, NY 10022

Provides all of the background needed for offering appropriate services to students with disabilities who are served in the regular classroom.

2922 Mainstreaming Exceptional Students

Jane B. Schultz, Author

Allyn & Bacon
160 Gould Street   800-852-8024
Needham Heights, MA 02194

Provides a clear overview of mainstreaming and public law.

2923 Mainstreamlining

R.D. Lavoie, Author

Connecticut Association for Children with LD
18 Marshall Street   203-838-5010
South Norwalk, CT 06854   FAX 203-866-6108

$ 7.00

2924 Managing Inappropriate Behavior in the Classroom

ERIC Clearinghouse on Disabled and Gifted Children
1920 Association Drive   703-620-3660
Reston, VA 22091

2925 Meeting the Needs of Able Learners Through Flexible Pacing

ERIC Clearinghouse on Disabled and Gifted Children
1920 Association Drive   703-620-3660
Reston, VA 22091

2926 Meeting the Needs of Special Students

Lawrence J. Johnson, Author

Corwin Press, Inc.
P.O. Box 2526   805-499-9774
Newbury Park, CA 91319   FAX 805-499-0871

The author gives administrators the information they need about the rights of students, federal guidelines and case law and precedents.

$ 11.05

2927 A National Forum for Schools: Partnerships in Education

American Speech-Language-Hearing Association
10801 Rockville Pike   301-897-5700
Rockville, MD 20852   800-638-8255

Addresses three major issues: identifying young children at risk for educational failure, ending literacy and meeting the needs of the growing number of multicultural students.

$ 75.00

2928 Neuropsychological Fundamentals in Learning Disabilities

Learning Disabilities Association of America
4156 Library Road   412-341-1515
Pittsburgh, PA 15234

2929 Opening the Door to Classroom Research

Mary Olson, Author

International Reading Association
800 Barksdale Rd., P.O. Box 8139   302-731-1600
Newark, DE 19714   800-336-READ
FAX 302-731-1057

Examines the concept of the teacher as researcher from various perspectives - the teachers, the administrators, and the university-based researchers.

$ 10.25

2930 Pre-Referral Intervention for Students with Learning Problems

The Council for Exceptional Children
1920 Association Drive   703-620-3660
Reston, VA 22091

2931 Preserving Special Education

L. Lieberman, Author

Connecticut Association for Children with LD
18 Marshall Street   203-838-5010
South Norwalk, CT 06854   FAX 203-866-6108
$ 10.95

2932 Preventing Academic Failure

Phyllis Bertin, Author

Monroe Associates
P.O. Box 332
Scarsdale, NY 10583

Offers a sequence of over 200 coordinated lessons with corresponding word lists, specific references to pages in readers and workbooks to reinforce wach lesson; instructions for teaching reading, spelling and handwriting with multisensory techniques and criterion-based tests to monitor children's progress.

$ 43.25

2933 Preventing Special Education...for Those Who Don't Need It

L. Lieberman, Author

Connecticut Association for Children with LD
18 Marshall Street   203-838-5010
South Norwalk, CT 06854   FAX 203-866-6108
$ 8.95

2934 Reading and Learning Disabilities: a Resource Guide

NICHCY
P.O. Box 1492   703-893-6061
Washington, DC 20013   800-999-5599

2935 Reading Research and Instruction

The College Reading Association
3340 South Danbury Avenue
Springfield, MO 65807

2936 Rehabilitation of Clients with Specific Learning Disabilities

Rehabilitation Research and Training Center
P.O. Box 1358   501-624-4411
Hot Springs, AR 71902

Functional definitions of SLD detail the changed definition that made adults eligible for vocational rehabilitation services.

$ 8.50

2937 Research in Learning Disabilities

Sharon Vaughn, Author

Pro-Ed
8700 Shoal Creek Blvd.   512-451-3246
Austin, TX 78758   FAX 512-451-8542

This important book for researchers and educators in learning disabilities addresses critical issues and future directions.

$ 29.00

2938 Resourcing: Handbook for Special Educators

Mary Yeomans Jackson, Author

The Council for Exceptional Children
1920 Association Drive   703-620-3660
Reston, VA 22091

Everything you need to know about how to be a "resource" for other teachers and support personnel who work with special education students. This book will teach how to be a resource to yourself, how to be a resource to others and how to access resources - people, telephone, parents, instructional materials and national resources.

$ 11.40

2939 Restructuring for Caring and Effective Education

R.A. Villa, Author

Books on Special Children
P.O. Box 305 914-638-1236
Congers, NY 10920 FAX 914-638-0847
Offers case studies on specific schools with inclusive systems.

$ 35.00

2940 Semantic Feature Analysis: Classroom Applications

Susan Pittelman, Author
International Reading Association
800 Barksdale Rd., P.O. Box 8139 302-731-1600
Newark, DE 19714 800-336-READ
FAX 302-731-1057

This practical and thorough guide to using semantic feature analysis is a welcome companion to Heimlich and Pittelman's earlier bestseller on semantic mapping.

$ 6.00

2941 Semantic Mapping: Classroom Applications

Joan Heimlich, Author
International Reading Association
800 Barksdale Rd., P.O. Box 8139 302-731-1600
Newark, DE 19714 800-336-READ
FAX 302-731-1057

Semantic mapping, a categorical structuring of information in graphic form, has been used successfully in many classroom applications.

$ 6.00

2942 Sensory Integration: Theory and Practice

Anne Fisher, Author
Therapro, Inc.
225 Arlington Street 508-872-9494
Framingham, MA 01701 FAX 508-875-2062

The very latest in sensory integration theory and practice.

$ 37.50

2943 Skillstreaming in Early Childhood

Ellen McGinnis, Author
Connecticut Association for Children with LD
18 Marshall Street 203-838-5010
South Norwalk, CT 06854 FAX 203-866-6108

$ 16.50

2944 Skillstreaming the Adolescent

A. Goldstein, Author
Connecticut Association for Children with LD
18 Marshall Street 203-838-5010
South Norwalk, CT 06854 FAX 203-866-6108

$ 16.50

2945 Skillstreaming the Elementary School Child

E. McGinnis, Author
Connecticut Association for Children with LD
18 Marshall Street 203-838-5010
South Norwalk, CT 06854 FAX 203-866-6108

$ 16.50

2946 Social Cognition

Doanl Carlston, PhD, Author
Guilford Publications, Inc.
72 Spring Street 212-431-9800
New York, NY 10012 800-365-7006
FAX 212-966-6708

Jody Falco, Managing Editor

A pioneer in this exciting area of the behavioral sciences. Distinguished by a superb group of expert contributors, SOCIAL COGNITION has become the definitive resource for professionals in the fields concerned. Featured are reports of empirical research, conceptual analyses and critical reviews of the role of cognitive processes in the study of personality, development and social behavior; occasional special issues are devoted to defined topics.

2947 Special Education in New York

Advocates for Children
24-16 Bridge Plaza South 718-729-8866
Long Island City, NY 11103 FAX 718-729-8931

Galen D. Kirkland, Executive Director

Highlights the fact that New York rates last among all states in inclusive education.

$ 14.50

2948 Special Education Programs

Ada L. Vallecorsa, Author
Corwin Press, Inc.
P.O. Box 2526 805-499-9774
Newbury Park, CA 91319 FAX 805-499-0871

A guide to evaluation of specail education programs.

$ 19.95

2949 The Special Education Sourcebook

Michael Rosenberg, Author
Woodbine House
5615 Fishers Lane 301-468-8800
Rockville, MD 20852 800-843-7323

A teacher's guide to programs, materials and information sources.

$ 21.95

2950 Special Education Teacher's Kit

Edmark Corporation
P.O. Box 3218 206-746-3900
Redmond, WA 98073 800-362-2890

Simulates and encourages learning with a potpourri of new teaching ideas.

$ 95.00

2951 Special Educators Guide to Regular Education

L. Lieberman, Author
Connecticut Association for Children with LD
18 Marshall Street   203-838-5010
South Norwalk, CT 06854   FAX 203-866-6108

$ 10.50

2952 Strategies for Teaching Learners with Special Needs, Fifth Edition

Edward A. Polloway, Author
Macmillan Publishing Company
866 Third Avenue
New York, NY 10022

An updated version that helps future special educators develop the full range of competencies they'll need to be effective.

2953 Strategy Assessment and Instruction for Students with Learning Disabilities

Lynn Meltzer, Author
Pro-Ed
8700 Shoal Creek Blvd.   512-451-3246
Austin, TX 78758   FAX 512-451-8542

The unifying theme of this volume is the view that strategic learning is a critical component of academic success and that inefficient strategy use characterizes many learning disabled students and prevents them from functioning at the level of their potential.

$ 36.00

2954 Student Teacher to Master Teacher

M.S. Rosenberg, Author
Books on Special Children
P.O. Box 305   914-638-1236
Congers, NY 10920   FAX 914-638-0847

Offers information on classroom management, programs, consultations and various legal and professionals involved in special education.

$ 34.00

2955 Students with Learning Disabilities

C.D. Mercer, Author
Books on Special Children
P.O. Box 305   914-638-1236
Congers, NY 10920   FAX 914-638-0847

New ediction including life-span coverage from preschool thru adulthood. Gives basic understanding of the learning disabled person from mildly to severely disabled.

$ 42.00

2956 Study Skills Handbook: a Guide for All Teachers

Kenneth Graham, Author
International Reading Association
800 Barksdale Rd., P.O. Box 8139   302-731-1600
Newark, DE 19714   800-336-READ
                                                      FAX 302-731-1057

Being able to study efficiently and effectively is vital to a student's academic success. Busy elementary and secondary teachers can use this guidebook to improve their competence in teaching study skills.

$ 8.00

2957 Support Groups for Practicing Special Education Professionals

Lynne Cook, Author
The Council for Exceptional Children
1920 Association Drive   703-620-3660
Reston, VA 22091

This resource provides suggestions on how to get support groups started as well as a variety of activities that help reduce the isolation of teaching and dealing with stress. Activities include providing immediate assistance and emotional support, fostering professional discussions, facilitating joint planning and design of curriculum, and promoting peer observation and feedback.

$ 10.00

2958 Support Networks for Inclusive Schooling

W. Stainbeck, Author
Books on Special Children
P.O. Box 305   914-638-1236
Congers, NY 10920   FAX 914-638-0847

Stainbeck Techniques for each child to learn in classroom with peers.

$ 30.00

2959 The Survival Manual: Case Studies and Suggestions for Learning Disabled

Learning Disabilities Association of America
4156 Library Road   412-341-1515
Pittsburgh, PA 15234

2960 Take Part Art

Bob Gregson, Author
Connecticut Association for Children with LD
18 Marshall Street   203-838-5010
South Norwalk, CT 06854   FAX 203-866-6108

$ 16.95

2961 Taking the First Step Toward Understanding of Good Mental Health and LD

Learning Disabilities Association of America
4156 Library Road   412-341-1515
Pittsburgh, PA 15234

2962 The Teacher Is the Key

Ken Weber, Author
Connecticut Association for Children with LD
18 Marshall Street   203-838-5010
South Norwalk, CT 06854   FAX 203-866-6108
$ 16.25

2963 Teaching Children and Adolescents with Special Needs

J. Olson, Author
Books on Special Children
P.O. Box 305   914-638-1236
Congers, NY 10920   FAX 914-638-0847

Specific planning techniques with lesson planning, assessment of progress and materials needed.
$ 34.00

2964 Teaching Learning Disabled Adolescents

G. Alley And D. Deshler, Author
The Council for Exceptional Children
1920 Association Drive   703-620-3660
Reston, VA 22091

Outlines strategies and methods useful to teachers working with learning disabled adolescents.
$ 36.95

2965 Teaching Learning Disabled Elementary School Children

The Council for Exceptional Children
1920 Association Drive   703-620-3660
Reston, VA 22091

This computerized search is a bibliography of other materials in print. It lists 97 abstracts of resources available in ERIC and ECER databases.

2966 Teaching Special Students the Mainstream

Rena Lewis, Author
Books on Special Children
P.O. Box 305   914-638-1236
Congers, NY 10920   FAX 914-638-0847

Overview of mainstream, classroom behavior, tips for teachers and more.
$ 40.00

2967 Teaching Students Ways to Remember

Drs. Margo Mastropieri & Thomas Scruggs, Author
Brookline Books
P.O. Box 1046   617-868-0360
Cambridge, MA 02238   FAX 617-868-1772

This book was written in response to the enormous interest in "mnemonic" instruction by teachers and administrators, telling them how it can be used with their students.
$ 21.95

2968 Teaching Students with Learning Problems, Fourth Edition

Cecil D. Mercer, Author
Macmillan Publishing Company
866 Third Avenue
New York, NY 10022

The leading text for preparing future teachers of pupils with mild disabilities in Grades K-12.

2969 Teaching the Learning Disabled Adolescent: Strategies and Methods

Learning Disabilities Association of America
4156 Library Road   412-341-1515
Pittsburgh, PA 15234

This book gives expert strategies and methods for teaching learning disabled adolescents.

2970 Teachnology in the Classroom: Listening and Hearing Module

American Speech-Language-Hearing Association
10801 Rockville Pike   301-897-5700
Rockville, MD 20852   800-638-8255
                                                FAX 301-571-0457

Cameron Werker, Mktg. Coordinator

Provides a brief background on assistive technology and thoroughly explains how it applies to children with listening and hearing communication disorders.
$ 18.00

2971 Technology in the Classroom: Communication Module

American Speech-Language-Hearing Association
10801 Rockville Pike   301-897-5700
Rockville, MD 20852   800-638-8255
                                                FAX 301-571-0457

Cameron Werker, Mktg. Coordinator

Provides a brief backgroun of assistive technology and a detailed discussion on augmentative communciation.

Contains technology and strategies aimed at giving children who have disabilities, another way to communicate when speaking is difficult or impossible.

$ 26.00

2972 Technology in the Classroom: Education Module

American Speech-Language-Hearing Association
10801 Rockville Pike   301-897-5700
Rockville, MD 20852   800-638-8255
                                        FAX 301-571-0457

Cameron Werker, Mktg. Coordinator

Offers in-depth discussion as to how assistive technology can be used in educational settings. The technology is geared for children who have severe disabilities and provides a discussion of how to assess a child's needs for assistive technology in order to perform both pre-academic and academic tasks.

$ 40.00

2973 Technology in the Classroom: Positioning, Access and Mobility Module

American Speech-Language-Hearing Association
10801 Rockville Pike   301-897-5700
Rockville, MD 20852   800-638-8255
                                        FAX 301-571-0457

Cameron Werker, Mktg. Coordinator

This manual emphasizes the importance of proper positioning that comfortably enables a child to perform activities of everyday life, and the technology which is available to help children move about when they are physically unable to do so.

$ 23.00

2974 Textbooks and the Students Who Can't Read Them

Jean Ciborowski, Author
Brookline Books
P.O. Box 1046   617-868-0360
Cambridge, MA 02238   FAX 617-868-1772

Based on a careful analysis of 10 textbook programs, 5 science and 5 social studies, the author concisely and sensibly indicates the proceduare that facilitate teacher's use of regular grade level textbooks with low-reading students.

2975 A Therapeutic Approach to Work-Related Tasks: An Activities Curriculum

Molly Campbell, Author
Therapro, Inc.
225 Arlington Street   508-872-9494
Framingham, MA 01701   FAX 508-875-2062

This manual contains ideas for improving cognitive, perceptual and motor skills through use of specific "work" tasks.

$ 22.50

2976 Three Approaches to Diagnosis and Education

Learning Disabilities Association of America
4156 Library Road   412-341-1515
Pittsburgh, PA 15234

2977 Tools for Transition

AGS
7201 Woodland Road   612-786-4343
Circle Pines, MN 55014   800-328-2560

The materials in this kit offer a curriculum that is not always included in learning disabled programs. Comes with a teacher's manual, complete with instructions for each unit and a Student Workbook filled with skill-building activities. The accompanying video presents a variety of scences to demonstrate plus an interview with college students who have learning disabilities.

2978 Topic Talk

Linda Carey, Author
The Speech Bin
1965 Twenty-Fifth Avenue   407-770-0007
Vero Beach, FL 32960   FAX 407-770-0006

Jan J. Binney, Editor In Chief
Barbara Hector, Office Manager

Designed to foster valuable interaction and cooperation to be used by both groups and individuals with a broad range of skills.

$ 58.50

2979 Transition for Adolescents with Learning Disabilities

Catherine Trapani, Author
Pro-Ed
8700 Shoal Creek Blvd.   512-451-3246
Austin, TX 78758   FAX 512-451-8542

Provides important information about academic, social and vocational planning for students with learning disabilities.

$ 24.00

2980 Understanding Adolescents and Young Adults with Learning Disabilities

E.F. Biller, Author
Charles C. Thomas Publisher
2600 South First Street   217-789-8980
Springfield, IL 62794

A guide for rehabiliation counselors.

2981 Vision and Learning Disabilities

Learning Disabilities Association of America
4156 Library Road   412-341-1515
Pittsburgh, PA 15234

2982 What Are Learning Disabilities?

M.M. Banbury, Author

American Federation of Teachers
555 New Jersey Avenue NW   202-879-4400
Washington, DC 20001

Adult

2983 Adults with Learning Disabilities: An Overview for the Adult Educator

Learning Disabilities Association of America
4156 Library Road   412-341-1515
Pittsburgh, PA 15234

A thorough and clear discussion of adult learning disabilities.

$ 38.00

2984 Contributor's Guide to Periodicals in Reading

International Reading Association
800 Barksdale Rd., P.O. Box 8139   302-731-1600
Newark, DE 19714   800-336-READ
          FAX 302-731-1057

An invaluable guide for authors who wish to publish in the field of reading.

2985 Fun and Fundamentals

M. Noyes, Author

Connecticut Association for Children with LD
18 Marshall Street   203-838-5010
South Norwalk, CT 06854   FAX 203-866-6108
          $ 3.00

2986 Handbook for the Teaching of Beginning Adult Learners

E.D. McAllister, Author

Learning Disabilities Association of America
4156 Library Road   412-341-1515
Pittsburgh, PA 15234

The purpose of this manual is to help literacy instructors to understand and teach learning disabled and learning different adults.

2987 Project Success: Meeting the Diverse Needs of Learning Disabled Adults

Richland College of the Dallas Community College
12800 Abrams Road   214-238-6194
Dallas, TX 75243

2988 Project Upgrade, Working with Adults Who Have Learning Disabilities

Manhattan Adult Learning and Resource Center
2031 Casement Road
Manhattan, KS 66502

2989 Reality Orientation

Lorna Rimmer, Author

The Speech Bin
1965 Twenty-Fifth Avenue   407-770-0007
Vero Beach, FL 32960   FAX 407-770-0006

Jan J. Binney, Editor In Chief
Barbara Hector, Office Manager

Helps treat memory loss, disorientation and confusion in adult patients.

$ 27.95

Attention Deficit Disorder

2990 ADHD - a Guide to Understanding and Helping Children

Lauren Braswell, Author

Connecticut Association for Children with LD
18 Marshall Street   203-838-5010
South Norwalk, CT 06854   FAX 203-866-6108

This guide is designed to help teachers and other professionals to understand and manage children with ADHD in school settings.

$ 12.95

2991 Attention Deficit Disorder: Current Understanding

Richard Elliott, Author

Connecticut Association for Children with LD
18 Marshall Street   203-838-5010
South Norwalk, CT 06854   FAX 203-866-6108

Comprehensive review of ADHD.

$ 2.50

2992 Attention Deficit Disorders and Hyperactivity

ERIC Clearinghouse on Disabled and Gifted Children
1920 Association Drive   703-620-3660
Reston, VA 22091

2993 Children with ADD: a Shared Responsibility

The Council for Exceptional Children
1920 Association Drive   703-620-3660
Reston, VA 22091

This book represents a consensus of what professionals and parents believe ADD is all about and how children with ADD may best be served. reviews the evaluation process under IDEA and 504 and presents effective classroom strategies.

$ 8.90

2994 Children's Learning and Attention Problems

M. Kisbourne, Author

Little Brown & Company
Boston, MA

An insight into attention deficit disorders.

2995 Educational Strategies for Students with Attention Deficit Disorder

Mark Sloane, Author

Connecticut Association for Children with LD
18 Marshall Street   203-838-5010
South Norwalk, CT 06854   FAX 203-866-6108

Common problems for studens with ADHD are discussed and interventions offered.

$ 2.00

2996 Medications for Attention Disorders and Related Medical Problems

Edna Copeland, Author

Connecticut Association for Children with LD
18 Marshall Street   203-838-5010
South Norwalk, CT 06854   FAX 203-866-6108

Covers the history, characteristics and causes of ADHD.

$ 35.00

2997 A New Look At Attention Deficit Disorder

Samuel Nichamin, Author

Connecticut Association for Children with LD
18 Marshall Street   203-838-5010
South Norwalk, CT 06854   FAX 203-866-6108

Defines ADHD and includes early warning signs of an ADHD problem.

$ 2.00

2998 Prognosis of Attention Deficit Disorder and Its Management in Adolescence

Rachel Gittelman Klein, Author

Connecticut Association for Children with LD
18 Marshall Street   203-838-5010
South Norwalk, CT 06854   FAX 203-866-6108

Discusses the long term outcome of children with ADHD and clinical management of the adolescent.

$ 3.00

College & the LD Student

2999 College and the Learning Disabled Student: Program Development

Simon and Schuster
P.O. Box 11071   515-284-6751
Des Moines, IA 50336

$ 40.95

3000 College Relations Recruitment Survey

College Placement Council, Inc.
62 Highland Avenue   215-868-1421
Bethlehem, PA 18017   800-544-5272

Gives hard data on practitioners, budgets, the college relations and recruitment function, entry-level hiring, on-campus recruitment, new hires and much much more.

$ 46.95

3001 Dispelling the Myths: College Students and Learning Disabilities

Learning Disabilities Association of America
4156 Library Road   412-341-1515
Pittsburgh, PA 15234

Written for college teachers, this book explains learning disabilities and tells what faculty members can do to help LD students succedd in college.

$ 4.75

3002 A Guide for Delivering Faculty Inservice on the LD College Student

HEATH Resource Center
One Dupont Circle NW, Ste. 800   202-939-9320
Washington, DC 20036   800-544-3284

The guide focuses on providing faculty inservice and training on how to work with students with learning disabilities.

$ 15.00

3003 Keymakers II, the Learning Disabled Postsecondary Student

MACLD
1821 University Avenue, Ste. 494-N   612-646-6136
St. Paul, MN 55104

Provides an overview of learning disabilities in postsecondary settings, primarily at technical colleges, with the ultimate goal of guiding postsecondary educators to create environments that maximize student potential.

$ 15.00

3004 The Postsecondary Learning Disabilities Primer, a Training Manual

LD Training Project - Western Carolina University
Cullowhee, NC 38723   704-227-7127

A one volume collection of service options and handouts for students/service providers.

$ 20.50

3005 Postsecondary Transition

Learning Disabilities Association of America
4156 Library Road   412-341-1515
Pittsburgh, PA 15234

3006 Programming for College Students with Learning Disabilities

Association on Higher Education and Disability
P.O. Box 21192   614-488-4972
Columbus, OH 43221   FAX 614-488-1174

This publication offers a model for institutions that are beginning support services components for students with learning disabilities.

$ 21.00

3007 Project T.A.P.E.: Technical Assistance for Postsecondary Education

Northern Illinois University
DeKalb, IL 60115   815-753-0659

Ernest Rose

Includes intervention strategies for persons with learning disabilities attending two-year community colleges.

3008 Secondary Schools and Beyond

Anna Gajar, Author
Macmillan Publishing Company
866 Third Avenue
New York, NY 10022

This comprehensive text presents a thorough study of transition for individuals with mild disabilities and the issues involved in its successful completion.

3009 A Study of Job Clubs for Two-Year College Students with Learning Disabilities

HEATH Resource Center
One Dupont Circle NW, Ste. 800   202-939-9320
Washington, DC 20036   800-544-3284

This report describes the results of a study of how job clubs help two-year college students with learning disabilities improve their job-seeking skills.

$ 15.00

3010 Teaching Reading and Study Strategies At the College Level

Rona Flippo, Author
International Reading Association
800 Barksdale Rd., P.O. Box 8139   302-731-1600
Newark, DE 19714   800-336-READ
          FAX 302-731-1057

Spanning a range of topics from vocabulary acquisition and instruction to strategies for taking tests.

$ 19.50

3011 Unlocking Potential: College and Other Choices for the Learning Disabled

Barbara Scheiber, Author
Adler and Adler Publications
5530 Wisconsin Avenue, Ste. 1460   301-654-6600
Bethesda, MD 20815

The goal of this book is to help students with learning disabilities achieve access to postsecondary campuses and to help postsecondary schools make accessibility a reality.

Counseling & Psychology

3012 Aphasia Rehabilitation Workbooks

Cheryl Traendly, Author
The Speech Bin
1965 Twenty-Fifth Avenue   407-770-0007
Vero Beach, FL 32960   FAX 407-770-0006

Jan J. Binney, Editor In Chief
Barbara Hector, Office Manager

Designed for moderately to mildly aphasics who can work independently or with a family member.

$ 32.00

3013 Behavior Management Applications for Teachers and Parents

Thomas J. Zirpoli, Author
Macmillan Publishing Company
866 Third Avenue
New York, NY 10022

A clear, extensive presentation of the technical basis and appropriate implementation strategies for managing behavior in classrooms, day care centers, even at home.

3014 Behavior Management System

Ethyl Papa, Author

Connecticut Association for Children with LD
18 Marshall Street 203-838-5010
South Norwalk, CT 06854 FAX 203-866-6108
$ 5.95

3015 Behavior Research and Therapy

Maxwell House
Fairview Park 914-524-9200
Elmsford, NY 10523 FAX 914-592-3625

3016 Brain/Mind Bulletin

Box 42111
Los Angeles, CA 90042

3017 Breaking Through the Unseen Barriers

Agency for Instructional Technology
1111 West 17th Street 812-339-2203
Bloomington, IN 47404

This title, which focuses on the role of both teachers and parents in identifying the student with learning disabilities and in planning an individualized educational program, is taken from a practical, eight-part series that also addressess the topics of emotional consequences and classroom management.

$ 995.00

3018 Counseling the Culturally Different

Derald Wing Sue, Author

Books on Special Children
P.O. Box 305 914-638-1236
Congers, NY 10920 FAX 914-638-0847

Offers information on whether or not a persons of a different culture can counsel successfully.

$ 34.95

3019 The Disabled and Their Parents: a Counseling Challenge

Leo Buscaglia, Author

Charles B. Slack, Inc.
6900 Grove Road
Thorofare, NJ 08086

$ 8.95

3020 Effective School Consultation: An Interactive Approach

George Sugai, Author

Brooks/Cole
511 Forest Lodge Road 408-373-0728
Pacific Grove, CA 93950

Practical text provides special educators with strategies they can actually use in solving academic and social behavior problems with other professionals and aprents.

3021 General Guidelines for Providers of Psychological Services

American Psychological Association
Order Dept., P.O. Box 2710 202-336-5510
Hyattsville, MD 20784 800-374-2721
FAX 202-336-5502

Offers information for the professional in the area of psychology.

3022 Journal of Child Psychology and Psychiatry

Pergamon Press, Inc.
Fairview Park 914-592-7700
Elmsford, NY 10523

3023 Learners At Risk

Linda Gambrell, Author

International Reading Association
800 Barksdale Rd., P.O. Box 8139 302-731-1600
Newark, DE 19714 800-336-READ
FAX 302-731-1057

This special journal issue focuses on reaching adolescents who may be at risk for school failure due to poor basic literacy skills.

$ 3.00

3024 Learning to Get Along

Jackson, Bennett & Farnya, Author

Edmark Corporation
P.O. Box 3218 206-746-3900
Redmond, WA 98073 800-362-2890

Helps adolescents and adults with developmental disabilities gain effective social behavior.

$ 35.95

3025 Managing Attention Disorders in Children: a Guide for Practitioners

Sam Goldstein, Author

Books on Special Children
P.O. Box 305 914-638-1236
Congers, NY 10920 FAX 914-638-0847

Offers information about human personality, structure and dynamics, assessment and adjustment.

$ 58.95

3026 Neuropsychological Fundamentals in Learning Disabilities

Learning Disabilities Association of America
4156 Library Road 412-341-1515
Pittsburgh, PA 15234

3027 Occupational Therapy: Overcoming Human Performance Deficits

Charles Christianson, Author

Therapro, Inc.
225 Arlington Street   508-872-9494
Framingham, MA 01701   FAX 508-875-2062

One book taking all the different components of occupational therapy and puts them together in one volume.

$ 65.00

3028 100 Ways to Enhance Self-Concept in the Classroom

Canfield & Wells, Author

Prentice-Hall
Englewood Cliffs, NJ

$ 45.00

3029 Overcoming Dyslexia in Children, Adolescents and Adults

Dale Jordan, Author

Connecticut Association for Children with LD
18 Marshall Street   203-838-5010
South Norwalk, CT 06854   FAX 203-866-6108

This book describes some forms of dyslexia in detail and then relates those problems to the social, emotional and personal development of dyslexic individuals.

$ 30.25

3030 Painful Passages: Working with Children with Learning Disabilities

Elizabeth Dane, Author

NCLD
99 Park Avenue   212-687-7211
New York, NY 10016

For social workers assisting learning disabled children.

$ 17.95

3031 Physicians Guide to Learning Disabilities

Learning Disabilities Association of America
4156 Library Road   412-341-1515
Pittsburgh, PA 15234

3032 Private Practice, Clinical Series 2

ASHA Fulfillment Operations
10801 Rockville Pike   301-897-5700
Rockville, MD 20852

Discusses the background and history of private practice, practitioner qualifications and case types.

3033 The Psychological Examination of the Child

Theodore Blass, Author

Books on Special Children
P.O. Box 305   914-638-1236
Congers, NY 10920   FAX 914-638-0847

Purposes and goals of basic psychological examination of the child.

$ 38.95

3034 Reflections Through the Looking Glass

Association on Higher Education and Disability
P.O. Box 21192   614-488-4972
Columbus, OH 43221   FAX 614-488-1174

A must for new professionals offering a philosophical review of the nature of the field written in first person by charter member and former Association President Richard Harris of Ball State University.

3035 Report Writing in the Field of Communication Disorders, Clinical 4

ASHA Fulfillment Operations
10801 Rockville Pike   301-897-5700
Rockville, MD 20852

Stresses the summarization and interpretation of vital information and highlights matters of ethics, privacy and more.

3036 Right Brain Lesson Plans for a Left Brain World

S. Rotalo, Author

Connecticut Association for Children with LD
18 Marshall Street   203-838-5010
South Norwalk, CT 06854   FAX 203-866-6108

$ 19.95

3037 Self Advocacy for Junior High School Students with Learning Disabilities

Utah Department of Special Education
160 Olpin Union   801-538-7500
Salt Lake City, UT 84112

A program designed to increase students verbal expressive skills in discussing learning disabilities, ADD and related characteristics.

3038 Self-Advocacy Handbook for the High School Student

Ann Jepsen, Author

Utah Department of Special Education
160 Olpin Union
Salt Lake City, UT 84112

This manual teaches the students to advocate for themselves.

3039 Spotlight on Speech-Language Services

The Speech Bin
1965 Twenty-Fifth Avenue   407-770-0007
Vero Beach, FL 32960   FAX 407-770-0006

Jan J. Binney, Editor In Chief
Barbara Hector, Office Manager

Book describes a step-by-step easy to implement, program for publicizing and promoting speech-language pathology and audiology services. It includes low-cost ideas and reproductible materials for a comprehensive public realtions program.

$ 25.00

3040 Stop and Think Workbook

Phillip Kendall, Author

Connecticut Association for Children with LD
18 Marshall Street   203-838-5010
South Norwalk, CT 06854   FAX 203-866-6108

Sixteen lessons a teacher or therapist must work through with a child.

$ 17.65

3041 Teaching Students with Learning and Behavior Problems

Donald Hammill, Author

Pro-Ed
8700 Shoal Creek Blvd.   512-451-3246
Austin, TX 78758   FAX 512-451-8542

This popular, classic text provides teachers with a comprehensive overview of the best practices in assessing and instructing students with mild-to-moderate learning and behavior problems.

$ 38.00

Language Arts

3042 Alternate Methods of Communication Disorders, Clinical Series 7

ASHA Fulfillment Operations
10801 Rockville Pike   301-897-5700
Rockville, MD 20852

Introduces students and professionals to nonspeech communication systems and provides readers with a basic understanding of the clinical variables that must be considered when treating the nonspeaker.

3043 Augmentative Communications: Implementation Strategies

American Speech-Language-Hearing Association
10801 Rockville Pike   301-897-5700
Rockville, MD 20852   800-638-8255

An in-depth manual of practical applications for the implementation of augmentative communication strategies in many settings.

$ 45.00

3044 The Clinical Interview: a Guide for Speech -Language Pathologists/Audiologists

ASHA Fulfillment Operations
10801 Rockville Pike   301-897-5700
Rockville, MD 20852

Integrates the components of the clinical interview within the context of the speech-language pathology and audiology helping process.

3045 Clinical Oral Language Sampling, Clinical Series 5

ASHA Fulfillment Operations
10801 Rockville Pike   301-897-5700
Rockville, MD 20852

Explains the procedures and skills necessary to sample and analyze a child's spontaneous speech in order to detect and diagnose a possible language disorder.

3046 Clues: Speech Reading for Adults

Pamela Jo Feehan, Author

The Speech Bin
1965 Twenty-Fifth Avenue   407-770-0007
Vero Beach, FL 32960   FAX 407-770-0006

Jan J. Binney, Editor In Chief
Barbara Hector, Office Manager

Teaches speedreading with the eclectic programmed approach.

$ 59.00

3047 A Cluster Approach to Elementary Vocabulary Instruction

Robert Marzano, Author

International Reading Association
800 Barksdale Rd., P.O. Box 8139   302-731-1600
Newark, DE 19714   800-336-READ
FAX 302-731-1057

This volume discusses the research on vocabulary instruction and then presents a new instructional method based on organizing words into semantically related clusters.

$ 10.50

3048 Cognitive Reorganization

Elizabeth Bressler, Author

The Speech Bin
1965 Twenty-Fifth Avenue   407-770-0007
Vero Beach, FL 32960   FAX 407-770-0006

Jan J. Binney, Editor In Chief
Barbara Hector, Office Manager

Meets the diverse needs of clients who cannot use their functional language skills in any organized, sequential or pragmatic way.

$ 59.00

3049 Counseling in Speech and Hearing Practice, Clinical Series 9

ASHA Fulfillment Operations
10801 Rockville Pike   301-897-5700
Rockville, MD 20852

Explains the nature and techniques of counseling, which can be used to maintain a focus on the client with a communication impairment and to assist the client in his or her efforts.

3050 Curriculum Guide for An Introductory Course/ Augmentative Communication

American Speech-Language-Hearing Association
10801 Rockville Pike   301-897-5700
Rockville, MD 20852   800-638-8255

A complete plan for conducting introductory courses in augmentative communication, including class outlines and teaching objectives.

$ 8.00

3051 Curriculum-Based Evaluation: Teaching and Decision Making, Second Edition

Kenneth W. Howell, Author

Brooks/Cole
511 Forest Lodge Road   408-373-0728
Pacific Grove, CA 93950

A philosophy of teaching and learning that does not blame the teacher.

3052 Dysarthria and Apraxia of Speech

Christopher Moore, Author

The Speech Bin
1965 Twenty-Fifth Avenue   407-770-0007
Vero Beach, FL 32960   FAX 407-770-0006

Jan J. Binney, Editor In Chief
Barbara Hector, Office Manager

A comprehensive discussion of motor speech disorders and effective techniques for treatment.

$ 45.00

3053 Handbook of Research on Teaching the English Language Arts

James Flood, Author

International Reading Association
800 Barksdale Rd., P.O. Box 8139   302-731-1600
Newark, DE 19714   800-336-READ
    FAX 302-731-1057

This handbook addresses new trends in research in the English language arts.

$ 65.00

3054 Help and Nature Developmental Skills: H.A.N.D.S. Program

Mary Jo Gilpin, Author

Therapro, Inc.
225 Arlington Street   508-872-9494
Framingham, MA 01701   FAX 508-875-2062

Contains a summary of pre-writing development, a discussion of good habits in handwriting, specific instructions on how to form letters correctly and instructions on which pages to use to compile a manual for training the implementers of the program.

$ 49.95

3055 Helping Young Writers Master the Craft

Karen R. Harris, Author

Brookline Books
P.O. Box 1046   617-868-0360
Cambridge, MA 02238   FAX 617-868-1772

This text will help the beginning writer, the unmotivated student and the learning disabled student to learn writing.

$ 24.95

3056 Instrumentation in the Speech Clinic, Clinical Series 3

ASHA Fulfillment Operations
10801 Rockville Pike   301-897-5700
Rockville, MD 20852

Describes the commercially available equipment that is most likely to be found in speech and hearing clinics.

3057 Language and Cognitive Facilitation

Lorie Dilton, Author

The Speech Bin
1965 Twenty-Fifth Avenue   407-770-0007
Vero Beach, FL 32960   FAX 407-770-0006

Jan J. Binney, Editor In Chief
Barbara Hector, Office Manager

Reproductible exercises giving the client in-depth treatment materials for language and cognitive deficits typically found in neurologically impaired adolescents and adults.

$ 29.95

3058 Language, Speech and Hearing Services in Schools

ASHA Fulfillment Operations
10801 Rockville Pike   301-897-5700
Rockville, MD 20852

Presents up-to-date information dealing with all aspects of clinical speech, language and hearing services to children.

3059 Multi-Sensory Approach to Language Arts

Beth H. Slingerland, Author
Educators Publishing Service, Inc.
75 Moulton Street   800-225-5750
Cambridge, MA 02138

This adaptation approach for classroom teachers is a multisensory, phonetically structured introduction to reading, writing and spelling.

$ 75.00

3060 Nonverbal Learning Disabilities

Byron Rourke, Author
Connecticut Association for Children with LD
18 Marshall Street   203-838-5010
South Norwalk, CT 06854   FAX 203-866-6108

$ 30.00

3061 Observing the Language Learner

Angela Jaggar, Author
International Reading Association
800 Barksdale Rd., P.O. Box 8139   302-731-1600
Newark, DE 19714   800-336-READ
    FAX 302-731-1057

This book builds on the knowledge base developed as a series of IRA/NCTE sponsored conferences and examines the implications for classroom practice.

$ 9.50

3062 Playing with Words

Learning Disabilities Association of America
4156 Library Road   412-341-1515
Pittsburgh, PA 15234

3063 Quick Tech Activities for Literacy

Peggi McNaim, Author
Don Johnston Developmental Equipment, Inc.
P.O. Box 639, 1000 N. Rand Road   708-526-2682
Wauconda, IL 60084   800-999-4660

New and easy ideas for the language arts curriculum for teachers of nonspeaking students.

$ 25.00

3064 School Issues: Effective Integration of Speech-Language Services

American Speech-Language-Hearing Association
10801 Rockville Pike   301-897-5700
Rockville, MD 20852   800-638-8255
    FAX 301-571-0457

Cameron Werker, Mktg. Coordinator

This set of 2-hour audiocassette teleconference tapes and accompanying manual presents successful strategies to integrate speech-language services into the school curricula.

$ 45.00

3065 Teachers and Research: Language Learning in the Classroom

Myna Matlin, Author
International Reading Association
800 Barksdale Rd., P.O. Box 8139   302-731-1600
Newark, DE 19714   800-336-READ
    FAX 302-731-1057

Teachers, teacher educators, researchers and staff developers must communicate and collaborate to achieve positive change in educational systems.

$ 8.00

3066 Visualizing and Verbalizing for Language Comprehension/ Thinking

Nanci Bell, Author
Academy of Reading Publications
1720 Filbert   805-238-2008
Paso Robles, CA 93446   800-233-1819
    FAX 805-541-8756

Anita Williamson
Ellen Lathrop

Provides theory and methodology for successfully developing concept imagery and language comprehension. This program consists of specific steps to develop gestalt imagery and comprehension. Sample dialogue is presented and summary pages after each step make it easy to implement the program in the classroom.

Math

3067 Developmental Teaching of Mathematics for the Learning Disabled

John Cawley, Author

263

Pro-Ed
8700 Shoal Creek Blvd.   512-451-3246
Austin, TX 78758   FAX 512-451-8542

Saves hours of preparation time in preparing learning disabled math students for the "real world".

$ 35.00

3068 Math and the Learning Disabled Student: a Practical Guide for Accommodations

P. Nolting, Author

Academic Success Press, Inc.
P.O. Box 25002-Box #132   800-444-2524
Bradenton, FL 34206

More and more learning disabled students are experiencing difficulty passing mathematics. The book is especially written for counselors and mathematics instructors of learning disabled students, and provides information on accommodations for students with different types of learning disabilities.

3069 Teaching Mathematics to the Learning Disabled

Nancy Bley, Author

Pro-Ed
8700 Shoal Creek Blvd.   512-451-3246
Austin, TX 78758   FAX 512-451-8542

Offers information on problem-solving, estimation and the use of computers in teaching mathematics to the child with learning disabilities.

$ 34.00

Pre-School

3070 Administrator's Policy Handbook for Preschool Mainstreaming

Barbara J. Smith, Author

Brookline Books
P.O. Box 1046   617-868-0360
Cambridge, MA 02238   FAX 617-868-1772

This handbook has been prepared specifically for the public school administrator who is developing the policies and procedures to place young children with disabilities in mainstreamed settings.

3071 The Carolina Curriculum for Preschoolers with Special Needs

N.M. Johnson, Author

Books on Special Children
P.O. Box 305   914-638-1236
Congers, NY 10920   FAX 914-638-0847

Lessons contain behavior patterns, materials, procedures and group activities.

$ 48.00

3072 Developing Motor Skills for Early Childhood Education

Learning Disabilities Association of America
4156 Library Road   412-341-1515
Pittsburgh, PA 15234

$ 5.00

3073 Does Early Intervention Help?

ERIC Clearinghouse on Disabled and Gifted Children
1920 Association Drive   703-620-3660
Reston, VA 22091

3074 Early Intervention for Infants and Toddlers

ERIC Clearinghouse on Disabled and Gifted Children
1920 Association Drive   703-620-3660
Reston, VA 22091

3075 Emerging Literacy: Young Children Learn to Read and Write

Dorothy Strickland, Author

International Reading Association
800 Barksdale Rd., P.O. Box 8139   302-731-1600
Newark, DE 19714   800-336-READ
                                     FAX 302-731-1057

Recognized experts in the field of children's literacy development have broken new ground in learning about emergent literacy. Contributors to this award-winning book share practical ideas for day care workers, classroom teachers and curriculum teachers.

$ 15.00

3076 Interdisciplinary Assessment of Infants

Elizabeth D. Gibbs, Author

Paul H. Brookes Publishing Company
P.O. Box 10624   410-337-8539
Baltimore, MD 21285   800-638-3775
                                FAX 410-337-8539

Presents state-of-the-art infant assessment methods and information on disciplinary infant assessment from such traditionally distinct disciplines as psychology, physical and occupational therapy.

$ 42.00

3077 Movement Is Fun

Susan Young, Author

Therapro, Inc.
225 Arlington Street   508-872-9494
Framingham, MA 01701   FAX 508-875-2062

A movement program developed for use with preschoolers. This movement program seeks to mesh elements of movement education programs with theories of sensory integration and development.

$ 17.50

3078 School Age Children with Special Needs

Dale Borman Fink, Author

Special Needs Project
1482 East Valley Road, #A-121   805-565-1914
Santa Barbara, CA 93108   800-333-6867

The most comprehensive survey to date of child care practice for school aged children with a wide range of disabilities.

$ 12.95

3079 Tips From Tots

Cindy Baker, Author

Therapro, Inc.
225 Arlington Street   508-872-9494
Framingham, MA 01701   FAX 508-875-2062

A series of 20 developmental activity pamphlets for parents and caregivers of infants and toddlers focusing on movement, cognition, language and safety and health.

$ 12.95

Reading

3080 Annals on Dyslexia

The Orton Dyslexia Society
Chester Bldg., #382, LaSalle Rd   410-296-0232
Baltimore, MD 21204

Yearly journal which reports on scientific research completed in teh previous year.

3081 Becoming a Nation of Readers: the Report of the Commission on Reading

Richard Anderson, Author

International Reading Association
800 Barksdale Rd., P.O. Box 8139   302-731-1600
Newark, DE 19714   800-336-READ
    FAX 302-731-1057

Current knowledge about reading and of the state of the art in teaching reading.

$ 7.50

3082 Beginning to Read: Thinking and Learning About Print, a Summary

Marilyn Jager Adams, Author

International Reading Association
800 Barksdale Rd., P.O. Box 8139   302-731-1600
Newark, DE 19714   800-336-READ
    FAX 302-731-1057

This summary delves deeply into important issues in beginning reading.

$ 7.50

3083 Behavior Modification and Beginning Reading

Learning Disabilities Association of America
4156 Library Road   412-341-1515
Pittsburgh, PA 15234

3084 Better Reading for Better Jobs

EBSCO Curriculum Materials
P.O. Box 486   205-991-6600
Birmingham, AL 35202   800-633-8623

Instructional materials to teach career/vocational education with emphasis on job skills and the necessary reading, writing, reasoning and computational skills.

$ 19.95

3085 Cases in Literacy: An Agenda for Discussion

International Reading Association
800 Barksdale Rd., P.O. Box 8139   302-731-1600
Newark, DE 19714   800-336-READ
    FAX 302-731-1057

This thought-provoking booklet from IRA and the National Council of Teachers of English uses case studies to clarify our understanding of what is meant by literacy in the world today.

$ 3.50

3086 Changing School Reading Programs: Principles and Case Studies

S. Jay Samuels, Author

International Reading Association
800 Barksdale Rd., P.O. Box 8139   302-731-1600
Newark, DE 19714   800-336-READ
    FAX 302-731-1057

Administrators responsible for developing and changing reading programs will find this book useful.

$ 13.50

3087 Children's Comprehension of Text: Research Into Practice

K. Denise Muth, Author

International Reading Association
800 Barksdale Rd., P.O. Box 8139   302-731-1600
Newark, DE 19714   800-336-READ
    FAX 302-731-1057

Focuses on ways to help students better understand the tests they read.

$ 13.00

3088 Children's Literature in the Reading Program

Bernice Cullinan, Author

International Reading Association
800 Barksdale Rd., P.O. Box 8139   302-731-1600
Newark, DE 19714   800-336-READ
                                      FAX 302-731-1057

Authorities in the field of children's literature are contributors to this best-selling volume. The book deals at length with ways of using various types of literature to enrich K-8 reading programs at all levels.

$ 12.00

3089 Clinical and Research Applications of the K-ABC

AGS
7201 Woodland Road   612-786-4343
Circle Pines, MN 55014   800-328-2560

A valuable resource, this book covers timely and key issues related to the use of K-ABC.

$ 43.00

3090 Counterpoint and Beyond: a Response to Becoming a Nation of Readers

Jane Davidson, Author

International Reading Association
800 Barksdale Rd., P.O. Box 8139   302-731-1600
Newark, DE 19714   800-336-READ
                                      FAX 302-731-1057

A research-supported response to Becoming a Nation of Readers: The Report of the Commission on Reading.

$ 7.25

3091 Disabled Readers: Insight, Assessment, Instruction

D.J. Sawyer, Author

Learning Disabilities Association of America
4156 Library Road   412-341-1515
Pittsburgh, PA 15234

$ 6.00

3092 Dyslexia - the Pattern of Difficulties

Learning Disabilities Association of America
4156 Library Road   412-341-1515
Pittsburgh, PA 15234

3093 Dyslexia: Theory and Practice of Remedial Instruction

D. Clark, Author

Connecticut Association for Children with LD
18 Marshall Street   203-838-5010
South Norwalk, CT 06854 FAX 203-866-6108

$ 23.00

3094 Dyslexia - Understanding Reading Problems

Learning Disabilities Association of America
4156 Library Road   412-341-1515
Pittsburgh, PA 15234

3095 The Dyslogic Syndrome

Learning Disabilities Association of America
4156 Library Road   412-341-1515
Pittsburgh, PA 15234

3096 Exemplary Practices in Literacy Development and Instruction

Peter Winograd, Author

International Reading Association
800 Barksdale Rd., P.O. Box 8139   302-731-1600
Newark, DE 19714   800-336-READ
                                      FAX 302-731-1057

The articles in this collection describe outstanding and innovative practices that promote integrated language arts and literacy abilities from elementary through middle school levels.

$ 5.00

3097 A Guide to Selecting Basal Reading Programs

International Reading Association
800 Barksdale Rd., P.O. Box 8139   302-731-1600
Newark, DE 19714   800-336-READ
                                      FAX 302-731-1057

This series of eight booklets plus a leader's manual provides guidelines that testbook adoption commitees and other groups can use in evaluating the content and instructional quality of basal reading programs.

$ 50.00

3098 Handbook for the Volunteer Tutor

Sidney Rauch, Author

International Reading Association
800 Barksdale Rd., P.O. Box 8139   302-731-1600
Newark, DE 19714   800-336-READ
                                      FAX 302-731-1057

This second edition details lessons for tutors to use in their work with individuals. The concepts, practices and materials discussed focus on the elementary and secondary student who can benefit from extra help in reading.

$ 10.50

3099 Handbook of Reading Research: Volume II

Rebecca Barr, Author

International Reading Association
800 Barksdale Rd., P.O. Box 8139   302-731-1600
Newark, DE 19714   800-336-READ
FAX 302-731-1057

This handbook containing 34 chapters by leading researchers, is completely different from Volume 1. It starts with the broadest possible societal view of literacy, then spans from the materials and tasks of literacy to the context of schooling, and concludes with a reflection on the progress in reading research.

$ 90.00

3100   How Children Construct Literacy: Piagetian Perspectives

Yetta Goodman, Author

International Reading Association
800 Barksdale Rd., P.O. Box 8139   302-731-1600
Newark, DE 19714   800-336-READ
FAX 302-731-1057

This book presents a wealth of information on children's literacy development.

$ 9.00

3101   How to Prepare Materials for New Literates

International Reading Association
800 Barksdale Rd., P.O. Box 8139   302-731-1600
Newark, DE 19714   800-336-READ
FAX 302-731-1057

This book describes a method for preparing reading materials for new literates, including principles that would be useful to educators in many parts of the world.

$ 7.00

3102   Informal Reading Inventories

Marjorie Seddon Johnson, Author

International Reading Association
800 Barksdale Rd., P.O. Box 8139   302-731-1600
Newark, DE 19714   800-336-READ
FAX 302-731-1057

This revised edition provides a comprehensive description of the construction and use of informal reading inventories.

$ 9.50

3103   Invitation to Read: More Children's Literature in the Reading Program

Bernice Cullinan, Author

International Reading Association
800 Barksdale Rd., P.O. Box 8139   302-731-1600
Newark, DE 19714   800-336-READ
FAX 302-731-1057

Teachers offer their ideas and practices regarding whole language.

$ 18.00

3104   New Directions in Reading Instruction

Jay Monahan, Author

International Reading Association
800 Barksdale Rd., P.O. Box 8139   302-731-1600
Newark, DE 19714   800-336-READ
FAX 302-731-1057

This handy flipchart provides a quick summary of recent research ideas relating to content area reading: comprehension instruction, cooperative learning, textbooks, questioning and more than 20 other topics of current concern to teachers.

$ 3.95

3105   Organizing for Instruction

Kathryn Au, Author

International Reading Association
800 Barksdale Rd., P.O. Box 8139   302-731-1600
Newark, DE 19714   800-336-READ
FAX 302-731-1057

Offprint of articles from a special themed journal issue exploring alternatives to conventional practices of teaching reading.

$ 3.00

3106   Parent Programs in Reading: Guidelines for Success

Anthony Fredericks, Author

International Reading Association
800 Barksdale Rd., P.O. Box 8139   302-731-1600
Newark, DE 19714   800-336-READ
FAX 302-731-1057

Parental involvement in reading curriculum can add an exciting dimension to an overall school program as it reinforces the home/school partnership.

$ 6.75

3107   Phonic Remedial Reading Lessons

Kirk E. Minskoff, Author

Learning Disabilities Association of America
4156 Library Road   412-341-1515
Pittsburgh, PA 15234

$ 15.00

3108   Phonology and Reading Disability

Donald Shankweiler, Author

University of Michigan Press
839 Greene Street   313-764-4392
Ann Arbor, MI 48106

Colin Day, Director
Mary Erwin, Assistant Director

Argues the association of words with the sounds they represent is crucial to the learning process.

$ 32.50

3109 Prereading Activities for Content Area Reading and Learning

David Moore, Author

International Reading Association
800 Barksdale Rd., P.O. Box 8139   302-731-1600
Newark, DE 19714   800-336-READ
                                          FAX 302-731-1057

This second edition describes the wealth of prereading activities and strategies designed to help teachers make unfamiliar, often unappealing material understandable to maturing readers.

$ 7.75

3110 Reading and the Special Learner

Carolyn Hedley, Author

Ables Publishing Corporation
355 Chestnut Street   201-767-8450
Norwood, NJ 07648   FAX 201-767-6717

Explores the needs of the special learner; compensatory methods and adaptive means.

$ 45.00

3111 The Reading Brain: the Biological Basis of Dyslexia

Learning Disabilities Association of America
4156 Library Road   412-341-1515
Pittsburgh, PA 15234

3112 Reading Comprehension Instruction 1783-1987: a Review of Trends

H. Alan Robinson, Author

International Reading Association
800 Barksdale Rd., P.O. Box 8139   302-731-1600
Newark, DE 19714   800-336-READ
                                          FAX 302-731-1057

Provides an in-depth analysis of the methods, materials, outcomes and technologies of comprehension instruction from the 1780's to the present day.

$ 9.00

3113 Reading Comprehension Instruction: Issues and Strategies

K. Maria, Author

Learning Disabilities Association of America
4156 Library Road   412-341-1515
Pittsburgh, PA 15234

3114 Reading Disabilities in College and High School

Aaron & Baker, Author

Learning Disabilities Association of America
4156 Library Road   412-341-1515
Pittsburgh, PA 15234

$ 21.00

3115 Reading in the Middle School

Gerald Duffy, Author

International Reading Association
800 Barksdale Rd., P.O. Box 8139   302-731-1600
Newark, DE 19714   800-336-READ
                                          FAX 302-731-1057

Completely revised and updated, this book combines both theory and practical suggestions for establishing effective middle school reading programs.

$ 13.00

3116 Reading Teacher

International Reading Association
800 Barksdale Rd., P.O. Box 8139   302-731-1600
Newark, DE 19714   FAX 302-731-1057

Professional journal directed toward preschool, primary and elementary school educators.

3117 Reading: What Can Be Measured?

Roger Farr, Author

International Reading Association
800 Barksdale Rd., P.O. Box 8139   302-731-1600
Newark, DE 19714   800-336-READ
                                          FAX 302-731-1057

This revision of an earlier volume organizes and describes the research literature on measurement and evaluation in reading.

$ 14.25

3118 Reading/Learning Disability An Ecological Approach

Bartoli & Botel, Author

Learning Disabilities Association of America
4156 Library Road   412-341-1515
Pittsburgh, PA 15234

$ 20.00

3119 Reading/Writing Connections: Learning From Research

Judith Irwin, Author

International Reading Association
800 Barksdale Rd., P.O. Box 8139   302-731-1600
Newark, DE 19714   800-336-READ
                                          FAX 302-731-1057

An excellent resource that presents current reviews of research on reading/writing connections. Issues such as awareness of context and examining reading and writing as processes are addressed.

$ 15.00

3120 Reading/Writing/Rage: the Terrible Price Paid By Victims of School Failure

D.F. Ungerleider, Author
B.L. Winch/Jalmar Press
45 Hitching Post Drive 310-547-1240
Rolling Hills Estates, CA 90274 800-662-9662

3121 Re-examining Reading Diagnosis: New Trends and Procedures

Learning Disabilities Association of America
4156 Library Road 412-341-1515
Pittsburgh, PA 15234

3122 Remediation of Learning Disabilities

Robert Valett, Author
Fearon/Janus
500 Harbor Blvd. 415-592-7810
Belmont, CA 94002

A guide to describing disabilities and providing remedial activities.

$ 23.40

3123 Responses to Literature Grades K-8

James Macon, Author
International Reading Association
800 Barksdale Rd., P.O. Box 8139 302-731-1600
Newark, DE 19714 800-336-READ
FAX 302-731-1057

A practical tool for teaching students how to respond to literature, this book provides classroom activities that encourage students to think more as they read and to focus on the literary elements of a story.

$ 4.50

3124 Roles in Literacy Learning: a New Perspective

Duane Tovey, Author
International Reading Association
800 Barksdale Rd., P.O. Box 8139 302-731-1600
Newark, DE 19714 800-336-READ
FAX 302-731-1057

The growing body of thought and research on children's emergent literacy has led to a greater understanding of language processing abilities.

$ 7.50

3125 Teaching Reading Skills Through the Newspaper, Third Edition

Arnold Cheyney, Author
International Reading Association
800 Barksdale Rd., P.O. Box 8139 302-731-1600
Newark, DE 19714 800-336-READ
FAX 302-731-1057

Chock-full of new teaching tips, this book along with a newspaper will provide teachers with enough materials to challenge and excite students for hours.

$ 6.00

3126 Teaching the Dyslexic Child

A. Griffiths, Author
Connecticut Association for Children with LD
18 Marshall Street 203-838-5010
South Norwalk, CT 06854 FAX 203-866-6108

$ 8.95

3127 Teaching Vocabulary to Improve Reading Comprehension

William Nagy, Author
International Reading Association
800 Barksdale Rd., P.O. Box 8139 302-731-1600
Newark, DE 19714 800-336-READ
FAX 302-731-1057

This practical book uses research based knowledge to show teachers how to utilize vocabulary instruction more effectively to improve reading comprehension.

$ 6.25

3128 Theoretical Models and Processes of Reading

Harry Singer, Author
International Reading Association
800 Barksdale Rd., P.O. Box 8139 302-731-1600
Newark, DE 19714 800-336-READ
FAX 302-731-1057

The theories, models and research in processes of reading are covered in this comprehensive collection of important studies.

$ 35.00

3129 Thinking and Learning Across the Curriculum

Thomas Estes, Author
International Reading Association
800 Barksdale Rd., P.O. Box 8139 302-731-1600
Newark, DE 19714 800-336-READ
FAX 302-731-1057

Offprint of articles from a special themed journal issue focusing on the connections among reading, thinking and learning.

$ 3.00

269

3130 Toward An Ecological Assessment of Reading Progress

Mary Jett-Simpson, Author

International Reading Association
800 Barksdale Rd., P.O. Box 8139   302-731-1600
Newark, DE 19714   800-336-READ
                                                        FAX 302-731-1057

This monograph offers valuable insights on key issues relating to assessment.

$ 8.00

3131 Toward Defining Literacy

Richard Venezky, Author

International Reading Association
800 Barksdale Rd., P.O. Box 8139   302-731-1600
Newark, DE 19714   800-336-READ
                                                        FAX 302-731-1057

This book is designed to raise awareness of the complex issues surrounding literacy.

$ 6.75

3132 Using Discussion to Promote Reading Comprehension

Donna Alverman, Author

International Reading Association
800 Barksdale Rd., P.O. Box 8139   302-731-1600
Newark, DE 19714   800-336-READ
                                                        FAX 302-731-1057

This book shows preservice and inservice teachers at the middle and high school levels how to use discussion to foster students' comprehension of assigned textbook materials.

$ 6.75

3133 What Research Has to Say About Reading Instruction, Second Edition

S. Jay Samuels, Author

International Reading Association
800 Barksdale Rd., P.O. Box 8139   302-731-1600
Newark, DE 19714   800-336-READ
                                                        FAX 302-731-1057

This new edition maintains the balance between theory and application while updating the contents to reflect changes in reading curriculum.

$ 16.00

3134 Writing for Publication in Reading and Language Arts

James Bauman, Author

International Reading Association
800 Barksdale Rd., P.O. Box 8139   302-731-1600
Newark, DE 19714   800-336-READ
                                                        FAX 302-731-1057

Provides novice and experienced writers with information on all aspects of publishing professional and instructional materials in literacy education.

$ 10.00

Science

3135 Improving Reading in Science

Judith Thelen, Author

International Reading Association
800 Barksdale Rd., P.O. Box 8139   302-731-1600
Newark, DE 19714   800-336-READ
                                                        FAX 302-731-1057

This handy booklet combines a solid theoretical base with practical suggestions for the science teacher.

$ 5.00

3136 Science Learning: Processes and Applications

Carol Minnick Santa, Author

International Reading Association
800 Barksdale Rd., P.O. Box 8139   302-731-1600
Newark, DE 19714   800-336-READ
                                                        FAX 302-731-1057

A collection of articles authored by science and reading teachers at all levels.

$ 18.00

Social Skills

3137 Can Social Skills for Employment Be Taught?

ERIC Clearinghouse on Disabled and Gifted Children
1920 Association Drive   703-620-3660
Reston, VA 22091

3138 Developing Social Vocational Skills in Handicapped Individuals

ERIC Clearinghouse on Disabled and Gifted Children
1920 Association Drive   703-620-3660
Reston, VA 22091

3139 Learning Disability: Social Class and the Construction of American Education

James Carrier, Author

Greenwood Publishing Group, Inc.
88 Post Road
Westport, CT 06881

Presents a detailed historical description of the social and education assumptions integral to the idea of learning disability.

$ 39.95

3140   1993 Teacher's Curriculum Guide: Exploring Your World with Newspapers

Leslie Gray, Author
International Reading Association
800 Barksdale Rd., P.O. Box 8139   302-731-1600
Newark, DE 19714   800-336-READ
                                                   FAX 302-731-1057

Six units focus on newspaper knowledge, community and world people, environmental and social issues, community resources and the arts.

$ 1.50

3141   Teaching Social Skills to Youngsters with Disabilities

Susan Lehr, Author
Federation for Children with Special Needs
95 Berkeley Street, Ste. 104   617-482-2915
Boston, MA 02116   800-331-0688

This Manual explains the importance of instruction and training to learn appropriate social behavior.

$ 5.00

3142   Training for Independent Living Curriculum: 4th Edition

RPM Press, Inc.
P.O. Box 31483   602-886-1990
Tucson, AZ 85751

Jan Stonebraker, Operations Manager

Provides educators and rehabilitation personnel with a 400 page curriculum designed to help teach developmentally disabled and other severly challenged persons essential independent living skills including; personal and social adjustment, money management, meal preparation, money handling, personal safety, grooming and more.

$ 79.95

Physical Education

3143   Social Perception and Learning Disabilities

Learning Disabilities Association of America
4156 Library Road   412-341-1515
Pittsburgh, PA 15234

Alabama

3144　Learning Specialists

526 Santolina Drive　　　　FAX 205-793-9542
Dothan, AL　36303

Martha Smith, B.S., M.S., CMA, LD Specialist

Provides learning disability assessment through diagnostic evaluation, testing by a licensed psychometrist, academic evaluation, and tutoring by licensed, certified christian instructors.

3145　Special Education Action Committee

P.O. Box 161274　　　　　205-478-1208
Mobile, AL　36616　　　　 800-222-7322

Parent Training and Information Program views parents as full partners in the educational process and a significant source of support and assistance to each other. Funded by the Division of Personnel Preparation, Office of Special Education Programs, these programs provide training and information to parents to enable such individuals to participate more effectively with professionals in meeting the educational needs of disabled children.

3146　Three Springs

247 Chateau Drive, Ste. A
Huntsville, AL　35801　　　205-880-3339

Mike Watson, President

Offers four private schools serving the resident population of the Three Springs Treatment Programs.

Alaska

3147　Center for Community

700 Katlian, Ste. B　　　　907-747-6960
Sitka, AK　99835　　　　　800-478-6970
　　　　　　　　　　　FAX 907-747-4868

Mark Jacobina, Assistive Tech.

A private, non-profit corporation provides comprehensive and individualized support and training services for people of all ages who have a developmental delay or disability. Programs include assistive technology services and vocational assessment, training and placement, as well as other residential and respite services.

3148　Parents As Resources Engaged In

P.O. Box 32198　　　　　907-790-2246
Juneau, AK　99803　　　　800-478-7678

Parent Training and Information Program views parents as full partners in the educational process and a significant source of support and assistance to each other. Funded by the Division of Personnel Preparation, Office of Special Education Programs, these programs provide training and information to parents to enable such individuals to participate more effectively with professionals in meeting the educational needs of disabled children.

3149　Slingerland Tutorial Service

1145 I Street　　　　　　907-272-3720
Anchorage, AK　99501

Hazel Smith, Consultant

Arizona

3150　Center for Neurodevelopmental Studies, Inc.

8434 North 39th Avenue　　602-934-7166
Phoenix, AZ　85051

Marilyn Cabay

3151　Devereux Arizona

6436 E. Sweetwater Avenue　602-998-2920
Scottsdale, AZ　85254

Residential and day programs for children and adolescents with emotional and/or learning disabilities.

3152　Henry Occupational Therapy Services

2432 West Peoria, Ste. 1241　602-371-1204
Phoenix, AZ　85029

Diana Henry, MS, OTR/L, O.T/Owner
Carla Norris, Parent Support Spec.

Emphasizes medical sensory integration diagnostic treatments in the clinic, and educational based O.T. services in private and public schools.

3153　LATCH School, Inc.

8145 North 27th Avenue　　602-995-7366
Phoenix, AZ　85051

Sandra Landy, Executive Director

Offers individual assessment for children with disabilities.

3154　Life Development Institute

1720 East Monte Vista　　　602-254-0822
Phoenix, AZ　85006　　　　FAX 602-253-6878

Robert Crawford, President

Serves older adolescents and adults with learning disabilities, ADD and related disorders. The purpose of the training is to enable program participants to pursue responsible independent living, enhance academic/ workplace literacy skills and facilitate placement in educational/employment opportunities commensurate with individual capabilities. Current efforts to open a stand alone, regionally accredited 2-year college are underway with projected opening in fall 1994.

3155   New Way School

2340 North Hayden Road   602-946-9112
Scottsdale, AZ 85252

3156   Pilot Parent Partnerships

2150 East Highland Avenue, Ste. 105   602-468-3001
Phoenix, AZ 85016

Parent Training and Information Program views parents as full partners in the educational process and a significant source of support and assistance to each other. Funded by the Division of Personnel Preparation, Office of Special Education Programs, these programs provide training and information to parents to enable such individuals to participate more effectively with professionals in meeting the educational needs of disabled children.

Arkansas

3157   Arkansas Disabilitiy Coalition

10002 West Markahm, Ste. B7   501-221-1330
Little Rock, AR 72205

Parent Training and Information Program views parents as full partners in the educational process and a significant source of support and assistance to each other. Funded by the Division of Personnel Preparation, Office of Special Education Programs, these programs provide training and information to parents to enable such individuals to participate more effectively with professionals in meeting the educational needs of disabled children.

California

3158   The Alamansor Center

1955 Fremont Avenue   818-282-6194
South Pasadena, CA 91030

3159   Ann Martin Children's Center

1250 Grand Avenue   415-655-7880
Piedmont, CA 94610

Suzie Thum

3160   Aria School (Program of San Francisco Educational Services)

2660 San Bruno   415-468-7055
San Francisco, CA 94134

Lorraine Petro

3161   Armstrong High School

797 Santa Margarita   415-873-7312
Millbrae, CA 94030

Jenny Munro

Full high school program for dyslexic students.

3162   Basic Skills Learning Center

650 Montecillo Road   415-499-0811
San Rafael, CA 94903

Jean Cook

3163   Bay Area Speech, Language and Learning Clinic

38218 Glenmmor Drive, Ste. A   415-794-5155
Fremont, CA 94536

Nancy Barcal

3164   Bay Center for Educational Services

2837 Claremont Blvd.   415-848-6868
Berkeley, CA 94705

Don De Rushia

3165   Brainard Vision Center

2562 State Street, Ste. E   619-434-5025
Carlsbad, CA 92008

Elliott Brainard

3166   Brislain Learning Center

1550 Humboldt Road, Ste. 3   916-352-2567
Chico, CA 95928

Judy Brislain

3167   Center for Adaptive Learning

3350 Clayton Road, Ste. A   510-827-3863
Concrod, CA 94519

Committed to creating and maintaining a holistic environment for neurologically impaired individuals which will promote dignity, and support a sense of community. The CAL program provides each participant with an opportunity to experience optimal growth. Further, CAL is committed to maintain a standard of the highest quality of living possible; this standard will allow each student to develop a sense of pride, to augment self-esteem and to foster a sense of self worth.

3168   Charles Armstrong School

1405 Solana Drive   415-592-7570
Belmont, CA 94002

Jean Reim, Executive Director

Strives to provide an appropriate educational experience for the SLD/dyslexic learner which enables the student not only to acquire necessary language skills but also instills joy for learning, enhances self-worth and allows each right to identify, understand and fulfill personal potential.

3169 The CHILD Center

100 Shaw Drive   415-456-0440
San Anselmo, CA 94960

Winifred Setrakian

3170 Children's Therapy Center

1371 Del Norte Road   805-988-9815
Camarillo, CA 93010

Jo Murphy Hyland

3171 Developmental Movement Laboratory

1100 5th Avenue   415-485-0879
San Rafael, CA 94901

Pat Hegerhorst

3172 Devereux Santa Barbara

P.O. Box 1079   805-968-2525
Santa Barbara, CA 93102

Residential, day and community programs for children and adults who have a wide range of developmental and/or emotional disorders.

3173 Division of Behavioral and Developmental Pediatrics & Learning Program

University of California
400 Parnassus Avenue, Room A203   415-476-4575
San Framcisco, CA 94143

W. Thomas Boyce

3174 Educational and Tutorial Services

655 Deep Valley Drive, Ste. 110   213-544-1555
Rolling Hills Estates, CA 90274

Patricia Shawaker, PhD, Director

Offers diagnostic services, educational consulting, school placement, educational therapy, tutoring and a reading clinic.

3175 Educational Psychology Clinic

California State University
1250 Bellflower Blvd.   213-985-4991
Long Beach, CA 90630

3176 Educational Tutoring Center

793-B Lomas Santa Fe Plaza   619-481-9919
Solana Beach, CA 92075

Ronald Rauckhorst

3177 Educators in Private Practice

8 Commercial Blvd.   415-925-0875
Novato, CA 94949

Beverly Tait, M.S., Educ. Therapist
Jean Cook, M.A., Educ. Therapist

An organization of educational therapists, tutors and evaluators who provide services to all ages and grades in all subject areas, including study skills.

3178 ERAS Center for Special Education

10101 West Jefferson Blvd.   213-838-1200
Culver City, CA 90232

Barbara Cull

3179 Escalon Center

536 East Mendocino Street   818-798-0744
Altadena, CA 91001

Marge Cravens

3180 Frostig School

971 North Altadena Drive   818-791-1255
Pasadena, CA 91107

Private school for learning disabled children without serious emotional problems.

3181 Full Circle Programs, Inc.

4 Joseph Court   415-499-3320
San Rafael, CA 94903

Timothy Tabernik, Executive Director

Provides residential treatment with on-site school services for 40 boys. Provides diagnostic assessments and special education for children who are severly emotionally disabled and learning disabled. Primary referrals are from mental health, social services and probation departments.

3182 Garden Sullivan Learning and Development Program

2750 Geary Blvd.   415-921-6171
San Francisco, CA 94118

Antje Shadoan

3183 Granada Hills One to One Reading and Educational Center

10324 Woodley Avenue   818-891-3090
Granada Hills, CA 91344

Paul Klinger, Owner/Director

Reading instruction on a 1-1 basis at all times. All types of reading problems, including dyslexia, ADD, etc. On request at times the Center offers test preparation, math and study skills.

3184 Help for Brain Injured Children, Inc.

The Cleta Harder Developmental School
981 North Euclid   213-694-5655
La Habra, CA 90631

Cleta Harder

3185 Hillside Developmental Learning Center

1223 Verdugo Blvd.   818-790-3044
La Canada, CA 91011

Elizabeth Campbell

3186 Irvine Optometric Group

33 Creek Road, Ste. 300   714-559-5905
Irvine, CA 92714

Julie Ryan

3187 Jean Weingarten Peninsula Oral School for the Deaf

2525 Buena Vista Avenue   415-593-1848
Belmont, CA 94002

Kathleen Daniel Sussman

3188 The Learning Center

1125 A St., #303, Garden Court Bldg   415-485-9737
San Rafael, CA 94901

Pamela Wilding, Co-Director
Joan Cayton, Co-Director

Provides diagnostic training, educational assessment, educational therapy services including remediation of learning disabilities, development of academic skills, compensatory strategies, coursework support, study skills, test taking strategies and comprehensive case management, content tutorial services, consultation and referral services for individuals, families and professionals serving children and adults with learning difficulties.

3189 The Learning Center: Redlands Psychological Group

440 Cajon Street
Redlands, CA 92373

3190 The Learning Clinics - Port Hueneme

227 East Channel Islands Blvd.   805-984-2355
Port Hueneme, CA 93041

Toby Forden

Provides diagnostic testing and individualized instruction for students of all ages who wish to improve their reading, writing, or math skills.

3191 The Learning Clinics (TLC)

484 Mobil Avenue, Ste. 12   805-482-3730
Camarillo, CA 93010

Paula Lopez

Provides diagnostic testing and individualized instruction for students of all ages who wish to improve their reading, writing, or math skills.

3192 The Learning Clinics - Ventura

5550 Telegraph Road, Ste. C-3   805-656-4654
Ventura, CA 93003

Toby Forden

Provides diagnostic testing and individualized instruction for students of all ages who wish to improve their reading, writing or math skills.

3193 Learning Styles Educational Therapy Services

26 Meadow Drive   415-485-1132
San Rafael, CA 94903

Sandra Zeichner

3194 LeeBill School and Learning Center

1411 Lincoln Avenue   415-454-6618
San Rafael, CA 94901

William Miller

3195 Lindamood Bell Learning Processes

416 Higuera   805-541-3836
San Luis Obispo, CA 93401   800-233-1819
                                   FAX 805-541-8756

Wendy Cook
Ellen Lathrop

A center specializing in diagnosing and treating learning disabilities in all ages of individuals. The Directors have authored programs to develop three sensory-cognitive processes: 1) Conceptualization for decoding and spelling; 2) Imagery for Language Comprehension and Thinking, and 3) Visual-Motor processing for fine motor skill development. These three areas underlie basic language processing. In providing services, the primary concern is the quality of personal interaction with clients.

3196 The Marianne Frostig Center of Educational Therapy

971 North Altadena Avenue   818-791-1255
Pasadena, CA 91107

Dennett Ross

3197 Marina Center for Therapy

4676 Admiralty Way, Ste. 515   213-390-7194
Marina Del Ray, CA 90292

Bruce Hirsch

3198 Melmed Learning Clinic

957 Dewing Avenue   415-283-6777
Lafayette, CA 94549

Paul Melmed

3199 Melvin-Smith Learning Center

4436 Engle Road   916-483-6415
Sacramento, CA 95821

Joan Smith

Provides a program for children and adults with learning disabilities. Population includes: learning disabled, dyzlexic and head trauma clients. Clinical inservice training is available for professionals interested in working with dyslexic and learning disabled students.

3200 Mission Reading Clinic

2701 Folsom Street   415-282-3800
San Francisco, CA 94110

Kenneth Romines

3201 Modesto Rehabilitation Services

929 Melinda Lane   209-522-9257
Modesto, CA 95350

Lorraine Vaille

Assessment, consultation and treatment, psychological testing, academic testing and screening for dyslexia and associated difficulties are provided upon appointment.

3202 Naness Family Center

7657 Winnetka Avenue, Ste. 348   818-99-TRUST
Canoga Park, CA 91306

Sue Naness

The center helps children with Attention Deficit Disorder, are achievers, lack motivation have learning, behavior or social problems. The family experiences stress due to these problems and needs to develop positive solutions by building a child's stregths while confronting negative learning/behavior patterns.

3203 Neuropsychological Development Center

2682 Royal Crest Drive   619-560-7245
Escondido, CA 92025

Mary Louise Scholl

3204 New Vistas Christian School

2073 Oak Park Blvd.   415-930-8894
Pleasant Hill, CA 94523

Bonnevieve Reynolds

3205 Newport Language, Speech and Audiology Center

24401 Calle De La Louisa, Ste. 310   714-581-2800
Laguna Hills, CA 92653

Sharlene Goodman

3206 The Open Book

2031 Bush Street   415-563-6732
San Francisco, CA 94115

David Whitmore

3207 Optometric Center of Fullerton

Southern California College of Optometry
2575 Yorba Linda Blvd.   714-449-7400
Fullerton, CA 92631

George Comer, O.D., Chief Of Staff
Michael Rouse, O.D., M.S. Ed., Chief, Vision Ther.

The Center provides comprehensive primary vision care for patients of all ages. The Vision Therapy Service specializes in complete diagnostic and therapeutic care of both children and adults presenting with visual and related learning problems. The primary goal is the diagnosis and management of visual and visual perceptual-motor difficulties that may interfere with efficient learning. Testing services are also available for the diagnosis of specific dyslexia. A sliding fee scale is available.

3208 Parents Helping Parents

535 Race Street, Ste. 140   408-288-5010
San Jose, CA 95126

Florene Stewart Poyadue

Parent Training and Information Program views parents as full partners in the educational process and a significant source of support and assistance to each other. Funded by the Division of Personnel Preparation, Office of Special Education Programs, these programs provide training and information to parents to enable such individuals to participate more effectively with professionals in meeting the educational needs of disabled children.

3209 Park Century School

2040 Stoner Avenue   310-478-5065
Los Angeles, CA 90025

Gail Spindler

Offers a comprehensive program which addresses the ever-changingh needs of bright children with learning disabilities and their families.

3210 Peninsula Associates

830 Menlo Avenue, Ste. 109   415-324-0648
Menlo Park, CA 94025

Maureen O'Connor

A speech and language therapy privcate practice which provides individual and group speech, language and learning services to individuals with communication and learning problems. Diagnostic and therapy services are provided for a wide range of communication problems and for ages infants, children, teens and adults.

3211 Perceptual Tutor

542 Mt. Dell Drive, P.O. Box 705   415-672-2305
Clayton, CA 94517

Linda Symons

Training to compensate and correct visual learning disabilities.

3212 Pine Meadows School

P.O. Box 5C   916-359-2211
French Gulch, CA 96033

David Hull

3213 Prentice Day School

2596 Willo   714-650-1115
Costa Mesa, CA 92627   FAX 714-631-6237

Nancy Royal, EdD, Executive Director
Debra Jarvis, MA, Dir. Of Education

A private, co-educational day school serving children in grades K-8 utilizing the Slingerland Classroom Adaptation of the Orton-Gillingham Multisensory Approach to Language Arts. At Prentice, each student is nurtured within a unique environment reflecting a keen understanding of individual students needs. Classroom sizes do not exceed 15 in grades K-5 or 16 in grades 6-8. Each class is taught by a fully credentialed, highly trained educators and aides.

3214 Providence Speech and Hearing Center

1301 Providence Avenue   714-639-4990
Orange, CA 92668

O.T. Kenworthy, PhD, Executive Director
Vicki Jax, PhD, Sir. Speech-Language

Accredited by the Professional Services Board of the American-Speech-Language-Hearing Association. Comprehensive services for testing and treatment of all speech, language and hearing problems. Individual and group therapy beginning with parent/infant programs.

3215 REACH for Learning

1221 Marin Avenue   510-524-6455
Albany, CA 94706

Corinne Gustafson

Educational services for children and adults including: diagnostic assessment, individual remediation/tutoring, small group workshops, and consulation for parents and professionals.

3216 Read: Write Professional Tutorial and Consulting Service

2701 Cottage Way, Ste. 16   916-484-6616
Sacramento, CA 95825

Bernard Goldberg

3217 The Reading Center of Bruno

9555 Garfield, Suite B   714-964-2434
Fountain Valley, CA 92708

Muriel Bruno

3218 Rincon Center for Learning

594 North Westwind Drive   619-442-2722
El Cajon, CA 92020

Lois Dotson

3219 Santa Barbara Center for Educational Therapy

2130 Mission Ridge Road   805-687-3711
Santa Barbara, CA 93103

Susan Hamilton, Dir., Educ. Ther.
Joyce Tolle, Dir., Educ. Ther.

Provides educational assessment to determine learning style and document learning disabilities. Also provided are one-to-one remedial or tutorial services for individuals specializing in dyslexia.

3220 The Santa Cruz Learning Center

720 Fairmount Avenue   408-427-2753
Santa Cruz, CA 95062

Eleanor F. Stitt, Director

Individualized one-to-one tutoring for individuals aged 5 to adults. Specializes in dyslexia, learning difficulties and gifted persons. Includes test preparation, math, reading, self confidence, study skills, time organization and related services.

3221 Second Start: Pine Hill School

1975 Cambrianna Drive   408-371-5881
San Jose, CA 95124

Betty Siemer

3222 The Stillman Dyslexia Center, Inc.

16133 Ventura Blvd., #905   818-789-1111
Encino, CA 91436

Earl Chappell

3223 Stockdale Learning Center

5405 Stockdale Highway, Ste. 205　　805-397-9559
Bakersfield, CA 93309

Andrew Barling

3224 Stowell Learning Center

3333 Brea Canyon Road, Ste. 210　　714-598-2482
Diamond Bar, CA 91765

Jill Stowell, Director

A diagnostic and teaching center for learning and attention disorders. Specialize in instruction for dyslexia or learning disabled children and adults. Our services include diagnostic evaluation, developmental evaluation, and educational therapy which is provided on a one-to-one basis.

3225 Switzer Center

1110 Sartori Avenue　　213-328-3611
Torrance, CA 90501

Janet Switzer

3226 Team of Advocates for Special Kids, Inc.

100 West Cerritos Avenue　　714-533-TASK
Anaheim, CA 92805　　FAX 714-533-2533

Joan Tellefsen, Director

Parent Training and Information Program views parents as full partners in the educational process and a significant source of support and assistance to each other. Funded by the Division of Personnel Preparation, Office of Special Education Programs, these programs provide training and information to parents to enable such individuals to participate more effectively with professionals in meeting the educational needs of disabled children.

3227 Vision Care Clinic of Santa Clara Valley

2730 Union Avenue　　408-377-1150
San Jose, CA 95124

V. Liane Rice

3228 Ygnacio Learning Center

200 La Caa Via　　415-937-7323
Walnut Creek, CA 94598

Sue Caputi

Colorado

3229 Havern Center, Inc.

4000 South Wadsworth　　303-986-4587
Littleton, CO 80123

Barbara Schulte

3230 Jefferson County Community Center for Developmental Disabilities

7456 West 5th Avenue　　303-233-3363
Lakewood, CO 80226

Arthur Hogling, Executive Director

3231 PEAK Parent Center, Inc.

6055 Lehman Drive, Ste. 101　　719-531-9400
Colorado Springs, CO 80918　　800-284-0251

Parent Training and Information Program for the State of Colorado views parents as full partners in the educational process and a significant source of support and assistance to each other. Funded by the Division of Personnel Preparation, Office of Special Education Programs, these programs provide training and information to parents to enable such individuals to participate more effectively with professionals in meeting the educational needs of children with disabilities.

3232 Timberline Trails Camp

Box 397　　303-469-0262
Almont, CO 81210

Art Pliner

Connecticut

3233 A.J. Pappanikou Center on Special

A University Affiliated Program
991 Main Street　　203-282-7050
East Hartford, CT 06108

Orv Karan, Director

3234 American School for the Deaf

139 North Main Street　　203-727-1300
West Hartford, CT 06107

Winfield McChord, Jr., Executive Director

3235 Boy's Village, Inc.

528 Wheelers Farm Road　　203-877-0300
Milford, CT 06460

Donald Gaskill, Director

A residential treatment for 37 emotionally disturbed/learning disabled childre.

3236 Boys Village Youth and Family Services, Inc.

528 Wheelers Farm Road　　203-877-0300
Milford, CT 06460

Steven Pynn, Director

Facility offering residential, educational and day treatment programs.

3237   Candee Hill, Inc.

122 Candee Hill Road   203-274-8332
Watertown, CT 06795

Frank Popkiewicz, Director

Emphasis on increasing client's self-sufficiency in areas of daily skills, community awareness and social interaction.

3238   Chapel Haven, Inc.

1040 Whalley Avenue   203-397-1714
New Haven, CT 06515   FAX 203-397-8004

Phyllis Monoson, Director

A comprehensive year-round program for young adults who desire independence. It is strictly a transitional experience involving a five-part program which is shaped around the individual needs of each student.

3239   Children's Home of Cromwell - the Learning Center

60 Hicksville Road   203-635-6010
Cromwell, CT 06416

Carole O'Neal, Director

Offers small group individualized instruction by certified special education teachers with a teacher/student ratio of 1:8.

3240   Community Child Guidance Clinic School

317 North Main Street   203-643-2101
Manchester, CT 06040

Tanash Atoynatan, M.D., Director

This School offers two educational programs for children who are autistic and developmentally delayed and children with learning disabilities.

3241   Connecticut Center for Augmentative

St. Vincent's Special Needs Center
95 Merritt Blvd.   203-375-6400
Trumbull, CT 06611

Provides persons of all ages with evaluation/training in augmentative aids/systems to facilitate communication, writing and computer access.

3242   COPE (Center of Progressive Education)

P.O. Box 626   203-426-3344
Newtown, CT 06470

Peter Rockholz, Director

An alternative, special education school serving substance abusing adolescents placed at the Alpha House Residential Treatment Facility.

3243   Curtis Home Children's Program

380 Crown Street   203-237-9526
Meriden, CT 06450

Michael Rhode, Director

3244   Curtis School

380 Crown Street   203-237-9526
Meriden, CT 06450

Michael Rohde, Director

Provides residential treatment, day treatment specialized foster care, aftercare and special education services.

3245   Devereux Glenholme

81 Sabbaday Lane   203-868-7377
Washington, CT 06793

Residential treatment center for children and adolescents, with emotional disorders and learning disabilities.

3246   The Devereux Glenholme School

81 Sabbaday Lane   203-868-7377
Washington, CT 06793

Gary Fitzherbert, Director

A complete psycho-educational residential treatment program serving children with special needs.

3247   Eagle Hill School

45 Glenville Road   203-622-9240
Greenwich, CT 06831

Mark Griffin, Director

Remedial language instruction for children with specific learning disabilities. Offers interscholastic athletic programs and a full range of related services.

3248   Eagle Hill-Southport

214 Main Street   203-254-2044
Southport, CT 06490

Leonard Tavormine, Director

A day program for learning disabled, transitional nongraded. Offers extra curricular activities and interscholastic athletic programs.

3249   Elizabeth Ives School for Special Children

700 Hartford Turnpike   203-281-1148
Hamden, CT 06517

Betty Sword, Director

The facility has a structured, individualized education program for children from preschool age through 15 years. A life skills program is included for appropriate students and speech therapy is provided on a regular basis.

3250   Elmcrest Schools

25 Marlborough Street   203-342-0480
Portland, CT 06480

Elaine Green, Director

Offers short-term treatment, long-term treatment and a day treatment program for the learning disabled and children with substance abuse problems.

3251   The Forman School

12 Norfolk Road, P.O. Box 80   203-567-8712
Litchfield, CT 06759   FAX 203-567-3501

Karen A. Lambert, Admissions Director

For over 60 years the Forman School has encouraged talented, creative and intelligent young men and women to make the best of their abilities. The comprehensive college prepatory program offered is designed to helkp students overcome academic frustrations and increase their self-esteem. The faculty helps the student build and strengthen their skills in one-on-one work with teachers who pay special attention to the way an individual student learns bests.

3252   Foundation School, Inc.

719 Derby-Milford Road   203-795-6075
Orange, CT 06477

Walter Bell, Director

Basic developmental skills address speech/language and perceptual/motor areas. Academic skills are reading, writing and arithmetic with social studies, science and career studies.

3253   Founders Cottage

188 Wolfpit Avenue   203-847-6760
Norwalk, CT 06851

Claire Balian, Director

3254   Gengras Center

Saint Joseph College   203-232-5616
West Hartford, CT 06117

Diane Goncalves, Director

A highly structured behaviorally oriented program providing academic, vocational evaluation/training and support services.

3255   Gray Lodge

105 Spring Street   203-522-9363
Hartford, CT 06105

Rose Alma Senatore, Director

3256   The Hartford Graduate Center

275 Windsor Street   203-548-2497
Hartford, CT 06120

Rebecca Danchak, Dean Of Students

3257   Highland Heights

651 Prospect Street   203-777-5513
New Haven, CT 06505

Sister Mary Frances McMahon, Director

A component of the residential treatment program which offers residential treatment, special education and day treatment programs.

3258   The Institute of Living Schools - Children's School

17 Essex Street   203-241-8093
Hartford, CT 06106

Rosemary Baggish, Director

A day program serving children with emotional distrubances, learning disabilities and pervasive developmental disorders.

3259   The Institute of Living Schools - Middle and High Schools

400 Washington Street   230-241-8093
Hartford, CT 06106

Rosemary Baggish, Director

Working with the belief that learning builds confidence, the Institute offers special educatrion programs for adolescents who are emotionally disturbed and learning disabled.

3260   Intensive Education Center, Inc.

27 Park Road   203-236-2049
West Hartford, CT 06119

Sister Helen Dowd, Director

A non-profit, non-sectarian school for learning disabled children, this program strives to help children reach their full potential by helping them gain confidence, recognize their strengths and weaknesses, set realistic goals and attain satisfaction by achieving these goals.

3261   Klingberg Family Centers

370 Linwood Street   203-224-9113
New Britain, CT 06052

Dr. Daniel O'Connell, Director

Provides structured programs for residential, day treatment and day school students in a therapeutic environment.

3262   Lake Grove Durham

459 R Wallingford Road   203-349-3467
Durham, CT 06422

Christopher Ezzo, Director

Non-graded educational program individualized to teach students falling within a wide spectrum of disabilities.

3263 The Learning Clinic, Inc.

P.O. Box 324　　　　　　　203-928-5274
Brooklyn, CT 06234　　　　FAX 203-928-1796

Raymond DuCharme, Director

A private, non-profit educational program that provides day and residential school focused on ADHD and learning and emotional issues. The program is coeducational and serves sixty students. The faculty is 50 in number including special and regular education certified staff. Academic, Young Apprentice and Wilderness programs are individualized and self-paced. College bound and vocationally oriented students are welcome.

3264 Lorraine D. Foster Day School

50 Shaw Road　　　　　　　203-484-2787
North Branford, CT 06471

Gerald LaBrec, Director

A psycho-educational day treatment program for students with social and emotional maladjustments and/or learning problems.

3265 Natchaug Hospital School Program

189 Storrs Road　　　　　　203-456-1311
Mansfield Center, CT 06250

Louis Haddad, Director

Offers educational services for students placed on the Adolescent Inpatient Unit and the Adolescent Partial Hospitalization Program, The Joshua Center. In addition, the School program operates a clinical day treatment program where psychoeducational and counseling services are provided on an outpatient basis.

3266 NCH School

450 Forbes Street　　　　　203-569-0140
East Hartford, CT 06118

Norman Turchi, Director

Operates a full-day program with a minimum calendar of 181 school days and provides educational services for students with social and emotional disturbances.

3267 The NCH School At East Hartford

450 Forbes Street　　　　　203-569-0140
East Hartford, CT 06118

Norman Turchi, Director

A comprehensive special education program for children from early childhood through high school. Diagnosis and treatment services are provided in the following areas: psychiatry, psychology, speech and language and adaptive physical education.

3268 Northwest Village School, Wheeler Clinic

91 Northwest Drive　　　　　203-747-6801
Plainville, CT 06062

John Mattas, Director

A special education day program for children with emotional problems, speech and language impairments, cognitive limitations and developmental delays.

3269 Regional School District One

Warren Turnpike Road　　　　203-824-5639
Falls Village, CT 06031

Theresa Terry, Spec. Ed. Supervisor

Offers a comprehensive program of pupil services for all students with special needs in the towns of Falls Village, Cornwall, Kent, North Canaan, Salisbury and Sharon. A wide range of services and programs are offered to meet individual needs in accordance with federal and state laws.

3270 Residential Education Center

474 School Street　　　　　203-289-8131
East Hartford, CT 06108

Richard Nowakowski, General Director

3271 Special Education Resource Center

25 Industrial Park Road　　　203-632-1485
Middletown, CT 06457

Serves as a centralized resource for professionals, families, and community members on early intervention, special education and pupil services for individuals with special needs.

3272 The University School

160 Iranistan Avenue　　　　203-579-0434
Bridgeport, CT 06606

Nicholas Macol, Director

Located at the University of Bridgeport campus at Seaside Park, the center has access to U.B. facilities as part of its program to serve the socially/emotionally maladjusted and the learning disabled srudents.

3273 Villa Maria Education Center

159 Sky Meadow Drive　　　　203-322-5886
Stamford, CT 06903

Sister Carol Ann, Director

A co-educational school serving children with specific learning disabilities in the areas of language arts, math and perception.

3274   Vitam Center, Inc.

57 West Rocks Road   203-846-2091
Norwalk, CT 06852

Leonard Kenowtiz, Director

An adolescent treatment program offering comprehensive medical, counseling, family and educational services to boys and girls who have experienced a wide range of difficulties including learning problems.

3275   Waterford Country Schools, Inc.

78 Hunts Brook Road   203-442-9454
Quaker Hill, CT 06375

David Moorehead, Director

A residential treatment and special education facility servicing special needs students.

3276   Wheeler Clinic, Inc.

91 Northwest Drive   203-793-0249
Plainville, CT 06062

Dennis Keenan, Director

Provides special education programs for students with severe behavior and learning problems. Services include speech and language, occupational therapy, individual, group and family counseling.

3277   Wilderness School

P.O. Box 298, Rte. 20   203-566-4146
East Hartland, CT 06027

Works with Connecticut youth and offers a three phas, high impact experience that closely involves a community referring agency with the students' Wilderness School Program. Adolescents male and female may participate. The School offers a referring agency handbook explaining the programs offered.

3278   Yale Child Study Center School

P.O. Box 3333   203-785-2513
New Haven, CT 06510

Lynne Doran Zimmerman, Director

Provides educational evaluation, diagnostic prescriptive teaching, and behavioral intervention to children hospitalized on the Children's Psychiatric Inpatient Service of Yale New Haven Hospital.

Delaware

3279   Au Clair Programs

4185 Kirkwood-St. Georges   302-834-7018
Bear, DE 19701

Kenneth Mazik, President

Private residential and educational treatment facilities for children and adults with developmental and emotional disturbances.

3280   Centreville School

6201 Kennett Pike   302-571-0230
Centreville, DE 19807

Victoria Yatzus, Head Of School
Kathleen Johnson, Admissions Director

A private day school serving children between 3 and 12 years of age who have learning disabilities. Through a multidisciplinary approach combining small class size, language therapy, occupational therapy and an intensive reading program students' weak areas are remediated in preparation for entry into regular school programs.

3281   Educational Service

1701 Augustine Cut-Off, Ste. 21   302-655-6283
Wilmington, DE 19803

Tina Masington, Director

Helps students both maximize their potentials adn improve their self-images through well-planned, individualized intervention in the form of diagnostic psycho-educational evaluation and/or remedial and supportive private tutoring.

3282   Parent Information Center of Delaware,

700 Barksdale Road, Ste. 6   302-366-0152
Dewark, DE 19711   FAX 302-366-0276

Parent Training and Information Program views parents as full partners in the educational process and a significant source of support and assistance to each other. Funded by the Division of Personnel Preparation, Office of Special Education Programs, these programs provide training and information to parents to enable such individuals to participate more effectively with professionals in meeting the educational needs of disabled children.

3283   The Pilot School

100 Garden Of Eden Road   302-478-1740
Wilmington, DE 19806

Doris LeStourgeon

District of Columbia

3284   Developmental Services Center

Adult Day Treatment Program
6045 16th Street NW   202-727-1089
Washington, DC 20011   FAX 202-576-8799

3285   Floc Learning Center

1401 Massachusetts Avenue NW   202-387-1143
Washington, DC 20005

3286   The Kingsbury Center

2138 Bancroft Street NW   202-232-5878
Washington, DC 20008   FAX 202-667-2290

Brenda E. Wilkes, Executive Assistant

3287   The Lab School of Washington

4759 Reservoir Road NW   202-965-6600
Washington, DC 20007

Offers individualized reading, spelling, math, writing, and study skills tutoring by master teachers. Students with learning disabilities can discover their strengths and exercise their creativity while working to overcome academic difficulties. Offers a primary program, extended primary program and an elementary/intermediate program. Also offers a career/counseling center, speech/language therapy, diagnostic testing and an adult night school.

3288   Paul Robeson School

3700 10th Street NW   202-576-7154
Washington, DC 20010

3289   Rap, Inc.

3451 Holmead Street NW   202-462-7500
Washington, DC 20010   FAX 202-462-7507

3290   Scottish Rite Center for Childhood

1630 Columbia Road NW   202-939-4703
Washington, DC 20009   FAX 202-939-4717

3291   Washington Ethical Society High School

7750 16th Street NW   202-829-0088
Washington, DC 20012

Florida

3292   Academic Achievement Center

313 Pruett Road   813-654-4198
Seffner, FL 33584

Lillian Stark

3293   Assistive Technology Network of Florida

434 North Tampa Avenue   407-849-3504
Orlando, FL 32805   FAX 407-849-3520

Sandra Osborn, Program Specialist
Kathleen Bastedo, OTR/L, Occupational Therap.

Provides state-wide services in the areas of assistive technology. Available services include: augmentative communication evaluations; follow up training for students, families and professionals working with them; support and training for a network of highly trained CSEC Local Augmentative Specialists and also offers a quarterly newsletter on the organization as well as a ference library of books, training manuals and videotapes available for short-term loans.

3294   Baptist Bible Institute

1306 College Drive   904-263-3261
Graceville, FL 32440

Martha Smith, Supervisor

3295   Barbara King's Center for Educational Services, Inc.

5005 West Laurel Street, Ste. 100   813-874-3918
Tampa, FL 33607

Barbara King, Director
Educational therapy services offered.

3296   Beach Learning Center, Inc.

444 4th Avenue   305-725-7437
Indialantic, FL 32903

Peggy Christ

3297   Brevard Learning Clinic, Inc.

1900 South Harbor City Blvd. #231   407-676-3024
Melbourne-Rockledge, FL 32901

Barbara Jeffers

Complete educational evaluation for K-adult. Remediation is 1:1, hourly. All cinicians have at least an M.A. and considerable experience with LD, dyslexia and gifted education.   Year-round individualized program focuses on strong foundations, organization and awareness to prepare student for independent success. Materials, equipment, and strategies vary to fit each student's skills, abilities and interests, study skills and S.A.T. preparation courses are available.

3298   Crossroads School

4650 SW 61st Avenue   305-584-1100
Fort Lauderdale, FL 33314

Joyce Fein

Offers residential, diagnostic testing and full time and part time programs for reading or learning difficulties.

3299   Developmental Resource Center Day School and Clinic

2751 Van Buren Street   305-920-2008
Hollywood, FL 33020

Deborah Levy

3300   The Edison-Russell School

10350 Riverside Drive   407-622-0401
Palm Beach Gardens, FL 33410

Robert Ballagh

Grades 1-12 day school, coed, college preparatory curriculum, including art, physical education etc., diagnostic prescriptive methologies, SLD mainstreamed, small classes (N 6-10), non-residential, founded in 1977.

3301 Family Network on Disabilities

1211 Tech Blvd., Ste. 105   813-623-4088
Tampa, FL 33619   800-825-5736

Parent Training and Information Program views parents as full partners in the educational process and a significant source of support and assistance to each other. Funded by the Division of Personnel Preparation, Office of Special Education Programs, these programs provide training and information to parents to enable such individuals to participate more effectively with professionals in meeting the educational needs of disabled children.

3302 The Kurtz Center

1201 Louisiana Avenue   407-740-5678
Winter Park, FL 32789

Gail Kurtz, Director/Owner
Denton M. Kurtz, School Psychologist

Provides a full diagnostic testing and cognitive therapy for reading, comprehension of oral and written language, written expression and motor output for those with learning difficulties, language difficulties and ADHD or UADD.

3303 Morning Star School

210 East Linebaugh Avenue   813-935-0232
Tampa, FL 33612

Jeanette Friedheim, Principal

3304 PACE Private School, Inc.

3221 Sand Lake Road   407-869-8882
Longwood, FL 32779   FAX scott

3305 PEAC: South

4131 Raynolds Avenue   305-665-1286
Coconut Grove, FL 33133

Susan Maynard

3306 Psychological and Educational Services

820 Prudential Drive, Ste. 208   904-399-0324
Jacksonville, FL 32207

Ruth Weinstein Klein

3307 Ralph J. Baudhuin Oral School of Nova University

3375 SW 75th Avenue   305-475-7324
Fort Lauderdale, FL 33314

Susan Talpins, Ed.D, Executive Director
Susan Kabot, M.S., Director

A humanistic learning environment for children birth through the eighth grade with communication disorders, learning disabilities and attention deficit disorders. Recognizing that all children benefit from a multifaceted approach to learning, the School provides each child with an individualized program that combines academics, physical education, social skills development and opportunities for creative expression. The goal is to provide every student with a solid educational experience.

3308 San Juan Reading Center, Inc.

5311 San Juan Avenue   904-388-4676
Jacksonville, FL 32210

Vida MacArthur

3309 T & M Ranch

P.O. Box 788   407-597-2315
Indiantown, FL 34956

Susan Padgett, Administrator

Emphasis is toward the development of prevocational skills and functional daily living skills.

3310 Tampa Reading Clinic and Day School

3020 Azeele Street   813-876-7202
Tampa, FL 33609

Joan Schabacker

Full time day school for children with learning disabilities and also tutoring services available for anyone ages 4-Adult. The Day School is available for children ages 6-12.

3311 Troywood School

1950 Prairie Road   407-969-3000
West Palm Beach, FL 33406

Sharon Tarlow

3312 The Vanguard School

2249 Highway 27 North   813-676-6091
Lake Wales, FL 33853

Harry Nelson

3313 Vanguard School of Coconut Grove, Florida

3939 Main Highway   305-445-7992
Coconut Grove, FL 33133

John Havrilla

3314 Wellington Learning Center

179 Wranglewood Drive   407-793-5936
West Palm Beach, FL 33414

Sandra Scritchfield

Georgia

3315 The Achievement Academy
4021 Macon Road   404-563-5581
Columbus, GA 31907

Beth Sawyer

3316 Atlanta Speech School
3160 Northside Parkway, NW   404-233-5332
Atlanta, GA 30327

Jane Blalock

3317 The Bedford School
2619 Dodson Drive   404-669-2083
East Point, GA 30344

Betsy E. Box, Director

Located in East Point, Georgia, This school serves students in grades 1-9 with specific learning disabilities and/or attention deficit disorder. Staff/student ratio of 10:1 in academic classes.

3318 Brandon Hall School
1701 Brandon Hall Drive   404-394-8177
Atlanta, GA 30350   FAX 404-804-8821

Paul R. Stockhammer, Dir. Admissions

College preparatory, co-ed day and boys' boarding school for students in grades 4-12. Designed for academically underachievers and students with learning disabilities, attention deficit disorders and dyslexia. Enrollment 150 students; faculty 70 with 100% college acceptances. Interscholastic sports and numerous co-curriculum activities and summer programs.

3319 Cloister Creek Educational Center, Inc.
P.O. Box 80310   404-483-6793
Conyers, GA 30208

Delia S. Heming, Director

A nonprofit residential school designed to meet the special education needs of young adults.

3320 The Davison School
1500 North Decatur Road NE   404-373-7288
Atlanta, GA 30306

Susan Smith

Offers a curriculum based language intervention, intensive speech language services and residential and day programs for mild to moderate language and speech learning disabled persons.

3321 The Howard Schools Central Campus
1246 Ponce De Leon Blvd.   404-377-7436
Atlanta, GA 30306

Jean Bowen

3322 The Howard Schools North Campus
9415 Willeo Road   404-642-9644
Roswell, GA 30075   FAX 404-998-1398

Gayle F. Born, Principal

The mission of the school is to provide the finest quality educational, diagnostic and counseling services for students with specific learning disabilities, attention deficit disorders and/or dyslexia, and for their families. Promotes quality education, supplement and complement other programs in the community and foster's the society's understanding of learning problems.

3323 The New School
6955 Brandon Mill Road   404-255-5951
Atlanta, GA 30328

Tweetie Moore

3324 Parents Educating Parents
ARC of Georgia
1851 Ram Runway, Ste. 104   404-761-2745
College Park, GA 30337

Parent Training and Information Program views parents as full partners in the educational process and a significant source of support and assistance to each other. Funded by the Division of Personnel Preparation, Office of Special Education Programs, these programs provide training and information to parents to enable such individuals to participate more effectively with professionals in meeting the educational needs of disabled children.

3325 Reading Success, Inc.
3720 Exec. Ctr., Ste. B, 130 Davis   706-863-8173
Augusta, GA 30907

Sandra Mashburn, Director

A locally owned and operated diagnostic and remedial program designed to help children succeed. It provides individualized programs in reading, math or written language for children and adults having learning difficulties. Diagnostic screening tests are required. A program is especially designed for each student based on strengths and weaknesses diagnosed in the testing. Homework program, SAT and GED prep are also available. The guarantee, your child will make progress.

Hawaii

3326 ASSETS School

Box 106
Pearl Harbor, HI 96860

808-423-1356

Ron Yoshimoto

3327 Hawaii Learning Disabilities Association

200 N. Vineyard Blvd, Ste. 310
Honolulu, HI 96817

808-536-2280

Parent Training and Information Program views parents as full partners in the educational process and a significant source of support and assistance to each other. Funded by the Division of Personnel Preparation, Office of Special Education Programs, these programs provide training and information to parents to enable such individuals to participate more effectively with professionals in meeting the educational needs of disabled children.

3328 Variety School

710 Palekaua Street
Honolulu, HI 96816

808-732-2835

Jennifer Dang

Idaho

3329 Idaho Parents Unlimited

4696 Overland Road, Ste. 478
Boise, ID 83705

208-342-5884
800-242-4785

Parent Training and Information Program views parents as full partners in the educational process and a significant source of support and assistance to each other. Funded by the Division of Personnel Preparation, Office of Special Education Programs, these programs provide training and information to parents to enable such individuals to participate more effectively with professionals in meeting the educational needs of disabled children.

Illinois

3330 The Achievement Centers, Inc.

1209 West Ogden Avenue
La Grange Park, IL 60525

708-579-9040

Kathryn Fouks

3331 Allendale

P.O. Box 277
Lake Villa, IL 60046

708-356-2351

Robert Holway

3332 Camelot Care Center - Illinois

1502 North NW Highway
Palatine, IL 60067

312-359-5600

Tom Dempsey, Principal

A psychiatric residential treatmetn center using a developmentally based treatment model called "Process Therapy".

3333 Catholic Children's Home

Special Education School
1400 State Street, Box 486
Alton, IL 62002

618-465-3826

Lawrence Drury, Executive Director

This program has three areas of focus: a structured residential setting, a short term emergency/diagnostic facility and an appropriate individualized educational environment.

3334 Center for Learning

1740 Lake Avenue
Wilmette, IL 60091

708-256-5150

Jodie Manes, Director

Offers remedial tutoring for children with learning disabilities, psychological, educational and neuropsychological evaluations and testing of gifted children.

3335 Center for Speech and Language Disorders

479 Spring Road
Elmhurst, IL 60126

708-530-8551

Sally Bligh, Co-Director

Offers hearing screening, speech and language evaluation and therapy and academic tutoring.

3336 Chicago Urban Day School

1248 West 69th Street
Chicago, IL 60636

312-483-3555

Georgia Jordan, Executive Director

3337 Children's Center for Behavioral Development

353 North 88th Street
Centreville, IL 62203

618-398-1152

Patricia Mayberry Vecchio, Executive Director

A special education program for children and adolescents with emotional disturbances, behavioral disorders and learning disabilities.

3338 The Cove School

520 Glendale Avenue
Winnetka, IL 60093

708-441-9300
FAX 708-441-9373

Elizabeth Noell, Executive Director

Offers a broad-based, integrated curriculum for students with dyslexia and other learning disabilities. The curriculum emphasizes critical thinking, language and study skills in the language arts, math, science and social studies classes. Cove's supportive learning environment enables students to learn at their own pace according to their own learning styles, and develop confidence as learners.

3339   Designs for Change

220 South State Street, Ste. 1900   312-922-0317
Chicago, IL 60604

Parent Training and Information Program views parents as full partners in the educational process and a significant source of support and assistance to each other. Funded by the Division of Personnel Preparation, Office of Special Education Programs, these programs provide training and information to parents to enable such individuals to participate more effectively with professionals in meeting the educational needs of disabled children.

3340   Educational Services of Glen Ellyn

444 North Main   708-469-1479
Glen Ellyn, IL 60137

Elizabeth Siebens, M.A.

Tutoring for all ages in all subject areas. Diagnostic testing, specializing in learning disabilities, career counseling for learning disabled adults is also offered.

3341   Elm Christian School and Workshop

13020 South Central Avenue   708-389-0555
Palos Heights, IL 60463

Greorge Groen, Executive Director

A school for the education and training of mentally handicapped, physically disabled and learning disabled student.

3342   Esperanza School

520 North Marshfield Avenue   312-243-6097
Chicago, IL 60622

Barbara Belletini Fields, Executive Director

Self-help educational services offered to children who are autistic or mentally disabled.

3343   Family Resource Center on Disabilities

20 East Jackson Blvd, Rm. 900   312-939-3513
Chicago, IL 60604   800-952-4199

Parent Training and Information Program views parents as full partners in the educational process and a significant source of support and assistance to each other. Funded by the Division of Personnel Preparation, Office of Special Education Programs, these programs provide training and information to parents to enable such individuals to participate more effectively with professionals in meeting the educational needs of disabled children.

3344   Greenrose Elementary School

5244 North Lakewood   312-728-5959
Chicago, IL 60640

Fran Rothman, Social Worker

Offers a therapeutic primary school focusing on social/emotional growth with therapy, counseling and groups for parents.

3345   Hammit School (of the Baby Fold)

108 East Willow Street   309-452-1170
Normal, IL 61761

Wendell Hess, Executive Director

Offers individualized approaches to instruction and intervention, regardless of disabling conditions.

3346   The Hope School

50 Hazel Lane   217-786-3350
Springfield, IL 62716

Thomas Jones, President

Offers individual educational and treatment programs for each resident.

3347   Illinois Center for Autism

548 South Ruby Lane   618-398-7500
Fairview Heights, IL 62208

Carol Madison

A non-profit community-based mental health treatment and educational center dedicated to serving persons afflicted with autism.

3348   KEEP (Kennedy Early Education Program)

420 Raynor
Joliet, IL 60435

3349   Kennedy Lt. Joseph P., Jr. School/

123rd & Wolf Road   708-448-6520
Palos Park, IL 60464

Wayne Kottmeyer, Executive Director

Offers residential and day comprehensive special education and training programs that focus on self-help and independent living.

3350   La Grange Area Department of Special Education

1301 West Cossitt   708-354-5730
La Grange, IL 60525

Dr. Howard Blackman

Offers programs for students with moderate to severe mental retardation, learning disabilities or behavior disorders.

3351 The LEARN Center Illinois Masonic Medical Center

836 Nelson 312-883-7132
Chicago, IL 60657

Bethany Graham

3352 The Reading Group

Box 4227, Lincoln Square Mall 217-367-0914
Urbana, IL 61801

Marilyn Kay

3353 South Central Community Center

8316 South Ellis 312-483-0900
Chicago, IL 60619

Felicia Blasingame, Executive Director
Offers special education, individual and family counseling services, adult program services and a community center.

3354 St. Joseph's Carondelet Child Center

739 East 35th Street 312-624-7443
Chicago, IL 60616

James McLaughlin, Executive Director

3355 Summit School

611 East Main Street, Rte. 72 312-428-6451
Dundee, IL 60118

A special education facility offering learning disabled, gifted, philosophy and pre-school programs.

Indiana

3356 Educational Enrichment Center

1450 Bellemeade Avenue 812-473-0651
Evansville, IN 47714

Janet Dill

3357 IN*SOURCE

833 East Northside Blvd. 219-234-7101
South Bend, IN 46617 800-332-4433

Parent Training and Information Program views parents as full partners in the educational process and a significant source of support and assistance to each other. Funded by the Division of Personnel Preparation, Office of Special Education Programs, these programs provide training and information to parents to enable such individuals to participate more effectively with professionals in meeting the educational needs of disabled children.

3358 Reading and Communication Skills

Indiana University
2805 East 10th Street 812-855-5847
Bloomington, IN 47408 FAX 812-855-7901

Offers information on Reading, English and communication skills, preschool through college.

Iowa

3359 National Education Center, National Institute of Technology Campus

1119 Fifth Avenue 515-223-1486
West Des Moines, IA 50265

John Hamilton, Special Services

Kansas

3360 Families Together

1023 SW Gage Avenue 913-273-6343
Topeka, KS 66604

Parent Training and Information Program views parents as full partners in the educational process and a significant source of support and assistance to each other. Funded by the Division of Personnel Preparation, Office of Special Education Programs, these programs provide training and information to parents to enable such individuals to participate more effectively with professionals in meeting the educational needs of disabled children.

3361 Heartspring

2400 Jardine Drive 800-835-1043
Wichita, KS 67219

Residential school for children with multiple disabilities. Provides a wide-range of assessment, and/or treatment options, ranging from a few days to several months in length. Assessments are made in areas of audiology, physical and occupational therapy, speech/language therapy and behavioral disorders.

3362 Menninger Center for Learning Disabilities

Menninger Clinic
Box 829 913-273-7500
Topeka, KS 66601 800-351-9056
FAX 913-232-6524

Michele Berg, Director
The Center offers the following services for children and adults: 1) Educational evaluations for learning disabilities, dyslexia, learning problems and other special needs 2) gifted evaluations 3) Workshops for parents and educators 4) reading assessments 5) training for teachers in multisensory remedial approaches and 6) group and individual tutoring.

Kentucky

3363   The dePaul School

1925 Duker Avenue   502-459-6131
Louisville, KY 40205

Sister Anne Rita Mauck, Executive Director
Anthony R. Kemper, Admissions Director

Since 1970, the School has provided acclaimed education-al programs for dyslexic students of all ages. All offerings provide highly structured, multisensory and individual-izes remediation in various subjects: linguistics, reading, math, writing, spelling, social values and auditory dis-crimination. A fulltime school is available for students of grades K-8 with tutorial programs available on weekends and in the summer.

3364   KY-SPIN

2210 Goldsmith Lane, Ste. 118   502-456-0923
Louisville, KY 40218   800-525-7746
                                             FAX 502-456-0893

Parent Training and Information Program views parents as full partners in the educational process and a significant source of support and assistance to each other. Funded by the Division of Personnel Preparation, Office of Special Education Programs, these programs provide training and information and support to parents and families fo chil-dren of all ages with all types of disabilities. We empower all parents to recognize and use the resouces that exist everywhere.

3365   Meredith-Dunn School

3023 Melbourne Avenue   502-456-5819
Louisville, KY 40220

Shirley K. Meredith, M.Ed., Executive Director
Barbara Toth, M.A., Principal

Helps children achieve and succeed by teaching them to cope with and overcome their learning differences. Class size is limited to 14 students, with a teacher and teaching assistant in each classroom. A variety of teaching meth-ods and activities are used to meet each child's learning style and needs. Meredith-Dunn School helps children gain the necessary skills to succeed academically in order to move into the mainstream program.

Louisiana

3366   Project Prompt

UCP of Greater New Orleans
1500 Edwards Avenue, Ste. O   504-734-7736
Harahan, LA 70123   800-766-7736

Parent Training and Information Program views parents as full partners in the educational process and a significant source of support and assistance to each other. Funded by the Division of Personnel Preparation, Office of Special Education Programs, these programs provide training and information to parents to enable such individuals to participate more effectively with professionals in meeting the educational needs of disabled children.

3367   Reading Research Foundation

P.O. Box 30185   318-984-7485
Lafayette, LA 70593

Sylvia Olinde

Maine

3368   Maine Parent Federation, Inc.

P.O. Box 2067   207-582-2504
Augusta, ME 04338   800-325-0220

Parent Training and Information Program views parents as full partners in the educational process and a significant source of support and assistance to each other. Funded by the Division of Personnel Preparation, Office of Special Education Programs, these programs provide training and information to parents to enable such individuals to participate more effectively with professionals in meeting the educational needs of disabled children.

Maryland

3369   Center for Unique Learners

11600 Nebel Street, Ste. 200   301-231-0115
Rockville, MD 20852

Patricia Williams, Executive Director

Services offered to students from elementary-school age through high school, college and adulthood include; diag-nosis and assessment, academic instruction, career coun-seling, personal counseling, advocacy and training semi-nars for the learning disabled.

3370   Chelsea School

711 Pershing Drive   301-585-1430
Silver Spring, MD 20910

3371   Children's Developmental Clinic

301 Largo Road   301-322-0519
Largo, MD 20772

Offers one-on-one gross and fine motor development, additional language or reading development, parent edu-cation and discussion.

3372   Developmental School Foundation

Broschart School
14901 Broschart Road   301-251-4624
Rockville, MD 20850

Mary Jane Kennelly, Executive Director

Provides a therapeutic day setting with a full school program that addresses the children's social/emotional and learning needs.

3373 Edgemeade-Raymond Rodgers, Jr. School

13400 Edgemeade Road   301-888-1330
Upper Marlboro, MD 20772

Donna Grubb, Executive Director

3374 The Forbush School

6501 North Charles Street   410-938-3000
Towson, MD 21285

Burton Lohnes, Educational Director

3375 The Frost Center

4915 Aspen Hill Road   301-933-3451
Rockville, MD 20853   FAX 301-933-3330

Sean McLaughlin, Center Director

3376 The Hannah More Center Schools

P.O. Box 370   410-526-5000
Reistertown, MD 21136

Mark Waldman, Executive Director
Educates seriously disabled students and provides therapeutic services so that the student may develop responsible patterns of behavior for their mainstreaming into society. A psycho educational approach consisting of a comprehensive combination of academic subjects, counseling programs and a behavioral management systems is designed to meet the individual needs of each student.

3377 The Harbour School

1933 Severen Grove Road   301-841-6410
Annapolis, MD 21401

Linda Jacobs

3378 Ivymount School

11614 Seven Locks Road   301-469-0223
Bethesda, MD 20854

Shari Gelman

3379 The Jemicy School

11 Celadon Road   301-653-2700
Owings Mills, MD 21117

Stephen Wilkins

3380 Optometry and Occupational Therapy Associates

6509 Democracy Blvd.   301-897-8484
Bethesda, MD 20817

Dr. Stanley Appelbaum, Co-Director
Barbara Bassin, Co-Director

Specializes in the diagnosis and treatment of children and daults with vision disorders, learning disabilities, sensory integration and behavioral disorders.

3381 Parents' Place of Maryland

7257 Parkway Drive, Ste. 210   301-379-0900
Hanover, MD 21076

Parent Training and Information Program views parents as full partners in the educational process and a significant source of support and assistance to each other. Funded by the Division of Personnel Preparation, Office of Special Education Programs, these programs provide training and information to parents to enable such individuals to participate more effectively with professionals in meeting the educational needs of disabled children.

3382 Queen Anne Learning Center At the Gunston School

P.O. Box 200   410-758-0620
Centreville, MD 21617

Kathleen White, Co-Director
Kathleen Garson, Co-Director
Provides tutoring for individuals from K through adult. It also offers intelligence and educational testing.

3383 School for Contemporary Education/Maryland

4906 Roland Avenue   410-235-9292
Baltimore, MD 21210

Martha Johansen, Director
Utilizes behavior management apppproaches with a therapeutic milieu designed to reinforce appropriate social behavior and enhance academic development.

3384 Specific Diagnosis

11600 Nebel Street, Ste. 130   301-468-6616
Rockville, MD 20852

Lynn O'Brien

3385 Youth Development Information Center

National Agricultural Library
10301 Baltimore Blvd.   301-344-3719
Beltsville, MD 20705

Provides services focused on all aspects of youth development.

Massachusetts

3386 Berkshire Children's Community

249 North Plain Road   413-528-2523
Housatonic, MA 02136

A private, non-profit residential school offering an innovative learning center with a unique curriculum for the learning disabled individual.

3387 Boston Higashi School

2618 Massachusetts Avenue   617-862-7222
Lexington, MA 02173

Robert Fantasia

The curriculum is designed for children who tend to be socially isolated. It is implemented in a group environment in order to foster the students' abilities to socialize and communicate.

3388 The Brightside for Families and Children

2112 Riverdale Street   413-788-7366
West Springfield, MA 01089

Richard Krzanowski, Educational Admin.

Offers a comprehensive co-educational program which serves students with learning disabilities and emotional disturbances.

3389 CAST

39 Cross Street   508-531-8555
Peabody, MA 01960   FAX 508-531-0192

A non-profit organization whose mission is to expand educational opportunities for all children through innovative uses of computer technology. CAST provides direct services to individuals, offers consultation and training organizations, conducts research and develops software and implementation models for education.

3390 Commonwealth Learning Center

145 Rosemary Street   617-444-5193
Needham, MA 02194

Donna Sullivan

3391 Communication Enhancement Center

Children's Hospital
Fegan Plaza, 300 Longwood Avenue   617-735-6486
Boston, MA 02115

Will evaluate children or adults with learning disabilities (among others) and recommend actions to take, especially in regards to the use of a computer and specific software titles.

3392 Cotting School

453 Concord Avenue   617-862-7323
Lexington, MA 02173

Carl Morse

Day school for boys and girls with physical and learning challenges.

3393 Curtis Blake Center

American International College
Springfield, MA 01109   413-737-7000

Dr. Cynthia Hall

3394 Devereux Massachusetts

60 Miles Road   503-886-4746
Rutland, MA 01543

A residential program for children and adolescents and young adults who have emotional disorders and developmental and learning disabilities.

3395 Doctor Franklin Perkins School

971 Main Street   508-365-7376
Lancaster, MA 01523

3396 Evergreen Center

345 Fortune Blvd.   508-478-2631
Milford, MA 01757

Robert Littleton, Jr., Executive Director

3397 F.L. Chamberlain School

1 Prospect Street   508-947-7825
Middleborough, MA 02346

Sarah Norfleet

3398 Landmark Outreach Program

Landmark School
Prides Crossing, MA 01965   508-927-4440

An internationally recognized leader in providing programs to meet the challenge of dyslexia.

3399 Landmark Preparatory Program

Landmark School
412 Hale Street   508-927-4440
Prides Crossing, MA 01965   FAX 508-927-7268

Meryl Doherty, Admissions Director

Offers a secondary school level curriculum emphasizing organizational and study skills development in a traditional classroom setting, and is designed for college bound boys and girls who have progressed within a year or two of expected grade level performance.

3400 Landmark School

412 Hale Street   508-927-4440
Prides Crossing, MA 01965   FAX 508-927-7268

Meryl Doherty, Admissions Director

A selective school working with a special group of children from all over American and around the world. The school accepts bright, emotionally sound young people who are floundering in regular classrooms because their reading, writing, spelling and math skills have not caught up with their thinking and problem solving capacities.

3401 Landmark Summer Marine Science Program

Landmark School
412 Hale Road   508-927-4440
Prides Crossing, MA 01965   FAX 508-927-7268

Meryl Doherty

Combines half-day of academic instruction, including a daily one-to-one tutorial, with a half-day of coastal marine science and ecology study.

$ 3050.00

3402 Landmark Summer Seamanship Program

Landmark School
412 Hale Road   508-927-4440
Prides Crossing, MA 01965   FAX 508-927-7268

Meryl Doherty

Combines a half-day of academic instruction, including a daily one-to-one tutorial, with a half-day of sailing instruction abroad school vessels.

$ 3050.00

3403 League School of Boston, Inc.

225 Nevada Street   617-964-3260
Newtonville, MA 02160   FAX 617-964-3264

Herman Fishbein, Executive Director

Offers transitional programs, pre-school programs and residential programs.

3404 The Learning Center - Massachusetts

411 Waverly Oaks Road   617-893-6000
Waltham, MA 02154

A community-based residential and day treatment program for autistic, mentally retarded and hearing impaired individuals.

3405 The Learning Disabilities Network

72 Sharp Street, Ste. A-2   617-340-5605
Hingham, MA 02043   FAX 617-340-5603

Polly Cowen, Administrative Dir.

3406 Living Independently Forever, Inc.

550 Lincoln Road Ext., P.O. Box 233   508-778-0228
Hyannis, MA 02601

Cre A. Dorey, Executive Director

The purpose of this organization, known as LIFE, is to foster independent living for learning disabled adults functioning on a lower level. LIFE provides individual and group support services on a contractual basis to all residents living in the LIFE program.

3407 Marine Science Program

Landmark School
Prides Crossing, MA 01965   508-927-4440
                                 FAX 508-927-7268

Offered to students who are curious about and interested in the natural and physical world.

3408 The May Institute, Inc.

100 Sea View Street, Box 708   508-945-1147
Chatham, MA 02633

Walter Christian, Executive Director

Provides educational and rehabilitative services for individuals with autism, developmental disabilities, neurological disorders and mental illness.

3409 Riverbrook School, Inc.

Ice Glen Road   413-298-4926
Stockbridge, MA 01262

Joan Burkhard

Individualized for females with moderate retardation developed according to learning strengths and weaknesses.

3410 Riverview School

551 Route 6A   508-888-0489
East Sandwich, MA 02537   FAX 508-888-1315

A residential, secondary level school for 110 boys and girls who, on entrance, are between the ages of 16-19, are marginally disabled mentally and have identifiable learning difficulties.

3411 Riverview School, Career Apprenticeship Program

551 Route 6A   508-888-0489
East Sandwich, MA 02537

Rochard Lavoie

3412 Stetson School, Inc.

455 South Street   508-355-4541
Barre, MA 01005

Richard Robinson, Executive Director

Campus consists of five living units and a learning center set amid 117 acres. Each unit is staffed by a treatment and education team consisting of a case manager, supervisor, moderate special needs teacher and a child care staff.

3413 Trantec

251 Harvard Street #1   617-232-3644
Brookline, MA 02146

Cecilia Gandolfo

3414 Unity College Learning Resource

Center Quaker Hill Road   207-948-3131
Unity, MA 04988

James Horan, Director

3415 Valleyhead, Inc.

P.O. Box 714   413-637-3635
Lenox, MA 01240

Matthew Merritt, Jr., Director

Provides a structured, ungraded academic program based on IEP. Emphasis is placed on language skills development and other skills necessary for successful independent living.

3416 Willow Hill School

98 Haynes Road   508-443-2581
Sudbury, MA 01776

Jane Jakuc

3417 Wilson Language Training Center

4-B Evergreen Lane, Rt. 140   508-478-8454
Hopedale, MA 01747   800-899-8454

Meets the needs of students with language-based learning disabilities.

3418 Wilson Learning Center

4-B Evergreen Lane   508-478-8454
Hopedale, MA 01747

Barbara Wilson

Michigan

3419 CAUSE

313 South Washington Square #040   517-485-4084
Lansing, MI 48933   800-221-9105

Parent Training and Information Program views parents as full partners in the educational process and a significant source of support and assistance to each other. Funded by the Division of Personnel Preparation, Office of Special Education Programs, these programs provide training and information to parents to enable such individuals to participate more effectively with professionals in meeting the educational needs of disabled children.

3420 Center for Human Development William Beaumont Hospital

3203 Coolidge Highway   313-551-3150
Royal Oak, MI 48072

Richard Galpin

3421 Educational Evaluation and Consultation Service

University of Michigan Medical Center
1500 East Medical Center Drive   313-764-1226
Ann Arbor, MI 48109

Anita Swift Miller, Coordinator
Carrie Fosselman, Director

A comprehensive diagnosticevaluation service is offered for children, adolescents and adults who are having difficulties in some are of their education or in the workplace. The individual's potential achievement, actual achievement and causes of any discrepancy between the two are identified.

3422 Erickson Learning Center

1621 West Michigan Avenue   517-787-8518
Jackson, MI 49202

Jan Williams

3423 Services for Students with Disabilities

University of Michigan
G-625 Haven Hall   313-677-3222
Ann Arbor, MI 48106

Phi; Banks, Program Manager

Offers information to parents and students.

3424 Specific Language Disability Center, Inc.

504 South Westnedge Avenue   616-345-2661
Kalamazoo, MI 49007

Louise Haas, Executive Director
Diane Van Zetten, Educational Director

Tutoring in reading, spelling, writing and math using the Orton-Gillingham approach. Testing and evaluations. Teacher/tutor training. Fees on a sliding scale, serving children adn adults. Also offers a Grand Rapids chapter.

Minnesota

3425 Educational Specialists, Inc.

105 Florida Court   612-545-5067
Minneapolis, MN 55426

Mildred Mastbaum

3426 The Wilson Center

P.O. Box 917   507-334-5561
Faribault, MN 55021

Kevin Mahoney

3427 Wilson Center

14th St. & Shumway Avenue   507-334-5561
Faribault, MN 55021

Kevin Mahoney, President
Long term inpatient care for adolescents with severe psychiatric illnesses and in many cases concomitant learning disabilities.

Mississippi

3428 Heritage School

P.O. Box 20434   601-969-0603
Jackson, MS 39289

Jeanie Muirhead

3429 Millcreek Schools, Inc.

P.O. Drawer 1160   601-849-4221
Magee, MS 39111

Margaret Tedford, Executive Director
A residential Treatment Center for children with emotional disturbances and an Intensive Care Facility for children with mental retardation.

3430 Mississippi Parent Advocacy Center

332 New Market Drive   601-922-3210
Jackson, MS 39209   800-231-3721

Parent Training and Information Program views parents as full partners in the educational process and a significant source of support and assistance to each other. Funded by the Division of Personnel Preparation, Office of Special Education Programs, these programs provide training and information to parents to enable such individuals to participate more effectively with professionals in meeting the educational needs of disabled children.

3431 Tougaloo College

Tougaloo, MS 39174   601-956-4941

H.E. Dockins

Missouri

3432 The Churchill School

1035 Price School Lane   314-997-4343
St. Louis, MO 63124

Sandra Gilligan

3433 College Reading Improvement

604 West Blvd. South   314-442-2396
Columbia, MO 65203

Dr. Margaret Henrichs, Chair CRI/IRA
Has four basic purposes: 1) Exchange information relating to the remedial and developmental reading and study skills programs of colleges and univerisities in areas of teaching strategies, analyses of students' reading and evaluations of the effectiveness of programs and teaching materials. 2) Proposes and encourages the adoption of certain specific qualifications for the teachers of college reading. 3) Resource to aid colleges in implementing study programs. 4) Sponsors national conferences.

3434 Gillis Center

8150 Wornall Road   816-363-1414
Kansas City, MO 64114

Barbara O'Toole, Executive Director

3435 The Metropolitan School

7281 Sarah   314-644-0850
St. Louis, MO 63143

Ann Larson

3436 The Miriam School

501 Bacon   314-968-5225
Webster Groves, MO 63119

Linda Shemwell, Director
Joan Holland, Coordinator
A non-profit day school for children between four and twelve years of age who are learning disabled and/or behaviorally disabled. Speech and language services and occupational therapy are integral components of the $11, 475 per year program. The focus of all the activities is to increase children's self-esteem and help them acquire the coping skills needed to successfully meet future challenges.

3437 Missouri Parents Act

1722-W South Glenstone #125   417-882-7434
Springfield, MO 65804   800-743-7634

Parent Training and Information Program views parents as full partners in the educational process and a significant source of support and assistance to each other. Funded by the Division of Personnel Preparation, Office of Special Education Programs, these programs provide training and information to parents to enable such individuals to participate more effectively with professionals in meeting the educational needs of disabled children.

3438 Speech Pathology Service

33 East Broadway, Ste. 150   314-449-5484
Columbia, MO 65203

Judith Harper

3439 Total Learning Clinic

1104 East Broadway, Ste. 8   314-442-5013
Columbia, MO 65201

John Houmes

Montana

3440 The Child Study Center

1224 North 28th Street   406-252-6620
Billings, MT 59101

Paul Crellin

3441 Parents Let's Unite for Kids

1500 North 30th   406-657-2055
Billings, MT 59101

Parent Training and Information Program views parents as full partners in the educational process and a significant source of support and assistance to each other. Funded by the Division of Personnel Preparation, Office of Special Education Programs, these programs provide training and information to parents to enable such individuals to participate more effectively with professionals in meeting the educational needs of disabled children.

Nebraska

3442 Nebraska Parents Information and Training

3610 Dodge Street, Ste. 102   402-346-0525
Omaha, NE 68131   800-284-8520

Parent Training and Information Program views parents as full partners in the educational process and a significant source of support and assistance to each other. Funded by the Division of Personnel Preparation, Office of Special Education Programs, these programs provide training and information to parents to enable such individuals to participate more effectively with professionals in meeting the educational needs of disabled children.

Nevada

3443 Nevada Technology Center

2860 E. Flamingo Road, Ste. I   702-735-2922
Las Vegas, NV 89121   800-435-2448

Parent Training and Information Program views parents as full partners in the educational process and a significant source of support and assistance to each other. Funded by the Division of Personnel Preparation, Office of Special Education Programs, these programs provide training and information to parents to enable such individuals to participate more effectively with professionals in meeting the educational needs of disabled children.

3444 Optimal-Ed Learning Center

1516 East Tropicana Avenue, #B-5   702-736-0706
Las Vegas, NV 89119

Sandra Obara

New Hampshire

3445 Cardigan Mt. School

Canaan, NH 03741   603-523-4321

Cameron Dewar

3446 Cedarcrest

91 Maple Avenue   603-358-3384
Keene, NH 03431

Sharon Kaiser, R.N., Director

A non-profit home, school and medical support facility for severe to rpofoundly multi-handicapped children. Serves up to 25 children, without regard to race, color, religious affiliation or financial standing. As a State Department of Education-approved school, Cedarcrest also serves as a placement option for any school district in the state.

3447 Hampshire Country School

Rindge, NH 03461   603-899-3325

William Dickerman, Admissions Director

A very small co-ed boarding school and summer camp designed to provide extra structure, direction and attention needed by some students in order to thrive. Usual entering ages 8 to 13. School Year: $23,500 and Summer Camp: $3,500.

3448 Parent Information Center

P.O. Box 1422   603-224-6299
Concord, NH 03302

Parent Training and Information Program views parents as full partners in the educational process and a significant source of support and assistance to each other. Funded by the Division of Personnel Preparation, Office of Special Education Programs, these programs provide training and information to parents to enable such individuals to participate more effectively with professionals in meeting the educational needs of disabled children.

3449 The Pike School, Inc.

Box 101   603-989-5862
Haverhill, NH 03765

Francis McCabe, Jr., Executive Director

Based upon a learning view of growth and development. The School devotes attention to academic, vocational and experiential education.

New Jersey

3450 American Self-Help Clearinghouse

St. Clares-Riverside Medical Center
Pocono Road   201-625-7101
Denville, NJ 07834

Provides information on a wide range of self-help groups and state/local self-help clearinghouses.

3451 Bancroft, Inc.

Hopkins Lane   609-429-0010
Haddonfield, NJ 08033

George W. Niemann

A private, non-profit organization offering educational/ vocational programs, therapeutic support services and full range of community living opportunities for children and adults with developmental disabilities and head injuries. Residential options include community living supervised apartments, specialized supervised apartments, group homes and supported living models.

3452 The Center School

319 North 3rd Avenue   908-249-3355
Highland Park, NJ 08904

Jeanne Prial, Director

A non-profit school providing for the special needs of youngsters with learning disabilities.

3453 The Children's Institute

51 Old Road   201-740-1663
Livingston, NJ 07039   FAX 800-248-0115

Bruce Ettinger, School Administrator
Terry O'Donnell, School Principal

Enrolls pre-school, handicapped, emotionally disturbed, and autistic children from northern and central New Jersey. Offers small ratio of students to staff, small class size, learning disabilities remediation, language/speech therapy, behavior management, family counseling, parent education program, career education and activities of daily living program, Extended School Summer Program and more.

3454 The Community School of Bergen County, Inc.

11 West Forest Avenue   201-837-8070
Teaneck, NJ 07666

Rita Rowan

3455 Craig School

215 Hill Street   201-334-4375
Boonton, NJ 07005

Alice Gleason

3456 Devereux Center for Autism

186 Roadstown Road   609-455-7200
Bridgeton, NJ 08302

A residential program for individuals who have mild to severe mental retardation.

3457 Devereux Deerhaven

230 Pottersville Road   908-879-4166
Chester, NJ 07930

Residential and day programs for females, who have emotional and behavioral disorders and learning disabilities.

3458 ECLC of New Jersey

Ho-Ho-Kus Campus, ECLC of New Jersey
302 North Franklin Turnpike   201-635-1705
Ho-Ho-Kus, NJ 07423

Dr. Dulcie A. Freeman, Executive Director

Offers support services in speech, language, physical and occupational therapy, psychological counseling and adaptive physical education.

3459 Eden Programs

One Logan Drive   609-987-0099
Princeton, NJ 08540   FAX 609-987-0243

David Holmes, Executive Director

The Eden Family of Programs offers a complete spectrum of behaviorally-oriented educational, residential, employment and outreach programming for both children and adults with autism.

3460 Family Resource Associates, Inc.

Family Resource Association
35 Haddon Avenue   908-747-5310
Shrewsbury, NJ 07702

Private, non-profit agency servicing children with disabilities and their families. Sibling support services are provided via newsletters and sibling groups.

3461 High Road Schools

Lower School
11 Lexington Avenue   908-238-7700
East Brunswick, NJ 08816

Ellyn Lerner, Co-Director

Offers programs serving the educational, social and emotional needs of children with specific learning disabilities, communication disorders and/or behavioral difficulties.

3462 Jewish Education for Special Children

JESC-at-JCC
411 East Clinton Avenue   201-569-7900
Tenafly, NJ 07670

Rabbi Gary Hoffman

Offers a Sunday morning supplemental program, adaptive physical education, music therapy and occupational therapy.

3463 Kingsway Learning Center

144 Kings Highway West   609-428-8108
Haddonfield, NJ 08033

David Panner

3464 Laboratory of Psychological Studies

Stevens Institute
Castle Point On The Hudson   201-420-5177
Hoboken, NJ 07030

H. Karl Springob

3465 The Lewis Clinic for Educational Therapy

53 Bayard Lane   609-924-8120
Princeton, NJ 08540

Marsha Gaynor-Lewis

3466 The Matheny School and Hospital

Main Street   201-234-0011
Peapack, NJ 07977

Robert Schonhorn

3467 Metropolitan Speech and Language Center

22 Old Short Hills Road, Ste 211   201-994-4468
Livingston, NJ 07039

Miriam Marzell, M.A., CCC-SLP, Director

Provides diagnostics and therapy for children and adults with speech, language, voice and stuttering problems.

3468 The Midland School

Readington Road   908-722-8222
North Branch, NJ 08876

Edward Scagliotta

3469 The Newgrange School

52 Lafaette Avenue   609-394-2255
Trenton, NJ 08610

Lois Young

3470 Perry Learning Center

Williamsburg Commons-7B Aver Court   201-390-9490
East Brunswick, NJ 08816

Jesse Perry

3471 Rock Brook School

432 Route 518   609-466-2989
Blawenburg, NJ 08504

Mary Caterson-Marshall

3472 The Rugby School

Woodfield Avenue & Belmar Blvd.   908-938-2442
Wall, NJ 07719   FAX 908-938-2499

Donald J. DeSanto, Executive Director
Anthony J. Aquilino, Asst. Director

Helps special students realize their potential and bring college admission a step closer. To do this, the college developed a program designed to meet the needs and maximize the unique talents of each individual. The staff consists of highly qualified teachers who see beyond labels and reach the person inside. By pacing scholastics to each students ability, the college increases undersztanding and makes learning a positive experience. Instruction is tailored to each individual.

3473 SEARCH Day Program, Inc.

73 Wickapecko Drive   201-531-0454
Ocean, NJ 07712

Kenneth Appenzeller, Jr., Executive Director

A multi-faceted agency designed to serve the comprehensive needs of children with autism from preschool through adult life.

3474 Speech/Language Therapy

188 Highwaood Avenue   201-569-5061
Tenafly, NJ 07670

Dorothy Unger

3475 Statewide Parent Advocacy Network

516 North Avenue East   908-654-7726
Westfield, NJ 07090   800-654-SPAN

Parent Training and Information Program views parents as full partners in the educational process and a significant source of support and assistance to each other. Funded by the Division of Personnel Preparation, Office of Special Education Programs, these programs provide training and information to parents to enable such individuals to participate more effectively with professionals in meeting the educational needs of disabled children.

New Mexico

3476 Brush Ranch School

P.O. Box 2450   505-757-6114
Santa Fe, NM 87504   FAX 505-757-6118

David Floyd, Director

A co-educational boarding school for children with learning difficulties. The school is fully licensed and accredited by both the New Mexico Board of Education and the North Central Association of Colleges and Schools. Situated on 283 acres in the Santa Fe national forest, the school offers a wide range of educational and recreational opportunities.

3477 Designs for Learning Differences School

2430 Juan Tabone, Ste. 156   505-822-0476
Albuquerque, NM 87112

Margaret Suber

3478 EPICS Parent Project

SW Community Resources
P.O. Box 788   505-876-3396
Bernalillo, NM 87004

Parent Training and Information Program views parents as full partners in the educational process and a significant source of support and assistance to each other. Funded by the Division of Personnel Preparation, Office of Special Education Programs, these programs provide training and information to parents to enable such individuals to participate more effectively with professionals in meeting the educational needs of disabled children.

3479 New Mexico Speech & Language Consultants

1000 West 4th   505-623-8319
Roswell, NM 88201

Eileen Grooms

Provides diagnostic and therapy services for communicatively impaired individuals.

3480 Parents Reaching Out to Help

1127 University Blvd. NE   505-842-9045
Albuquerque, NM 87102   800-524-5176

Parent Training and Information Program views parents as full partners in the educational process and a significant source of support and assistance to each other. Funded by the Division of Personnel Preparation, Office of Special Education Programs, these programs provide training and information to parents to enable such individuals to participate more effectively with professionals in meeting the educational needs of disabled children.

New York

3481 Advocates for Children

24-16 Bridge Plaza South   718-729-8866
Long Island City, NY 11101   FAX 718-729-8931

Galen D. Kirkland, Executive Director

Parent Training and Information Program that views parents as full partners in the educational process and a "significant source" of support and assistance to each other. Funded by the Division of Personnel Preparation, Office of Special Education Programs, these programs provide training and information to parents to enable such individuals to participate more effectively with professionals in meeting the educational needs of disabled children.

3482 Anderson School

875 Route 9   914-889-4034
Staatsburg, NY 12580

Frank Mulhern, Director

3483 Bailin-Mann Associates Learning Center

603 East 23rd Street   718-859-3367
Brooklyn, NY 11210

Amy Bailin, Director
Marcia Mann, Director

A private learning center offering educational therapy/remediation for children and adults with Dyslexia and other learning difficulties. Orton-Gillingham techniques of multisensory teaching are employed. Services included educational consultation and advisement, parent counseling and support, teacher training and professional development and speech and language therapy.

3484 Baker Hall/Our Lady of Victory Infant Home Nursery School

Baker Hall
777 Ridge Road   716-828-9737
Lackawanna, NY 14218

J. Brad Herman, Executive Director

Offers a certified special education program and a full range of classroom options, in-house, pre-vocational training and BOCES school placements are avilable to students dependening on need.

3485 Berrent Learning and Reading Center

1025 Northern Blvd.   516-365-7691
Roslyn, NY 11576

Howard Berrent, PhD, Director

Individual instruction for children, adolescents and adults. Established in 1971, offers a full assessment and coordination with schools when necessary.

3486 The Child Center for Developmental Service

251 Manetto Hill Road   516-938-3788
Plainview, NY 11803

Iris Lesser

3487 Children's Evaluation and Rehabilitation Center - Rose F. Kennedy Center

1410 Pelham Parkway South   212-430-2434
Bronx, NY 10461

Herbert Cohen

3488 Community Based Services, Inc.

P.O. Box 247   914-277-4771
Purdys, NY 10578

Kevin McCarthy

Six intermediate care facilities for people with autism and learning disabilities.

3489 Diagnostic Learning Center

416 Ridge Road   518-793-0668
Queensbury, NY 12804

Jan Bishop

3490 EAC, Inc. Developmental Learning Program

300 Park Avenue   516-242-7130
Deer Park, NY 11729

C. Leonard Davis

3491 EAC, Inc. Developmental Program - Port Washington

382 Main Street   516-883-3006
Port Washington, NY 11050

Nadine Heyman

3492 Eden II School for Autistic Children, Inc.

Vanderbilt Ave. & Bay Street   718-816-1422
Staten Island, NY 10304

Fred West, Executive Director

Offers a school for children with autism and an adult day training program.

3493 Educational Interventions for Learning Differences

2810 East Cedar Bayou Lynchburg 713-421-4660
Baytown, NY 77523

Nancy Robeson, Director

Blends academic programs and special multi-sensory programs to attain successful learning.

3494 Environmental Science and Forestry - State University of New York College

110 Bray Hall   315-470-6660
Syracuse, NY 13210

Thomas Slocum, Special Services

3495 The Gateway School of New York

921 Madison Avenue   212-628-3560
New York, NY 10021

Davida Sherwood

3496 The Gow School

Emery Road   716-652-3450
South Wales, NY 14139

J. William Adams

3497 The Hallen School

1310 Harrison Avenue   914-381-2006
Mamaroneck, NY 10543

Carol LoCascio, Executive Director

A special education school offering a sound academic program in a therapeutic setting.

3498 The Hartsdale School

15 Oakland Avenue   914-961-0640
Tuckahoe, NY 10707

Myrna Block

3499 Healing Arts Group

R.D. #2, Box 229   518-672-7108
Harlemville-Ghent, NY 12075

Russell Klavun

3500 Hudson Valley Learning Center

17 Collegeview Avenue   914-545-4769
Poughkeepsie, NY 12603

Glenn Nystrup

3501 ICD - International Center for the Disabled

340 East 24th Street   212-679-0100
New York, NY 10010

Barbara Kligerman

3502 Julia Dyckman Andrus Memorial

1156 North Broadway   914-965-3700
Yonkers, NY 10701

Gary Carman, Executive Director

Residential treatment for youngsters who have moderate to severe emotional problems.

3503 Just Kids: Early Childhood Learning Center

P.O. Box 12   516-924-0008
Middle Island, NY 11953

Steven Held, Executive Director
A family focused early intervention program for young children with disabilities.

3504 The Karafin School, Inc.

111 Radio Circle
Mt. Kisco, NY 10549

Dr. Albert Karafin

3505 Learning Diagnostic Program

Schneider Children's Hospital
Long Island Jewish Medical Center   212-477-4633
New York, NY 10003

3506 Little Village School

Bayberry Avenue   516-746-5575
Garden City, NY 11530

Caryl Bank, Educational Director
Provides a year round program to children with developmental delays.

3507 Manhattan Center for Learning

590 West End Avenue, Ste. 1A   212-787-5712
New York, NY 10024

Judith Baumrin, Psychologist
Services for the learning disabled includes: tutoring, remediation, cognitive therapy, psychoeducational testing and parent counseling.

3508 Maplebrook School

P.O. Box 118, Rte. 22   914-373-8191
Amenia, NY 12501   FAX 914-373-7029

Roger A. Fazzone, Headmaster
Lori S. Hale, Admissions
A private boarding school for students with learning differences and low average abilities. day programming is available. Focus is on individual learning styles in academic areas. High school diploma available. Wonderful athletic program and enrichment programs to develop social skills competencise and self-esteem.

3509 The New Interdisciplinary School

One Scouting Blvd.   516-924-5583
Medford, NY 11763

Claire Salant, Director
Describes the integration into the classroom and home of professionals from a variety of disciplines: special education, language development, gross and dine motor, sensory integration, mental health, audiology and nursing.

3510 Norman Howard School

220 Idlewood Road   716-461-1600
Eochester, NY 14618

William Elberty

3511 North Shore Learning Associates, Inc.

37 Milburn Lane   516-625-1008
Rosyln Heights, NY 11577

Howard Boll

3512 Para-Educator Center for Young Adults

PEC for Young Adults
One Washington Place   212-598-3906
New York, NY 10003

Judith Kranes, Director

3513 Para-Educator Center for Young Adults At New York University

One Washington Place   212-998-5800
New York, NY 10003

Dr. Jane E. Herzog, Director
Sharon Morando, Admissions Coord.
Trains students with learning disabilities for careers in the human services and for independent living. All areas of the program are integrated with special emphasis on social skills, speech, language development and life skills, as well as specific vocational training which can lead to competitive employment and independence. Upon successfully completing two years of study, students earn a PEC certificate and 6 credits from the School of Continuing Education at N.Y.U..

3514 Parent Network Center

1443 Main Street   716-885-1004
Buffalo, NY 14209   800-724-7408

Joan Watkins, Executive Director
Views parents as full partners in the educational process and a significant source of support and assistance to each other. These programs provide training and information to parents to enable such individuals to participate more effectively with professionals in meeting the educational needs of disabled children, and ongoing needs as they "age out" of mandated services and require independent help to live inclusive lives and experience full citizenship.

3515 The Preschooler's Place for Learning

P.O. Box 123, Route 25A   516-929-3833
Wading River, NY 11792

Helene Greenberg, Executive Director

Offers two types of programs: the Early Intervention and the Special Education Preschool for disabled children.

3516 Program for Learning Disabled College Students Adelphi Unviersity

Eddy Hall-lower Level   516-877-4710
Garden City, NY 11530

Sandra Holzinger

3517 Resources for Children with Special

200 Park Avenue South, Ste. 816   212-677-4650
New York, NY 10003

Parent Training and Information Program views parents as full partners in the educational process and a significant source of support and assistance to each other. Funded by the Division of Personnel Preparation, Office of Special Education Programs, these programs provide training and information to parents to enable such individuals to participate more effectively with professionals in meeting the educational needs of disabled children.

3518 Robert Louis Stevenson School

24 West 74th Street   212-787-6400
New York, NY 10023

3519 The Russell Clinic

1417 Avenue P
Brooklyn, NY 11229

George Russell

3520 Stephen Gaynor School

22 West 74th Street   212-787-7070
New York, NY 10023

Miriam Michael

3521 West Side Psychological Service

27 West 95th Street   212-662-1111
New York, NY 10025

Maury Neuhaus

3522 Windward School

Windward Avenue   914-949-6968
White Plains, NY 10605

Judith Hochman

3523 Winston Preparatory School

4 West 76th Street   212-496-8400
New York, NY 10023

Roberta Michaels

North Carolina

3524 Carstens Psychological Associates

3025 Sunset Ave., Ste. 3   919-937-2596
Rocky Mount, NC 27804

Andrea Carstens, PhD, President

Psychological, psychoeducational and neuropsychological evaluations, psycotherapy, parent training and school consultations.

3525 Eastern Associates Speech and Language Services, Inc.

2501-B Wayne Memorial Drive   919-731-2234
Goldsboro, NC 27534   FAX 919-731-2306

Rhonda Sutton-Merritt

A private practice clinic providing diagnosis and treatment of speech and language disorders/differences. All speech pathologists hold a master's degree, are licensed by the NC Board of Examiners for Speech Pathologists and Audiologists and hold a Certificate of Clinical Competence issued by the American Speech-Language and Hearing Association.

3526 Exceptional Children's Assistance Center

P.O. Box 16   704-892-1321
Davidson, NC 28036

Parent Training and Information Program views parents as full partners in the educational process and a significant source of support and assistance to each other. Funded by the Division of Personnel Preparation, Office of Special Education Programs, these programs provide training and information to parents to enable such individuals to participate more effectively with professionals in meeting the educational needs of disabled children.

3527 Families First Coalition

300 Enola Road   704-433-2661
Norganton, NC 28655

Parent Training and Information Program views parents as full partners in the educational process and a significant source of support and assistance to each other. Funded by the Division of Personnel Preparation, Office of Special Education Programs, these programs provide training and information to parents to enable such individuals to participate more effectively with professionals in meeting the educational needs of disabled children.

3528 Hill Learning Development Center of Durham Academy

3130 Pickett Road   919-489-7464
Durham, NC 27705

Sharon Maskel

3529 The Patterson School

Route 5, Box 170   800-367-4921
Lenoir, NC 28645

Sherri Stafford

3530 The Piedmont School, Inc.

108 W. Farris Avenue   919-883-0992
High Point, NC 27262

Susan Gottfried

Works collaboratively with public schools to offer alternative opportunities for learning disabled students. The half-day program provides instruction in reading, written language and math with teacher/pupil ratios of 1:3. The primary goal of the School is to close the gap between the student's academic performance and his potential as quickly as possible. In addition to the core program, the school also offers after-school remediation tutoring and study ahll programs.

3531 Raleigh Learning and Language Clinic

216 West Milbrook Road   919-870-0664
Raleigh, NC 27609

Stan Kant

3532 The Thomas Jefferson Academy

1360 Lyndale Drive   919-924-4908
Winston-Salem, NC 27106

Vea Snyder

3533 Tutoring Services, Inc.

6401 Carmel Road, Ste. 101   704-542-6471
Charlotte, NC 28226

Rosanne Manus

Ohio

3534 Akron Reading and Speech Center

700 Ghent Road   216-666-1161
Akron, OH 44333

Ardath Franck, PhD, Director

Remedial, developmental and enrichment reading, speech therapy services.

3535 Bellefaire

22001 Fairmount Blvd.   216-932-2800
Shaker Heights, OH 44118

Sam Kelman

3536 Center for the Advancement of Learning

PLUS Program
Montgomery Hall   614-826-8246
New Concord, OH 43762

Jen Navicky, Associate Director

Academic support services for learning disabled students consisting of intensive tutoring, out class testing, and other reasonable accommodations.

3537 Child Advocacy Center

SOC Information Center
106 Wellington Place   513-381-2400
Cincinnati, OH 45219

Parent Training and Information Program views parents as full partners in the educational process and a significant source of support and assistance to each other. Funded by the Division of Personnel Preparation, Office of Special Education Programs, these programs provide training and information to parents to enable such individuals to participate more effectively with professionals in meeting the educational needs of disabled children.

3538 Cincinnati Center for Developmental Disorders

3300 Elland Avenue   513-559-4623
Cincinnati, OH 45229

Jack Rubinstein

3539 Cincinnati Occupational Therapy Institute for Services and Study, Inc.

4440 Carver Woods Drive   513-791-5688
Cincinnati, OH 45242

Elizabeth Newcomer

3540 Cleveland Institute of Art

11141 East Blvd., University Circle   216-421-7462
Cleveland, OH 44106   800-223-4700
      FAX 216421-7438

No student whould be discouraged from attending CIA because of a learning disability. A student working on their B.F.A. degree at the Institute of Art can get academic support from the tutoring director in the Office of Academic Services. Service include books-on-tape, one-on-one tutoring, alternative curriculum advising, notetaking services, alternative test taking and assignment arrangements. Services outside the scope of the program can be arranged at the student's expense.

3541 Developmental Clinic, Inc.

5669 Mahoning Avenue   216-792-1085
Austintown, OH 44515

James LaPolla

3542 Developmental Clinic, Inc./ Warren

875 Howland-Wilson Road NE   216-856-5858
Warren, OH 44484

Jams LaPolla

3543 The Educational Clinic, Inc.

867 South James Blvd.   614-236-1604
Columbus, OH 43227

Gerald Pruzan

3544 Hobart School of Welding Technology

Trade Square East
Troy, OH 45373

Raymond Dunlavy, Supervisor

3545 Mary F. Och Learning Center

3591 Templeton Road, NW   216-898-3591
Warren, OH 44481

3546 North Coast Tutoring Services

27346 Santa Clara Drive   216-892-0967
Westlake, OH 44145

Carole Ricahrds

3547 Ohio Coalition for the Education Of

1299 Campbell Road, Ste. B   614-431-1307
Marion, OH 43302

Parent Training and Information Program views parents as full partners in the educational process and a significant source of support and assistance to each other. Funded by the Division of Personnel Preparation, Office of Special Education Programs, these programs provide training and information to parents to enable such individuals to participate more effectively with professionals in meeting the educational needs of disabled children.

3548 The Olympus Center

38 East Hollister Street   513-621-4606
Cincinnati, OH 45219   FAX 513-721-0959

Sandy Sanborn Martin

A private, non-profit diagnostic agency providing comprehensive psychoeducational and language evaluations for children, adolescents and adults who are experiencing learning difficulties. A multi-disciplinary team is coordinated by a case manager. Extensive school or work follow-up is an integral part of each evaluation.

3549 The Springer School

2121 Madison Road   513-871-6080
Cincinnati, OH 45208   FAX 513-871-6428

Corrine Thaler, Admissions Director
Nancy Ike, Placement Director

An independent elementary day school for children with diagnosed learning disabilities. In school services include academic language, motor, social and psychological therapies. Average length of enrollment is 3 years.

Oklahoma

3550 Pro-Oklahoma

UCP of Oklahoma
1917 South Harvard Avenue   405-681-9710
Oklahoma City, OK 73128

Parent Training and Information Program views parents as full partners in the educational process and a significant source of support and assistance to each other. Funded by the Division of Personnel Preparation, Office of Special Education Programs, these programs provide training and information to parents to enable such individuals to participate more effectively with professionals in meeting the educational needs of disabled children.

3551 Town and Country School

1515 South 71st East Avenue   918-665-3113
Tulsa, OK 74112

J. Elaine Minson, EdD, Executive Director

A private school for learning disabled students, with or without attention deficit disorder. Class size limited to 12 persons, a certified teacher and an aide.

Oregon

3552 Cornell Vision Center

1010 NE Cornell Road   503-640-8530
Hillsboro, OR 97124

William Ludlam

3553 Learning Disabled Student SIG

Chemetka Community College
P.O. Box 14007   503-399-2556
Salem, OR 97309

A special interest group concerned with the educational needs of college-level learning disabled students.

3554 Oregon COPE Project, Inc.

999 Locust Street NE   503-373-7477
Salem, OR 97303

Parent Training and Information Program views parents as full partners in the educational process and a significant source of support and assistance to each other. Funded by the Division of Personnel Preparation, Office of Special Education Programs, these programs provide training and information to parents to enable such individuals to participate more effectively with professionals in meeting the educational needs of disabled children.

3555 Salem Eye Clinic

1097 Liberty Street SE   503-581-4411
Salem, OR 97302

Jordan Brown

3556 Tree of Learning High School

9000 SW Beaverton Highway   503-297-2336
Portland, OR 97225

Jocelyn Tuthill

Pennsylvania

3557 The Abraxas Foundation, Inc.

Box 59   814-927-6615
Marienville, PA 16239

Daniel Heit, President

3558 Center for Alternative Learning

P.O. Box 716   215-525-8336
Bryn Mawr, PA 19010

A non-profit organization designed to provide direct services to learning disabled adults and teacher training to adult learning disabled practitioners.

3559 Center for Psychological Services

125 Coulter Avenue   215-642-4873
Ardmore, PA 19003

Moss Jackson

Individual, family and group therapy psychoeducational evaluation and school consultation.

3560 The Crossroads School

Box 730 North Valley Road   215-296-6765
Paoli, PA 19301

Norman Jason

3561 Devereux Brandywine

P.O. Box 69   215-942-5900
Glenmoore, PA 19343   FAX 215-942-9572

Kenneth Ferro, Executive Director
Kathleen Deeming, Admissions Director

Residential treatment for emotionally disturbed males consisting of five distinct programs based upon age and diagnostic criteria. Includes program for the "deaf". Services provided include: psychiatric; therapeutic; milieu with integrated behavior management system; intermediate; high school with 12-month educational program and more. Offers a 350 acre campus, including stocked lake, swimming pool, playing fields and more.

3562 The Devereux Foundation

Philadelphia, PA   215-964-3045
        800-345-1292
        FAX 215-971-4600

Offers residential and community-based treatment centers nationwide. Provides comprehensive services to individuals of all ages.

3563 Devereux Mapleton Center

655 Sugartown Road   215-296-6970
Malvern, PA 19355

Residential and in-patient program for children, adolescents and young adults with emotional disorders and learning disabilities.

3564 Dr. Gertrude A. Barber Center, Inc.

136 East Avenue   814-453-7661
Erie, PA 16507

Gertrude Barber, President

An individualized educational program designed to meet the needs of preschool and school-aged students.

3565 The Hillside School

2697 Brookside Road   215-967-5449
Macungie, PA 18062

Linda Whitney

3566 The Institute for the Achievement of Human Potential

8801 Stenton Avenue
Philadelphia, PA 19118

Neil Harvey, President

3567 KidsPeace

5300 KidsPeace Drive   215-799-8000
Orefield, PA 18069   800-25-PEACE

John Peter, President

Offers various programs including: community residential care, residential care, specialized group homes, child and family guidance center and student assistance programs.

3568 The Learning Center - State College

1315 West College Avenue, Ste. 303   814-234-3450
State College, PA 16801

Cynthia Miller

3569 New Castle School of Trades

RD #1
Pulaski, PA 16143

Joseph Clavelli

3570 Parent Education Network

333 East Seventh Avenue   717-845-9722
York, PA 17404

Parent Training and Information Program views parents as full partners in the educational process and a significant source of support and assistance to each other. Funded by the Division of Personnel Preparation, Office of Special Education Programs, these programs provide training and information to parents to enable such individuals to participate more effectively with professionals in meeting the educational needs of disabled children.

3571 Parents Union for Public Schools

311 South Juniper Street, Ste. 602   215-546-1212
Philadelphia, PA 19107

Parent Training and Information Program views parents as full partners in the educational process and a significant source of support and assistance to each other. Funded by the Division of Personnel Preparation, Office of Special Education Programs, these programs provide training and information to parents to enable such individuals to participate more effectively with professionals in meeting the educational needs of disabled children.

3572 The Pathway School

162 Egypt Road   215-277-0660
Jeffersonville, PA 19403

Ted Enoch, Ed.S., Admissions Coord.

Provides services for individuals, ages 5-21, with learning , developmental, neurological and behavioral disorders using a multidisciplinary team approach. All students have individualized educational and treatment plans.

3573 The Rehabilitation Institute of Pittsburgh

6301 Northumberland Street   412-521-9000
Pittsburgh, PA 15217

John Wilson, President

Offers quality services to young people with moderate to severe disabilities with different levels of physical, cognitive and emotional functioning.

3574 Stratford Friends School

Darby And Llandillo Roads   215-446-3144
Havertown, PA 19083

Dorothy Flanagan

3575 Thaddeus Stevens State School of Technology

750 East King Street   717-299-7791
Lancaster, PA 17602

Patricia DeWitt, Special Services

3576 The Woods Schools

Residential Center
Route 213   215-750-4000
Langhorne, PA 19047

Robert Griffith, President

Provides a full range of residential, special education, habilitation, rehabilitation, recreation and vocational training.

Rhode Island

3577 Behavior Research Institute

240 Laban Street   401-944-1186
Providence, RI 02909   800-231-3405
    FAX 401-946-4190

Penny Potter, Dir. Student Service
Rose Silva, Asst. Dir. Students

A nationally recognized residential/educational treatment program for children and adults with behavior disorders. The students here have autism, mental retardation, brain damage, emotional disturbances or have been in trouble with the law. Often their problems are so severe that it has been impossible for them to be accepted by, or successfully educated and treated by, other programs. The average student at BRI has been expelled from 5 programs and rejected by 9 others.

3578 Harmony Hill School, Inc.

63 Harmony Hill Road   401-949-0690
Chepachet, RI 02814   FAX 401-949-2060

Terrence Leary, Executive Director

Committes to providing a residential or day treatment program for youngsters with behavioral disorders and learning disabilities.

3579 Rhode Island Parent Information Network

500 Prospect Street   401-727-4144
Pawtucket, RI 02860   800-464-3399

Parent Training and Information Program views parents as full partners in the educational process and a significant source of support and assistance to each other. Funded by the Division of Personnel Preparation, Office of Special Education Programs, these programs provide training and information to parents to enable such individuals to participate more effectively with professionals in meeting the educational needs of disabled children.

South Carolina

3580 Camperdown Academy

1457 Cleveladn Street   803-250-1023
Greenville, SC 29607

Michael Miller

3581 The Mashburn School, Inc.

105 Lancaster Street   803-642-5067
Aiken, SC 29801

Sandra Mashburn

3582 Parents Reaching Out to Parents of South

2712 Middleburg Drive, Ste. 102   803-779-3859
Columbia, SC 29204

Colleen M. Lee, Program Director
Parent Training and Information Program views parents as full partners in the educational process and a significant source of support and assistance to each other. Funded by the Division of Personnel Preparation, Office of Special Education Programs, these programs provide training and information to parents to enable such individuals to participate more effectively with professionals in meeting the educational needs of disabled children.

3583 Pine Grove

P.O. Box 100   803-438-3011
Elgin, SC 29045

Carl Herring, Executive Director
Offers an intensive academic, social skills and behavior modification program designed to return the child to his/her home area as soon as possible.

South Dakota

3584 South Dakota Parent Connection, Inc.

P.O. Box 84118   605-335-8844
Sioux Falls, SD 57118   800-640-4553

Parent Training and Information Program views parents as full partners in the educational process and a significant source of support and assistance to each other. Funded by the Division of Personnel Preparation, Office of Special Education Programs, these programs provide training and information to parents to enable such individuals to participate more effectively with professionals in meeting the educational needs of children with disabilities.

Tennessee

3585 The Bodine School

2432 Yester Oaks Drive   901-754-1800
Germantown, TN 38139

Rene Friemoth Lee

3586 Camelot Care Center - Tennessee

Route 3, Box 267C   615-376-2296
Kingston, TN 37763

James Spicer, Executive Director

A psychiatric residential treatment center serving children with emotional disturbances and learning disabilities.

3587 Devereux Genesis Learning Centers

430 B Allied Drive   615-832-4222
Nashville, TN 37211

Day school and treatment programs for adolescents and young adults who have emotional disorders and learning disabilities.

3588 Support and Training for Exceptional

1805 Hayes Street, Ste. 100   615-327-0294
Nashville, TN 37203

Parent Training and Information Program views parents as full partners in the educational process and a significant source of support and assistance to each other. Funded by the Division of Personnel Preparation, Office of Special Education Programs, these programs provide training and information to parents to enable such individuals to participate more effectively with professionals in meeting the educational needs of disabled children.

3589 Tomlinson College

Cleveland, TN 37311   615-476-3271

Buford Johnson, Special Services

Texas

3590 The Bridges School

4408 North Stanton   915-532-6647
El Paso, TX 79902

Victoria Ives-Adamson

3591 Crisman Preparatory School

2455 North Eastman Road   214-758-9741
Longview, TX 75601

Lucy Peacock, Director

3592 Diagnostic and Remedial Reading Clinic

622 Isom Road   512-341-7417
San Anotnio, TX 78217

Lola Austin

3593 Gateway School

7200 John T. White Road   817-496-5066
Fort Worth, TX 76120

Harriet Walber, Director
An alternative school for students designed for the student who has average or above average intelligence yet has experienced little or no success previously in school.

3594 Kenley School

1434 Matador   915-698-3220
Abilene, TX 79605

Rosalind Shields

3595 Kids Are VIP's

3445 Executive Center Dr., Ste. 102   512-345-9274
Austin, TX 78731

Roberta Rosen

3596 Overton Speech and Language Center

4763 Barwick Drive, Ste. 103   817-294-8408
Fort Worth, TX 76132

Valerie Johnson

3597 The Parish School

11059 Timberline   713-467-4696
Houston, TX 77043

Robbin Parish, Director/Founder
Amy Hammett, Admissions

Private school, language based curriculum for children 18 months through fifth grade with language and learning differences.

3598 PATH

6465 Calder, Ste. 202   409-866-4726
Beaumont, TX 77706   800-678-9638

Parent Training and Information Program views parents as full partners in the educational process and a significant source of support and assistance to each other. Funded by the Division of Personnel Preparation, Office of Special Education Programs, these programs provide training and information to parents to enable such individuals to participate more effectively with professionals in meeting the educational needs of disabled children.

3599 Project FIT

Tri-co., Co-op Commerce Public
Commerce, TX 75428

Dr. Elaine Adams

3600 Psychoeducational Diagnostic Services

7233 Brentfield   214-931-5299
Dallas, TX 75248

Harrian Stern, Educ. Diagnostician

Psychoeducational diagnostic assessment of intellectual, academic learning modality, dyslexia, ADD, gifted, consulations with parents, schools, etc..

3601 Psychology Clinic of Fort Worth

4100 South Hulen, Ste. 230   817-731-0888
Fort Worth, TX 76109

William Barry Norman

3602 Shelton School and Evaluation Center

5002 West Lovers Lane   214-352-1772
Dallas, TX 75209   FAX 214-352-1851

Joyce S. Pickering, B.S., M.A., Executive Director
Diann Slaton, B.A., Admissions Director

A coeducational day school serving 250 students. The School focuses on the development of "learning disabled" students of average to above average intelligence to enable them to succeed in conventional classroom settings. Services include on-site Evaluation Center for diagnostic testing, a Speech, Language and Hearing Clinic, an Early Childhood Program and more.

3603 SHIP Resource Center

University United Methodist Church
5084 DeZavala Road   512-822-0995
San Antonio, TX 78249

3604 Star Ranch

Star Programs, Inc.
HCR 7, Box 39C   210-367-4868
Ingram, TX 78025   FAX 210-367-2814

Stevend Hamilton, Development Director
Rand Southard, Administrative Dir.

Operates two programs at Star Ranch. One is a recreational/educational summer camp for children with larning difficulties. Boys and girls ages 7-18 attend one or two week sessions during the summer. Traditional summer camp activities as well as academic tutoring are offered. The second is a residential tratment center for boys ages 7-17 who are diagnosed as learning disabled and emotionally disturbed. Preference is given to younger boys as placement is long term.

3605 Starpoint School

Texas Christian University
2829 Stadium Drive   817-921-7141
Fort Worth, TX 76109

Henry Patterso

3606 The Winston School

5707 Royal Lane   214-691-6950
Dallas, TX 75229

Rita Sherbenou, PhD, Head Of School
Ellen D. Cassidy, Admissions Director

Founded in 1975, Winston is a 1-12 grade (plus College Bridge for Freshmen) school for children of average to above average intelligence who have trouble in school because they learn differently. Fully accredited curriculum includes art, athletics, drama, computer camping and photography. Student teacher ration is 7 to 1.

Utah

3607 Mountain Plains Regional Resource Center

Utah State University
1780 N. Research Parkway, Ste. 112   801-752-0238
Logan, UT 84321   FAX 801-753-9750

Glenn Latham, Director

A federally funded project which provides technical assistance to BIA, Colorado, Iowa, Kansas, Missouri, Montana, Nebraska, North Dakota, South Dakota, Utah and Wyoming on how to serve disabled infants, toddlers, children, youth and their families. Learning disabled children constitute a large block of our service population. A major component of our technical assistance is in the form of information drawm from thousands of documents ranging from published research studies to newsletters.

3608 Reid School

3310 South 2700 East   801-486-5083
Salt Lake City, UT 84109

Ethna Reid

3609 Specialized Educational Programming Services, Inc.

1760 South 1100 East   801-467-2122
Salt Lake City, UT 84105   FAX 801-467-2148

AvaJane Pickering, PhD

Offers case management, services to rural areas, one-to-one tutorials and consultations.

3610 Utah Parent Center

2290 East 4500 South, Ste. 110   801-272-1051
Salt Lake City, UT 84117   800-468-1160

Parent Training and Information Program views parents as full partners in the educational process and a significant source of support and assistance to each other. Funded by the Division of Personnel Preparation, Office of Special Education Programs, these programs provide training and information to parents to enable such individuals to participate more effectively with professionals in meeting the educational needs of disabled children.

Vermont

3611 The Greenwood School

R.R. 2, Box 270   802-387-4545
Putney, VT 05346

Thomas Scheidler

3612 Pine Ridge School

1075 Williston Road   802-434-2161
Williston, VT 05495   FAX 802-434-5512

Mary Jean Thielen

Serves students who have been diagnosed with a primary, specific language disability. They are in the average range of intelligence and want to use those strengths in their remediation of their language weaknesses.

3613 Stern Center for Language and Learning

81 West Canal Street   802-655-2332
Winooski, VT 05404   FAX 802-655-2332

Blanche Podhajski, PhD, Director

Founded in 1983, the center is a non-profit organization providing comprehensive services for children and adults with learning disabilities. The Center is also an educational resource serving all of Northern New England. Programs include; educational testing, individual instruction, psychotherapy, school consultation, professional training for educators and a parent/professional resource library.

3614 Vermont Information and Training Network

Champlain Mill   802-655-4016
Winooski, VT 05404

Parent Training and Information Program views parents as full partners in the educational process and a significant source of support and assistance to each other. Funded by the Division of Personnel Preparation, Office of Special Education Programs, these programs provide training and information to parents to enable such individuals to participate more effectively with professionals in meeting the educational needs of disabled children.

Virginia

3615 Accolink Academy

8519 Tuttle Road   703-451-8041
Springfield, VA 22152   FAX 703-569-5365

3616 The Achievement Center - Virginia

P.O. Box 12368   703-982-0128
Roanoke, VA 24025

Barbara Ann Whitwell

3617 The Dominion School Day Program

370 South Washington Street   703-536-6103
Falls Church, VA 22046

Debra Kae Pell, Director

Provides a structured and individualized psychoeducation program designed for students who are currently experiencing emotional and/or behavioral problems.

3618   Fairfax House

3300 Woodburn Road   703-560-6116
Annandale, VA 22003

3619   Grafton School

P.O. Box 112   703-955-2400
Berryville, VA 22611   FAX 703-955-3496

Robert Stieg, Jr.

3620   The Learning Center - Virginia

1602 Gordon Avenue   804-977-6006
Charlottesville, VA 22903

Anne McGann, Med Director

3621   The Learning Resources Center

909 First Colonial Road   804-428-3367
Virginia Beach, VA 23454

Rosalind Foer

3622   Leary School, Inc.

6349 Lincolnia Road   701-573-5400
Alexandria, VA 22312

3623   Little Keswick School

P.O. Box 24   804-295-0457
Keswick, VA 22947

Marc Columbus, Headmaster

A residential special education school for 30 boys with emotional disturbances, learning disabilities and educable mental retardation with highly structured academic and behavioral programs.

3624   The New Community School

4211 Hermitage Road   804-266-2494
Richmond, VA 23227

Julia Ann Greenwood

3625   New Vistas School

520 Eldon Street   804-846-0301
Lynchburg, VA 24501

Lucy Ross

3626   Oakland School

Oakland Farm   804-293-9059
Boyd Tavern, VA 22947

Joanne Dondero, Director
Judith Edwards, Asst. Director

A coed school for students of normal or better intelligence who have not succeeded in a regular classroom. Most of the students are learning disabled and the curriculum goes through grade 9 with Oakland specializing in the teaching of reading, writing, study skills and written language. Facilities include a new gymnasium, horse back riding included in P.E. program and more.

3627   Oakwood School

7210 Braddock Road   703-941-5788
Annandale, VA 22003   FAX 703-941-4186

Robert McIntyre, Executive Director

A co-educational day school for children of average to above average potential with mild to moderate learning disabilities. Special education and related services are provided by this private, non-profit school founded in 1971.

3628   The Pines Residential Treatment Center

825 Crawford Parkway   804-398-0300
Portsmouth, VA 23704

Lenard Lexier

3629   Riverside School, Inc.

2110 McRae Road   804-320-3465
Richmond, VA 23235

Patricia DeOrio

3630   School for Contemporary Education/Virginia

7010 Braddock Road   703-941-8810
Annandale, VA 22003

Sally Sibley, Administrative Dir.

A private day school offering quality special education to exceptional children.

3631   Seton Centers, Inc.

307 Annandale Road, Ste. 100 703-533-7670
Falls Church, VA 22042

Mary Doherty

3632   Speech and Language Center of Northern Virginia

888 Dolley Madison Blvd.   202-356-2833
McLean, VA 22101

Marilyn K. Johnson, MA, CCC-SLP, Director

A private, nonprofit organization designed to offer a full range of speech-language diagnostic and therapy services to the community at a reasonable rate. The CENTER serves preschool and school-aged children with speech and language delays, articulation, phonological and fluency problems, as well as language-based learning difficulties.

3633 StoneBridge Schools Riverview Learning Center

P.O. Box 9247, 4225 Portsmouth   804-488-7586
Blvd
Chesapeake, VA 23321

Martha B. Shirley, Director

Staff 4; day; remedial tutoring; diagnostic testing; educational therapy; fee-fixed and more.

Washington

3634 Hamlin Robinson School

10211-12th Avenue South   206-763-1167
Seattle, WA 98168

Beverly Wolf, Director

A non-profit, state approved elementary day school for children with Specific Language Disability (Dyslexia), providing a posititve learning environment, meeting individual needs and nurtures the whole child. Small classes use the Slingerland multi-sensory classroom approach in reading, writing, spelling and all instructional areas. It helps students discover the joy of learning, build positive self-esteem, and explore their full creative potential while preparing them for the classroom.

3635 Specialized Training for Military Parents

12208 Pacific Highway SW   206-588-1741
Tacoma, WA 98499

Parent Training and Information Program views parents as full partners in the educational process and a significant source of support and assistance to each other. Funded by the Division of Personnel Preparation, Office of Special Education Programs, these programs provide training and information to parents to enable such individuals to participate more effectively with professionals in meeting the educational needs of disabled children.

3636 Westside Place

1310 North 45th Street   206-634-0782
Seattle, WA 98103

Rosemarie Morris

West Virginia

3637 Children's Therapy Clinic Project GLUE

2345 Chesterfield Avenue   304-340-3546
Charleston, WV 25304

Provides physical, occupational and speech therapy. Also augmentative communication, assistive devices, a swimming program and horseback riding for the disabled individual.

3638 West Virginia Parent Training And

229 Washington Avenue   304-624-1436
Clarksburg, WV 26301   800-281-1436

Parent Training and Information Program views parents as full partners in the educational process and a significant source of support and assistance to each other. Funded by the Division of Personnel Preparation, Office of Special Education Programs, these programs provide training and information to parents to enable such individuals to participate more effectively with professionals in meeting the educational needs of disabled children.

Wyoming

3639 Wyoming Parent Information Center

270 Fort Street   307-684-5461
Buffalo, WY 82834

Parent Training and Information Program views parents as full partners in the educational process and a significant source of support and assistance to each other. Funded by the Division of Personnel Preparation, Office of Special Education Programs, these programs provide training and information to parents to enable such individuals to participate more effectively with professionals in meeting the educational needs of disabled children.

Colleges

Alabama

3640 Alabama Aviation and Technical College

P.O. Box 1209   205-774-5113
Ozark, AL 36361

Carol Parker, Student Support

A public two-year college with 2 special education students out of a total of 582. Tuition: $900.

3641 Alabama Southern Community College

P.O. Box 2000   205-575-3156
Monroeville, AL 36460

Theada Samuel

A public two-year college with 1 special education students out of a total of 1117. Tuition: $981.

3642 Auburn University At Montgomery

9th Floor, Library Tower   205-244-3468
Montgomery, AL 36193

Gerri Wolfe, Director

3643 Bishop State Community College

351 North Broad Street   205-690-6423
Mobile, AL 36603

Carrie Moore, Counselor

A public two-year college with 2 special education students out of a total of 2144. Tuition: $891.

3644 Brimingham-Southern College

Birmingham, AL 35234   205-328-5250

Robert Dortch, VP Administrative

3645 Chattahoochee Valley State Community College

2602 Savage Drive   205-297-4981
Phenix City, AL 36867

Doug Chambers

3646 Douglas MacArthur State Technical College

P.O. Box 649   205-493-3573
Opp, AL 36467   FAX 205-493-7003

Deanna L. Culbertson, Learning Specialist
Peggy Linton, Dir. Of Development

A public two-year college with 100 special education students out of a total of 632. Tuition: $729.

3647 George County Wallace State Communty College

P.O. Drawer 1049   205-875-2634
Selma, AL 36702

Effell Williams, Special Services

3648 Jacksonville State University

147 Daugette Hall   205-782-5093
Jacksonville, AL 36265

Daniel Miller, Director

3649 James H. Faulkner State Junior College

Highway 31 South   205-937-9581
Bay Minette, AL 36507

Lena Dexter, Director

A public two-year college with 14 special education students out of a total of 3449. Tuition: $900.

3650 John M. Patterson State Technical College

3920 Troy Highway   205-288-1080
Montgomery, AL 36116

Jerry Joyce, Coordinator

A public two-year college with 91 special education students out of a total of 785. Tuition: $1056.

3651 Marion Military Institute

P.O. Box 420   205-683-2303
Marion, AL 36756

Col. Joe Berry, Academic Dean

An independent two-year college with 6 special education students out of a total of 140. Tuition: $9790.

3652 Miles College

Birmingham, AL 35208   205-923-2771

Elaine Williams

3653 Northeast Alabama State Junior College

P.O. Box 159   205-638-4418
Rainsville, AL 35986

Elaine Marshall, Academic Dean

A public two-year college with 13 special education students out of a total of 1367. Tuition: $819.

3654 S.D. Bishop State Junior College

351 North Broad Street
Mobile, AL 36603

M. Dillard

3655 Troy State University At Dothan

P.O. Box 8368   205-792-8783
Dothan, AL 36304

Pamela Williamson, Special Services

3656 University of Alabama

P.O. Box 87304   205-348-5175
Tuscaloosa, AL 35487

Pat Friend, Special Services
A public four-year college with 130 special education students out of a total of 15943. Tuition: $1436.

3657 University of Alabama At Birmingham UAB Horizons Program

Room 157, Education Bldg.   205-975-6770
Birmingham, AL 35294

Dr. Jade Carter, Special Services
A public four-year college with 250 special education students out of a total of 11752. Tuition: $1860.

3658 University of Montevallo

Station 6250   205-665-6250
Montevallo, AL 35115

Elaine Elledge, Special Services

3659 University of South Alabama

Room 120, 120 Alpha East   205-460-7212
Mobile, AL 36688

Ana Maria Ramirez, Special Services

Alaska

3660 John Brown University

Siloam Springs, AK 72761   501-524-3131

Jeff Tabor

3661 Ketchikan Campus, University of Alaska Southeast

2600 7th   907-225-6177
Ketchikan, AK 99901

L. Lee Naugen, Asst. Professor

3662 Sitka Campus, University of Alaska Southeast

1332 Seward Avenue   907-747-6653
Sitka, AK 99835

Teresa Holt, Adult Education

3663 University of Alaska, Anchorage

2533 Providence Drive   907-786-1570
Anchorage, AK 99508

Doran Vaughan, Special Services

3664 University of Alaska Fairbanks

Fairbanks, AK 99775   907-474-7043

Diane Preston, Special Services
A public four-year college with 25 special education students out of a total of 3999. Tuition: $1320.

Arizona

3665 Eastern Arizona College

Thatcher, AZ 85552   602-428-1133

Beverly Teague, Student Services

3666 Glendale Community College

6000 West Olive Avenue   602-435-3080
Glendale, AZ 85302

Mark Ferris, LD Specialist
A public two-year college with 200 special education students out of a total of 15126.

3667 Grand Canyon College

P.O. Box 11097   602-249-3300
Phoenix, AZ 85017

Dr. Jane Castillo, Instructor Education

3668 Mesa Community College

1833 West Southern Avenue   602-461-7449
Mesa, AZ 85202

Judith Taussig, Special Services

3669 Northern Arizona University

Box 6045   602-523-2261
Flagstaff, AZ 86011

Jane Mulrooney, Special Services
A public four-year college with 17 special education students out of a total of 13488. Tuition: $1590.

3670   Phoenix College

1202 West Thomas Road   602-285-7476
Phoenix, AZ 85013

Ginny Bugh, Special Services

A public two-year college with 20 special education students out of a total of 14319. Tuition: $832.

3671   Pima Community College

200 North Stone Avenue   602-884-6986
Tucson, AZ 85702

Dr. Patricia Richard, Learning Specialist

A public two-year college with 340 special education students out of a total of 29088. Tuition: $576.

3672   Scottsdale Community College

9000 East Chaparral Road   602-423-6517
Scottsdale, AZ 85250

Dee Duggan, Dis. Student Service
Offers disabled student services.

3673   South Mountain Community College

7050 South 24th Street   602-243-8064
Phoenix, AZ 85040

Henrietta Harris, Special Services

3674   The University of Arizona S.A.L.T. Center for LD

Student Counseling Services
Old Main, Room 117   602-621-1242
Tucson, AZ 85721   FAX 602-621-9448

Susan Williams Wilemon, Assistant Director
Shirley Ramsey, Admissions Counselor

A public four-year college with 360 special education students out of a total of 26826. There is a $1100 fee for the special education program in addition to the regular tuition of $1590.

3675   University of Arizona

Tucson, AZ 85721   602-621-1242

Susan Wilemon, Asst. Director

3676   Yavapai College

1100 E. Sheldon Street   602-776-2088
Prescott, AZ 86301

Dr. Merrill Elastrom, Director

A public two-year college with 12 special education students out of a total of 5499. Tuition: $652.

Arkansas

3677   Arkansas Baptist College

1600 Martin Luther King, Jr. Drive   501-372-1637
Little Rock, AR 72202

Dr. Nile Smith, Director

An independent four-year college with 34 special education students out of a total of 408. Tuition: $4258.

3678   Arkansas State University

P.O. Box 119   501-972-2034
State University, AR 72467

Dr. Jennifer Rice Mason, Dir. Disabled Srvcs.

Dr. Jennifer Rice Mason, the University's Coordinator of Services to the Disabled is the compliance coordinator of Section 504 of the rehabilitation Act of 1973 and the Americans with Disabilities Act. In this capacity, Dr. Mason arranges for academic adjustments and auxiliary aids to be provided to qualified students and coordinates workplace accommodations. The University will provide auxiliary aids, without cost, to those students with verified disabilities who require such services.

3679   Arkansas Tech University

Russellville, AR 72801   501-968-0272

Dr. C.C. Smith

3680   Garland County Community College

400 College Drive   501-767-9371
Hot Springs, AR 71913

Annette Smelser-Turk

3681   Harding University

P.O. Box 2235   501-279-4416
Searcy, AR 72149   800-477-4407

Linda Thompson, Student Services Dir

An independent four-year college with 25 special education students out of a total of 3122. Tuition: $8736.

3682   Henderson State University

Arkadelphia, AR 71923   501-246-5511

Dr. William Inman

3683   Mississippi County Community College

Blytheville, AR 72316   501-762-1020

Myles Jeffers, Special Services

3684 Philander Smith College

812 West 13th   501-370-5366
Little Rock, AR 72202

Dr. Dorothy Arnett, Director

3685 Southern Arkansas University

P.O. Box 1250   501-235-4160
Magnolia, AR 71753

Dr. Robert Terry, Special Services

3686 University of Arkansas

113 ARU   501-575-3104
Fayetteville, AR 72701

Dr. Riqua Serobrein, Special Services

3687 University of the Ozarks

Jones Learning Center
415 College Avenue   501-754-3839
Clarksville, AR 72830

Emma Lee Morrow

An independent four-year college with 90 special education students out of a total of 634. There is a $6100 fee for the special education program in addition to the regular tuition of $6920.

California

3688 Allan Hancock College

800 South College Drive   805-922-6966
Santa Maria, CA 93454

Mark Malangko, DSS Director

Offers special courses in learning styles and strategies, assessment, specific skills and counseling services to the learning disabled student.

3689 Antelope Valley College

3041 West Avenue K   805-943-3241
Lancaster, CA 93536

David Greenleaf

A public two-year college with 225 special education students out of a total of 11000.

3690 Bakersfield College

1801 Panorama Drive   805-395-4557
Bakersfield, CA 93305

Joyce Kirst, LD Specialist

A public two-year college with 200 special education students out of a total of 12300.

3691 Barstow C. College

Disabled Student Program and Services
2700 Barstow Road   619-252-2411
Barstow, CA 92311   FAX 619-252-1875

Gene Pfeifer, Counselor
Gordon L. Smith, LD Specialist

Educational support program for disabeld students including special classes and support services for all disabled students.

3692 Biola University

13800 Biola Avenue   310-903-4874
La Mirada, CA 90639

Marylucia Arace, Assistant Dean

Christian liberal arts university responsible for all programs related to students with disabilities.

3693 Butte College

3536 Butte Campus Drive   916-895-2455
Oroville, CA 95965

Richard Dunn, LD Specialist

A public two-year college with 215 special education students out of a total of 12838.

3694 California Lutheran University

60 West Olsen Road   805-493-3260
Thousand Oaks, CA 91360

Gerald Swanson

3695 California Polytechnic State University, San Luis Obispo

San Luis Obispo, CA 93407   805-756-1395

Harriet Clendenen, Dis. Student Service
Ann Fryer, Dis. Student Service

Comprehensive program of academic advising and support services. Due to budgetary contraints, primarily for California residents.

3696 California State Polytechnic University, Pomona

3801 West Temple Avenue   714-869-3333
Pomona, CA 91768

Carol Goldstein

3697 California State University, Chico

Chico, CA 95929   916-898-5959

Laurel Ittleson, LD Director

A public four-year college with 250 special education students out of a total of 13720.

3698 California State University, Dominguez Hills

1000 East Victoria Street   310-516-3660
Carson, CA 90747   FAX 310-516-3846

Patricia Ann Wells, Coordinator
A public four-year college with 77 special education students out of a total of 6908.

3699 California State University, Fullerton

Counseling and Learning Disabilities
Fullerton, CA 92634   714-773-3117

John Liverpool, Counseling
A public four-year college with 35 special education students out of a total of 21274.

3700 California State University, Hayward

25800 Carlos Bee Blvd.   510-881-3868
Hayward, CA 94542

Douglas Worley
A public four-year college with 100 special education students out of a total of 9778.

3701 California State University, Sacramento

Services to Students with Disabilities
6000 J Street   916-278-6955
Sacramento, CA 95819

Susan Eiland-Rickman, LD Specialist
Diane Helvig, LD Counselor

3702 California State University, San Bernadino

5500 University Parkway   714-880-5238
San Bernadino, CA 92407

Barbara Sovereign
A public four-year college with 49 special education students out of a total of 9050.

3703 California State University, Stanislaus

801 West Monte Vista Avenue   209-667-3381
Turlock, CA 95380

Karen Mendonca, Director
A public four-year college with 21 special education students out of a total of 4290.

3704 Canada College

Building 3, Room 117   415-306-3421
Redwood City, CA 94061

Judy Colson, LD Specialist
A public two-year college with 50 special education students out of a total of 7355.

3705 Cerritos College

11110 East Alondra Blvd.   213-860-2451
Norwalk, CA 90650

Al Spetrino, Program Head
A public two-year college with 60 special education students out of a total of 20676.

3706 Chaffey Community College District

Educational Resource Center
5885 Haven Avenue   714-941-2332
Alta Loma, CA 91737

Zenia Loggins, LD Director
A public two-year college with 350 special education students out of a total of 15000.

3707 Chapman College

Orange, CA 92666   714-997-6828

Anthony Garcia

3708 Christ College Irvine

1530 Concordia   714-854-8002
Irvine, CA 92715

Dian Vieselmeyer

3709 College of Alameda

555 Atlantic Avenue   510-748-2388
Alameda, CA 94501

Pat Smith, LD Specialist
Accommodations, assessment and special classes are provided for learning disabled students enrolled at College Alameda, a 2 year college located by San Francisco Bay.

3710 The College of San Mateo

1700 West Hilldale Blvd.   415-574-6433
San Mateo, CA 94002

Marie Paparelli, LD Specialist
Primary objective of the Disabled Students Program-Learning Disabilities Center is to assist the student in achieving academic, vocational, personal and social success. This is best accomplished by integration into the mainstream of college classes and services. The learning disabilities program provides support services in the following areas: assessment and evaluation, specialized tutoring, test accommodations, computer access and more.

3711 College of the Canyons

26455 North Rockwell Canyon Road 805-259-7800
Valencia, CA 91355

Dr. Nina Nashur, Coordinator

A public two-year college with 42 special education students out of a total of 6250.

3712 College of the Desert

43-500 Monterey 619-346-8041
Palm Desert, CA 92260

Dr. Frank Siehien, LD Specialist

3713 College of the Redwoods Learning Skills Center

7351 Tompkins Hill Road 707-445-6862
Eureka, CA 95501 800-641-0400
FAX 707-445-6990

Gail J. Conrad, LD Specialist
Sonja Velasco, Lead LD Specialist

Offers the Center for the accommodations and devices offered for the learning disabled students on campus.

3714 College of the Sequoias

Enabler Program
915 South Mooney Blvd. 209-730-3805
Visalia, CA 93277 FAX 209-730-3894

Don Mast, Associate Dean

A public two-year college with 94 special education students out of a total of 9289.

3715 Columbia College

P.O. Box 1849 209-533-5133
Columbia, CA 95310

Patricia Harrelson, LD Specialist

3716 Contra Costa College

2600 Mission Bell Drive 415-235-7800
San Pablo, CA 94806

Peggy Fleming, Learning Specialist

3717 Cosumnes River College

8401 Center Parkway 916-686-7275
Sacramento, CA 95823

Carol Rustigan, LD Director

A public two-year college with 85 special education students out of a total of 12039.

3718 Crafton Hills College

11711 Sand Canyon Road 714-794-2161
Yucaipa, CA 92399

Kristen Colvey, LD Specialist

A public two-year college with 50 special education students out of a total of 5738.

3719 Cuesta College

Learning Skills Services
P.O. Box 8106 805-546-3148
San Luis Obispo, CA 93403

Dr. Lynn Frady, Dis. Services

A public, two-year community college, offering instruction and services to students with learning disabilities since 1973. A comprehensive set of services and special classes are available. Contact the program for further information.

3720 Cypress College

9200 Valley View 714-826-2220
Cypress, CA 90630

Cindy Owens, LD Specialist

A public two-year college with 190 special education students out of a total of 14792.

3721 De Anza College

21250 Stevens Creek 408-996-4838
Cupertino, CA 95014

Karen Halliday, Director

A public two-year college with 300 special education students out of a total of 25200. There is a $120 fee for the special education program in addition to the regular tuition.

3722 Diablo Valley College

Plesant Hill, CA 94523

3723 East Los Angeles College

1301 Brooklyn Avenue 213-265-8787
Monterey Park, CA 91754

Marilyn Hutchens

A public two-year college with 44 special education students out of a total of 14587. There is a $60 fee for the special education program in addition to the regular tuition.

3724 El Camino College

16007 South Crenshaw Blvd. 213-715-3435
Torrance, CA 90506

Bill Hoanzel, LD Specialist

3725 Evergreen Valley College

3095 Yerba Buena Road 408-270-6447
San Jose, CA 95135

Bonnie Clark, LD Specialist

A public two-year college with 60 special education students out of a total of 11849.

3726 Feather River College

P.O. Box 1110   916-283-0202
Quincy, CA 95971

Maureen McPhee

3727 Foothill College

Student Tutorial Evaluation Program
12345 El Monte Road   415-949-7447
Los Altos Hills, CA 94022

Dr. Charlene Maltzman, Coordinator

3728 Fresno City College

1101 East University Avenue   209-442-4600
Fresno, CA 93741

Jeanette Imperatrice, LD Specialist

A public two-year college with 250 special education
students out of a total of 17941.

3729 Fullerton College

Learning Resource Services
321 East Chapman Avenue   714-992-7270
Fullerton, CA 92634

Thomas Cantrell

A public two-year college with 280 special education
students out of a total of 20736.

3730 Gavilan College

5055 Santa Teresa Blvd.   408-848-4871
Gilroy, CA 95020

Dr. Carol Cooper, Coordinator

3731 Golden Gate University

San Francisco, CA 94105   415-442-7000

Char Hamada, Dean

3732 Hartnell College

Learning Disability Services
156 Homestead   408-755-6760
Salinas, CA 93901

Deborah Shulman, Enabler

A public two-year college with 75 special education students out of a total of 7594.

3733 Humboldt State University

Arcata, CA 95521   707-826-4678

Theresa Jordan

A public two-year college with 193 special education
students out of a total of 6814.

3734 Imperial Valley College

P.O. Box 158   619-352-8320
Imperial, CA 92251

Norma Nava-Pinuleas, Instructional Spec.

A public two-year college with 40 special education students out of a total of 5226.

3735 Institute for the Redesign of Learning

1955 Fremont Avenue   213-257-3006
South Pasadena, CA 91030

Nancy Lavelle

A full day school serving 100 boys and girls, at-risk infants
and children and a Vocational Program serving adults and
includes Supported Employment Services and an
Indepdndent Living Program.

3736 Irvine Campus, University of California

105 Administration Bldg.   714-856-7494
Irvine, CA 92717

Dr. Ron Blosser, Director

3737 Irvine Valley College

5500 Irvine Center Drive   714-559-3243
Irvine, CA 92720

Julie Willard, LD Specialist

3738 Kings River Community College

995 North Reed Avenue   209-638-3641
Reedley, CA 93654

Lynn Mancini, Student Services

A public two-year college with 95 special education students out of a total of 5149.

3739 La Monte Academie

27801 La Paz Road   714-643-0313
Laguan Niguel, CA 92677

Sister Paula Jane Tupa

3740 Laney College

900 Fallon Street   510-464-3534
Oakland, CA 94607

Sondra Neiman, LD Specialist

A public two-year college with 55 special education students out of a total of 11800.

3741 Long Beach City College

1305 East Pacific Coast Highway   310-599-7926
Long Beach, CA 90806   FAX 310-599-7912

Mark Matsui, Dis. Student Service
Marvin Mastros, LD Specialist

A public two-year college with 52 special education students out of a total of 29465.

3742 Los Angeles City College

Learning Disabilities Program
855 North Vermont Avenue   213-953-4515
Los Angeles, CA 90029

Susan Matranga, LD Specialist

A public two-year college with 150 special education students out of a total of 17500.

3743 Los Angeles Mission College

13356 Eldridge Avenue   818-364-7732
Sylmar, CA 91342

Dr. Rick Scuderi, LD Specialist

A public two-year college with 103 special education students out of a total of 7272.

3744 Los Angeles Pierce College

6201 Winnetka Avenue   818-719-6430
Woodland Hills, CA 91371

David Phoenix

A public two-year college with 250 special education students out of a total of 19201.

3745 Los Angeles Valley College

Disabled Student Programs
5800 Fullerton Avenue   818-781-8542
Van Nuys, CA 91401

Kathleen Sullivan, Coordinator

A public two-year college with 100 special education students out of a total of 19838.

3746 Los Medanos College

2700 East Leland Road   510-439-2181
Pittsburg, CA 94565

Dorrie Fisher

A public two-year college with 175 special education students out of a total of 7779.

3747 Marin Community College

Disabled Students Program   415-485-9406
Kentfield, CA 94904

Marie Castoldi, Coordinator

3748 Master's College

Box 878   805-259-3082
Newhall, CA 91322

Donna Hall

An independent two-year college with 5 special education students out of a total of 850. There is a $1900 fee for the special education program in addition to the regular tuition of $11950.

3749 Merced College

3600 M Street   209-384-6155
Merced, CA 95340

Robert Lenz, Dir. Disabled Srvc.

A public two-year college with 92 special education students out of a total of 7835.

3750 Merritt College

Disabled Student Programs and Services
12500 Campus Drive   510-436-2579
Oakland, CA 94619

Mary McGrath, LD Specialist

A public two-year college with 75 special education students out of a total of 6683.

3751 Miracosta College

1 Barnard Drive   619-757-2121
Oceanside, CA 92056

Lorreta Bohl, Coordinator

A public two-year college with 75 special education students out of a total of 9137.

3752 Modesto Junior College

435 College Avenue   209-575-6225
Modesto, CA 95350

Bob Williams, Dirctor

A public two-year college with 190 special education students out of a total of 8164.

3753 Monterey Peninsula College

980 Fremont Avenue   408-646-4069
Monterey, CA 93940

Bill Jones, LD Coordinator

A public two-year college with 200 special education students out of a total of 8500.

3754 Moorpark College

7075 Campus Road   805-378-1461
Moorpark, CA 93021

Joanna Dillon

A public two-year college with 150 special education students out of a total of 12412.

3755　Mt. San Antonio College

Handicapped Student Services
1100 North Grand Avenue　　　　714-594-5611
Walnut, CA 91789

Mayne Thornton, Director

A public two-year college with 275 special education students out of a total of 23119.

3756　Mt. San Jacinto College

1499 North State Street　　　　909-654-8011
San Jacinto, CA 92583

Marcia Krull, LD Specialist

A public two-year college with 77 special education students out of a total of 6652.

3757　Napa Valley College

2277 Napa-Vallejo Hwy.　　　　707-253-3283
Napa, CA 94558

Dr. Gwynne Katz, LD Specialist

3758　Ohlone College

43600 Mission Blvd.　　　　415-659-6140
Fremont, CA 94539

Fred Hilke, Special Services

3759　Orange Coast College

2701 Fairview Road　　　　714-457-5042
Costa Mesa, CA 92628

Dr. Ken Ortiz, Associate Dean

A public two-year college with 350 special education students out of a total of 27960. There is a $3 fee for the special education program in addition to the regular tuition of $0.

3760　Oxnard College

4000 South Rose Avenue　　　　805-9865830
Oxnard, CA 93033

Carole Frick, LD Specialist
Offers disabled student services.

3761　Palomar College

1140 West Mission Avenue　　　　619-744-1150
San Marcos, CA 92069

Ronald Haines, Student Program

A public two-year college with 150 special education students out of a total of 23901.

3762　Pasadena City College

1570 East Colorado Blvd.　　　　818-585-7127
Pasadena, CA 91106

Dr. Emy Lu Weller

A public two-year college with 400 special education students out of a total of 24033.

3763　Porterville College

900 South Main　　　　209-781-3130
Porterville, CA 93257

Carol Wilkins, LD Specialist

A public two-year college with 80 special education students out of a total of 2754.

3764　Rancho Santiago College

1530 West 17th Street　　　　714-564-5250
Santa Ana, CA 92706

Mary Kobane, LD Specialist

A public two-year college with 318 special education students out of a total of 26379.

3765　Raskob Learning Institute & Day School

3520 Mountain Blvd.　　　　510-436-1275
Oakland, CA 94619

John M. Davis, PhD, Director

A non-profit, non-denominational services for children and adults with learning problems in the areas of reading, spelling, writing, language and mathematics. Diagnostic Evaluation, remedial instruction, full-time comprehensive educational program.

3766　San Diego City College

1313 12th Avenue　　　　619-230-2513
San Diego, CA 92101

Ken Mayer, Counselor

3767　San Diego Mesa College

7250 Mesa College Drive　　　　619-560-2780
San Diego, CA 92111

Glenyth Turner, LD Specialist

A public two-year college with 135 special education students out of a total of 27000.

3768　San Diego Miramar College

10440 Black Mountain Road　　　　619-536-7362
San Diego, CA 92126

Cindy Donahue, Advisor

A public two-year college with 39 special education students out of a total of 8438. Tuition: $3060.

3769　San Diego State University

Disabled Student Services　　　　619-265-6473
San Diego, CA 92182

Dr. Frank Siehien, Coordinator

A public four-year college with 670 special education students out of a total of 26134.

3770 San Francisco State University

1600 Holloway Avenue   415-338-2472
San Francisco, CA 94132

Molly Brodie, Director

A public four-year college with 250 special education students out of a total of 20516.

3771 San Jose City College

2100 Moorpark Avenue   408-298-2181
San Jose, CA 95128

Martha Glazer, LD Specialist

3772 Santa Ana College

17th At Bristol   714-835-3000
Santa Ana, CA 92706

Cheryl Dunn-Hoanzl

3773 Santa Barbara City College

721 Cliff Drive   805-965-0581
Santa Barbara, CA 93109   FAX 805-963-7222

Mary Lawson, LD Specialist
Gerry Lewin, LD Specialist

A public two-year college with 300 special education students out of a total of 11981.

3774 Santa Clara University

Disabled Student Resources   408-554-4109
Santa Clara, CA 95053   FAX 408-554-2700

Christine Remy, Assistant Director

An independent four-year college with 14 special education students out of a total of 3998. Tuition: $17706.

3775 Santa Monica College

1900 Pico Blvd.   310-452-9265
Santa Monica, CA 90405

Mary Weil, Counselor

A public two-year college with 300 special education students out of a total of 26360.

3776 Santa Rosa Junior College

1501 Mendocino Avenue   707-527-4278
Santa Rosa, CA 95401

Elizabeth Carlson, Department Chair

A public two-year college with 250 special education students out of a total of 28844.

3777 Shasta College

P.O. Box 6006   916-225-4710
Redding, CA 96049

Parker Pollock, Handicapped Director

A public two-year college with 103 special education students out of a total of 12820.

3778 Sierra College

5000 Rocklin Road   916-624-3333
Rocklin, CA 95677

Denise Stone, LD Specialist

A public two-year college with 350 special education students out of a total of 14490.

3779 Skyline College

Developmental Skills Program
3300 College Drive   415-738-4280
San Bruno, CA 94066

Linda Van Sciver, Coordinator

A public two-year college with 100 special education students out of a total of 9028.

3780 Solano Community College

4000 Suisun Valley Road   707-864-7000
Suisun City, CA 94585

Ruth Miller, LD Specialist

The LD Center offers eligibility assessment (students with average to above average intelligence with severe processing deficit(s), severe aptitude-achievement discrepancies), and instruction in strategies and interventions to help the student become more successful in regular college classes. Academic and personal counseling from Disabled Student Programs Counselors are available. Support services such as notetaking, extended test time and other modifications are available.

3781 Sonoma State University

Rohnert Park, CA 94928   707-664-2677

Bill Clopton, Special Services

A public four-year college with 140 special education students out of a total of 6098.

3782 Southwestern College

Diagnostic Learning Center
900 Otay Lakes Road   619-421-6700
Chula Vista, CA 92010

Diane Branman

A public two-year college with 90 special education students out of a total of 17080.

3783 Spraings Academy

89 Moraga Way   510-253-1906
Orinda, CA 94563

Violet Spraings, PhD, Director
Diane Emberlin, Asst. Director

A State of California Certified School for Students with learning disabilities, dyslexia, and other language disorders. The Diagnostic Center provides psychological, psycho-educational, speech & language, prevocational assessments as well as therapy and tutorial programs.

3784 Springall Academy

6550 Soledad Mountain Road 619-459-9047
La Jolla, CA 92037

3785 Stanford University

123 Meyer Library 415-723-1039
Stanford, CA 94305

Molly Sandperl, Special Services

An independent four-year college with 100 special education students out of a total of 6527. Tuition: $22849.

3786 Taft College

29 Emmons Park Drive 805-763-4282
Taft, CA 93268

Jeff Ross, Disabled Services

A public two-year college with 54 special education students out of a total of 954.

3787 Tuba College

Disabled Student Services
Room 1103, 2088 N. Beale Rd. 916-742-7351
Marysville, CA 95901

Helen David Shaw

3788 University of Califonria, Irvine

105 Administration Building 714-856-7151
Irvine, CA 02717

Dr. Ron Blosser, Special Services

3789 University of California At Berkeley

230 Golden Bear Center 510-642-0518
Berkeley, CA 94720

Ward Newmeyer, LD Director

A public four-year college with 300 special education students out of a total of 21660.

3790 University of California At San Francisco

Division of Behavioral & Developmental Pediatrics
Room A203, Box 0314 415-476-4575
San Francisco, CA 94143 FAX 415-476-2300

W. Thomas Boyce, M.D., Director
Lane Tanner, M.D., Assistant Director

The Division (formerly the Child Study Limit) is a multi-disciplinary program within the Deparmtnet of Pediatrics. It serves children and adolescents of all ages. A particular focus is the comprehensive evaluation - medical, psychological and psychosocial - of children with school and learning problems.

3791 University of California, Davis

Davis, CA 95616 916-752-3184

Christine O'Dell, Special Services

3792 University of California, Los Angeles

A-255 Murphy Hall, 405 Hilgard 310-825-1501
Los Angeles, CA 90024

Dr. Arline Halper, Special Services

A public four-year college with 56 special education students out of a total of 24368.

3793 University of California - Pernaid - L.A.

405 Hilgard Avenue 213-825-2140
Los Angeles, CA 90024

Linda Taylor

3794 University of California, Riverside

900 University Avenue 714-787-4538
Riverside, CA 92521

Marcia Theise Schiffer, Special Services

A public four-year college with 14 special education students out of a total of 7310.

3795 University of California, San Diego

Office for Students with Disabilities
9500 Gilman Drive 619-534-4382
La Jolla, CA 92093 FAX 619-534-4650

Roberta Gimblett, Director/Office Dis.

A public four-year college with 60 special education students out of a total of 14529.

3796 University of California, Santa Barbara

Santa Barbara, CA 93106 805-893-8897

Michele Bass, Special Services

A public four-year college with 85 special education students out of a total of 16176. Tuition: $2980.

3797 University of California, Santa Cruz

140 Hahn 408-429-2089
Santa Cruz, CA 95064

Sharyn Martin, Special Services

A public four-year college with 88 special education students out of a total of 9161.

3798 University of Redlands

P.O. Box 3080   714-793-2121
Redlands, CA 92373

Judy Strack, Special Services

3799 University of San Diego

Alcala Park   619-260-4655
San Diego, CA 92110

Dr. Tyler Gabriel, Academic Counseling
An independent four-year college with 25 special education students out of a total of 3901. Tuition: $17530.

3800 University of Southern California

University Park   213-740-0776
Los Angeles, CA 90089

Dr. Janet Eddy
An independent four-year college with 117 special education students out of a total of 14668. Tuition: $22280.

3801 University of the Pacific

Academic Skills Center
Learning Disability Support   209-946-3219
Stockton, CA 95207

Howard Houck, Coordinator

3802 Ventura College

4667 Telegraph Road   805-654-6300
Ventura, CA 93003

Dr. Jeff Barsch, LD Director
A public two-year college with 421 special education students out of a total of 12158.

3803 Victor Valley College

18422 Bear Valley Road   619-245-4271
Victorville, CA 92392

Susan Tillman, LD Specialist

3804 West Hills College

300 Cherry Lane   209-935-0801
Coalinga, CA 93210

Tom Winters
A public two-year college with 60 special education students out of a total of 3500.

3805 West Los Angeles College

4800 Freshmen Drive   310-287-4423
Culver City, CA 90230

Frances Israel
A public two-year college with 100 special education students out of a total of 8958.

3806 West Valley College

14000 Fruitvale Avenue   408-867-2200
Saratoga, CA 95070

Susan Bunch, LD Specialist
A public two-year college with 200 special education students out of a total of 1424.

Colorado

3807 Alms Community College

P.O. Box 69
Greeley, CO 80631

Donna Wright, LD Center

3808 Arapahoe Community College

5900 South Santa Fe Drive   303-797-5651
Littleton, CO 80160

Dr. Alex Labak

3809 Colorado Mountain College

Central Admissions Office
Box 10001DT   800-621-8559
Glenwood Springs, CO 81602

3810 Colorado Northwestern Community College

Box 21   303-675-3244
Rangley, CO 81648

Mark Mascarenas, LD Director
A public two-year college with 5 special education students out of a total of 505.

3811 Colorado State University

116 Student Services Building   303-491-6385
Ft. Collins, CO 80524   FAX 303-491-5010

P.J. McGuire, Counselor/Coord.
Rosemary Kreston, Director
A public four-year college with 239 special education students out of a total of 17460. Tuition: $1982.

3812 Community College of Aurora

16000 East Centre Tech Pkwy. A-102   303-360-4790
Aurora, CO 80011

Theresa Campbell

3813 Community College of Denver

Special Learning Support Programs
Campus Box 600, P.O. Box 173363   303-556-3406
Denver, CO 80217   FAX 303-556-8555

Dr. Gary Macdonald, Coordinator

A public two-year college with 100 special education students out of a total of 6000. There is a $4950 fee for the special education program in addition to the regular tuition of $1485.

3814　Denver Academy

1101 South Race Street　　　303-777-5870
Denver, CO　80210

Paul Knott

3815　Fort Lewis College

Durango, CO　81301　　　303-247-7459

Tim Slane, Disabled Student Dir
Coordinate services at Fort Lewis for those stduents with disabilities, acts a liaison between students and faculty programs.　Advises and directs those students to the appropriate services and academic advisors.

3816　Front Range Community College Progressive Learning

3645 West 112th Avenue　　　303-466-8811
Westminster, CO　80030

Karol Janice Bennett, Education Assistant
Karen Hossack, Faculty
A public two-year college with 55 special education students out of a total of 10477. There is a $900 fee for the special education program in addition to the regular tuition of $1032.

3817　Lamar Community College

2401 South Main　　　719-336-2248
Lamar, CO　81052

Cynthia Baer, Director

3818　Morgan Community College

17800 Road 20　　　303-867-3081
Fort Morgan, CO　80701

Maxine Weimer, Developmental Ed.
A public two-year college with 1 special education students out of a total of 887. Tuition: $1190.

3819　Northeastern Junior College

100 College Drive　　　303-522-6600
Sterling, CO　80751

Nancy Mann, Special Services
A public two-year college with 35 special education students out of a total of 2040.

3820　Pikes Peak Community College

5675 South Academy Blvd.　　　719-540-7128
Colorado Springs, CO　80906

William Flynn, Coordinator
A public two-year college with 100 special education students out of a total of 6517. Tuition: $1032.

3821　Pueblo Community College

900 West Orman Avenue　　　719-549-3228
Pueblo, CO　81004

Bob Van Alstyne

3822　Red Rocks Community College

13300 West 6th Avenue　　　303-988-6160
Lakewood, CO　80401

Theona Hammond-Harns, Special Services
A public two-year college with 30 special education students out of a total of 6300. Tuition: $1032.

3823　Regis College

West 50th And Lowell Blvd.　　　303-458-4146
Denver, CO　80221

An independent four-year college with 60 special education students out of a total of 1125. Tuition: $16470.

3824　Trinidad State Junior College

600 Prospect　　　719-846-5557
Trinidad, CO　81082

John Giron, Special Services

3825　University of Colorado At Boulder

Campus Box 107　　　303-492-8671
Boulder, CO　80309

Terri Bodhaine
A public four-year college with 225 special education students out of a total of 20495. There is a $150 fee for the special education program in addition to the regular tuition of $2080.

3826　University of Colorado At Colorado Springs

Library 131, 1420 Austin Bluffs Pk.　　　719-593-3650
Colorado Springs, CO　80933

Merril Boruchin, LD Coordinator
A public four-year college with 70 special education students out of a total of 333. Tuition: $1770.

3827　University of Denver

Special Services
1870 South High Street　　　303-871-2000
Denver, CO　80208

Lisa Switzer, Director
An independent four-year college with 79 special education students out of a total of 2778. There is a $1200 fee for the special education program in addition to the regular tuition of $18026.

3828 University of Northern Colorado

Office of Resource for the Disabled
Candelaria Hall 232   303-351-2289
Greeley, CO 80639

Dr. James Bowen

3829 University of Southern Colorado

2200 Bonforte Blvd.   719-549-2581
Pueblo, CO 81001

Sam Clay, Special Services

A public four-year college with 5 special education students out of a total of 3960. Tuition: $1428.

3830 Western State Collge of Colorado

Gunnison, CO 81230   303-943-2130

Jill Martinez, Advisor

A public four-year college with 58 special education students out of a total of 2450. Tuition: $1206.

Connecticut

3831 Albertus Magnus College

Director of the Academic Development Center
700 Prospect Street   203-773-8590
New Haven, CT 06511

Antonia Lewandowski

3832 Asnuntuck Community Technical College

170 Elm Street   203-253-3164
Enfield, CT 06082

Hassan Babatunji, Learning Lab Coord.

The Learning Lab is offered to students with learning disabilities.

3833 Ben Bronz Academy

139 North Main Street   203-236-5807
West Hartford, CT 06107

Aileen Stan-Spence, Director

Day program for the learning disabled focusing on developing independent learning strategies through metacognitive and metalinguistic processes.

3834 Briarwood College

2279 Mt. Vernon Rd   203-628-4751
Southington, CT 06489

Barbara Mackay, Dean Of Students

An independent two-year college with 16 special education students out of a total of 288. Tuition: $8300.

3835 Central Connecticut State University

1615 Stanley Street, Willard Hall   203-827-7651
New Britain, CT 06050

George Tenney, Director

3836 Connecticut College

Director Of The Writing Center   203-447-1911
New London, CT 06375

Theresa Ammirati, LD Coordinator

3837 Connecticut College Program for Children with Special Needs

Box 5574   203-447-7545
New London, CT 06320

Margaret Sheridan, Director

A preschool program for special needs children. This program is in session from early September to June for a 4-week summer session.

3838 Eastern Connecticut State Unviersity

83 Windham Street   203-456-5448
Willimantic, CT 06226

Shirley Doiron, Counselor

A public four-year college with 24 special education students out of a total of 4071. Tuition: $1518.

3839 Fairfield University

North Benson Road   203-254-4000
Fairfield, CT 06430

Rv. Lawrence O'Neil, Dean Of Students

3840 Greater Hartford Community College

61 Woodland Street   203-520-7817
Hartford, CT 06105

Virginia Foley-Psillas

3841 Greater New Haven State Technical College

88 Bassett Road   203-234-3340
North Haven, CT 06473

Richard Muniz, Dean Of Students

A public two-year college with 7 special education students out of a total of 850. Tuition: $1368.

3842 Hartford College for Women

1265 Asylum Avenue   203-236-1215
Hartford, CT 06105

Louise Loomis

3843 Hartford State Technical College

401 Flatbush Avenue   203-527-4111
Hartford, CT 06106

Joseph Mandell, Dean Of Students

3844 Housatonic Community College

Learning Disabilities Services   203-579-6427
Bridgeport, CT 06608

Natalie Bieber, Director
A public two-year college with 82 special education students out of a total of 2383. Tuition: $1128.

3845 Manchester Community College

60 Bidwell Street   203-647-6113
Manchester, CT 06040

Dr. Mary White-Edger, LD Director
A public two-year college with 67 special education students out of a total of 6134. Tuition: $1276.

3846 Mattatuck Community College

Chase Parkway   203-575-8052
Waterbury, CT 06708

Dr. Carolyn Curtiss, Coordinator
A public two-year college with 85 special education students out of a total of 4270. Tuition: $1276.

3847 Mitchell College - Learning Resource Center

Learning Resource Center
437 Pequot Avenue   203-443-2811
New London, CT 06320   800-223-2769

Susan L. Duques, PhD, Director, LRC
An independent two-year college with 52 special education students out of a total of 525. There is a $3400 fee for the special education program in addition to the regular tuition of $15396.

3848 Mount Saint John

135 Kirtland Street   203-526-5391
Deep River, CT 06417

Rev. K.F. Macdonald, Director
This special education program offers individualized and small group instruction for boys who are socially/emotionally disabled and/or learning disabled.

3849 Northwestern Connecticut Community College

Park Place   203-379-8543
Winsted, CT 06098

Beverly Chrzan Banks, Educational Support

3850 Norwalk Community College

188 Richards Avenue   203-857-7192
Norwalk, CT 06854

Dr. Stephen Spillane, LD Specialist
A public two-year college with 53 special education students out of a total of 3866. Tuition: $984.

3851 Norwalk State Technical College

181 Richards Avenue   203-855-6638
Norwalk, CT 06854

Joseph Karpowich, Dean Of Students

3852 Paier College of Art

60 Prospect Court   203-776-5622
Hamden, CT 06511

Sante Graziani, Academic Dean

3853 Post College

800 Country Club Road   203-755-0121
Waterbury, CT 06708

Eleanor Gersman, Admissions Director

3854 Quinebaug Valley Community College

742 Upper Maple Street   203-774-1160
Danielson, CT 06239

Gary Hottinger, Director LD Center
Pam Abel, Learning Specialist
The Learning Assistance Center provides academic support for students with disabilities. Such support may include untimed tests, readers, proctors, note-takers, tape recorders and so on. There is a Peer Advocate for Students with Disabilities to assist disabled students; therre is also a Learning Specialist available ten hours a week to counsel and tutor disabled students.

3855 Quinnipiac College

555 New Road   203-281-8722
Hamden, CT 06518

Donald Blumenthal, Counseling Director

3856 Sacred Heart University

Bridgeport, CT 06606   203-371-7880

Louise Summa, Special Services

3857 South Central Community College

60 Sargent Drive 203-789-6928
New Haven, CT 06511

Roxann Riskin, LD Specilist

3858 Southern Connecticut State University

501 Crescent Street 203-397-4362
New Haven, CT 06515

Deborah Fairchild, Disability Director
A public four-year college with 400 special education students out of a total of 9201. Tuition: $2570.

3859 St. Joseph College

1678 Asylum Avenue 203-232-4572
West Hartford, CT 06117

Judy Arzt, Director

3860 Thames Valley Campus of Three Rivers Community Technical College

574 New London Turnpike 203-886-0177
Norwich, CT 06360

Dr. Linda Jacobsen, Dir. Of Research
Margaret Stroup, Technical Admissions
Offers Associate degrees in computers, industrial management and engineering technologies (chemical, civil, electrical, general, manufacturing, mechanical and nuclear) and one-year cerificates in Industrial Electronics, architectural and industrial/CADD drafting and data processing.

3861 Trinity College

300 Summit Street 203-297-2000
Hartford, CT 06106

Kirk Peters, Dean Of Student

3862 Tunxis Community College

Routes 6 & 177 203-677-7701
Farmington, CT 06032

Dr. David Smith, LD Director

3863 University of Bridgeport

380 University Avenue 203-576-4000
Bridgeport, CT 06602

Janet Shepro, Director

3864 University of Connecticut

249 Glenbrook Road 203-486-0178
Storrs, CT 06269

Dr. Joan McGuire, LD Director

A public four-year college with 90 special education students out of a total of 12621. Tuition: $3160.

3865 University of Hartford

Auerbach Hall 213 203-243-4312
West Hartford, CT 06117

Helen Apthorp, Coordintor

3866 University of New Haven

300 Orange Avenue 203-932-7409
West Haven, CT 06516

David Kmetz, LD Director
An independent four-year college with 49 special education students out of a total of 3399. Tuition: $14314.

3867 Waterbury State Technical College

750 Chase Parkway 203-575-8081
Waterbury, CT 06479

Dorothy Pierson-Hubeny, Dean Of Students

3868 Wesleyan University

Middletown, CT 06457 203-344-7950

Denise Darrigrand, Dean Of Student Life

3869 Western Connecticut State University

181 White Street 203-797-4392
Danbury, CT 06810

H. Richard Dozier, Dean Of Students

3870 Yale University

80 Wall Street 203-432-2324
New Haven, CT 06520

Dr. Rita Brackman, LD Director

Delaware

3871 Brandywine College of Widener University

P.O. Box 7139 302-478-3000
Wilimington, DE 19803

Linda Baum, Program Coordinator

3872 Delaware Technical and Community College, Terry Campus

1832 North DuPont Parkway 302-736-5390
Dover, DE 19901

Wilma Mishoe Sudler, Student Support

3873 University of Delware

Department of Educational Studies
Newark, DE 19716   302-831-2325

3874 American University

Learning Services Program
4400 Massachusetts Avenue NW   202-885-2161
Washington, DC 20016

Helen Steinberg, Coordinator

An independent four-year college with 130 special education students out of a total of 5120. There is a $1000 fee for the special education program in addition to the regular tuition of $20566.

3875 George Washington University

Rice Hall 401   202-994-8250
Washington, DC 20052

Christy Willis, Coordinator

An independent four-year college with 79 special education students out of a total of 6285. Tuition: $22395.

3876 Howard University

Room 211, M.W. Johnson Bldg.   202-636-7506
Washington, DC 20059

Vincent Johns, Dean

3877 Southeastern University

501 I Street SW   202-488-8162
Washington, DC 20024   FAX 202-488-8093

James Kutz

An independent four-year college with 55 special education students out of a total of 445. Tuition: $5688.

3878 University of the District of Columbia

4200 Connecticut Avenue NW   202-364-6037
Washington, DC 20008

Henry Wilcox, Coordinator

Florida

3879 Beacon College

105 East Main Street   904-787-7660
Leesburg, FL 34748   FAX 904-787-0721

Leilani Crafts, Admissions

A unique four year college for students with learning disabilities offering field placement programs, students services and interdisciplinary academics.

3880 Brevard Community College

1519 Clear Lake Road   407-632-1111
Cocoa, FL 32922

Brenda Fettrow

A public two-year college with 175 special education students out of a total of 15033. Tuition: $960.

3881 Broward Community College

3501 SW Davis Road   305-475-6528
Fort Lauderdale, FL 33314

3882 Central Florida Community College

P.O. Box 1388   904-237-2111
Ocala, FL 32678

Chuck Corcoran

A public two-year college with 19 special education students out of a total of 5616. Tuition: $937.

3883 Chipola Junior College

3094 Indian Circle   904-526-2761
Marianna, FL 32446

Wanda Haynie, Dean Of Students

A public two-year college with 7 special education students out of a total of 2883. Tuition: $680.

3884 Eckerd College

St. Petersburg, FL 33733   813-867-1166

Patricia Bowman

3885 Edison Community College

College Parkway SW   813-489-9274
Fort Myers, FL 33906

Andrea Anderson

3886 Embry-Riddle Aeronautical University

600 Clyde Morris Blvd.   904-226-6036
Daytona Beach, FL 32114

Maureen Bridger, Director

An independent four-year college with 17 special education students out of a total of 4672. Tuition: $10010.

3887 Florida A&M University/ Learning Development and Evaluation Center

555 Orr Drive, FAMU Campus   904-599-3180
Tallahassee, FL 32307   FAX 904-561-2513

Dr. Sharon Wooten, Director, LDEC

A public four-year college with 56 special education students out of a total of 8264. There is a $600 fee for the special education program in addition to the regular tuition of $1545.

3888 Florida Atlantic University

P.O. Box 3091   305-393-3880
Boca Raton, FL 33431

Dee Davis, Coordinator

3889 Florida Community College At Jacksonville

501 West State Street   904-766-6769
Jacksonville, FL 32218

Lucretia Childers, Disabled Student

A public two-year college with 71 special education students out of a total of 19866. Tuition: $900.

3890 Florida International Unviersity

University House 340, University Pk   305-348-3532
Miami, FL 33199

Jennifer King, Coordinator

A public four-year college with 118 special education students out of a total of 19095. Tuition: $1404.

3891 Florida State University

303 Bryan Hall   904-644-1741
Tallahassee, FL 32306

Dr. Robin Leach, Director

A public four-year college with 140 special education students out of a total of 21300. Tuition: $1492.

3892 Gulf Coast Community College

5230 West Highway 98   904-872-3834
Panama City, FL 32401

Linda Van Dalen, Coorindator

A public two-year college with 61 special education students out of a total of 7375. Tuition: $787.

3893 Indian River Community College

3209 Virginia Avenue   407-462-4328
Fort Pierce, FL 34981

Rhoda Brant, Counselor

Two-year community college providing services for learning disabled students (i.e., unlimited tests, notetakers, etc.).

3894 Jacksonville University

Jacksonville, FL 32211   904-744-3950

Nick Speckman

3895 Lake City Community College

Box 7, Route 3   904-752-1822
Lake City, FL 32055

Ronald Johnsrud, Director

A public two-year college with 28 special education students out of a total of 2551. Tuition: $840.

3896 Lynn University

3601 North Military Trail   407-994-0770
Boca Raton, FL 33431

Marsha Glines

An independent two-year college with 28 special education students out of a total of 860. There is a $900 fee for the special education program in addition to the regular tuition of $16900.

3897 Manatee Community College

5840 26th Street West   813-755-1511
Bradenton, FL 34207

Paul Nolting, Director

3898 Matlock Academy

2491 Homewood Road   407-687-0327
West Palm Beach, FL 33415

Daphne Grad, President

Designs its program to meet the specific needs of the student who underacheives, seeks to fulfill their needs through a comprehensive student centered philosophy and offers a very successful educational program.

3899 Miami-Dade Community College

11380 Northwest 27th Avenue   305-347-1276
Miami, FL 33132

Dianne Rossman, Coordinator

A public two-year college with 300 special education students out of a total of 30000. Tuition: $919.

3900 Oklaoosa-Walton Community College

100 College Blvd.   904-729-5372
Niceville, FL 32578

Ann James, Student Services

3901 Oklaoosa-Walton Junior College

Niceville, FL 32578   904-678-5111

Inez Bailey, Special Services

3902 Palm Beach Atlantic College

P.O. Box 24708   407-650-7611
West Palm Beach, FL 33416

Mary Ann Taylor-Hardwell, Special Services

3903 Pensacola Junior College

1000 College Blvd.   904-484-2094
Pensacola, FL 32504

Linda Sheppard, Special Services

3904 Pine Bayou Academy

6533 9th Avenue North   813-345-7592
St. Petersburg, FL 33710

Ronald Cirksena

3905 Polk Community College

999 Avenue H NE   813-297-1041
Winter Haven, FL 33881

James Dowdy, Special Services

3906 Santa Fe Community College

3000 NW 83rd Street   904-395-5836
Gainesville, FL 32602

Dr. Al Block, Special Services

A public two-year college with 60 special education students out of a total of 11728. Tuition: $928.

3907 Seminole Community College

Sanford, FL 32773   407-323-1450

Dorothy Paishon, Special Services

3908 Southeastern College of the Assemblies of God

1000 Longfellow Blvd.   813-665-4404
Lakeland, FL 33801

Gary Yost, Director

3909 St. Johns River Community College

5001 St. Johns Avenue   904-328-1571
Palatka, FL 32177

Annette Jones, Special Services

A public two-year college with 2 special education students out of a total of 3344. Tuition: $800.

3910 St. Petersburg Junior College

2465 Drew Street   813-791-2710
Clearwater, FL 34619

Dr. Susan Blacnchard, LD Specialist

A public two-year college with 125 special education students out of a total of 19271. Tuition: $798.

3911 Tallahassee Community College

444 Appleyard Drive   904-922-8138
Tallahassee, FL 32304

Margaret Rivenbark, Educational Services

A public two-year college with 320 special education students out of a total of 10400. Tuition: $744.

3912 Tampa Bay Academy

12012 Boyette Road   813-677-6700
Riverview, FL 33569

Malcolm Harriman

3913 University of Central Florida

Orlando, FL 32816   305-275-2511

Louise Friderchi

3914 University of Florida

10205 Peabody Hall   904-392-1261
Gainesville, FL 32611

Kenneth Oldsfield, Special Services

A public four-year college with 92 special education students out of a total of 26860. Tuition: $1475.

3915 University of Miami

5513 Merrick Drive   305-284-5927
Coral Gables, FL 33124

3916 University of North Florida

Jacksonville, FL 32216   904-646-2766

Gary Albritton, Special Services

3917 University of Tampa

401 W. Kennedy Blvd.   813-253-3333
Tampa, FL 33606

Dr. Helene Silverman, Special Services

An independent four-year college with 5 special education students out of a total of 2177. Tuition: $15922.

3918 University of West Florida

11000 University Parkway   904-474-2387
Pensacola, FL 32514

Barbara Fitzpatrick, Special Services

A public four-year college with 4 special education students out of a total of 6784. Tuition: $1463.

3919 Valencia Community College

710 North Econlockhatchee Trail   305-299-5000
Orlando, FL 32802

Walter Johnson, Special Services

A public two-year college with 85 special education students out of a total of 20816. Tuition: $908.

3920   Webber College

P.O. Box 96
Babson Park, FL 33827

Dr. Deborah Milliken, Student Development

An independent four-year college with 35 special education students out of a total of 347. Tuition: $8120.

3921   Woodland Hall Academy - Dyslexia Research Institute

4745 Centreville Road   904-893-2216
Tallahassee, FL 32308

Patricia Hardman

Georgia

3922   Andrew College

413 College Street   912-732-2171
Cuthbert, GA 31740

Carol Trieble

3923   Berry College

Mount Berry Station   404-236-2259
Rome, GA 30149

Dr. Marshall Jenkins, Director

3924   Brenau University

Learning Disability Program
1 Centennial Circle
Gainesville, GA 30501   404-534-6134

Dr. Vince Yamilkoski, Dir. Learning Center
Dr. John Upchurch, Admissions Director

The Brenau Learning Center is a program for students with a diagnosed learning disability and who have average to above average intellectual potential. The program is designed to provide support services for learning disabled students as they attend regular college courses. This program offers a more structured learning environment, as well as the freedom associated with college living.

3925   Brewton-Parker College

Highway 280, Box 144   912-583-2241
Mt. Vernon, GA 30445

Mitch McClure, Director

An independent four-year college with 5 special education students out of a total of 1942. Tuition: $6075.

3926   Chatham Academy, Inc.

6412 Waters Avenue   912-355-0583
Savannah, GA 31406

Carolyn Hannaford

3927   Clayton State College

P.O. Box 285   404-961-3515
Morrow, GA 30260

Michelle Settle

A public four-year college with 30 special education students out of a total of 4551. Tuition: $1290.

3928   Columbus College

Columbus, GA 31993   404-568-2196

Dr. Joseph Petite, Developmental Study

3929   Devry Institute of Technology

250 North Arcadia   404-292-7900
Decatur, GA 30030

Andrea Rutherford, Academic Support

3930   East Georgia College

Swainsboro, GA 30401   912-237-7831

Bennie Brinson, Student Services

3931   Emory University

Atlanta, GA 30322   404-727-3300

Lelia Crawford, Asst. Dean Campus

An independent four-year college with 19 special education students out of a total of 4974. Tuition: $20612.

3932   Gables Academy

1337 Fairview Road NE   404-377-1721
Atlanta, GA 30306

Ajmes Meffen

3933   Georgia College

Milledgeville, GA 31061   912-453-4027

Dr. Helen Hill, Student Support

3934   Georgia Institute of Technology

Room 221, Student Services   404-894-2564
Atlanta, GA 30332

RoseMary Watkins

A public four-year college with 8 special education students out of a total of 9487. Tuition: $1722.

3935   Georgia Southern College

Landrum Box 8024   912-681-5541
Statesboro, GA 30460

Regina Blok, Director

3936   Georgia State University

University Plaza   404-651-1487
Atlanta, GA   30303   FAX 404-651-1404

Dr. Carole Pearson
A public four-year college with 46 special education
students out of a total of 16925. Tuition: $1778.

3937   Mercer University

Macon, GA   31207   912-744-2778

Linda Conrads, Coordinator

3938   Mercer University, Atlanta

Teaching Learning Center   404-451-0331
Atlanta, GA   30341

Dorothy Roberts, Director

3939   Mill Springs Academy

Special Education Systems
6955 Brandon Mill Road   404-255-5951
Atlanta, GA   30328   FAX 404-255-5938

Tweetie L. Moore, Executive Director
Robert Moore, Administrator

A small, structured, accredited day school combining
learning disability teaching techniques within the therapeutic milieu. Integral components include supportive
services for parents and consistent communication with
other professionals working with our students. The K-12
program includes an after school program for younger
stduents and an athletic program for older students. mark
trail Camp is a 7 week summer program for K-7th grades
which includes academics and camp activities.

3940   Piedmont College

P.O. Box 626   404-778-4144
Demorest, GA   30535

Nancy Adams, Special Services

3941   Reinhardt College

P.O. Box 128   404-479-1454
Waleska, GA   30183

Sylvia Robertson, Academic Support

An independent two-year college with 45 special education students out of a total of 600. There is a $1200 fee for
the special education program in addition to the regular
tuition of $7515.

3942   Shorter College

315 Shorter Avenue   706-291-2121
Rome, GA   30165

Dr. Margaret Davis

3943   South Georgia College

Douglas, GA   31533   912-383-4276

Tommaline Key, Special Services

3944   Southern College of Technology

112 Clay Street   404-424-7226
Marietta, GA   30060

Dr. Patricia Soper, Special Services

3945   University of Georgia

Handicapped Student Services
537 Aderhold   706-542-4589
Athens, GA   30602

Vicki Martin, Coodinator

A public four-year college with 121 special education
students out of a total of 22385. There is a $900 fee for the
special education program in addition to the regular
tuition of $1791.

3946   Valdosta State College

Valdosta, GA   31698   912-245-2498

Marsha Reed, Special Services

A public four-year college with 70 special education
students out of a total of 6254. Tuition: $108.

3947   West Georgia College

137 Mandeville Hall   404-836-6428
Carrollton, GA   30118

Dr. Ann Phillips, Special Services

A public four-year college with 32 special education
students out of a total of 5521. Tuition: $1704.

Hawaii

3948   Brigham Young University - Hawaii

Oahu, HI   96762   808-293-3519

3949   University of Hawaii At Manoa

244 Dole Street   808-948-7511
Honolulu, HI   96822

Ann C. Ito, Special Services

A public four-year college with 36 special education
students out of a total of 13025. Tuition: $1340.

3950   University of Hawaii - Honolulu Community College

874 Dillingham Blvd.   808-845-9228
Honolulu, HI   96817

Rosa Wong, Special Services

3951 University of Hawaii - Kapiolani Community College

4303 Diamond Head Road   808-734-9552
Honolulu, HI 96816

Mary Joan Haverly, Special Services

A public two-year college with 18 special education students out of a total of 6526. Tuition: $456.

3952 University of Hawaii - Kauai Community College

3-1901 Kaumuali Highway   808-245-8261
Lihue, HI 96766

Frances Dinnan, Special Services

3953 University of Hawaii - Leeward Community College

Program for Adult Achievement
96-045 Ala Ike   808-455-0421
Pearl City, HI 96782

C. Lynne Douglas

A public two-year college with 150 special education students out of a total of 6342. Tuition: $440.

3954 University of Hawaii - Maui Community College

310 Kaahumanu Avenue   808-242-1241
Kahului, HI 96732

G. Robert Converse, Director

A public two-year college with 5 special education students out of a total of 2589. Tuition: $440.

Idaho

3955 Boise State Unviersity

1910 University Drive   208-385-1583
Boise, ID 83725

Roger Gossi

A public four-year college with 34 special education students out of a total of 12810.

3956 College of Southern Idaho

P.O. Box 1238   208-733-9554
Twin Falls, ID 83301

Jim Palmer

3957 North Idaho College

Coeur d'Alene, ID 83814   208-769-3392

Kristine Wold, Special Services

3958 University of Idaho

Room 302, Phinney Hall   208-885-6746
Moscow, ID 83843

Meredyth Goodwin, Special Services

A public four-year college with 47 special education students out of a total of 7368.

Illinois

3959 Aurora University

347 South Gladstone   312-844-5520
Aurora, IL 60506

Maureen Connolly, Director

An independent four-year college with 14 special education students out of a total of 1616. Tuition: $12680.

3960 Barat College

Learning Opportunities Program
700 Westleigh   312-234-3000
Lake Forest, IL 60045

Dr. Pamela Adelman, Learning Opp. Dir.

An independent four-year college with 46 special education students out of a total of 719. There is a $1000 fee for the special education program in addition to the regular tuition of $13140.

3961 Belleville Area College

2500 Carlyle Road   618-235-2700
Belleville, IL 62221

Patricia Brian, Director

3962 Blackburn College

700 College Avenue   217-854-3231
Carlinville, IL 62626

Patricia Kowal, Directyor

3963 Brehm Preparatory School

1245 East Grand Avenue   618-457-0371
Carbondale, IL 62901

Richard Collins, Executive Director

A private boarding school for learning disabled students providing a comprehensive range of services, which include: instruction in core academic areas; remedial services and compensatory strategies for skill deficit areas; social skills development and more.

3964 Chicago State University

Office of Student Development, Adm. 303
9500 King Drive   312-995-2015
Chicago, IL 60628   FAX 312-995-4456

Dr. Sandra Westbrooks, Assist Provost
Bridget L. Mason, Research Assistant

The Office of Student Development has just implemented a Student Support Services Program for the Disabled Students on the campus. Seeking to meet the needs and concerns of the Disabled. Services, sources and suggestions are welcomed.

3965 College of DuPage

22nd Street & Lambert 312-858-2800
Glen Ellyn, IL 60136

Mary Van DeWarker

3966 Danville Area Commuity College

2000 East Main Street 217-443-8853
Danville, IL 61832

Karen Davis, Special Pop. Program

3967 Depaul University - PLUS

Productive Learning Strategies
2323 North Seminary 312-362-6897
Chicago, IL 60614

Karen L. Wold, Director

An independent four-year college with 48 special education students out of a total of 9757. There is a $1200 fee for the special education program in addition to the regular tuition of $14179.

3968 Elgin Community College

1700 Spartan Drive 708-697-1000
Elgin, IL 60123

Annabelle Rhoades, Director Of LD

3969 Governors State University

University Park, IL 60466 312-534-5000

Peggy Woodard, Coordinator

Provides assistance to GSU students with learning disabilities. Assistance includes coordination of untimed tests, notetakers, test readers, computerized testing and other assistance that will allow students equal access to the learning environment.

3970 Highland Community College

2998 West Pearl City Road 815-235-6121
Freeport, IL 61032

Sue Wilson, Director

A public two-year college with 20 special education students out of a total of 3258. Tuition: $900.

3971 Illinois Central College

1 College Drive 309-694-5131
East Peoria, IL 61635

Denise Cioni, Special Needs

A public two-year college with 65 special education students out of a total of 13930. Tuition: $1100.

3972 Illinois Eastern Community College/Lincoln Trail College

Route 3 618-544-8657
Robinson, IL 62454

Searoba Mascher, Learning Skills

A public two-year college with 4 special education students out of a total of 1040. Tuition: $768.

3973 Illinois Eastern Community College/Olney Central College

Olney, IL 62450 618-395-4351

Teresa Tagler, Learning Skills

3974 Illinois Eastern Community Colleges, Frontier Community College

Fairfield, IL 62837 618-842-3711

Beverly Fisher

3975 Illinois Eastern Community College/Wabash Valley College

Mount Carmel, IL 62863 618-262-8641

Marj Doty, Learning Skills

3976 Illinois State University

324 Fairchild 309-438-5853
Normal, IL 61761

Toni McCarty, Executive Director
Donella Hess-Grabill, Co-Director

A public two-year college with 110 special education students out of a total of 22361. Tuition: $1800.

3977 Illinois Technical College

33 East Congress Parkway 312-922-9000
Chicago, IL 60605

Dr. Aminul Karim, Education Dean

3978 John A. Logan College

Carterville, IL 62918 618-985-3741

Dr. Dollean York, Director

A public two-year college with 40 special education students out of a total of 4635. Tuition: $713.

3979 John Wood Community College

150 South 48th Street 217-224-6500
Quincy, IL 62301

Sandra Hutton Thomas, Director

A public two-year college with 220 special education students out of a total of 4005. Tuition: $1120.

3980 Joliet Junior College

1216 Hubolt Avenue 815-729-9020
Joliet, IL 60436

Jeanne Legan, Special Needs

3981 Joseph Academy, Inc.

8257 Harrison 708-966-1080
Miles, IL 60648

Michael Schack, Executive Director
Co-educational private therapeutic day school.

3982 Kaskaskia College

27210 College Road 618-532-1981
Centralia, IL 62801

Lisa Oelze, SNAP Coordinator

3983 Kendall College

2408 Orrington 312-866-1305
Evanston, IL 60201

Peter Pauletti, Admissions
An independent four-year college with 55 special education students out of a total of 390. Tuition: $12024.

3984 Kishwaukee College

Malta, IL 60150 818-825-2086

Frances Loubere, Coordinator
Community college services for students with special needs. Students will be counseled and appropriate accommodations made on an individual basis.

3985 Knox College

Box 109 309-343-0112
Galesburg, IL 61401

Karyn Halloran, Director

3986 Lake Land College

5001 Lake Land Blvd. 217-235-3131
Mattoon, IL 61938

Donna Beno, Special Needs
A public two-year college with 30 special education students out of a total of 4835. Tuition: $1024.

3987 Lewis and Clark Community College

Godfrey, IL 62035 618-466-3411

Patricia Dunn-Horn, Coordinator

3988 Lexington Institute of Hospitality Careers

10840 South Western Avenue 312-779-3800
Chicago, IL 60643

Theresa Wisniewski, Controller
An independent two-year college with 1 special education students out of a total of 39. Tuition: $6950.

3989 Lincoln College

Lincoln, IL 62656 217-732-3155

Michael Riley, Admissions Director

3990 Lincoln Land Community College

Shepherd Road 217-786-2224
Springfield, IL 62708

Pamela Beck, Special Needs
A public two-year college with 70 special education students out of a total of 7877. Tuition: $960.

3991 MacMurray College

447 East College 217-479-7123
Jacksonville, IL 62650

Gloria Hale, Coordinator
An independent four-year college with 5 special education students out of a total of 668. Tuition: $12100.

3992 McHenry County College

Rte. 14 & Lucas Road
Crystal Lake, IL 60014

Ed Eisner

3993 Moraine Valley Community College

Diagnostic Test Center
10900 South 88th Avenue 708-974-5711
Palos Hills, IL 60465

Laura Vonborstel, Director
A public two-year college with 120 special education students out of a total of 13938. Tuition: $1110.

3994 Morton College

3801 South Central Avenue 312-656-8000
Cicero, IL 60650

Patricia Valente, Special Services
A public two-year college with 60 special education students out of a total of 5036. Tuition: $1085.

3995 National College of Education

18 South Michigan   312-621-9650
Evanston, IL 60603

Carol Eckerman, Special Services

3996 National-Louis University

2840 Sheridan Road   312-621-9650
Evanston, IL 60201

Ann Kim, L.D. Coordinator
Regina Jones, Admissions Counselor
An independent four-year college with 5 special education students out of a total of 3400. There is a $1200 fee for the special education program in addition to the regular tuition of $13039.

3997 North Central College

30 North Brainard   708-420-3300
Naperville, IL 60566

Rich Wilders, Asst. Vice President

3998 Northeastern Illinois University

5500 North Street   312-583-4050
Chicago, IL 60625

Victoria Amey-Flippin, Special Services
A public four-year college with 31 special education students out of a total of 7712. Tuition: $1656.

3999 Northwestern University

Evanston, IL 60201

Dr. Doris Johnson

4000 Northwestern University Communicative Disorders

2299 Sheridan Road   708-491-3066
Evanston, IL 60201   FAX susan

Mulhern Director
Offers speech/language and voice services, learning disabilities center and a hearing service.

4001 Oakton Community College

1600 East Golf Road   312-635-1655
Des Plaines, IL 60016

4002 Parkland College

2400 West Bradley Avenue   217-351-9620
Champaign, IL 61821

Norm Lambert, Special Services
Services are provided to disabled students.

4003 Quincy College

1830 College
Quincy, IL 63201

Joseph Quinn

4004 Richland Community College

One College Park   217-875-7200
Decatur, IL 62521

Crystal Sargent, Coordinator
A public two-year college with 4 special education students out of a total of 3850. Tuition: $840.

4005 Rockford College

5050 E. State Street   815-226-4087
Rockford, IL 61108

Jeanne Grey, Director

4006 Roosevelt University

Learning and Support Services Program
430 South Michigan Avenue   312-341-3870
Chicago, IL 60605

Dr. Margaret Policostro, Director
An independent four-year college with 25 special education students out of a total of 4258. There is a $2000 fee for the special education program in addition to the regular tuition of $13096.

4007 Rosary College

River Forest, IL 60305   312-366-2490

Dr. Molly Burke, Special Services

4008 Saint Xavier College

103rd Street & Central Park Avenue   312-779-3300
Chicago, IL 60655

Sister Joan Fleming

4009 Sangamon State University

Springfield, IL 62794   217-786-6581

Homer Butler, VP Student Services
A public four-year college with 16 special education students out of a total of 2645. Tuition: $1644.

4010 School of the Art Institute of Chicago

Chicago, IL 60603   312-899-5100

Judy Watson, Learning Center
Offers courses in reading and writing to students who need additional work to bring these skills up to a college level. In addition, there is a Learning Center available to give academic support to all students. Assistance is offered to learning disabled students who need a scribe for their

writing assignments, books on tape, special arrangements for testing, an advocate, or counselling about course selection or career placement.

4011 Shawnee College

Ullin, IL 62992 618-634-2242

Don Slayter, Special Services

4012 Shimer College

P.O. Box A500 312-623-8400
Waukegan, IL 60079

Bobbie Groth, Special Services

A public four-year college with 5 special education students out of a total of 88. Tuition: $9500.

4013 Southeastern Illinois College

Route 4 618-252-6376
Harrisburg, IL 62946

Catherine Packard, Special Services

A public two-year college with 5 special education students out of a total of 3445. Tuition: $672.

4014 Southern Illinois University At Edwardsville

Box 1640 618-692-3701
Edwardsville, IL 62026

Jane Dabbs, Special Services

A public four-year college with 47 special education students out of a total of 2165. Tuition: $1726.

4015 Southern Illinois University At Carbondale

Clinical Center Achieve Program
Carbondale, IL 62901 618-453-2361

Ellen Bradley

A public four-year college with 58 special education students out of a total of 20485. Tuition: $1638.

4016 Spoon River College

RR 1 309-647-4645
Canton, IL 61520

Bradley Clark, SNAP/CAED

A public two-year college with 55 special education students out of a total of 2300. Tuition: $1248.

4017 Springfield College in Illinois

1500 North Fifth Street 217-525-1420
Springfield, IL 62702

Dr. Karen Hunter Anderson

4018 University of Illinois At Chicago

Counseling Center M/C 333, Box 4838 312-413-2183
Chicago, IL 60680

Jean Gorman, Coordinator

A public four-year college with 40 special education students out of a total of 15837. Tuition: $2032.

4019 University of Illinois At Urbana - Champaign

1207 Oak Street 217-333-4602
Champaign, IL 61820

4020 Waubonsee Community College

Route 47 At Harter Road 708-466-4811
Sugar Grove, IL 60554

Iris Jorstad, LD Specialist

A public two-year college with 149 special education students out of a total of 7402. Tuition: $1184.

4021 Western Illinois University

University Advising Center-Memorial 309-298-1846
Macomb, IL 61455

Candace McLaughlin, Special Services

A public four-year college with 73 special education students out of a total of 11127. Tuition: $1656.

4022 William Rainey Harper College

1200 W. Algonquin Road 708-397-3000
Palatine, IL 60067

Pascuala Herrera

A public two-year college with 150 special education students out of a total of 15604. Tuition: $900.

Indiana

4023 Ancilla College

Union Road 219-936-8898
Donaldson, IN 46513

Kathryn Bigley, Director

An independent two-year college with 4 special education students out of a total of 661. Tuition: $2220.

4024 Anderson University

Special Educational Services
1100 East Fifth Avenue 317-641-4226
Anderson, IN 46012 FAX 317-641-3851

Rinda Smith, Director

An independent four-year college with 15 special education students out of a total of 2050. Tuition: $11900.

4025 Ball State University

Handicapped Services   317-285-5293
Muncie, IN 47306

Richard Harris

4026 Bethel College - Indiana

1001 West McKinley Avenue 219-259-8511
Mishawaka, IN 46544

4027 Butler University

4600 Sunset Avenue   317-283-9255
Indianapolis, IN 46208

Rick Tirman

4028 Earlham College

Richmond, IN 47374   317-983-1316

Kathy Bryne

4029 Franklin College of Indiana

501 East Monroe Street   317-738-8080
Franklin, IN 46131

Dana Giles, Asst. Director
An independent four-year college with 2 special education students out of a total of 904. Tuition: $13230.

4030 Goshen College

1700 South Main Street   219-535-7535
Goshen, IN 46526

Marty Hooley, Director
An independent four-year college with 13 special education students out of a total of 1039. Tuition: $11810.

4031 Indiana Institute of Technology

1600 East Washington Blvd. 219-422-5561
Fort Wayne, IN 46803

Russell Baker, Dir. Student Support
A program of academic support services, including appropriate tutoring, peer mentoring and academic assistance, which is provided to students meeting specific federal eligibilitym guidelines.

4032 Indiana State University

Stalker Hall Room 119   812-237-2300
Terre Haute, IN 47809

Rita Worrell, Coordinator

4033 Indiana University At Kokomo

2300 South Washington Street 317-455-9316
Kokomo, IN 46904

Gerry Stroman, Director
A combination of attitudes assistance, accommodations, classroom arrangements and technological aids that make it possible for learning disabled and physically disabled students to succeed in a degree program for which they are qualified.

4034 Indiana University At South Bend

South Bend, IN 46615   219-237-4455

Karen Goepfrich

4035 Indiana University Bloomington

Franklin Hall 096   812-855-7578
Bloomington, IN 47405

Steve Morris, Dis. Student Service
A public four-year college with 88 special education students out of a total of 26728. Tuition: $2582.

4036 Indiana University East

2325 Chester Blvd.   317-966-8261
Richmond, IN 47374

Sabrina Pennington, Student Support
A public four-year college with 11 special education students out of a total of 2157. Tuition: $1915.

4037 Indiana University Northwest

3400 Broadway   219-980-6798
Gary, IN 46408

Ronald Thornton, Student Coordinator
A public four-year college with 24 special education students out of a total of 4952. Tuition: $1915.

4038 Indiana University Southeast

4201 Grantline Road   812-941-2309
New Albany, IN 47129

Patricia Ramsey, Director

4039 Indiana University-Purdue University At Indianapolis

425 N. University Blvd.   317-274-3241
Indianapolis, IN 46202

Pamela King, Director
A public four-year college with 155 special education students out of a total of 21157. Tuition: $2240.

4040 Indiana Vocational Technical College - Kokomo

1815 East Morgan   317-459-0561
Kokomo, IN 46901

Russ Ragland, Support Services
A public two-year college with 100 special education students out of a total of 5376. Tuition: $1509.

4041 Indiana Vocational Technical College, Columbus

4475 Central Avfenue   812-372-9925
Columbus, IN 47203

Nancy Olsen, Special Needs Coun.

A public two-year college with 4 special education students out of a total of 2614. Tuition: $1509.

4042 Indiana Vocational Technical College- Central Indiana

1 West 26th Street   317-921-4983
Indianapolis, IN 46206

Dianne Noe, Special Needs Srvcs.

A public two-year college with 1 special education students out of a total of 1662. Tuition: $1509.

4043 Indiana Wesleyan University

4201 South Washington   317-674-6901
Marion, IN 46953

Ruth DeGroff, Asst. Professor

4044 Martin Center College

P.O. Box 18567   317-543-3249
Indianapolis, IN 46205

Sr. Judith Mangin, Director

4045 Northcentral Campus, Indiana Vocational Technical College

1534 West Sample   219-289-7001
South Bend, IN 46619

Connie Johnston, Program Coordinator

4046 Northcentral Indiana Vocational Technical College

1534 West Sample   219-289-7001
South Bend, IN 46619

Christine Brooks-Leonard

4047 Northeast Indiana Vocational Technical College

3800 North Anthony   219-482-9171
Fort Wayne, IN 46805

Karen Limkemann, Counselor

4048 Purdue University

Schleman Hall   317-494-1144
West Lafayette, IN 47907

Sarah Templin, Special Services

A public four-year college with 229 special education students out of a total of 29663. Tuition: $2520.

4049 Rose-Hulman Institute of Technology

5500 Wabash Avenue   812-877-8319
Terre Haute, IN 47803

Susan Smith, Director

4050 Saint Josephs College

Rensselaer, IN 47978   219-866-7111

Diane Jennings, Special Services

4051 Saint Mary-Of-The-Woods College

Saint-Mary-of-the-Woods, IN 47876   812-535-5106

Kate Satchwill, Vice President

4052 Southcentral Indiana Vocational Technical College

8204 Highway 311
Sellersburg, IN 47172

Jack Womack

4053 Southeast Campus, Indiana Vocational Technical College

Ivy Tech Drive   812-265-2580
Madison, IN 47250

Margaret Seifert, Chair

4054 Southeast Indiana Vocational Technical College

Ivy Tech Drive   812-265-2580
Madison, IN 47250

Jane Vire, Support Services

4055 Southwest Campus, Indiana Vocational Technical College

3501 First Avenue   812-426-2865
Evansville, IN 47710

Peg Ehlen, Special Needs

Ivy Tech Southwest provides reasonable accommodations including notetakers, use of cassettes, speaking spellchecks, etc. to students with recent certification of learning disabilities.

4056 University of Evansville

1800 Lincoln Avenue   812-479-2500
Evansville, IN 47722

Dr. Richard Nicholas, Special Services

An independent four-year college with 6 special education students out of a total of 2679. Tuition: $14670.

4057   University of Southern Indiana

8600 University Blvd.   812-464-1867
Evansville, IN 47712

Leslie Morrow, Special Services

4058   Vincennes University

1002 North 1st   812-885-4209
Cincennes, IN 47591

Jane Kavanaugh

A public two-year college with 38 special education students out of a total of 7211. There is a $500 fee for the special education program in addition to the regular tuition of $1750.

4059   Whitewater, Indiana Vocational Technical College

Chester Blvd.   317-966-2656
Richmond, IN 47374

Patricia Rush, Skills Advancement

Iowa

4060   Clinton Community College

1000 Lincoln Blvd.   319-242-6841
Clinton, IA 52732

Marilyn Lyons

4061   Coe College

1220 1st Avenue NE   319-399-8508
Cedar Rapids, IA 52402

Lois Kabela

4062   Cornell College

Mount Vernon, IA 52314   319-895-4477

An independent four-year college with 9 special education students out of a total of 1111. Tuition: $17300.

4063   Drake University

College of Eudcation
Special Services   515-271-3125
Des Moines, IA 50311

Steve Schodde, Dir. Student Srvcs.

Consultation and advocacy for students at Drake University with learning disabilities.

4064   Ellsworth Community College

1100 College Avenue   515-648-4611
Iowa Falls, IA 50126

Lori Mulford

4065   Graceland College

Lamoni, IA 50140   515-784-5226

J.R. Smith, Director

An independent four-year college with 27 special education students out of a total of 968. There is a $1650 fee for the special education program in addition to the regular tuition of $11200.

4066   Grand View College

1200 Grandview Avenue   515-263-2884
Des Moines, IA 50316

A. Jane Molden, Director

An independent four-year college with 19 special education students out of a total of 1420. Tuition: $12350.

4067   Grinnell College

P.O. Box 805   515-269-3702
Grinnell, IA 50112

Jo Calhoun, Academic Advising

An independent four-year college with 3 special education students out of a total of 1291. Tuition: $18670.

4068   Hawkeye Institute of Technology

P.O. Box 8015   319-236-1013
Waterloo, IA 50704

Mary Jensen, Director

4069   Indian Hills Community College/Transition Program

525 Grandview   515-683-5125
Ottumwa, IA 52501   800-726-2585

Judy Brickey, Coordinator
Mary Stewart, Dir. Special Needs

A public two-year college with 5 special education students out of a total of 3176. There is a $130 fee for the special education program in addition to the regular tuition of $1200.

4070   Iowa Central Community College

330 Avenue M   515-576-7201
Fort Dodge, IA 50501

Barbara McClannahan, Coordinator

A public two-year college with 33 special education students out of a total of 2500. Tuition: $1568.

4071   Iowa Lakes Community College, North Attendance Center

Estherville, IA 51334   713-362-2604

Roy Weigert, Director

4072 Iowa Lakes Community College, South Attendance Center

3200 College Drive   712-852-3554
Emmetsburg, IA 50536

Carl Heilman, Special Needs

4073 Iowa Wesleyan College

601 North Main Street   319-385-6332
Mount Pleasant, IA 52641

Linda Widmer, Director

An independent four-year college with 3 special education students out of a total of 994. Tuition: $11200.

4074 Iowa Western Community College

Box 4C, 2700 College Road   712-325-3209
Council Bluffs, IA 51502

Mary Pape, Coordinator

A public two-year college with 50 special education students out of a total of 3478. Tuition: $1470.

4075 Linn Academy, Inc.

23rd Street And 3rd Avenue   319-373-0187
Marion, IA 52302

Theresa Petersen

4076 Loras College

Box 31, 1450 Alta Vista   319-588-7134
Dubuque, IA 52001

Dianne Gibson, LD Specialist

An independent four-year college with 63 special education students out of a total of 1542. There is a $800 fee for the special education program in addition to the regular tuition of $13370.

4077 Luther College

Decorah, IA 52101   319-387-1269

Myung Kim, Director

4078 Marshalltown Community College

3700 South Center Street   515-752-3161
Marshalltown, IA 50158

William Martin, Director

A public two-year college with 22 special education students out of a total of 1363. Tuition: $1540.

4079 Morningside College

Sioux City, IA 51106   712-274-5104

Tim Orwig, Special Services

4080 Mount Saint Clare College

400 Nolrth Bluff Blvd.   319-242-4023
Clinton, IA 52732

Diane Cornilsen, Director

4081 Muscatine Community College

152 Colorado Street   319-263-8250
Muscatine, IA 52761

Gloriann Hart, Special Needs

A public two-year college with 25 special education students out of a total of 1186. Tuition: $1008.

4082 North Campus, Southeastern Community College

Drawer F, 1015 South Gear Ave.   319-752-2731
West Burlington, IA 52655

Dana Feinberg, Admissions Coord.

Offers special services and students services to the learning disabled.

4083 North Iowa Community College

500 College Drive   515-421-4254
Macon City, IA 50401

Sue Norton, Special Services

4084 Northwestern College

Orange City, IA 51041   712-737-4821

Marcia Olson, Special Services

4085 Scott Community College

500 Belmont Road   319-359-7531
Bettendorf, IA 52722

Jerri Crabtree, Director

A public two-year college with 50 special education students out of a total of 3600. Tuition: $1416.

4086 Southwestern Community College

1501 Townline Road   515-782-7081
Creston, IA 50801

Gary O'Daniels, Special Services

4087 St. Ambrose College

Davenport, IA 52803   319-383-8888

An independent four-year college with 30 special education students out of a total of 1701. Tuition: $12790.

4088 University of Iowa

3101 Burge Hall   319-335-1462
Iowa City, IA 52242

Donna Chandler, Special Services

A public four-year college with 181 special education students out of a total of 18917. Tuition: $2088.

4089 University of Northern Iowa

Cedar Falls, IA 50613   319-273-2281

Dr. Larry Steinhauser

4090 Waldorf College

106 South 6th Street   515-582-8207
Forest City, IA 50436

Rebecca Hill

An independent two-year college with 17 special education students out of a total of 593. There is a $800 fee for the special education program in addition to the regular tuition of $11360.

4091 Wartburg College

222 9th Street NW   319-352-8260
Waverly, IA 50677

Debbie Heida, Vice President

An independent four-year college with 6 special education students out of a total of 1453. Tuition: $13720.

4092 Western Iowa Tech Community College

P.O. Box 265   712-274-6337
Sioux City, IA 51002

Ann Brodersen, Coordinator

Kansas

4093 Allen County Community College

1801 North Cottonwood   316-365-5116
Iola, KS 66749

Rochelle Smith

4094 Barton County Community College

Route 3, Box 1362   316-792-2701
Great Bend, KS 67530

Jan Felton

A public two-year college with 10 special education students out of a total of 4460. Tuition: $624.

4095 Bethel College, Kansas

300 East 27th   316-283-0656
North Newton, KS 67117

Sandee Zerger

4096 Butler County Community College

901 South Haverhill Road   316-321-2222
El Dorado, KS 67042   FAX 316-321-5122

Lora Rozeboom, Special Needs

A public two-year college with 90 special education students out of a total of 5599. Tuition: $944.

4097 Colby Community College

1255 South Range   913-462-3984
Colby, KS 67701

Joyce Washburn, Academic Services

4098 Cowley County Community College

Arkansas City, KS 67005   316-442-0430

Chris Vollweider

4099 Donnelly College

608 North 18th Street   913-621-6070
Kansas City, KS 66102

Lee Stephenson, Dir. Support Service

An independent two-year college with 2 special education students out of a total of 377. Tuition: $2790.

4100 Emporia State University

1200 Commercial   316-343-1200
Emporia, KS 66801

Dr. Keith Frank, Coordinator

4101 Fort Scott Community College

2108 South Horton   316-223-2700
Fort Scott, KS 66701

Connie Corbett-Williams, Special Services

A public two-year college with 30 special education students out of a total of 1918. Tuition: $810.

4102 Hutchison Community College

1300 North Plum   316-665-3563
Hutchinson, KS 67501

Mary Coplen, Director

4103 Kansas City, Kansas Community College

7250 State Avenue   913-334-1100
Kansas City, KS 66112

Linda Wildgen, Supervisor

A public two-year college with 25 special education students out of a total of 5466. Tuition: $750.

4104   Kansas Newman College

Wichita, KS 67213   316-942-4291

Dr. Roger Sorochty, Vide President

4105   Kansas State University

Disabled Students
201 Holton Hall   913-532-6441
Manhattan, KS 66506

Gretchen Holden, Director
A public four-year college with 63 special education students out of a total of 17105. Tuition: $1456.

4106   Kansas Technical Institute

2409 Scanlan Avenue
Salina, KS 67401

Charles Scott, Director

4107   Labette Community College

200 South 14th   316-421-6700
Parsons, KS 67357

Viv Metcalf, Director
A public two-year college with 80 special education students out of a total of 2598. Tuition: $690.

4108   Neosho County Community College

1000 South Allen   316-431-6222
Chanute, KS 66720

John Messenger, Instructor

4109   Ottawa University

1001 South Cedar   913-242-5200
Ottawa, KS 66067

Karen Ohnesorge-Fick, Academic Achievement
An independent four-year college with 8 special education students out of a total of 536. Tuition: $10076.

4110   Pittsburg State University

1701 South Broadway   316-231-8464
Pittsburg, KS 66762

Dr. Nick Henry, Special Services
A public four-year college with 19 special education students out of a total of 4476. Tuition: $1132.

4111   Saint Mary College

4100 South Fourth Street Trafficway   913-682-5151
Leavenworht, KS 66048

Dr. Carol Hinds, Academic Dean

4112   Seward County Community College

1801 North Kansas   316-624-1951
Liberal, KS 67905

Larry Philbeck, Academic Ahievement
A public two-year college with 11 special education students out of a total of 1519. Tuition: $864.

4113   Tabor College

Hillsboro, KS 67063   316-947-3121

Judy Heibert

4114   Washburn University of Topeka

University Of Topeka   913-231-1625
Topeka, KS 66621

Greg Moore

4115   Wichita State University

1845 Fairmount   316-689-3309
Wichita, KS 67208

Grady Landrum, Special Services
A public four-year college with 9 special education students out of a total of 13100. Tuition: $1875.

Kentucky

4116   Berea College

Berea, KY 40404   606-986-9341

John Cook

4117   Brescia College

7171 Frederica Street   502-686-4259
Owensboro, KY 42301

Teresa Riley
An independent four-year college with 7 special education students out of a total of 840. Tuition: $9050.

4118   Clear Creek Baptist Bible College

300 Clear Creek Road   606-337-3196
Pineville, KY 40977

Georgia Mink
An independent four-year college with 8 special education students out of a total of 139. Tuition: $4110.

4119   Eastern Kentucky University

Richmond, KY 40475   606-622-1500

Dr. James H. Allen

4120 Kentucky State University

Frankfort, KY 40601   502-564-2550

Patricia Jones

4121 Lindsey Wilson College

Columbia, KY 42728   502-384-2126

Barbara Peterson, Director

4122 Madisonville Community College, University of Kentucky

200 College Dirve   502-821-2250
Madison, KY 42431

Nancy Douglas, Instructor

4123 Northern Kentucky University

Highland Heights, KY 41076   606-572-5180

A. Dale Adams, Special Services

4124 Pikeville College

Pikeville, KY 41501   606-432-9322

William Little

4125 Shedd Academy

346 Central Ave., P.O. Box 493   502-247-8007
Mayfield, KY 42066

Dr. Paul Thompson, Executive Director
Debbie Taylor, Office Manager
Works with children and adolescents who have dyslexia, learning disabilities and Attention Deficit Disorders. The Academy works with students from all over the country in its full-time school, summer school and tutorial programs. Shedd has had much success through its efforts with students.

4126 Thomas More College

Student Support Services
333 Thomas More Parkway   606-344-3521
Crestview Hills, KY 41017   FAX 606-344-3342

Dr. Ray Hebert, Dean Academic Affair
Barbara Davis, Students Support Dir
An independent four-year college with 120 special education students out of a total of 1268. Tuition: $12110.

4127 University of Kentucky, Lexington Community College

103F Oswald Building, Cooper Dr.   606-257-6068
Lexington, KY 40506

Marlene Huff, Special Services
A public two-year college with 105 special education students out of a total of 4398. Tuition: $1620.

4128 University of Kentucky, Paducah Community College

Box 7380   502-554-9200
Paducah, KY 42002

Gail Ridgeway, Special Services
A public two-year college with 23 special education students out of a total of 3187. Tuition: $700.

4129 University of Louisville

Robbins Hall   502-588-6938
Louisville, KY 40292

Cathy Patus, Special Services
A public four-year college with 50 special education students out of a total of 18333. Tuition: $1880.

4130 Woodbridge Academy/Academic Edge

2675 Regency Road   606-277-1099
Lexington, KY 40503

Elizabeth Goldsworthy

Louisiana

4131 Crescent Acadmey

926 Milan Street   504-895-3952
New Orleans, LA 70115

Barbara Leggett

4132 Louisiana State Uniersity At Eunice

P.O. Box 1129   318-457-7311
Eunice, LA 70535

Dr. Marvette Thomas Smith, Director

4133 Louisiana State University Agricultural and Mechanical College

Johnston Hall   504-388-4423
Baton Rouge, LA 70803

Tina Schultz
A public four-year college with 80 special education students out of a total of 21243. Tuition: $2058.

4134 Louisiana State University At Alexandria

8100 Highway 71 South   318-473-6451
Alexandria, LA 71302

Eloise Andries, Learning Center

4135 Louisiana State University At Eunice

P.O. Box 1129   318-457-7311
Eunice, LA 70535

Dr. Marvette Thomas, Director Of TRIO

A public two-year college with 25 special education students out of a total of 2590. Tuition: $912.

4136 McNeese State University

P.O. Box 92687   318-475-5444
Lake Charles, LA 70609   800-622-3352

Sena Theall, Dir. Special Project
Jessica McCauley, Academic Coord.

Provides academic advising, arrangements for individual accommodations for disabilities, tutoring and computers and word processing equipment. All services are available to the students at no charge.

4137 University of New Orleans

260 University Center   504-286-6222
New Orleans, LA 70148

Cheryl Tate

A public four-year college with 40 special education students out of a total of 12435. Tuition: $1924.

4138 University of Southwestern Louisiana

Drawer 41650   318-231-5252
Lafayette, LA 70504

Carmen Charles, Special Services

A public four-year college with 55 special education students out of a total of 14667. Tuition: $1578.

Maine

4139 Bates College

102 Lane Hall   207-786-6219
Lewiston, ME 04240

F. Celeste Branham, Dean

An independent four-year college with 14 special education students out of a total of 1500. Tuition: $22850.

4140 Bowdoin College

Brunswick, ME 04011   207-725-3145

Mary McCann

4141 Eastern Maine Vocational-Technical Institute

Bangor, ME 04401   207-941-4658

Phillip Pratt

4142 Kennebec Valley Technical College

92 Western Avenue   207-453-9762
Fairfield, ME 04937

Pat Ross, Students Services

A public two-year college with 9 special education students out of a total of 1080. Tuition: $1152.

4143 Mid-State College

Auburn, ME 04210   207-783-1478

Richard Gross, Special Services

4144 Nasson College

Office Of Admissions   207-324-5340
Springvale, ME 04083

4145 Northern Maine Technical College

33 Edgen Drive   207-769-2461
Presque Isle, ME 04769

Iris Brewer, Special Services

A public two-year college with 30 special education students out of a total of 813. Tuition: $1440.

4146 Southern Maine Technical College

South Portland, ME 04106   207-767-9536

Gail Rowe, Learning Center Dir.

A public two-year college with 42 special education students out of a total of 1271. Tuition: $1728.

4147 Unity College

Unity, ME 04988   207-948-3131

James Horan, Special Services

4148 University of Maine

Orono, ME 04469   207-581-2319

Ann Smith, Special Services

A public four-year college with 100 special education students out of a total of 9503. Tuition: $2670.

4149 University of Maine At Fort Kent

Pleasant Street   207-834-3162
Fort Kent, ME 04743

Dian Burns, Special Services

A public four-year college with 5 special education students out of a total of 603. Tuition: $2130.

4150 University of Maine At Machias

9 O'Brien Avenue   207-255-3313
Machias, ME 04654

Dave Baldwin, Special Services

A public four-year college with 8 special education students out of a total of 966. Tuition: $2130.

4151 University of New England

Hills Beach Road   207-283-0171
Biddeford, ME 04005

Ann Rousselle, Admissions Director

An independent four-year college with 33 special education students out of a total of 800. There is a $1250 fee for the special education program in addition to the regular tuition of $15280.

4152 University of Southern Maine

96 Falmouth Street   207-780-4706
Portland, ME 04103

Joyce Branaman, Counselor

A public four-year college with 51 special education students out of a total of 8645. Tuition: $2310.

4153 Westbrook College

Portland, ME 04103   207-797-7261

Maryland

4154 Bowie State College

Support Services For Disabled   301-464-3363
Bowie, MD 20715

Johanna Fisher

4155 Catonsville Community College

800 South Rolling Road   301-445-4356
Catonsville, MD 21228

Marjorie Zensky

4156 Charles County Community College

P.O. Box 910   301-934-2251
La Plata, MD 20646

M. Penelope Appel

A public two-year college with 25 special education students out of a total of 5143. Tuition: $1300.

4157 Chesapeake College

P.O. Box 8   301-822-5400
Wye Mills, MD 21679

Becky Rader

4158 Columbia Union College

7600 Flower Avenue   301-891-4106
Takoma Park, MD 20912

Betty Howard, Assistant Dean

4159 Community College of Baltimore

Baltimore, MD 21215   301-396-0004

L. Rowena Wingfield, Disabled Services

4160 Frostburg State University

113 Pullen Hall   301-689-4481
Frostburg, MD 21532

Beth Hoffman, Coordinator

A public four-year college with 149 special education students out of a total of 4468. Tuition: $2222.

4161 Hagerstown Junior College

11400 Robinwood Drive   301-790-2800
Hagerstown, MD 21742

Lynn Schlossberg, Coordinator

A public two-year college with 12 special education students out of a total of 3361. Tuition: $1614.

4162 Harford Community College

401 Thomas Run Road   410-836-4414
Bel Air, MD 21015   FAX 410-836-4198

Leigh Marshall, Coordinator

A public two-year college with 30 special education students out of a total of 5348. Tuition: $1290.

4163 Howard Community College

Little Patuxent Parkway   301-992-4822
Columbia, MD 21044

Janice Marks, Director Support

A public two-year college with 72 special education students out of a total of 4883. Tuition: $1740.

4164 Johns Hopkins University

235 Mergenthaler Hall   410-516-8216
Baltimore, MD 21218

Martha Rosemann

An independent four-year college with 15 special education students out of a total of 3125. Tuition: $23305.

4165 Montgomery Community College

51 Mannakee Street   301-279-5058
Rockville, MD 20850

Lynne Harrison Martin

A public two-year college with 45 special education students out of a total of 14128. Tuition: $1560.

4166 New Community College of Baltimore

2901 Liberty Heights Avenue   410-333-5332
Baltimore, MD 21215

L. Rowena Wingfield, Student Services

4167 Prince George's Community College

Largo, MD 20772   301-366-6000

Carrier Johnson, Special Services

4168 School for Contemporaty Education

4906 Roland Avenue   301-235-9292
Baltimore, MD 21210

Artha Johnson

4169 Towson State University

Dowell Hall-Second Level   410-830-2638
Towson, MD 21204

Margaret Warrington, Special Services

A public four-year college with 134 special education students out of a total of 13757. Tuition: $1846.

4170 University of Maryland, Baltimore County

Baltimore, MD 21228   301-455-2459

Sadie Fletcher, Special Services

4171 University of Maryland, College Park

Shoemaker Bldg., Room 0126   301-314-7682
College Park, MD 20742

Dr. William Scales

4172 University of Maryland, Eastern Shore

Box 1088   301-651-2200
Princess Anne, MD 21853

Dr. Diann Showell, Special Services

4173 Western Maryland College

2 College Hill   410-857-2504
Westminster, MD 21157

Thomas Gibbon, Special Services

An independent four-year college with 40 special education students out of a total of 1224. There is a $900 fee for the special education program in addition to the regular tuition of $18280.

4174 Westminster College/Maryland

Learning Disabilities Program   314-642-3361
Fulton, MD 20759

Henry Ottinger

4175 Wor-Wic Tech Community College

1409 Wesley Drive   410-749-8181
Salisbury, MD 21801

Karen Goyer, Counseling Director

A public two-year college with 8 special education students out of a total of 1692. Tuition: $1320.

Massachusetts

4176 American International College Support, Learning Services Program

1000 State Street   413-737-7000
Springfield, MA 0109

Mary Saltus

An independent four-year college with 95 special education students out of a total of 1433. There is a $2700 fee for the special education program in addition to the regular tuition of $12711.

4177 Amherst College

Box 2206, Converse Hall   413-542-2529
Amherst, MA 01002

Frances Tuleja, Director

4178 Anna Maria College

Sunset Lane   617-757-4586
Paxton, MA 01612

Olivia Tarleton, Director

An independent four-year college with 15 special education students out of a total of 681. Tuition: $15025.

4179 Aquinas College At Newton

15 Walnut Park   617-969-4400
Newton, MA 02158

Sr. Elenor Shea, Director

An independent two-year college with 7 special education students out of a total of 210. Tuition: $6800.

4180　Bentley College

175 Forest Street	617-891-2274
Waltham, MA 02154	

Dr. Brenda Hawks

An independent four-year college with 11 special education students out of a total of 5177. Tuition: $17015.

4181　Boston College

140 Commonwelaht Avenue	617-552-3310
Chestnut Hill, MA 02167	

Dr. David John Smith

An independent four-year college with 195 special education students out of a total of 14230. There is a $2600 fee for the special education program in addition to the regular tuition of $23157.

4182　Boston University

19 Deerfield Street	617-353-6880
Boston, MA 02215	

Dr. Loring Brinckerhoff, Director Of LD

4183　Bradford College

South Main Street	508-372-7161
Bradford, MA 01835	

William Dunfey, Dean Of Admissions

An independent four-year college with 35 special education students out of a total of 500. There is a $3500 fee for the special education program in addition to the regular tuition of $18650.

4184　Brandeis University

415 South Street	617-736-3677
Waltham, MA 02254	

Dr. Walter Anthony, Jr., Assistant Dean

An independent four-year college with 64 special education students out of a total of 2898. Tuition: $24227.

4185　Bridgewater State College

Bridgewater, MA 02325	508-697-1276

Martha D. Jones

4186　Bristol Community College

777 Elsbree Street	508-678-2811
Fall River, MA 02720	

Sue Boissoneault

A public two-year college with 60 special education students out of a total of 3056. Tuition: $1320.

4187　Cape Cod Community College

Route 132	503-362-2131
West Barnstable, MA 02668	

Dr. Richard Sommers, LD Specialist

A public two-year college with 130 special education students out of a total of 2137. Tuition: $1008.

4188　Clark University

950 Main Street	617-793-7468
Worcester, MA 01610	

Dr. Martin Patwell

An independent four-year college with 84 special education students out of a total of 2151. Tuition: $20680.

4189　Curry College

Learning Center	617-333-0500
Milton, MA 02186	

Barbara Wilczewski, Secretary

An independent four-year college with 160 special education students out of a total of 968. There is a $3000 fee for the special education program in addition to the regular tuition of $18345.

4190　Eastern Nazerene College

23 East Elm Avenue	617-773-6350
Quincy, MA 02170	

Lois Nox, Director

4191　Endicott College

376 Hale Street	508-927-0585
Beverly, MA 01915	

Jane Lang, Student Support

An independent two-year college with 40 special education students out of a total of 783. Tuition: $15920.

4192　Essex Agricultural and Technical Institute

562 Maple Street	617-774-0050
Hawthorne, MA 01937	

Craig Gray, Coordinator

A public two-year college with 64 special education students out of a total of 543. Tuition: $1050.

4193　Framingham State College

South Pierce Hall	508-626-4509
Framingham, MA 01701	

4194　Harvard University

20 Garden Street	617-496-8707
Cambridge, MA 02138	

Louise Russell, Student Disability

An independent four-year college with 35 special education students out of a total of 6622. Tuition: $23514.

4195 Lesley College

Threshold Program
29 Everett Street
Cambridge, MA 02238

Dr, Arlyn Roffman

4196 Massachusetts Bay Community College

50 Oakland Street   617-237-1100
Wellsley Hills, MA 02181

Gail Stanton-Hammond, LD Specialist

A public two-year college with 34 special education students out of a total of 4674. Tuition: $1008.

4197 Massasoit Community College

1 Massasoit Blvd.   617-588-9100
Brockton, MA 02402

Peter Johnston, Director

A public two-year college with 160 special education students out of a total of 6421. Tuition: $1008.

4198 Middlesex Community College

Programs for the Learning Disabled
Terrace Hall Avenue   617-272-7342
Burlington, MA 01803

Karen Muncaster, Director

A public two-year college with 298 special education students out of a total of 4028. Tuition: $1100.

4199 Mount Ida College, Learning Opportunities Program

777 Dedham Street   617-969-7000
Newton Center, MA 02173

Jill Mehler, Dir. Of LD Program

Designed and developed to provide additional support for students with learning disabilities. Services include: Individual tutoring by professional learning specialties; reduced course load; credit study skills course; specialized accommodations and community functions.

4200 Mount Wachusett Community College

444 Green Street   617-632-6600
Gardner, MA 01440

Francine Meigs, Special Services

A public two-year college with 175 special education students out of a total of 2200. Tuition: $1008.

4201 Newbury College

129 Fisher Avenue   617-739-0510
Brookline, MA 02146

Donald Cocci, Special Services

An independent two-year college with 70 special education students out of a total of 992. Tuition: $14950.

4202 North Adams State College Learning Center

Church Street   413-664-4511
North Adams, MA 01247   FAX 413-663-3300

Terry Miller, Assistant Director

A public four-year college with 12 special education students out of a total of 2007. Tuition: $1610.

4203 North Shore Community College

1 Ferncroft Road   508-762-4000
Danvers, MA 01923

Helen Halloran, Special Services

A public two-year college with 275 special education students out of a total of 3305. Tuition: $1008.

4204 Northeastern University

360 Huntington Avenue   617-437-2675
Boston, MA 02115

G. Ruth Bork, Dean

4205 Northern Essex Community College

Eliot Way   617-374-5808
Havehill, MA 01830

Jan Scherer, Special Services

4206 Pine Manor College

400 Heath Street   617-731-7104
Chestnut Hill, MA 02167

Laura McPhie, Special Services

An independent four-year college with 43 special education students out of a total of 500. Tuition: $21136.

4207 Regis College, Massachusetts

2135 Wellesley Street   617-893-1820
Weston, MA 02193

S. Marilyn MacGregor

4208 Simmons College

300 The Fenway   617-738-2105
Boston, MA 02115

Carolyn Holland, Special Services

An independent four-year college with 43 special education students out of a total of 1380. Tuition: $21284.

4209 Smith College

College Hall 7   413-585-2071
Northampton, MA 01063

Mary Jane Maccardini, Special Needs Srvcs.

An independent four-year college with 32 special education students out of a total of 2607. Tuition: $23070.

4210 Southeastern Massachusetts University

Old Wesport Road   617-999-8711
North Dartmouth, MA 02747

Carole Johnson, Special Services

4211 Springfield Technical Community College

1 Armory Square   413-781-7822
Springfield, MA 01105

Deena Shriver, Special Services

4212 Stonehill College

Washington Street   508-230-1306
North Easton, MA 02357

Richard Grant, Special Services

An independent four-year college with 41 special education students out of a total of 1964. Tuition: $16539.

4213 Suffolk University

8 Ashburton Place   617-573-8239
Boston, MA 02108

Zegenu Tsige, Special Services

4214 Tufts University

72 Professors Row   617-628-5000
Medford, MA 02155

Jean Herbert, Special Services

4215 University of Lowell

1 University Avenue   617-452-5000
Lowell, MA 01854

Dr. Noel Cartwright, Special Services

4216 University of Massachusetts At Amherst

Amherts, MA 01003   413-545-4602

Dr. Patricia Gillespie-Silver, Special Services

A public four-year college with 190 special education students out of a total of 17170. Tuition: $2134.

4217 University of Massachusetts, Boston

020-3/435   617-287-5820
Boston, MA 02125

Mary Beth Maneen

A public four-year college with 150 special education students out of a total of 8589. Tuition: $2052.

4218 Wellesley College

Wellesley, MA 02181   617-283-2641

An independent four-year college with 35 special education students out of a total of 2319. Tuition: $22900.

4219 Wheaton College

East Main Street   617-285-7722
Norton, MA 02766

Susan Dearing, Special Services

An independent four-year college with 40 special education students out of a total of 1302. Tuition: $22600.

Michigan

4220 Adrian College

Academic Services Program
Jones Hall   517-265-5161
Adrian, MI 49221

Dr. Mary Anne Stibbe, Academic Services

An independent four-year college with 24 special education students out of a total of 1194. Tuition: $13355.

4221 Alma College

614 West Superior   517-463-7225
Alma, MI 48801

Dr. Robert Perkins, Director

An independent four-year college with 6 special education students out of a total of 1224. Tuition: $15462.

4222 Andrews University

Counseling & Testing
Berrien Springs, MI 49104

Marion Swanpoel, Director

4223 Aquinas College

AB-320   616-459-8281
Grand Rapids, MI 49506

Jane McCloskey, Director

An independent four-year college with 22 special education students out of a total of 2138. Tuition: $13792.

4224 Bay De Noc Community College

2001 North Lincoln Road   906-786-5802
Escanaba, MI 49829   800-221-2001

Marlene Paavilainen, Special Pop. Dir.

A public two-year college with 6 special education students out of a total of 2255. Tuition: $1302.

4225 Central Michigan University

150 Foust Hall   517-774-3465
Mount Pleasant, MI 48859

Carol Wojcik, Dis. Student Service

Handicapped Student Services provides services, assistance and advisement to enrolled students with disabilities.

4226 Charles Stewart Mott Community College

1401 East Court Street   313-762-0399
Flint, MI 48502

Delores Williams

4227 College of Art and Design, Center for Creative Studies

201 East Kirby   313-872-3118
Detroit, MI 48202

Rochana Koach

4228 Concordia College

4090 Geddes Road   313-995-7300
Ann Arbor, MI 48105

Grace Dolak, Development Dir.

An independent four-year college with 10 special education students out of a total of 593. Tuition: $12430.

4229 Delta College

University Center, MI 48710   517-686-9096

David Murley, Special Needs

4230 Detroit College of Business

4801 Oakman Blvd.   313-581-4400
Dearborn, MI 48126

Fran Jarvis, Director

4231 Detroit College of Business, Warren Campus

27500 Dequindre   313-558-8700
Warren, MI 48092

Mary Cross, Associate Dean

4232 Eton Academy

1755 Melton   313-642-1150
Birmingham, MI 48009   FAX 313-642-3670

Mary Bramson Van der Tuin, Headmistress

An independent, nondenominational day school for students with specific learning disabilities including dyslexia. Eton enrolls 136 boys and 46 girls with classes being comprised of fewer than 9 students. Students with average or above average academic potential are accepted for enrollment. Students are taught learning strategies and to be their own advocates.

4233 Glen Oaks Community College

62249 Shimmel Road   616-467-9945
Centreville, MI 49032

Connie Nofz, Special Needs Adv.

A public two-year college with 175 special education students out of a total of 1416. Tuition: $1209.

4234 Grand Rapids Junior College

143 Bostwick NE   616-456-3798
Grand Rapids, MI 49503

Catha Jane Galante, Coordinator

4235 Henry Ford Community College

5101 Evergreen   313-845-9617
Dearborn, MI 48128

Theodore Hunt, Jr., Program Manager

A public two-year college with 32 special education students out of a total of 15510. Tuition: $1209.

4236 Hope College

Academic Support Center   616-394-7830
Holland, MI 49423

Jacqueline Heisler, Director

An independent four-year college with 20 special education students out of a total of 2746. Tuition: $14718.

4237 Jackson Community College

2111 Emmons Road   517-787-0800
Jackson, MI 49201

Chris Kane, Chair

4238 Kalamazoo College

1200 Academy Street   616-337-7209
Kalamazoo, MI 49006

Dr. Marilyn LaPlante, Dean Of Students

A selective, independent and undergraduate liberal arts college. The unique curricular plan weaves career development internships, study abroad programs and senior independent research projects with traditional liberal arts on-campus programs.

4239 Kellogg Community College

450 North Avenue   616-965-4150
Battle Creek, MI 49017

Janice McNearney, Support Services

A public two-year college with 35 special education students out of a total of 7662. Tuition: $960.

4240 Kendall College of Art and Design

111 Division Avenue North   616-451-2787
Grand Rapids, MI 49503

Kathy Jordan, Counselor

An independent four-year college with 7 special education students out of a total of 652. Tuition: $8620.

4241 Lake Michigan College

2755 East Napier   616-927-8100
Benton Harbor, MI 49022

Jean Christensen, Special Populations

A 2-year community college offering students vocational/technical programs in business, health science, technology and the first two years of college credit toward transfer in a bacca-laureate program. 3,700 students attend each semester. Tutors, readers, notetakers and other support services are available to eligible disabled students.

4242 Lake Superior State Uniersity

Brown Hall   906-635-2453
Sault Sainte Marie, MI 49783

David Castner, Couneling

4243 Lansing Community College

P.O. Box 40010   517-483-1207
Lansing, MI 48901

Karen Holt, Coordinator

4244 Mercy College of Detroit

8200 West Outer Drive   313-592-6068
Detroit, MI 48219

Elizabeth Church, Director

4245 Michigan State University

East Lansing, MI 48854   517-255-8332

Dr. Elaine Cherney

4246 Michigan Technological University

152 Administration Building   906-487-2212
Houghton, MI 49931

Richard Drenovsky, Special Services

A public four-year college with 8 special education students out of a total of 6355. Tuition: $2781.

4247 Mid Michigan Community College

1375 South Clare Avenue   517-386-7792
Harrison, MI 48625

Susan Cobb, Special Services

A public two-year college with 25 special education students out of a total of 2266. Tuition: $1116.

4248 Monroe County Community College

155 South Rainesville Road   313-242-7300
Monroe, MI 48161

Kim Hripko-Jacob, Special Services

4249 Montcalm Community College

2800 College Drive   517-328-2111
Sidney, MI 48885

Charlotte Fokens, Special Needsces

4250 Nazareth College

Nazareth, MI 49074   616-349-7783

Ken Morgan

4251 Northern Michigan University

Marquette, MI 49855   906-227-1550

Darlene Buck, Special Services

A public four-year college with 52 special education students out of a total of 7649. Tuition: $2318.

4252 Northwestern Michigan College

Instructional Support Center
1701 East Front Street   616-922-1139
Traverse City, MI 49684

Denny Everett, Instructional Center

A public two-year college with 30 special education students out of a total of 4428. Tuition: $1551.

4253 Oakland Community College

27055 Orchard Lake Road   313-471-7616
Farmington Hills, MI 48018

Dr. Lawrence Gage, Special Services

4254 Oakland University

Rochester, MI 48309   313-370-3266

Iris Johnson, Interim Director

4255 Reformed Bible College

3333 East Beltline NE   616-363-2050
Grand Rapids, MI 49505

Glenda Droogsma, Dean Of Students

An independent four-year college with 3 special education students out of a total of 176. Tuition: $8199.

4256 Schoolcraft College

18600 Haggerty   313-591-6400
Livonia, MI 48152

Dr. Sirkka Gudan, Special Services

A public two-year college with 75 special education students out of a total of 9551. Tuition: $1095.

4257 St. Clair County Community College

323 Erie   313-984-3881
Port Huron, MI 48061

Nancy Pecorilli, Special Services

A public two-year college with 24 special education students out of a total of 4534. Tuition: $1426.

4258 Suomi College

601 Quincy Street   906-487-7258
Hancock, MI 49930

Carol Bated, LD Coordiantor

An independent two-year college with 16 special education students out of a total of 535. Tuition: $11100.

4259 University of Michigan

300 North Ingalls Building   313-763-3000
Ann Arbor, MI 48109

Emily Singer, Special Services

A public four-year college with 58 special education students out of a total of 23126. Tuition: $3710.

4260 University of Michigan, Dearborn

4901 Evergreen Road   313-593-5430
Dearborn, MI 48128

Dr. Mary Ann Zawada, Counseling Director

A public four-year college with 24 special education students out of a total of 5977. Tuition: $112.

4261 University of Michigan, Flint

Flint, MI 48502   313-762-3456

JoAnn Shabazz, Director

A public four-year college with 3 special education students out of a total of 6168. Tuition: $2380.

4262 Washtenaw Community College

4800 Huron River Drive   313-973-3483
Ann Arbor, MI 48106

Dr. Francie Helm Moorman, Special Services

A public two-year college with 58 special education students out of a total of 10776. Tuition: $1140.

4263 Western Michigan University

West Michigan Avenue   616-387-4440
Kalamazoo, MI 49008

Kate Wesler, LD Director

A public four-year college with 88 special education students out of a total of 20928. Tuition: $2200.

Minnesota

4264 Alexandria Technical Institute

1601 Jefferson   612-762-0221
Alexandria, MN 56308

Renee Larson, Support Services

4265 Anoka-Ramsey Community College

11200 Mississippi Blvd.   612-427-2600
Coon Rapids, MN 55433

Nancy Edwards, Coordinator

A public two-year college with 43 special education students out of a total of 6830. Tuition: $1704.

4266 Augsburg College

731 21st Avenue South   612-330-1053
Minnespolis, MN 55454

Diane Glorvigen, Educational Director

An independent four-year college with 98 special education students out of a total of 2940. Tuition: $14883.

4267 Austin Community College Center for Student Success

1600 Eighth Avenue NW   507-433-0558
Austin, MN 55912   800-747-6941
                                  FAX 507-433-0515

Mindi Federman Askelson, Co-Director, Center

A public two-year college with 6 special education students out of a total of 1318. Tuition: $1704.

4268 Bemidji State University

12 Sanford Hall   218-755-2595
Bemidji, MN 56601

Ann Austad, Coordinator

4269 Bethel College

3900 Bethel Drive   612-638-6353
St. Paul, MN 55112

Lucie Johnson, Chairperson

An independent four-year college with 65 special education students out of a total of 576. Tuition: $10976.

4270   College of Associated Arts

344 Summitt Avenue   612-224-3416
St. Paul, MN 55102

Barbara Davis, Associate Professor

4271   College of Saint Scholastica

1200 Kenwood Avenue   218-723-6552
Duluth, MN 55811

Jay Newcomb, Director

4272   College of St. Catherine, St. Paul Campus

O'Neill Learning Center
2004 Randolph Street   612-690-6563
St. Paul, MN 55105

Elaine McDonough, Assistant Director
Academic support services for students with disabilities of the College.

4273   Fergus Falls Community College

1414 College Way   218-739-7555
Fergus Falls, MN 56537

Dr. David Seyfried, Director
A public two-year college with 10 special education students out of a total of 1300. Tuition: $1750.

4274   Gustavus Adolphus College

800 West College Avenue   507-933-7027
St. Peter, MN 56082

Bob Carlson, Asst. Academic Adv.
An independent four-year college with 5 special education students out of a total of 2305. Tuition: $12835.

4275   Hibbing Community College

1515 East 25th Street   218-262-6712
Hibbing, MN 55746

Barbara Anderson, Coordinator
A public two-year college with 10 special education students out of a total of 1115. Tuition: $1704.

4276   Hutchinson Area Vo-Tech Institute

200 Century Avenue
Hutchison, MN 55350

4277   Inver Hills Community College

8445 College Trail   612-450-8628
Inver Grove Heights, MN 55075

Gini Spurr
A public two-year college with 170 special education students out of a total of 5444. Tuition: $1600.

4278   Itasca Community College

1851 Highway 169 East   218-327-4210
Grand Rapids, MN 55744

Sally Velzen, Learning Skills
A public two-year college with 12 special education students out of a total of 1240. Tuition: $1800.

4279   Lakewood Community College

3401 Century Avenue   612-779-3355
White Bear Lake, MN 55110

Vicki Johnson, Coord. Disabled Ctr.
Willie Nesbit, Dean Of Students
The disabilities access center provided by the college is a liaison service for students with disabilities to provide access to educational and student programs at the college.

4280   Mankato State University

Mankato, MN 56001   507-389-2422

Dr. Daniel Beebe

4281   Mesabi Community College

Virginia, MN 55792   218-479-7763

Ann Jahonen, Coordinator

4282   Minneapolis Community College

1501 Mannepin Avenue   612-341-7205
Minneapolis, MN 55403

Dr. Melissa Russell, DirectorServices
A public two-year college with 100 special education students out of a total of 4055. Tuition: $1598.

4283   Moorhead State University

112 Comstock Memorial Union   218-299-5859
Moorhead, MN 56563

Paula Ahless
A public four-year college with 35 special education students out of a total of 8441. Tuition: $2033.

4284   Normandale Community College

9700 France Avenue South   612-832-6422
Bloomington, MN 55431

Mary Jibben, DEEDS Coordinator
A public two-year college with 160 special education students out of a total of 9317. Tuition: $1688.

4285 North Hennepin Community College

7411 85th Avenue North   612-424-0725
Minneapolis, MN 55445

Sue Smith, Special Services

A public two-year college with 20 special education students out of a total of 6300. Tuition: $1800.

4286 Northwestern Electronics Institute

825 41st Avenue NE   612-781-4881
Columbia Heights, MN 55421

John Salma, Director Of Evening

4287 Pillsbury Baptist Bible College

315 South Grove   507-451-2710
Owatonna, MN 55060

Larry Tindall, Admissions Director

An independent four-year college with 3 special education students out of a total of 326. Tuition: $6890.

4288 Rainy River Community College

1801 3rd Street   218-285-2238
International Falls, MN 56649

Carol Grim, Disability Services

A public two-year college with 5 special education students out of a total of 738. Tuition: $1778.

4289 Rochester Community College

Highway 14 East   507-285-7261
Rochester, MN 55904   800-383-5421

Bonnie Mercer, Dir. Support Service

A public two-year college with 45 special education students out of a total of 3987. Tuition: $1704.

4290 Saint John's University

Box 2000   612-363-2248
Collegeville, MN 56321

Rev. Anthony Hellenberg, Special Services

An independent four-year college with 26 special education students out of a total of 1873. Tuition: $14361.

4291 Saint Mary's College

P.O. Box 1495   507-457-1421
Winona, MN 55987

Jane Ochrymowcyz, Special Services

4292 Southwest State University

Marshall, MN 56258   507-537-6286

Marilyn Leach

4293 St. Cloud University

222 H Atwood   612-255-3004
St. Cloud, MN 56301

Patricia Borgert, Special Services

A public four-year college with 45 special education students out of a total of 14955. Tuition: $1882.

4294 St. Mary's Campus of the College of St. Catherine

2500 South Sixth Street   612-332-5521
Minneapolis, MN 55454

Dr. Karen Hilgers, Special Services

4295 St. Olaf College

Northfield, MN 55057   507-663-3288

Kathy Quaid, Special Services

4296 St. Paul Technical College

235 Marshall Avenue   612-228-4300
St. Paul, MN 55102

Margie Warrington, Transition Director

A public two-year college with 75 special education students out of a total of 3570. Tuition: $1550.

4297 University of Minnesota, Crookston

Bede Student Center   218-281-6510
Crookston, MN 56716

Laurie Wilson, Coordinator

A public two-year college with 20 special education students out of a total of 1336. Tuition: $2475.

4298 University of Minnesota, Duluth

Learning Disabilities Program
10 University Drive   218-726-7965
Duluth, MN 55812

Judy Bromen, Coordinator

A public four-year college with 100 special education students out of a total of 7411. Tuition: $2475.

4299 University of Minnesota Morris

362 Briggs Library   612-589-6178
Morris, MN 56267

Ferolyn Angell, Special Services

4300 University of Minnesota Technical College, Crookston

Bede Student Center   218-281-6510
Crookston, MN 56716

Laurie Wilson, Special Services

4301 University of Minnesota, Twin Cities Campus

30 Nicholson Hall, 216 Pillsbury   612-624-4037
Minneapolis, MN 55455

Susan Aase, LD Specialist

A public four-year college with 400 special education students out of a total of 25515. Tuition: $2829.

4302 University of St. Thomas

2115 Summit Avenue   612-647-4048
St. Paul, MN 55105

Stephanie Zurek, Coordinator

An independent four-year college with 50 special education students out of a total of 5279. Tuition: $14168.

4303 Willmar Community College

Box 797   612-231-5176
Willmar, MN 56201

Bernice Grabber-Tintes, Special Services

A public two-year college with 11 special education students out of a total of 1379. Tuition: $1704.

4304 Willmar Technical College

2101 15th Avenue NW   612-235-5114
Wilmar, MN 56201

Mary Casey Allen, Department Chair

A public two-year college with 50 special education students out of a total of 1336. Tuition: $1692.

4305 Worthington Community College

1450 College Way   507-372-2107
Worthington, MN 56187

Esther Klein, Special Services

A public two-year college with 15 special education students out of a total of 860. Tuition: $1704.

Mississippi

4306 Hinds Community College

P.O. Box 10400   601-857-3386
Raymond, MS 39154

Ginger Manchester, Director

4307 Holmes Community College

P.O. Box 369   601-972-2312
Goodman, MS 39079

Julia Williams, Instructor

4308 Itawamba Community College

602 West Hill Street   601-862-3101
Fulton, MS 38843

Betty Heaton, Chariperson

4309 Northeast Mississippi Community College

Cunningham Blvd.   601-728-7751
Booneville, MS 38829

Sarah Rhodes, Director

A public two-year college with 3 special education students out of a total of 3041. Tuition: $950.

4310 University of Mississippi

Room 110-C, J.D. Williams Library   601-232-7128
University, MS 38677

Ardessa Milor, Special Services

A public four-year college with 69 special education students out of a total of 8791. Tuition: $2435.

4311 William Carey College

Box 181   601-582-6208
Hattiesburg, MS 39401

Brenda Waldrip, Special Services

Missouri

4312 Central Methodist College

Fayette, MO 65248   816-248-3391

Charlotte O'Brien

4313 Central Missouri State University

Union 215   816-429-4421
Warrensburg, MO 64093

Alice Gower

4314 East Central College

P.O. Box 529   314-583-5193
Union, MO 63084

Michael Knight, Assessment Director

4315 Evangel College

1111 North Glenstone   417-865-2811
Springfield, MO 65802

Dr. Eleanor Syler, Assoc. Professor

An independent four-year college with 10 special education students out of a total of 1440. Tuition: $9440.

4316　Jefferson College

P.O. Box 1000　　　　　　　　314-942-3000
Hillsboro, MO 63050

Tom Burke, Director

4317　Kansas City Art Institute

4415 Warwick　　　　　　　　816-561-4852
Kansas City, MO 64111

Patty Jachowicz, Director

4318　Lindenwood College

St. Charles, MO 63301
　　　　　　　　　　　　　　314-949-2000

V. Peter Pitts, Director

4319　Longview Community College

500 Longview Road　　　　　　816-672-2366
Lee's Summit, MO 64081

Mary Ellen Jenison, Project ABLE Coord.

A public two-year college with 22 special education students out of a total of 9844. There is a $80 fee for the special education program in addition to the regular tuition of $1110.

4320　Maple Woods Community College

2601 Northeast Barry Road　　　816-437-3192
Kansas City, MO 64156　　　FAX 816-437-3049

Kathy Acosta, Disabled Specialist
Janet Weaver, Outreach Counselor

A public two-year college with 30 special education students out of a total of 5007. Tuition: $1110.

4321　Missouri Southern State College

Joplin, MO 64801
　　　　　　　　　　　　　　417-625-9373

Myrna Dolence, Special Services

4322　Missouri Valley College

500 East College　　　　　　　816-886-6924
Marshall, MO 65340

Marilyn Ehlert, Director

An independent four-year college with 5 special education students out of a total of 1032. Tuition: $13050.

4323　North Central Missouri College

1301 Main Street　　　　　　　816-359-3948
Tranton, MO 64683

Ginny Wickoff, Counselor

4324　Northwest Missouri State University

Maryville, MO 64468　　　　　816-562-1219

W.C. Dizney, Special Services

4325　Rockhurst College

1100 Rockhurst Road　　　　　816-926-4052
Kansas City, MO 64110

Deborah Spickelmier, Special Services

An independent four-year college with 5 special education students out of a total of 2081. Tuition: $12260.

4326　Southwest Missouri State University

901 South National　　　　　　417-836-4787
Springfield, MO 65804

A public four-year college with 62 special education students out of a total of 17941. Tuition: $1966.

4327　St. Louis Community College At Florissant Valley - Accessibility Services

3400 Pershall Road　　　　　　314-595-4551
St. Louis, MO 63135　　　FAX 314-595-4544

Suelaine Matthews, Manager

A public two-year college with 65 special education students out of a total of 10233. Tuition: $1184.

4328　St. Louis Community College At Forest Park

5600 Oakland Avenue　　　　　314-644-9243
St. Louis, MO 63110

Monica Heibert, Special Services

A public two-year college with 50 special education students out of a total of 7469. Tuition: $1280.

4329　St. Louis Community College At Meramec

11333 Big Bend Blvd.　　　　　314-984-7673
Kirkwood, MO 63122

Judy Ryan

A public two-year college with 286 special education students out of a total of 15566. Tuition: $1140.

4330　University of Missouri - Columbia

407 General Classroom Building　314-882-4826
Columbia, MO 65211

Drew Love, Special Services

4331 University of Missouri, Kansas City

Kansas City, MO 64110   816-932-4444

Paul Arena

4332 University of Missouri - Rolla

Rolla, MO 65401   314-341-4211

Dr. Debra Robinson, Special Services

4333 Washington University

Campus Box 1134   314-889-5970
St. Louis, MO 63130

Dr. Leon Ashford, Special Services

4334 Webster University

470 East Lockwood Street   314-968-7495
St. Louis, MO 63119

Karin Niemeyer, Special Services

4335 Westminster College

Westminster Hall   314-642-3361
Fulton, MO 65251

Henry Ottinger, Director

An independent four-year college with 28 special education students out of a total of 746. There is a $2200 fee for the special education program in addition to the regular tuition of $12700.

Montana

4336 College of Great Falls

1301 20th Avenue South   406-761-8210
Great Falls, MT 59405   800-848-3431
                               FAX 406-761-8210

Bonnie Steele

An independent four-year college with 15 special education students out of a total of 1018. Tuition: $4200.

4337 Dull Knife Memorial College

Box 98   406-477-6215
Lame Deer, MT 59043

Juanita Lonebear

4338 Flathead Valley Community College

777 Grandview Drive   406-756-3882
Kalispell, MT 59901

Brian Bechtold, Counselor/Advocate

LD testing and learning styles assessment is available in the Learning Center. Advocates for Students with Disabilities works with faculty and staff to provide appropriate accommodations for students with learning disabilities.

4339 Great Falls Commercial College

Ebronix Learning Center
905 First Avenue
N. Great Falls, MT 59403

Dennis Wingen, Director

4340 Montana State University

Disabled Student Services
Bozemann, MT 59717   406-994-2824

Laurie Gaffey, Program Specialist

4341 Northern Montana College

P.O. Box 77511   406-265-3783
Havre, MT 59501

Linda Hoines, Learning Specialist

A public four-year college with 14 special education students out of a total of 1571. Tuition: $1440.

4342 Rocky Mountain College

Services for Academic Success
1511 Poly Drive   406-657-1070
Billings, MT 59102   800-877-6259
                           FAX 406-259-9751

Dr. Jane Van Dyk, Director

An independent four-year college with 31 special education students out of a total of 705. Tuition: $11495.

4343 Western Montana College

710 South Atlantic   406-683-7330
Dillon, MT 59725

Clarence Kostelecky, Special Services

A public four-year college with 9 special education students out of a total of 1106. Tuition: $1274.

Nebraska

4344 Chadron State College

Chadron, NE 69337   308-432-4451

Mabel Muller

4345 Concordia Teachers College

800 North Columbia   402-643-3651
Seward, NE 68434   800-535-5494

Dr. Gayle Grotjan, Director

A co-educational institute of higher learning committed to the Christian growth of its students. As a means of maximizing the learning experience and meeting the special needs individual students require. Concordia offers the services of a coordinator for those students. The coordinator acts as a liasion between students and instructors to identify accommodations that would meet the student's learning needs. Through the Learning Center, the school provides peer tutoring programs in academics.

4346   Creighton University

2500 California   402-280-2749
Omaha, NE 68178

Joel Scherling, Associate Director

An independent four-year college with 3 special education students out of a total of 4113. Tuition: $13670.

4347   Dana College

2848 College Drive   402-426-9000
Blair, NE 68008

Dr. Bernard Matthies, Academic V.P.

4348   Doane College

1014 Boswell Avenue   402-826-8554
Crete, NE 68333

Sherri Hanigan

An independent four-year college with 3 special education students out of a total of 740. Tuition: $11470.

4349   Hastings College

7th and Turner   402-461-7386
Hastings, NE 68902   800-LEARN-HC

Kathleen Haverly, Director Of Center
Sam Remnick, Admissions Director

Learning disabled students are provided with a personalized accommodation plan. Students must be verified prior to enrollment and submit a psychological review profile prior to being served. Services include: study skills instruction, academic, career and vocational counseling services, note takers, tutors, professionals and testing accommodations.

4350   Southeast Community College, Beatrice Campus

Route 2, Box 35A   402-228-3468
Beatrice, NE 68310

Jim Rakers, Special Services

A public two-year college with 5 special education students out of a total of 843. Tuition: $1002.

4351   Southeast Community Collge, Lincoln Campus

8800 'O' Street   402-436-2625
Lincoln, NE 68520   800-642-4075
                                   FAX 402-437-2404

Darlene Williams, Counselor/Coord.

A two year vocational/technical college with approximately 4,000 full/part time students. Assommodations for students with disabilities are made through the Counselor/Coordinator of Services for Students with Disabilities.

4352   Union College

3800 South 48th   402-486-2506
Lincoln, NE 68506

Jennifer Forbes

An independent four-year college with 52 special education students out of a total of 614. There is a $275 fee for the special education program in addition to the regular tuition of $10610.

4353   University of Nebraska - Lincoln

132 Administration Building   402-472-3787
Lincoln, NE 68588

Christy Horn, Special Services

A public four-year college with 138 special education students out of a total of 19884. Tuition: $1718.

4354   University of Nebraska, Omaha

Omaha, NE 68182   402-554-2393

Dr. John Hill

4355   Wayne State College

200 East 10th   402-375-7496
Wayne, NE 68787

Dorothy Weber, Special Services

4356   Western Nebraska Community College, Scottsbluff Campus

1601 East 27th Street   308-635-3606
Scottsbluff, NE 69361

Vanessa Harrison, Special Services

Nevada

4357   Truckee Meadows Community College

7000 Dandini Blvd.   702-673-7060
Reno, NV 89512

Tom Tooke, Special Services

A public two-year college with 140 special education students out of a total of 9742. Tuition: $840.

4358   University of Nevada, Las Vegas

4505 South Maryland Parkway   702-739-3781
Las Vegas, NV 89154

Janice Hurtubise

A public four-year college with 42 special education students out of a total of 16812. Tuition: $1665.

4359 University of Nevada - Reno

Reno, NV 89557   702-784-6801

Nancye Pierce, Special Services

4360 Western Nevada Community College

2201 West Nye Lane   702-887-3092
Carson City, NV 89703

Connie Capurro, Counselor

New Hampshire

4361 Colby-Sawyer College

100 Main Street   603-526-2010
New London, NH 03257

Ellen Ross-Mims, Learning Specialist
Dr. Thomas Mooney, Learning Specialist
An independent four-year college with 26 special education students out of a total of 611. Tuition: $17895.

4362 Dartmouth College

6 College Hall   603-646-2014
Hanover, NH 03755

Nancy Pompian, Coordinator

4363 Franklin Pierce College

College Road   603-899-4107
Rindge, NH 03461

Anna Carlson, Academic Resources
An independent four-year college with 50 special education students out of a total of 1298. Tuition: $16410.

4364 Keene State College

229 Main Street   603-358-2353
Keene, NH 03431

Dwight Fischer, Director
Deborah Merchant, Asst. Director
A public four-year college with 95 special education students out of a total of 3793. Tuition: $114.

4365 Learning Skills Academy

1247 Washington Road   603-964-9560
Rye, NH 03870

Carol Cook

4366 Nathaniel Hawthorne College

Antrim, NH 03440

R. Rachie

4367 New England College

7 Main Street   603-428-2218
Henniker, NH 03242

Joanne MacEachran, Special Services
An independent four-year college with 191 special education students out of a total of 1000. Tuition: $16960.

4368 New Hampshire College

2500 River Road   603-645-9606
Manchester, NH 03104

Francis Doucette, Special Services

4369 New Hampshire Technical College

277R Portsmouth Avenue   603-772-1194
Stratham, NH 03885

David Veno, Dean Of Students
A public two-year college with 26 special education students out of a total of 428. Tuition: $2088.

4370 New Hampshire Vocational Technical College

Prescott Hill, Route 106   603-524-3207
Laconia, NH 03246

Maria Dreyer, Special Services

4371 Notre Dame College

Manchester, NH 03104   603-699-4298

Dr. Robert Cray-Andrews

4372 Rivier College

420 South Main Street   603-888-1311
Nashua, NH 03060

Annette Mayo Pagano, Special Needs
An independent four-year college with 7 special education students out of a total of 1647. Tuition: $14070.

4373 University of New Hampshire

200 Memorial Union Bldg.   603-862-2607
Durham, NH 03824

Donna Marie Sorrentino, Special Services

4374 White Pines College

40 Chester Street   603-887-4401
Chester, NH 03036

Dr. John Hoar, Special Services

New Jersey

4375 Caldwell College

Learning Center
9 Ryerson Avenue   201-228-4424
Caldwell, NJ 07006

Harriet Schenk

An independent four-year college with 8 special education students out of a total of 1306. Tuition: $12360.

4376 College of Saint Elizabeth

Convent Station, NJ 07961   201-292-6318

Sr. Marie MacNamee, Dean Of Studies

4377 Fairleigh Dickinson University, Teaneck- Hackensack Campus

1000 River Road   201-692-2808
Teaneck, NJ 07666

Dr. Mary Farrell, Director

An independent four-year college with 90 special education students out of a total of 2094. Tuition: $15692..

4378 Felician College

260 South Main Street   201-778-1190
Lodi, NJ 07644

Sandra Van Dyk, Director Admission

4379 Gloucester County College

Tanyard Road   609-468-5000
Sewell, NJ 08080

Edward Hudak, Jr., Coordiantor

A public two-year college with 25 special education students out of a total of 4755. Tuition: $1320.

4380 Hudson County Community College

900 Bergen Avenue   201-714-4497
Jersey City, NJ 07306

Ellen O'Shea, Coordinator

4381 Jersey City State College

Learning Center   201-547-3368
Jersey City, NJ 07305

Dr. Myrna Ehrlich, Director

4382 Kean College of New Jersey

Morris Avenue   908-527-2380
Union, NJ 07083

Dr. Marie Segal, Director

Operates a number of clinics, each of which may function inter-disciplinary to provide services, such as speech, audiology, psychology, reading, learning, social work and special education.

4383 Middlesex County College

Mill Road   908-906-2507
Edison, NJ 08818

Joan Ikle, Director

A public two-year college with 150 special education students out of a total of 11218. Tuition: $1254.

4384 Monmouth College

West Long Branch, NJ 07764   201-222-6600

Robert Andreach

4385 New Jersey Institute of Technology

University Heights   201-596-3414
Newark, NJ 07102

Dr. Phyllis Bolling, Special Services

A public four-year college with 14 special education students out of a total of 4896. Tuition: $3628.

4386 Ocean County College

Project Academic Skills Support
P.O. Box 2001, College Drive   908-255-0456
Toms River, NJ 08754

Maureen Reustle, Director, PASS
Anne Hammond, Counselor, PASS

A public two-year college with 195 special education students out of a total of 8117. Tuition: $108.

4387 Princeton University

303 West College   609-452-3054
Princeton, NJ 08544

Stephen Cochrane, Special Services

4388 Ramapo College

Office of Specialized Services
505 Ramapo Valley Road   201-825-2800
Mahwah, NJ 07430

Pamela Bischoff

4389 Raritan Valley Community College

Box 3300   908-526-1200
Somerville, NJ 08876

Patricia Kretschy, LD Specialist

A public two-year college with 100 special education students out of a total of 5638. Tuition: $1308.

4390 Round Lake Camp of the N.J. YM-YWHA Camps

21 Plymouth Street   201-575-3333
Fairfield, NJ 07004

Eugene Bell

4391 Rutgers, the State University of New Jersey, Rutgers College

Center for Cognitive Training
Rutgers College   201-648-5845
Newark, NJ 07102

Dr. Elaine Dolinsky, Co-Director
A public four-year college with 2 special education students out of a total of 437. Tuition: $3254.

4392 Salem Community College

460 Hollywood Avenue   609-299-2100
Carneys Point, NJ 08069

Teresa Haman, Coordinator

4393 Stockton State College

Pomona, NJ 08240   609-652-4723

Thomasa Gonzalez, Special Services

4394 Trenton State College

P.O. Box 4700   609-771-2572
Trenton, NJ 08650

Dr. Juneau Gary, Special Services
A public four-year college with 24 special education students out of a total of 6018. Tuition: $3761.

4395 Upsala College

East Orange, NJ 07019   206-266-7191

Robert Nilan, Special Services

4396 William Paterson College of New Jersey

300 Pompton Road   201-595-2491
Wayne, NJ 07470

Barbara Milne, Special Services

New Mexico

4397 Albuquerque Technical Vocational Institute

525 Buena Vista SE   505-224-3259
Albuquerque, NM 87106

A. Paul Smarrella, Special Services
Provides or coordinates services for students with all disabilities. For students with learning disabilities can

arrange for special testing situations, notetaker/scribes, tape recorders, use of wordprocessors or other accommodations based on individual needs.

4398 Eastern New Mexico University, Roswell

P.O. Box 6000   505-624-7289
Roswell, NM 88202

Linda Green, Special Services
A public two-year college with 24 special education students out of a total of 2074. Tuition: $612.

4399 Institute of American Indiana Arts

P.O. Box 20007   505-988-6432
Santa Fe, NM 87504

Karen Roberts Strong, Learning Resources
A public two-year college with 5 special education students out of a total of 227. Tuition: $5061.

4400 New Mexico Institute of Mining and Technology

Box 3527, Campus Station   505-835-5208
Socorro, NM 87801

Dr. Judith Raymond, Special Services
A public four-year college with 5 special education students out of a total of 1126. Tuition: $1666.

4401 New Mexico Junior College

5317 Lovington Highway   503-392-4510
Hobbs, NM 88240

Georgia Jordan, Special Services
A public two-year college with 159 special education students out of a total of 2438. Tuition: $380.

4402 New Mexico State University

Box 30001, Department 4149   505-646-1921
Las Cruces, NM 88003

Mary Thumann, Coordinator
A public four-year college with 15 special education students out of a total of 12922. Tuition: $1708.

4403 Northern New Mexico Community College

1002 Onate   503-753-7141
Espanola, NM 87532

Millie Lowry, Special Services
If you have a learning disability, support services include: reading class, readers of tests, notetakers, taped texts, tutoring, math class, recorders for classroom use, library assistance, extra time for tests, self-esteem counseling, resume' assistance and kurzweil reading computers.

4404 San Juan College

4601 College Blvd.   505-599-0271
Farmington, NM 87402

Sandra Conner, Counselor
Ken Kernagis, Counseling Director

A public two-year college with 20 special education students out of a total of 3650. Tuition: $360.

4405 University of Albuquerque

Albuquerque, NM 87106   505-821-1111

Dr. Sandra Pitts

4406 University of New Mexico

Albuquerque, NM 87131   505-277-0111

Juan Candelaria

4407 University of New Mexico, Los Alamos Branch

4000 University Drive   505-662-5919
Los Alamos, NM 87544

Juliana Pufal, Coordinaotr

4408 University of New Mexico, Valencia Campus

280 La Entrada   505-865-1630
Los Lunas, NM 87031

Sharon Matthews, Coordinator

A public two-year college with 15 special education students out of a total of 1317. Tuition: $600.

4409 Western New Mexico University

Silver City, NM 88061   505-538-6310

Tony Machias, Special Services

New York

4410 Adelphi University

Box 701, Eddy Hall   516-877-4710
Garden City, NY 11530

Sandra Holzinger, Director Of LD

An independent four-year college with 140 special education students out of a total of 4599. There is a $3500 fee for the special education program in addition to the regular tuition of $17680.

4411 Albert Einstein College of Medicine, Rose F. Kennedy Institute

1410 Belham Parkway South   212-430-3397
Bronx, NY 10461

Ruth Gottesman, Ed.D., Director Adult Lit.

Provides evaluation and psychoeducational treatment to adults with severe reading difficulties.

4412 Alfred Campus, State University of New York College

Alfred, NY 14802   607-587-4122

Kathryn Fosegan, Coordinator

An independent four-year college with 22 special education students out of a total of 1936. Tuition: $19733.

4413 Bank Street College - Graduate School of Education

610 West 1112th Street   212-663-7200
New York, NY 10025

Sylvia Ross

For learning disabled college students who are highly motivated to become teachers of children and youth with learning problems and who wish to earn a masters degree in Special Education.

4414 Bramson Ort Technical Institute

6930 Austin Street   718-261-5800
Forest Hills, NY 11375

Susan Davidovic, Student Counselor

4415 Broome Community College

P.O. Box 1017   607-771-5234
Binghamton, NY 13902

Bruce Pomeroy, Director

A public two-year college with 65 special education students out of a total of 6400. Tuition: $1630.

4416 Buffalo - State University of New York College

1300 Elmwood Avenue   716-878-6711
Buffalo, NY 14222

Joseph Luzio, Special Services

A public four-year college with 37 special education students out of a total of 15439. Tuition: $2650.

4417　Canisius College

Academic Development Center
Buffalo, NY 14208　　716-883-7000

David Lauerman

4418　Canton - State University of New York College of Technology

Canton, NY 13617　　315-386-7121
　　　　　　　　　　　800-388-7123

Debora Camp, Accommodative Srvcs.

A public four-year college with 68 special education students out of a total of 2297. Tuition: $2650.

4419　Cazenovia College

Cazenovia, NY 13035　　315-655-9446

Faith Cobb, PhD, Special Services
Margery Pinet, Dir. Learning Ctr.

An independent two-year college with 50 special education students out of a total of 1071. Tuition: $13417.

4420　College of New Rochelle, New Resources Division

29 Castle Place　　914-654-5364
New Rochelle, NY 10805

Joan Bristol

4421　College of Staten Island of the City University of New York

2800 Victory Blvd.　　718-390-7626
Staten Island, NY 10314

Dr. Audrey Glynn, Director
Margaret Venditti, Assistant

A public four-year college with 32 special education students out of a total of 11133. Tuition: $1850.

4422　Columbia-Greene Community College

P.O. Box 1000　　518-828-4181
Hudson, NY 12534

June Blake, Chairperson

A public two-year college with 25 special education students out of a total of 1661. Tuition: $1580.

4423　Cornell University

234 Day Hall　　607-255-3976
Ithaca, NY 14853

Joan Fisher, Disability Services

An independent four-year college with 74 special education students out of a total of 12915. Tuition: $22940.

4424　Corning Community College

One Academic Drive　　607-962-9459
Corning, NY 14830

Charles Hollister, Director
Judy Northrop, Counselor

A public two-year college with 70 special education students out of a total of 3540. Tuition: $1750.

4425　Delhi - State University of New York College of Technology

Bush Hall　　607-746-4364
Delhi, NY 13753

Ellenn D'Acquisto, Srvcs For LD Student

A public four-year college with 80 special education students out of a total of 2332. Tuition: $21500.

4426　Dutchess Community College

Dutchess Hall 204　　914-471-4500
Poughkeepsie, NY 12601

Mary Staskel, Coordinator

A public two-year college with 47 special education students out of a total of 7509. Tuition: $1550.

4427　Elizabeth Seton College

1061 North Broadway　　914-969-4000
Yonkers, NY 10701

Sandi Galst, Director

4428　Erie Community College, South Campus

Main And Young Roads　　716-634-0800
Williamsville, NY 14221

Nancy Bailey, Counselor

A public two-year college with 200 special education students out of a total of 3485. Tuition: $3660.

4429　Farmingdale - State University of New York College of Technology

Roosevelt Hall　　516-420-2450
Farmingdale, NY 11735

Anita Triell, Special Services

A public four-year college with 200 special education students out of a total of 9684. Tuition: $2150.

4430　Fashion Institute of Technology

Seventh Ave. At 27th Street　　212-760-7994
New York, NY 10001

Gail Ballard, Tutoring Program

A public four-year college with 103 special education students out of a total of 12007. Tuition: $36.

4431 Finger Lakes Community College

4355 Lake Shore Drive   716-394-3500
Canandaigua, NY 14424

Patricia Malinowski, Chairperson

Provides services such as pre-admission counseling, academic advisement, tutoirlas, computer assistance, workshops, peer couseling and support groups. The College does not offer a formal program but aids students in arranging appropriate accommodations.

4432 Fiorello H. Laguardia Community College of the City University of New York

The Learning Project
31-10 Thomson Avenue   718-482-5278
Long Island City, NY 11101

Carol DeSantis, Director

A public two-year college with 59 special education students out of a total of 9270. Tuition: $1750.

4433 Fordham University

McGinley Center 224   212-579-2152
Bronx, NY 10458

Gregory Pappas, Student Services

An independent four-year college with 20 special education students out of a total of 7089. Tuition: $17625.

4434 Fredonia - State University of New York College

2130 Thompson Hall   716-673-3461
Fredonia, NY 14063

Marion Steese, Special Services

4435 Fulton-Montgomery Community College

Johnstown, NY 12095   518-762-4651

Harold Morell, Coordinator

A public two-year college with 74 special education students out of a total of 1745. Tuition: $1750.

4436 Genesco Campus, State University of New York College

Fraser 107, 1 College Circle   716-245-5492
Geneseo, NY 14454

Paula Melendrez, Associate Dean

A public four-year college with 3 special education students out of a total of 5140. Tuition: $2650.

4437 Genesee Community College

1 College Road   716-343-0055
Batavia, NY 14020

Dr. Ann Marie Malachowski, Dean Of Students

A public two-year college with 72 special education students out of a total of 3210. Tuition: $1800.

4438 Herkimer County Community College

Herkimer, NY 13350   315-866-0300

Michele Weaver, Assistant Dean

A public two-year college with 120 special education students out of a total of 2330. Tuition: $1700.

4439 Hofstra University

Program for Academic Learning Skills
202 Roosevelt Hall   516-560-5840
Hempstead, NY 11550

Dr. Ignacio Gotz, Director

4440 Houghton College

Houghton, NY 14744   716-567-9622

Mary Jayne Allen, Counseling Services

An independent four-year college with 18 special education students out of a total of 1146. Tuition: $12534.

4441 Hudson Valley Community College

80 Vandenburgh Avenue   518-270-7554
Troy, NY 12180

Maryo Archibee Blake

A public two-year college with 18 special education students out of a total of 9766. Tuition: $1300.

4442 Hunter College of the City University of New York

695 Park Avenue   212-772-4888
New York, NY 10021

Sandra LaPorta, Student Services

4443 Iona College

College Assistance Program
715 North Avenue   914-378-8014
New Rochelle, NY 10801   800-800-IONA

Elsa Brady-DeVita, Director CAP

The College Assistance Program is a comprehensive support program for stduents with learning disabilities. The students in CAP receive services including tutoring, advocacy, priority registration, reduced course load, counseling and career services. Students can matriculate for either an associate's degree or bachelor's degree.

4444 Ithaca College, Speech and Hearing Clinic

Smiddy Hall, Ithaca College   607-274-3714
Ithaca, NY 14850

Richard Schissel

4445 Jamestown Community College

525 Falconer Street   716-665-5220
Jamestown, NY 14701

Nancy Callahan, Disability Support

A public two-year college with 39 special education students out of a total of 4529. Tuition: $1600.

4446 Jefferson Community College

Outer Coffeen Street   315-782-5250
Watertown, NY 13601

Ted Hogancamp, Coordinator

A public two-year college with 24 special education students out of a total of 2100. Tuition: $1400.

4447 John Jay College of Criminal Justice of the City University of New York

445 West 59th Street   212-237-8122
New York, NY 10019

Farris Forsythe, Coordinator

An independent two-year college with 60 special education students out of a total of 7900. Tuition: $1850.

4448 Long Island University, Southampton Campus

Southampton, NY 11968   516-283-4000

Pamela Topping, Director

4449 Long Island University - the Brooklyn Center

Special Education Services Program   212-834-6045
Brooklyn, NY 11201

Robert Nathanson, Director

4450 Manhattan College

Manhattan College Parkway   212-920-0409
Riverdale, NY 10471

Dr. Sheila Meindl, Administrator

An independent four-year college with 5 special education students out of a total of 3071. There is a $3000 fee for the special education program in addition to the regular tuition of $17562.

4451 Manhattanville College

Purchase, NY 10577   914-694-2200

Joyce French, Director

4452 Maria College

700 New Scotland Avenue   518-438-3111
Albany, NY 12208

Margie Byrd, Chair

An independent two-year college with 10 special education students out of a total of 860. Tuition: $4200.

4453 Marist College

290 North Road   914-575-3274
Poughkeepsie, NY 12601   FAX 914-471-6213

Dr. Diane Perriera, Director

An independent two-year college with 50 special education students out of a total of 3692. There is a $1800 fee for the special education program in addition to the regular tuition of $16096.

4454 Marymount Manhattan College

221 East 71st Street   212-517-0501
New York, NY 10021

Dr. Joan Shapiro

An independent four-year college with 10 special education students out of a total of 1300. There is a $3000 fee for the special education program in addition to the regular tuition of $9820.

4455 Mater Dei College

RR 2, Box 445   313-393-5930
Ogdensburg, NY 13669

Anthony Puccia, Coordinator

Support Services offered include accommodations, DSS office, registration assistance, on-campus housing, counseling, disability-specific assessment, referrals, adapted equipment, learning skills center lab, notetakers, readers, tutors, scribes, taped texts, alternative testing methods, course substituion, waiver, basic cognitive and achievement testing.

4456 Medaille College

18 Agassiz Circle   716-884-3281
Buffalo, NY 14214

Jacqueline Smuckler

4457 Mercy College

Program for Learning Disabled College Students
555 Broadway   914-693-4500
Dobbs Ferry, NY 10522

Dr. Peter Schnecker, Director

4458 Mohawk Valley Community College

1101 Sherman Drive   315-792-5413
Utica, NY 13501

Joseph A. Zizzi, Special Services

4459 Molloy College

1000 Hempstead Avenue   516-678-5000
Rockville Centre, NY 11570

Sr. Therese Forker, Disabled Students

An independent four-year college with 5 special education students out of a total of 1428. There is a $600 fee for the special education program in addition to the regular tuition of $8190.

4460 Morrisville - State University of New York College of Agriculture/Technology

Counseling Center   315-684-6071
Morrisville, NY 13408

Lisa Oristian, Special Services

4461 Nassau Community College

1 Education Drive   516-222-7138
Garden City, NY 11530

Dr. Victor Margolis, Coord. Disabled Srv.

A public two-year college with 188 special education students out of a total of 17621. Tuition: $1650.

4462 Nazareth College of Rochester

4245 East Avenue   716-586-2525
Rochester, NY 14618

Joan Anderson, Residential Director

4463 New College At Hofstra University

Hempstead, Long Island, NY 11550   516-560-0500

4464 New York City Technical College of the City University of New York

300 Jay Street #A237   718-643-7230
Brooklyn, NY 11201

Joann Mischianti, Special Services

4465 New York Institute of Technology

Old Westbury, NY 11568   516-686-7655

Dr. Judith Amster

An independent four-year college with 39 special education students out of a total of 7623. There is a $4000 fee for the special education program in addition to the regular tuition of $12695.

4466 New York University

Access to Learning
Room 701, 566 LaGuardia Place   212-998-4980
New York, NY 10011

Georgeann du Chossois, Coordinator

An independent four-year college with 125 special education students out of a total of 15092. Tuition: $23430.

4467 New York University Medical Center, Learning Diagnostic Center

525 East 68th   212-263-7753
New York, NY 10021   FAX 212-263-7721

Ruth Nass, Dir., Assoc. Prof.

Assessment team, neurology, neuro-psychology, psychiatry services are offered.

4468 Niagara County Community College

3111 Saunders Settlement Road   716-731-3271
Sanborn, NY 14132

Karen Drilling, Special Services

A public two-year college with 67 special education students out of a total of 5480.

4469 Niagara University

Alumni Hall   716-285-1212
Niagara University, NY 14109

Linda McGrath, Special Services

An independent four-year college with 25 special education students out of a total of 2410. Tuition: $13746.

4470 North Country Community College

20 Winona Avenue   518-891-2915
Saranac Lake, NY 12983

Jo Ann K. Branch, Director

A public two-year college with 15 special education students out of a total of 1604. Tuition: $1600.

4471 Oneonta Campus, State University of New York College

1 Alumni Hall   607-436-2137
Oneonta, NY 13820

Sandra Denicore, Academic Services

A public four-year college with 60 special education students out of a total of 1016. Tuition: $2650.

4472 Onondaga Community College

Services for Students with Special Needs
Onondaga Hill, Ste. 173   315-469-2245
Syracuse, NY 13215

Linda Koslowsky, Administrative Aids

A public two-year college with 200 special education students out of a total of 8389. Tuition: $1540.

4473 Orange County Community College

Middletown, NY 10940   914-343-1121

Marilynn Brake, Special Services Cd.

The Office of Special Services for the Disabled provides support services to meet the individual needs of students with disabilities. Such accommodations include oral testing, extended time testing, tape recorded textbooks, writing lab, note-takers and others. Pres-admission counseling ensure accessibility for the qualified student.

4474 Oswego Campus, State University of New York College

501 Culkin Hall   315-341-2240
Oswego, NY 13126

Kathleen Evans, Coordinator

A public four-year college with 28 special education students out of a total of 7621. Tuition: $2650.

4475 Paul Smith's College

Paul Smiths, NY 12970   518-327-6425

Carol McKillip, LD Specialist

4476 Plattsburgh - State University of New York College

Angell Center 110   518-564-2810
Plattsburgh, NY 12901

Michele Little, Special Services

A public four-year college with 90 special education students out of a total of 5530. Tuition: $2650.

4477 Polytechnic University, Farmingdale Campus

333 Jay Street   718-260-3560
Farmingdale, NY 11735

Haang Fung, Special Services

4478 Potsdam Campus, State University of New York College

Room 120, 555P   315-267-2795
Potsdam, NY 13676

Susan Romeo, Accommodative Coun.

A public four-year college with 54 special education students out of a total of 4162. Tuition: $2650.

4479 Purchase - State University of New York College

Humanities 2077   914-253-5156
Purchase, NY 10577

Dr. Marjorie Miller, Special Services

4480 Queens College of the City University of New York

Kiely 171   718-520-7636
Flushing, NY 11367

Debra Cole, Special Services

A public four-year college with 90 special education students out of a total of 14704. Tuition: $2200.

4481 Queensborough Community College of the City University of New York

56th Ave. & Springfield Road   718-631-6257
Bayside, NY 11364

Elliot Rosman, Special Services

A public two-year college with 350 special education students out of a total of 12300. Tuition: $2100..

4482 Rensselaer Polytechnic Institute

Room 200, Troy Building   518-276-2746
Troy, NY 12180

Debra Hamilton, Special Services

An independent four-year college with 24 special education students out of a total of 4450. Tuition: $21870.

4483 Rochester Business Institute

1850 East Ridge Road   716-266-0430
Rochester, NY 14622

Eva Wallace, Student Advisor

An independent two-year college with 10 special education students out of a total of 525. Tuition: $4500.

4484 Rochester Institute of Technology

1 Lomb Memorial Drive   716-475-2215
Rochester, NY 14623

Jacqueline Lynch Czamanske, Chair Learning Dept.

An independent four-year college with 110 special education students out of a total of 11150. Tuition: $18006.

4485 Rockland Community College

145 College Road   914-356-4650
Suffern, NY 10901

Marge Zemek, Special Services

A public two-year college with 250 special education students out of a total of 8271. Tuition: $1750.

4486 Schenectady County Community College

78 Washington Avenue   518-346-6211
Schenectady, NY 12305

Jo Fenton-Bird, Dis. Student Service

Access for All program is designed to make programs and facilities accessible to all students in pursuit of their academic goals. Disabled Student Services seeks to ensure accessible educational opportunities in accordance with individual needs. Offers general support services, program services such as: exam assistance, special scheduling, adaptive equipment, readers, taping assistance and more.

4487 St. Bonaventure University

Teaching & Learning Center
Room 26, Doyle Hall   716-375-2066
St. Bonaventure, NY 14778

Janet Medina, Student Services

An independent four-year college with 25 special education students out of a total of 1559. Tuition: $14333.

4488 St. Lawrence University

Canton, NY 13617   315-379-5104

Jim Cohn, Director

An independent four-year college with 113 special education students out of a total of 1997. Tuition: $22120.

4489 St. Thomas Aquinas College

The STAC Exchange
Rte. 340   914-359-9500
Sparkhill, NY 10976

Dr. Marijane Doonan, Director

An independent four-year college with 82 special education students out of a total of 1989. There is a $2250 fee for the special education program in addition to the regular tuition of $11850.

4490 State University of New York At Albany

1400 Washington Avenue   518-442-5491
Albany, NY 12222

Nancy Belowich-Negron, Special Services

4491 State University of New York At Binghamton

Box 6000, Lecture Hall B 51   607-777-2686
Binghamton, NY 13902   FAX 607-777-6515

B. Jean Fairbairn, Coordinator

A public four-year college with 17 special education students out of a total of 8928. Tuition: $2650.

4492 State University of New York At Buffalo

272 Capen Hall   716-636-2608
Buffalo, NY 14260   FAX 716-645-3116

James J. Gruber, Interim Director

A public four-year college with 37 special education students out of a total of 15439. Tuition: $2650.

4493 State University of New York At Stony Brook

Disabled Student Services, Room 133   516-632-6748
Stony Brook, NY 11794

Carol Dworkin, LD Coordinator

A public four-year college with 63 special education students out of a total of 11058. Tuition: $2650.

4494 State University of New York - Cobbleskill

Cobbleskill, NY 12043

4495 State University of New York College At Brockport

101 Rakov Center   716-395-5409
Brockport, NY 14420

Karen Phelps, Special Services

4496 State University of New York College of Agriculture and Technology

Cobleskill, NY 12043   518-234-5211

Wayne Morris, Special Services

A public four-year college with 130 special education students out of a total of 9874. Tuition: $2650.

4497 State University of New York - Farmingdale

Memorial Hall   516-420-2411
Farmingdale, NY 11735

Malka Edelman

4498 Suffolk County Community College - Selden Campus

533 College Road   516-451-4046
Selden, NY 11784

Dr. Elmira Johnson, Special Services

A public two-year college with 235 special education students out of a total of 12693. Tuition: $1570.

4499 Suffolk County Community College, Eastern Campus

Speonk-Riverhead Road   516-548-2525
Riverhead, NY 11901

Judith Koodin, Counselor

The Eastern Campus is an accessible, open admissions institution. Services are provided to Learning Disabled Students to allow them the same or equivalent educational experiences as non-disabled students have.

4500 Suffolk County Community College - Western Campus

Brentwood, NY 11717   516-434-6715

Judith Taxier-Reinauer, Special Services

4501 Sullivan County Community College

Department of Developmental Studies
Loch Sheldrake, NY 12759   914-434-5750

Dennis Rowen, Director

4502 Syracuse University

804 University Avenue   315-423-4498
Syracuse, NY 13244

Joanne Heinz, Special Services

An independent four-year college with 235 special education students out of a total of 11495. Tuition: $20025.

4503 Trocaire College

110 Red Jacket   716-826-1200
Buffalo, NY 14220

Norine Truax, Coordinator

An independent two-year college with 4 special education students out of a total of 1049. Tuition: $4850.

4504 Ulster County Community College

Stone Ridge, NY 12484   914-687-5091

James Quirk, Special Services

A public two-year college with 40 special education students out of a total of 2088. Tuition: $1650.

4505 Utica College of Syracuse University

1600 Burrstone Road   315-792-3032
Utica, NY 13502

Stephen Pattarini, Special Services

An independent four-year college with 26 special education students out of a total of 1707. Tuition: $15780.

4506 Utica/Rome Campus, State University of New York College

P.O. Box 3050   315-792-7208
Utica, NY 13504

Roger Sullivan, Admissions Director

4507 Vassar College

Box 294   914-452-7000
Poughkeepsie, NY 12601

Karen Getter, Special Services

4508 Villa Maria College of Buffalo

240 Pine Ridge Road   716-896-0700
Buffalo, NY 14225

Bonnie Clark, Special Services

4509 Wagner College

Staten Island, NY 10301   718-390-3340

Ruth Ann Perri, Director

An independent four-year college with 25 special education students out of a total of 1272. There is a $50 fee for the special education program in addition to the regular tuition of $16250.

4510 Westchester Community College

75 Grasslands Road   914-285-6735
Valhalla, NY 10595

Dr. Alan Seidman, Special Services

A public two-year college with 200 special education students out of a total of 11145. Tuition: $1750.

North Carolina

4511 Anson Community College

P.O. Box 68   704-826-8333
Ansonville, NC 28007

Algie Gatewood, Dean Of Students

4512　Appalachian State University

Learning Disability Program
Boone, NC　28608　　　　　　704-262-2291

Arlene Lundquist, Coordinator

A public four-year college with 105 special education students out of a total of 10545. Tuition: $1239.

4513　Bennett College

900 East Washington Street　　　919-370-8782
Greensboro, NC　27401

Thelma Copeland, Support Services

An independent four-year college with 10 special education students out of a total of 568. Tuition: $11275.

4514　Blue Ridge Community College - Virginia

Rt. 2, Box 133A　　　　　　　704-692-3572
Flat Rock, NC　28731

Victoria McKee, Director

A public two-year college with 21 special education students out of a total of 3064. Tuition: $1312.

4515　Caldwell Community College and Technical Institute

1000 Hickory Blvd.　　　　　704-724-4323
Hudson, NC　28638

Teena McRary

A public two-year college with 10 special education students out of a total of 2730. Tuition: $552.

4516　Catawba College

2300 West Innes Street　　　　704-637-4410
Salisbury, NC　28144

Sara Welch, Master Learner

An independent four-year college with 7 special education students out of a total of 936. Tuition: $11980.

4517　Catawba Valley Community College

Box 283, Rte. 3　　　　　　704-327-9129
Hickory, NC　28602

Dr. Dan Gwaltney, Director

A public two-year college with 10 special education students out of a total of 3427. Tuition: $483.

4518　Central Carolina Community College

1105 Kelly Drive　　　　　　919-775-5401
Sanford, NC　27330

Dr. Frances Andrews, Associate Dean

4519　Central Piedmont Community College

P.O. Box 35009　　　　　　704-342-6621
Charlotte, NC　28235

Norma-Jean Arey, LD Specialist

A public two-year college with 130 special education students out of a total of 15871. Tuition: $483.

4520　Chowan College

Murfreesboro, NC　27855　　　919-398-4101

Bobbi Wooten

An independent four-year college with 45 special education students out of a total of 748. Tuition: $9380.

4521　Craven Community College

P.O. Box 885　　　　　　　919-638-4131
New Bern, NC　28563

Edna Barrett, Director

4522　Davidson County Community College

P.O. Box 1287　　　　　　702-249-8186
Lexington, NC　27293

Dr. Ed Morse, Vice President

4523　Dore Academy

1727 Providence Road　　　　704-365-5490
Charlotte, NC　28207

Mary Dore

4524　East Carolina University

212 Whichard Building　　　　919-757-6799
Greenville, NC　27858

C.C. Rowe, Coordinator

A public four-year college with 57 special education students out of a total of 13883. Tuition: $676.

4525　Forsyth Technical Community College

2100 Silas Creek Parkway　　　919-723-0371
Winston-Salem, NC　27103

Laura Wyatt, Chairperson

4526　Guilford Technical Community College

P.O. Box 309　　　　　　　919-292-1101
Jamestown, NC　27282

Dr. James Ggripper

4527 Isothermal Community College

P.O. Box 804 704-286-3636
Spindale, NC 28160

Ruth Boehning, LD Specialist

4528 Lees-Mcrae College

P.O. Box 128 704-898-5241
Banner Elk, NC 28604

Pat Smith, Chair

4529 Lenoir Community College

P.O. Box 188 919-527-6223
Kinston, NC 28501

Carl Farmer, Director
A public two-year college with 15 special education students out of a total of 2174. Tuition: $483.

4530 Mars Hill College

Mars Hill, NC 28754 704-689-1186

Gail Sawyer, Director
An independent four-year college with 5 special education students out of a total of 1323. Tuition: $10550.

4531 Maryland Community College

P.O. Box 547 704-765-7351
Spruce Pine, NC 28777

Nancy Godwin, Special Services

4532 McDowell Technical Community College

Box 170, Route 1 704-652-6021
Marion, NC 28752

James Robinson, Counseling Director
A public two-year college with 15 special education students out of a total of 857. Tuition: $483.

4533 Montgomery Community College, North Carolina

P.O. Box 787 919-572-3691
Troy, NC 27371

Dr. Virginia Morgan, Dept. Chairperson

4534 North Carolina State University, Handicapped Student Services

Box 7312 919-515-7653
Raleigh, NC 27695

Lelia Brettmann, LD Coordinator
Academic accommodations and services are provided for students at the University who have documented learning disabilities. Admission to the University is based on academic qualifications and learning disabled students are considered in the same manner as any other student.

4535 North Carolina Wesleyan College

Rocky Mount, NC 27804 919-977-7171

Lisa Singletary, Special Services

4536 Pitt Community College

Greenville, NC 27835 919-756-3130

Lynda Wilms, Special Services

4537 Randolph Community College

Box 1009 919-629-1471
Asheboro, NC 27204

Rebekah Megerian, Special Services
A public two-year college with 20 special education students out of a total of 1480. Tuition: $483.

4538 Rockingham Community College

P.O. Box 38 919-342-4261
Wentworth, NC 27375

Jack Darber, Special Services

4539 Salem College - North Carolina

Center For Special Education 919-723-7961
Winston-Salem, NC 27108

Dudley Shearburn, Director

4540 Sampson Community College

P.O. Drawer 318 919-592-8081
Clinton, NC 28328 FAX beth

4541 Sandhills Community College

2200 Airport Road 919-695-3733
Pinehurst, NC 28374

Peggie Chavis, Special Services

4542 Southwestern Community College, North Carolina

275 Webster Road 702-586-4091
Sylvia, NC 28779

Drucilla Shelton, Director
A public two-year college with 20 special education students out of a total of 1522. Tuition: $483.

4543   Summitt Academy

P.O. Box 682   704-452-0944
Hazelwood, NC 28738

James Jones

4544   Surry Community College

P.O. Box 304   919-386-8121
Dobson, NC 27017

Larry Rooks, Developmental Study

4545   Tri-County Community College

P.O. Box 40   704-837-6810
Murphy, NC 28906

Sarah Harper, Special Services

4546   University of North Carolina At Chapel Hill

Campus Box 5100, 05 Steele Bldg.   919-966-4041
Chapel Hill, NC 27599

Laura Thomas, Coordinator
A public four-year college with 120 special education students out of a total of 15439. Tuition: $1248.

4547   University of North Carolina At Charlotte

105 Winningham, Hwy. 49   704-547-4354
Charlotte, NC 28223

Susanne McWilliams, Special Services
A public four-year college with 57 special education students out of a total of 12791. Tuition: $676.

4548   University of North Carolina At Greensboro

157 Elliott University Center   919-334-5440
Greensboro, NC 27412

Patricia Bailey
A public four-year college with 120 special education students out of a total of 8921. Tuition: $1492.

4549   University of North Carolina At Wilmington

Student Development Center   919-395-3746
Wilmington, NC 28403

Phillip Sharp, Special Services

4550   Wake Forest University

P.O. Box 7838   919-761-5929
Winston-Salem, NC 27109

Dr. Sandra Chadwick, Special Services

4551   Wake Technical Community College

9101 Fayetteville Road   919-772-0551
Raleigh, NC 27603

Sheila Hite, Director Access Svc.

4552   Western Carolina University

H.F. Robinson Administration Bldg.   704-227-7234
Cullowhee, NC 28723

Dr. Bonita Jacobs, Special Services
A public four-year college with 98 special education students out of a total of 5439. Tuition: $676.

4553   Wilkes Community College

P.O. Box 120   919-651-8753
Wilkesboro, NC 28697

Dr. Barbara Holt, Special Services
A public two-year college with 5 special education students out of a total of 2100. Tuition: $483.

4554   Wilson County Technical College

P.O. Box 4305   919-291-1195
Wilson, NC 27893

William James, Special Services

4555   Wingate College

Wingate, NC 28174   704-233-8203

Patricia LeDonne, V.P. Academic Affair
An independent four-year college with 50 special education students out of a total of 1372. There is a $1000 fee for the special education program in addition to the regular tuition of $9750.

4556   Winston-Salem State Unviersity

601 Martin Luther King Dr.   919-750-5000
Winston-Salem, NC 27006

Maurice Johnson, Directopr

North Dakota

4557   Anne Carlsen School

301 7th Avenue NW   701-252-3850
Jamestown, ND 58401

Michael Numrich, Administrator
Offers education, therapy, medical care and social and psychological services for children and youth with disabilities.

4558 Bismarck State College

1500 Edwards Avenue   701-224-5426
Bismarck, ND 58501

Jason Karch

4559 Fort Berthold Community College

Box 490   701-627-3665
New Town, ND 58763

Delores Wilkinson, Dean Of Students

An independent two-year college with 3 special education students out of a total of 179. Tuition: $1440.

4560 Mayville State University

330 3rd Street   701-786-2301
Mayville, ND 58257

Deb Glennon, Coordinator

4561 North Dakota State College of Science

Counseling Center   701-671-2327
Wahpeton, ND 58076   800-342-4325

Georgia Vosberg, Resource Program

A public two-year college with 78 special education students out of a total of 2144. Tuition: $1599.

4562 North Dakota State University

Ceres Hall 212   701-237-7671
Fargo, ND 58105

Elizabeth Sepe, LD Specialist

Provides comprehensive services for students who have learning disabilities.

4563 North Dakota State University, Bottineau Branch and Institute of Forestry

First And Simrall   701-228-2277
Bottineau, ND 58318

Jan Nahinurk, Special Services

4564 Standing Rock College

Fort Yates, ND 58538   701-954-3862

Linda Ivan, Special Services

4565 University of North Dakota

Box 8256, University Station   701-777-3425
Grand Forks, ND 58202

A public four-year college with 108 special education students out of a total of 10119. Tuition: $1860.

4566 Art Academy of Cincinnati

1125 St. Gregory Street   513-562-8766
Cincinnati, OH 45202

Jane Stanton, Dean Of Students

4567 Baldwin-Wallace College

Berea, OH 44017   216-826-2222

J. Edward Warner

4568 Bowling Green State University

705 Administration Bldg.   419-372-8495
Bowling Green, OH 43403

Robert Cunningham

4569 Case Western Reserve University

4 Yost Hall   216-368-5230
Cleveland, OH 44106

Mayo Bulloch, Director

An independent four-year college with 11 special education students out of a total of 3227. Tuition: $19725.

4570 Central Ohio Technical College

Developmental Education
University Drive   614-366-9246
Newark, OH 43055

Dr. Phyllis Thompsen, Coordinator

A public two-year college with 50 special education students out of a total of 1716. Tuition: $1764.

4571 Cincinnati Technical College

3520 Central Parkway   513-569-1613
Cincinnati, OH 45223

David Cover

A public two-year college with 48 special education students out of a total of 5500. Tuition: $4230.

4572 Clark State Community College

P.O. Box 570   513-328-6081
Springfield, OH 45501

Deborah Titus, Counselor

4573 Cleveland Institute of Art

11141 East Blvd.   216-229-0989
Cleveland, OH 44106

Leila Flores

An independent four-year college with 87 special education students out of a total of 464. Tuition: $15190.

4574   Cleveland State University

1935 Euclid Avenue   216-687-2015
Cleveland, OH 44115

Michael Zuccaro

A public four-year college with 44 special education students out of a total of 13050. Tuition: $2790.

4575   College of Mount St. Joseph

Project EXCEL
Cincinnati, OH 45051   513-244-4819

Dollie Kelly

An independent four-year college with 41 special education students out of a total of 2388. There is a $1800 fee for the special education program in addition to the regular tuition of $12820.

4576   College of Mt. St. Joseph on the Ohio

5701 Delhi Road   513-244-4623
Cincinnati, OH 45233   FAX 513-244-4222

Dollie Kelly, Coordinator, LD

Learning disabled staff offers intensive instruction in reading, writing and study skills.

4577   The College of Wooster

Wooster, OH 44691   216-246-1234

Dr. Carol Roose

4578   Columbus State Community College

550 East Spring Street   614-227-2629
Columbus, OH 43215

Linda Wetters, Director

A public two-year college with 65 special education students out of a total of 15209. Tuition: $1656.

4579   Cuyahoga Community College, Eastern Campus

4250 Richmond Road   216-987-2034
Highland Hills Village, OH 44122

Mary Syarto, Student Advisor

A public two-year college with 76 special education students out of a total of 5764. Tuition: $1350.

4580   Cuyahoga Community College, Western Campus

11000 West Pleasant Valley Road   216-987-5079
Parma, OH 44130

Connie Henderson, Assistant Director

A public two-year college with 125 special education students out of a total of 12285. Tuition: $1350.

4581   Defiance College

Defiance, OH 43512   419-784-4010

Jo McCormick, Associate Professor

4582   Denison University

Box H   614-587-6666
Granville, OH 43023

Theron Snell, Educational Services

4583   Findlay College

100 North Main Street   419-424-4697
Findlay, OH 45840

Donna Smith, Director

4584   Franklin University

201 South Grant Avenue   614-224-6237
Columbus, OH 43215

Linda Turley, CoordinatorS

An independent four-year college with 21 special education students out of a total of 3990. Tuition: $3319.

4585   Heldelberg College

Tiffin, OH 44883   419-448-2404

John Nelson

4586   Hiram College

Hinsdale Hall   216-569-5125
Hiram, OH 44234

Dr. Vivian Makosky, Counseling Director

4587   Hocking Technical College

Nelsonville, OH 45764   614-753-3591

Kim Forbes Shaner, Support Specialist

4588   ITT Technical Institute

655 Wick Avenue   216-747-5555
Youngstown, OH 4501

Sara Sofia, Educational Director

4589   Jefferson Technical College

4000 Sunset Blvd.   614-264-5591
Steubenville, OH 43952

Theresa Fernandes, Director

4590   Kent State University

Disabled Student Services
181 Michael Schwartz Center   216-672-3391
Kent, OH 44242

Barbara Haugland, LD Prog. Coord.
Services offered to learning disabled students.

4591 Kent State University, Tuscarawas Campus

University Drive NE   216-339-5391
New Philadelphia, OH 44663

Joyce Belknap, Developmental Ed.

4592 Kenyon College

Gambier, OH 43022   614-427-5145

Elizabeth Keeney, Academic Affairs
An independent four-year college with 11 special education students out of a total of 1507. Tuition: $21180.

4593 Lorain County Community College

1005 N. Abbe Road   216-365-4191
Elyria, OH 44035   800-995-5222
                           FAX 216-265-6519

Ruth Porter, Coordinator
A public two-year college with 25 special education students out of a total of 7746. Tuition: $1617.

4594 Malone College

515 25th Street NW   216-471-8222
Canton, OH 44709

Dr. Patricia Long, Advising Director
An independent four-year college with 11 special education students out of a total of 1601. Tuition: $11640.

4595 Marburn Academy

1860 Walden Drive   614-433-0822
Columbus, OH 43229

Earl Oremus

4596 Marietta College

Marietta, OH 45750   614-374-4784

Bruce Peterson, Resident Director
An independent four-year college with 5 special education students out of a total of 1231. Tuition: $15990.

4597 Marion Technical College

1467 Mount Vernon Avenue   614-389-4636
Marion, OH 43302

Lori Thomas, Spec. Pop.
A public two-year college with 2 special education students out of a total of 1653. Tuition: $1656.

4598 Miami University

20 Campus Avenue Building   513-529-1375
Oxford, OH 45056

Lois Philips, Coordinator

A public four-year college with 83 special education students out of a total of 14688. Tuition: $3764.

4599 Miami University, Middletown Campus

4200 East University Blvd.   513-424-4444
Middletown, OH 45042

June Fening, Special Services

4600 Northwest Technical College

Box 246A, Route 1   419-267-5511
Archibold, OH 43502

Dennis Gable, Special Services

4601 Notre Dame College of Ohio

4545 College Road   216-381-1680
South Euclid, OH 44121

Sr. Helene Marie Gregos, Special Services

4602 Oberlin College

Room 6, Peters Hall   216-775-8467
Oberlin, OH 44074

Dr. Dean Kelly, Coordinator
An independent four-year college with 45 special education students out of a total of 2843. Tuition: $23093.

4603 Ohio State University Agricultural Technical Institute

1382 Dover Road   216-264-3911
Wooster, OH 44691   800-647-8283

Tanya Kunze, LD Specialist
Jay Clevenger, Learning Assistance
A public two-year college with 73 special education students out of a total of 691. There is a $150 fee for the special education program in addition to the regular tuition of $2064.

4604 Ohio State University, Marion Campus

1465 Mount Vernon Avenue   614-389-6786
Marion, OH 43302

Margaret Hazelett, LD Specialist
A public four-year college with 14 special education students out of a total of 971. There is a $150 fee for the special education program in addition to the regular tuition of $2064.

4605 Ohio State University, Newark Campus

University Drive   614-366-9246
Newark, OH 43055

Phyllis Thompson, Coordinator

A public four-year college with 19 special education students out of a total of 1552. Tuition: $2064.

4606 Ohio University

101 Crewson House 614-593-2620
Athens, OH 45701

Susan Wagner, Off. Afirmative Act.

A public four-year college with 110 special education students out of a total of 15000. Tuition: $2967.

4607 Ohio University, Chillicothe

Rooms 231 And 233 Bennett Hall 614-774-7200
Chillicothe, OH 45601

Dr. Diane Diekroger, Student Support

A public four-year college with 5 special education students out of a total of 1660. Tuition: $2397.

4608 Otterbein College

106 Towers Hall 614-898-1413
Westerville, OH 43081

Ellen Kasualis, Special Services

An independent four-year college with 7 special education students out of a total of 2397. Tuition: $14712.

4609 Owens Technical College

30335 Oregon Road 419-666-0580
Toledo, OH 43699

Ann Ferguson, Disability Resources

A public two-year college with 70 special education students out of a total of 8286. Tuition: $1484.

4610 Shawnee State University

240 2nd Street 614-335-2456
Portsmouth, OH 45662

Patty Gilmore, Coordinator

4611 Sinclair Community College

444 West Third Street 513-226-2752
Dayton, OH 45402

Lisa Shook, LD Specialist

A public two-year college with 150 special education students out of a total of 20417. Tuition: $1395.

4612 Southern Ohio College, Fairfield Campus

Fairfield Campus 513-829-7100
Fairfield, OH 45014

Jane Ann Benson, Special Services

4613 Southern Ohio College, Northeast Campus

2791 Mogadore Road 216-735-8766
Akron, OH 44312

Kathy Antonucci, Special Services

4614 Southern State Community College

200 Hobart Drive 513-393-3431
Hillsboro, OH 45133

Carl Vertona, Special Services

4615 University of Akron Wayne College

10470 Smucker Road 216-683-2010
Orrville, OH 44667

Julia Beyeler

A public two-year college with 5 special education students out of a total of 1538. Tuition: $2525.

4616 University of Cincinnati

69 Beecher Hall 513-475-6813
Cincinnati, OH 45221

Larry Goodall, Special Services

A public four-year college with 159 special education students out of a total of 13506. Tuition: $2622.

4617 University of Cincinnati, Raymond Walters General and Technical College

9555 Plainfield Road 513-475-5730
Cincinnati, OH 45236

Carol Robinson, Special Services

4618 University of Dayton

300 College Park 513-229-2229
Dayton, OH 45469

L.B. Fred, Special Services

An independent four-year college with 16 special education students out of a total of 6985. Tuition: $14140.

4619 The University of Findlay

1000 North Main Street 419-424-4697
Findlay, OH 45840

Donna Smith, Director

An independent four-year college with 13 special education students out of a total of 2505. Tuition: $14554.

4620   University of Toledo

2801 South Bancroft Street   419-537-2624
Toledo, OH 43606

Carl Earwood, Special Services

A public four-year college with 275 special education students out of a total of 21620. Tuition: $3008.

4621   Urbana University

597 College Way   513-652-1301
Urbana, OH 43078

Sheri Holmes, Director

An independent four-year college with 8 special education students out of a total of 945. Tuition: $12035.

4622   Walsh College

2020 Easton Street NW   216-499-7090
North Canton, OH 44720

Jim Korcusler, Special Services

An independent four-year college with 11 special education students out of a total of 1338. Tuition: $10672.

4623   Washington State Community College

710 Colegate Drive   614-374-8716
Marietta, OH 45750

Ann Hontz, Director

A public two-year college with 35 special education students out of a total of 2097. Tuition: $2160.

4624   Wilmington College of Ohio

319 College Street   513-382-6661
Wilmington, OH 45177

Laurel Eckels, Special Services

4625   Wright State University

Colonel Glenn Highway   513-873-2140
Dayton, OH 45435

Ron Lofton, Asst. Director

A public four-year college with 124 special education students out of a total of 13831. Tuition: $2694.

4626   Xavier University

201 Joseph Building   513-745-3655
Cincinnati, OH 45207

Dr. Sally Pruden, Coordinator

An independent four-year college with 14 special education students out of a total of 4079. Tuition: $14780.

4627   Bacone College

Muskogee, OK 74801

Paul Travis, Director

4628   Carl Albert Junior College

1507 South McKenna   918-647-8660
Poteau, OK 74953

Gail Booth, Director

4629   Central State University

100 N. University Drive
Edmond, OK 73034

4630   East Central University

East 14th Street   405-332-8000
Ada, OK 74820

Dwain West, Director

A public four-year college with 15 special education students out of a total of 3833. Tuition: $1350.

4631   Moore-Norman Vo-Tech

4701 12th Avenue NW
Norman, OK 73069

Bill Henderson

4632   Oklahoma City Community College

7777 South May   405-682-7535
Oklahoma City, OK 73159

Pam Davenport, Special Services

4633   Oklahoma State University

315 Student Union   405-744-7116
Stillwater, OK 74078

Maureen McCarthy, Special Services

A public four-year college with 45 special education students out of a total of 14595. Tuition: $1395.

4634   Oklahoma State University, Tech Branch, Oklahoma City

900 North Portalnd   405-945-3224
Oklahoma City, OK 73107

Mark Ames, Special Services

4635 Oklahoma State University, Technical Branch, Okmulgee

4th And Mission   918-756-6211
Okmulgee, OK 74447

Billie L. Coakley, Special Services

4636 Rogers State College

Will Rogers & College Hill   918-341-7510
Claremore, OK 74017

Dr. Penny Coggins, Director
A public two-year college with 2 special education students out of a total of 3875. Tuition: $983.

4637 Rose State College

6420 SE 15th   405-733-7407
Midwest City, OK 73110

Linda Jansen, Special Services

4638 Seminole Junior College

2701 State Street   405-382-9950
Seminole, OK 74868

Dr. Martha Steger, Academic Assistance

4639 Southwestern Oklahoma State University

100 Campus Drive   405-774-3233
Wetherford, OK 73096

Donnell Alexander, Student Development

4640 Tulsa Junior College

909 South Boston   918-587-6561
Tulsa, OK 74119

Yolanda Williams, Special Services

4641 University of Oklahoma

Room 318, 731 Elm   405-325-1459
Norman, OK 73019

Suzette Dyer, Special Services
A public four-year college with 23 special education students out of a total of 14685. Tuition: $1705.

Oregon

4642 Blue Mountain Community College

Box 100   503-276-1260
Pendleton, OR 97801

Cynthia Hilden, Special Services
A public two-year college with 50 special education students out of a total of 3256. Tuition: $900.

4643 Central Oregon Community College

Bend, OR 97701

R.R. Meedish, Registrar

4644 Clackamas Community College

19600 South Molalla Avenue   503-657-6958
Oregon City, OR 97045

Caroline Cate
A public two-year college with 55 special education students out of a total of 7025. Tuition: $972.

4645 Columbia Christian College

9101 East Burnside Street   503-255-7060
Portland, OR 97216

James Bean, Administrator

4646 George Fox College

414 North Meridian #6097   503-538-8383
Newberg, OR 97132

Bonnie Jerke, Academic Success
An independent four-year college with 11 special education students out of a total of 1137. Tuition: $13540.

4647 Lane Community College

4000 East 30th   503-747-4501
Eugene, OR 97405

Dolores May, Coordinator

4648 Linfield College

McMinnville, OR 97128   503-472-4121

Dr. Judith Haynes, Director
An independent four-year college with 68 special education students out of a total of 1418. Tuition: $15780.

4649 Linn-Benton Community College

6500 SW Pacific Blvd.   503-967-8836
Albany, OR 97321   FAX 503-967-6550

Paula Grigsby, Coordinator
A public two-year college with 41 special education students out of a total of 6767. Tuition: $936.

4650 Mount Hood Community College

Eastern Oregon State College
Lagrande, OR 97850

Dr. Bill Wells, Academic Reading Ctr

4651 Mount Olive School for Dyslexic Children

15351 SE Johnson Road   503-650-8277
Clackamas, OR 97015

Sharon Smith

4652 Mt. Hood Community College

26000 SE Stark Street   503-667-7650
Gresham, OR 97030   FAX 503-667-7388

Debbie Derr, MS, LPC, NCC, Counselor
Mika Greenup, Special Services
A commitment to providing educational opportunities for all students forms the foundation of the Special Services Program at Mt. Hood College. If you are a student with a disability, Special Servcices will help you overcome potential obstacles so that you may be successful in your area of study. Special Services gives you the needed support to help you meet your goals without separating you and other students with disabilities from existing programs.

4653 Oregon Institute of Technology

3201 Campus Drive   503-885-1015
Klamath Falls, OR 97601

Jane Pickett, Coordinator
A public four-year college with 15 special education students out of a total of 2661. Tuition: $2002.

4654 Oregon State University

Services for Students with Disabilities
A200 Administration Bldg.   503-737-3661
Corvallis, OR 97331   FAX 503-737-2400

Tracy Bentley, Director
A public four-year college with 66 special education students out of a total of 12070. Tuition: $2505.

4655 Portland Community College

P.O. Box 19000   503-244-6111
Portland, OR 97219

Carolee Schmeer, LD Specialist

4656 Reed College

3203 SE Woodstock   503-777-7521
Portland, OR 97202

Betsy Emerick, Assoc. Dean Students

4657 Rogue Community College

3345 Redwood Highway   503-471-3500
Grants Pass, OR 97527

Bonnie Breeden, Support Services
A public two-year college with 50 special education students out of a total of 2544. Tuition: $900.

4658 Southern Oregon State College

Counseling Center, Britt 205   503-482-6213
Ashland, OR 97520

4659 Southwestern Oregon Community College

1988 Newark Avenue   503-888-2525
Coos Bay, OR 97420

Margaret McGuire, ABE Coordiantor
Ann Fauss, Counsellor
The college will provide reasonable accommodation for students with learning disabilities. Some instructors in Academic Skills have special training in working with learning disabled students.

4660 Treasure Valley Community College

650 College Blvd.   503-889-6493
Ontario, OR 97914

Cleo Dyer, Department Chair

4661 Umpqua Community College

P.O. Box 967   503-440-4600
Roseburg, OR 97470

Mary Sharp, Special Services
A public two-year college with 31 special education students out of a total of 1846. Tuition: $1176.

4662 University of Oregon

164 Oregon Hall   503-686-3211
Rugene, OR 97403

Dr. Hilary Gerdes, Special Services
A public four-year college with 100 special education students out of a total of 13074. Tuition: $2598.

4663 Warner Pacific College

Portland, OR 97215   503-775-4368

Judy Witt

4664 Western Oregon State College

345 North Monmouth Avenue   503-838-8250
Monmouth, OR 97361

Martha Smith, Special Services
A public four-year college with 13 special education students out of a total of 3593. Tuition: $2478.

4665 Willamette University

Salem, OR 97301

James Sumner, Admissions Office

Pennsylvania

4666 Albright College

P.O. Box 15234   215-921-2381
Reading, PA 19612

R. Jane Williams, Counseling Director

An independent four-year college with 17 special education students out of a total of 1090. There is a $450 fee for the special education program in addition to the regular tuition of $18095.

4667 Bloomsburg University

Bloomsburg, PA 17815   717-389-3316

Dr. Jesse Bryan

4668 Boyce Campus of the Community College of Allegheny County

595 Beatty Road   412-733-4220
Monroeville, PA 15146

Dr. Renee Clark, Director

4669 Cabrini College

Radnor, PA 19087   215-687-2100

Barbara Rubin

4670 California University of Pennsylvania

Center for Academic Research and Enhancement
California, PA 15419   412-938-4142

Dheryl Bilitski, Coordinator

A public four-year college with 46 special education students out of a total of 5865. There is a $2570 fee for the special education program in addition to the regular tuition of $2628.

4671 Clarion University

Clarion, PA 16214   814-226-2347

Gregory K. Clary

4672 College Misericordia

Alternative Learners Project
Lake Street   717-675-2181
Dallas, PA 18612

Dr. Joseph Rogan, Driector

An independent four-year college with 60 special education students out of a total of 1463. Tuition: $14370.

4673 Community College of Allegheny County Allegheny Campus

Library Room 404, 808 Ridge Ave.   412-237-4612
Pittsburgh, PA 15212

Lisa Tellers, Disability Director

A public two-year college with 250 special education students out of a total of 12041. Tuition: $1344.

4674 Community College of Allegheny County, College Center, North Campus

8701 Perry Highway   412-369-3686
Pittsburgh, PA 15237

Kathleen White, Special Services Dir

Support services for students with disabilities are provided according to individual needs. Services include assistance with testing, advisement, registration, classroom accommodations, professor and agency contact.

4675 Community College of Philadelphia

1700 Spring Garden Street   215-751-8050
Philadelphia, PA 19130

Jay Segal, Coordinator

A public two-year college with 125 special education students out of a total of 17547. Tuition: $1770.

4676 Delaware County Community College

Media, PA 19063   215-359-5390

Stuart Dix

4677 Delaware Valley College of Science and Agriculture

Doylestown, PA 18901   215-345-6473

Joseph Fulcoly, Jr., Counseling Director

4678 Dickinson College

P.O. Box 1773   717-245-1740
Carlisle, PA 17013

Dr. Kate Brooks, Director

An independent four-year college with 10 special education students out of a total of 2029. Tuition: $21475.

4679 Drexel University

32nd And Chestnut Streets   215-895-2523
Philadelphia, PA 19104

Ina Ellen, Director

An independent four-year college with 29 special education students out of a total of 8341. Tuition: $16969.

4680 Edinboro University of Pennsylvania

Office for Students with Disabilities
Shafer Hall   814-732-2462
Edinboro, PA 16444   FAX 814-732-2866

Kathleen Strosser, Asst. To Director
Janet Jenkins, LD Coordinator

A public four-year college with 129 special education students out of a total of 7464. There is a $1600 fee for the special education program in addition to the regular tuition of $2628.

4681 Geneva College

Beaver Falls, PA 15010   412-847-6605

Dr. James Boelkins, Vice President

4682 Gettysburg College

Box 414   717-337-6579
Gettysburg, PA 17325

Tim Dodd, Associate Dean

4683 Gwynedd-Mercy College

Sunneytown Pike   215-641-5566
Gwynedd Valley, PA 19437

Catherine McMahon, Director

4684 Harcum Junior College

Montgomery Avenue   215-526-6034
Bryn Mawr, PA 19010

Dr. Tania Bailey, Director

An independent two-year college with 46 special education students out of a total of 809. There is a $2400 fee for the special education program in addition to the regular tuition of $10704.

4685 Harrisburg Area Community College

3300 Cameron Street Road   717-780-2401
Harrisburg, PA 17110

N. Lorraine Basonic, Assistant Dean

A public two-year college with 70 special education students out of a total of 10444. Tuition: $1200.

4686 Immaculata College

Immaculata, PA 19345   215-647-4400

Sr. Kathleen McKee, Vice President

An independent four-year college with 3 special education students out of a total of 2120. Tuition: $13650.

4687 Indiana University of Pennsylvania

106 Pratt Hall   412-357-4067
Indiana, PA 15705

Catherine Dugan, Director

4688 Keystone Junior College

LaPlume, PA 18440   717-945-5141

Dan Rosenfield

4689 Kutztown University of Pennsylvania

220 Administration Building   215-683-4108
Kutztown, PA 19530

Barbara Peters, Director

A public four-year college with 36 special education students out of a total of 7317. Tuition: $2628.

4690 Lehigh County Community College

2370 Main Street   215-799-1140
Schnecksville, PA 18078

Karen Goode-Ferguson, Director

A public two-year college with 52 special education students out of a total of 4649. Tuition: $1300.

4691 Lock Haven University of Pennsylvania

Lock Haven, PA 17745   717-893-2324

Nathaniel Hosley, Special Services

A public four-year college with 26 special education students out of a total of 3332. Tuition: $2628.

4692 Luzerne County Community College

Nanticoke, PA 18634   717-829-7410

Regina Antonini, Director

4693 Lycoming College

Box 144   717-321-4052
Williamsport, PA 17701

Dr. Diane Bonner, Director

An independent four-year college with 15 special education students out of a total of 1405. Tuition: $16300.

4694 Manor Junior College

Jenkintown, PA 19046   215-783-2360

John Boyd, Director

4695 Mansfield University of Pennsylvania

202 South Hall   717-662-4693
Mansfield, PA 16933

Celeste Burns Sexauer, Director

4696 Mercyhurst College

Glenwood Hills   814-824-2202
Erie, PA 16546   800-825-1926
    FAX 814-824-2071

Noreen Herlihy, Adm. Asst. Admission
Barbara Weiger, PhD, Director LD Program

An independent four-year college with 42 special education students out of a total of 2156. There is a $750 fee for the special education program in addition to the regular tuition of $12831.

4697 Messiah College

Grantham, PA 17027   717-691-6041

Dr. Miriam Sailers, Associate Dean

An independent four-year college with 10 special education students out of a total of 2259. Tuition: $13530.

4698 New Castle Business College

316 Rhodes Place
New Castle, PA 16101

Samuel Haycock

4699 New England Trade and Technical Institute

P.O. Box 716   215-275-7211
Bryn Mawr, PA 19010

Richard Cooper

4700 Northampton County Area Community College

3835 Green Pond Road   215-861-5346
Bethlehem, PA 18017

Cheryl Ashcroft, LD Specialist

4701 Pennsylvania Institute of Technology

Media, PA 19063   215-565-7900

Dr. Robert Zabek, Special Services

4702 Pennsylvania State University, Worthington Scranton Campus

120 Ridge View Drive   717-963-4128
Dunmore, PA 18512

Michele Steele, Special Services

4703 Pennsylvania State University, Mont Alto Campus

301 General Studies Building   717-749-3111
Mont Alto, PA 17237

Norene Moskalski, Special Services

A public two-year college with 26 special education students out of a total of 863. Tuition: $4332.

4704 Pennsylvania State University, Schuylkill Campus

P.O. Box 308   717-385-4500
Schuylkill Haven, PA 17972

Nancy Stumhofer, Special Services

4705 Pennsylvania State University, Shenango Valley Campus

147 Shenango Avenue   412-983-5847
Sharon, PA 16146

Julie Persing, Special Services

4706 Pennsylvania State University, University Park Campus

Services for Students with Disabilities
105 Bouke Building   814-863-2291
University Park, PA 16802   FAX 814-865-3815

Marianne Karwacki, LD Specialist

Offers academic support services in a mainstreamed setting for students with learning disabilities. Services include: 1) providing students with information on locating audiotaped textbooks; 2) helping students arrange course substitutions when essential degree requirements are not involved; 3) arranging test accommodations as needed; 4) providing individual counseling to students so they can plan a reasonable course load in light of their strengths and weaknesses.

4707 Philadelphia College of Bible

200 Manor Avenue   215-752-5800
Langhorne, PA 19047

Barry Yoder, Special Services

An independent four-year college with 3 special education students out of a total of 685. Tuition: $10594.

4708 Pierce Junior College

1420 Pine Street   215-545-6400
Philadelphia, PA 19102

Leslie Daughtry, Special Services

A public two-year college with 10 special education students out of a total of 1016. Tuition: $5840.

4709 Point Park College

201 Wood Street   412-392-3870
Pittsburgh, PA 15222

Dr. Charles Quillin, Student Development

4710 Reading Area Community College

P.O. Box 1706   215-372-4721
Reading, PA 19603

Cathy Hunsicker, Tutorial Coordinator
A public two-year college with 41 special education students out of a total of 2957. Tuition: $1560.

4711 Robert Morris College

Narrows Run Road   412-262-8290
Coraopolis, PA 15108

Caryl Sheffield, Special Services

4712 Rosemont College

Rosemont, PA 19010   215-525-6420

Linda De Simone, Admissions Director

4713 Rosemont: the Hill Top Preparatory School

S. Ithan Ave. & Clyde Road   215-527-3230
Bryn Mawr, PA 19010

Elissa Fisher, Director

4714 Saint Francis College

Loretto, PA 15940   814-472-7000

Sharon Donovan-Sheridan, Special Services

4715 Spring Garden College

7500 Germantown Avenue   215-248-7910
Philadelphia, PA 19119

Peter Rondianaro, Special Services

4716 Swarthmore College

500 College Avenue   215-328-8300
Swarthmore, PA 19081

4717 Temple University

Center For The Disabled   215-787-1280
Philadelphia, PA 19122

Mary Stampone, Director

4718 University of Pennsylvania

34th And Spruce Streets   215-898-6993
Philadelphia, PA 19104

Alice Nagle, Special Services

An independent four-year college with 58 special education students out of a total of 9541. Tuition: $23168.

4719 University of Pittsburgh

4200 Fifth Avenue   412-648-7890
Pittsburgh, PA 15260

Sabina Bilder, Special Services
A public four-year college with 14 special education students out of a total of 18250. Tuition: $4546.

4720 University of Pittsburgh At Bradford

Academic Development Center   814-362-7533
Bradford, PA 16701

Joanne Cree Burgart, Special Services

4721 University of Pittsburgh At Greensburg

1150 Mount Pleasant Road   412-836-9879
Greensburg, PA 15601

Helen Connors, Counselor

4722 University of the Arts

Broad And Pine Streets   215-875-2254
Philadelphia, PA 19102

Stephanie Bell, LD Director
An independent four-year college with 25 special education students out of a total of 1269. Tuition: $11200.

4723 Ursinus College

Collegeville, PA 19426   215-489-4111

Richard DiFeliciantonio, Director

4724 Villa Maria College

2551 West Eigth Street   814-838-1966
Erie, PA 16505

Sr. Joyce Lowrey
An independent two-year college with 27 special education students out of a total of 429. Tuition: $5050.

4725 Washington and Jefferson College

Washington, PA 15301   412-223-6008

Mary Jane Jones, Assistant Dean
An independent four-year college with 7 special education students out of a total of 1126. Tuition: $17110.

4726 Waynesburg College

Act 101   412-627-8191
Waynesburg, PA 15370

Charles Beiter, Special Services

4727 Westmoreland County Community College

Youngwood, PA 15697   412-925-4186

Mark Wallace, Special Services

4728 Widener University, Pennsylvania Campus

One Unviersity Place   215-499-1270
Chester, PA 19013

Linda Baum, Special Services

An independent four-year college with 10 special education students out of a total of 5400. Tuition: $16000.

4729 Williamsport Area Community College

Williamsport, PA 17701   717-327-4765

Kathy Ferrence, Special Services

Rhode Island

4730 Brown University

Providence, RI 02912   401-863-2315

Robert Shaw

An independent four-year college with 85 special education students out of a total of 5906. Tuition: $23353.

4731 Bryant College

1150 Douglas Pike   401-232-6045
Smithfield, RI 02917

William Phillips

An independent four-year college with 8 special education students out of a total of 4124. Tuition: $17732.

4732 Community College of Rhode Island

400 East Avenue   401-825-2305
Warwick, RI 02886

Elizabeth Dalton

A public two-year college with 114 special education students out of a total of 11344. Tuition: $1298.

4733 Johnson & Wales College

Abbott Park Place   401-456-4689
Providence, RI 02903

Meryl Berstein, Special Needs Coord.

An independent four-year college with 200 special education students out of a total of 7096. Tuition: $13110.

4734 Providence College

Providence, RI 02918   401-865-2141

Frances Shipps

4735 Roger Williams College

Old Ferry Road   401-254-3038
Bristol, RI 02809

An independent four-year college with 37 special education students out of a total of 2111. Tuition: $16650.

4736 University of Rhode Island

332 Memorial Union   401-792-2101
Kingston, RI 02881

Barbara Roberts, Special Services

South Carolina

4737 Aiken Technical College

P.O. Drawer 696   803-593-9231
Aiken, SC 29802

Richard Weldon, Supervisor

A public two-year college with 2 special education students out of a total of 2187. Tuition: $750.

4738 Beaufort Technical College

Room 233, Coleman Hall   803-525-8221
Beaufort, SC 29902

Carolyn Banner, Career Development

4739 The Citadel, the Military College of South Carolina

Department Of Education   803-792-5097
Charleston, SC 29409

Gordon Wallace

4740 College of Charleston

66 George Street   803-792-5981
Charleston, SC 29424

4741 Erskine College

Due West, SC 29639   803-379-8867

Katharine Chandler

4742 Francis Marion College

P.O. Box 100547   805-661-1290
Florence, SC 29501

Kenneth Dye

A public four-year college with 8 special education students out of a total of 3666. Tuition: $2140.

4743　Greenville Technical College

P.O. Box 5616　　　　　　803-250-8104
Greenville, SC　29606

Owen Perkins, Associate Dean

A public two-year college with 20 special education students out of a total of 8690. Tuition: $900.

4744　Lander College

Greenwood, SC　29646　　　803-229-8797

Carol Walker, Counselor

4745　Limestone College

1115 College Drive　　　　803-489-7151
Gaffney, SC　29340

Sherry Horton

An independent four-year college with 7 special education students out of a total of 860. There is a $3000 fee for the special education program in addition to the regular tuition of $10200.

4746　Midlands Technical College

Columbia, SC　29202　　　803-738-1400

Annie Porterfield, Special Services

4747　North Greenville College

Tigerville, SC　29688　　　803-895-1410

Dr. Robert Greenwood, Special Services

4748　Sandhills Academy

4335 Timberlane Drive　　　803-787-2441
Columbia, SC　29205　　FAX 803-787-0103

Joan Hathaway

A private, nonprofit school for children with learning disabilities. Serves students from grades 1-8 and also offer diagnostic evaluations, summer school and educational therapy for all ages. Boarding with local families is also available.

4749　Spartanburg Methodist College

1200 Textile Road　　　　803-587-4272
Spartanburg, SC　29301

Sharon Porter, Director

An independent two-year college with 12 special education students out of a total of 1100. Tuition: $9850.

4750　Trident Academy

1455 Wakendaw Road　　　803-884-7046
Mt. Pleasant, SC　29464　FAX 803-881-8320

Myron C. Harrington, Jr., Headmaster
Julie Ravenel-Lee, Director Admissions

Private school for children with learning disabilities grades K5 through 12th, boarding and day students accepted.

4751　Trident Technical College

P.O. Box 10367　　　　　803-572-6102
Charleston, SC　29411

Vincent Ashby, Jr., Special Services

A public two-year college with 50 special education students out of a total of 7588. Tuition: $1020.

4752　University of South Carolina

1625 College Street　　　803-777-6742
Columbia, SC　29208

Deborah Haynes, Special Services

A public four-year college with 50 special education students out of a total of 16059. Tuition: $2818.

4753　University of South Carolina At Aiken

171 University Parkway　　803-648-6851
Aiken, SC　29801

Randy Duckett, Special Services

A public four-year college with 6 special education students out of a total of 3108. Tuition: $1950.

4754　University of South Carolina At Beaufort

800 Carteret Street　.　　803-521-4100
Beaufort, SC　29902

Vince Mesaric, Associte Dean

A public two-year college with 1 special education students out of a total of 1050. Tuition: $130.

4755　University of South Carolina At Lancaster

P.O. Box 889　　　　　　803-285-7471
Lancaster, SC　29721

4756　University of South Carolina - Coastal Carolina College

P.O. Box 1954　　　　　803-347-0939
Conway, SC　29526

Dr. Joe Mazurkiewicz, Special Services

4757　Winthrop College

Rock Hill, SC　29733　　　803-323-3191

James McCammon, Director

4758　Yankton College

Academic Skills Center　　　605-665-3661
Yankton, SC　57078

Nancy Reddy, Director

South Dakota

4759　Black Hills State College

1200 University　　　605-642-6622
Spearfish, SD　57799

Sharon Hemmingson

A public four-year college with 6 special education students out of a total of 2698. Tuition: $1336.

4760　Mount Marty College

Yankton, SD　57028
　　　　　800-843-3724

Sister Marie Krantz

4761　National College

P.O. Box 1780　　　605-394-4820
Rapid City, SD　57709

Keith Carylyle, Special Services

Tennessee

4762　Austin Peay State Unviersity

P.O. Box 4476　　　615-648-7612
Clarksville, TN　37044

Dr. Carlette Hardin, Director

4763　Brookhaven College

3939 Valley View Lane　　　214-620-4844
Farmers Branch, TN　75234

Jeri Evans

A public two-year college with 75 special education students out of a total of 8041. Tuition: $358.

4764　Bryan College

P.O. Box 7000　　　615-775-7225
Dayton, TN　37321　　　800-277-9522
　　　　　FAX 615-775-7330

Donna Poole, Counseling Director
Dr. William E. Brown, President

Committed to providing quality education for those who meet admission standards but learn differently from others.　Modifications are made in the learning environemnt to enable LD students to succeed.　Some of the modifications made require documentation of the specific disability while other adaptations do not.　In addition to modifications the small teacher-student ratio allows the school to provide much individual attention to those with learning difficulties.

4765　Carson-Newman College

Box 1873　　　615-475-4549
Jefferson City, TN　37760

John Gibson, Associate Professor

An independent four-year college with 4 special education students out of a total of 1972. Tuition: $9990.

4766　Knoxville Business College

720 North Fifth Avenue　　　615-524-3043
Knoxville, TN　37917

Judy Ferguson, Dean Of Students

4767　Lambuth College

Jackson, TN　38301
　　　　　901-427-1500

Robert McLendon

4768　Lee College

North Ocoee Street　　　615-478-7475
Cleveland, TN　37311

Bill Winters, Director

An independent four-year college with 2 special education students out of a total of 1827. Tuition: $7282.

4769　Memphis State University

215 Scates Hall　　　901-678-2880
Memphis, TN　38152

Traci Sallinger, Director

A public four-year college with 164 special education students out of a total of 15782. Tuition: $1748.

4770　Middle Tennessee State University

P.O. Box 7　　　615-898-2783
Murfreesboro, TN　37132

John Harris, Dir. Dis. Services

The college believes that every member of society has the right to an education commensurate with his or her ability and interests.　Disabled Student Services is the coordinating body at MTSU which distributes information concerning services available to students with disabilities.　The office acts as an advocate for disabled students at the University, surveying the needs of these students and developing programs to meet those needs.　The office assists students with learning disabilities.

4771　Milligan College

Milligan College, TN　37604　　　615-461-8946

Nancy Ross, Assistant Professor

4772 Morristown College

417 North James Street
Morristown, TN 37814

Lanny Bowers

4773 Motlow State Community College

P.O. Box 88100   615-455-8511
Tullahoma, TN 37388

Nellie Gerwe

A public two-year college with 3 special education students out of a total of 3033. Tuition: $840.

4774 Northeast State Technical Community College

P.O. Box 246   615-323-3191
Blountville, TN 37617

Patrick Sweeney, Associate Dean

A public two-year college with 8 special education students out of a total of 3133. Tuition: $912.

4775 Pellissippi State Technical Community College

10915 Hardin Valley Road   615-694-6453
Knoxville, TN 37933   FAX 615-694-6435

Joan Newman, Dir. Academic Assess

A public two-year college with 55 special education students out of a total of 7200. Tuition: $840.

4776 Rhodes College

2000 N Parkway   901-726-3849
Memphis, TN 38112

Dr. Libby Robertson, Counseling Services

4777 Southern College of Seventh-Day Adventists

P.O. Box 370   615-238-2779
Collegedale, TN 37315

George Babcock, Chairman

An independent four-year college with 4 special education students out of a total of 1532. Tuition: $10700.

4778 State Technical Institute At Memphis

5983 Macon Cove   901-377-4123
Memphis, TN 38134

Paul Dudenhefer, Special Services

A public two-year college with 150 special education students out of a total of 10100. Tuition: $840.

4779 Tusculum College

P.O. Box 5078   615-638-1111
Greenville, TN 37743

Annette Harmon, Special Services

4780 University of Tennessee At Chattanooga

520 Oak Street   615-755-4006
Chattanooga, TN 37403

Dr. Patricia Snowden, Coordinator

A public four-year college with 130 special education students out of a total of 6840. There is a $1000 fee for the special education program in addition to the regular tuition of $1558.

4781 University of Tennessee, Knoxville

900 Volunteer Blvd.   615-974-6087
Knoxville, TN 37996

Jan ScottBey, Special Services

4782 Vanderbilt University

P.O. Box 1809, Station B   615-322-4705
Nashville, TN 37235

Michael Miller, Special Services

An independent four-year college with 34 special education students out of a total of 5547. Tuition: $22035.

4783 William Jennings Bryan College

Box 7000   615-775-7225
Dayton, TN 37321

Donna Poole, Counseling Director

A public four-year college with 4 special education students out of a total of 478. Tuition: $10660.

Texas

4784 Alvin Community College

3110 Mustang Road   713-388-4636
Alvin, TX 77511

Eileen Cross

A public two-year college with 25 special education students out of a total of 3914.

4785 Amarillo College

P.O. Box 447   806-371-5439
Amarillo, TX 79178

Deana Milliron, Coordinator

4786 American Technological University

P.O. Box 1416   817-526-1278
Kileen, TX 76541

Richard Putman, Admissions Director

4787 Angelina College

P.O. Box 1768   409-639-1301
Lufkin, TX 75901

Dr. Barbara Flournoy, Director
A public two-year college with 15 special education students out of a total of 3074. Tuition: $420.

4788 Bee County College

3800 Charco Road   512-358-3130
Beeville, TX 78102

Patricia Myers, Counseling Director
A public two-year college with 101 special education students out of a total of 2267. Tuition: $424.

4789 Central Texas College

P.O. Box 1800   817-526-1339
Kileen, TX 76540

Jose Apotte, Counselor

4790 Cisco Junior College

Route 3, P.O. Box 3   817-442-2567
Cisco, TX 76437

Debora Robinson
A public two-year college with 4 special education students out of a total of 2101. Tuition: $570.

4791 College of the Mainland

8001 Palmer Highway   409-938-1211
Texas City, TX 77591

Dr. Marcella Derrick

4792 Collin County Community College

2800 East Spring Creek Pkwy.   214-881-5898
Plano, TX 75074

Audrey Newsome, Director
A public two-year college with 55 special education students out of a total of 9729. Tuition: $540.

4793 Concordia Lutheran College

3400 IH 35 North   512-406-3189
Austin, TX 78705

Nancee Lottmann, Director
An independent four-year college with 3 special education students out of a total of 688. Tuition: $9440.

4794 Dallas Academy

950 Tiffany Way   214-342-1481
Dallas, TX 75218

Jim Richardson

4795 Dallas County Community College

701 Elm Street
Dallas, TX 75202

4796 East Texas Baptist University

707 Van Zandt   214-935-1779
Marshall, TX 75670

Charles Taylor, Directort

4797 East Texas State University

East Texas Station   214-886-5000
Commerce, TX 75428

Tom Lynch

4798 Eastfield College

3737 Motley Drive   214-324-7032
Mesquite, TX 75150

Reva Rattan, Coordinator

4799 El Centro College

Main And Lamar Streets   214-746-2073
Dallas, TX 75202

Jim Handy
A public two-year college with 30 special education students out of a total of 5954. Tuition: $358.

4800 El Paso Community College

Valle Verde Campus
P.O. Box 20500   915-594-2426
El Paso, TX 79998   FAX 915-594-2155

Ann Lemke, Director
Joyce Whiteside, Instructor For CSD
The Center for Students with Disabilities is a support service for students enrolled at the College who have a verified temporary or permanent disability. Support Services offered include: advisiong, tutoring, notetaking, test assistance and more.

4801 Frank Phillips College

P.O. Box 5118   806-274-5311
Borger, TX 79008

Kristy Blodgett, Spec. Pop. Director

4802 Galveston College

4015 Avenue Q
Galveston, TX 77550

409-763-6551

Dr. Gaynelle Hayes, Vice President
A public two-year college with 18 special education students out of a total of 2115. Tuition: $256.

4803 Gulf Coast Bible College

911 West 11th Street
Houston, TX 77008

W. Maurice Slater, Admissions Director

4804 Hill College of the Hill Junior College District

P.O. Box 619
Hillsboro, TX 76645

817-582-2555

Louis Allen, Dean Of Students

4805 Houston Community College System

320 Jackson Hill
Houston, TX 77270

713-868-8166

Dr. Weldon Elbert, Counselor

4806 Jarvis Christian College

P.O. Drawer G
Hawkins, TX 75765

903-769-2174

Mary Berry, Director
Student Support Services is a federally funded program whose purpose is to improve the retention and graduate rate of program participants. Eligible program participants include low income, first generation college students and students with learning and physical disabilities. A variety of support services are provided.

4807 Lamar University-Port Arthur

P.O. Box 310
Port Arthur, TX 77641

409-727-0886

Sherly Hopper, Director
A public two-year college with 20 special education students out of a total of 2039. Tuition: $720.

4808 Laredo Junior College

West End Washington Street
Laredo, TX 78040

512-722-0521

Jose Miranda, Jr., Counselor

4809 Lubbock Christian College

Lubbock, TX 79407

4810 McLennen Community College

1400 College Drive
Waco, TX 76708

817-750-3573

Dr. Patsy White, Director
A public two-year college with 150 special education students out of a total of 5704. Tuition: $450.

4811 Midwestern State University

3400 Taft Blvd.
Wichita Falls, TX 76308

817-689-4618

Debra Higginbotham, Director
A public four-year college with 21 special education students out of a total of 4824. Tuition: $720.

4812 North Harris County College

2700 W. W Thorne Drive
Houston, TX 77073

713-443-5481

Sandi Patton, Special Services

4813 North Lake College

5001 North MacArthur
Irving, TX 75038

214-659-5237

Mary Ciminello, Special Services
A public two-year college with 65 special education students out of a total of 6855. Tuition: $430.

4814 Oak Hill Academy

6464 East Lovers Lane
Dallas, TX 75214

214-368-0664

Carole Hill
A private special school for bright and talented students who have language learning differences. The focus is on developing the whole child. A wide range of educational methodologies are implemented in a structured environment by professional, caring teachers and therapists. Individualized programming allows students to progress at their own rate using multisensory/interactive learning experiences. The Academy also provides speech/language therapy and a summer program.

4815 Pan American Uniersity

1201 West University Drive
Edinburg, TX 78539

512-381-2585

Arturo Ramos, Special Services

4816 Richland College

12800 Abrams Road
Dallas, TX 75243

214-238-6353

Jeanne Brewer, LD Director

4817 Sam Houston State University

Box 2059
Huntsville, TX 77343

409-294-1720

Dr. Patsy Copeland, Director

4818 San Antonio College

Programs for the Handicapped
1300 San Pedro
San Antonio, TX 78284

512-733-2352

Thomas Hoy, Counselor

A public two-year college with 295 special education students out of a total of 19908. Tuition: $510.

4819 San Jacinto College - Central Campus

8060 Spencer Highway
Pasadena, TX 77505

713-476-1501

Mary Battarbee, Special Services

4820 San Jacinto College - South Campus

13735 Beamer Road
Houston, TX 77089

713-922-3453

Bonnie Bereck, Special Populations

A public two-year college with 50 special education students out of a total of 5619. Tuition: $384.

4821 Schreiner College

2100 Memorial Avenue
Kerrville, TX 78028

210-896-5411
800-343-4919

Dewayne Bannister, Admissions Director

An independent four-year college with 69 special education students out of a total of 637. There is a $2390 fee for the special education program in addition to the regular tuition of $13635.

4822 South Plains College

Loveland, TX 79336

Bill Powell, Studies Program

4823 Southern Methodist University

Box 355
Dallas, TX 75275

214-692-4563

Dr. Patricia Terrell, Special Services

An independent four-year college with 41 special education students out of a total of 5309. Tuition: $13950.

4824 Southwest Texas State University/Office of Disabled Students Services

601 University Drive
San Marcos, TX 78666

512-245-3451

Tom Hutson, Coordinator
Rhonda Alm, Student Development

The goal of the DSS Office is to assist students with disabilities to achieve their educational goals and enhance their leadership development. By identifying and assessing students needs, DSS provides direct services and refers students to appropriate resources on and off campus. DSS also promoted awareness of the special needs and abilities of students with disabilities through educational events and outreach activities.

4825 Southwestern Junior College of the Assemblies of God

1200 Sycamore
Waxhachie, TX 75165

214-937-4010

Mary Savell, Special Services

4826 St. Edwards University

3001 South Congress
Austin, TX 78704

512-448-8561

Bunny Smith, Special Services

An independent four-year college with 35 special education students out of a total of 2653. Tuition: $12040.

4827 St. Mary's University of San Antonio

San Antonio, TX 78284

5124363203

Barbara Biassiolli, DirectorServices

4828 Stephen F. Austin State University

P.O. Box 6130
Nacogdoches, TX 75942

409-568-1340

Linda Blassingame, Coordinator

4829 Tarrant County Junior College

828 Hartwood Road
Hurst, TX 76053

817-281-7860

Joyce Brewer

4830 Texas A&I University

Room 130, Eckhardt Hall
Kingsville, TX 78363

512-595-3991

Gary Low, Special Services

4831　Texas A&M University

College Station, TX　77843　　　409-845-1247

Gail Walters, Special Services

A public four-year college with 93 special education students out of a total of 30000. Tuition: $809.

4832　Texas Southern University

3100 Cleburne　　　　　710-527-4210
Houston, TX　77004

Minnine Simmons, Counselor

A public four-year college with 12 special education students out of a total of 8331. Tuition: $600.

4833　Texas State Technical College At Amarillo

Box 11197　　　　　　806-335-2316
Amarillo, TX　79111

Carolyn Allen, Program Chairman

4834　Texas State Technical Institute, Sweetwater Campus

300 College Drive　　　　912-235-7300
Sweetwater, TX　79556

Phyllis Morris, Special Services

4835　Texas Woman's University

Box 22305　　　　　　817-898-3626
Denton, TX　76204

Tricia Behle Hurter, Special Services

A public four-year college with 29 special education students out of a total of 5319. Tuition: $556.

4836　Tyler Junior College

Box 9020　　　　　　214-531-2388
Tyler, TX　75711

Vickie Geisel, Special Services

4837　University of Houston - Downtown

One Main Street, Rm. 903-S　　713-221-8430
Houston, TX　77002

Duraese Hall, Coordinator

A public four-year college with 11 special education students out of a total of 8702. Tuition: $600.

4838　University of North Texas

NT Box 5356　　　　　817-565-4323
Denton, TX　76203

Steve Pickett, Special Services

A public four-year college with 181 special education students out of a total of 20215. Tuition: $600.

4839　University of Texas At Arlington

Box 19156　　　　　　817-273-3670
Arlington, TX　76019

Dr. Cheryl Cardell, Counselor

A public four-year college with 40 special education students out of a total of 20889. Tuition: $600.

4840　University of Texas At Brownsville

80 Fort Brown　　　　　512-544-8292
Brownsville, TX　78520

Stephen Wilder, Dis. Student Srvcs.

A public four-year college with 17 special education students out of a total of 1118. Tuition: $480.

4841　University of Texas At Dallas

Box 830688　　　　　214-690-2098
Richardson, TX　75083

Gloria Williams, Special Services

4842　University of Texas At El Paso

500 West University Avenue　　915-747-5366
El Paso, TX　79968

Dr.Margarita Calderon, Special Services

A public four-year college with 26 special education students out of a total of 14201. Tuition: $768.

4843　University of Texas At Pan American

1201 West University Drive　　512-381-2585
Edinburg, TX　78539

Arturo Ramos, Asst. Director

4844　University of Texas At San Antonio

6900 North Loop 1604 West　　512-691-4157
San Antonio, TX　78249

Dr. Lynn Flinders, Special Services

A public four-year college with 17 special education students out of a total of 13849. Tuition: $582.

4845　West Texas State University

Canyon, TX　79016　　　806-656-2392

Kay Kropff, Special Services

A public four-year college with 15 special education students out of a total of 5122. Tuition: $720.

4846　Wharton County Junior College

911 Boling Highway
Wharton, TX　77427

4847 Wiley College
711 Roseborough Spring Road
Marshall, TX 75670

4848 Williams Academy
4767 Cockrell   817-921-6884
Fort Worth, TX 76133

Leigh Williams

Utah

4849 Brigham Young University
149 Spencer W. Kimball Tower   801-378-6020
Provo, UT 84602

Norman Roberts

4850 College of Eastern Utah
451 East 400 North   801-637-2120
Price, UT 84501

Colleen Quigley, Counselor

A public two-year college with 365 special education students out of a total of 2800. Tuition: $837.

4851 Latter-Day Saints Business College
411 East South Temple Street   801-363-2765
Salt Lake City, UT 84111

Tina Van Orden, Dean Of Students

4852 Salt Lake Community College
P.O. Box 30808   801-964-4659
Salt Lake City, UT 84130

Kay Fulton, Dir. Disability Ctr.

A public two-year college with 75 special education students out of a total of 15374. Tuition: $954.

4853 Snow College
150 East College Avenue   801-283-4021
Ephraim, UT 84627

Cyndi Crabb, Special Services

A public two-year college with 40 special education students out of a total of 2158. Tuition: $822.

4854 Southern Utah State College
Box 9375   801-586-7848
Cedar City, UT 84720

Pamela France, Special Services

A public four-year college with 26 special education students out of a total of 4280. Tuition: $1138.

4855 University of Utah
160 Union   801-581-5020
Salt Lake City, UT 84112

Olga Nadeau

A public four-year college with 317 special education students out of a total of 21018. Tuition: $1751.

4856 Utah State University
University Hill   801-750-2444
Logan, UT 84322

Diane Craig Brown, Special Services

A public four-year college with 175 special education students out of a total of 13783. Tuition: $1821.

4857 Utah Technical College - Salt Lake
P.O. Box 31808
Salt Lake City, UT 84131

4858 Utah Valley Community College
800 West 1200 South   801-222-8000
Orem, UT 84058

Curtis Pendleton, Disabled Services

4859 Weber State College
3750 Harrison Blvd.
Odgen, UT 84408

LaMar Kap

4860 Westminster College of Salt Lake City
1840 South 1300 East   801-488-4135
Salt Lake City, UT 84105

Bill Simmons, Special Services

Vermont

4861 Burlington College
95 North Avenue   802-862-9616
Burlington, VT 05401

Larry Lewack, Director Admissions

An independent four-year college with 10 special education students out of a total of 145. Tuition: $7200.

4862 Community College of Vermont
P.O. Box 120   802-241-3535
Waterbury, VT 05676

John Anderson, Director

A public two-year college with 200 special education students out of a total of 1912. Tuition: $2130.

4863 Goddard College

Learning Skills Center
Plainfield, VT 05667   802-454-8311

Fran Toomey, Director

4864 Green Mountain College

Poultney, VT 05764   802-287-9313

Harriet McCuen

4865 Johnson State College

Johnson, VT 05656   802-635-2356

Patricia Scott

A public four-year college with 50 special education students out of a total of 1298. Tuition: $2760.

4866 Norwich University

203 Harmon Hall   802-485-2130
Northfield, VT 05663

Paula Gills, Special Services

An independent four-year college with 110 special education students out of a total of 2086. Tuition: $17840.

4867 Saint Michael's College

Winooski Park   802-654-2347
Colchester, VT 05439

An independent four-year college with 46 special education students out of a total of 1728. Tuition: $16100.

4868 Southern Vermont College

Monument Avenue   802-442-5427
Bennington, VT 05201

Virginia Sturevant, LD Director

An independent four-year college with 69 special education students out of a total of 726. Tuition: $12202.

4869 St. Josephs College

Rutland, VT 05701   802-773-5900

Charles Bruckerhoff

4870 University of Vermont

146 South Williams Street   802-656-3340
Burlington, VT 05405

Susan Krasnow, Special Services

A public four-year college with 175 special education students out of a total of 8029. Tuition: $5740.

4871 Vermont Technical College

Randolph Center, VT 05061   802-728-3391

Wendy Duquette, Special Services

Virginia

4872 Augusta Psychological Associates

436 South Linden Avenue   703-949-4202
Waynesboro, VA 22980

Maya Layman

4873 Blue Ridge Community College

Special Populations Office
P.O. Box 80   703-234-9261
Weyers Cave, VA 24486   FAX 704-692-2441

Emily Sterrett, Coordinator

A public two-year college with 15 special education students out of a total of 1586. Tuition: $483.

4874 Chesapeake Bay Academy

5721 Sellger Avenue   804-459-2300
Norfolk, VA 23502

Katherine Shannon

4875 College of William and Mary

Room 209, James Blair Hall   804-253-4247
Williamsburg, VA 23185

Dr. Carroll Hardy, Director

4876 Commonwealth College, Virginia Beach

4160 Virginia Beach Blvd.   804-340-0222
Virginia Beach, VA 23452

Gardiner Haight, Dean, Academic

4877 Emory & Henry College

Emory, VA 24327   703-944-3121

Georgeanna Driver, Advisement Director

4878 Ferrum College

Ferrum, VA 24088   703-365-4270

Brenda Newcombe, Reading Specialist

An independent four-year college with 50 special education students out of a total of 1211. Tuition: $11850.

4879 Hampden-Sydney College

Mapden-Sydeny, VA 23943   804-223-4381

Dr. Tony Campbell, Director

4880 James Madison University

Harrisonburg, VA 22807   703-568-6705

Tracy Hakala, Coordinator

A public four-year college with 67 special education students out of a total of 9946. Tuition: $3576.

4881 John Tyler Community College

Chester, VA 23831   804-796-4167

Dr. Charles Garren, Counselor

A public two-year college with 10 special education students out of a total of 5287. Tuition: $1050.

4882 Liberty University

Box 20000   804-582-2226
Lynchburg, VA 24506

Denton McHaney, Faculty Advisor

An independent four-year college with 37 special education students out of a total of 10549. Tuition: $10320.

4883 Longwood College

Farmville, VA 23909   804-395-2391

L. Scott Lissner, Coordinator

A public four-year college with 78 special education students out of a total of 2884. Tuition: $2154.

4884 Lord Fairfax Community College

P.O. Box 47   703-869-1120
Middletown, VA 22645

Paula Dean

A public two-year college with 20 special education students out of a total of 2857. Tuition: $1312.

4885 Mary Washington College

1301 College Avenue   703-899-4694
Fredericksburg, VA 22401

Patricia Tracy, Coordinator

A public four-year college with 37 special education students out of a total of 3426. Tuition: $1864.

4886 New River Community College

Southwest Virginia Regional Center for the LD
Box 1127   703-674-3600
Dublin, VA 24084

Jeananne Dixon, Coordinator

A public two-year college with 115 special education students out of a total of 2365. Tuition: $1312.

4887 Northern Virginia Community College

8333 Little River Turnpike   703-323-3209
Annandale, VA 22003

Karen Wray, Coordinator

A public two-year college with 400 special education students out of a total of 30000. Tuition: $1312.

4888 Old Dominion University, Disability Services

111 Old Administration Bldg.   804-683-4655
Norfolk, VA 23529   FAX 804-683-5357

Nancy Olthoff, PhD, Coordinator

Works with students to provide access to higher education. Reasonable accommodations are identified to address specific individual needs. Accommodations may include extended testing time, permission to tape record classes, distraction-free test setting, etc..

4889 Patrick Henry Community College

P.O. Drawer 5311   703-638-8777
Martinsville, VA 24115

Carolyn Byrd, Special Services

4890 Paul D. Camp Community College

530 East Piner Street   804-925-2429
Franklin, VA 23434

Carol Able, Student Support

A public two-year college with 8 special education students out of a total of 1557. Tuition: $1050.

4891 Piedmont Virginia Community College

Route 6, Box 1   804-977-3900
Charlottescille, VA 22902

Marlene Herakovich, Counselor

A public two-year college with 53 special education students out of a total of 4249. Tuition: $1130.

4892 Radford University

P.O. Box 5705   703-831-5439
Radford, VA 24142

Stanley Jones, Dean, College Of Ed.

Special Education Porgram - B.S. and M.S. in mental retardation, learning disabilities and emotional disturbances.

4893 Randolph-Macon Women's College

2500 Rivermount Avenue   804-947-8100
Lynchburg, VA 24503

James C. Kughn, Jr., Special Services

An independent four-year college with 6 special education students out of a total of 769. Tuition: $18070.

4894 Rappahannock Community College

Box 287   804-758-5324
Glenns, VA 23149

Alan Harris, Special Services

4895 South Virgnia Community College

Alberta, VA 23947

John Sykes

4896 Southern Seminary College

Buena Vista, VA 24416   703-761-8420

Jack Turregano, Special Services

4897 Southwest Virginia Community College

P.O. Box SVCC   703-964-2555
Richlands, VA 24641

Julie Mayrose, Special Services

4898 St. Colletta School

1305 North Jackson Street   703-525-4433
Arlington, VA 22201

4899 Thomas Nelson Community College

P.O. Box 9407   804-825-2827
Hampton, VA 23670

Thomas Kellen, Special Services
A public two-year college with 7 special education students out of a total of 7900. Tuition: $1230.

4900 Tidewater Community College, Chesapeake Campus

1428 Cedar Road   804-547-9271
Chesapeake, VA 23320

Michael Barton, Special Services
A public two-year college with 40 special education students out of a total of 2847. Tuition: $1050.

4901 Tidewater Community College, Portsmouth Campus

State Route 135   804-484-2121
Portsmouth, VA 23703

Andrew Love, Special Services

4902 Tidewater Community College, Virginia Beach Campus

1700 College Crescent   804-427-7211
Virginia Beach, VA 23456

Gary Medlin, Special Services
A public two-year college with 78 special education students out of a total of 11239. Tuition: $1050.

4903 University of Virginia

B012 Brooks Hall   804-924-3139
Charlottesville, VA 22906

Dr. Eleanore Westhead, Special Services

4904 Virginia Commonwealth University

Richmond, VA 23284   804-257-1222

Ellen Pearson

4905 Virginia Highlands Community College

P.O. Box 828   703-628-6094
Abingdon, VA 24210

Charlotte Faris
A public two-year college with 20 special education students out of a total of 2295. Tuition: $1312.

4906 Virginia Intermont College

1013 Moore Street   703-669-6101
Bristol, VA 24201

Barbara Holbrook, Special Services
An independent four-year college with 22 special education students out of a total of 641. Tuition: $11300.

4907 Virginia Polytechnic Institute and State University

105 Brodie Hall   703-231-3787
Blacksburg, VA 24061

Wayne Speer, Special Services
A public four-year college with 68 special education students out of a total of 19308. Tuition: $3538.

4908 Virginia Western Community College

P.O. Box 14007   703-857-7786
Roanoke, VA 24038

Michael Henderson, Special Services
A public two-year college with 106 special education students out of a total of 7368. Tuition: $1050.

Washington

4909 Bellevue Community College

3000 SE Landerholm Circle   206-641-0111
Bellevue, WA 98007

Harold VanAuken, Coordinator

4910 Central Washington University

Ellensburg, WA 98926   509-963-2171

David Brown

A public four-year college with 90 special education students out of a total of 6726. Tuition: $1698.

4911 Centralia College

600 West Locust   206-736-9391
Centralia, WA 98531

Kay Odegaard, Cooridinator

4912 Clark College

1800 East McLoughlin Blvd.   206-699-0260
Vancouver, WA 98663

Duane Henry, Director

A public two-year college with 10 special education students out of a total of 9100. Tuition: $996.

4913 Columbia Basin College

2600 North 20th Avenue   509-547-0511
Pasco, WA 99301

Peggy Buchmiller, Coordinator

A public two-year college with 154 special education students out of a total of 6842. Tuition: $999.

4914 Cornish College of the Arts

710 East Roy Street   206-323-1400
Seattle, WA 98102

Bill Oye, Counselor

An independent four-year college with 14 special education students out of a total of 529. Tuition: $8650.

4915 Eastern Washington University

Mail Stop 180   509-359-2293
Cheney, WA 99004

Karen Raver, Student Services

A public four-year college with 11 special education students out of a total of 6990. Tuition: $2085.

4916 Edmonds Community College

20000 68th Avenue West   206-771-1536
Lynwood, WA 98036

Marva Brown, Coordinator

4917 Everett Community College

801 Wetmore
Everett, WA 98201

W.J. Deller

4918 Evergreen State College

Olympia, WA 98505   206-886-6000

Linda Murphy

A public four-year college with 19 special education students out of a total of 3224. Tuition: $1785.

4919 Fort Stellacoom Community College

9401 Farwest Drive SW
Tacoma, WA 98449

Pearl Rose

4920 Green River Community College

12401 SE 320th   206-833-9111
Auburn, WA 98002

Karen Bruno, Educational Planning

Services to suppoort education for students with disabilities that include but are not limited to early registration, specialized equipment including speech synthesizers, enlargers, brailling system, with support services such as tutoring, interpreters, court reporters, notetakers, mobility orientation and extended time lines. All programs are accessible.

4921 Highline Community College

Des Moines, WA 98198   206-878-3710

Pam Arsenault-Goldsmith, Program Coordinator

4922 North Seattle Community College

9600 College Way   206-527-3658
Seattle, WA 98103

Karen Iverson, Special Services

4923 Olympic College

16th And Chester   206-478-4607
Bremerton, WA 98310

Anna Hoey-Dorsey, Special Services

4924 Seattle Central Community College

1718 Broadway
Seattle, WA 98122

Stanley Traxler

4925   Seattle Pacific University

3307 3rd Avenue West   206-281-2486
Seattle, WA 98119

Brian Bosse, Disabled Services

An independent four-year college with 21 special education students out of a total of 2224. Tuition: $15579.

4926   South Puget Sound Community College

2011 Mottman Road SW   206-754-7711
Olympia, WA 98502

Laurie Tremblay, Special Services

4927   South Seattle Community College

6000 16th Avenue SW   206-764-5335
Seattle, WA 98106

Tim Walsh, LD Director

A public two-year college with 30 special education students out of a total of 6500. Tuition: $1174.

4928   Spokane Community College

N1810 Greene Street, MS 2160   509-553-8679
Spokane, WA 99207

Melody Weins, Special Services

4929   Spokane Falls Community College

3410 West Fort George Wright Dr.   509-459-3543
Spokane, WA 99204

Ben Webinger, Special Services

4930   St. Christopher Academy

318 Third Avenue South   206-852-1515
Kent, WA 98032

Darlene Jones

4931   University of Puget Sound

1500 North Warner Street   206-756-3395
Tacoma, WA 98416

Dorothy Lee

4932   University of Washington

PB-07   206-543-8924
Seattle, WA 98195

Judy Lonergan, Special Services

A public four-year college with 45 special education students out of a total of 25092. Tuition: $2274.

4933   Walla Walla Community College

500 Tausick Way
Walla Walla, WA 99362

Hilda Thompson, Coordinator

4934   Washington State University

Room 57, Cleveland   509-335-1566
Pullman, WA 99164

Marshall Mitchell, Special Services

A public four-year college with 138 special education students out of a total of 14893. Tuition: $2274.

4935   Western Washington University

275 Old Main   206-676-3083
Bellingham, WA 98225

Dorothy Crow, Special Services

A public four-year college with 160 special education students out of a total of 9179. Tuition: $1785.

4936   Whatcom Community College

237 West Kellogg Road   206-676-2170
Bellingham, WA 98226

Tony Navarro, Counselor

A public two-year college with 20 special education students out of a total of 2074. Tuition: $990.

4937   Whitworth College

#38   509-466-3271
Spokane, WA 99251

Pat Coleman, Special Services

4938   Yakima Valley College

P.O. Box 1647
Yakima, WA 98907

Gaye Hickraw

West Virginia

4939   Bethany College

Special Advising
Bethany, WV 26032   304-829-7000

Christine Sampson, Director

An independent four-year college with 3 special education students out of a total of 631. Tuition: $10669.

4940   Bluefield State College

219 Rock Street   304-327-4098
Bluefield, WV 24701

Dr. Claudius Oni, Director

A public four-year college with 10 special education students out of a total of 2907. Tuition: $1726.

4941   Davis & Elkins College

Davis & Elkins College
201 Albert Hall   304-636-1900
Elkins, WV 26241

Dr. Margaret Turner, LD Specialist

An independent four-year college with 56 special education students out of a total of 855. There is a $1100 fee for the special education program in addition to the regular tuition of $12090.

4942   Fairmont State College

200 Jaynes Hall   304-367-4299
Fairmont, WV 26554

Martha French

4943   Marshall University H.E.L.P. Program

Myers Hall
520 18th Street   304-696-6252
Huntington, WV 25755

Dr, Barbara Guyer, Director

A tutoring and support program for learning disabled college students. Applications must be made to H.E.L.P. one year in advance. Interview is required. H.E.L.P. has approximately 180 students, 40 graduate assistants, 15 remediation tutors, along with a director, assistant director and 8 other staff members. This program sees that students receive modifications guaranteed under Section 504.

4944   Parkersburg Community College

Parkersburg, WV 26101   304-424-8000

James Cook, Special Services

4945   Salem College

Salem, WV 26426   304-782-5292

Cynthia Calise, Special Services

4946   Salem-Teikyo University

233 West Main Street   304-782-5261
Salem, WV 26426

Paris Herbert Roland, Dir. Student Support

Student Support Services grant program funded by the US Dept of Education for 125 college students who are identified as disadvantaged and/or disabled. On staff are a counselor, a learning disabled specialist in math and science and a learning specialist in reading adn writing.

4947   Southern West Virginia Community College

Logan, WV 25601   304-792-4300

Walter Adams, Special Services

4948   West Virginia Northern Community College

College Square   304-233-5900
Wheeling, WV 26003

Bonnie Ellis, Special Services

A public two-year college with 7 special education students out of a total of 2903.

4949   West Virginia State College

Box 178   304-766-3083
Institute, WV 25112

Jacqueline Burns, Special Services

A public four-year college with 22 special education students out of a total of 4986. Tuition: $1578.

4950   West Virginia University/ Department of Speech Pathology & Audiology

P.O. Box 6122   304-293-4242
Morgantown, WV 26506   FAX 304-293-7565

Dennis Ruscello, Director

Offers a clinic for people with special hearing and speech needs.

4951   West Virginia Wesleyan College

Buckhannon, WV 26201   303-473-8000

Phyllis Coston, LD Director

An independent four-year college with 237 special education students out of a total of 1529. There is a $3700 fee for the special education program in addition to the regular tuition of $15955.

Wisconsin

4952   Alverno College

3401 South 39th Street   414-382-6353
Milwaukee, WI 53215

Nancy Bornstein

An independent four-year college with 10 special education students out of a total of 2499. Tuition: $10582.

4953   Beloit College

Beloit, WI 53511   608-365-3391

John Lind

4954   Blackhawk Technical College

6004 Prairie Road   608-756-4121
Janesville, WI 53547

Christine Flottum

A public two-year college with 50 special education students out of a total of 2600. Tuition: $1312.

4955   Cardinal Stritch College

6801 North Yates Road   414-352-5400
Milwaukee, WI 53217

Marica Laskey

An independent four-year college with 12 special education students out of a total of 2520. Tuition: $10710.

4956   Carthage College

Academic Support Program
2001 Alford Park Drive
Kenosha, WI 53140   414-551-8500

Laura Busch, Director

An independent four-year college with 11 special education students out of a total of 1925. Tuition: $14995.

4957   Chippewa Valley Technical College

620 West Clairemont Avenue   715-833-6280
Eau Claire, WI 54701

Robert Benedict

A public two-year college with 105 special education students out of a total of 3750. Tuition: $1230.

4958   Edgewood College

855 Woodrow   608-257-4861
Madison, WI 53711

Kathie Moran, Academic Dean Asst.

An independent four-year college with 10 special education students out of a total of 1226. Tuition: $11000.

4959   Fox Valley Technical College

1825 North Bluemond Drive   414-735-5682
Appleton, WI 54913

Lori Weyers, Dean General Studies

A public two-year college with 65 special education students out of a total of 4810. Tuition: $1312.

4960   Gateway Technical College

3520 30th Avenue   414-656-6958
Kenosha, WI 53144

Jo Bailey, Learning Skills

A public two-year college with 235 special education students out of a total of 7844. Tuition: $1285.

4961   Marian College of Fond Du Lac

45 South National Avenue   414-923-8117
Fond Du Lac, WI 54933

Gretchen Gall, Director

4962   Marquette University

1324 West Wisconsin Avenue   414-288-1645
Milwaukee, WI 53233

Patricia Almon, Coordinator

An independent four-year college with 2 special education students out of a total of 8409. Tuition: $14284.

4963   Mid-State Technical College

500 32nd Street North   715-423-5650
Wisconsin Rapids, WI 54494

Dr. John Bellanti, Special Services

4964   Milwaukee Area Technical College

700 West State Street   414-278-6594
Milwuakee, WI 53233

Brenda Benton, Guidance Counselor

A public two-year college with 200 special education students out of a total of 23099. Tuition: $1245.

4965   Mt. Denario College

College Avenue   715-532-5511
Lodysmith, WI 54848

Victor Macaruso

4966   Nicolet Area Technical College

Box 518   715-365-4430
Rhinelander, WI 54501

Robert Weber, Special Needs

A public two-year college with 26 special education students out of a total of 1500. Tuition: $1312.

4967   Northcentral Technical College

1000 Campus Drive   715-675-3331
Wausau, WI 54401

Lois Gilliland, Special Services

4968   Northeast Wisconsin Technical College

Special Services Program
P.O. Box 19042, 2740 W. Mason St.   414-498-5470
Green Bay, WI 54307   800-272-2740
                                   FAX 414-498-6260

Jerome Miller, Special Services

A public two-year college with 88 special education students out of a total of 7682. Tuition: $1230.

4969 Ripon College

300 Seward Street 414-748-8107
Ripon, WI 54971

Dan Krhin, Special Services

An independent four-year college with 16 special education students out of a total of 838. Tuition: $17175.

4970 University of Wisconsin Center, Marshfield /Wood County

2000 West 5th Street 715-389-6529
Marshfield, WI 54449

Linda Gleason, Associate Director

A public two-year college with 11 special education students out of a total of 540. Tuition: $1426.

4971 University of Wisconsin, Eau Claire

P.O. Box 4004 715-836-4542
Eau Claire, WI 54701

Thomas Bouchard, Director

4972 University of Wisconsin, La Crosse

1725 State Street 608-785-8535
La Crosse, WI 54601

June Reinert, Special Services

4973 University of Wisconsin, Madison

500 Lincoln Drive 608-263-2741
Madison, WI 53715

Cathleen Trueba, Special Services

4974 University of Wisconsin, Milwaukee

P.O. Box 413 414-229-6239
Milwaukee, WI 53201

Laurie Gramatzki, Coordinator

A public four-year college with 100 special education students out of a total of 20557. Tuition: $2200.

4975 University of Wisconsin, Oshkosh

Box #69, Nursing Education Bldg. 414-424-1033
Oshkosh, WI 54901

Dr. Robert Nash, Director

A public four-year college with 145 special education students out of a total of 9525. Tuition: $1822.

4976 University of Wisconsin, Platteville

453 Gardner Hall 608-342-1816
Platteville, WI 53818

Dale Bernhardt, Special Services

4977 University of Wisconsin, River Falls

25 Hathorn Hall 715-425-3884
River Falls, WI 54022

Dr. John Hamann, Special Services

4978 University of Wisconsin, Whitewater

Room 2019 414-472-4788
Whitewater, WI 53190

Dr. Connie Dalke, Director

A public four-year college with 100 special education students out of a total of 9069. There is a $550 fee for the special education program in addition to the regular tuition of $1914.

4979 Viterbo College

815 South 9th Street 608-791-0354
La Crosse, WI 54601

Jane Eddy, Program Director

An independent four-year college with 6 special education students out of a total of 1160. Tuition: $11550.

4980 Waukesha County Technical College

800 Main Street 414-691-5392
Pewaukee, WI 53072

Judy Jorgenson

4981 Western Wisconsin Technical College

Sixth And Vine Street 608-785-9144
La Crosse, WI 54602

Keith Valiquette, Special Services

4982 Wisconsin Indianhead Tech College, Rice Lake Campus

1900 College Drive 715-234-7082
Rice Lake, WI 54868

Patricia Peters, Special Needs

A public two-year college with 30 special education students out of a total of 1097. Tuition: $1310.

4983 Wisconsin Indianhead Technical College, Ashland Campus

2100 Beaser Avenue   715-682-4591
Ashland, WI 54806

Cindy Utities-Heart, Special Services

A public two-year college with 38 special education students out of a total of 386. Tuition: $1310.

Wyoming

4984 Laramie County Community College

1400 E. College Drive   307-778-5222
Cheyenne, WY 82007   FAX 307-778-1399

Dr. Caron Mellbolm, Center Coordinator

A public two-year college with 130 special education students out of a total of 4400. Tuition: $624.

4985 Sheridan College

P.O. Box 1500   307-674-6446
Sheridan, WY 82801

Tena Hanes, Special Services

A public two-year college with 50 special education students out of a total of 2896. Tuition: $756.

4986 University of Wyoming

Box 3808, University Station   307-766-6189
Laramie, WY 82071

Chris Primus, Special Services

An independent four-year college with 49 special education students out of a total of 9444. Tuition: $1426.

4987 Wheeling Jesuit College

Wheeling, WY 26003   304-243-2428

Leslie Frankovitch, Special Services

Information for the College-Bound

4988 Above and Beyond

Jade Ann Gingerich, Author
AASCU
One Dupont Circle, Ste. 700   202-293-7070
Washington, DC 20036

Describes winning college services for students with learning disabilities.

$ 8.00

4989 American Trade Schools Directory

Croner Publications, Inc.
34 Jericho Turnpike   516-333-9085
Jericho, NY 11753   800-441-4033
                             FAX 516-338-4986

Carol Sixt, Editor

Offers a cost-effective way of facilitating access to more than 12,000 trade, technical and vocational schools in the United States. The newly revised and completely updated edition remains the most authoritative resource profiling facilities in your community, as well as every major population center in all fifty states.

$ 79.95

4990 The Association of Schools and Agencies Serving Persons with Special Needs

The Forum School
107 Wyckoff Avenue   201-444-5882
Waldwick, NJ 07463

Steve Krapes, President

4991 Campus Access for Learning Disabled Students

Closer Look
1201 16th Street NW
Washington, DC 20036

A very useful practical guide for college bound SLD persons.

$ 17.95

4992 Campus Opportunities for Students with Learning Differences

Octameron Associates
P.O. Box 3437   703-823-1882
Alexandria, VA 22302

A booklet for young adults about the various types of learning disabilities.

4993 College and the Learning Disabled Student

Charles T. Mangrum, III, Author
Learning Disabilities Association of America
4156 Library Road   412-341-1515
Pittsburgh, PA 15234

A book describing what college learning disabled students are like.

$ 38.95

4994 College Reading and Study Strategy Programs

Rona Flippo, Author

International Reading Association
800 Barksdale Rd., P.O. Box 8139   302-731-1600
Newark, DE 19714   800-336-READ
                                          FAX 302-731-1057

A companion book providing a review of the theoretical, empirical and programmatic issues involved in managing and assessing college reading programs.

$ 8.00

4995 College Students with Learning Disabilities

Learning Disabilities Association of America
4156 Library Road   412-341-1515
Pittsburgh, PA 15234

4996 Colleges/Universities That Accept Students with Learning Disabilities

Learning Disabilities Association of America
4156 Library Road   412-341-1515
Pittsburgh, PA 15234

List of colleges by state.

$ 4.00

4997 Directory of Catholic Special Education Programs and Facilities

National Catholic Education Association
1077 30th Street NW, Ste. 100   202-337-6232
Washington, DC 20007

NCEA Publications Sales

A valuable resource for anyone seeking appropriate placements in Catholic settings.

$ 8.00

4998 Directory of Disability Support Services in Community Colleges

Lynne Barnett, Author
American Association of Community Colleges
P.O. Box 1737   410-546-0391
Salisbury, MD 21802

Michele Jackman, Marketing Coord.

Funded by the US Department of Education, this brand new and updated directory provides information from more than 600 institutions on services and accommodations available to individuals with disabilities. It contains specific information on each institution, a "spreadsheet" of services and accommodations by institution and a special features index. Includes a list of community college with learning disability support services as well.

$ 20.00

4999 Directory of Educational Facilities for Learning Disabled Students

Learning Disabilities Association of America
4156 Library Road   412-341-1515
Pittsburgh, PA 15234

5000 Directory of Technical Assistants

Independent Living Research Utilization Project
P.O. Box 20095   713-666-6244
Houston, TX 77225

$ 5.00

5001 Four Year College Databook

CGP - Chronicle Guidance Publications, Inc.
P.O. Box 1190   800-622-7284
Moravia, NY 13118

Offers information on more than 2,000 colleges and universities, 963 school majors or occupational career programs.

$ 19.96

5002 From Access to Equality

Association on Higher Education and Disability
P.O. Box 21192   614-488-4972
Columbus, OH 43221   FAX 614-488-1174

This resource manual is for service providers who want to take concrete action toward integrating women with disabilities into the mainstream of college life.

$ 9.95

5003 Getting LD Students Ready for College

HEATH Resource Center
One DuPont Circle NW   202-939-9329
Washington, DC 20036   800-544-3284

Carol Sullivan, Counselor

List offering parents, counselors, teachers and learning disabled students a reminder of helpful skills and necessary steps to take as a high school student with a learning disability moves toward college.

5004 Guide Lines for Learning Disabled College Students

Learning Disabilities Association of America
4156 Library Road   412-341-1515
Pittsburgh, PA 15234

5005 A Guide to Colleges for Learning Disabled Students

Academic Success Press, Inc.
P.O. Box 25002-Box #132   800-444-2524
Bradenton, FL 34206

Mary Ann Liscio, Editor

5006 Guide to Community Colleges Serving Students with Learning Disabilities

Sonja Burnham, Author

**Project We Can, Mississippi State University
Department Of Counselor Education**

A list by state of two-year community colleges in Mississippi, Alabama, Georgia, Tennessee and Florida, describing services and accommodations provided for students with learning disabilities.

$ 1.50

5007 HEATH Resource Directory

**National Clearinghouse on Postsecondary Education
One Dupont Circle, Ste. 800**   202-939-9300
Washington, DC 20036

Annotated listings of over 150 national organizations which can provide additional information about postsecondary education and individuals with disabilities.

5008 High School/College Connection: a Guide for the Transition of LD Students

Pearl Seidenberg, Author

**Long Island University Transition Project
Long Island University
Brooklyn, NY 11201**

5009 Higher Education Information Center

**Boston Public Library
666 Boylston Street**   617-536-0200
Copley Square, Boston, MA 02116   800-442-1171

Offers information on colleges and universities, vocational/technical schools, financial aid and careers, counseling on school selection and paying for educational costs and offers a toll-free hotline.

5010 How to Succeed in College, a Handbook for Students with Learning Disabilities

**The National Center on Employment and Disability
I.U. Willets Road**   516-747-5400
Albertson, NY 11507

These two volumes demonstrate the advantages of cooperation between vocational rehabilitation and education.

$ 15.00

5011 How to Succeed in College with Dyslexia

J. Woods, Author

**Learning Disabilities Association of America
4156 Library Road**   412-341-1515
Pittsburgh, PA 15234

5012 Issues in College Learning Centers: a Collection of Articles

**Long Island University
Brooklyn Campus
Brooklyn, NY 11201**

Elaine Caputo, Associate Director

5013 The K & W Guide to Colleges for the Learning Disabled

**Connecticut Association for Children with LD
18 Marshall Street**   203-838-5010
South Norwalk, CT 06854   FAX 203-866-6108

$ 17.50

5014 Learning Disabilities: Coping in College

**Handicapped Student Services
Wright State University**   513-873-2140
Dayton, OH 45435

5015 Learning to Care

**ACTION
1100 Vermont Avenue NW**   202-606-5135
Washington, DC 20525

A national directory of student community service programs.

5016 List of Colleges/Universities That Accept Students with Learning Disabilities

**Learning Disabilities Association of America
4156 Library Road**   412-341-1515
Pittsburgh, PA 15234

$ 4.00

5017 Lovejoy's College Guide for the Learning Disabled

Charles T. Straughn, II, Author

**Special Needs Project
1482 East Valley Road #A-121**   805-565-1914
Santa Barbara, CA 93108   800-333-6867

Information about 270 college and universities, mostly four-year.

$ 12.95

5018 The National Association of Private Schools for Exceptional Children

**NAPSEC
1522 K Street NW, Ste. 1032**   202-408-3338
Washington, DC 20005   FAX 202-408-3340

*Sherry Kolbe, Executive Director
Mara Miller, Administrator*

A membership directory listing all the private schools, nationwide for exceptional children. Information given includes: disabilities served, program descriptions, school profiles, admissions procedures and funding approval.
$ 28.00

5019 A National Directory of Four Year, Two Year Colleges & High Schools for LD

Partners in Publishing
1419 West First   918-584-5906
Tulsa, OK 74127

P.M. Fielding, Editor

Gathered through questionaires, this directory offers school name, size, type, address, telephone, contact person and what programs are offered for the learning disabled students.

5020 1993 College Placement Council Directory

College Placement Council, Inc.
62 Highland Avenue   215-868-1421
Bethlehem, PA 18017   800-544-5272

Offers the who's who in the college placement/recruitment field.
$ 47.95

5021 Peterson's Guide to Colleges with Programs for Students with LD

Peterson's Guides
202 Carnegie Center, P.O. Box 2123   800-338-3282
Princeton, NJ 08543   FAX 609-452-0966

Ruth Lewis, Publicity Director

A comprehensive guide to more than 1,000 colleges offering special academic programs for learning-disabled students.
> *"...a valuable tool in NCLD's Information and Referral Service. I am pleased to recommend it."*
> -Anne Ford, Chair Nat'l Ctr. for LD
$ 24.95

5022 Postsecondary LD Network News

University of Connecticut
U-64, 249 Glenbrook Road   202-486-2020
Storrs, CT 06269

Focuses on a variety of topics concerning college students with learning disabilities.
$ 20.00

5023 Questions to Aid in Selecting An Appropriate College Program for LD

Connecticut Association for Children with LD
18 Marshall Street   203-838-5010
South Norwalk, CT 06854   FAX 203-866-6108

A collection of five one page information sheets, each from a different source.
$ 2.00

5024 School Search: Guide to Colleges with Programs for the Learning Disabled

Midge Lipkin, Author
Connecticut Association for Children with LD
18 Marshall Street   203-838-5010
South Norwalk, CT 06854   FAX 203-866-6108

Offers information on admissions, information, special services, expenses and summer programs.
$ 33.00

5025 A Shopper's Guide to Colleges Serving the Learning Disabled College Students

Fred Barbaro, Author
Learning Disabilities Association of America
4156 Library Road   412-341-1515
Pittsburgh, PA 15234
$ 3.00

5026 A Talking Mouth Speaks About Learning Disabled College Students

Learning Disabilities Association of America
4156 Library Road   412-341-1515
Pittsburgh, PA 15234
$ 3.50

5027 Two-Year College Databook

CGP - Chronicle Guidance Publications, Inc.
P.O. Box 1190   800-622-7284
Moravia, NY 13118

Offers information on 2,361 colleges, 963 occupational-career programs or majors and information on the college decision process.
$ 19.95

5028 Vocational School Manual

CGP - Chronicle Guidance Publications, Inc.
P.O. Box 1190   800-622-7284
Moravia, NY 13118

Offers information on more than 4,100 accredited schools and 904 programs of study.
$ 19.98

5029 When College Is Appropriate

Connecticut Association for Children with LD
18 Marshall Street   203-838-5010
South Norwalk, CT 06854   FAX 203-866-6108

Four, one page information sheets from different sources useful to the learning disabled student pondering a college education.

$ 2.00

5030 A World of Options for the 90's: a Guide to International Education

Mobility International USA
P.O. Box 3551   503-343-1284
Eugene, OR 97403

Offers information on international education and travel for persons with disabilities.

$ 14.00

Financial Aid

5031 Chronicle Student Aid Annual 1992-1993

P.O. Box 1190   800-622-7284
Morovia, NY 13118

A comprehensive listing of more than 1900 programs of financial aid for undergraduate and graduate study.

5032 Federal Student Aid Fact Sheet

U.S. Department of Education
Student Financial Assistance   800-433-3243
Washington, DC 20202

Describes basic federal programs for undergraduate and graduate students and their families.

5033 Federal Student Aid Information Center

800-4-FEDAID

Helps students file applications or correct a SAR, checks on whether a school takes part in Federal student aid programs, or if a school has a high default rate, explains student eligibility requirements, mails publications and explains the process of determining financial aid awards.

5034 Foundation Center

79 Fifth Avenue   212-620-4230
New York, NY 10003

Operates four libraries offering index books of foundations and grants made to organizations serving disabilities.

Centers & Publishers

5035   ACT Test Administration

P.O. Box 168   319-337-1332
Iowa City, IA 52243

Responds to needs for special arrangements at its regular testing centers.

5036   ATP Services for Handicapped Students

CN 6400   609-734-5350
Princeton, NJ 08541

Offers information on testing and college testing for students.

5037   Clinical Classroom for Learning Problems Center

University of Kansas Medical Center
4001 H.C. Miller Bldg.   913-588-5951
Kansas City, KS 66103

Dr. Floyd Hudson, Coordinator

The CCLP provides diagnostic assessment of the learning problems of school-aged children who exhibit moderate-to-severe learning problems within their current school setting. The CCLP's ultimate goal is the student's return to the home school, equipped with descriptions of specific strengths and concerns for each academic or social area diagnosed, and relevant instructional recommendations.

5038   College Board Testing for Learning Disabled Students

Princeton, NJ 08540

Learning disabled students can be tested under special conditions such as extended time, seperate text rooms, a reader or a scribe.

5039   Educational and Diagnostic Resources, Inc.

Traveling Tutors
1420 Beverly Road, Ste. 3000   703-893-9010
McLean, VA 22101   FAX 703-734-0910

5040   Educational Record Bureau

37 Cameron Street   617-235-8920
Wellsley, MA 02181

5041   Educational Study Center

353-A Robinson Hall I   703-993-2044
Fairfax, VA 22030   FAX 703-993-2564

5042   Educational Testing Service

Test Collection
Rosedale Road   609-734-1622
Princeton, NJ 08541

An educational measurement and research organization providing tests and related services for schools, colleges and government agencies.

5043   GED Test Accommodations for Candidates with Specific Learning Disabilities

GED Testing Service
One Dupont Circle   202-939-9490
Washington, DC 20036

A publication that describes the policies and procedures for obtaining special accommodations on the GED tests.

5044   General Educational Development - GED Testing Service

American Council on Education
One Dupont Circle   202-939-9490
Washington, DC 20036

Administers the GED tests and provides information on disability-related adaptations/accommodations for the GED tests to prospective examiners and instructors.

5045   Georgetown University Child Development Center

3800 Reservoir Road NW   202-687-8635
Washington, DC 20007   FAX 202-687-1954

Debra Folberg, Clinical Care

Developmental testing for children ages up to 21 years.

5046   Hawaii Early Learning Profile

The Speech Bin
1965 Twenty-Fifth Avenue   407-770-0007
Vero Beach, FL 32960   FAX 407-770-0006

Jan J. Binney, Editor In Chief
Barbara Hector, Office Manager

Comprehensive assessment and service delivery system for the whole child.

$ 36.00

5047   Initial Preparation Program for the GED Test

Aquarius Instructional
P.O. Box 128   813-595-7890
Indiana Rocks Beach, FL 34635   800-338-2644
     FAX 813-595-2685

Offers computer programs, audio cassettes and duplicate worksheets for the GED test.

$ 1495.00

5048   Plano Child Development Center

2830 South Indiana Avenue   312-326-4488
Chicago, IL 60616

Stephanie Johnson, Executive Director

Surveys children with visually related learning disabilities and offers vision education seminars geared to learning disabilities.

5049 Scholastic Aptitude Test

Admissions Testing Program for Handicapped Student
CN 6603   215-750-8147
Princeton, NJ 08541

5050 Vocational Entry-Skills Student Worksheets

W. Washburn, Author
Connecticut Association for Children with LD
18 Marshall Street   203-838-5010
South Norwalk, CT 06854   FAX 203-866-6108
$ 7.75

Behavior & Self-Esteem

5051 AAMD Adaptive Behavior Scale - Residential and Community Education

Kazuo Nihira, Author
Western Psychological Services Corporation
12031 Wilshire Blvd.   213-478-2061
Los Angeles, CA 90025   800-648-8857
                                                    FAX 213-478-7838

A behavior rating scale for mentally retarded and emotionally maladjusted children. By providing information crucial for those planning education, training and rehabilitation programs, the scale enables workers to describe more clearly and comprehensively an individual daily functioning.

$ 26.00

5052 AAMD Adaptive Behavior Scale - School Edition

Nadine Lambert, Author
Pro-Ed
8700 Shoal Creek Blvd.   512-451-3246
Austin, TX 78758   FAX 512-451-8542

Assesses children whose behavior indicates possible mental retardation, emotional disturbances or other learning difficulties.

$ 34.00

5053 Adaptive Behavior Inventory (ABI)

Western Psychological Services Corporation
12031 Wilshire Blvd.   213-478-2061
Los Angeles, CA 90025   800-648-8857
                                                    FAX 213-478-7838

Measures adaptive behavior. This test can be an increasingly important component of psychological and school-based evaluations and can be extremely useful in diagnosing mental retardation and indentifying students who may qualify for special education programs.

$ 72.00

5054 AEPS: Assessment, Evaluation and Programming Systems for Infants

Diane Bricker, Author
The Speech Bin
1965 Twenty-Fifth Avenue   407-770-0007
Vero Beach, FL 32960   FAX 407-770-0006

Jan J. Binney, Editor In Chief
Barbara Hector, Office Manager

Gives you an easy-to-use comprehensive interdisciplinary assessment tool to measure the young child's functional skills in the six key domains of fine motor, gross motor, adaptive and social development.

$ 39.00

5055 Autism Screening Instrument for Education Planning

The Speech Bin
1965 Twenty-Fifth Avenue   407-770-0007
Vero Beach, FL 32960   FAX 407-770-0006

Jan J. Binney, Editor In Chief
Barbara Hector, Office Manager

Helps you test vocal behavior, interaction, autism behaviors and prognosis of the learnin g rate.

$ 194.00

5056 Behavior Evaluation Scale

Stephen McCarney, Author
Pro-Ed
8700 Shoal Creek Blvd.   512-451-3246
Austin, TX 78758   FAX 512-451-8542

Assists school personnel in making decisions about eligibility, placement and programming for students with behavior problems who have been referred for evaluation.

$ 59.00

5057 Behavior Rating Profile

Linda Brown, Author
Pro-Ed
8700 Shoal Creek Blvd.   512-451-3246
Austin, TX 78758   FAX 512-451-8542

A global measure of behavior providing student, parent, teacher and peer scales. It helps to identify behaviors that may cause a student's learning problems.

$ 147.50

5058 The Child Behavior Checklist

Achenbach, University of Vermont
1 South Prospect Street
Burlington, VT 05405

5059   Child Behavior Rating Scale

Russell Cassel, Author

Western Psychological Services Corporation
12031 Wilshire Blvd.   213-478-2061
Los Angeles, CA 90025   800-648-8857
                                                   FAX 213-478-7838

This test is a popular assessment of behavior and personality. It provides a profile of a child's adjustment in five areas: self, home, social, school and physical.

$ 22.00

5060   Children's Apperceptive Story-Telling Test

Mary Schneider, Author

Pro-Ed
8700 Shoal Creek Blvd.   512-451-3246
Austin, TX 78758   FAX 512-451-8542

Employs apperceptive stories to evaluate the emotional functioning of school-age children.

$ 98.00

5061   Communication and Symbolic Behavior

Amy Wetherby, Author

The Speech Bin
1965 Twenty-Fifth Avenue   407-770-0007
Vero Beach, FL 32960   FAX 407-770-0006

Jan J. Binney, Editor In Chief
Barbara Hector, Office Manager

Assess preverbal infants and toddlers at developmental ages.

$ 489.00

5062   Comprehensive Tests of Adaptive Behavior

Gary Adams, Author

The Psychological Corporation
P.O. Box 839954   800-228-0752
San Antonio, TX 78283   FAX 512-299-2722

An individually administered instrument for evaluating how well students with physical and mental handicaps function independently in their environments.

$ 80.00

5063   Conners' Rating Scales - Teacher and Parent Rating Series

C. Keith Conners, Author

Pro-Ed
8700 Shoal Creek Blvd.   512-451-3246
Austin, TX 78758   FAX 512-451-8542

The Teacher rating scales was originally designed to help identify hyperactive children and have been proven to be useful for characterizing numerous other clinical patterns of behavior. The Parent rating scales are widely used for clinical and research purposes.

$ 109.00

5064   Culture-Free Self-Esteem Inventories

James Battle, Author

Pro-Ed
8700 Shoal Creek Blvd.   512-451-3246
Austin, TX 78758   FAX 512-451-8542

A series of self-report scales used to determine the level of self-esteem in children and adults.

$ 98.00

5065   Draw a Person: Screening Procedure for Emotional Disturbance

Pro-Ed
8700 Shoal Creek Blvd.   512-451-3246
Austin, TX 78758   FAX 512-451-8542

A screening test that helps identify children and adolescents who have emotional problems and require further evaluation.

$ 59.00

5066   Index of Personality Characteristics

Linda Brown, Author

Pro-Ed
8700 Shoal Creek Blvd.   512-451-3246
Austin, TX 78758   FAX 512-451-8542

The test results provide critical information for the identification and diagnosis of emotionally disturbed students.

$ 64.00

5067   Inventory for Client and Agency Planning

Robert Bruininks, Bradley Hill & Richard Woodcock, Author

DLM Assessment Catalog
P.O. Box 4000, One DLM Park   800-527-4747
Allen, TX 75002

A short standardized assessment test that measures adaptive and maladaptive behavior. It's strong psychometric properties make it a valuable tool for: determing eligibility, service planning, evaluation, reporting progress or for funding reports.

$ 80.00

5068   Marshalltown Behavioral Developmental Profile

The Marshalltown Project
507 East Anson Street
Marshalltown, IA 50158

5069 Minnesota Multiphasic Personality Inventory

Western Psychological Services Corporation
12031 Wilshire Blvd.   213-478-2061
Los Angeles, CA 90025   800-222-2670
    FAX 213-478-7838

Offers two reports: Report –1: Computer Scoring and Interpretation provides what many regard as being the best scoring service available, used each year by thousands of professionals. and Report –2: Diagnostic Classification Report allows the professional to take greater advantage of the vast body of empirical data accumulated on the MMPI over the past 30 years. Unlike other computer analyses, this test compares client's profiles to those of clinically relevant groups.

$ 58.00

5070 Multidimensional Self Concept Scale

Bruce Bracken, Author
Pro-Ed
8700 Shoal Creek Blvd.   512-451-3246
Austin, TX 78758   FAX 512-451-8542

A thoroughly researched, developed and standardized clinical instrument. It assesses global self-concept and six context-dependent self-concept domains that are functionally important in the social-emotional adjustment of youth and adolescents.

$ 64.00

5071 Personality Inventory for Children

Robert Wirt, Ph.D., Author
Western Psychological Services Corporation
12031 Wilshire Blvd.   213-478-2061
Los Angeles, CA 90025   800-222-2670
    FAX 213-478-7838

Satisfies the clinician's needs for both relevant information and administrative flexibility. Offers comprehensive assessment services, flexible application, computer administration and interpretation and more for the professional.

5072 Psychological and Family Problems Associated with Learning Disability

Learning Disabilities Association of America
4156 Library Road   412-341-1515
Pittsburgh, PA 15234

5073 The Pyramid Scales

John Cone, Author
Pro-Ed
8700 Shoal Creek Blvd.   512-451-3246
Austin, TX 78758   FAX 512-451-8542

Asseses adaptive behavior in moderately to severely disabled persons. The scales are administered in one or all three different modes: By interview, informant, or by direct observation. The language of the administration procedures is simple, and the test is easily administered in 30-45 minutes.

$ 46.00

5074 Revised Behavior Problem Checklist

Quay-Peterson, University of Miami
Box 248074
Coral Gables, FL 33124

5075 Roberts Apperception Test for Children

Glen Roberts, Author
Western Psychological Services Corporation
12031 Wilshire Blvd.   213-478-2061
Los Angeles, CA 90025   800-222-2670
    FAX 213-478-7838

Gives you all the clinical benefits of a projective test, along with an objective scoring system and norms. Designed to overcome the limitations of the older Thematic Apperception Test. The RATC test shows realistic, up-to-date illustrations of children and adults engaged in everyday interaction, offer supplementary Test Pictures designed specifically for black children, provides an objective scoring system and provides norms for a sample of 200 well-adjusted children.

5076 Scales of Independent Behavior

Robert H. Bruininks, Richard Woodcock, Author
DLM Teaching Resources
One DLM Park, P.O. Box 4000   214-248-6300
Allen, TX 75002   800-527-4747

The leader in measuring adaptive and problem behavior. It provides an easy-to-administer, structrured interview format that collects useful information for measuring personal and community independence.

$ 135.00

5077 Self-Esteem Index

Linda Brown, Author
Pro-Ed
8700 Shoal Creek Blvd.   512-451-3246
Austin, TX 78758   FAX 512-451-8542

A new, multidimensional, norm-referenced measure of the way that individuals perceive and value themselves.

$ 69.00

5078 Social Prevocational Information Battery

McGraw-Hill
2500 Garden Road
Monterey, CA 93940

5079 Social-Emotional Dimension Scale

Jerry Hutton, Author

Pro-Ed
8700 Shoal Creek Blvd.   512-451-3246
Austin, TX 78758   FAX 512-451-8542

A quick, well-standardized rating scale that can be used by teachers, counselors and psychologists to screen students who are at risk for conduct disorders or emotional disturbances.

$ 49.00

5080   SSRS: Social Skills

AGS
7201 Woodland Road   612-786-4343
Circle Pines, MN 55014   800-328-2560

A nationally standardized series of questionnaires that obtain information on the social behaviors of children and adolescents from teachers, parents and the students themselves.

5081   System of Multicultural Pluralistic Assessment

The Psychological Corporation
555 Academic Court   800-228-0752
San Antonio, TX 78204   FAX 512-299-2720

This comprehensive test determines the cognitive abilities, sensorymotor abilities and adaptive behavior of children ages 5-11 years of age.

5082   Test of Early Socioemotional Development

Wayne Hresko, Author

Pro-Ed
8700 Shoal Creek Blvd.   512-451-3246
Austin, TX 78758   FAX 512-451-8542

A battery of four components designed to evaluate the behavior of children. The test can be used to identify young children suspected of having behavior problems, to document the degree of behavioral difficulty observed in these children and to identify specific settings in which problem behaviors most often occur.

$ 74.00

5083   Vineland Behavior Tests: Adaptive Behavior Scales

Sara Sparrow, David Balla & Domenic Cicchetti, Author

Pro-Ed
8700 Shoal Creek Blvd.   512-451-3246
Austin, TX 78758   FAX 512-451-8542

Identifies personal and social skills with a comprehensive, yet flexible manner. Offers the Interview Edition, Survey Form which includes 297 items and provides general assessment of adaptive behavior. Administration Time 20-60 minutes; The Interview Edition, Expanded Form including 577 items and yields a more comprehensive assessment of adaptive behavior and gives a systematic approach for preparing individuals, educational, habilitative or treatment programs. Administration Time 60-90 minutes.

5084   Walker Problem Behavior Identification Checklist

Hill M. Walker, PhD, Author

Western Psychological Services Corporation
12031 Wilshire Blvd.   213-478-2061
Los Angeles, CA 90025   800-648-8857
          FAX 213-478-7838

The checklist allows the elementary school teacher to identify quickly and economically, children with behavior problems who should be referred for further psychological evaluation or treatment.

$ 50.00

5085   Walker-McConnell Scale of Social Competence & School Adjustment

Hill Walker, Author

Pro-Ed
8700 Shoal Creek Blvd.   512-451-3246
Austin, TX 78758   FAX 512-451-8542

A 43-item teacher rating scale of social skills for students.

$ 49.00

Reading

5086   Assess a Revised Diagnostic Test

Lexia Learning Systems, Inc.
P.O. Box 466   617-259-8751
Lincoln, MA 01773   800-435-3942

A computerized diagnostic oral reading test of basic recognition skills.

$ 150.00

5087   Assess B Diagnostic Test

Lexia Learning Systems, Inc.
P.O. Box 466   617-259-8751
Lincoln, MA 01773   800-435-3942

A computerized diagnostic oral reading test of specific word recognition skills.

$ 150.00

5088   Bankson-Bernthal Test of Phonology

Nicholas Bankson, Author

The Speech Bin
1965 Twenty-Fifth Avenue   407-770-0007
Vero Beach, FL 32960   FAX 407-770-0006

Jan J. Binney, Editor In Chief
Barbara Hector, Office Manager

Survey phonological processes and individual phonemes in 20 minutes or less using interesting full-color pictures.

$ 112.50

5089 Construction Versus Choice in Cognitive Measurement

Randy Elliot Bennett, Author
Lawrence Erlbaum Associates, Inc.
365 Broadway   201-666-4110
Hillsdale, NJ 07642   FAX 201-666-2394

This book brings together psychometric, cognitive science, policy and content domain perspectives on new approaches to educational assessment.

$ 69.95

5090 Doren Diagnostic Reading Test of Word Recognition Skills

AGS
7201 Woodland Road   612-786-4343
Circle Pines, MN 55014   800-328-2560

A measure of basic word recognition skills. Administration Time: 1-3 hours.

5091 DRS-81: Diagnostic Reading Scales

AGS
7201 Woodland Road   612-786-4343
Circle Pines, MN 55014   800-328-2560

A measure of reading comprehension providing an accurate diagnosis of the nature and extenet of oral reading errors, an estimate of silent reading comprehension and a measure of auditory comprehension.

5092 Durrell Analysis of Reading Difficulty

Donald Durrell, Author
The Psychological Corporation
555 Academic Court   800-228-0752
San Antonio, TX 78204   FAX 512-299-2720

A diagnostic test which examines a child's reading behavior.

5093 Formal Reading Inventory

J. Lee Wiederholt, Author
Pro-Ed
8700 Shoal Creek Blvd.   512-451-3246
Austin, TX 78758   FAX 512-451-8542

A national test for assessing silent reading comprehension and diagnosing reading miscues.

$ 69.00

5094 Gray Oral Reading Tests

J. Lee Wiederholt, Author
Pro-Ed
8700 Shoal Creek Blvd.   512-451-3246
Austin, TX 78758   FAX 512-451-8542

The latest revision provides an objective measure of growth in oral reading and an aid in the diagnosis of oral reading difficulties.

$ 109.00

5095 Gray Oral Reading Tests - Diagnostic

Brian Bryant, Author
Pro-Ed
8700 Shoal Creek Blvd.   512-451-3246
Austin, TX 78758   FAX 512-451-8542

Uses two alternate, equivalent forms to assess students who have difficulty reading continuous print and who require an evaluation of specific abilities and weaknesses.

$ 109.00

5096 Reading Comprehension for Aphasia

Leonard LaPointe, Author
The Speech Bin
1965 Twenty-Fifth Avenue   407-770-0007
Vero Beach, FL 32960   FAX 407-770-0006

Jan J. Binney, Editor In Chief
Barbara Hector, Office Manager

Systematically evaluates the nature and degree of reading impairments in aphasic adolescents and adults.

$ 79.00

5097 Reading Tests: Do They Help Or Hurt Your Child

Ann Cook, Author
North Dakota Study Group on Evaluation Center
University Of North Dakota
Grand Forks, ND 58202

5098 SORTS Test

Richard Slosson, Author
Western Psychological Services Corporation
12031 Wilshire Blvd.   213-478-2061
Los Angeles, CA 90025

Measures reading ability for students in primary grades through high school.

5099 Standardized Reading Inventory

Phyllis Newcomer, Author
Pro-Ed
8700 Shoal Creek Blvd.   512-451-3246
Austin, TX 78758   FAX 512-451-8542

An instrument for evaluating students' reading ability.

$ 69.00

5100 TERA-2: Test of Early Reading Ability-2

AGS
7201 Woodland Road   612-786-4343
Circle Pines, MN 55014   800-328-2560

Ideal for screening children's early reading abilities. Specifically the test measures knowledge of contextual meaning, the alphabet and conventions such as reading from left to rights.

5101 Test of Early Reading Ability

D. Kim Reid, Author
Pro-Ed
8700 Shoal Creek Blvd.   512-451-3246
Austin, TX 78758   FAX 512-451-8542

Unique test in that it measures the actual reading ability of young children. Items measure knowledge of contextual meaning, alphabet and conventions.

$ 119.00

5102 Test of Reading Comprehension

Virginia Brown, Author
Pro-Ed
8700 Shoal Creek Blvd.   512-451-3246
Austin, TX 78758   FAX 512-451-8542

A multidimensional test of silent reading comprehension for students. The test reflects current psycholinguistic theories that consider reading comprehension to be a constructive process involving both language and cognition.

$ 102.00

5103 Test of Word-Finding

DLM Teaching Resources
One DLM Park   214-248-6300
Allen, TX 75002

5104 WRMT-R: Woodcock Reading Mastery Tests- Revised

AGS
7201 Woodland Road   612-786-4343
Circle Pines, MN 55014   800-328-2560

An individual assessment of reading skills for children and adults. Administration Time: 10-30 minutes.
$ 235.00

Speech & Language Arts

5105 Adolescent Language Screening Test

Denise Morgan, Author
Pro-Ed
8700 Shoal Creek Blvd.   512-451-3246
Austin, TX 78758   FAX 512-451-8542

Provides speech/language pathologists and other interested professionals with a rapid thorough method for screening adolescents speech and language.

$ 89.00

5106 Aphasia Language Performance Scales

Joseph Keenan, Author

The Speech Bin
1965 Twenty-Fifth Avenue   407-770-0007
Vero Beach, FL 32960   FAX 407-770-0006

Jan J. Binney, Editor In Chief
Barbara Hector, Office Manager

Enables physicians to examine most patients completely within a half an hour. Measures language impairment, prognosis, plan treatment, recovery levels and comprehensive reports.

$ 43.00

5107 Arizona Articulation Proficiency Scale

Western Psychological Services Corporation
12031 Wilshire Blvd.   213-478-2061
Los Angeles, CA 90025

This test rapidly measures the articulatory skill in children from 1 1/2 through 13 years of age.

5108 Assessment of Fluency in School-Age Children

Julia Thompson, Author
Pro-Ed
8700 Shoal Creek Blvd.   512-451-3246
Austin, TX 78758   FAX 512-451-8542

A diagnostic, criterion-referenced instrument to be used with children, to determine which stutterers would benefit from early intervention.

$ 59.00

5109 Assessment of Intelligibility of Dysarthric Speech

Kathryn Yorkston, Author
The Speech Bin
1965 Twenty-Fifth Avenue   407-770-0007
Vero Beach, FL 32960   FAX 407-770-0006

Jan J. Binney, Editor In Chief
Barbara Hector, Office Manager

Quickly and efficiently quantify the intelligibility of single words and sentences and the speaking rates of adolescents and adults.

$ 89.00

5110 Assessment of Nonverbal Communication

Robert Duffy, Author
The Speech Bin
1965 Twenty-Fifth Avenue   407-770-0007
Vero Beach, FL 32960   FAX 407-770-0006

Jan J. Binney, Editor In Chief
Barbara Hector, Office Manager

Assesses the gestural abilities of language disordered adults and adolescents who have experienced brain injury, determine appropriate treatment to enhance their language skills and measure treatment gains.

$ 69.00

5111 The Assessment of Phonological Processes Revised Edition

Barbara Williams Hodson, Author
Pro-Ed
8700 Shoal Creek Blvd.   512-451-3246
Austin, TX 78758   FAX 512-451-8542

Allows virtually all speech deviations to be categorized and logically explained, thereby providing the speech-language pathologist with an efficient diagnostic tool and giving the student clinician a practical guide for identifying and understanding phonological processes.

$ 69.00

5112 Bankson Language Test - 2

Nicholas Bankson, Author
The Speech Bin
1965 Twenty-Fifth Avenue   407-770-0007
Vero Beach, FL 32960   FAX 407-770-0006

Jan J. Binney, Editor In Chief
Barbara Hector, Office Manager

Measures the psycholinguistic and perceptual skills of young children.

$ 89.00

5113 Bedside Evaluation and Screening Test of Aphasia

Joyce Fitch-West, Author
Pro-Ed
8700 Shoal Creek Blvd.   512-451-3246
Austin, TX 78758   FAX 512-451-8542

Examines language competence and deficits in speaking, comprehension and reading.

$ 139.00

5114 The Boone Voice Program for Children

Pro-Ed
8700 Shoal Creek Blvd.   512-451-3246
Austin, TX 78758   FAX 512-451-8542

Provides a cognitive approach to voice therapy and is designed to give useful step-by-step guidelines and materials for diagnosis and remediation of voice disorders in children.

$ 179.00

5115 Boston Assessment of Severe Aphasis

Nancy Helm-Estabrooks, Author

The Speech Bin
1965 Twenty-Fifth Avenue   407-770-0007
Vero Beach, FL 32960   FAX 407-770-0006

Jan J. Binney, Editor In Chief
Barbara Hector, Office Manager

Identifies and quantifies the preserved abilities of severly aphasic patients.

$ 198.00

5116 Boston Diagnostic Aphasia Exam

Harold Goodglass, Author
The Speech Bin
1965 Twenty-Fifth Avenue   407-770-0007
Vero Beach, FL 32960   FAX 407-770-0006

Jan J. Binney, Editor In Chief
Barbara Hector, Office Manager

A helpful addition to assessing word retrieval.

$ 55.00

5117 Children's Articulation Test

George Haspiel, Author
The Speech Bin
1965 Twenty-Fifth Avenue   407-770-0007
Vero Beach, FL 32960   FAX 407-770-0006

Jan J. Binney, Editor In Chief
Barbara Hector, Office Manager

Profiles specific articulation errors or obtains a scored phonological analysis of phonemic skills with their delightfully illustrated articulation test.

$ 32.95

5118 Children's Auditory Verbal Learning Test

Jack Talley, Author
The Speech Bin
1965 Twenty-Fifth Avenue   407-770-0007
Vero Beach, FL 32960   FAX 407-770-0006

Jan J. Binney, Editor In Chief
Barbara Hector, Office Manager

This normed test measures immediate memory span, level of learning, immediate and delayed recall, recognition accuracy and total intrusions in percentiles and standard scores.

$ 43.00

5119 Clark-Madison Test of Oral Language

John B. Clark, Author
Pro-Ed
8700 Shoal Creek Blvd.   512-451-3246
Austin, TX 78758   FAX 512-451-8542

Evaluates the expressive capacity of children for using the structural components of language.

$ 79.00

5120 Communication Abilities Diagnostic Test

Elizabeth Johnston, Author

The Speech Bin
1965 Twenty-Fifth Avenue   407-770-0007
Vero Beach, FL 32960   FAX 407-770-0006

Jan J. Binney, Editor In Chief
Barbara Hector, Office Manager

This standardized test uses naturalistic contexts to sample pragmatic, semantic, and syntactic language.

$ 180.00

5121 Communication Abilities in Daily Activities

Audrey Holland, Author

The Speech Bin
1965 Twenty-Fifth Avenue   407-770-0007
Vero Beach, FL 32960   FAX 407-770-0006

Jan J. Binney, Editor In Chief
Barbara Hector, Office Manager

The first truly practical test of functional communicative adequacy for aphasic adults.

$ 119.00

5122 Communicative Abilities in Daily Living

Audrey Holland, Author

Pro-Ed
8700 Shoal Creek Blvd.   512-451-3246
Austin, TX 78758   FAX 512-451-8542

Designed as a supplemental aphasia tool that assesses the functional communication skills of aphasic adults.

$ 114.00

5123 Early Language Milestone Scale

James Coplan, Author

The Speech Bin
1965 Twenty-Fifth Avenue   407-770-0007
Vero Beach, FL 32960   FAX 407-770-0006

Jan J. Binney, Editor In Chief
Barbara Hector, Office Manager

The first norm-referenced validated language screening instrument for children.

$ 79.00

5124 Edinburgh Functional Communication Profile

Catherine Skinner, Author

The Speech Bin
1965 Twenty-Fifth Avenue   407-770-0007
Vero Beach, FL 32960   FAX 407-770-0006

Jan J. Binney, Editor In Chief
Barbara Hector, Office Manager

Assesses spoken, gestural, facial, verbal and written communication skills in requesting, acknowledging, greeting, problem solving and propositional contexts.

$ 54.95

5125 Evaluation Criteria

Learning Systems Technologies
45 Tioga Way   617-639-0114
Marblehead, MA 01945

Test offering information on conceptual vocabulary.

5126 Expressive and Receptive One-Word Picture Vocabulary Tests

Morrison Gardner, Author

Pro-Ed
8700 Shoal Creek Blvd.   512-451-3246
Austin, TX 78758   FAX 512-451-8542

Measures a child's verbal expression of language by means of a child's ability to make word-picture associations. Administration Time: 5-10 minutes.

$ 69.00

5127 Expressive One-Word Picture Vocabulary Test

Morrison Gardner, Author

The Speech Bin
1965 Twenty-Fifth Avenue   407-770-0007
Vero Beach, FL 32960   FAX 407-770-0006

Jan J. Binney, Editor In Chief
Barbara Hector, Office Manager

Best-selling individual picture vocabulary measures verbal intelligence.

$ 75.00

5128 Frenchay Dysarthria Assessment

Pamela Enderby, Author

The Speech Bin
1965 Twenty-Fifth Avenue   407-770-0007
Vero Beach, FL 32960   FAX 407-770-0006

Jan J. Binney, Editor In Chief
Barbara Hector, Office Manager

Easy to use, requires few materials, scores quickly and provides a bar graph profile of the skills and characteristics of the dysarthric patient.

$ 34.00

5129 Fullerton Language Test for Adolescents

Consulting Psychologists Press
577 College Avenue
Palo Alto, CA 94306

5130 Iowa's Severity Rating Scales

Iowa Department Of Education, Author
Pro-Ed
8700 Shoal Creek Blvd.   512-451-3246
Austin, TX 78758   FAX 512-451-8542

This test determines the severity of the speech or language disorder and the likelihood that the deficiencies will be remedied with appropriate interventions.

$ 29.00

5131 Kindergarten Language Screening Test

The Speech Bin
1965 Twenty-Fifth Avenue   407-770-0007
Vero Beach, FL 32960   FAX 407-770-0006

Jan J. Binney, Editor In Chief
Barbara Hector, Office Manager

Samples kindergartners' ability to follow directions, give information and use spontaneous speech in just five minutes.

$ 44.00

5132 K-TEA: Kaufman

Pro-Ed
8700 Shoal Creek Blvd.   512-451-3246
Austin, TX 78758   FAX 512-451-8542

An individually administered diagnostic battery that measures reading, math and spelling skills. Offers two varieties the brief form and the comprehensive form for in-depth analysis. Administration Time: 20-30 minutes (Brief), and 30-60 minutes (Comprehensive).

5133 Lindamood Auditory Conceptualization Test

Charles Lindamood, Author
DLM Assessment Catalog
P.O. Box 4000, One DLM Park   800-527-4747
Allen, TX 75002

This test measures auditory discrimination as well as perception of number and order of speech sounds in sequence.

$ 49.50

5134 Malcomesius

Learning Disabilities Association of America
4156 Library Road   412-341-1515
Pittsburgh, PA 15234

A screening test for specific language disability.

5135 Matrix Analogies Test - Short Form

Jack Naglieri, Author
The Psychological Corporation
555 Academic Court   800-228-0752
San Antonio, TX 78204   FAX 512-299-2720

This test predicts academic learning problems in students.

5136 Miller-Yoder Language Comprehension Test

Jon Miller, Author
Pro-Ed
8700 Shoal Creek Blvd.   512-451-3246
Austin, TX 78758   FAX 512-451-8542

Provides speech clinicians with a quick look at young children's understanding of short, simple sentences in a variety of grammatical structures.

$ 89.00

5137 Minnesota Test for Differential Diagnosis of Aphasia

Hildred Schuell, Author
The Speech Bin
1965 Twenty-Fifth Avenue   407-770-0007
Vero Beach, FL 32960   FAX 407-770-0006

Jan J. Binney, Editor In Chief
Barbara Hector, Office Manager

Comprehensive adult aphasia exam measures language disturbances resulting from brain damage, including auditory, visual and reading, speech and language and numerical disturbances.

$ 56.00

5138 The Nonspeech Test

Don Johnston Developmental Equipment, Inc.
P.O. Box 639, 1000 N. Rand Rd.   708-526-2682
Wauconda, IL 60084   800-999-4660
          FAX 708-526-4177

A standardized test of receptive and expressive language abilities for nonspeaking children.

$ 179.00

5139 Oral Speech Mechanism Screening Examination

D.M. Ruscello, Author
Pro-Ed
8700 Shoal Creek Blvd.   512-451-3246
Austin, TX 78758   FAX 512-451-8542

Speech mechanism exam that is readable, easy to score, and quick to administer.

$ 46.00

5140 Preschool Language Assessment Instrument

Marion Blank, Author

The Psychological Corporation
555 Academic Court
San Antonio, TX 78204
800-228-0752
FAX 512-299-2720

Provides a profile of a child's language skills in order to match teaching with the students competence. The test is ideal for children ages 3 to 6 and is available in Spanish.

5141 Preschool Language Scale 3

The Psychological Corporation
555 Academic Court
San Antonio, TX 78204
800-228-0752
FAX 512-299-2720

This tool measures a broad range of receptive and expressive language skills. A Spanish version is also available.

5142 The Primary Language Screen

Diane Eger, Author

The Speech Bin
1965 Twenty-Fifth Avenue
Vero Beach, FL 32960
407-770-0007
FAX 407-770-0006

Jan J. Binney, Editor In Chief
Barbara Hector, Office Manager

Expressive skills are judged individually but can be administered to an entire classroom.

$ 29.95

5143 Prueba Del Desarrollo Inicial Del Lenguaje

Wayne Hresko, Author

The Speech Bin
1965 Twenty-Fifth Avenue
Vero Beach, FL 32960
407-770-0007
FAX 407-770-0006

Jan J. Binney, Editor In Chief
Barbara Hector, Office Manager

Measures the sematic, syntactic and cognitive aspects of language and the spoken language abilities of Spanish speaking children.

$ 49.00

5144 Quick Screen of Phonology

Nicholas Bankson, Author

The Speech Bin
1965 Twenty-Fifth Avenue
Vero Beach, FL 32960
407-770-0007
FAX 407-770-0006

Jan J. Binney, Editor In Chief
Barbara Hector, Office Manager

Samples both phonological processes and individual consonants.

$ 57.00

5145 Receptive One-Word Picture Vocabulary Test

Morrison Gardner, Author

The Speech Bin
1965 Twenty-Fifth Avenue
Vero Beach, FL 32960
407-770-0007
FAX 407-770-0006

Jan J. Binney, Editor In Chief
Barbara Hector, Office Manager

At last you can accurately and meaningfully compare receptive and expressive vocabulary scores.

$ 65.00

5146 Receptive-Expressive Emergent Language Tests

Kenneth Bzoch, Author

Pro-Ed
8700 Shoal Creek Blvd.
Austin, TX 78758
512-451-3246
FAX 512-451-8542

Designed to use with at risk infants and toddlers to provide a multidimensional analysis of emergency language skills.

$ 56.00

5147 Rhode Island Test of Language Structure

Elizabeth Engen, Author

The Speech Bin
1965 Twenty-Fifth Avenue
Vero Beach, FL 32960
407-770-0007
FAX 407-770-0006

Jan J. Binney, Editor In Chief
Barbara Hector, Office Manager

This test, which focuses on syntax, has sufficient depth and range to allow for educational planning.

$ 98.00

5148 Rules Phonologcial Evaluation

Jane Webb, Author

The Speech Bin
1965 Twenty-Fifth Avenue
Vero Beach, FL 32960
407-770-0007
FAX 407-770-0006

Jan J. Binney, Editor In Chief
Barbara Hector, Office Manager

Assesses speech sound production in young children with unintelligible speech.

$ 49.95

5149 Screening Kit of Language Development

The Speech Bin
1965 Twenty-Fifth Avenue
Vero Beach, FL 32960
407-770-0007
FAX 407-770-0006

Jan J. Binney, Editor In Chief
Barbara Hector, Office Manager

Assesses language comprehension, story comprehension, sentence repetition with and without pictures, comprehension of commands and vocabulary in three age ranges.

$ 55.00

5150 Screening Test for Developmental Apraxia of Speech

Robert Blakely, Author

The Speech Bin
1965 Twenty-Fifth Avenue   407-770-0007
Vero Beach, FL 32960   FAX 407-770-0006

Jan J. Binney, Editor In Chief
Barbara Hector, Office Manager

Offers eight subtests to help assess developmental apraxia of speech.

$ 59.00

5151 Sequenced Inventory of Communication Development

Dona Lea Hedrick, Author

The Speech Bin
1965 Twenty-Fifth Avenue   407-770-0007
Vero Beach, FL 32960   FAX 407-770-0006

Jan J. Binney, Editor In Chief
Barbara Hector, Office Manager

Assesses communication skills of normal and retarded children functioning between four months and four years of age, including children who have sensory impairments of hearing or vision.

$ 295.00

5152 Slingerland

Learning Disabilities Association of America
4156 Library Road   412-341-1515
Pittsburgh, PA 15234

Screening test for identifying children with specific language disabilities.

5153 Slosson Articulation, Language Test with Phonology

The Speech Bin
1965 Twenty-Fifth Avenue   407-770-0007
Vero Beach, FL 32960   FAX 407-770-0006

Jan J. Binney, Editor In Chief
Barbara Hector, Office Manager

Screens the phonological, articulatory and language skills.

5154 Spanish Articulation Measures

Larry Mattes, Author

The Speech Bin
1965 Twenty-Fifth Avenue   407-770-0007
Vero Beach, FL 32960   FAX 407-770-0006

Jan J. Binney, Editor In Chief
Barbara Hector, Office Manager

Evaluates speech sound production of school-age Spanish-speaking children with this comprehensive criterion-referenced test that has a variety of informal spontaneous and elicited tasks.

$ 36.00

5155 Speech and Language

Learning Systems Technologies
45 Tioga Way   617-639-0114
Marblehead, MA 01945

Test offering information on students articulation processes.

5156 Speech and Language Evaluation Scale

D.R. Fressola, Author

The Speech Bin
1965 Twenty-Fifth Avenue   407-770-0007
Vero Beach, FL 32960   FAX 407-770-0006

Jan J. Binney, Editor In Chief
Barbara Hector, Office Manager

Offers 68 items easily observed and documented by teachers to tell if children need additional testing and treatment services in articulation, voice, fluency and language form, content and use.

$ 112.00

5157 Speech-Ease Screening Inventory

The Speech Bin
1965 Twenty-Fifth Avenue   407-770-0007
Vero Beach, FL 32960   FAX 407-770-0006

Jan J. Binney, Editor In Chief
Barbara Hector, Office Manager

Screens articulation, vocabulary and auditory comprehension.

$ 59.00

5158 Spellmaster Assessment and Teaching System

Claire Greenbaum, Author

Pro-Ed
8700 Shoal Creek Blvd.   512-451-3246
Austin, TX 78758   FAX 512-451-8542

This revolutionary test is comprised of a series of examinations whose results supply tailored instructional plans for students.

5159 Structured Photographic Language Test

Janelle Publications
P.O. Box 12
Sandwich, IL 60548

5160 Stuttering Severity Instrument for Children and Adults

Glyndon Riley, Author

Pro-Ed
8700 Shoal Creek Blvd.   512-451-3246
Austin, TX 78758   FAX 512-451-8542

With these easily administered tools you can determine whether to schedule a child for therapy using the Stuttering Prediction Instrument or to evaluate the effects of treatment using the Stuttering Severity Instrument.

$ 49.00

5161 TELD-2: Test of Early Language Development , Second Edition

Pro-Ed
8700 Shoal Creek Blvd.   512-451-3246
Austin, TX 78758   FAX 512-451-8542

An individually administered test of spoken language abilities. This test fills the need for a well-constructed, standardized instrument, based on a current theory, that can be used to assess spoken language skills at early ages. Administration Time: 20 minutes.

$ 107.80

5162 Templin-Darley Articulation Test

Mildred Templin, Author

The Speech Bin
1965 Twenty-Fifth Avenue   407-770-0007
Vero Beach, FL 32960   FAX 407-770-0006

Jan J. Binney, Editor In Chief
Barbara Hector, Office Manager

This revised version includes two forms, one for screening and a complete diagnostic test.

$ 20.00

5163 Test of Early Language Development

Wayne Hresko, Author

The Speech Bin
1965 Twenty-Fifth Avenue   407-770-0007
Vero Beach, FL 32960   FAX 407-770-0006

Jan J. Binney, Editor In Chief
Barbara Hector, Office Manager

An overall language score and an expanded diagnostic profile.

$ 109.00

5164 Test of Early Written Language

Wayne Hresko, Author

Pro-Ed
8700 Shoal Creek Blvd.   512-451-3246
Austin, TX 78758   FAX 512-451-8542

Measures the merging written language skills of young children and is especially useful in identifying mildy disabled students.

$ 79.00

5165 Test of Legible Handwriting

Stephen Larsen, Author

Pro-Ed
8700 Shoal Creek Blvd.   512-451-3246
Austin, TX 78758   FAX 512-451-8542

The only nationally standardized, reliable and valid test of legibility reports its results in terms of standard scores and percentiles.

$ 49.00

5166 Test of Oral and Limb Apraxia

Nancy Helm-Estabrooks, Author

The Speech Bin
1965 Twenty-Fifth Avenue   407-770-0007
Vero Beach, FL 32960   FAX 407-770-0006

Jan J. Binney, Editor In Chief
Barbara Hector, Office Manager

Assesses apraxia in 10-15 minutes, obtaining a thorough analysis of both oral and limb deficits.

$ 36.00

5167 Test of Oral Structures and Functions

Gary Vitalli, Author

The Speech Bin
1965 Twenty-Fifth Avenue   407-770-0007
Vero Beach, FL 32960   FAX 407-770-0006

Jan J. Binney, Editor In Chief
Barbara Hector, Office Manager

Assesses oral structures, nonverbal and verbal oral functioning, and oral motor integraity in a standardized systematic way to establish the nature of disorders.

$ 60.00

5168 Test of Pragmatic Language

Dian Phelps-Terasaki, Author

The Speech Bin
1965 Twenty-Fifth Avenue   407-770-0007
Vero Beach, FL 32960   FAX 407-770-0006

Jan J. Binney, Editor In Chief
Barbara Hector, Office Manager

Measures the ability of children to use language in social situations and in context.

$ 84.00

5169 Test of Syntactic Abilities

Stephen Quigley, Author

Pro-Ed
8700 Shoal Creek Blvd.   512-451-3246
Austin, TX 78758   FAX 512-451-8542

Consists of a battery of 20 individual diagnostic tests each containing 70 multiple-choice items. The tests pinpoint a user's strengths and weaknesses.

$ 179.00

5170   Test of Written Spelling

Stephen Larsen, Author

Pro-Ed
8700 Shoal Creek Blvd.   512-451-3246
Austin, TX 78758   FAX 512-451-8542

Assesses students ability to spell words whose spellings are readily predictable in sound-letter patterns, words whose spellings are less predictable and both types of words considered together.

$ 44.00

5171   TOAL-2: Test of Adolescent Language, Second Edition

Pro-Ed
8700 Shoal Creek Blvd.   512-451-3246
Austin, TX 78758   FAX 512-451-8542

This test is a measure of receptive and expressive language skills. In this revision easier items were added to the subtests, making them more appropriate for testing disabled stduents. Administration Time: 1 hour and 45 minutes.

$ 114.40

5172   TOLD-2: the Test of Language Development Primary and Intermediate

The Psychological Corporation
555 Academic Court   800-228-0752
San Antonio, TX 78204   FAX 512-299-2720

An individually administered language battery. Primary assesses the understanding and meaningful use of spoken words, aspects of grammar, word pronounciation and the ability to distinguish between similar sounding words.

$ 130.90

5173   Tongue Thrust

Donald Rampp, Author

The Speech Bin
1965 Twenty-Fifth Avenue   407-770-0007
Vero Beach, FL 32960   FAX 407-770-0006

Jan J. Binney, Editor In Chief
Barbara Hector, Office Manager

Includes a diagnostic checklist, intraoral examination protocol, and articulation test.

$ 59.00

5174   TOWL-2: Test of Written Language, Second Edition

Pro-Ed
8700 Shoal Creek Blvd.   512-451-3246
Austin, TX 78758   FAX 512-451-8542

Offers a measure of written language skills to identify students who need help improving their writing skills. Administration Time: 65 minutes.

$ 136.40

5175   Utah Test of Language Development - 3

Merlin Mecham, Author

The Speech Bin
1965 Twenty-Fifth Avenue   407-770-0007
Vero Beach, FL 32960   FAX 407-770-0006

Jan J. Binney, Editor In Chief
Barbara Hector, Office Manager

This classic measures expressive and receptive langauge skills.

$ 79.00

5176   Voice Assessment Protocol for Children and Adults

Rebekah Pindzola, Author

Pro-Ed
8700 Shoal Creek Blvd.   512-451-3246
Austin, TX 78758   FAX 512-451-8542

Easily guides the speech pathologist through a systematic evaluation of vocal pitch, loudness, quality, breath features and rate/rhythm.

$ 39.00

5177   Word Finding Referral Checklist

Diane German, Author

The Speech Bin
1965 Twenty-Fifth Avenue   407-770-0007
Vero Beach, FL 32960   FAX 407-770-0006

Jan J. Binney, Editor In Chief
Barbara Hector, Office Manager

This systematic observation tool shelps you identify persons who need to be evaluated for disorders in word finding.

$ 25.00

5178   The Word Test

Lingui Systems
1630 Fith Ave., Ste. 806
Moline, IL 61265

5179   Written Language

Learning Systems Technologies
45 Tioga Way   617-639-0114
Marblehead, MA 01945

Test offering information on students ability to form and identify sentences.

Learning Disability Screening

5180 Adaptive Behavior Scales

Pro-Ed
8700 Shoal Creek Blvd.   512-451-3246
Austin, TX 78758   FAX 512-451-8542

Includes 244 items that assess adaptive behavior in the classroom. The edition is administered in the form of a questionnaire completed by a teacher. A qualified professional is needed to interpret the scores.

$ 79.00

5181 Basic School Skills Inventory - Screen and Diagnostic

Donald Hammill, Author

Pro-Ed
8700 Shoal Creek Blvd.   512-451-3246
Austin, TX 78758   FAX 512-451-8542

Can be used to locate children tho are high risk for school failure, who need more in-depth assessment and who should be referred for additional study.

$ 21.00

5182 BASIS - Basic Achievement Skills Individual Screener

The Psychological Corporation
P.O. Box 839954   800-228-0752
San Antonio, TX 78283   FAX 512-299-2722

An individually administered achievement test of reading, mathematics and spelling skills. Also includes an optional writing exercise. The first step in a diagnostic assessment of a student's academic strengths and needs.

$ 88.00

5183 Battelle Developmental Inventory

DLM Teaching Resources
One DLM Park   214-248-6300
Allen, TX 75002

5184 Boehm Test of Basic Concepts

Ann Boehm, Author

The Psychological Corporation
555 Academic Court   800-228-0752
San Antonio, TX 78204   FAX 512-299-2720

The Boehm test measures a child's mastery of those basic concepts considered essential for achievement during the early years of schooling.

5185 Brackin Basic Concept Scale

The Psychological Corporation
P.O. Box 839954   800-228-0752
San Antonio, TX 78283   FAX 512-299-2722

A comprehensive system of basic concept assessment, consisting of two instruments: a Diagnostic Scale that measures 258 basic concepts, and a set of eight short, easily administered Screening Tests. This test is appropriate in both regular and special education settings.

$ 130.00

5186 Burks' Behavior Rating Scales Preschool and Kindergarten Editions

Harold Burks, PhD, Author

Western Psychological Services Corporation
12031 Wilshire Blvd.   213-478-2061
Los Angeles, CA 90025   800-648-8857
FAX 213-478-7838

This proven and widely accepted instrument identifies behavior problems. Both editions are specifically designed to facilitate differential diagnosis rather than to screen large groups of children performing adequately.

$ 100.00

5187 CELF-R

Eleanor Simel, Author

The Psychological Corporation
555 Academic Court   800-228-0752
San Antonio, TX 78204   FAX 512-299-2720

Aids professionals in evaluating school children who lack basic language skills (semantics, syntax and memory.

5188 Clinical Assessment of Learning Problems

Marion Sanders, Author

Brookline Books
P.O. Box 1046   617-868-0360
Cambridge, MA 02238

Offers models, processes and remedial planning information for children with learning disabilities.

5189 Cognitive Abilities Scale

Sharon Bradley Johnson, Author

The Speech Bin
1965 Twenty-Fifth Avenue   407-770-0007
Vero Beach, FL 32960   FAX 407-770-0006

Jan J. Binney, Editor In Chief
Barbara Hector, Office Manager

Uses toys to engage children who will not or cannot talk or whose speech is unintelligible so you can accurately assess their concept and skill development.

$ 114.00

5190 COGREHAB

Life Science Associates
1 Fenimore Road   516-472-2111
Bayport, NY 11705

Divided into six groups for diagnosis and treatment of attention, memory and perceptual disorders to be used by and under the guidance of a professional.

$ 250.00

5191 Columbia Mental Maturity Scale

The Psychological Corporation
555 Academic Court   800-228-0752
San Antonio, TX 78204   FAX 512-299-2720

This kit tests mental abilities without stipulating verbal response. It is ideal for children who are entering nursery school or kindergarten, especially those individuals with impaired physical or verbal functioning.

5192 Comprehensive and Basic Learning Disabilities Assessments

Learning Disabilities Association of America
2104 Park Avenue South   612-871-9011
Minneapolis, MN 55404

Offers various assessment tests for the learning disabled.

5193 Comprehensive Tests of Basic Skills

McGraw-Hill
2500 Garden Road
Monterey, CA 93940

5194 DABERON Screening for School Readiness

Virginia Danzer, Author
Pro-Ed
8700 Shoal Creek Blvd.   512-451-3246
Austin, TX 78758   FAX 512-451-8542

Provides a standardized assessment of school readiness in children with learning or behavior problems.

    $ 24.00

5195 Detroit Tests of Learning Aptitude-Primary

Donald Hammill, Author
Western Psychological Services Corporation
12031 Wilshire Blvd.   213-478-2061
Los Angeles, CA 90025   800-648-8857
    FAX 213-478-7838

A standardized instrument to identify children who may be deficient in general and specific aptitudes.

    $ 115.00

5196 Detroit Tests of Learning Aptitude-2

Donald Hammill, Author
Western Psychological Services Corporation
12031 Wilshire Blvd.   213-478-2061
Los Angeles, CA 90025   800-648-8857
    FAX 213-478-7838

A revision and restandardization of one of the most widely used and respected tests of specific abilities. It is used to isolate individual strengths and weaknesses and to identify students who are deficient in general and specific aptitudes.

    $ 130.00

5197 Developmental Assessment for the Severely Disabled

Mary Kay Dykes, Author
Pro-Ed
8700 Shoal Creek Blvd.   512-451-3246
Austin, TX 78758   FAX 512-451-8542

DASH offers diagnostic and programming personnel concise information about individuals who are funtioning between birth and 18 years of age developmentally.

    $ 98.00

5198 Developmental Profile II (DP-II)

Western Psychological Services Corporation
12031 Wilshire Blvd.   213-478-2061
Los Angeles, CA 90025   800-648-8857
    FAX 213-478-7838

An easy standardized assessment of a child's development. The inventory accesses five key areas. These are profiled to clearly indicate the child's functional developmental deviations, both advanced and delayed, according to age norms in each of the five areas assessed.

    $ 85.00

5199 Developmental Programming for Infants and Young Children

D. Sue Schafer, Author
The Speech Bin
1965 Twenty-Fifth Avenue   407-770-0007
Vero Beach, FL 32960   FAX 407-770-0006

Jan J. Binney, Editor In Chief
Barbara Hector, Office Manager

Here's how to assess and treat children functioning in various developmental age ranges.

    $ 50.00

5200 Diagnostic Achievement Battery

Phyllis Newcomer, Author
Western Psychological Services Corporation
12031 Wilshire Blvd.   213-478-2061
Los Angeles, CA 90025   800-648-8857
    FAX 213-478-7838

The latest version of one of the most popular and useful individual achievement tests available today. Twelve subtests measure performance in areas key to learning disabled assessment: story comprehension, characteristics, synonyms, reading comprehension, writing composition and math calculation.

    $ 135.00

5201 Educational Developmental Series

STS, Inc.
480 Meyer Road
Bensenville, IL 60106

708-766-7150
800-642-6STS
FAX 708-766-8054

A standardized battery of ability and achievement tests.

5202 GED Test Accommodations for Candidates with Specific Learning Disabilities

The GED Testing Service
One Dupont Circle, Ste. 20
Washington, DC 20036

202-439-9490

Learning disabled adults who cannot be fairly tested by the regular edition of the GED test may apply for special editions of the GED test.

5203 Goldman-Fristoe-Auditory Skills Test Battery

Ronald Goldman, Author

Pro-Ed
8700 Shoal Creek Blvd.
Austin, TX 78758

512-451-3246
FAX 512-451-8542

An individually administered measure of a broad range of auditory skills. Administer the full battery to receive a total picture of an individual's auditory skills using the Battery Profile. Administer a single test or a cluster of tests as needed.

5204 Goodenough-Harris Drawing Test

Florence Goodenough, Author

The Psychological Corporation
555 Academic Court
San Antonio, TX 78204

800-228-0752
FAX 512-299-2720

This test focuses on mental maturity without requiring verbal skills. The fifteen-minute examination provides standard scores for children ages 3-15..

5205 Hudson Education Skills Inventory

Floyd Hudson, Author

Pro-Ed
8700 Shoal Creek Blvd.
Austin, TX 78758

512-451-3246
FAX 512-451-8542

A curriculum-based assessment series for use in planning instruction with dysfunctional learning patterns.

$ 198.00

5206 Illinois Test of Psycholinguistic Abilities

Samuel Kirk, Author

Western Psychological Services Corporation
12031 Wilshire Blvd.
Los Angeles, CA 90025

213-478-2061

This widely recognized diagnostic instrument identifies specific abilities and disabilities.

5207 The Instructional Environment Scale

James Ysseldyke, Author

Pro-Ed
8700 Shoal Creek Blvd.
Austin, TX 78758

512-451-3246
FAX 512-451-8542

A comprehensive methodology that enables professionals to gain essential information for designing instructional interventions for individual students.

$ 59.00

5208 Instructional Environmental Scale

James Ysseldyke, Author

Pro-Ed
8700 Shoal Creek Blvd.
Austin, TX 78758

512-451-3246
FAX 512-451-8542

This tool provides information on how to modify a students instruction.

5209 Language Structured Auditory Retention Test

Luis Carlson, Author

The Speech Bin
1965 Twenty-Fifth Avenue
Vero Beach, FL 32960

407-770-0007
FAX 407-770-0006

Jan J. Binney, Editor In Chief
Barbara Hector, Office Manager

Assesses short-term memory for linguistically significant information and determine optimum length of auditory messages from which a learner may profit.

$ 45.00

5210 Matrix Analogies Test Expanded Form

Jack Nagueri, Author

The Psychological Corporation
555 Academic Court
San Antonio, TX 78204

800-228-0752
FAX 512-299-2720

This test provides a more exclusive insight to the non-verbal reasoning ability of a student.

5211 McCarthy Scales of Children's Abilities

Dorothea McCarthy, Author

The Psychological Corporation
555 Academic Court
San Antonio, TX 78204

Determines the cognitive and motor development of children ages 3-9.

5212 Metropolitan Achievement Tests

The Psychological Corporation
555 Academic Court
San Antonio, TX 78204

5213 Monitoring Basic Skills Progress

Lynn Fuchs, Author

Pro-Ed
8700 Shoal Creek Blvd.   512-451-3246
Austin, TX 78758   FAX 512-451-8542

A computer-assisted measurement program that tests and monitors progress in three academic areas: basic reading, basic math and basic spelling.

$ 279.00

5214 Oral Motor Assessment and Treatment

Glyndon Riley, Author

The Speech Bin
1965 Twenty-Fifth Avenue   407-770-0007
Vero Beach, FL 32960   FAX 407-770-0006

Jan J. Binney, Editor In Chief
Barbara Hector, Office Manager

This three-part program gives you an oral training program with 14 difficulty levels and performance criteria.

$ 69.00

5215 Peabody Individual Achievement Test

AGS
7201 Woodland Road   612-786-4343
Circle Pines, MN 55014   800-328-2560

A thorough and updated individual measure of academic achievement. PIAT also provides a written language composite, obtained by combining scores on the spelling and written expression subtests.

5216 Photo Articulation Test

Kathleen Pendergast, Author

The Speech Bin
1965 Twenty-Fifth Avenue   407-770-0007
Vero Beach, FL 32960   FAX 407-770-0006

Jan J. Binney, Editor In Chief
Barbara Hector, Office Manager

Assess the production of consonants and vowels in single words and connected speech.

$ 79.00

5217 PIAT-R: Peabody Individual Achievement Test-Revised

AGS
7201 Woodland Road   612-786-4343
Circle Pines, MN 55014   800-328-2560

A thorough and updated individual measure of academic achievement. Administration Time: 60 minutes.

5218 Picture Articulation and Language Screening Test

William Rodgers, Author

Pro-Ed
8700 Shoal Creek Blvd.   512-451-3246
Austin, TX 78758   FAX 512-451-8542

An efficient and effective test that uses picture stimuli to elicit sounds spontaneously.

$ 29.00

5219 PPVT-R: Peabody Test-Picture Vocabulary Test Revised

AGS
7201 Woodland Road   612-786-4343
Circle Pines, MN 55014   800-328-2560

A measure of hearing vocabulary for Standard American English, Administration Time: 10-20 minuts.

5220 Preschool Evaluation Scale

Stephen McCarney, Author

The Speech Bin
1965 Twenty-Fifth Avenue   407-770-0007
Vero Beach, FL 32960   FAX 407-770-0006

Jan J. Binney, Editor In Chief
Barbara Hector, Office Manager

A standardized instrument that can be easily completed by parent or child care professional in 20 minutes.

$ 60.00

5221 Problem-Solving

Dworkin And Dworkinb, Author

Center for Unique Learners
11600 Nebel Avenue   301-231-0115
Rockville, MD 20852

Patricia Williams, Executive Director

A test that deals with focusing on the processing of selecting strategies, rather than on the content of the tasks themselves.

5222 Quick Neurological Screening Test

The Psychological Corporation
555 Academic Court   800-228-0752
San Antonio, TX 78204   FAX 512-299-2720

This test is a rapid way to determine if a child is learning disabled. In general it is appropriate for all ages.

5223 Quick-Score Achievement Test

Donald Hammill, Author

Pro-Ed
8700 Shoal Creek Blvd.   512-451-3246
Austin, TX 78758   FAX 512-451-8542

A quick, individually administered test of basic school achievement that measures student proficiency in reading, writing, arithmetic and factual information relating to science, social studies, health and language arts.

$ 69.00

5224 Rating Inventory for Screening Kindergardners

J. Michael Coleman, Author

Pro-Ed
8700 Shoal Creek Blvd.   512-451-3246
Austin, TX 78758   FAX 512-451-8542

Effectively screens kindergarten students in a school district.

$ 190.00

5225 Ross Information Processing Assessment

Deborah Ross, Author

The Speech Bin
1965 Twenty-Fifth Avenue   407-770-0007
Vero Beach, FL 32960   FAX 407-770-0006

Jan J. Binney, Editor In Chief
Barbara Hector, Office Manager

Diagnose processing deficits and establish severity ratings in ten areas.

$ 69.00

5226 Scholastic Aptitude Scale

Brian Bryant, Author

Pro-Ed
8700 Shoal Creek Blvd.   512-451-3246
Austin, TX 78758   FAX 512-451-8542

Designed for use with students as an independent measure of cognitive ability or as a supplement to the Diagnostic Achievement Battery-Second Edition or Diagnostic Achievement Test for Adolescents-Second Edition.

$ 74.00

5227 School Readiness Test

STS, Inc.
480 Meyer Road   708-766-7150
Bensenville, IL 60106   800-642-6STS
FAX 708-766-8054

Students beginning first grade differ considerably in readiness for formal education. Therefore it is important that the teacher learn as much as possible about every entering student's total readiness for formal learning. This hand-scored group test is designed to be administered by the classroom teacher at the end of kindergarten of before the third full week of first grade.

5228 Screening Children for Related Early Educational Needs

Wayne Hresko, Author

Pro-Ed
8700 Shoal Creek Blvd.   512-451-3246
Austin, TX 78758   FAX 512-451-8542

A new academic screening test for young children that provides both global and specific ability scores that can be used to identify individual abilities.

$ 69.00

5229 Selective Auditory Attention Test

Rochelle Cherry, Author

The Speech Bin
1965 Twenty-Fifth Avenue   407-770-0007
Vero Beach, FL 32960   FAX 407-770-0006

Jan J. Binney, Editor In Chief
Barbara Hector, Office Manager

Identifies poor auditory attending and offers two lists of audiotaped monosyllabic words in quiet and two in semantically distracting competing messages.

$ 81.00

5230 Slosson Intelligence Test-Revised

Richard Slosson, Author

Pro-Ed
8700 Shoal Creek Blvd.   512-451-3246
Austin, TX 78758   FAX 512-451-8542

One of the most widely used individual screening tests of its kind. This test is used by teachers, psychologists, guidance counselors and special educators who need to evaluate the mental ability of individuals.

$ 59.00

5231 Specific Diagnostics

11600 Nebel Street, Ste. 130   301-468-6616
Rockville, MD 20852   FAX 301-230-1454

5232 Stanford Achievement Tests

The Psychological Corporation
555 Academic Court
San Antonio, TX 78204

5233 Stanford-Binet Intelligence Scale

Learning Disabilities Association of America
4156 Library Road   412-341-1515
Pittsburgh, PA 15234

An individually administered test of intelligence.

5234 TEMAS (Tell-Me-A-Story)

Giuseppe Costantino, Author

Western Psychological Services Corporation
12031 Wilshire Blvd.   213-478-2061
Los Angeles, CA 90025   800-222-2670
FAX 213-478-7838

A multicultural apperception test for children giving clinicians full-color Stimulus Cards that both minority and nonminority children.

5235 Test of Auditory Analysis Skills

Jerome Rosner, Author

The Speech Bin
1965 Twenty-Fifth Avenue   407-770-0007
Vero Beach, FL 32960   FAX 407-770-0006

Jan J. Binney, Editor In Chief
Barbara Hector, Office Manager

Assesses a child's skill in processing sequences of sounds and syllables within common words and the associated auditory skills necessary for efficient learning.

$ 10.00

5236 Test of Auditory Reasoning and Processing Skills

Morrison Gardner, Author

The Speech Bin
1965 Twenty-Fifth Avenue   407-770-0007
Vero Beach, FL 32960   FAX 407-770-0006

Jan J. Binney, Editor In Chief
Barbara Hector, Office Manager

A standardized test that evaluates how children understand, interpret and draw conclusions.

$ 39.00

5237 Test of Auditory-Perceptual Skills

Morrison Gardner, Author

The Speech Bin
1965 Twenty-Fifth Avenue   407-770-0007
Vero Beach, FL 32960   FAX 407-770-0006

Jan J. Binney, Editor In Chief
Barbara Hector, Office Manager

Measures the auditory-perceptual skills of processing, sequential memory and interpretation of oral directions.

$ 69.50

5238 Test of Memory and Learning

Pro-Ed
8700 Shoal Creek Blvd.   512-451-3246
Austin, TX 78758   FAX 512-451-8542

This kit provides ten subtests that evaluate general and specific memory functions.

$ 159.00

5239 Test of Nonverbal Intelligence

Linda Brown, Author

Pro-Ed
8700 Shoal Creek Blvd.   512-451-3246
Austin, TX 78758   FAX 512-451-8542

A language-free measure of reasoning and intelligence presents a variety of abstract problem solving tasks.

$ 129.00

5240 Test of Practical Knowledge

J. Lee Wiederholt, Author

Pro-Ed
8700 Shoal Creek Blvd.   512-451-3246
Austin, TX 78758   FAX 512-451-8542

Comprised of three subtests: Personal Knowledge, Social Knowledge and Occupational Knowledge.

$ 59.00

5241 Token Test for Children

DLM Teaching Resources
One DLM Park   214-248-6300
Allen, TX 75002

5242 TONI-2: Test of Nonverbal Intelligence-2

AGS
7201 Woodland Road   612-786-4343
Circle Pines, MN 55014   800-328-2560

A language-free assessment of nonverbal intelligence and reasoning abilities. Administration Time: 20 minutes.

$ 136.50

5243 T.O.V.A.

Universal Attention Disorders, Inc.
4281 Katella Avenue, Ste. 215   714-229-8770
Los Alamitos, CA 90720   800-729-2886

This is an objective standardized test for children and adults. The test resembles a computer game, whenever the correct stimulus is presented the subject presses a firing button, and reactions are recorded for interpretation later. Variables include errors of omission, errors of commission, reaction time, variability, post-commission reaction time and multiple responses.

5244 Upper Extension: Expressive One-Word Picture Vocabulary Test

Morrison Gardner, Author

The Speech Bin
1965 Twenty-Fifth Avenue   407-770-0007
Vero Beach, FL 32960   FAX 407-770-0006

Jan J. Binney, Editor In Chief
Barbara Hector, Office Manager

Assesses expressive vocabulary.

$ 65.00

5245 Upper Extension - Receptive One-Word Picture Vocabulary Test

Rock Brownell, Author

The Speech Bin
1965 Twenty-Fifth Avenue   407-770-0007
Vero Beach, FL 32960   FAX 407-770-0006

Jan J. Binney, Editor In Chief
Barbara Hector, Office Manager
Assess adolescents vocabulary in just 10 minutes.

$ 65.00

5246   Wechsler Intelligence Scale of Children - Revised

The Psychological Corporation
555 Academic Court
San Antonio, TX 78204

5247   Wechsler Preschool and Primary Scale of Intelligence

Learning Disabilities Association of America
4156 Library Road   412-341-1515
Pittsburgh, PA 15234

This test consists of 12 subtests, five of which form the basis for the verbal intelligence and five are used for the performance intelligence.

5248   Wepman's Auditory Discrimination Test

Western Psychological Services Corporation
12031 Wilshire Blvd.   213-478-2061
Los Angeles, CA 90025   800-648-8857
          FAX 213-478-7838

A quick, economical means of individually screening children for auditory discrimination. This test uses a very simple procedure to assess the child's ability to recognize the fine differences between phonemes.

$ 70.00

5249   Wide Range Achievement Test

Sarah Jastak, Author

The Psychological Corporation
P.O. Box 839954   800-228-0752
San Antonio, TX 78283   FAX 512-229-2722

Uses two levels to assess the reading, spelling and arithmetic abilities of persons ages 5 to 75. Three subtests focus on reading, spelling and arithmetic calculation.

$ 70.00

5250   WISC-R

The Psychological Corporation
555 Academic Court   800-228-0752
San Antonio, TX 78204   FAX 512-299-2720

By performing a series of tasks, the individual shares his/her capacity to understand and cope with the cognitive demands of the environment.

5251   Woodcock-Johnson Psychoeducational Battery Revised

DLM Teaching Resources
One DLM Park, P.O. Box 4000   214-248-6300
Allen, TX 75002   800-527-4747

This battery contains 9 tests and provides examiners with achievement scores in the areas of reading, math, written language and knowledge.

$ 175.00

5252   WPPSI-R

The Psychological Corporation
555 Academic Court   800-228-0752
San Antonio, TX 78204   FAX 512-299-2720

A standardized measure of intellectual abilities of young children while incorporating the most current theory and practice.

Visual & Motor

5253   Bender-Gestalt

Learning Disabilities Association of America
4156 Library Road   412-341-1515
Pittsburgh, PA 15234

This test measures visual-motor coordination for all ages.

5254   Benton Revised Visual Retention Test

The Psychological Corporation
555 Academic Court   800-228-0752
San Antonio, TX 78204   FAX 512-299-2720

This kit tests visual perception and visual memory.

5255   Berry ·

Learning Disabilities Association of America
4156 Library Road   412-341-1515
Pittsburgh, PA 15234

A developmental test of visual motor integration skills.

5256   DeGrange-Berk TSI

Western Psychological Services Corporation
12031 Wilshire Blvd.   213-478-2061
Los Angeles, CA 90025

This test is a highly regarded measure of overall sensory integration, covering postural, control, bilateral motor and reflex integration.

5257   Development Test of Visual Perception

Pro-Ed
8700 Shoal Creek Blvd.   512-451-3246
Austin, TX 78758   FAX 512-451-8542

Standardized on 1,972 children from 12 states. This test measures visual perception through its 8 sub-tests.

$ 114.00

5258 Developmental Test of Visual-Motor Integration

Keith Beery, Author

Pro-Ed
8700 Shoal Creek Blvd.   512-451-3246
Austin, TX 78758   FAX 512-451-8542

The most highly acclaimed measure of students' visual-motor skills.

$ 98.00

5259 Frostig Developmental Test of Visual Perception

Marianne Frostig, Author

Pro-Ed
8700 Shoal Creek Blvd.   512-451-3246
Austin, TX 78758   FAX 512-451-8542

A test for evaluating basic perceptual and perceptual-motor skills in children, this test has been administered to more than 6 million children since its publication.

5260 KLPA: Khan-Lewis Phonological Analysis

Pro-Ed
8700 Shoal Creek Blvd.   512-451-3246
Austin, TX 78758   FAX 512-451-8542

An in-depth measure of phonological processes for assessment and remediation planning. Administration Time: 5-10 minutes.

$ 52.00

5261 Learning Efficiency Test

Raymond Webster, Author

Western Psychological Services Corporation
12031 Wilshire Blvd.   213-478-2061
Los Angeles, CA 90025

This test surveys the visual and auditory memory of students.

5262 Motor

Learning Systems Technologies
45 Tioga Way   617-639-0114
Marblehead, MA 01945

Test offering information on a student's fine motor skills.

5263 Motor-Free Visual Perception

Western Psychological Services Corporation
12031 Wilshire Blvd.   213-478-2061
Los Angeles, CA 90025

This test furnishes results on overall visual perception processing for children.

5264 Pennsylvania Bi-Manual Worksample

AGS
7201 Woodland Road   612-786-4343
Circle Pines, MN 55014   800-328-2560

Assesses speed and dexterity in skills integrating the use of fingers, hands and arms. Administration Time: 12 minutes.

5265 Perceptual Training

Learning Disabilities Association of America
4156 Library Road   412-341-1515
Pittsburgh, PA 15234

5266 Test of Gross Motor Development

Dale Urlich, Author

Pro-Ed
8700 Shoal Creek Blvd.   512-451-3246
Austin, TX 78758   FAX 512-451-8542

Assesses the common motor skills that are appropriate for preschool and elementary grade students. The test is designed for children and was standardized on 908 children in eight states.

$ 49.00

5267 Visual Skills Appraisal

Gary Oppenheim, Author

Western Psychological Services Corporation
12031 Wilshire Blvd.   213-478-2061
Los Angeles, CA 90025

An individually administered screening, this test identifes visual problems in children.

Math

5268 Diagnostic Test of Arithmetic Strategies

Herbert Ginsburg, Author

Pro-Ed
8700 Shoal Creek Blvd.   512-451-3246
Austin, TX 78758   FAX 512-451-8542

Measures the procedures elementary school children use to perform arithmetic calculation in addition, subtraction, multiplication and division.

$ 84.00

5269 Key-Math: a Diagnostic Inventory

AGS
7201 Woodland Road   612-786-4343
Circle Pines, MN 55014   800-328-2560

An updated measure of understanding and application of important mathematics concepts and skills. Administration Time: 35-50 minutes.

$ 290.00

5270 Measurement

Learning Systems Technologies
45 Tioga Way   617-639-0114
Marblehead, MA 01945

Test offering information on students ability to comprehend money and counting.

5271   QUIC Tests

STS, Inc.
480 Meyer Road
Bensenville, IL 60106
708-766-7150
800-642-6STS
FAX 708-766-8054

Innovative testing instruments which enable you to establish and verify functional levels of student competency in Math or Communicative Arts.

$ 41.95

5272   Sequential Assessment of Mathematics

Fredricka Reigman, Author
The Psychological Corporation
555 Academic Court
San Antonio, TX 78204
800-228-0752
FAX 512-299-2720

Assesses a students overall standing in a mathematics curriculum, including strengths and weaknesses.

5273   Stanford Diagnostic Mathematics Test Third Edition

Leslie Beatty, Author
The Psychological Corporation
555 Academic Court
San Antonio, TX 78204
800-228-0752
FAX 512-299-2720

This reputable test is designed to trace pupils' progress in basic math concepts and skills.

5274   Test of Early Mathematics Ability

Pro-Ed
8700 Shoal Creek Blvd.
Austin, TX 78758
512-451-3246
FAX 512-451-8542

The latest version of the popular test of early math functioning. It measures the math performance of children and is also useful for older children experiencing learning problems.

5275   Test of Mathematical Abilities

Virginia Brown, Author
Pro-Ed
8700 Shoal Creek Blvd.
Austin, TX 78758
512-451-3246
FAX 512-451-8542

Hase been developed to provide standardized information about story problems and computation, attitude, vocabulary and general cultural application.

$ 59.00

5276   Academic Therapy Publications

High Noon Books, Ann Arbor Division
20 Commercial Blvd.
Novato, CA 94949
415-883-3314
800-422-7249
FAX 415-883-3720

Offers various texts, curriculum materials, parent/teacher resources adn assessment tests for the special educator.

5277   Assessing Students with Special Needs

Robert A. Gable, Author
Longman Publishing Group
95 Church Street
White Plains, NY 10601
914-993-5000

Step-by-step guide to informal, classroom assessment of students with special needs.

5278   Assessing Vocational Teachers

Center on Education and Training for Employment
Ohio State - 1900 Kenny Road
Columbus, OH 43210
614-292-4353
800-848-4815

Examines seven approaches to teacher education, teacher interviews, student achievement, classroom observations, peer reviews and self-evaluation.

$ 8.00

5279   Assessment and Application: Volume 1 Developmental Rpogramming

University of Michigan Press
839 Green Street
Ann Arbor, MI 48106
313-764-4388
800-876-1922
FAX 313-936-0456

Provides detailed instruction for the use of Early Intervention Developmental Profile.

$ 13.95

5280   Assessment of Learners with Special Needs

Richard L. Luftig, Author
Allyn & Bacon
160 Gould Street
Needham Heights, MA 02194
800-852-8024

The central goal of this book is to help teachers become sophisticated, informed test consumers in terms of choosing and interpreting commercially prepared tests for their special needs students.

5281   Assessment of Students with Handicaps in Vocational Education

L. Albright, Author

American Vocational Association
1410 King Street
Alexandria, VA 22314   703-683-3111

5282 Assessment Update

Jossey-Bass, Inc.
350 Sansome Street, 5th Floor   415-433-1740
San Francisco, CA 94104

Trudy Banta, Editor

Covers the latest developments in higher education assessment.

5283 Career Education for Special Needs Individuals

D.E. Berkell, Author

The Council for Exceptional Children
1920 Association Drive   703-620-3660
Reston, VA 22091

Offers strategies in the vocational assessment of students with severe disabilities.

5284 Computer Scoring Systems for PRO-ED Tests

Pro-Ed
8700 Shoal Creek Blvd.   512-451-3246
Austin, TX 78758   FAX 512-451-8542

Allows test users to accurately, conveniently and quickly score the TOLD-2 Primary, TOLD-2 Intermediate, TOWL-2, ABI, Q-SAT and SCREEN tests.

5285 Diagnostique

The Council for Exceptional Children
1920 Association Drive   703-620-3660
Reston, VA 22091

Offers information on preparation for postsecondary success.

5286 GED Items

GED Testing Service
One Dupont Circle   202-939-9490
Washington, DC 20036

A newsletter for GED examiners and teachers.

5287 A Guide to 65 Tests for Special Education

Carolyn Compton, Author

Pittman Learning, Inc.
6 Davis Drive
Belmont, CA 94002

$ 14.95

5288 Handbook on the Assessment of Learning Disabilities

Learning Disabilities Association of America
4156 Library Road   412-341-1515
Pittsburgh, PA 15234

5289 Individual Learning Objectives Manual

Learning Systems Technologies
45 Tioga Way   617-639-0114
Marblehead, MA 01945

Contains upwards of 22,000 behavioral objectives in IEP Development.

5290 K-SOS: Kaufman Sequential and Simultaneous

AGS
7201 Woodland Road   612-786-4343
Circle Pines, MN 55014   800-328-2560

Shows teachers how to use K-ABC scores for planning intervention. The K-SOS workshop helps teachers understand the difference between sequential and simultaneous processing.

$ 60.50

5291 Parents Can Understand Testing

Henry Dyer, Author

National Committee for Citizens in Education
Suite 410, Wilde Lake Village Green
Columbia, MD 21044

5292 Pre GED/GED Computer and Multimedia Program

Aquarius Instructional
P.O. Box 128   813-595-7890
Indiana Rocks Beach, FL 34635   800-338-2644
                                   FAX 813-595-2685

Combines all of the curriculum areas included in the GED test.

$ 1495.00

5293 Request for ACT Assessment Special Testing

ACT Test Administration
P.O. Box 168   319-337-1000
Iowa City, IA 52243

Pamphlet offering information on eligibility for special testing, requesting and arranging for special testing and how to test students with disabilities.

5294 Skirting the Perils of Testing: How Standardized Tests Affect Children

Jayne DeLawter, Author

Pittman Learning, Inc.
530 University Avenue
Palo Alto, CA 94301

5295 Spelling Words for Writing

Robert G. Forest, Ed.D., Author

Curriculum Associates, Inc.
5 Esquire Road   508-667-8000
North Billerica, MA 01862   FAX 508-667-5706

Offers students who still need to mater spelling and writing skills, a fresh start.

5296   Standards and Procedures Manual for Certification/ Vocational Evaluation

CCWAVES
1156 Shure Drive
Arlington Heights, IL 60004

5297   Teaching Test Taking Skills

Thomas Scruggs, Author
Brookline Books
P.O. Box 1046   617-868-0360
Cambridge, MA 02238   FAX 617-868-1772

This text aims to improve the validity of the test. It makes scores more accurateyl reflect what students really know by making sure that students lose points only because they do not know the information, not because they marked an answer choice incorrectly or misinterpreted the test directions. This text teaches about the test format or other conditions of testing, not to specific items on the test.

5298   Testing Accommodations for Students with Disabilities

Association on Higher Education and Disability
P.O. Box 21192   614-488-4972
Columbus, OH 43221   FAX 614-488-1174

This guide is written for the service provider who is responsible for arranging testing accommodations for students with disabilities in higher education.

5299   Tests, Measurement and Evaluation

American Institutes for Research
3333 K Street NW   202-342-5060
Washington, DC 20007

5300   Truths and Consequences of Testing

Perceptions, Inc.
P.O. Box 142   201-376-3766
Millburn, NJ 07041

Bebe Antell, Editor
Offers information on special testing, test results, assessing intelligence and more.

5301   Wordly Wise Tests

Kenneth Hodkinson, Author

Educators Publishing Service, Inc.
75 Moulton Street   800-225-5750
Cambridge, MA 02138

These tests contain questions in a variety of formats that test students' knowledge of the words taught in the Wordly Wise series.

Adult

5302   Apraxia Battery for Adults

Barbara Dabul, Author
The Speech Bin
1965 Twenty-Fifth Avenue   407-770-0007
Vero Beach, FL 32960   FAX 407-770-0006

Jan J. Binney, Editor In Chief
Barbara Hector, Office Manager
Assesses the presence and severity of apraxia in adolescents and adults.

       $ 69.00

5303   The Boone Voice Program for Adults

Daniel Boone, Author
Pro-Ed
8700 Shoal Creek Blvd.   512-451-3246
Austin, TX 78758   FAX 512-451-8542

Provides for diagnosis and remediation of adult voice disorders. This program is based on the same philosophy and therapy as The Program for Children but is presented at an adult interest level.

       $ 17.90

5304   Scholastic Abilities Test for Adults

Brian Bryant, Author
Pro-Ed
8700 Shoal Creek Blvd.   512-451-3246
Austin, TX 78758   FAX 512-451-8542

Measures scholastic competence, aptitude and academic achievement for persons with learning difficulties.

       $ 109.00

5305   Wechsler Adult Intelligence Scale

David Wechsler, Author
The Psychological Corporation
555 Academic Court   800-228-0752
San Antonio, TX 78204   FAX 512-299-2720

Intended for use by trained clinical examiners, this test measures a person's capacity for intelligent behavior. It is the most widely used intelligence scale for adults.

Toys & Games

5306 ABC Mazes

Therapro, Inc.
225 Arlington Street   508-872-9494
Framingham, MA 01701   FAX 508-875-2062

Enhances visual perceptual abilitiy and promotes eye-hand coordination and figure ground with many of the mazes as a letter of the alphabet.

$ 7.00

5307 The Able Child

P.O. Box 250   516-563-7176
Bohemia, NY 11716

5308 Ask Me Anything Games

Lakeshore Learning Materials
2695 East Dominguez Street   310-537-8600
Carson, CA 90749   800-421-5354
                FAX 310-537-5403

Hundreds of questions ranging from fact-oriented questions to fun questions challenging students in these unique games.

$ 13.95

5309 Beads and Baubles

Therapro, Inc.
225 Arlington Street   508-872-9494
Framingham, MA 01701   FAX 508-875-2062

100 pieces in various shapes, colors and sizes to string on a lace.

$ 4.95

5310 Beads and Pattern Cards

Therapro, Inc.
225 Arlington Street   508-872-9494
Framingham, MA 01701   FAX 508-875-2062

Colorful wooden beads in 6 colors and 3 shapes to string on a lace.

$ 24.95

5311 Big Pegboard

Therapro, Inc.
225 Arlington Street   508-872-9494
Framingham, MA 01701   FAX 508-875-2062

One inch pegs in different colors fit easily into the durable plastic board.

$ 18.95

5312 Big-Little Peg Board and Peg Sets

Therapro, Inc.
225 Arlington Street   508-872-9494
Framingham, MA 01701   FAX 508-875-2062

Hardwood pegs with a durable rubber board.

$ 12.95

5313 BUSY BOX Activity Centers

Toys for Special Children
385 Warburton Avenue   800-TEC-TOYS
Hastings-on-Hudson, NY 10706

Offers a full line of activity centers for the learning disabled, hearing impaired, visually impaired and multisensory impaired.

5314 Childswork/Childsplay Catalogue

Center for Applied Psychology, Inc.
P.O. Box 1587   215-277-4020
King Of Prussia, PA 19406   800-962-1141
                FAX 215-277-4088

Hennie Shore, Marketing

The most complete source for toys, books and games to help children with their mental health needs, including hundreds of items that deal with ADD, behavior problems, learning disabilities, physical disabilities, sleep disorders, stress and more.

5315 Circus Wagon

Therapro, Inc.
225 Arlington Street   508-872-9494
Framingham, MA 01701   FAX 508-875-2062

Six colorful pegs of the same size can be placed at random in the holes of this pull-toy circus wagon. Great for "in-out" play, early eye-hand coordination and pulling.

$ 19.00

5316 Colored Counting Cubes

Therapro, Inc.
225 Arlington Street   508-872-9494
Framingham, MA 01701   FAX 508-875-2062

Hardwood, one inch cubes come in six bright colors.

$ 15.95

5317 Computer Training Devices

Toys for Special Children
385 Warburton Avenue   800-TEC-TOYS
Hastings-on-Hudson, NY 10706

Offers a full line of switches, adapters and keyboard covers for special children.

5318 Count My Fingers

Therapro, Inc.
225 Arlington Street   508-872-9494
Framingham, MA 01701   FAX 508-875-2062

Counting Fingers is a basic, but challenging task made of foam rubber.

$ 11.95

5319 Creative Disks

Therapro, Inc.
225 Arlington Street   508-872-9494
Framingham, MA 01701   FAX 508-875-2062

These large disks are great for basic hand-eye coordination and bilateral integration skills.

$ 8.50

5320   Crinkling Pals

Therapro, Inc.
225 Arlington Street   508-872-9494
Framingham, MA 01701   FAX 508-875-2062

These bright, eye catching, soft toys are easy to grasp.

$ 3.95

5321   Electronic Boards and Resistors

Therapro, Inc.
225 Arlington Street   508-872-9494
Framingham, MA 01701   FAX 508-875-2062

An electronic board and package of resistors are provided. Clients poke wire ends of the resistors through appropriately spaced holes.

$ 12.95

5322   Entertainment Electronics

Toys for Special Children
385 Warburton Avenue   800-TEC-TOYS
Hastings-on-Hudson, NY 10706

Offers a full line of specially adapted electronics from radios to tape recorders for special children.

5323   Eye-Hand Coordination Boosters

Therapro, Inc.
225 Arlington Street   508-872-9494
Framingham, MA 01701   FAX 508-875-2062

A book of 92 masters that can be used over and over again with worksheets that are appropriate for all ages. These are perceptual motor activities that involve copying and tracing in the areas of visual tracking, discrimination and spatial relationships.

$ 12.50

5324   Familiar Things

Therapro, Inc.
225 Arlington Street   508-872-9494
Framingham, MA 01701   FAX 508-875-2062

Identify and match shapes of common objects with these square, rubber pieces.

$ 16.95

5325   Fishing!

Therapro, Inc.
225 Arlington Street   508-872-9494
Framingham, MA 01701   FAX 508-875-2062

Encourages eye-hand coordination.

$ 5.95

5326   Flagship Carpets, Inc.

P.O. Box 1189   404-695-4055
Chatsworth, GA 30705   800-848-4055
                                             FAX 404-695-6632

Offers a variety of capeting that offers games life hopscotch, the alphabet, geography maps and more.

5327   Form Peg Wagon

Therapro, Inc.
225 Arlington Street   508-872-9494
Framingham, MA 01701   FAX 508-875-2062

An early spacial/perceptual toy. Four differently shaped forms fit into one side of the base.

$ 21.00

5328   From Toys to Computers

Christine Wright, Author
Don Johnston Developmental Equipment, Inc.
P.O. Box 639, 1000 N. Rand Road   708-526-2682
Wauconda, IL 60084   800-999-4660

Easy-to-follow guide with practical ideas and instructions on how to adapt commercially available toys with switches and simple devices.

$ 24.00

5329   Geoboards

Therapro, Inc.
225 Arlington Street   508-872-9494
Framingham, MA 01701   FAX 508-875-2062

Teach eye/hand coordination skills while strengthening pincher grasp with rubber bands.

$ 11.00

5330   Geosafari

Lakeshore Learning Materials
2695 East Dominguez Street   310-537-8600
Carson, CA 90749   800-421-5354
                                             FAX 310-537-5403

A fast-paced electronic game teaching geography in an exciting new way.

$ 99.50

5331   Golf Tee Pegboards and Tees

Therapro, Inc.
225 Arlington Street   508-872-9494
Framingham, MA 01701   FAX 508-875-2062

Six different color pegboards with matching tees. 16 holes in each board, this task can improve eye-hand coordination and color discrimination.

$ 34.95

5332   Half and Half Design and Color Series

Therapro, Inc.
225 Arlington Street   508-872-9494
Framingham, MA 01701   FAX 508-875-2062

Geometric designs appropriate for all ages. The client draws over dotted lines to finish the other half of the printed design.

$ 9.00

5333 Hook Board and Washers

Therapro, Inc.
225 Arlington Street   508-872-9494
Framingham, MA 01701   FAX 508-875-2062

A board with a horizontal row of hooks mounted on it and a base to support it.

$ 32.50

5334 Jigsaw Number Puzzle

Therapro, Inc.
225 Arlington Street   508-872-9494
Framingham, MA 01701   FAX 508-875-2062

Teach numbers, motor skills, and counting. Wonderfully constructed wooden box and pieces, appropriate for all ages.

$ 15.95

5335 Kinetic Learning Book

Therapro, Inc.
225 Arlington Street   508-872-9494
Framingham, MA 01701   FAX 508-875-2062

Loaded with ideas for using Wikki Stix.

$ 1.98

5336 Kitchen Magnets

Therapro, Inc.
225 Arlington Street   508-872-9494
Framingham, MA 01701   FAX 508-875-2062

Pre-cut wooden shapes with easy to paint designs outlined on the wood plus self-stick magents. Offers four full-color packages; Hearts and Geese, Country Collection, real Butterflies, and Real Songbirds.

$ 4.95

5337 Lace-A-Puppet

Therapro, Inc.
225 Arlington Street   508-872-9494
Framingham, MA 01701   FAX 508-875-2062

Great craft items for singles or groups. Sew, decorate and use them as hand puppets when creations are complete.

$ 9.95

5338 Lacing Activities

Therapro, Inc.
225 Arlington Street   508-872-9494
Framingham, MA 01701   FAX 508-875-2062

Offers various activities such as lacing pads, lacing shapes and animal lacing boards providing training in coordination skills.

$ 12.95

5339 Lacing Board

Therapro, Inc.
225 Arlington Street   508-872-9494
Framingham, MA 01701   FAX 508-875-2062

A board with eye hooks secured to it which form a simple geometric pattern. The client threads the attached brightly colored lace through each eye hook in succession.

$ 19.95

5340 Link N' Learn Activity Book

Therapro, Inc.
225 Arlington Street   508-872-9494
Framingham, MA 01701   FAX 508-875-2062

A nice accompaniment to the color rings. There are great cognitive activities included.

$ 7.95

5341 Link N' Learn Activity Cards

Therapro, Inc.
225 Arlington Street   508-872-9494
Framingham, MA 01701   FAX 508-875-2062

Learn patterning, sequencing and color discrimination by using this set of 20 cards that show the links as life-sized.

$ 6.95

5342 Link N' Learn Color Rings

Therapro, Inc.
225 Arlington Street   508-872-9494
Framingham, MA 01701   FAX 508-875-2062

Easy to hook and separate colorful plastic rings.

$ 6.95

5343 Lumberjacks

Therapro, Inc.
225 Arlington Street   508-872-9494
Framingham, MA 01701   FAX 508-875-2062

Nine wooden lumberjacks stack by interlocking or by being placed head to head. Brightly painted with non-toxic paints, they fit together beautifully into many different designs.

$ 12.95

5344 The Magical World of Animation

MindPlay
Unit F92, P.O. Box 36491   602-322-6365
Tucson, AZ 85740   800-221-7911

The magician performs magic tricks and demonstrates why animation looks like magic.
"Animation video builds self-confidence and strengthens skills."

-Curriculum Product Review

5345 Magnetic Fun

Therapro, Inc.
225 Arlington Street   508-872-9494
Framingham, MA 01701   FAX 508-875-2062

One swipe of the magic wand, and the client can pick up small objects without the need for a refined pincer grasp.

$ 13.95

5346   Marvelous Mosaics Set

Therapro, Inc.
225 Arlington Street   508-872-9494
Framingham, MA 01701   FAX 508-875-2062

Creates simple to difficult designs with these plastic traezoids.

$ 18.95

5347   The Maze Book

Therapro, Inc.
225 Arlington Street   508-872-9494
Framingham, MA 01701   FAX 508-875-2062

Significantly more challenging that the ABC Mazes; rich in perceptual activities.

$ 15.00

5348   MORE Basic Kit

Therapro, Inc.
225 Arlington Street   508-872-9494
Framingham, MA 01701   FAX 508-875-2062

Collection of 11 essential items ideal for treating children with sensorimotor problems. These toys stimulate oral-motor functions of sucking, blowing and biting, while providing integrating tactile, proprioceptive, visual and auditory input.

$ 11.50

5349   MORE Deluze Kit

Therapro, Inc.
225 Arlington Street   508-872-9494
Framingham, MA 01701   FAX 508-875-2062

These more durable items increase the challenge and complexity of oral-motor tasks.

$ 35.00

5350   MORE Variety Kit

Therapro, Inc.
225 Arlington Street   508-872-9494
Framingham, MA 01701   FAX 508-875-2062

Valuable addition to a therapist's oral motor equipment allowing children to experiment with a variety of whistles with visual and auditory stimuli which facilitates gradation of respiration and oral motor control.

$ 22.50

5351   Nesting Cup Cart

Therapro, Inc.
225 Arlington Street   508-872-9494
Framingham, MA 01701   FAX 508-875-2062

This is a unique, pull-toy that has many uses. In addition to being pulled, it requires some early eye-hand coordination skills.

$ 19.00

5352   Occluded Vision Manual Dexterity Board

Therapro, Inc.
225 Arlington Street   508-872-9494
Framingham, MA 01701   FAX 508-875-2062

The threaded ends of bolts appear on the under side of a supported board.

$ 29.95

5353   Paint By Piece Kits

Therapro, Inc.
225 Arlington Street   508-872-9494
Framingham, MA 01701   FAX 508-875-2062

A perfect activity for groups as well as individuals. The picture is divided into die cut wooden pieces that are painted separately and then reassembled into a professional looking wood-painting. Complete kit includes pre-cut wooden parts, paints, brush, glue and complete instructions. Eight kits are available.

$ 11.95

5354   Parquetry

Therapro, Inc.
225 Arlington Street   508-872-9494
Framingham, MA 01701   FAX 508-875-2062

Blocks and pattern cards that challenge a person's sense of design and color as well as encouraging visual perception skills.

$ 25.95

5355   Pattern Block Activity Pack

Therapro, Inc.
225 Arlington Street   508-872-9494
Framingham, MA 01701   FAX 508-875-2062

Everything needed to stimulate visual perceptual skills.

$ 19.95

5356   Pattern Block Party

Therapro, Inc.
225 Arlington Street   508-872-9494
Framingham, MA 01701   FAX 508-875-2062

For independent work or competitive challenges, individuals assemble block pattern puzzles and emplore color and geometric shape relationships.

$ 19.95

5357   Patternables

Therapro, Inc.
225 Arlington Street   508-872-9494
Framingham, MA 01701   FAX 508-875-2062

Activity book providing plans for building pictures of objects with pattern blocks.

$ 7.95

5358   Pegboard Activity Cards

Therapro, Inc.
225 Arlington Street   508-872-9494
Framingham, MA 01701   FAX 508-875-2062

20 colorful, double-sided task cards, designed for use with pegs and pegboard.

$ 11.95

5359 Perceptual Activities

Therapro, Inc.
225 Arlington Street   508-872-9494
Framingham, MA 01701   FAX 508-875-2062

Activity sheets to practice matching, copying, figure-ground, drawing and tracing. Offers Level 1, Beginning and Level 2, Advanced.

$ 6.50

5360 Pin Ups

Judy Pankratz, Author

The Speech Bin
1965 Twenty-Fifth Avenue   407-770-0007
Vero Beach, FL 32960   FAX 407-770-0006

Jan J. Binney, Editor In Chief
Barbara Hector, Office Manager

A collection of games to be displayed and played over an extended period of time.

$ 16.95

5361 Playshapes

Therapro, Inc.
225 Arlington Street   508-872-9494
Framingham, MA 01701   FAX 508-875-2062

Explore visual discrimination, shape and size recognition, and sorting activities. Colorful sheets with 22 patterns assist design construction.

$ 24.95

5362 Primer Pak

Therapro, Inc.
225 Arlington Street   508-872-9494
Framingham, MA 01701   FAX 508-875-2062

A challenging sampler of manipulatives: lacing shapes, form structures and space disks.

$ 11.95

5363 Programming Concepts, Inc.

5221 McCullough   512-824-5949
San Antonio, TX 78212   800-594-GAME
          FAX 512-824-8055

Janie Haugen, Developer

Offers 8 programs in a gameboard format to improve life and social skills including; Cooking Class, You Tell Me, Community Skills, All About You, Looking Good, Eating Skills, Workplace Skills and Behavior Skills.

$ 49.95

5364 Puzzlers

Therapro, Inc.
225 Arlington Street   508-872-9494
Framingham, MA 01701   FAX 508-875-2062

A great bilateral activity that is visually stimulating. Use either hand to create endless designs, even if the puzzle cannot be solved. Comes in Novice, Challenger or Avenger.

$ 6.25

5365 Rainbow Numbers

Therapro, Inc.
225 Arlington Street   508-872-9494
Framingham, MA 01701   FAX 508-875-2062

This matching and stacking stimulates coordination, number sequencing, counting and color recognition.

$ 12.95

5366 Reading, Writing and Rummy

Learning Disabilities Association of America
4156 Library Road   412-341-1515
Pittsburgh, PA 15234

5367 Rub-A-Dub Pegs

Therapro, Inc.
225 Arlington Street   508-872-9494
Framingham, MA 01701   FAX 508-875-2062

Made out of wood, each of the "three Men" ride in a bright colored tub of his own.

$ 13.00

5368 Sailor Boy Peg Boat

Therapro, Inc.
225 Arlington Street   508-872-9494
Framingham, MA 01701   FAX 508-875-2062

Another great pull toy! Six differently colored peg "sailors" have removable, colored caps so not only does the child learn color matching, but the pieces require beginning sequencing skills.

$ 26.00

5369 Sesame Street Toys

Toys for Special Children
385 Warburton Avenue   800-TEC-TOYS
Hastings-on-Hudson, NY 10706

Offers a full line of specially adapted toys from the Sesame Street series.

5370 Shape and Color Sorter

Therapro, Inc.
225 Arlington Street   508-872-9494
Framingham, MA 01701   FAX 508-875-2062

A simple and safe task of perception. 25 crepe foam rubber pieces to sort by shape or colors.

$ 11.95

5371 Shape Form Board

Therapro, Inc.
225 Arlington Street   508-872-9494
Framingham, MA 01701   FAX 508-875-2062

Ideal basic puzzle. Large knobs for easy manipulation of the puzzle pieces providing practice in shape recognition.

$ 16.95

5372 Size Discrimination Nut and Bolt Board

Therapro, Inc.
225 Arlington Street 508-872-9494
Framingham, MA 01701 FAX 508-875-2062

Nine bolts of various sizes are mounted on a board. Clients develop size discrimination skills by matching nuts to appropriately sized bolts.

$ 29.95

5373 Small Plastic Peg Board Kit

Therapro, Inc.
225 Arlington Street 508-872-9494
Framingham, MA 01701 FAX 508-875-2062

Set includes plastic peg board with 100 holes, small plastic pegs and a very useful manual.

$ 15.00

5374 Soft Toy

Therapro, Inc.
225 Arlington Street 508-872-9494
Framingham, MA 01701 FAX 508-875-2062

Soft, textured toy that is easily grasped and contains a rattle for sensory stimulation.

$ 3.95

5375 Talkabout Bag

Cindy Drolet, Author

The Speech Bin
1965 Twenty-Fifth Avenue 407-770-0007
Vero Beach, FL 32960 FAX 407-770-0006

Jan J. Binney, Editor In Chief
Barbara Hector, Office Manager

Offers an innovative collection of toys teaching important language skills for young children.

$ 179.50

5376 Tangram Kit

Therapro, Inc.
225 Arlington Street 508-872-9494
Framingham, MA 01701 FAX 508-875-2062

Spatial planning, shape recognition, pattern replication and pattern design are encouraged with these brightly colored 7 piece geometric puzzle.

$ 7.95

5377 Tangramables

Therapro, Inc.
225 Arlington Street 508-872-9494
Framingham, MA 01701 FAX 508-875-2062

Offers 75 reproductible activity sheets and 7 piece tangram set.

$ 7.95

5378 Terry Tangram

Therapro, Inc.
225 Arlington Street 508-872-9494
Framingham, MA 01701 FAX 508-875-2062

Shape recognition and spatial relationships are fun with this delightful character.

$ 15.95

5379 TFH Achievement & Special Needs

4449 Gibsonia Road 412-444-6400
Gibsonia, PA 15044

5380 Therapro, Inc.

225 Arlington Street 508-872-9494
Framingham, MA 01701 FAX 508-875-2062

Offers a catalog with a variety of toys and games for teaching the learning disabled coordination, perception, sensation and motor skills.

5381 Tic-Tac-Toe

Therapro, Inc.
225 Arlington Street 508-872-9494
Framingham, MA 01701 FAX 508-875-2062

Large bright board and pieces make this classic game easy to see and manipulate while encouraging motor coordination.

$ 7.50

5382 Toddler Tote

Therapro, Inc.
225 Arlington Street 508-872-9494
Framingham, MA 01701 FAX 508-875-2062

Offers one Junior Fit-A-Space panel that has large geometric shapes; 4 Shape Squares providing basic shapes in a more challenging size; 2 Peg Play Vehicles and Pegs introducing early peg board skills; 3 Familiar Things present 2 piece puzzles and a handy take-along bag.

$ 11.95

5383 Whistle Set

Therapro, Inc.
225 Arlington Street 508-872-9494
Framingham, MA 01701 FAX 508-875-2062

Set of six whistles and a one foot length of Theratubing. Whistles included are; race car, aircraft, rooster, mini mouth harmonica, space ship and river boat.

$ 5.95

5384 Wikki Stix

Therapro, Inc.
225 Arlington Street 508-872-9494
Framingham, MA 01701 FAX 508-875-2062

Colorful, non-toxic waxed strings which are easily molded to create various forms, shapes and letters. Combine motor planning skill with fine motor skill by following simple shapes with Wikki Stix and then coloring in the shape.

$ 4.25

5385 Wingo-Wordo

Caroline Peck, Author
Educators Publishing Service, Inc.
75 Moulton Street   800-225-5750
Cambridge, MA 02138

Follows the classic bingo game pattern, with six large game cards.

5386 Wooden Pegboard

Therapro, Inc.
225 Arlington Street   508-872-9494
Framingham, MA 01701   FAX 508-875-2062

Lacquer finished wooden board with 100 drilled holes.

$ 6.95

5387 Wooden Pegs

Therapro, Inc.
225 Arlington Street   508-872-9494
Framingham, MA 01701   FAX 508-875-2062

Smooth pegs in 6 colors for use in design and pattern making with the wooden pegboard.

$ 4.95

Major Toy Catalogs

5388 Advantage Bag Company

22633 Ellinwood Drive   213-540-8197
Torrance, CA 90505

5389 Aquatic Therapy

123 Hymac Street   616-349-9049
Kalamazoo, MI 49004

5390 BeeBop, Inc.

P.O. Box 9245   509-965-8211
Yakima, WA 98907

5391 Cliftcraft Manufacturing, Inc.

6400 East Eldorado Circle   800-458-7400
Tucson, AZ 85719

5392 Easy Access Corporation

1989 Sherwood Street   813-441-3279
Clearwater, FL 34625

5393 Equipment Shop

P.O. Box 172   617-275-7681
Bedford, MA 01730

5394 Flaghouse, Inc.

150 North MacQuestern Parkway   800-793-7900
Mt. Vernon, NY 10550

Over 4000 rehabilitation and recreation products.

5395 Flying Rich Kraft

8131 Allport Avenue   310-693-6372
Santa Fe Springs, CA

5396 Gametime, Inc.

P.O. Box 121   205-845-8610
Fort Payne, AL 35967

5397 Innovative Products, Inc.

830 South 48th Street   701-772-5185
Grand Forks, ND 58201

5398 Kimbo Educational

P.O. Box 477   800-631-2187
Long Branch, NJ 07740

5399 McLain Cycle Products

12786 North Garfield Road   616-694-9704
Travers City, MI 49684

5400 Mobility International USA

P.O. Box 3551   503-343-1284
Eugene, OR 97403

5401 Novei Products, Inc.

P.O. Box 408   800-323-5143
Rockton, IL 61072

5402 Over the Rainbow

186 Mehani Circle   808-879-5521
Kihei Maui, HI 96753

5403 PCA Industries

5642 Natural Bridge   314-389-4140
St. Louis, MO 63120

5404 PlayDesigns

P.O. Box 427   800-327-7571
New Berlin, PA 17855

5405 Programming Concepts

5221 McCullough
San Anotnio, TX 78212

5406 Quickie Designs

2842 Business Park   800-456-8168
Fresno, CA 93727

5407 Racing Strollers

P.O. Box 2189   509-457-0925
Yakima, WA 98907

5408 Radventure, Inc.

20755 SW 238th Place   503-628-2895
Sherwood, OR 97140

5409   TFH (USA), Ltd.

4449 Gibsonia Road   412-444-6400
Gibsonia, PA 15044   FAX 412-444-6411

Offers entertainment, stimulation and education products for people with special needs. Offers over 300 products that range in use from Activity to Multi Sensory Stimulation.

5410   Therapeutic Toys, Inc.

34 North Moodus   203-873-2003
Moodus, CT 06469

5411   Toys for Special Children

385 South Warburton Avenue   914-478-0960
Hastings-on-Hudson, NY 10706

5412   Turfking, Inc.

9310 North 16th Street   813-933-8894
Tampa, FL 33612

5413   T-Wheeler, Inc.

7467 Mission Gorge #16   619-449-8783
Santee, GA 92071

5414   Woodset

657 Printers Court   301-932-8200
White Plains, MD 20695

Arizona

5415 Life Development Institute/ Summer Sessions

1720 East Monte Visa   602-254-0822
Phoenix, AZ 85006

Robert Crawford

Vocational/career exploration, independent living skills and a residential program offered.

California

5416 Odyssey Academic Camp

P.O. Box 38   415-687-6851
Castella, CA 96017   800-642-2014

Don Smith

An academic summer camp located in the mountains, it offers an individualized program and a variety of recreational activities.

5417 Technology and Persons with Disabilities

California State University, Northridge
18111 Nordhoff Street   818-885-2578
Northridge, CA 91330

Dr. Harry Murphy

Colorado

5418 Timberline Trails

P.O. Box 397   303-641-1562
Tincup, CO 81210

Art Pliner

This mountain camp is designed especially for children with specific learning disabilities. Primary goals include improving self-concepts, social skills and interpersonal communication abilities as well as providing fun and recreation.

Connecticut

5419 Adaptive Aquatic Camp

Brookfield Parks & Recreation Department
P.O. Box 5106 - Pocono Road   203-775-2444
Brookfield, CT 06804

Kevin Walsh
Julie Schiller

Offers all level swimming lessons and aquatic adjustment safety taught on an individual basis by certified instruc-

tors. These lessons are offered to the mentally disabled, physically disabled, learning disabled and emotionally disturbed.

$ 15.00

5420 Becket Academy

River Road   203-873-8658
East Haddam, CT 06423

Donald Hirth

Educational facility and summer camp program offering day and residential programs.

5421 Camp Crystal, Camp Friendship, Camp Fun Time and Camp Pee-Wee

Middletown Parks and Recreation Department
319 Butternut Street   203-344-3473
Middletown, CT 06457

Colleen F. Maniscalco, Program Services

Each of these camps offer a variety of recreational and social activities. Each camp will be integrated with at least 12% population of children with disabilities.

5422 Camp Hemlocks

P.O. Box 198   203-228-9496
Hebron, CT 06248

Sunny P. Ku, Program Director

Offers various travel and trips, arts and crafts, boating, fishing and more.

5423 Camp Horizons Support Services

Camp Horizons
P.O. Box 323   203-456-1032
South Windham, CT 06266   FAX 203-456-4721

Marcella Curry, Support Manager

Supports provided by professionals experienced in: Positive program design, Working with people who present challenging behaviors, Sign Language, Mobility Training, Training parents, teachers and staff to use effective teaching strategies, supporting families of people with special needs. Supports assist a person to: participate in a community-based daily routine, be successful in home or school despite challenging behaviors and more.

5424 Camp Kennedy

41 Center Street   203-647-3084
Manchester, CT 06040

Laura Dunfield

A day camp offering out-door wooded areas with shelter, a main indoor recreation facility, swimming and more for the learning disabled camper.

5425   Camp Lark

Litchfield County Association for Retarded Citizen
84-R Main Street   203-482-9364
Torrington, CT   06790

Katherine Marchand-Beyer

Program offers arts and crafts, swimming, field sports, archery, outdoor education, music and drama and adventure courses. Once a week overnights are offered and the program runs in conjunction with the Torrington YMCA camp.

5426   Camp Sequassen

Boy Scouts of America
1861 Whitney Avenue   203-288-6211
New Haven, CT   06517

David Maher

Program offered includes swimming, rowing, canoeing, leatherwork, basketry, rifle, archery and nature education.

5427   Camp Tepee

Route 59, Box 89   203-261-2566
Monroe, CT   06468

Donna Denesha

A day camp offering programs including arts and crafts, sports, swimming, nature lore, boating, archery, riflery and special events.

5428   Computer Creatives

The Learning Incentive, Inc.
139 North Main Street   203-236-5807
West Hartford, CT   06107

Martha Harthan

Offers computer lessons and remedial academic classes including remediation and recreation.

5429   CREC Summer School

River Street School
601 River Street   203-298-9079
Windsor, CT   06095

Thomas Parvenski

Offers an educationally-oriented program with recreational opportunities, strong behavior management and highly structured groupings.

5430   Eagle Hill - Southport

214 Main Street   203-254-2044
Southport, CT   06490

Carolyn Lavender

This program is designed for boys and girls who are experiencing academic difficulties and would benefit from an individualized program of skill development.

5431   Eagle Hill Summer Program

45 Glenville Road   203-622-9240
Greenwich, CT   06831

Tom Cone, Director

Offers a language based academic program including two tutorials each morning as well as three additional skill classes. A program designed for children with a specific learning disability and/or needing additional support in specific academic skill areas is also a part of the program.

5432   East Hartford Special Education Camp

Gorman Park, May Road   203-291-7350
East Hartford, CT   06118

Greg Fox

A day camp offering swimming, sports, arts and crafts, projects, music and field trips.

5433   Exceptional Kids on the Block Program

Easter Seal Rehab Center of Central Connecticut
158 State Street   203-237-7835
Meriden, CT   06450

Debora Mesite

The purpose of this day camp is to allow children to experience social relationships as they work, play, and have fun together.

5434   Haddam-Killingworth Recreation Department

Little City Road   203-345-8334
Higganum, CT   06441

Frank Sparks

Programs offered include; arts and crafts, games, sports workshops, field trips, movies, special events and a carnival.

5435   Hall-Brooke School

47 Long Lots Road   203-277-1251
Westport, CT   06880

Alan Rudolph

Offers a school program of math, English, history, science and physical education.

5436   Kiwanis Easter Seal Day Camp

Easter Seal Rehabilitation Center
76 Westbury Park Road   203-879-2343
Watertown, CT   06795

Alice Hubbell
Ronnie Genova

Program offered includes swimming, athletics, camping, hiking, outdoor education, camp music activities, arts and crafts and special day activities.

5437   The Learning Clinic Camp

Route 169, Box 324   203-928-5274
Brooklyn, CT 06234

Raymond DuCharme

A day and residential camp offering children with learning disabilities individual and small group instruction with supported services through a variety of sports including horseback riding, sailing and other recreational activities.

5438   Marvelwood Summer

Cornwall, CT 06753   203-672-6612

William Austin

The emphasis in this summer program is on diagnosis and remediation of individual reading, spelling, writing, math and study problems.

5439   Milford Recreation Department

Parsons Complex
70 West River Street   203-783-3280
Milford, CT 06460

Edward Austin

A day camp offering a program of recreational games, trips and educational experiences.

5440   Newington Children's Hospital School

NCH School
450 Forbes Street   203-569-0140
East Hartford, CT 06118

Ed Gorman

A day program with the primary emphasis being on a continuation of the school year program. Individual and small group instruction is provided and all related services such as counseling, occupational therapy, physical therapy and speech/language therapy are provided.

5441   Norwalk Public Schools Special Education Summer Programs

125 East Avenue   203-854-4133
Norwalk, CT 06852

Oneita Haynes

Offers pre-school/elementary students developmental and remedial academics.

5442   Oxford Academy

1393 Boston Post Rd, P.O. Drawer P   203-399-6247
Westbrook, CT 06498

Philip Davis

Individualized education prepares academically deficient students for college or further secondary work.

5443   Redding Park and Recreation Summer Playground

P.O. Box 71   203-938-2551
Redding, CT 06875

Maura Callahan

Program offers organized play activities with arts and crafts, special guest artists and a weekly trip to various attractions and shows.

5444   Shadybrook Learning Center

P.O. Box 365   203-873-8800
Moodus, CT 06469   800-666-4752

Les Kershnar, Director

Offers clinical (remedial academics, speech and langauge, rap sessions, optional OT and PT), recreational (aquatics, crafts, creative dramatics, non-competitive games, adaptive sports), and vocational (paid supervised job experience for all ages) services. Programs are individualized and promote independent, self-esteem and socialization.

5445   Shriver Summer Developmental Program

Nathan Hale School
Taylor Road   203-741-3701
Enfield, CT 06082

Maria Bonney

Academic/recreational program including instructional swimming for the learning disabled.

5446   Timber Trails Camps

Connecticut Valley Girl Scout Council
74 Forest Street   203-522-0163
Hartford, CT 06105

Linda Miller, LD Specialist
Eric Munson, Jr., Director Of Camps

Program offered includes gymnastics, arts and carfts, aquatics, photography, project adventure, video, equestrian, riding lessons, sailing and canoeing.

5447   Valley Shore YMCA Live Y'ers

P.O. Box Y   203-399-9622
Westbrook, CT 06498

Valerie Moore

Program describes music, arts and crafts, swimming, hiking, sports, games, nature study, archery and overnight campouts.

5448   Wilderness Challenge

The Wheeler Clinic
91 Northwest Drive   203-747-6801
Plainville, CT 06062

Phil Colston

A three week program offering therpetic outdoor education programs which include a variety of non-competitive group games and activities.

Florida

5449 Camp Chanyahah

Route Box 242
Arcadia, FL 33821

813-494-4917

Founded in 1964, campers here are mainstreamed with regular campers: serves children with learning disabilities.

Georgia

5450 Camp Howard

Rabun Gap, GA 30568

404-377-7436

Pamela Helms

Camp Howard is designed for children of average intelligence with specific learning problems.

5451 Squirrel Hollow, Inc.

1831 Walker Avenue
College Park, GA 30337

404-762-7896

Betsy E. Box, Director

Located in East Point, Georgia, this camp serves children ages 6-17 with specific learning disabilities and/or Attention Deficit Disorder. Held in Atlanta Christian College in East Point with 1-week at Unicoi State Park. Staff/student ratio of 1:2. Tutoring in language arts, math, auditory discrimination, social values, word processing and physical education.

Illinois

5452 Western Du Page Special Recreation Association

671 Crescent Blvd.
Glen Ellyn, IL 60137

708-790-9370

Jane Hodgkinson, Executive Director
Peg Wilson, Superintendent

Offers year-round services to special residents of its eight member communities.

Indiana

5453 Worthmore Academy

609 East 29th Street
Indianapolis, IN 46205

317-925-2101

Serving children with dyslexia, this camp offers a six week summer program, providing one-to-one tutoring in reading, writing, spelling and arithmetic.

Maine

5454 Camp Waban

Waban's Projects, Inc.
RR 1, Box 2405
Sanford, ME 04073

207-324-7955

Gervaise Fecteau, Program Director

Boating, swimming, arts and crafts, music, creative crafts and special events.

Maryland

5455 Camp Stonehenge

Chevy Chase, MD

301-652-0760

Located in Maryland, this camp combines academics and recreation.

Massachusetts

5456 Camp Calumet Lutheran

New England Synod
90 Madison Street #303
Worcester, MA 01608

603-539-4773

Don Johnson, Program Director

Offers swimming, crafts, volleyball and more.

5457 Camp Favorite

Patriots' Trail Girl Scout Council, Inc.
985 Berkeley Street
Boston, MA 02116

617-482-1078

Canoeing, swimming, windsurfing, life saving, sailing, biking and trips.

5458 Camp Freedom

Nichols House
Harvard University
Cambridge, MA 02138

Serves learning disabled boys and girls.

5459 Camp Holiday

Everett Recreation Center
Elm Street
Everett, MA 02149

617-394-2390

Flora Formosi, Program Director

Arts and crafts, physical fitness and more.

5460 Camp Joy

C/O Boston Community Schools
1010 Massachuseets Ave.
Boston, MA 02174

617-725-3469

Ed Nazzaro, Program Director

Therapeutic recreational activities, field trips and more.

5461   Camp Lapham

South Road   617-386-5633
Ashby, MA 01431

Kathy Lozano, Program Director
Many recreational activities with mainstreaming available.

5462   Camp Polywog

Malden YMCA
83 Pleasant Street   617-324-7680
Malden, MA 02148

Robert Fiske, Program Director
Offers a gym, swimming, city tours and more.

5463   Camp Ramah

New England Tikvah Program
Round Pond   413-283-9771
Palmer, MA 01069

Sleep-away camp with an integrated program of special education in Judaica.

5464   Camp Reach

422 Summer Street   617-641-5492
Arlington, MA 02174   FAX 617-641-5495

Andrea McKenney, Program Director
Swimming, arts and crafts, games, fieldtrips and special events.

5465   Camp Rice-Moody

Patriots' Trail Girl Scout Council, Inc.
95 Berkeley Street   617-482-1078
Boston, MA 02116

Hdonna Gibson, Program Director
Offers many different programs including discoverers, explorers, entertainers, day trippers, rainbow of cultures and more.

5466   Camp Six Acres

475 Winthrop Street   617-391-2220
Medford, MA 02155

Roz Abukasis, Program Director
Offers swimming, athletics, arts and crafts, preschool program and extended day programs.

5467   Camp Vacations

P.O. Box 740   508-778-1810
W. Hyannisport, MA 02672

Kathleen Kelly, Program Director
Community-based, normalized program with mainstrewaming available.

5468   Camp Wing-Duxbury Stockade

742 Keene Street   617-837-6144
Duxbury, MA 02332

Mike Lazano, Program Director
Boating, swimming, sports, nature classes, arts and crafts and more.

5469   The Carroll School Summer Program

Baker Bridge Road, Box 280   617-259-8342
Lincoln, MA 01773

Catherine Callahan
One-to-one and small-group tutoring in reading, math, spelling, vocabulary, handwriting and study skills is available to students not achieving their potential.

5470   Eagle Hill School

Old Petersham Road   413-477-6000
Hardwick, MA 01037

George Thomson
For the child with a specific learning disability, this summer program offers a structured curriculum designed to build a basic foundation of academic competence. Extracurricular and outdoor activities.

5471   Half Moon Camps, Inc.

P.O. Box 188   413-528-0940
East Barrington, MA 02130

Edward Mann, Director
Sleep-away camp offering sports, creative arts and clubs.

5472   Kolburne School Camp

Southfield Road   413-229-8787
New Marlborough, MA 02130

Jeane Weinstein
Offers an academic and camp program for those with learning, emotional and social problems.

5473   Landmark Summer School

Landmark School
412 Hale Road   508-927-4440
Prides Crossing, MA 01965   FAX 508-927-7268

Meryl Doherty, Admissions Director
A coed, residential and day, six-week summer program for emotionally stable students who have been diagnosed as having a learning disability or dyslexia.

$ 3050.00

5474 Tower Program At Regis College

235 Wellesley Street   617-893-1820
Weston, MA 02193

S. Marilyn MacGregor

The TOWER Program helps average and above-average college-bound students, having a diagnosed dyslexic learning disability, to adjust to a college setting. Daily outdoor challenge activities are offered.

5475 Tufts University Summer Learning Program

108 Packard Street   617-381-3568
Medford, MA 02155

Gabriella Goldstein

This program is designed for students who wish to improve writing, spelling, organizational and study skills, or attention span. Offers a full sports program with swimming and sailing.

5476 Valleyhead

Box 714   413-637-3635
Lenox, MA 01240

Matthew Merritt, Jr.

A program of remediation and retraining is designed to help girls with specific learning and emotional problems, with emphasis on the basic skills of math.

5477 Zoo Camp

Council for Greater Boston Camp Fire
380 Green Street   617-876-9800
Cambridge, MA 02139

Peggy Burke, Program Director

Emphasis is on learning about animals and the environment through arts and crafts, drama small group activities and free play.

Michigan

5478 Camp Fowler

2315 Harmon Lake Blvd.   517-673-3666
Mayville, MI 48744   FAX 517-673-5865

Al Breidenbach, Executive Director
Stephen Gredine, Director

36 years of camping programs for campers with special needs and their families and friends. Some of the camping programs offered include; backpacking, camping, nature education, arts and crafts, sports, swimming, boating, hiking, dancing and activity workshops. Offers social skills training, cooking, life and daily skills and more for the learning disabled, autistic and head injured campers.

5479 Camp Gitchimich

8789 Williams Road   517-467-7711
DeWitt, MI 48820

This one week residential summer camping program has been developed to create a better self-image and an improved feeling of self-worth for youths with learning and adjustment problems.

5480 Camp Night of the Pines

Methodist Children's Home
26645 West Six Mile Road   313-531-4060
Detroit, MI 48240

Jane Scheff

For learning disabled and emotionally impaired youngsters.

5481 Camp Niobe

19620 Cherry Hill   313-540-9329
Southfield, MI 48076

Joanne Mandel, Director

A five week summer resident camp program for boys and girls whose learning and behavior styles have made successful participation in the traditional camp program difficult. Emphasis is on creative arts, outdoor living skills and developing social skills.

5482 Grand Valley State University Summer Camp

121 AuSable Hall
Allendale, MI 49401

Dr. Jame O. Grant, Director

This program is designed for persons who have learning disabilities.

Minnesota

5483 Camp Buckskin

3811 West Broadway   612-536-9749
Minneapolis, MN 55422

Thomas Bauer, CCD, Assistant Director

Buckskin operates a therapeutic summer program for youth with ADD/ADHD and related difficulties. We have two 32 day sessions which utilize a combination of traditional camp activities and academics to develop self confidence and improves self esteem. Ample numbers of staff provide individualized instruction and attention. The program is supportive, yet provides adequate structure to improve social skills, particularly peer realtions.

5484 Chi Rho Camp

Route 1, Box 274   612-827-4406
Annandale, MN 55302

Clair Lohmann, Camp Director

For learning disabled students who have completed third, fourth or fifth grade.

5485 Confidence Learning Center

6260 Mary Fawcett Memorial Drive   218-828-2344
Brainerd, MN 56401   FAX 218-828-2618

Edward Scinto, Executive Director
Jeff Olson, Camp Director

A nonprofit organization that provides year-round education and camping services FREE-OF-CHARGE for the mentally retarded and developmentally disabled. The Center offers services and facilities to over 3,000 citizens of all ages from Minnesota and surrounding states. The camp provides cabins for year-round housing and is open seven days a week year-round.

5486 Creative Options

C/O Friendship Ventures
10509 108th Street NW   612-274-8376
Annandale, MN 55302   FAX 612-274-3238

Offers sports and games, crafts, dancing, music, biking, hiking, fishing, campfires, paddle boats, haywagon rides, canoeing, sledding, snowmobiling, ice fishing, ice skating and cross-country skiing.

5487 Groves Learning Center

3200 Highway 100 South   612-920-6377
St. Louis Park, MN 55416

Sue Kirchhoff, MEd

Offers diagnostic testing, speech and language counseling, summer school and day school.

5488 Learning and Language Specialists

1405 Lilac Drive, Ste. 200   612-545-7708
Minneapolis, MN 55422

Childrens groups, teen groups and parent groups.

Missouri

5489 Camp Happy Day

6493 Rhodes Avenue   314-332-0289
St. Louis, MO 63109

Jane Hannekan, Executive Director

This unique 6-7 week summer program is specifically designed to meet the needs of the Learning Disabled, Behaviorally Disordered and Attention Deficit Disordered Students.

Montana

5490 Spring Creek Community Summer Programs

1342 Blue Slide Road   406-827-4344
Thompson Falls, MT 59873

Dusti Scovel

The curriculum is a year-round wilderness school including therapy, academics, community service and a strong element of survival training.

Nebraska

5491 Project Explore Summer Camp

12001 Douglas   404-334-1677
Omaha, NE 68154

D'Arcy Goodrich, Coordinator

Specifically designed for children with communication, social, coordination or other learning disabilities who have average or above average potential without primary emotional or behavioral problems.

5492 Seraaj Family Homes Summer Camp - Lewistown

4924 Evans Street
Omaha, NE 68104

Abdul Seraaj, Director

This camp is available to youth from multi-cultural backgrounds and handicapped youth.

5493 Star Chapter ACLD - Annual Summer Camp

Rt. 1, Box 164   402-551-5292
Gretna, NE 68028

Mary Milota

Especially designed for those with communication, social, coordination or other learning disability problems.

New Hampshire

5494 Camp Runels

Little Island Road   603-635-2366
Pelham, NH 03076

Nancy Hartman, Program Director

General camping aquatics, arts, drama, hiking, sailing and more.

5495 Hampshire County - Summer Program

Rindge, NH 03461   603-889-3325

Peter Ray

Offers therapeutic camping.

New York

5496   Camp Cummings

The Educational Alliance
197 East Broadway   212-475-6061
New York, NY 10002

LOEB specialized service camp, back to nature camps and vacation programs.

5497   Camp Huntington

56 Bruceville Road   914-687-7840
High Falls, NY 12440

A co-ed residential camp for learning disabled, ADD and neurologically impaired.

5498   Camp Northwood

10 West 66th Street   212-799-4089
New York, NY 10023

Jim Rein, Director

A seven week overnight camp for children with learning disabilities.

5499   Dunnabeck At Kildonan

RR 1, Box 294   914-373-8111
Amenia, NY 12501

Diana King

Dunnabeck specializes in helping intelligent children with specific reading, writing and spelling disabilities. Camp activities include windsurfing and rock climbing.

5500   Gow Summer Programs

Emery Road   716-652-3450
South Wales, NY 14139   800-322-4691
                                         FAX 716-652-3457

Michael P. Holland, Director
J. William Adams, Headmaster

A co-educational, well-balanced programs combining morning academics, afternoon traditional camping activities and weekend overnight trips. The weekly program is a blend of structure and focus with flexibility and choice. The purpose of the the summer programs is to develop the skills and natural abilities of each camper student, while encouraging a sense of enthusiasm and positive self image.

5501   Northwood

Remsen, NY 13438   212-799-4089

Emphasis is on development of a positive self-image. Remedial work is conducted in language arts and math.

5502   Queens Nyabic - Blue Castle Day Camp

ANIBIC Center
212-12 26th Avenue   718-423-9550
Bayside, NY 11360

John Zielonka, Director
Marsha Owen, President

Children will participate in swimming, sports, music, arts and crafts, trips, all geared to meeting the child's needs.

$ 1250.00

5503   The Summit Camp Program

Summit Camp Program New York Office
339 North Broadway   914-358-7772
Upper Nyack, NY 10960

Mayer Stiskin, Director
Ninette Stiskin, Director

A therapeutic camping program for boys and girls with learning disabilities and/or attention deficit disorders.

5504   Summit Travel Program

Summit Travel
110-45 71st Road, Ste. 1G   718-268-0020
Forest Hills, NY 11375   800-323-9908

Dr. Gil Skyer, Director

Represents the logical extension of the camping program for Young Adults who have outgrown the traditional camping experience, but still require opportunities for structured and supervised social experiences as well as recreational opportunities of a more "adult" nature. This program offers 1,2,3 and 6 week programs of domestic and/or foreign travel.

North Carolina

5505   Camp Loquastee

679 Charles Lane   803-327-5227
Rock Hill, NC 29730

This camp provides a summer school for learning disabled/dyslexic boys and girls.

5506   Camp Winding Gap

Route 1, Box 46   704-966-4520
Lake Toxaway, NC 28747

Marg Shephard

Emphasis on nature, camping and farm chores.

5507   Project SOAR

P.O. Box 388   704-456-3435
Balsam, NC 28707

Jonathan Jones, Executive Director

Emphasis here is success-oriented, high adventure outdoor activities, emphasizing developing self-confidence, peer-interaction, problem solving techniques and willingness to try new things. Course sites include North Carolina, Florida Keys and Colorado.

Ohio

5508   Camp Nuhop

404 Hillcrest Drive   419-289-2227
Ashland, OH 44805

Jerry Dunlap

Founded on the premise that all children thrive when successful. Camp Nuhop centers its activities around developing a positive self-concept in an out-of-doors setting. Emphasis in each individualized camper program is placed on strengths, abilities and talents. There are ten unique programs from which to choose: Exploration Camp, Crusoe Camp, Wilderness Camp, Sports Skills Camp, Acclimatization Camp, Canoe Camp, Bike Camp, Backpack Camp, Sailing Camp and Jr. Leader Camp.

$ 475.00

5509   Exploring Wright Connections

Office Pf Pre-College Programs
140 East Monument Avenue   513-224-9720
Dayton, OH 45402

Elaine Waugh, Asst. Director

A comprehensive series of summer camps for motivated students entering grades K-11.

Oklahoma

5510   Ecology Camp

5436 NE Grand Blvd.   405-427-0144
Oklahoma City, OK 73111

John Preston

Residential outdoor, environmental science program and recreational activities with Camp Classen YMCA camp.

5511   Kamp Paddle Trails

Route 1, Box 210   918-723-3546
Watts, OK 74964

Katherine Pickel

Swimming, canoeing, nature study, arts and crafts, cookouts and overnight campouts to build successful self-esteem in children with dyslexia.

Pennsylvania

5512   Camp Kaleidiscope

200 Camp Hill Road   215-643-4142
Fort Washington, PA 19034

Judy Cooper

Remedial reading, english and mathematics.

5513   Camp Lee Mar

Route 590   717-685-7188
Lackawaxen, PA 18435

Sleep away camp for brain injured children.

5514   Camphill Special Schools

RD 1, Box 240   215-469-9236
Glenmoore, PA 19343

For children with mental handicaps and learning disabilities.

5515   Lee Mar Summer Camp and School

Lackawaxen, PA 18435   717-685-7188

Lee Morrone

This camp for educable mentally retarded and neurologically impaired children has a program of academics, speech therapy, vocational training and recreation.

5516   Phelps School Summer Session

Sugartown Road   215-644-1754
Malvern, PA 19355

Barry Parney, Assoc. Head Master

Enables boys to make up academic deficiencies, complete course requirements, remedial and developmental reading and improve study skills.

5517   Rock Creek Farm

RD 1, Box 53   717-756-2706
Thompson, PA 18465

Bernard Wray

Children with learning disabilities and accompanying difficulties learn to adjust socially in a community atmosphere.

5518   Round Lake

Route 247   717-798-2551
Lake Como, PA 18437

Eugene Bell

Providing individualized academics in reading, language development and math for children with minor learning disabilities. Offers therapeutic recreation, Jewish cultural values and traditional camp activities.

5519   A Summer Experience

Vanguard Middle School
Box 730   215-647-4110
Paoli, PA 19301

For students who are experiencing learning or retention difficulties.

5520 Summer Gain

KLS Educational Systems, Inc.
27 Conestoga Woods Road   814-466-7676
Lancaster, PA 17602

John Salvia, Director

Program provides very intensive academic instruction for about 1 1/2 hours a day for six weeks to learning disabled individuals.

5521 Wesley Woods

RD #1   814-436-7802
Grand Valley, PA 16420

Herb West, Director

Exceptional children's camp for children with emotional or intellectual handicaps.

Texas

5522 Austin Wilderness Counseling Services

1300 West Lynn Street, Ste. 200   512-472-2927
Austin, TX 78703

Nelda Beard

Day camps and wilderness trips for children and adolescents who can benefit from structured activities led by trained counselors.

5523 C.A.M.P., Inc.

P.O. Box 999
Cedar Point, TX 78010

Pat Kozar

Children with medical/physical handicaped that cannot attend any other camps are given first choice.

5524 Camp-I-Can

Brykerwood Community School
3302 Kerby Lane   512-478-2581
Austin, TX 78703

Connie Clark

Day camps geared toward children with special needs, but also with a strong emphasis on mainstreaming.

5525 Dallas Academy - Summer

950 Tiffany Way   214-324-1481
Dallas, TX 75218

Jim Richardson, Director

Provides a seven week summer session for students who are having difficulty in "regular" school classes.

5526 El Paso ACLD Vacation Adventure

8929 Viscount #112   915-591-8080
El Paso, TX 79925

Rosalie Avara

Summer developmental learning program for children currently placed in Special Education.

5527 Girl Scout Camp La Jita

10443 Gulfdale   512-349-2404
San Anotnio, TX 78216

Cathy Ritchie

A mainstream camp, open to children with disabilities.

5528 Rocking L Ranch Camp

Route 6, Box 825   214-560-0246
Wills Point, TX 75169

Charlene Larsen

Residential camp with horseback riding classes, swimming, volleyball and more.

5529 Star Ranch - Summer Program

HCR 7, Box 39C   210-367-4868
Ingram, TX 78025   FAX 210-367-2814

Steve Hamilton, Development Director
Rand Southard, Admin. Director

Operates two programs at Star Ranch. One is a recreational/education summer camp for children with learning differences. Boys and girls ages 7-18 attend one or two week sessions during the summer. Traditional summer camps as well as academic tutoring are offered. The second program is a residential treatment center for boys 7-17 who are diagnosed as learning disabled and emotionally disturbed. Preference is given to younger boys as placement is long term.

5530 Summer Sands Beach Camp

44214 Lexington Avenue   409-962-5805
Port Arthur, TX 77642

Della Borel, Director

Six one-week sessions offering developmental recreation with discovery marine science.

5531 Vacation Adventure Summer Developmental Program

El Paso ACLD, 8929 Viscount #112   915-591-8080
El Paso, TX 79925

Barbara Lino

Utah

5532   Reid Ranch

Winter: Reid Ranch
3310 South 2700 East   801-486-5083
Salt Lake City, UT 84109   800-468-3274
                                       FAX 801-485-0561

Dr. Ethna R. Reid, Director
Dr. Mervin R. Reid, President

Students can have fun while they learn at the Reid Ranch in the Unitach Mountains. This is the 27th year of outstanding achievement gains for students who need to experience success in reading. Teachers at the reid Ranch use teaching techniques developed by Dr. Ethna R. Reid, Director of the Exemplary Center for reading Instruction. These techniques have assured success in learning to read, write and spell for hundreds of students. Students may register for one to four week sof instruction.

$ 125.00

Vermont

5533   Bennington School

19 Fairview Street   802-447-0773
Bennington, VT 05201

Judith Fun

Designed to meet the needs of students with learning disabilities and emotional and/or behavioral problems.

5534   Pine Ridge Summer Program

1075 Williston Road   802-434-2161
Williston, VT 05495

Karen Lyons

The summer session is conducted for students, average or above intelligence and emotionally sound, who have encountered difficulties in school because of specific learning disabilities. Activities, day trips and special events are offered.

Virginia

5535   Oakland School and Camp

Boyd Tavern, VA 22947   804-293-8965

Joanne Dondero

A highly individualized program that stresses improtant and improved reading ability. Subjects taught are reading, English composition, math and word analysis.

Wisconsin

5536   Camp Algonquin

4151 Camp Bryn Afon Road   715-369-1277
Rhinelander, WI 54501

Donald McKinnon, Director

Offers a full recreation program and a reading and learning disability diagnostic and remediation clinic.

5537   Timbertop Nature Adventure Camp

7920 Country MM   715-824-2428
Amherst Junction, WI 54407

For children who can benefit from an individualized program of learning in a non-competitive out-door setting under the skilled leadership of people who understand the environment and the unique potential of these children.

Camp Directories

5538   A Directory of Summer Camps for Children with Learning Disabilities

Learning Disabilities Association of America
4156 Library Road   412-341-1515
Pittsburgh, PA 15234

Offers a full range of listings for the learning disabled.

5539   Learning Disabilities - Guide for Directors of Specialized Camps

Learning Disabilities Association of America
4156 Library Road   412-341-1515
Pittsburgh, PA 15234

5540   Learning Disabled - Camp Directors Guide on Integration

Learning Disabilities Association of America
4156 Library Road   412-341-1515
Pittsburgh, PA 15234

5541   Learning Disabled - Parents Guide to Camping

Learning Disabilities Association of America
4156 Library Road   412-341-1515
Pittsburgh, PA 15234

5542   1993/94 Guide to Accredited Camps

American Camping Association
5000 State Road 67 North   317-342-8456
Martinsville, IN 46151   800-428-2267
                                       FAX 317-342-2065

Over 2,100 of the best camps in the country. Listings of day and residential camps, programming for children, teens, adults, seniors and families. Also listing of site approved facilities that lease their facilities. Special populations listing and activity chart. Articles are also available on finding a job.

5543 Access Expo and Conference

The Fairfield Factor, Inc.
13 Obtuse Rocks Road   203-775-0422
Brookfield, CT 06804

Offers information on the latest technology, assistive devices and more for the disabled.

5544 Adaptive Technology Training

Pugliese, Davey and Associates
5 Bessom Street, Ste. 175   617-639-1930
Marblehead, MA 01945

Information on talking software, toys, keyboard emulators and computer equipment.

5545 AHEAD '93

Association on Higher Education and Disability
P.O. Box 21192   614-488-4972
Columbus, OH 43227

One of the largest gatherings of disability service providers in higher education internationally.

5546 American Association of School Administrators

1801 North Moore Street   703-528-0700
Arlington, VA 22209

5547 American Occupational Therapy Association Convention

1383 Piccard Drive   301-948-9626
Rockville, MD 20850

5548 American Speech-Language-Hearing Association Conference

10801 Rockville Pike   301-897-5700
Rockville, MD 20852

Mona Thomas, Public Relations

Hundreds of sessions for speech-language pathologists and audiologists and speakers on various topics concerned with communication disorders.

5549 ARCA/AACD Convention

AACD Membership Division
5999 Stevenson Avenue   800-347-6647
Alexandria, VA 22304

Offers programs, publications, speakers and workshops in various areas of disability.

5550 Assessing Learning Problems

Learning Disabilities Resources
P.O. Box 716   215-525-8336
Bryn Mawr, PA 19010   800-869-8336

This workshop includes behavioral manifestations of information processing problems and how to relate these to learning processes.

5551 Assistive Device Conference for Students, Parents and Educators

Pennsylvania Assistive Technology Center
6340 Flank Dr., Ste. 600e   717-541-4960
Harrisburg, PA 17112   800-360-7282

5552 Association for Applied Interactive Multimedia Conference

S.C. Board for Technical/Comprehensive Education
111 Executive Center Drive   803-737-9351
Columbia, SC 29210   800-553-7702

Ronald Plemmons, Special Events Dir.

Offers one and three day preconference skill training, half day workshops and 45 to 90 minute concurrent sessions. Exhibits will feature major vendors of hardware, software and services and will be open for all registered conference and preconference workshop attendees.

5553 CACLD Annual Conference

Connecticut Association for Children with LD
18 Marshall Street   203-838-5010
South Norwalk, CT 06854

Offers speakers, workshops, presentations and more for professionals and parents dealing with learning disability in their daily life.

5554 CAST Seminar Series

39 Cross Street   508-531-8555
Peabody, MA 01960

A series of seminars to introduce disabled persons and professionals working with the disabled into using the Macintosh to support learning.

5555 Closing the Gap Conference

P.O. Box 68   612-248-3294
Henderson, MN 56044   FAX 612-248-3810

5556 College Students with Learning Disabilities

Learning Disabilities Resources
P.O. Box 716   215-525-8336
Bryn Mawr, PA 19010   800-869-8336

This workshop is designed to provide both information and motivation to either students of college personnel.

5557 ConnSENSE 93'

University of Connecticut
249 Glenbrook Road U-64   203-486-0165
Storrs, CT 06269

Chauncy Rucker

Annual conference on technology for people with specail needs.

5558 Council for Educational Diagnostic Services Conference

CEDS Topical Conference
6810 Bellaire Drive
New Orleans, LA 70124

Gale Szubinski, Program Chair

5559 Council for Exceptional Children Annual Convention

1920 Association Drive   703-620-3660
Reston, VA 22091

Jamie Casamento

Offers booths on the latest technology for the disabled individual, professional and parents. Offers seminars, workshops, books, assistive devices and more.

5560 Counseling Individuals with Larning Disabilities

Learning Disabilities Resources
P.O. Box 716   215-525-8336
Bryn Mawr, PA 19010   800-869-8336

In this workshop, Dr. Cooper discusses reasons why some individuals with learning disabilities often do respond well to traditional therapies.

5561 Eleventh Annual National Conference, Technology, Reading & Learning

Educational Computer Conferences
1070 Crows Nest Way   510-222-1249
Richmond, CA 94083

5562 F.A.T. City

Connecticut Association for Children with LD
18 Marshall Street   203-838-5010
South Norwalk, CT 06854   FAX 203-866-6108

Nationally acclaimed workshop designed to sensitize adults to the frustration, anxiety and tension that the learning disabled child experiences daily.

5563 Foreign-Language Learning and Learning Disabilities Conference

English Language Institute/American University
4400 Massachusetts Avenue NW   202-885-2147
Washington, DC 20016

Robin Schwarz, Coordinator

5564 Fourth New England Joint Conference on Specific Learning Disabilities

Linda C. Downer
340 Foster Street   508-682-6154
North Andover, MA 01845   FAX 508-682-4351

A dynamic, informative conference with the goal being to improve services for language/learning-disabled individuals by encouraging dialogue among the many disciplines, organizations and professions involved in the field of learning disabilities.

5565 Handicapped Student Program Postsecondary Education Association

Box 21192   614-488-4972
Columbus, OH 43221

Jane Jarrow, Executive Director

5566 Independence Center for Young Adults with Learning Disabilities

11600 Nebel Street, Ste. 200   301-468-8810
Rockville, MD 20852

Offers evening workshops and fall services to the learning disabled.

5567 Innovative Instructional Techniques

Learning Disabilities Resources
P.O. Box 716   215-525-8336
Bryn Mawr, PA 19010   800-869-8336

In this workshop, Dr. Cooper provides an overview of the various techniques he has developed for helping students with learning problems in reading, writing, spelling and math.

5568 Interest Driven Learning

71 Laurie Circle   901-668-5812
Jackson, TN 38305   800-354-2950

Offers workshops, on-site training and software for the learning disabled and professionals working with the learning disabled.

5569 International Counseling Center "Preparing for the Future"

3000 Connecticut Avenue, Ste. 438   202-483-0700
Washington, DC 20008

5570 International Medical Device Expo & Conference

SEMCO Medical Expositions
1130 Hightower Trail   404-998-9800
Atlanta, GA 30350

5571 International Reading Association Convention

800 Barksdale Road   302-731-1600
Newark, DE 19714   FAX 302-731-1057

Offers the latest in educational programs and materials.

5572   International Society for Augmentative and Alternative Communication

A.I. duPont Institute
P.O. Box 269   302-651-6830
Wilmington, DE 19899

5573   Language Learning and Learning Disabilities Conference

The Orton Dyslexia Society
8600 LaSalle Road   410-296-0232
Baltimore, MD 21204   800-222-3123

Teaching Spanish using the Orton-Gillingham technique.

5574   LDA International Conference

1993 LDA Conference
4156 Library Road   412-341-1515
Pittsburgh, PA 15234

Frank Kline

This conference offers bridges into basic information regarding learning disabilities such as: definitions, how to obtain services and current issues in the field. Provides opportunities to make contacts with respected professionals and parents from all across the nation and several other countries. This conference offers a full array of information, provocative and interactive sessions including 12 topical workshops dealing with a variety of subjects.

5575   Learning Disabilities and the World of Work

Learning Disabilities Resources
P.O. Box 716   215-525-8336
Bryn Mawr, PA 19010   800-869-8336

This workshop is designed for employers, parents or professionals working with individuals with learning disabilities.

5576   Learning Disabilities Network Annual Spring Conference

72 Sharp Street, Ste. A-2   617-340-5605
Hingham, MA 02043   FAX 617-340-5603

Polly Cowen, Administrative Dir.
Cynthia Christopher, Asst. Director

4 day conference covering all aspects of learning disabilities.

5577   Learning Problems and Adult Basic Education

Learning Disabilities Resources
P.O. Box 716   215-525-8336
Bryn Mawr, PA 19010   800-869-8336

This workshop for adult educators discusses the manifestations of learning problems in adults.

5578   Linkages Conference

Illinois State University
Normal, IL 61761   209-438-3627

Toni McCarty

5579   Mainstreaming Students with Learning Disabilities

Learning Disabilities Resources
P.O. Box 716   215-525-8336
Bryn Mawr, PA 19010   800-869-8336

This workshop provides teachers with practical suggestions and techniques for mainstreaming students with learning problems.

5580   Minspeak Conference

Minspeal Conference Coordinator
1022 Heyl Road   800-262-1984
Wooster, OH 44691

Offers a primary focus on the latest in technology, mainstreaming, support groups and classroom devices for the disabled learner.

5581   National Adolescent Conference: Programs for Adolescents - Learning Disabled

Institute for Adolescents with Behavioral Disorder
1153 Benton Way   612-627-3175
Arden Mills, MN 55112

Information on programs for the developmental needs of adolescents with behavioral disorders.

5582   National Educational Computing Conference

P.O. Box 5155   817-565-3983
Denton, TX 76203

5583   National Symposium on Information Technology

University of South Carolina
Benson Bldg., 1st Floor   803-777-4435
Columbia, SC 29208   FAX 803-777-6058

Donna Lesse

5584   Non-Conference for Adaptive Technologists

Veterans Hospital
Blind Center, 124   708-531-7966
Hines, IL 60141

5585 **11th Annual TRLD Conference/Technology, Reading & Learning Difficulties**

ECC
1070 Crows Nest Way   510-222-1249
Richmond, CA 94803   800-255-2218

Diane Frost

Offers featured speakers, 100 workshops, sessions, special events and specific, practical use of technology in special education.

5586 **1993 Technology Fair Exhibition for Human DisAbilities**

George Mason University
4400 University Drive   703-993-3670
Fairfax, VA 22030

Annette Carr

5587 **Partners for Independence: the North American Concept of Rehabilitation**

U.S. Council on International Rehabilitation
1825 I Street NW, Ste. 400   202-429-2706
Washington, DC 20006

Offers information for professionals in the areas of rehabilitation research, assistive technology and more.

5588 **PDA Adaptive Technology Institutes**

Pugliese, Davey and Associates
5 Bessom Street   617-639-1930
Marblehead, MA 01945

Offers computer lab courses for Apple IIGS and Macintosh LC.

5589 **Project ACTT: Activating Children Through Technology**

Western Illinois University
27 Horrabin Hall   309-298-1014
Macomb, IL 61455

A technology conference for parents, teachers and other professionals working with young children with disabilities.

5590 **Remember the Past...Celebrate the Future**

TAM 93' - Special Education Resource Center
25 Industrial Park Road   203-638-4265
Middletown, CT 06547

5591 **Second Annual Conference on Multimedia in Education & Industry**

State Board of Technical & Comprehensive Education
111 Executive Center Drive   803-737-9351
Columbia, SC 29210   800-553-7702

Created to support professionals using and developing interactive multimedia.

5592 **Serving College Students with Learning Disabilities**

University of Connecticut/A.J. Pappanikou Center
U-64 Glenbrook Rd.   203-486-0163
Storrs, CT 06269

Patricia Anderson, Coordinator

This three-and-a-half day training institute is specifically designed for postsecondary learning disabled service providers, administrators and faculty, educational consultants and counselors. The focus of the Institute is to help concerned professionals meet the specialized needs of college students with learning disabilities. participants will be able to select from a variety of strands. Each strand will meet three times during the Institute to provide participants with in-depth info..

5593 **Seventh Annual National Symposium on Information Technology**

Center for the Developmentally Disabled
U.S.C. Benson Bldg., 1st Floor   803-777-4435
Columbia, SC 29208

Donna Lesser

5594 **So You Know the ADA: Now What? Conference**

Mainstream, Inc.
#3 Bethesda Metro Center, Ste. 830   301-654-2400
Besthesda, MD 20814

Offers information on the ADA, books, resources, videos, presentations for professionals and more.

5595 **Social Skills**

Learning Disabilities Resources
P.O. Box 716   215-525-8336
Bryn Mawr, PA 19010   800-869-8336

This workshop can be directed to individuals with learning disabilities, parents or professionals.

5596 **Speech and Language Technology for Disabled Persons**

Royal Institute of Technology
Box 70014, S-100 44   46-8-7906000
Stockholm, Sweden

Bjorn Granstrom

5597 Speech Communication Association

5105 Backlick Road, Bldg. E   703-750-0533
Annandale, VA 22003

5598 Stimulating Learning Through Mobility and Communication Technology

Children's Specialized Hospital
150 New Providence Road   908-233-3720
Mountainside, NJ 07092

Salley Comey

5599 Success with Technology: Transforming Learning for Special Needs Students

Macro International, Inc.
8630 Fenton Street, Ste. 300   FAX 301-585-3180
Silver Spring, MD 20910

A video teleconference.

5600 Taking Charge: Full Inclusion in California Schools

City Community Services
1346 Foothill Blvd., Ste. 301   818-952-2489
La Canada, CA 91011

Richard Rosenberg

5601 TAM Conference on Special Education and Technology

Center for Human disAbilities
4400 University Drive   703-993-3670
Fairfax, VA 22030

Chauncy Rucker, Conference Chair

110 presentations by educators and leaders in the field of special education technology, exhibits of new developments and poster sessions by fellow educators. Offers demonstrations and hands-on experience with technology applications for people with disabilities.

5602 Teacher Training Workshop

Learning Disabilities Resources
P.O. Box 716   215-525-8336
Bryn Mawr, PA 19010   800-869-8336

This two hour workshop provides teachers with instruction in Tic Tac Toe Math and how to teach it.

5603 Teaching Math

Learning Disabilities Resources
P.O. Box 716   215-525-8336
Bryn Mawr, PA 19010   800-869-8336

A workshop for teachers on how to teach math to individuals with learning problems.

5604 Teaching Reading

Learning Disabilities Resources
P.O. Box 716   215-525-8336
Bryn Mawr, PA 19010   800-869-8336

This workshop explains how to teach indviduals with reading problems, dyslexia, ADD, and specific learning disabilities.

5605 Teaching Spelling

Learning Disabilities Resources
P.O. Box 716   215-525-8336
Bryn Mawr, PA 19010   800-869-8336

Spelling is a problem which directly affects an individual's ability to write.

5606 Transition Into Tomorrow's Workplace, Education & Employing the Disabled

Intermediate District 287
1820 Xenium Lane   800-345-3655
North Plymouth, MN 55441

Jane Kist

5607 Voice '93

Medical Expositions
1130 Hightower Trail   404-641-8181
Atlanta, GA 30350

Offers information on assistive technology for the learning disabled and visually impaired.

5608 What Are Learning Disabilities, Problems and Differences

Learning Disabilities Resources
P.O. Box 716   215-525-8336
Bryn Mawr, PA 19010   800-869-8336

In this workshop, Dr. Cooper draws on personal experiences with a learning disability and on his clinical work with thousands of individuals with a wide variety of learning problems to provide the participants with an understanding of the positive and negative aspects of being living and learning different.

5609 With a Little Help From Our Friends

Federation for Children with Special Needs
95 Berkeley Street, Ste. 104   617-482-2915
Boston, MA 02116   800-331-0688

A statewide conference for parents of children with special needs, regular and special educators and other friends.

5610 **Young Adult Institute**
Conference on Developmental
Disabilities
YAI
460 West 34th Street   212-563-7474
New York, NY 10001

Nicole Landon

5611 Academic Year Abroad

Howard Edrice, Author
International Education
809 United Nations Plaza
New York, NY 10017

Describes over 18,000 study abroad programs, at both the undergraduate and graduate levels, conducted during the academic year by US colleges and universities in some 60 countries around the world.

$ 29.95

5612 American Institute for Foreign Study

100 Greenwich Avenue   203-625-0755
Greenwich, CT 06830

Anthony Cook, Executive Director

Provides summer travel programs overseas and in the US ranging from one week to a full academic year.

5613 American Universities International Program

Colorado University
Aylesworth Hall   303-491-5917
Fort Collins, CO 80523

100 colleges and universities throughout the USA and Canada participate in theis student exchange program.

5614 American-Scandinavian Foundation

725 Park Avenue   212-879-9779
New York, NY 10021

Jean Prahl, Executive Director

Offers young US citizens the opportunity ot live in Scandinavia and train in their professional field.

5615 Association for International Practice Training

10 Corporate Center, Ste. 250
Columbis, MD 21044

Robert Sprinkle, Executive Director

Non-profit organization dedicated to encouraging and facilitating the exchange of qualified individuals between the US and other countries so they may gain practical work experience.

5616 Basic Facts on Study Abroad

Barbara Cahn, Author
International Education
809 United Nations Plaza
New York, NY 10017

Information book including foreign study planning, educational choices, finances and study abroad programs.

$ 35.00

5617 CDS International

425 Park Avenue   212-593-3030
New York, NY 10022

John Early, Director

Provides exchange programs between the US and the Federal Republic of Germany. The programs combine language training with the opportunity for practical on-the-job training for up to a year and a half.

5618 Earthstewards Network

P.O. Box 10697   206-842-7986
Bainbridge, WA 98110

Diana Glasgow, Director

Hundreds of active, caring people in the US, Canada and other countries. Puts North American teenagers working alongside Northern Irish teenagers and more.

5619 Educational Foundation for Foreign Study

One Memorial Drive   617-494-0122
Cambridge, MA 02142

Offers an opportunity to study and live for a year in a foreign country for students between the ages of 15 and 18.

5620 Friends World College

Plover Lane   516-549-1102
Huntington, NY 11743

Arthur Meyer

Encourages people to "treat the world as a university, to make the most urgent human problems as their curriculum, to seek designs for a more humane future and to consider all of humanity as their ultimate loyalty".

5621 Friendship Force, Inc.

5755 South Omni International   404-522-9490
Atlanta, GA 30303

David Luria

Private, non-profit exchange program for persons of all ages and backgrounds.

5622 Higher Education Consortium of Urban Affairs

Hamline University   612-646-8831
St. Paul, MN 55104

Sherry Dunn

Organization of 17 midwest colleges and universities offering undergraduate opportunities for international and domestic field study internships.

5623 International Education Forum

P.O. Box 5107   415-866-9696
San Ramon, CA 94583

Brigitte Larin

Believes in building a foundation for world peace and international cooperation through direct, interpersonal relationshps between young people and families.

5624 International Summerstays

520 SW 6th, Ste. 800   503-274-1776
Portland, OR 97204

Offers summer homestays in a different country for teenagers from the US, Spain, Germany and Ireland.

5625 International University Partnerships

University of Pennsylvania
103E Keith Annex   412-357-2295
Indiana, PA 15705

Dr. Robert Morris

Offers a variety of international educational exchange programs to students who wish to study overseas.

5626 Lions Club International Youth Exchange

300 West 22nd Street   312-571-5466
Oak Brook, IL 60570

Audrey VanStockum

Provides international exchange programs to young adults for more than 80 countries.

5627 The Lisle Fellowship

433 West Sterns Road   313-847-7126
Temperance, MI 48182

Educational organization which works toward world peace and better quality of human life through increased understanding between persons of similar and different cultures.

5628 National Society for Internships

3509 Haworth Drive, Ste. 207   919-787-3263
Raleigh, NC 27609

Sally Migilore

National non-profit organization which advocates experimental learning and exchange programs.

5629 No Barriers to Study

Lock Haven University
Lock Haven, PA 17745
     717-893-2157

Dr. Peter Matthews

Offers opportunities fo disabled students to study in Anglo-US academic programs.

5630 Open Door Student Exchange

250 Fulton, P.O. Box 71   516-486-7330
Hempstead, NY 11511   800-366-OPEN

Provides exchanges for high school students in 33 countries.

5631 People to People International

501 East Armour Blvd.   816-531-4701
Kansas City, MO 64109

Alan Warner

Non-political, non-profit organization working outside the government to advance the cause of international understanding through international contact.

5632 Rotary International Youth Exchange

1600 Ridge Avenue
Evanston, IL 60201

Run by volunteers so that students must apply through local Rotary Clubs and District chapters.

5633 United States Information Agency

301 4th Street SW   207-485-2556
Washington, DC 20547

Programs are designed to increase mutual understanding between the people of the US and the people of other countries.

5634 Vermont Overseas Study Program

513 Waterman Building   802-656-1366
Burlington, VT 05405

Kate Perry

Program of studies at the University of Nice, France administered by the Department of Romance Languages and the University of Vermont.

5635 World Experience

2440 S. Hacienda Blvd., Ste. 116   818-336-3638
Hacienda Heights, CA 91745   800-633-6653

Non-profit organization which sponsors, develops and carries out international student exchange programs for study and service abroad.

5636 Youth for Understanding International

3501 Newark Street NW   800-USA-0200
Washington, DC 20016

One of the largest and oldest non-profit international exchange programs for high school students is dedicated to international understanding and world peace.

5637 Adult Basic Education and General Educational Development Programs

Free Library of Philadelphia
919 Walnut Street   215-925-3213
Philadelphia, PA 19107   800-222-1754
For disabled adults.

5638 Adult Learning

American Assoc. for Adult & Continuing Education
2101 Wilson Blvd., Ste. 925   202-463-6333
Arlington, VA 22201

Janet Smith, Editor

Contains articles relevant to adults with special learning needs as well as information useful to those who educate the learning disabled.

$ 27.00

5639 Adult Literacy Education: Program Evaluation and Learner Assessment

Susan Lytle, Author

Center on Education and Training for Employment
1900 Kenny Road   614-292-4353
Columbus, OH 43210   800-848-4815

Provides information to shape the design of evaluation, beginning with considerations of adults as learners, concepts of literacy and educational contexts.

$ 8.75

5640 Another Chance - the Comprehensive Learning Program for Adults with LD

HEATH Resource Center
One Dupont Circle NW, Ste. 800   202-939-9320
Washington, DC 20036   800-544-3284

An account of a model program designed to meet the educational needs of adults with learning disabilities.

$ 13.50

5641 Education's Castaways - Literacy Problems of Learning Disabled Adults

Helen Girandes, Author

Connecticut Association for Children with LD
18 Marshall Street   203-838-5010
South Norwalk, CT 06854   FAX 203-866-6108

$ 7.50

5642 Ends Or Means: An Overview of the History of the Adult Education Act

Amy D. Rose, Author

Center on Education and Training for Employment
1900 Kenny Road   614-292-4353
Columbus, OH 43210   800-848-4815

A review of 25 years of federal funding for adult education demonstrates the AEA's instrumental role in the growth of adult basic education in the United States.

$ 5.25

5643 Family and Intergenerational Literacy Programs

Ruth Nickse, Author

Center on Education and Training for Employment
1900 Kenny Road   614-292-4353
Columbus, OH 43210   800-848-4815

Depicts the context of family and intergenerational literacy, examines an interdisciplinary research base and describes existing programs.

$ 8.75

5644 The Hidden Problem - a Guide to Saving the Problem of Literacy

Learning Disabilities Association of America
4156 Library Road   412-341-1515
Pittsburgh, PA 15234

5645 It's Never to Late

N. Star, Author

Connecticut Association for Children with LD
18 Marshall Street   203-838-5010
South Norwalk, CT 06854   FAX 203-866-6108

Gives details of a program which tries to teach adults with learning disabilities how to improve their social communication skills.

5646 Laubach Literacy Action

P.O. Box 131   315-422-9121
Syracuse, NY 13210

The largest network of adult literacy programs in the United States. The programs provide literacy instruction through the use of trained volunteers.

5647 Learning and Reality: Reflections on Trends in Adult Learning

Gary J. Conti, Author

Center on Education and Training for Employment
1900 Kenny Road   614-292-4353
Columbus, OH 43210   800-848-4815

Observes the focus of the adult education field.

$ 5.25

5648 National Association for Adults with Special Learning Needs

Wallingford Adult Education
Hope Hill Road   203-294-5933
Wallingford, CT 06492

5649 National Network of Learning Disabled Adults

P.O. Box 32611   602-941-5112
Phoenix, AZ 85064

Bill Butler, Newsletter Editor

A clearinghouse that helps learning disabled adults find and network with each other in their communities.

5650 PLUS Research

WQED
4802 Fifth Avenue   412-622-1335
Pittsburgh, PA 15213   FAX 412-622-3443

Herb Stein, Author

This group seeks to address the issue of adult literacy problems.

5651 Project Enhance

Minneapolis Public Schools Community Education
1006 West Lake Street   612-627-2925
Minneapolis, MN 55408

Manny Boeser

An outreach and integration services serving adults with disabilities.

5652 The Rebus Institute

198 Taylor Blvd., Ste. 201   415-697-7424
Millbrae, CA 94030

A nonprofit research institute devoted to the study and dissemination of information related to adults with learning differences.

5653 Report on Literacy Programs

Business Publishers
951 Pershing Drive   301-587-6300
Silver Spring, MD 20910   800-274-0122
                              FAX 301-585-9075

David Speights, Editor

Focuses on adult literacy programs, legislation, funding and adgencies. Covers all areas of literacy including the learning disabled.

$ 234.00

5654 Resources for Adults with Learning Eisabilities

HEATH Resource Center
One Dupont Circle, Ste. 800   202-939-9320
Washington, DC 20036

5655 The Right to Read and Write: a Guide to Literacy and People with a Handicap

L'institute Roeher Institute
York University, 4700 Keele Street   416-661-9611
North York, Ontario, M3 J 1P3   FAX 416-661-5701

This book talks about reading and giving more people the chance to learn how to read including the disabled.

5656 Trends and Issues in Adult Education

Susan Imel, Author

Center on Education and Training for Employment
1900 Kenny Road   614-292-4353
Columbus, OH 43210   800-848-4815

Reviews two groups of trends and issues in adult education.

$ 4.75

Classroom Materials

5657 Ability Magazine

Jobs Information Business Service
1682 Langley   714-854-8700
Irvine, CA 92714   800-453-JOBS

Provides an electronic classified system which allows employers to recruit qualified individuals with disabilities, and people with disabilities to locate employment opportunities.

5658 After School...Then What? the Transition to Adulthood

Susan Lehr, Author

Federation for Children with Special Needs
95 Berkeley Street, Ste. 104   617-482-2915
Boston, MA 02116   800-331-0688

This monograph offers four sections including information and suggestions about when and how to plan for transition; to find adult services, including vocational rehabilitation; to evaluate programs and to form a transition planning team.

$ 5.00

5659 Alpha/Numerical Work Samples

Edmark Corporation
P.O. Box 3218   206-746-3900
Redmond, WA 98073   800-362-2890

Teaches basic clerical skills with work related exercises.

$ 110.00

5660 Articulation Models for Vocational Education

Mary Robertson-Smith, Author

Center on Education and Training for Employment
1900 Kenny Road   614-292-4353
Columbus, OH 43210   800-848-4815

Highlights the vital role of articulations in vocational education today.

$ 5.25

5661 Basic Hand Tools

Edmark Corporation
P.O. Box 3218   206-746-3900
Redmond, WA 98073   800-362-2890

Develops transitional skills through safe and correct use of hand tools.

$ 189.95

5662 The Bottom Line: Basic Skills in the Workplace

U.S. Department of Labor
200 Constitution Ave. NW, Rm.   202-535-0236
52307
Washington, DC 20210

Discusses the issues of meeting basic literacy needs and meeting them within the context of employment.

5663 Career Awareness Plus

Edmark Corporation
P.O. Box 3218   206-746-3900
Redmond, WA 98073   800-362-2890

Prepares students for entry level jobs.

$ 63.80

5664 Career Development for Exceptional Individuals

The Council for Exceptional Children
1920 Association Drive   703-620-3660
Reston, VA 22091

Articles on career awareness, exploration, preparation and assimilation for exceptional individuals of all ages.

$ 7.00

5665 Career Education for Handicapped Individuals

Charles Kokaska, Author

Books on Special Children
P.O. Box 305   914-638-1236
Congers, NY 10920   FAX 914-638-0847

Offers a way for the professional and business sector to become familiar with education, daily living skills and occupational abilities.

$ 55.00

5666 Career Planner: a Guide for Students with Disabilities

Learning Disabilities Association of America
4156 Library Road   412-341-1515
Pittsburgh, PA 15234

5667 Career Skills

Edmark Corporation
P.O. Box 3218   206-746-3900
Redmond, WA 98073   800-362-2890

This comprehensive program contains ten units designed to prepare students for jobs.

$ 99.50

5668 Careers and the Handicapped

Equal Opportunity Publications, Inc.
44 Broadway   516-261-8899
Greenlawn, NY 11740

Provides employment and career-oriented information for college graduating and young professionals.

$ 7.00

5669 CDM: the Harrington-O'Shea Career Decision-Making System

AGS
7201 Woodland Road   612-786-4343
Circle Pines, MN 55014   800-328-2560

A comprehensive career interest survey. Administration Time: 20-30 minutes.

5670 Center on Education and Training for Employment

The Ohio State University
1900 Kenny Road   614-292-4353
Columbus, OH 43210   800-848-4815

Offers assessment testing resource,s books and videos on career awareness and employment opportunities for the disabled.

5671 Checklist of Vocational Tips for Young Adults

Learning Consultants, Treehouse Associates
Box 1992   303-949-1088
Avon, CO 61620

Contains concise questions to put a young adult in touch with real strengths and weakness of a person with learning disabilities.

5672 Cognitive Theory-Based Teaching and Learning in Vocational Education

Ruth Thomas, Author

Center on Education and Training for Employment
1900 Kenny Road   614-292-4353
Columbus, OH 43210   800-848-4815

This research review explores the relevance to vocational curriculum and instruction of theories of cognition.

$ 8.75

5673 Collating, Sorting and Filing Program

Edmark Corporation
P.O. Box 3218   206-746-3900
Redmond, WA 98073   800-362-2890

Provides students with simulated on-the-job training.

$ 275.00

5674 Deluxe Transition Skills Center

Edmark Corporation
P.O. Box 3218   206-746-3900
Redmond, WA 98073   800-362-2890

Creates a comprehensive, hands-on job training program.

$ 1613.00

5675 Developing the Functional Use of a Telephone Book

Carol Jorgenson, Author

The Speech Bin
1965 Twenty-Fifth Avenue   407-770-0007
Vero Beach, FL 32960   FAX 407-770-0006

Jan J. Binney, Editor In Chief
Barbara Hector, Office Manager

Motivating activities emphasizing functional living skills: communication, organization and problem-solving to teach adolescents and adults to use phoen books.

$ 24.00

5676 Economics, Industry and Disability William E. Kiernan

Paul H. Brookes Publishing Company
P.O. Box 10624   410-337-8539
Baltimore, MD 21285   800-638-3137

An analysis of the movement toward nonsheltered employment, this book addresses the expanding opportunities and economic changes surrounding efforts of employing the disabled.

$ 42.00

5677 Eden Institute Curriculum, Vocational Education, Volume III

Eden Programs
One Logan Drive   609-987-0099
Princeton, NJ 08540   FAX 609-987-0243

David Holmes, EdD, Executive Director
Anne Holmes, M.S., C.C.C., Outreach Director

Vocationally oriented teaching programs for students with autism.

$ 125.00

5678 ERIC Information Analysis Products

Center on Education and Training for Employment
1900 Kenny Road   614-292-4353
Columbus, OH 43210

Products and books for the improvement of adult, career and vocational education programs.

5679 A Focus on Employability and Career Placement

Learning Disabilities Association of America
4156 Library Road   412-341-1515
Pittsburgh, PA 15234

5680 For Employers...A Look At Learning Disabilities

Learning Disabilities Association of America
4156 Library Road   412-341-1515
Pittsburgh, PA 15234

Helps employers understand learning disabilities.

5681 A Framework for Evaluating Local Vocational Education Programs

N.L. McCaslin, Author

Center on Education and Training for Employment
1900 Kenny Road   614-292-4353
Columbus, OH 43210   800-848-4815

Presents a comprehensive, systematic approach that draws information from the needs for vocational education of students, employers and society.

$ 4.75

5682 Fundamentals of Job Placement

James Costello, Author

RPM Press, Inc.
P.O. Box 31483   602-886-1990
Tucson, AZ 85751

Jan Stonebraker, Operations Manager

Provides step-by-stepo guidance for educators, special counselors and vocational rehabilitation personnel on how to develop job placement opportunities for special needs students and adults.

$ 64.95

5683 Fundamentals of Vocational Assessment

RPM Press, Inc.
P.O. Box 31483   602-886-1990
Tucson, AZ 85751

Jan Stonebraker, Operations Manager

Provides step-by-step guidance for educators, counselors and vocational rehabilitation personnel on how to conduct professional vocational assessments of special needs students.

$ 64.95

5684 Handbook for Developing Community Based Employment

RPM Press, Inc.
P.O. Box 31483   602-886-1990
Tucson, AZ 85751

Jan Stonebraker, Operations Manager

Provides step-by-step guidance for educators and vocational rehabilitation personnel on how to develop community-based employment training programs for severly challenged workers.

$ 44.95

5685 How to Hold Your Job

Edmark Corporation
P.O. Box 3218   206-746-3900
Redmond, WA 98073   800-362-2890

Helps students retain jobs through positive work attitudes and values.

$ 34.00

5686 Job Accommodation Handbook

Paul McCray, Author

RPM Press, Inc.
P.O. Box 31483   602-886-1990
Tucson, AZ 85751

Jan Stonebraker, Operations Manager

Provides how-to-do-it for counselors, job placement specialists, educators and others on how to modify jobs for special needs workers.

$ 44.95

5687 Job Accommodations Network

West Virginia University
809 Allen Hall   304-293-7186
Morgantown, WV 26506   800-526-7234

An international information network and consulting resource which issues to employers, rehabilitation professionals and persons with disabilities.

5688 Job Interview PracticePak

Edmark Corporation
P.O. Box 3218   206-746-3900
Redmond, WA 98073   800-362-2890

A culminating course in pre-employment training, this program contains everything you need to create complete job interview role-play simulations.

$ 64.50

5689 Job Interview Tips for People with Learning Disabilities

LDA Of Canada, Author

Learning Disabilities Association of America
4156 Library Road   412-341-1515
Pittsburgh, PA 15234

5690 Job Seeker's Workbook/Job Seeking Skills

Lee Ann Boerner, Author

Books on Special Children
P.O. Box 305   914-638-1236
Congers, NY 10920   FAX 914-638-0847

Offers lessons, goals, methods and materials used to help persons get employment.

$ 10.00

5691 J.O.B.S. II

PESCO International
21 Paulding Street   914-769-4266
Pleasantville, NY 10570   800-431-2016
                                   FAX 914-769-2970

A microcomputer matching disabled people with job training, employment, local employers and giving job outlooks for the year 2000.

5692   Know and Grow

Edmark Corporation
P.O. Box 3218   206-746-3900
Redmond, WA 98073   800-362-2890

Develops basic plant care skills while providing therapy.

$ 145.00

5693   Life Beyond the Classroom

Paul Wehrman, Author

Paul H. Brookes Publishing Company
P.O. Box 10624   410-337-8539
Baltimore, MD 21285   800-638-3775

This textbook is an essential guide to planning, designing and implementing successful transition programs for students with disabilities.

$ 44.00

5694   Life Centered Career Education: Occupational Guidance & Preparation

Richard T. Roessler & Donn E. Brolin, Author

The Council for Exceptional Children
1920 Association Drive   703-620-3660
Reston, VA 22091

The skills in this Domain prepare students to explore occupational possibilities; make appropriate choices; find a job; and exhibit appropriate behavior, work habits and physical dexterity on the job.

$ 300.00

5695   Life Centered Careere Education: Assessment Batteries

Donn E. Brolin, Author

The Council for Exceptional Children
1920 Association Drive   703-620-3660
Reston, VA 22091

The LCCE Batteries are curriculum-based assessment instruments designed to measure the career education knowledge and skills of regular and special education students. There are two alternative forms of a Knowledge Battery and two forms of the Performance Batteries. These assessment tools can be combined with instruction to determine the instructional goals most appropriate for a particular student.

$ 300.00

5696   Measuring Skills

Edmark Corporation
P.O. Box 3218   206-746-3900
Redmond, WA 98073   800-362-2890

Develops measuring skills with hands-on activities.

$ 185.00

5697   Moving On: Transition for Youth with Behavioral Disorders

Michael Bullis & Robert Gaylord-Ross, Author

The Council for Exceptional Children
1920 Association Drive   703-620-3660
Reston, VA 22091

Preparing students with behavioral disorders for long-term life adjustment is one of the education's greatest challenges. This book describes a vocational assessment that can help to focus skill training needed for the workplace.

5698   National Association of Trade and Technical Schools

2251 Wisconsin Avenue NW   202-333-1021
Washington, DC 20007

Describes the process of choosing a career school.

5699   National Clearinghouse of Rehabilitation Training Materials

Oklahoma State University
816 West Sixth Street   405-624-7650
Stillwater, OK 74078

Disseminates information on vocational rehabilitation with primary concentration on training materials for use by educators of rehabilitation practitioners and in-service training personnel.

5700   NICHCY Transition Summary

NICHCY
P.O. Box 1492   703-893-6061
Washington, DC 20013   800-999-5599

A newsletter offering information on vocational assessment, books and more for the disabled.

5701   Occupational Aptitude Survey Interest Schedule

Randall Parker, Author

Pro-Ed
8700 Shoal Creek Blvd.   512-451-3246
Austin, TX 78758   FAX 512-451-8542

Determines the skills and abilities of its clients by measuring six broad aptitude factors: general ability, verbal aptitude, numerical aptitude, spacial aptitude, perceptual aptitude and manual dexterity.

5702   Occupational Literacy Education

Learning Disabilities Association of America
4156 Library Road   412-341-1515
Pittsburgh, PA 15234

$ 5.50

5703 The Oregon Special Education Employment Clearinghouse

Oregon Federation of CEC
345 North Monmouth Avenue   503-838-8015
Monmouth, OR 97361

Assists the disabled individual in locating the special education employment opportunity right for them.

5704 Pre-Employment Skills Training for the Learning Disabled

Cindy Newell, Author

Department of Human Resources, Rehabilitation Div.
Reno, NV

This manual defines learning disability, who are the learning disabled, what is a viable format for the learning disabled in a job seeking skills class and what adaptations are appropriate for the specific learning disabled.

$ 26.50

5705 Preparing Personnel to Work with Persons with Severe Disabilities

A.P. Kaiser, Author

Books on Special Children
P.O. Box 305   914-638-1236
Congers, NY 10920   FAX 914-638-0847

Discusses the current perspectives, needs and resources for personnel preparation.

$ 36.00

5706 Preventing Obsolescence Through Retraining Contexts, Policies and Programs

Jeanne Prial Gordus, Author

Center on Education and Training for Employment
1900 Kenny Road   614-292-4353
Columbus, OH 43210   800-848-4815

Examines the adequacy of workers' skills by focusing on the retraining currently provided to employed and dislocated workers.

$ 7.00

5707 Prevocational Tasks

Edmark Corporation
P.O. Box 3218   206-746-3900
Redmond, WA 98073   800-362-2890

Teaches entry level job skills to the developmentally disabled.

$ 17.95

5708 Put That Person to Work! a Manual for Implementers

HEATH Resource Center
One Dupont Circle NW, Ste. 800   202-939-9320
Washington, DC 20036   800-544-3284

These documents and two accompanying videotapes are written for employers of persons with mental retardation or developmental disabilities in supported employment settings.

5709 PWI Profile

Goodwill Industries of America
9200 Wisconsin Avenue   301-530-6500
Bethesda, MD 20814

Newlsetter on employment of persons with disabilities.

5710 Reading-Free Vocational Interest Inventory

Edmark Corporation
P.O. Box 3218   206-746-3900
Redmond, WA 98073   800-362-2890

Determines vocational interests for special education students.

$ 13.50

5711 The Rehabilitation Research and Training Center on Supported Employment

Main St., VCU Box 2011   804-367-1851
Richmond, VA 23284

Helps disabled persons with finding and holding a job.

5712 Right Job

Sunburst Communications, Inc.
39 Washington Ave.   914-769-5030
Pleasantville, NY 10570

Helps students match interests, skills and working preferences with the best-suited job.

$ 189.00

5713 The Role of Vocational Education in the Development of Academic Skills

Sandra Pritz, Author

Center on Education and Training for Employment
1900 Kenny Road   614-292-4353
Columbus, OH 43210   800-848-4815

Highlights the current focus on integration of academic skills and vocational skills as a response to educational reform movements.

$ 5.25

5714 School to Adult Life Transition Bibliography

Special Education Resource Center
25 Industrial Park Road   203-632-1485
Middletown, CT 06457

A bibliography of references and resources at the Special Education Resource Center.

5715 Self Advocacy As a Technique for Transition

KUAF - University of Kansas
311 Haworth Hall   913-864-2700
Lawrence, KS 66045

A joint effort involved in researching the effect of self-advocacy training upon adolescents with learning disabilities.

$ 17.00

5716 Self-Directed Search

John Hiolland, Author

The Psychological Corporation
555 Academic Court   800-228-0752
San Antonio, TX 78204   FAX 512-299-2720

This self-administered, self-scored and self-interpreted test enables the individual to make education and career choices.

5717 Self-Supervision: a Career Tool for Audiologists, Clinical Series 10

ASHA Fulfillment Operations
10801 Rockville Pike   301-897-5700
Rockville, MD 20852

Describes concepts of supervision, defines and presents strategies for self-supervision, discusses supervisory accountability and covers some issues of self-supervision within a supervisor format.

5718 Shop Talk

Edmark Corporation
P.O. Box 3218   206-746-3900
Redmond, WA 98073   800-362-2890

Develops social skills and communication skills needed for the work place.

$ 25.95

5719 Small Parts Training Program

Edmark Corporation
P.O. Box 3218   206-746-3900
Redmond, WA 98073   800-362-2890

Develops job-related skills with hands-on training.

$ 269.00

5720 Social Skills for the World of Work and Beyond

Learning Disabilities Association of America
4156 Library Road   412-341-1515
Pittsburgh, PA 15234

5721 Steps to Independence for People with Learning Disabilities

NICHCY
P.O. Box 1492   703-893-6061
Washington, DC 20013

An excellent booklet whose purpose is to help learning disabled adults become economically independent and reach their full potential.

5722 Technology Education: Industrial Arts in Transition

David McCrory, Author

Center on Education and Training for Employment
1900 Kenny Road   614-292-4353
Columbus, OH 43210   800-848-4815

Exploires the transition of industrial arts into technology education through the following aspects: history, philosophy and objectives.

$ 7.00

5723 Telephone Skills Cassettes

Edmark Corporation
P.O. Box 3218   206-746-3900
Redmond, WA 98073   800-362-2890

Simulates job skills using the telephone in business.

$ 89.95

5724 Tele-Trainer

Edmark Corporation
P.O. Box 3218   206-746-3900
Redmond, WA 98073   800-362-2890

Teaches contact ways to use the telephone for work, pleasure and emergencies.

$ 249.00

5725 Third National Forum on Issues in Vocational Assessment

R.R. Fry, Author

MCD, Stout Vocational Rehabilitation Institute
University Of Wisconsin-Stout   715-232-2195
Menomonie, WI 54751

The impact potential curriculum-based vocational assessment in our schools.

5726 Time Incentive Program

Edmark Corporation
P.O. Box 3218   206-746-3900
Redmond, WA 98073   800-362-2890

Improves work performance by relating pay to time and amount of work completed.

$ 405.00

5727 Toward Productive Living: Second Edition

Doreen Kronick, Author
Connecticut Association for Children with LD
18 Marshall Street   203-838-5010
South Norwalk, CT 06854   FAX 203-866-6108

$ 5.80

5728 Training and Educating the Work Force in the Nineties

Thomas J Smith & Carolyn Trist, Author
Center on Education and Training for Employment
1900 Kenny Road   614-292-4353
Columbus, OH 43210   800-848-4815

Considers the changing context of skills training, which is making partnerships between the public and private sectors a necessity.

$ 6.00

5729 Transition From School to Work

Paul H. Brookes Publishing Company
P.O. Box 10624   410-337-8539
Baltimore, MD 21285   800-638-3137

A hands-on guide to planning and implementing successful transition programs for adolescents with learning disabilities.

> "...valuable to occupational therapists preparing to become mebers of the transitional team..."
> The Amer. Journal of Occupational Therap

$ 25.00

5730 Transition Goals for Adolescents with Learning Disabilities

Catherine Trapani, Author
Pro-Ed
8700 Shoal Creek Blvd.   512-451-3246
Austin, TX 78758   FAX 512-451-8542

Provides important information about academic, social and vocational planning for students with learning disabilities.

$ 24.00

5731 Transition of Adolescents with Learning Disabilities

Catherine Trapani, Author
Pro-Ed
8700 Shaol Creek Blvd.   512-451-3246
Austin, TX 78758   FAX 512-451-8542

Provides important information about academic, social and vocational planning for students with learning disabilities.

$ 24.00

5732 Transition Services Language Survival Guide for California

Transition Services and WorkAbility
721 Capitol Mall, 6th Floor   916-657-3373
Sacramento, CA 95814

Jeff Jeffers
Patricia Dougan
Short manual offering clear instructions, suggestions and guidelines for transition professionals.

5733 Transitional Apartment Program

18 Park Street   413-243-2256
Lee, MA 01238

An independent living program for learning disabled adults offering full clinical services, vocational training and the opportunity to earn a GED or to go on to college amd a residential program.

5734 Trends and Issues in Vocational Education

Wesley Burke, Author
Center on Education and Training for Employment
1900 Kenny Road   614-292-4353
Columbus, OH 43210   800-848-4815

Traces the influence of social, economic and technological changes on the vocational education and training enterprise.

$ 4.75

5735 Vocational Assessment of Special Students for Vocational Education

Center on Education and Training for Employment
Ohio State - 1900 Kenny Road   614-292-4353
Columus, OH 43210   800-848-4815

Clarifies issues on assessment of special needs students, including disabled and disadvantaged.

$ 8.00

5736 Vocational Entry Skills for Secondary Students

Learning Disabilities Association of America
4156 Library Road   412-341-1515
Pittsburgh, PA 15234

5737 Vocational Evaluation and Traumatic Brain Injury

Dr. S.W. Thomas, Author

Books on Special Children
P.O. Box 305   914-638-1236
Congers, NY 10920   FAX 914-638-0847
Contains definition and techniques for vocational evaluation strategies.

$ 18.00

5738   Vocational Mainstreaming

Winifred Washburn, Author

Academic Therapy Publications
20 Continental Blvd.   415-883-3314
Novato, CA 94949

A manual for teachers of learning disabled students.

$ 8.00

5739   Vocational Rehabilitation Services Handbook

SC Vocational Rehab. Dept./State Offic Bldg.
1410 Boston Avenue   803-734-6772
West Columbia, SC 28171

This booklet offers information on vocational programs for the disabled, evaluation, treatment and rehabilitation planning.

5740   Vocational Training and Employment of Autistic Adolescents

Charles C. Thomas Publisher
2600 South First Street   217-789-8980
Springfield, IL 62794   FAX 217-789-9130

Professionals and parents are now advocating, demanding and arranging that persons receive vocational training and equal rights for the disabled.

5741   A Way to Work

Edmark Corporation
P.O. Box 3218   206-746-3900
Redmond, WA 98073   800-362-2890

Prepares for students for the transition to working in the community.

$ 229.00

5742   What Do You Do After High School?

Learning Disabilities Association of America
4156 Library Road   412-341-1515
Pittsburgh, PA 15234

5743   Worklife

President's Committee for Employment of Disabled
1111 20th Street NW, Ste. 636   202-653-5044
Washington, DC 20036

Reports on progress in employment opportunities for people with disabilities.

5744   Workplace

Mainstream, Inc.
1030 5th Avenue NW   202-898-1400
Washington, DC 20005

This manual was designed for professionals in preparing company managers and supervisors in integrating people with disabilities into the workplace.

$ 89.95

5745   Writing for the World of Work

Ellen Kaplan, Author

Educational Design, Inc.
47 West 13th Street   800-221-9372
New York, NY 10011

An instructional material with over 100 exercises with emphasis on writing skills, survival reading, business writing and job applications.

$ 7.50

Alabama

5746   Coffee County Training Center

College Street Extension   205-393-1732
Enterprise, AL 36330

Vickie Florence, Director

Clients 21 years and up receive training in Independent Living Skills, Self-Care, Language Skills and more.

5747   Easter Seal Occupational Center

1616 Sixth Avenue South   205-939-5800
Birmingham, AL 35233

Phillip Johnson

5748   Opportunity Center - Easter Seal

P.O. Drawer 2247   205-237-0381
Anniston, AL 36291

Mike Almaroad

5749   Wireglass Rehabilitation Center, Inc.

805 Ross Clark Circle   205-792-0022
Dothan, AL 36503

Dorothy Morris, Administrator

5750   Workshops, Inc.

4244 Third Avenue South   205-592-9683
Birmingham, AL 35222

J.E. Crim, Executive Director

Funded by the public, community chest and workshop sales this center provides evaluation, employment, prevocational training and sheltered workshops to the disabled areas of Birmingham, Jefferson County, Northern Alabama and Shelby County.

5751   YES Work Center

311 Guff Avenue North   205-845-9367
Fort Payne, AL 35967

Kenny Maness, Work Adjustment

Arizona

5752   CAD Institute

The CAD Center
4100 East Broadway   602-437-0405
Phoenix, AZ 85040   800-658-5744
                                  FAX 602-437-5695

Daniel P. Edwards, National Admissions

The Career Development Division offers a 15-month Diploma program as well as an extended 19-month program for Associates of Applied Sciences and a 31-month program for Bachelors of Applies Sciences in CAD technology. Vocational training is offered in manufacturing/Electro-mechanical engineering, geographical information systems/civil, architectural engineering and construction and virtual reality.

5753   Life Development Institute

1720 East Monte Vista   602-254-0822
Phoenix, AZ 85006   FAX 602-253-6878

Robert Crawford, President

Serves older adolescents and adults with learning disabilities, ADD and related disorders. The purpose of the training is to enable program participants to pursue responsible independent living, enhance academic/workplace literacy skills and facilitate placement in educational/employment opportunities commensurate with individual capabilities. Current efforts to open a stand alone, regionally accredited 2-year college are underway with projected opening in fall 1994.

5754   Phoenix Union Adult Basic Education

Learning Disabilities Association of America
P.O. Box 15525   602-224-5269
Phoenix, AZ 85060

Dr. Claire Tarte

Offers free classes for adults with learning disabilities.

5755   TETRA Corporation

308 West Glenn   602-622-4874
Tucson, AZ 85703

Steven King

Work hardening andd disciplinary programs.

5756   Valpar International Corporation

P.O. Box 5767   602-293-1510
Tucson, AZ 85703   800-528-7070
                                  FAX 602-292-9755

P. Alex Swartz, President

Occupational Assessment and Career Exploration Products featuring SYSTEM 2000 used to evaluate students' physical and mental capabilities to determine the careers for which they are best suited and which educational or vocational training program they should follow to enhance their future potential.

5757   Yavapal Rehabilitation Center

436 N. Washington Street   602-445-0991
Prescott, AZ 86301

Bradley Newman

Arkansas

5758   Easter Seal Work Center

11801 Fairview Road   501-663-8331
Little Rock, AR 72212

Renee Hubbard

California

5759   CAR Contract and Employment Services

2751 Marine Way, Ste. A   415-961-3332
Mountain View, CA 94043   FAX 415-961-8835

Denise Carey

Adults 18 and over with developmental disabilities are served in 65 person workshop. Clients are also served in individual competitive employment placements and in small group placements throughout Santa Clara and Southern San mateo counties.

5760   Career Development Program

1523 East Valley Parkway   619-745-9999
Escondido, CA 92027

Dr. Richard Brady

5761   Desert Haven Training Center

P.O. Box 2119   805-948-8402
Lancaster, CA 93539

Roy Williams

5762   Imperial County Work Training Center

361 East Highway 80   619-352-6181
El Centro, CA 92243

5763 Independence Center, California

3640 S. Sepulveda Blvd., Ste. 102   310-202-7102
Los Angeles, CA 90034

Carol Hirshfield Goodman, Director
Christy Byrne, Job Developer

The program provides help in facilitating the transition to independent living, including job preparation and placement, social and recreational activities and apartment living for the learning disabled.

5764 Marin Puzzle People, Inc.

17 Buena Vista Avenue   415-383-8763
Mill Valley, CA 94941

Jo Ann Haseltine, Executive Director

Assisting adults with learning disabilities to reach their potential for social and vocational success through workshops, social events, public outreach and informational materials.

5765 Mt. Diablo Vocational Services

2325 Clayton Road, Ste. 300   415-687-9675
Concord, CA 94520

Bob Bennett
Work hardening and disciplinary programs.

5766 NCI Affiliates, Inc.

2125 Golden Hill Road   805-238-6630
Paso Robles, CA 93447

Laura Simpson, Executive Director
Judy Jacobson, Services Director

Provides independent living skills and vocational training to the disabled.

5767 Oakland Work Activity Area

6315 San Leandro Street   415-636-0751
Oakland, CA 94621

Greg Whalley

5768 Opportunities for the Handicapped, Inc.

3340 Marysville Blvd.   916-925-3522
Sacramento, CA 95838

Kathy Dodd

5769 Pomona Valley Workshop

4650 Brooks Street   714-624-3555
Montclair, CA 91763

Lucian Marchio

5770 Porterville Sheltered Workshop

97 North Main Street   209-784-7187
Porterville, CA 93257

5771 Project Independent Supported Employment

300 South Harbor Blvd., Ste. 716   714-772-5061
Anaheim, CA 92805

5772 Ramona Training Center

2138 San Vincente Road   619-789-5910
Ramona, CA 92065

Charlene Wutthe

5773 Sacramento Vocational Services

6950 21st Avenue   916-381-1300
Sacramento, CA 95820

Diane De Rodeff, Director

5774 Saddleback Community Enterprises

25701 Taladro Circle   714-837-7280
Mission Valley, CA 92691

Kathryn Hebel, Director

5775 Salinas Valley Training Center

P.O. Box 453
Salinas, CA 93902

Rosemary Anderson, Day Activity Manager

5776 Shasta County Opportunity Center

1265 Redwood Blvd.   916-225-5781
Redding, CA 96003

Carol Keating, Executive Director

5777 Social Vocational Services, Inc.

23822 Hawthorne Blvd., Ste. 200   213-375-5788
Torrance, CA 90505

Dr. Dale Dutton, Executive Director

5778 Unyeway, Inc.

2330 Main Street, Ste. E   619-789-5960
Ramona, CA 92065

Hank Newman, Director

5779 Work Training Programs, Inc.

20931 Nordhoff Street   818-773-9000
Chatsworth, CA 91311

Stephen Miller

Colorado

5780 Laradon Vocational Center

5100 Lincoln Street   303-296-3444
Denver, CO 80216

Toni Martin, Executive Director

5781 NORESCO Workshop

903 East Burlington Street   303-867-5702
Fort Morgan, CO 80701

Robert Duffield

5782 Sedgwick County Workshop

113 South Elm   303-747-2446
Julesburg, CO 80737

Robert Christansen

5783 Valley Industries

330 State Street   719-589-3123
Alamosa, CO 81101

Tim Johnson

Connecticut

5784 Area Cooperative Educational Services

205 Skiff Street   203-288-9119
Hamden, CT 06517

5785 CCARC Work Services Center

111 Franklin Square   203-229-6665
New Britain, CT 06037

Julie Erickson

5786 Cheshire Occupational and Career Center

615 West Johnson Avenue, Bldg #3   203-272-5607
Cheshire, CT 06410

Peter Mason

5787 Valley Memorial Health Center, Inc.

435 East Main Street   203-736-2601
Ansonia, CT 06401

Marilyn Cormack, Director
Provides remunerative work.

5788 Vista Program

Captain Spencer Homestead
1356 Old Clinton Road   203-399-8080
Westbrook, CT 06498

A private, post secondary program for young adults with learning disabilities. VISTA is designed for individuals who would like to succeed in work and independent living and need a non-traditional program to address their needs.

Delaware

5789 Opportunity Center, Inc.

200 Ruthar Drive   302-738-6650
Newark, DE 19711

Marianne Lego

District of Columbia

5790 AFL-CIO Human Resources Development Institute

815 16th Street NW, Room 405   202-638-3912
Washington, DC 20006

A program that places workers with various disabilities such as learning disabilities in training programs and jobs.

5791 Centers for Independent Living Program Rehabilitation Services Admin.

330 C Street SW
Washington, DC 20202

Offers individuals with severe disabilities to live and function independently. Centers offer individuals with disabilities a variety of services, including independent living skills training, counseling and advocacy services on income benefits and legal rights, information and referral, peer counseling, education and training, housing.

5792 Comprehensive Learning Center, Inc.

6017 Chillum Place NE   202-882-9525
Washington, DC 20011   FAX 202-882-9480

Offers psychiatric occupational therapy, computer program, dance therapy, art program, therapeutic recreation and special education.

5793 Job Training Partnership Act Programs Office of Job Training Programs

U.S. Department of Labor
200 Constitution Ave NW, Rm N-4709   202-535-0580
Washington, DC 20210

Trains and places economically disadvantaged adults and youth facing significant barriers to employment, including persons wtih disabilities, in permanent, unsubsidized jobs. More than 600 local JTPA programs offer individuals with disabilities who meet the Act's eligibility criteria a range of employment services.

5794 Mainstream, Inc.

1030 15th Street NW, Ste. 1010   202-898-1400
Washington, DC 20005

Works with employers and service providers around the country to increase employment opportunities for persons with disabilities.

5795 Office of Personnel Management

Office of Affirmative Recruiting and Employment
1900 E Street NW, Room 6336   202-606-0870
Washington, DC 20415

The central personnel agency of the Federal Government, provides information on the selective placement program for persons with disabilities.

5796 70001, Training and Employment, Ltd.

501 School Street SW, Ste. 600   202-484-0103
Washington, DC 20024

A national organization operating local programs for at-risk youth DC between 18 and 21 years of age in many cites across the country.

Florida

5797 MAClown Vocational Rehabilitation Workshop

6390 NE Second Avenue   305-758-2758
Miami, FL 33138

Pat Chavis
Provides remunerative work.

Georgia

5798 Creative Community Services

49B Lenox Pointe NE   404-814-1775
Atlanta, GA 30324

Nancy Elliott, Adult Program Dir.
Creates living arrangements for people with a range of learning disabilities who want to lead an adult lifestyle but still need some support and assistance. Program includes living, recreation, social and vocational supports.

Idaho

5799 High Reachers Employment and Training

245 East 6th Street   208-587-5804
Mountain Home, ID 83647

Joe McNeal, Executive Director

Illinois

5800 Att-P'tach Special Education Program

2828 West Pratt   312-973-2828
Chicago, IL 60645

Rabbi Harvey Well, Superintendent
Offers mainstreaming, independent skills, therapeutic swim classes and psychological services are available.

5801 Carle Vocational Rehabilitation Program

726 Killarney   217-337-3460
Urbana, IL 61801

Rock Boerema, Executive Director

5802 Illinois Technical Assistance for Special Populations Program

University of Illinois Site - NCRVE
1310 South Sixth Street   217-333-0807
Champaign, IL 61820

A service designed to assist in the improvement of vocational education programs for youth and adults with special needs.

5803 JoDavies Workshop, Inc.

706 West Street   815-777-2211
Galena, IL 61036

Intake and referrals, early intervention for children only, vocational education and work adjustment training services are offered.

5804 National Center for Research in Vocational Education

University of Illinois
345 Education Bldg., 1310 S. Sixth   217-333-0807
Champaign, IL 61820

Sheri Kallembach, Assistant Director
Federal vocational education legislation has provided funding of programs and support services designed to enhance the participation of special population students in secondary and postsecondary vocational education programs.

5805 Northwest Suburban Special Education Organization

799 West Kensington Road   708-577-7749
Mt. Peospect, IL 60056

Offers assessment behavior training, work skill training and vocational counseling.

5806 Owens Vocational Training Center

2639 North Kildare   312-486-3232
Chicago, IL 60639

5807 Secondary Transition Intervention Institute

University of Illinois At Urbana
1310 South 6th Street   217-333-0807
Champaign, IL 61820

5808 Technical Assistance for Special Population Programs

University of Illinois At Urbana
345 Education Bldg., 1310 S. 6th St   217-333-0807
Champaign, IL 61820   FAX 217-244-5632

Dr. Carolyn Maddy-Bernstein, Director

Works nationally to increase vocational program accessibility, quality, and availability for youth and adults from special populations.

5809 Time Out to Enjoy

P.O. Box 1084   212-444-9484
Evanston, IL 60204

Collects and disseminates information on educational and employment services and programs, provides referrals to learning disabled adults and sponsors mutual support groups.

5810 Transition Research Institute

61 Children's Ctr., 51 Gerty Drive   FAX 217-244-0851
Champaign, IL 61820

Paula D. Kohler, Associate Director

The Institute provides technical assistance on transition-focused projects, policy analysis concerning legislation focused on education and transition services for youths with disabilities, and a wealth of information for teachers, service providers and researchers.

5811 Washington County Vocational Workshop

P.O. Box 273   618-327-4461
Nashville, IL 62263

Keith Currin, Executive Director

5812 Clay Center - Adult Training Center

701 Fourth Street   913-632-5357
Clay Center, KS 67432

Lillian Bosch, Executive Director

5813 Learning Resources Network

1554 Hayes   913-539-5376
Manhattan, KS 66502

This network for educators provides resources to adult education and adult basic education service providers.

5814 Work Enhancement Center of Western Kentucky

803 Poplar Street   502-762-1137
Murray, KY 42071   FAX 502-762-1599

Steve Passmore, Director

This center has been established in order to service industry in three state areas surrounding Kentucky. This service includes job/skill evaluation, job design consultation, pre-employment employee evaluation and economic evaluation.

5815 Baton Rouge Evaluation and Testing Center

2097 Beaumont Drive   504-925-4985
Baton Rouge, LA 70806

A non-residential facility serving multi-disabled clients from the 9 parish Baton Rouge regional area with short-term vocational evaluation and assessment.

5816 The Adult Living Internship

Center for Unique Learners
11600 Nebel Street, Ste. 200   301-231-0115
Rockville, MD 20852

Patricia Williams, Executive Director

Provides transitional residential training in independent living skills to adults with learning difficulties. Based on a independent living skills assessment, each individual is placed in the program at a point that matches their skill levels.

5817 Career Development Center

Apprenticeship Program
1933 Severn Grove Road   301-841-6438
Annapolis, MD 21401

This Center serves a small number of young adults requiring counseling to continue their training or education.

5818 Independence Center for Young Adults with Learning Disabilities

11600 Nebel Street, Ste. 200   301-468-8810
Rockville, MD 20852

Judy Kramer, Project Director

Develop and implement projects to minimize participant long-term support needs through initial self-advocacy training and meet remaining support needs through grass roots peer support and social network training.

5819 Job Opportunities for the Blind

National Federation of the Blind
1800 Johnson Street   301-659-9314
Baltimore, MD 21230   800-638-7518

A nationwide job listing and job referral system of the NFB, a service available without charge.

Massachusetts

5820 Career Apprenticeship Program

335 Oakland Road   617-778-1488
Hyannis, MA 02601

Independent living skills are taught in a supportive, group home environment.

5821 Disability Rights in Voter Empowerment

2054 Main Street   800-462-8493
Concord, MA 01742

Presidential transition team working for the employment and rights of the disabled.

Minnesota

5822 Vocational Support Services

Learning Disabilities Association of America
2104 Park Avenue South   612-871-9011
Minneapolis, MN 55404

Provides employment services to meet the needs of adult clients.

Missouri

5823 Wx: Work Capacities, Inc.

17331 East 40th Highway, Ste. 103   816-478-2333
Independence, MO 64055

Carol Lett, Executive Director

New Jersey

5824 Camden County Occupational Training Center

215 West White Horse Pike   609-768-0845
Berlin, NJ 08009

Joseph Scardilli, Executive Director

5825 The First Occupational Center of New Jersey

391 Lakeside Avenue   201-672-5800
Orange, NJ 07050   800-894-6232
                          FAX 201-672-0065

Rocco Meola, President
Gerard Gannon, Vice President

A priavte, multi-service vocational training center. Services are offered to the developmentally disabled and include vocational evaluation and training, respite care, basic and remedial education and job placement.

5826 M.A.C.L.D. Apartment Residence

1501 Park Avenue   201-774-4737
Asbury Park, NJ 07712

A transitional living facility providing alternative education and experiential training to residents.

New York

5827 National Center on Disability Services

201 I.U. Willets Road   516-747-5400
Albertson, NY 11507

Engages in education, research, vocational counseling, job training and placement for children and adults with disabilities.

North Carolina

5828 Rutherford Vocational Workshop

200 Fairground Road   704-286-4352
Spindale, NC 28160

Judith Toney, Executive Director

5829 Transylvania Vocational Services, Inc.

P.O. Drawer 1115   704-884-3195
Brevard, NC 28712

Nancy Stricker, Executive Director

5830 Western Regional Vocational Rehabilitation Facility

P.O. Box 1443   704-433-2423
Morganton, NC 28655

Carroll Franklin, Executive Dirctor

Ohio

5831 The Center on Education and Training for Employment

1900 Kenny Road   614-292-4353
Columbus, OH 43210   800-848-4815
FAX 614-292-1260

Offers training for employment, adult education, career preparation, job skills enhancement and workplace literacy.

5832 Great Oaks Joint Vocational School

3254 East Kemper Road   513-771-8840
Cincinnati, OH 45241

Dr. Harold Carr, Executive Director

5833 Hearth Day Treatment and Vocational Services

8301 Detroit Avenue   216-281-2660
Cleveland, OH 44102

Ralph Fee, Executive Director

5834 Highland Unlimited Business Enterprises

65 West McMillen Street   513-569-4730
Cincinnati, OH 45202

Debbie Dutton, Executive Director

Pennsylvania

5835 Adult Literacy and Technology Project

Institute for the Study of Adult Literacy
203 Rackley Bldg.   814-863-3777
University Park, PA 16802

Studies and promotes high technology learning tools such as computer aided instruction and interactive videodisc, in adult basic education.

5836 Institute for the Study of Adult Literacy

The Pennsylvania State University College of Ed.
248 Calder Way, Ste. 209   814-863-3777
State College, PA 16801

Renee Atchison Ziegler

A research institute that works with government agencies and private corporations to develop educational materials to aid learning disabled people secure employment.

5837 Technology and Employment Services- TECenter

University of Pennsylvania
4212 Chestnut Street   215-898-8108
Philadelphia, PA 19104

Texas

5838 The Assessment of Learning Disabilities

Larry Silver, Author
Pro-Ed
8700 Shoal Creek Blvd.   512-451-3246
Austin, TX 78758   FAX 512-451-8542

This book provides a scholarly and comprehensive review of the current status of assessment for learning disabilities for each age group.

$ 26.00

5839 Handbook on the Assessment of Learning Disabilities

H. Lee Swanson, Author
Pro-Ed
8700 Shoal Creek Blvd.   512-451-3246
Austin, TX 78758   FAX 512-451-8542

This handbook delves into theories and research that are the underpinnings of the assessment process.

$ 34.00

5840 Independent Living Research Utilization Program

P.O. Box 20095   713-666-6244
Houston, TX 77225

A national resource center for independent living.

5841 Occupational Aptitude Survey and Interest Schedule

Randall Parker, Author
Pro-Ed
8700 Shoal Creek Blvd.   512-451-3246
Austin, TX 78758   FAX 512-451-8542

Consists of two related tests: the OASIS-2 Aptitude Survey and the OASIS-2 Interest Schedule. The tests were normed on the same national sample of 1,505 students from 13 states. The Aptitude Survey measures six broad aptitude factors that are directly related to skills and abilities required in over 20,000 jobs and the Interest Schedule measures 12 interest factors directly related to the occupations listed in Occupational Exploration.

$ 296.00

5842 Transitional Learning Community

1528 Postoffice Street   800-TLC-GROW
Galveston, TX 77550

Specializes in the vocational evaluation and community mainsteaming of brain injured adults.

5843 Vineland ASSIST

Pro-Ed
8700 Shoal Creek Blvd.   512-451-3246
Austin, TX 78758   FAX 512-451-8542

A fast and easy score conversion now available for IBM users. Survey and Expanded Forms are available. The new IBM program contains expanded features and lets you convert raw scores quickly, receive a narrative report of basic score information, and save the report to an ASCII file for later word processing.

$ 107.95

Virginia

5844 Fairfax Opportunities Unlimited, Inc.

3510 Port Royla Road   703-321-8890
Springfield, VA 22151   FAX 703-321-8963

Donald Hinkel
Offers vocational assessment to determine overall employability of the disabled.

Wisconsin

5845 Materials Development Center

Stout Vocational Rehabilitation Institute
University Of Wisconsin-Stout   715-232-1342
Menomonie, WI 54751

This Center develops and disseminates information to professionals about vocational rehabilitation and training of students with disabilities.

5846 Architects Limited

2120 Arch Street 215-568-8250
Philadelphia, PA 19103

James J. Foley, Jr., President

Provides architectural and interior design services to the health care community and has had considerable experience in the design of educational, residential and medical facilities for children with disabilities.

5847 Baker, Linda Saag, MS

17 Gleneden Avenue 415-549-2911
Oakland, CA 94611

5848 Baren, Martin, MD

805 West La Veta Avenue, Ste. 210 714-633-3695
Orange, CA 92668

5849 Bing, Janis, Assistive Technology Specialist

Education Service Center, Region VI
3332 Montgomery Road 409-295-9161
Huntsville, TX 77340

Consultant offering information to the learning disabled.

5850 Bowman, Ray L., PhD, PA

933 Oleander Way, South 813-347-4747
St. Petersburg, FL 33707

5851 Brainard, Elliott L., OD, FCOVD

23371 Mulholland Drive 818-347-1910
Woodland Hills, CA 91364

5852 Buchman, Stuart M., MS

7 Long Bow Lane 516-368-0400
Commack, NY 11725

5853 Carroll, Mary C., OD

2225 East Flamingo Road, Ste. 100 702-349-0225
Las Vegas, NV 89119

5854 Comprehensive Services for the Disabled

5105 Highway 33/34 South 908-938-7730
Wall, NJ 07727 FAX 908-938-2499

Donald DeSanto, Director

Offers services for public school pupils involving independent child study team evaluations and/or child study team diagnostic services to supplement existing local district services and for nonpublic school pupils, evaluation, determination of eligibility for special education and/or related services, classification and the development of an individualized education program; and supplementary instruction, speech correction and home instruction for pupils eligible for such services.

5855 Deich, Ruth F., PhD. and Associates

219 North Indian Hill Blvd., #101 909-626-2770
Claremont, CA 91711

Ruth F. Deich, PhD, Psychologist

Psychodiagnostic testing, assessment and evaluation, cognitive and behavioral approaches, tools and techniques for learning disabled and ADD children and adults.

5856 Developmental Evaluation Clinic Health Services for Children/Special Needs

DC General Hospital
19th And Massachusetts Avenue SE 202-675-5214
Washington, DC 20003 FAX 202-544-5945

5857 Developmental Learning Therapy

918 South Fillmore Way 303-778-7883
Denver, CO 80209

Jeanine Matney

A private practice for children with learning disabilities.

5858 Diversified Consultants Associates

34 Peachtree Street, NW. Ste. 2570 404-523-2744
Atlanta, GA 30303

David Skillen, Vice President

Offers consulting services in the areas of strategic/long range planning and fund-raising. Emphasis is on building sound, comprehensive programs that have sustaining value and contribute to meaningful governance and administrative leadership.

5859 Doran-Benyon, Sheila, MS

3333 Eastside 713-665-3939
Houston, TX 77098

5860 Education RX Associates, Inc.

4615 Backgate Property 803-293-1411
Myrtle Beach, SC 29577

Alice D'Antoni, Representative

Offers individual/small group therapy, consultation with parents and professionals and career planning/counseling services.

5861 Ellingsen & Associates, Inc.

3823 East Calle DeSoto 602-750-9811
Tucson, AZ 85716 800-851-1788

Learning disabled consultants.

5862 Engle, Elaine Dunn, PhD, Ltd.

636 Church Street 708-328-5923
Evanston, IL 60201

5863 Eugene Myer Treatment Center of the Washington School of Psychiatry

1610 New Hampshire Avenue NW   202-797-8740
Washington, DC 20009   FAX 202-667-8542

5864 Eye, Physician and Surgeons of Washington Circle Clinic of Washington, DC

3 Washington Circle NW, Ste. 209   202-466-7711
Washington, DC 20037

Visual evaluation, treatment, medical and surgical procedures performed.

5865 Feiner and Associates

2291 North University Drive   305-962-3855
Pembroke Pines, FL 33024

Arnold Feiner

Specializing in Attention Deficit Disorder.

5866 Geller, Marc D., PsyD

245 Union Avenue, Ste. 1B   908-725-9090
Bridgewater, NJ 08807

5867 Greenburg, Robert M.

11365 Sunset Hills Road   703-471-4600
Reston, VA 22090

Robert Greenburg, OD

5868 Hancock, Dr. Betsy J., OD, MS

21 East 5th Street   717-784-2131
Bloomsburg, PA 17815

5869 Harris, Arlene B., MA

225 East 26th Street   212-684-6546
New York, NY 10010

Arlene B. Harris, M.A., Educational Ther.

Comprehensive educational tutoring, therapy and counseling for individuals of all ages; seminars and workshops tailored to an organizations interests in the fields of learning disabilities; consulting services and more.

5870 Hattie B. Monroe Augmentative Communication Center

University of Nebraska Medical Center
600 South 42nd Street   402-559-6460
Omaha, NE 68198

A clinical program to train speech pathologists. Acts as a consultant for the state and those individuals who need more assistance in speech and language disorders.

5871 H2L2 Architects/Planners

714 Market Street   215-925-5300
Philadelphia, PA 19106

Robert Breading

Offers campus master planning, architectural and interior design services for schools, colleges and universities and facilities designed for the educational and care of exceptional children.

5872 Jablon, E.G., MEd, Educational Specialist

808 Hastings Drive   407-847-8816
Kissimmee, FL 34744

Remedial and tutorial services, diagnostic testing, perceptual, motor training, vocational and career counseling, and more.

5873 Kay, Margaret J. & Associates

2818 Lititz Pike   717-569-6223
Lancaster, PA 17601   800-750-6223
   FAX 717-560-9931

Margaret J. Kay, Lic. Psychologist

Provides comprehensive psychoeducational evaluations for children and adults with learning disabilities, dyslexia and other types of developmental disorders. Individualized, on-site tutorial services as well as cognitive retraining for individuals who have sustained traumatic brain injury, are also offered as adjunct services. Advocacy for children in public schools and or adults in the workplace is provided in addition to community and business training programs.

5874 Lane's Learning Center

One Gustafson Court   415-892-7706
Movato, CA 94947

Michele Lane, M.S., Director

Opened in 1980 and offers a supportive atmosphere which meets the individual needs of children and adults who experience difficulty in learning. With over 21 years of experience in the field of education, Michele works with families, schools, students and outside agencies involved. The center offers educational assessment, consultation and tutoring in academic areas, as well as swimming and computer instruction.

5875 Language Skills Therapy

2525 NW Lovejoy Street, Ste. 200   503-227-0671
Portland, OR 97210

Provides testing, consultation and tutoring services for children and for adults with specific language disabilities (dyslexia).

5876 Learning and Language Specialists

5555 East 71st Street, Ste. 6300   918-481-6150
Tulsa, OK 74136

Carole Stoen

5877 Learning Assessment Clinic Cleveland Clinic Foundation

9500 Euclid Ave., S 71   216-444-1993
Cleveland, OH 44195

Gerald Erenberg, M.D., Director Of Clinic
Karen Dakin, M.Ed., Co-Director

Offers multi-disciplinary assessment services for children with school learning problems. The goal is to provide a specific educational plan for the school and parents which leads towards remediation of the child's problems.

5878 Learning Associates

20 Community Place   201-540-0995
Morristown, NJ 07960

Holly Blumenstyk, M.Ed., LDT, Director

A private practice serving children and adults with larning problems. Services include comprehensive Learning Evaluations, consultations, remedial tutoring programs. Tutotirng is available for reading, writing, math, study skills, content subjects and test preparation. The Director is a certified Learning Disabilities Teacher-Consultant and Teacher of the Disabled.

5879 Learning Disabilities Association

2104 Park Avenue South   612-871-9011
Minneapolis, MN 55404

Jeannie Piekos, Marketing
Offers consulting services for the disabled.

5880 Learning Disabilities Consultants

P.O. Box 716   215-525-8336
Bryn Mawr, PA 19010

5881 Learning Therapy Associates, Inc.

207 South Ninth Street   317-742-4388
Lafayette, IN 47901

5882 Lehrhoff, Irwin, PhD & Associates, Inc.

1888 Century Park East #1900   310-477-2497
Los Angeles, CA 90067   FAX 310-477-5469

Irwin Lehrhoff, Representative

Offers psychological, educational and speech/language evaluations, educational consulting and placement of children into private day boarding schools.

5883 Luber, Carol Horwich, M.S., ED. Educational Consulting & Advocacy

2864 Club Drive   310-202-8145
Los Angeles, CA 90064   FAX 310-202-1204

Provides educational consulting and advocacy services to families with children who have special education needs. Services provided include program assessment and recommendations, IEP preparation and meeting participation, advice and support through due process procedures and guidance to access other support agencies and planning for the child's future.

5884 Maier, Arlee S., PhD.

1855 San Miguel Drive, Ste. 23   510-947-5765
Walnut Creek, CA 94596

Assessment of children and adults with learning, neurological, psychological and/or behavior disorders. Consultation for school placement, remedial programs and behavior management.

5885 Marlowe, Wendy B., PhD, ABPP

901 Boren Avenue, Ste. 610   206-623-5217
Seattle, WA 98104

5886 MTB Banking Corporation

90 Broad Street   212-858-3366
New York, NY 10004

Paul Schuldiner, Vice President

Offers working capital loans that are collateralized by accounts receivables from State and Local Government Agencies. Offers financing to non-profit schools which enable schools to generate positive cash flow.

5887 Oak Hill Youth Center

3201 Oak Hill Drive   301-497-8250
Laurel, MD 20724

5888 Parent Consultation and Child Evaluation Service, Counseling Center

University of Maryland
College Park, MD 20742   301-314-7673
   FAX 301-314-9206

5889 Peterson, Janice L., PhD

2660 Carmen Crest Drive   213-850-5456
Los Angeles, CA 90068

5890 Pugliese, Davey and Associates

5 Bessom Street, Ste. 175   617-639-1930
Marblehead, MA 01945

Offers highly respected training and support services in adaptive microcomputer technology.

5891 Reynolds, Ann, MS, Educational Consultant

P.O. Box 20086   415-547-1334
Oakland, CA 94620

5892 Ross, Richard E., OD, Inc.

1026 Oak Grove Road   415-682-2434
Concord, CA 94518

5893 Salkowitz, Bobbe Banks, MA, CCC, SLP

118 North Croft Avenue   213-655-6839
Los Angeles, CA 90048
Speech/language/voice pathologist.

5894 Severtson, Robert L., OD, and Getz, Nina C., O.D. - Behavioral Optometry

121 South Del Mar Avenue, Ste. A   818-287-0401
San Gabriel, CA 91776   FAX 818-287-1457

Dr. Severtson
Dr. Getz

Optimal Learning is dependent on efficient vision. "Vision" is the learned ability to identify, interpret, understand and act on what is seen. Individuals with learning problems frequently have undiagnosed "vision" problems such as focusing, eye movement adn eye teaming skills. Specialize in detection and treatment of learning-related "vision" problems.

5895 Sillman, Adrienne P., EdD

3816 Hollywood Blvd.   305-966-1300
Hollywood, FL 33021

5896 Starr, Nonnie CSW, Learning Specialist for Children and Adults

131 Main Street   516-374-9285
East Rockaway, NJ 11518

Nonnie Star, Dir. Of Educ. Srvcs.

Social skills remediation combined with free phonics tutoring if needed for school or work, individually or in groups, work and independent living readiness skills also provided.

5897 Synergy-Adaptive Innovations

55 Hale Road   508-668-7424
East Walpole, MA 02032

A company dedicated to empowering persons with physical, language and learning disabilities.

5898 Techspress

409 Columbia Street   315-797-4642
Utica, NY 13502   FAX 315-797-4747

Russ Holland, Director

Provides awareness, access and application for technology. Runs seminars, consultations and training. The organization newsletter is free with membership.

5899 Ungerleider, Dorothy, CET, MA

16800 Adlon Road   818-784-6561
Encino, CA 91436

5900 Wells, Elaine F., MA, Speech Pathologist

1844 San Miguel Drive, Ste. 108   415-933-6152
Walnut Creek, CA 94596

523

531

533

Subject Index

T

Tape Recorders, 5322
Teleconference, 5599
Testing Resources, 991, 1671, 1716, 1719, 2387, 2403, 2404, 2408, 2467, 5042, 5043, 5290, 5293, 5298, 5300, 5841
Tourette Syndrome, 766
Transition, 876, 882, 1112, 1119, 1133, 1179, 1339, 2659, 2888, 2897, 3005, 5008, 5606, 5658, 5661, 5693, 5696, 5700, 5714, 5715, 5729, 5730, 5731, 5732, 5733, 5741, 5742, 5763, 5810, 5826

V

Visually Impaired, 20, 25, 89, 739, 1479, 1546, 1547, 1548, 1572, 1581, 1591, 1592, 1618, 1631, 1792, 1968, 2264, 2619, 2650, 2653, 2654, 2981, 5313, 5819
Vocabulary, 1185
Vocational Counseling, 1059
Vocational Education, 33, 144, 160, 180, 205, 247, 325, 334, 341, 342, 386, 1042, 1057, 1077, 1083, 1084, 1094, 1104, 1105, 1106, 1107, 1109, 1110, 1111, 1353, 1471, 1663, 1973, 1995, 1997, 2022, 2024, 2025, 2026, 2027, 2028, 2070, 2072, 2073, 2094, 2152, 2365, 2391, 2596, 2708, 2805, 2936, 3084, 5028, 5050, 5575, 5618, 5657, 5659, 5660, 5662, 5663, 5664, 5665, 5666, 5667, 5668, 5669, 5670, 5671, 5672, 5673, 5674, 5676, 5679, 5680, 5681, 5682, 5683, 5684, 5685, 5686, 5687, 5688, 5689, 5690, 5692, 5694, 5695, 5699, 5701, 5703, 5704, 5705, 5706, 5708, 5709, 5710, 5711, 5712, 5713, 5716, 5718, 5719, 5723, 5724, 5727, 5728, 5734, 5735, 5736, 5737, 5739, 5743, 5744, 5746, 5747, 5748, 5749, 5750, 5751, 5752, 5753, 5755, 5757, 5758, 5760, 5761, 5762, 5764, 5765, 5766, 5767, 5768, 5769, 5770, 5771, 5772, 5773, 5774, 5775, 5776, 5777, 5778, 5779, 5780, 5781, 5782, 5783, 5784, 5785, 5786, 5787, 5788, 5789, 5790, 5791, 5792, 5793, 5795, 5796, 5797, 5799, 5801, 5802, 5803, 5804, 5806, 5807, 5808, 5811, 5814, 5815, 5817, 5820, 5822, 5823, 5824, 5825, 5827, 5828, 5829, 5830, 5831, 5832, 5833, 5834, 5837, 5842, 5844, 5845, 5872, 5897

W

Women's Resources, 961, 5002
Writing, 852, 887, 890, 897, 903, 913, 930, 952, 953, 956, 959, 960, 1197, 1354, 1395, 1468, 1469, 1470, 1472, 1566, 1630, 1650, 1675, 1680, 1684, 1685, 1686, 1687, 1693, 1695, 1702, 1723, 1725, 1735, 1737, 1754, 1756, 1757, 1759, 1776, 1783, 1802, 1803, 1820, 1821, 1822, 1833, 1837, 1838, 1849, 1863, 1864, 1872, 1881, 1898, 1913, 1914, 1915, 1916, 1922, 1926, 1929, 1958, 1962, 2019, 2048, 2049, 2050, 2051, 2052, 2053, 2090, 2091, 2257, 2422, 2468, 2482, 2491, 2532, 2569, 2598, 2622, 2631, 2635, 2638, 2647, 2655, 2656, 2664, 2666, 2667, 2668, 2669, 2670, 2671, 2672, 2673, 2674, 2675, 2676, 2677, 2679, 2680, 2681, 2683, 2684, 2685, 2686, 2687, 3054, 3055, 3119, 3134, 5745